OLDEST COLLEGE DAILY FOUNDED JANUARY 28, 1878

Yale Daily News
Guide to
Summer Programs

Third Edition

By Sara Schwebel
and the staff of the *Yale Daily News*

Simon & Schuster

NEW YORK · LONDON · SINGAPORE · SYDNEY · TORONTO

Kaplan Publishing
Published by Simon & Schuster
1230 Avenue of the Americas
New York, NY 10020

For bulk sales to schools, colleges, and universities, please contact:
Order Department, Simon & Schuster, 100 Front Street, Riverside, NJ 08075.
Phone: (800) 223-2336. Fax: (800) 943-9831.

Project Editor: Eileen Mager
Contributing Editors: Trent Anderson and Seppy Basili
Assistant Editor: Supurna Banerjee
Cover Design: Cheung Tai
Production Artist: Laurel Douglas
Production Editor: Maude Spekes
Production Manager: Michael Shevlin
Editorial Coordinator: Dea Alessandro
Executive Editor: Del Franz

Special thanks to Dave Chipps, Larissa Shmailo, and Kate Moran.

The material in this book is up-to-date at the time of publication. Changes may have occurred after this book was published. Please contact individual programs to obtain updated information.

Manufactured in the United States of America
Published simultaneously in Canada

November 2001
10 9 8 7 6 5 4 3 2 1

ISBN: 0-7432-1426-9
ISSN: 1096-8121

Table of Contents

About the Author viii
Acknowledgments ix
About Yale Daily News x
How to Use This Book xi

PART I: THE BASICS

Chapter 1: Let the Fun Begin 3

Chapter 2: Getting Organized, Getting In .13

PART II: TYPES OF PROGRAMS

Chapter 3: Academic Programs
    Overview 27
    List of Programs 40
    Enriching Your Summer 56

Chapter 4: Study Abroad and International Travel Programs
    Overview 63
    List of Programs 78
    Enriching Your Summer 83

Chapter 5: Community Service Programs
    Overview 89
    List of Programs 98
    Enriching Your Summer 99

Chapter 6: Outdoor Adventure and Travel Programs
    Overview 103
    List of Programs 111
    Enriching Your Summer 113

Chapter 7: Athletic Programs
    Overview 117
    List of Programs 128
    Enriching Your Summer 132

Table of Contents

Chapter 8: Arts Programs
 Overview 137
 List of Programs 148
 Enriching Your Summer 155

Chapter 9: Leadership Programs
 Overview 163
 List of Programs 170
 Enriching Your Summer 173

Chapter 10: Thy Eternal Summer Shall Not Fade 179

PART III: PROGRAM DIRECTORY

Program Directory 187

PART IV: INDEXES

Index by Subject Area 457

Index by Cost of Program 499

Index by Location of Program 517

Index by Duration of Program 539

In loving memory of my father, who inspired me to write.

About the Author

Sara Schwebel graduated from Yale with honors in 1998, where she was a history major and features editor of the *Yale Daily News*. After two years of teaching eighth grade history in Alexandria, Virginia, she is now a doctoral student in the History of American Civilization at Harvard University. She continues to plan her summers carefully, searching for just the right mixture of adventure, learning, and fun.

Acknowledgments

Most books are a collaborative effort, and this one is no exception. I want to thank the many people who helped make the *Yale Daily News Guide to Summer Programs* possible.

Yale Daily News reporters Mackenzie Barris, Shane Dizon, Stephanie Hanes, Glenn Hurowitz, Connie Ing, Nicole Itano, Sara Leitch, James McGuire, Kara Miller, Ace Padian, Zak Pines, Emily Saslow, and Isaiah Wilner each interviewed students about their summer program experiences. The quotes and anecdotes they contributed add much color and depth to the book. Thanks are also due to members of the YDN Board of 1999, who shared their reporters' valuable time and skill.

I am grateful to the many high school and college students who shared their stories, and to their teachers—the high school guidance counselors, independent educational consultants, college admissions officers, coaches, arts specialists, and summer program directors—who so generously gave of their time and wisdom.

I would like to thank the Kaplan/Simon & Schuster team for its help, support, and understanding of busy college lives. Rich Christiano, Del Franz, and Brent Gallenberger at Kaplan and Annaliza Martinez, Maureen McMahon, and Jennifer Shore at Simon & Schuster made writing this book a pleasure from start to finish. Special thanks to Kaplan editor Eileen Mager, who made the second and third editions of this book possible.

The *Yale Daily News* business staff deserves recognition for balancing the demands of book publishing with those of a daily newspaper. I would especially like to thank Susan Zucker for her patience and warm smile. Thanks also to Ali Mohamadi, YDN sports editor (1996–97), for reading a draft of the Athletics chapter and to former YDN editors-in-chief, Jake Sullivan, Kevin O'Connell, and Isaiah Wilner for steering this project.

Heartfelt thanks to my friends Zoë Allen-Pohle, Teri Niadna, Alex Robbins, and Heather Vanderhoof, who always knew the perfect moment to pull me away from my computer, and to Lynne Rogers, Sarah Voss, and Abby Williamson, with whom I shared my golden high school summers.

I could never thank my family enough for its love, support, and encouragement. I am so grateful to my mother, who brainstormed with me during countless phone calls and e-mails; to my brother, grandfather, and Uncle Bob, who carefully read and commented upon drafts of this manuscript; to my grandmother, who wisely told me to sleep; and to my Aunt Claudia and cousins Frank and Henry, who made my writing vacations so much fun.

Founded on January 28, 1878, the *Yale Daily News* is the oldest college daily paper in the United States. The all-student staff publishes a 10- to 16-page newspaper five nights a week, reporting stories related to the Yale and New Haven communities. Financially independent from the university, the *Yale Daily News* supports its own production through student-sold advertising.

Boasting an alumni list that includes Henry Luce, Sargent Shriver, Potter Stewart, William F. Buckley Jr., Garry Trudeau, Calvin Trillin, and Shelley Fisher Fishkin, the *Yale Daily News* has been called the best unofficial undergraduate school of journalism. Today's *Yale Daily News* remains committed to the mission of teaching journalism, conducting skills workshops, and hosting alumni speakers.

In addition to the daily newspaper, the *Yale Daily News* publishes a weekly news magazine, a monthly compilation of stories, and the *Insider's Guide to the Colleges*—a guidebook to the nation's colleges created by interviewing current undergraduates.

Most recently, the *Yale Daily News* has entered a joint venture with Kaplan Publishing and Simon & Schuster to produce a series of guide books to assist and advise students throughout their college careers. Titles include the *Yale Daily News Guide to Succeeding in College*, *Yale Daily News Guide to Writing College Papers*, *Yale Daily News Guide to Internships*, *Yale Daily News Working Knowledge*, and this publication, the *Yale Daily News Guide to Summer Programs*. Authored by staff members of the *Yale Daily News*, all the books offer valuable tips for college and career success drawn from the experiences of actual students.

Part I: The Basics

Let the Fun Begin

1

So you're determined to make the most of your summer vacation—to return to school in the fall smarter, happier, and more tan? Summer programs might just be your answer. Whether you're a high school freshman with an eye on school leadership positions or a high school senior eager to get out and see the world, summer programs offer a range of adventures and opportunities. From hiking in the Grand Canyon to biking across Africa, studying at Yale to dancing at the Edinburgh festival, summer programs can be the perfect cure for high school boredom, the ideal antidote for summertime's living-at-home claustrophobia.

——— **Expert Advice** ———

"It is important for students to have a meaningful summer experience. Selective colleges want to know how students spend their time outside the classroom."

—Barbara Aronson, career center coordinator, Miramonte High School

Few 15-year-olds know where they want to go to college; few 18-year-olds know exactly what they want to do with their lives. And that's a good thing. Ask any college student—high school is way too early to worry about "the real world." But as many a guidance counselor will tell you, it is not too soon to get serious about yourself. Regardless of what college you ultimately rank as your first choice, you can be sure its admissions officers look at more than SAT I, SAT II, and ACT scores. They look at more than grades and letters of recommendation. Each year, the admissions team scours stacks of student essays looking for those that speak honestly, passionately, and confidently about the world. Their interest is piqued by applicants who have sought unique experiences and strived to profit from them.

We all know that high schools are not created equal. Yet even the very best schools—ones providing a diverse community of teachers and students and classes ranging from Russian political history to Hindu literature—are still isolated communities. It's important to expose yourself to life outside of high school. Personal confidence, breadth of experience, and intriguing ideas often stem from contact with new and different people and environments. Many summer programs foster just that.

But, you say, there are hundreds of summer programs. How can I choose one from the pages and pages of listings in this book? I'll admit it's not easy (good thing you have enough summers to try a few), but here are some basic considerations to keep in mind.

Guava and Kiwi, Not Apples and Oranges

Before you look at cost, before you study dates, before you scrutinize location, ask yourself this one key question:

"Is this an experience I could only get if I attended the summer program, or are these activities available during the academic year at my school or in my community?"

Summertime is precious, so use it wisely. One of the biggest mistakes people make is investing their time and money in a summer program that provides more of the same. Be adventurous—stretch yourself! Take advantage of unique and crazy opportunities. That may mean backpacking across South America, dribbling down court under the eyes of Big Ten coaches, or running rats in a state-of-the-art university lab. It definitely does not mean gathering together ten of your closest friends and signing up for basketball camp at the high school across town.

THE BALANCING ACT

Summer programs range from two-day conferences to eight-week, all-out adventures. Some offer several length-of-stay options while others have one starting and ending date for all participants each summer. Which kind is best? There are many personal factors to consider. Do you need to attend the family reunion in June? Do you want to be home to celebrate the Fourth of July with high school buddies? Do you have to be back mid-August for the beginning of varsity soccer practice?

Shorter summer programs, especially those situated at the beginning and end of the summer, give you more flexibility. They also allow you to hold a summer job, which can be extremely advantageous. Granted, 14-, 15- and 16-year-olds usually don't pull large paychecks. But money aside, summer employment is a valuable experience. Most U.S. states and territories allow employers to hire students beginning at age fourteen. This means high school students can get "real" jobs, ones requiring them to complete an application, file social security, and don a uniform, or at least respectable clothes. Quite a difference from the informal babysitting or yard work you may have done in middle school or junior high.

Most college counselors, guidance counselors, and college admission officers agree that this real-world work experience looks good on college applications: It demonstrates not only one's initiative and responsibility, but also a familiarity with the adult world. Employment in high school makes getting your first job and internship as a college student much easier (Hint: Be sure to ask your employer to write you a letter of recommendation). And the high school student who begins building a résumé and learning how to handle personal finances—no matter how small—is one step ahead of the game when it comes to adjusting to college life.

But beware, there is a down side. Unless you secure an interesting and well-paying summer job, which is difficult to do when you are in high school, you will probably learn and grow more from a carefully selected summer program. If you flipped burgers or bussed tables the summer after your freshman year, are you going to learn anything new by doing it again the summer after your sophomore year? Probably not. If you can't bear to give up a summer salary entirely, consider taking three weeks off to invest in yourself by doing a summer program. Sure, you may lose out on $600 (before taxes), but you'll gain much, much more in personal growth and development. Think about what you would spend the money on. Is it really necessary, or is the opportunity to meet exciting students, see new parts of the world, and work with scientific experts more valuable? ("But," you say, "this is not a fair comparison. What about the cost of the summer program? That should be added to the $600." Good point. We'll discuss. Many summer programs offer financial aid for those who qualify, and some excellent opportunities are completely free of charge.)

Longer summer programs—those that run several weeks—allow you to travel farther from home. This means you are more likely to be surrounded by people with backgrounds and experiences different from your own. Moreover, the extra days give you

Expert Advice

"We sometimes ask ourselves why students are working over the summer. I think there is a difference between students who are working because they have to and students who are working because there are luxuries they want to afford. And of course, some students work both for the money and for the experience."

—Christoph Guttentag, director of undergraduate admissions, Duke University

Student Scoop

"I needed to earn money for school and had to choose a program that accommodated that. The cancer fellowship gave me the opportunity to do research without sacrificing a paying job. It also allowed me to stay home my last summer before college."

—Kelly Wilhelm, participant, University of Colorado/American Cancer Society Student Cancer Fellowship

time to really get to know and become friends with other participants. The pay off is considerable. During a multiple-week program, you are able to hone leadership skills and develop confidence that can come only from adapting to a new environment and knowing you are thriving in it.

Short programs and long programs. Fast food jobs and family vacations. Weeklong overnight stays and weekly Saturday baseball games. It's not easy; there are choices galore. With careful planning, however, you can make your high school summers fun, meaningful, and profitable—in both senses of the word.

Ideally, your summers should provide a combination of work experience, volunteer experience, short summer programs, and longer two-, three-, or four-week programs, not to mention time for pure relaxation. All boost the college application and enrich your life experiences. Remember that when planning your summers, it is important to show both consistency and breadth. You don't want to do the same thing every summer. For one thing, it's boring. For another, it suggests a lack of initiative and willingness to take risks. On the other hand, if you hold a summer job the summer after your freshman year and then never work again, admissions officers (and later, employers) might think you couldn't handle the responsibility.

You get the picture: Summer activities, like extracurricular projects and life in general, are about balance, balance, and more balance.

AROUND THE CORNER OR ACROSS THE OCEAN

Geography is an important factor when selecting a summer program. Do you want to commute from home? Stay in state? Try life on the opposite side of the country? Travel to another part of the world? All provide perks, if different ones. If you've grown up in Cleveland and always known you wanted to play football for the Wolverines, it might make sense to attend Michigan's football camp. It will let you meet the coaching staff and let them get an eye for your game. But if you live in St. Paul, plan to attend the University of Minnesota, and want a pre-college academic experience, it may make sense to stay near home and take classes at your future school. You'll earn college credit, learn your way around campus, and make sure it's the

Expert Advice

"Regardless of subject matter, participating in a summer program can definitely influence a student's decision to remain interested in the campus or not. If you have to choose a school you know nothing about or a school where you can picture yourself, the school where you have spent time is often more comfortable."

—Traevena Potter-Hall, director of scholar recruitment, University of Iowa

right place for you. But remember the rule to live by when scheduling your summer: A summer program should provide something new and different, something not available in your daily high school life. If you live in the Midwest far from an ocean, consider a summer program that flies you to the East or West Coast to study marine biology. You might just end up calling your favorite pop "soda," or joining the Beach Boys in their veneration of California girls.

In the end, it is a personal choice. Just like choosing colleges, some people are ready to venture far from home; others feel safer if they know mom and dad are within an hour's drive. Programs near and far can provide fun and rewarding experiences. Regardless of how close you stay to home, however, consider looking for some programs with national or international participation. Meeting people of vastly different experiences and backgrounds often proves to be the most exhilarating part of a summer program experience. In many cases, it matters less what you are doing or where you are doing it than whom you are doing it with.

MEETING A GOAL

With hundreds of summer programs to choose from, it is important that you sit down and set some goals. What is your primary motivation for attending a summer program: to experience campus life, to polish leadership skills, to escape a limited or homogenous high school and neighborhood community, to take academic classes that will help you pass out of annoying freshmen requirements in college, or to get recruited by top college athletic coaches? Ask yourself how this particular summer will fit into your larger high school experiences, and how it can affect life after high school. Remember: balance, balance, and more balance.

All well-run summer programs will expand your horizons, introduce you to a diverse group of high schoolers, cultivate leadership skills, and increase your sense of independence. But the specific skills gained vary. Some programs emphasize frivolity and fun. Others closely mirror college life—a balance of

Student Scoop

"There were kids from all over the country, but mostly from the South. It was kind of funny, because being from the Midwest, everything I said had an accent and everything they said had an accent. I got to learn all the slang words they used on the trip."

—Matt Moran, participant, Moondance Adventures

(considerable) work and (moderate) play. You'll want to decide what's best for you. Are you using the summer program to train under the best teachers in the country, or are you using it simply to meet new friends, experience life in New England, and pick up a few new skills? Will studying on a boarding school campus for eight weeks in the summer reawaken your interest in learning or leave you dreading the first day of classes in the fall? Everyone has a different vision of the ideal summer. Make sure whatever program you choose works with, rather than against, your dream vacation.

TALKIN' DOLLARS AND CENTS

There is a great range in program costs. While some local, in-state programs like the *Yale Daily News* Summer Journalism Program are entirely funded and ask participants to pay for only personal expenses, some international travel programs cost $7,000 or more. Some programs—both low- and high-price ones—provide considerable need-based financial aid; others offer no monetary assistance. So be a smart consumer.

When selecting a program, remind yourself and your parents that summer program price tags are an investment in your education. Paying big bucks for a summer program is not the same as shelling out hundreds for a Disney World vacation. When you return from Disney, you'll look the same, give or take a Mickey Mouse hat. But when you return from a summer program, your parents, teachers, and friends will see and feel a significant difference. So will you. But don't mistake high prices for high quality. The most expensive program is not necessarily the best one out there, and free, in-state programs can provide life-changing experiences. If cost plays a role in your decision, there are plenty of ways to save money without sacrificing quality.

Sometimes factors that don't necessarily affect a program's quality (such as location) can influence cost. For example, a top-notch drama program in Georgia will probably have a lower tuition than a similar program in New York City: the cost of living is simply less. Since the highest quality programs tend to recruit instructors nationally, location shouldn't matter much.

How can you gauge a program's relative quality? Gather information about its operation and compare it to that of its competitors. Are its teachers/guides/counselors of equal ability (inquire into their education, age, and experience)? How long has the program been in operation? Does it fill up every year, or is the program routinely canceled for lack of applicants? How do

program facilities measure up? What do their safety records (especially for athletic and outdoor adventure programs) look like? Are references of past participants available?

Make sure you look for hidden costs! Large discrepancies between similar programs can often be explained by the fact that some programs include airfare to the site while others expect participants to purchase their own tickets to the Caribbean or London or Quito (a call to your local travel agent can help determine which will be more cost-effective). When comparing programs that involve wilderness survival or extensive camping and backpacking, check to see if equipment—tents, backpacks, rain gear, mess kits—are included. If not, this can add considerable expense to your summer adventures. Do your research! Some programs provide necessary "extras," but others don't.

THE TEENYBOPPER FACTOR

There is a big difference between summer camp and summer programs. Or at least there should be. Summer camp is for kids; summer programs are for teenagers. When you select a program, make sure you choose one that understands and respects the difference. (Hint: You know you're in trouble if lights out is before 10:00 P.M.) Whether the focus is on sports, academics, community service, or the arts, summer programs should give you a taste of college life and the independence that blessed high school diploma brings. This is not possible in programs where some participants have yet to finish the seventh grade.

Don't, however, be scared off by brochures that advertise for kids as young as 11 or 12. Many of the best summer programs run separate trips for middle and high school students, adjusting the

───── Quick Tips ─────

Choosing a Program That's Right for You

Questions to ask yourself:

- Do the programs I'm considering offer unique opportunities unavailable to me during the school year?

- Do I want a shorter program that will let me plan other activities for the summer or a longer program that will allow me to immerse myself completely?

- Do I want a paying job this summer? Is it worth it to me to sacrifice the money for the benefits of a longer summer program?

- Do I prefer to stay close to home? Or am I ready to jet off to another country?

- What type of experience do I hope to gain from this summer (e.g., college prep vs. outdoor adventure)?

- Does the program fit my budget? Are there any hidden costs not included in the price the program advertises (like airfare or room and board)? Can I get financial aid?

activities, rules, and regulations accordingly. By separating age groups, these programs demonstrate that they know the difference between children and teenagers. Their staff will treat you like a young adult.

HITTING THE BOOKS OR TAKING TO THE TRAILS

Summer programs fall into many different categories, and this guidebook addresses each of the most common in turn. But from the viewpoint of a high school or college, there are two main types: academic and nonacademic. Is there an advantage to pursuing one over another? Different people have different opinions, and you won't get the same answer from every college admissions officer, high school guidance counselor, psychologist, parent, or high school student. Ultimately, you have to ask and answer the question for yourself. But first, let's take a minute to see what the experts have to say.

The Yale Daily News and Kaplan, Inc., conducted a survey of high school guidance and college counselors as well as independent educational consultants, people who specialize in finding the right schools for each of their students and then making sure they get in. Sixty-seven percent of these professionals said they recommend academic summer programs to their students more often than summer programs of any other kind. Seventy-three percent of survey-respondents said academic programs are also the most popular among their students. What does this mean? Well for starters, it suggests that students trust their advisors and take their advice. Does this mean you should select an academic summer program? Not necessarily.

It is essential to choose a summer program for the right reason: because it is interesting and offers you new and exciting opportunities. Don't select an academic summer program at a prestigious university simply because you think it will help you get in. It might, but it is clear that successful completion of another meaningful program can have just as much bearing on that acceptance letter's landing in your mailbox. So choose a program that will bring you the most pleasure and the best opportunity for novel experiences. The benefits will be evident in your character and in the way you think—two factors than can make you or break you in the college admissions game.

Expert Advice

"I must state a bias away from academics in the summer unless such is needed to make up a deficiency. I really am concerned about the amount of pressure students put on themselves and try not to add to this pressure if at all possible."

—Susan J. Bigg, independent educational consultant

Expert Advice

"I think that summer programs offer an opportunity for enrichment and personal growth. For many, it is their first chance to live away from home and to meet students from around the country. It gives them an edge in life, never mind college applications. Students should pursue their interests, not what they think will interest a college."

—Ann Maureen Penny, director of college guidance, Convent of the Sacred Heart

College admissions officers hold fairly consistent views about applicants' summer program enrollment: It is not the name of the summer program or the institution it is associated with that matters, it is the quality of the experience and what an individual student gets out of it. Admissions officers say they like to see high school students use their summers in one of two ways—to further pursue an interest or passion (anything from wilderness trailblazing to fighting lead poisoning) or to branch out and try something new. Obviously, attending a university, college, or boarding school summer session is not the only way, and in some cases not the preferred way, to do either. Specialized camps, volunteer work, and summer jobs can help fulfill these goals as well. So if you don't want to write papers or balance equations this summer, smile. You don't have to.

CHECKIN' IT TWICE

Summer programs are a big commitment, financially and time-wise. Brochures may look and sound alike, but we all know looks can be deceiving. Don't be hasty in choosing your program—it's a big investment. Flip through the pages at the back of this book and use the contact information to send away for brochures and promotional videos. When you get them, call people on the reference list and ask them about their experiences. Talk to your high school counselor about what programs other students have enjoyed. Attend local summer program fairs and speak with program organizers directly. Go back to this book's listings and look up program websites.

——— **Expert Advice** ———

"Summer is a good time for a little risk taking. None of us grows without pushing our boundaries a little bit. I like to see a student who has a curiosity about an area and wants to pursue it. Or a student who does something that is a little different from what they have ever done before. A lot of important things happen to us through serendipity. Students discover concepts, experiences, and other people through happenstance. Being open to that sort of experience is positive."

—Christoph Guttentag, director of undergraduate admissions, Duke University

——— **Expert Advice** ———

"Every bit of information we can assemble about a candidate is helpful. The overriding questions is, 'Who are you anyway?' How you spend your time—after school and in the summers—is a critical question that we always ask. Sometimes summer programs can help us answer that question. There is no automatic response, but we are very eager to understand, as fully as we can, how a person spends his or her time. ...We start with who the candidate is. For a person who says she is very interested in archaeology, for example, a summer program related to archeology [is one way to] illustrate that assertion. That relates to the developing picture of who she is."

—Marlyn McGrath Lewis, director of undergraduate admissions, Harvard University

──────── **Quick Tips** ────────

Making the Grade

What makes a program good?
Do your research:

- Call the programs that interest you and request brochures.

- Ask for references from past participants.

- Compare faculty credentials.

- Look at past popularity.

- Browse through program websites.

- Check safety records for any outdoor or study abroad programs.

- Talk to program directors and *ask questions*.

Most important, call or e-mail summer program directors directly (many of them even have toll-free numbers in their listings). They will be happy to discuss their program, and in a matter of five minutes, you may well be able to cross it off your list or send out your application. Ask what a typical day is like. Ask who attends their program. Ask if the food is good. It doesn't much matter what you ask, as long as you get them talking. A disorganized, inarticulate staff is easily detectable, as is an enthusiastic, caring teaching faculty.

As you finalize your plans, watch out for the parent trap. This is your summer. That's right, yours. So don't be afraid to pick up the phone and call yourself. You are the one attending, not your parents. If you are nervous about calling, it may help to remember that you are the consumer; the staff is trying to sell their program to you. Don't worry if you don't sound perfectly polished on the phone; few people do. And rest assured: If you are calling a Duke University summer program and really want to be a Blue Devil, the admissions officers would never think of noting that you sounded like an idiot on the phone. They have much better things to do than file away such memos in case you decide to apply for admission two years down the road. So get on that phone! If nothing else, it's good practice for arranging college tours and interviews during your junior year.

Taking the initiative can also help demonstrate to your parents that you care enough about your summer experience to choose a program wisely. So if your parents are pushing for Harvard Summer School and you're set on Outward Bound, doing advance research will make it easier to explain your preference to them—and will reassure them that you're making a mature decision that's right for you.

Getting Organized, Getting In

Unfortunately, great summer programs don't just fall in your lap. But once you have done your research and selected the program(s) to which you want to apply, you're well on your way. Congratulations. Now all you have to do is get in.

Unlike the college admissions process, which your high school will probably walk you through step-by-step, you're most likely going to be on your own here, especially if you attend a large public high school. The good news is that many summer programs have an open-door, rolling admissions policy. In other words, as long as you have planned ahead and sent a check well before the registration deadline, you're good to go: They process applications as they arrive. Programs that frequently have this no-sweat registration procedure include travel, outdoor adventure programs, and—because of NCAA regulations—even sports programs advertised for "elite" athletes. Occasionally some of these pay-and-you're-in programs request character references in the form of a name and phone number. But the key to getting in is simple: Apply early.

Other types of summer programs, often ones featuring academic course work, leadership training, organized community service activities, and the fine and performing arts, have a competitive admissions process. They demand a more extensive application, usually with a required writing sample. This is also good news. Granted, it can be a pain to write an essay about why you want to attend a particular program and what you expect to get out of it, but completing such an application is actually great practice. While summer program applications are not nearly as extensive as college applications, they often follow the same format: high school transcript, letters of recommendation, list of school and community activities, and personal statement on a designated topic. Think of your summer program application as a "trial

──── **Expert Advice** ────

"This is something [students] do all on their own. There's a large bulletin board post starting in February. There are notices in the parent newsletter, and over the bulletin every morning. At ninth-grade orientations, I also mention that they should be looking at programs between their junior and senior year. The hard part is getting the word out."

—Susan Cox, college and career advisor, Agoura High School

Quick Tips

Steps to Success

- Do your research.
- Apply early.
- Start a list of school and community activities.
- Choose references and recommendation writers with care.
- Write thank-you letters.

run." The stakes are not nearly as high as they will be senior year; in fact, they are almost nonexistent. So relax. If you don't get in, it's no big deal.

But rejection never feels good. So, here are some ways to maximize your application's potential. The earlier you learn this application etiquette, the better prepared you will be. The same basic principles will apply to college applications, scholarship applications, and, farther down the road, job applications. So here it goes.

THE EARLY BIRD GETS THE WORM

It's good policy to know what time your post office closes and how long it takes to get from your front door to the friendly mail carrier behind the counter. But also remember that this information is for emergencies only: You should never, never be applying for something important at the last minute. Remember Murphy's Law? "Nothing is as easy as it looks. Everything takes longer than you expect. And if anything can go wrong, it will. At the worst possible moment." We've all been there: Your essay is finished, but your computer freezes and your printer refuses to print. Your application is typed and sitting ready to go on the kitchen table, but a glass of orange juice somehow tips right onto it. You're on your way to the post office, sailing along at 60 mph ... until you hit a massive traffic jam halfway between home and the mail meter.

So give yourself a break. If your program has a firm deadline, finish and mail the application at least a week in advance. For programs featuring something called *rolling admissions*, the above advice is even more important. When it comes to summer programs, rolling admissions basically means first come, first served, as long as your application meets minimum standards (i.e., it's filled out completely, health requirements are met, references are provided, and a check is "in the mail"). Obviously, then, the earlier you submit your application, the greater the chances of acceptance.

REFERENCES AND RECOMMENDATIONS

Summer program directors often want to know a bit about who will be participating in their workshop, camp, or trip. In order to gain insight into applicants' character, ability, and level of motivation, they may ask for a reference or letter of recommendation.

A *reference* is simply the name and contact information (address, phone number) of an adult who knows you well and is willing to vouch for you. By tradition, family members usually cannot be used as references. Acceptable references include your guidance or college counselor, and depending on the type of program, teachers, private instructors (music, tennis, etcetera), coaches, an employer, a religious leader, a coordinator of volunteer work, and/or a youth group leader. A *letter of recommendation*, sometimes called a *reference form* if the program provides a list of questions for the letter writer to answer, is a more substantive testimony to your character, ability, and motivation. The same category of people suggested above for references can serve as recommenders.

While references may never even be contacted by your program's admissions committee (and if they are, the conversation is usually short), recommenders must compose a personal, individualized letter about you. Therefore, choose someone who has shown real interest in you, your activities, and your future. Such people will be willing to devote sufficient time to writing a stellar letter. Also, remember that whom you choose as a letter writer is a reflection on you. Being able to choose an appropriate person demonstrates your maturity and judgment. Choose someone who writes well.

The Three-Step Process: Ask, Inform, Thank

So you have thought through possible references and letter writers. Now it's time to gather the recommendation. To simplify the process, we'll consider three steps: asking, informing, and thanking.

Asking

It can sometimes be difficult to ask for a letter or recommendation. If you feel a little shy or embarrassed, you're not alone. When you ask someone who has repeatedly expressed interest in your personal development and success, however, chances are the person will be more than happy to help. She'll want to see you shine.

This comes with a caveat. Even if you ask a teacher who would normally bend over backwards for you, she will not be pleased if you hand her the recommendation form and ask that it be sent by the end of the week. There's a right and a wrong way to ask your favor. First, ask well in advance. I cannot emphasize that enough. Teachers, coaches, religious leaders—they are all busy people. If possible, give them a minimum of three weeks to write and send the letter. Second, do not assume they will say yes. It's bad form to ask, hear the answer, then whip out the recommendation form. Ask first, then bring or send them the form within the next two to three days.

Finally, ask at an appropriate time. By now you have had lots of practice asking your parents for things—CDs, money, a later curfew. There are good times and bad times to spring a request, right? The same goes for letters of recommendation. Try to avoid both hectic moments and hectic times of year. For example, teachers tend to be particularly

busy at the end of each grading period. If you have planned ahead, you should have time to wait until the beginning or middle of a quarter to ask for your letter. Similarly, two minutes before the beginning of your group tennis clinic is not the best time to ask your instructor to serve as a reference. He is gearing up for practice and has other things on his mind. Wait until after the session.

Keep the time commitment involved in writing a letter of recommendation in mind when you ask someone to serve as a recommender. Be considerate of their busy schedules. When you ask, you might consider saying something like the following: "I know you're extremely busy, but . . . ." Important people are always busy, and most like to hear that others recognize their many commitments. Also, you should ask for a letter only in private. If 10 other people are standing around when you ask, your teacher or coach might feel like he's being put on the spot. If he's surrounded by other people, he may be apprehensive about getting a flood of requests from the other people if he says "yes" to you at that moment.

Informing

Once you have obtained a yes, it's all in their hands, right? Wrong. Letters of recommendation are confidential, so you cannot directly influence what they say, but you can nevertheless do much to improve their quality. Your goal is to make writing a letter of recommendation absolutely as easy as possible for the person you have selected. Here are some tips on how to do that:

- Complete your portion of the recommendation form (usually your name and signature) and give that to your letter writer with a stamped envelope addressed to the summer program. Be sure to put a Post-it™ note on the envelope clearly marking the submission deadline.

- If possible, provide your letter writer or reference with a copy of the summer program brochure. If you're unable to obtain a copy, type out a brief description of the program and an outline of its admission criteria.

- Supply your letter writer or reference with any information about yourself that will help him or her in writing a letter or speaking to the summer program staff. For a general academic program, this might include a copy (official or unofficial) of your high school transcript, a list of honors and awards won, and a description of your major extracurricular activities in and out of school. Even if your letter writer or reference is aware of your school activities and academic course work, having a list handy can make things easier.

- Ensure that your letter writer or reference understands why you chose this particular summer program. The better informed he or she is, the better he or she can advocate on your behalf.

- Ask if there is anything else you can provide to make things easier.

Thanking

This step is simple, but important: Thank the person for her help. Thanking someone over and over again during the course of a five-minute conversation will make anyone but an egomaniac feel self-conscious. Three simple thank-yous, however, will ensure the person feels appreciated and will be willing to help you again in the future.

You should give one short, verbal "thank you" immediately after the person agrees to serve as a recommender. Thank-you number two, which should be both written and verbal, comes when you hand the person your recommendation form and/or supplementary information about the program and yourself. Thank-you number three, a formal, written thank-you note, should be mailed (yes, mailed) just after the submission deadline or immediately following a conversation in which the person informs you that he has sent off the recommendation letter. For bonus points, you can send the person a postcard from your summer program telling him what you're doing and what you enjoy most. This shows that you're truly appreciative of his help, and that you're making good use of the summer opportunity. Your teachers, coaches, and leaders work hard for you. Take the time to show you're appreciative.

THE WRITING SAMPLE

Sooner or later you will face an application with a required essay and/or short-answer questions. Many students see it and cringe. But before you break into a cold sweat, consider this. You have been turning out essays and writing samples since you wrote your first book report back in elementary school. You know how to write. As for writing about yourself, yes, it can be difficult. But it helps to know that there's no one right way to write an essay (repeat this over and over again to yourself). Successful personal statements cover an incredible range of topics and are composed in an impressive array of literary styles. Speaking honestly, clearly, and succinctly about your passions is the surest way to success.

During the course of your academic career, you will be writing more of these essays than you care to count. Colleges and universities require up to three for admissions. Almost every scholarship worth winning requires at least one. You may find you even have to write one for your first postcollege job. So what's the point? Do not reject a summer program simply because it requires a personal statement. You might as well get into the habit now, because the more you write, the better they get. And who knows, an essay you write for summer program admission may well serve as your ticket into college.

—— **Quick Tips** ——
To Type or Print?

When possible, a typewritten essay is preferred. If you compose the essay on a computer, it's perfectly acceptable to either write "please see attached" on the application or neatly cut the computer page and paste it directly on the application form.

If you handwrite your essay, write extremely neatly and be sure to proofread for spelling and grammar mistakes.

─────── **Quick Tips** ───────

The Dreaded Writing Sample

- Read the essay question carefully and make sure you address it fully in your essay.

- Draw from your own experiences, preferably highlighting a unique activity or episode from your life.

- Make sure your introduction and conclusion summarize your essay's central ideas.

- Use your own voice and a writing style you're comfortable with.

- Have a friend or a teacher read your essay so they can offer suggestions.

- Spell-check and carefully proofread your essay after your final draft.

There's no foolproof method for writing a winner essay, but there are a few basic strategies you can employ. Read the essay question carefully, and make sure you answer it. Write about something you know about and care about—it will make your statement more believable. And when possible, choose a topic that is unique or out-of-the-ordinary. Admissions committees review stacks and stacks of essays, and they quickly tire of reading the same old story.

Paying attention to language as well as content is key. Use your own voice. Trying to sound like a stodgy old English teacher will give your essay an awkward feel and will prevent the admissions committee from getting to know the real you. After all, it is a *personal* statement and should reflect who you are as faithfully as possible. The following editing tools may seem like common sense, but they're easy to forget when your mind is dreaming of summer adventure: polish openings and closings, they leave lasting impressions; check every paragraph for transitions; read your essay aloud; ask a friend, teacher, or parent to peruse your essay and offer suggestions. Put the statement aside for several days and look at it again with fresh eyes. And of course, spellcheck and proofread. Remember, neatness counts.

There are entire books written about the dreaded personal statement. If you're really nervous or really stuck and find yourself staring into a blank computer screen for hours, you may want to hit the library or bookstore and check out one of these books. They often provide sample essays. But remember, you're the best person to help yourself. Looking at sample essays for hints about structure is fine, but if you're looking to them for sources of essay topics, you're in trouble. You have to come up with that by yourself or your essay will sound trite and cliché.

TRANSCRIPTS

Many summer programs, especially ones with academic components, will ask for high school transcripts—a composite list of all the classes you have taken thus far and the grades you received in each. Transcripts often list academic honors earned as a result of your grade point average as well. At most schools, transcripts are very easy to obtain. Your guidance or college counselor can tell you how to get one—a secretary will probably prepare it for you. Make friends with that secretary. You will need to get transcripts for many college and scholarship applications down the road.

INTERVIEWS

The vast majority of summer programs, even ones with competitive admissions, do not require an interview. However, there are some that do. If you find yourself applying to a program that requires an interview, rejoice. You not only have a chance to elaborate on your personal statement, you also get unbeatable practice for college and job interviews a few years hence.

Preparing for the Interview

The key to a good interview is being prepared, enthusiastic, and confident. To prepare, read the summer program brochure carefully and speak to students who have participated in the program during the past two years. This will give you a clear sense of the program's philosophy and goals, and therefore the personal talents and experience you want to emphasize during your interview. Next, review the list of extracurricular activities, honors, and awards you have compiled for the people serving as your references and letter writers. Which most closely relate to the summer program for which you're interviewing? It's important not to barrage your interviewer with an endless stream of activities. This makes your commitment to each one come across as superficial. Instead, select two or three important activities and prepare to talk about these. Depending on the length of your interview and your interviewer's interest in a particular activity, award, or experience, you may not even get to them all. That is perfectly fine.

Next, generate a list of questions you think the interviewer might ask, and prepare your responses. It's always easier to answer an anticipated question. If you're applying for a leadership program, possible questions might include: What is your definition of a leader? What are the strengths and weaknesses of your personal leadership style? How do you think you could benefit from this program? Regardless of what summer program you're applying for, most interviewers will say "tell me about yourself." This is a tough one. Again, being prepared helps. Think about two or three things you can highlight and practice your answer. Don't memorize it word for word—you want to come across as natural—but have a pretty good idea of what you're going to say.

Once you have thoroughly prepared, practice. Out loud. Draft a friend or family member and ask her to help you role play the interview. "Interviewers" should ask the questions you have prepared—as well as several of their own—in random order. You may feel somewhat silly, but try to maintain your roles throughout the exercise. It's much less embarrassing and far more productive if you catch problems or areas for improvement during a practice run. When you have completed the mock interview, ask your "interviewer" to provide feedback. Did you sound confident and enthusiastic? Did you make eye contact and smile? Did you use any word or phrase too frequently? After receiving feedback, repeat the exercise.

If you have access to a video camera, you might want to try videotaping your mock interviews. It's amazing how quickly you can catch errors like slumping shoulders and an excess of "umms" or "likes" when you rewind the tape and press "Play." Many people find it easier to address weaknesses when they see exactly what they are doing wrong.

If all else fails and you cannot find someone with whom to role-play and/or videotape, write your questions on note cards, shuffle them, and stand before a full-length mirror. As you will soon discover, having answers prepared in your head is not quite the same as speaking them aloud.

Once you have prepared for the interview, it's time to select something to wear. No matter how informal the interview, you should look your best. Once again, neatness counts. Be sure to select an outfit that makes you look and feel your age, and of course, make sure you're clean and well groomed. How dressed-up should you be? It will depend on the program, the setting for your interview, and your own personal preference. For young women, a dress, skirt, or nice dress pants should be fine. For young men, slacks and a dress shirt, possibly with a tie, are appropriate. It's always better to be overdressed than underdressed, but you should also wear something that makes you feel comfortable. The last thing you need is to be tripping over high heels.

Surviving the Interview

You're well prepared, so relax. Some feelings of nervousness are inevitable and will work to your advantage—it may prevent you from slipping into casual speech. If you allow yourself to get overanxious, however, you're likely to stumble over your words. So take a deep breath before you begin, and another one whenever you feel your stomach start to tighten. Breathing will loosen your body, and that is key because body language is vital to an interview. To come off as confident and interested, sit up straight, look people in the eye, shake hands firmly. This helps in multiple ways. If you adopt good posture, you embrace that "adult mode" and will be less likely to slip into slang. And if you look your interviewer in the eye, you will be able to sense when you should elaborate on your answer and when you should pause for another question.

Interviews can be difficult because you need to strike a balance between being modest and being conceited. It's essential that you talk about your accomplishments and awards, but you must do so in a way that does not make you sound arrogant (which presumably you aren't). How can you do this? Each person must find a way that works with his or her personality. Often you can express awareness of your fortune (having the opportunity to attend a superb school, having the benefit of early exposure to music, etc.), and of your efforts to help others achieve. You might also describe personal sacrifices you have made to improve yourself and your skills over the years. You'll impress the interviewer with your self-awareness, a sign of maturity.

One more word of caution: When you discuss your activities, remember not to be self-centered. In other words, you may know that EHEC stands for the East High Environmental Club, but someone outside your small school community will not. Even honors from national organizations may be unfamiliar to some interviewers. If you say you organized a weekend nutrition workshop for teenagers as part of your Girl Scout Gold Award, you may need to explain that the Gold Award is the highest award in Girl Scouting, similar to the Eagle Award for Boy Scouts.

When the interviewer pauses to allow you to ask questions, seize the opportunity. This will show the interviewer that you have thought seriously about the program and that you're as interested as she is in determining whether it's the right program for you. You will also get useful information missing from brochures and websites.

Where do parents fit in? Well, that is a good question. Again, it will depend on the nature and setting of the interview. Some programs may specify that parents should be available for questions. Others may request that parents refrain from participating. If the program provides no such information, consider this: Students who confidently stride in by themselves look more mature than those who cling to their parents' side. The very nature of summer programs encourages independence, so it's probably best to arrive solo, or at least leave your parents in the car. Know that they are supportive of you even in their absence. If Mom or Dad insists on coming, do not scowl or make excuses when you greet your interviewer. Interviews are an opportunity to demonstrate confidence and adult behavior. You cannot afford to jeopardize that.

Follow Up

You've heard it before: Thank-you notes are a must. It's best to write a thank you note as soon as you return home from the interview, when your memory is still fresh. However, if you're feeling down because you don't feel you performed to your potential, wait a few hours or even a day until your mood lightens. Then compose a (positive) thank you.

Thank-you notes can be simple. You merely want to show that you're interested in the opportunity, enjoyed meeting the interviewer, and are a responsible and considerate teenager. Handwritten notes are fine. In fact, they are more personable than typed ones. Make sure that you spell the name of your interviewer correctly and that you:

- Mention something discussed in the interview (this should trigger the interviewer's memory).

- Express appreciation that the interviewer took time to meet with you.

- Reiterate your interest in the summer program and your eagerness to hear the final decision.

The Phone Interview

If you're asked to do an interview by phone, prepare in advance as you would for an in-person interview: Generate a list of potential questions, think about the key strengths you want to convey, and enlist friends or family members to assist with a mock interview. In addition, you may want to jot down the main ideas of your anticipated answers. Since you will be out of the interviewer's sight, you can refer to these prompts during your interview—a real plus. Be careful not to become dependent on your notes, however. You'll want to sound natural on the phone, which you definitely won't do if you read prepared statements.

Because phone interviews eliminate the element of body language, you should also try to articulate nonverbal cues. Where a nod or smile may do the trick during an in-person interview, they get you nowhere on the phone. Try saying "mm-hmm" or "I agree" instead. And since you won't be able to watch your interviewer for clues on when to expand or curtail your answer, listen closely; voice intonation can provide similar clues.

Don't forget your thank-yous! Make sure to thank the interviewer before you hang up, and write a prompt thank-you note after the phone call.

Quick Tips
The Interview

- Be prepared. Think of questions the interviewer might ask and practice your responses.
- Make a list of the activities and personal traits you want to mention during the interview.
- Have a friend play the role of the interviewer, and go through a mock interview.
- Wear neat clothing to the interview. If you're a girl, make sure your hair is out of your face. If you're a boy, remember to shave.
- If you're not sure whether or not to invite your parents along for the ride, remember that independence is a key element that most summer programs look for in their participants.
- Make eye contact with the interviewer and maintain good posture throughout the interview.
- Don't dwell on one subject for too long. You want to be able to touch on more than one or two of your admirable qualities.
- Temper your list of accomplishments with a dose of modesty. Don't toot your own horn too loud, or the interviewer might become deaf to your strong points as an applicant.
- Make sure your interviewer is always clear on what you're talking about and its relevance to the interview. Give him all the necessary background on your activities.
- Ask a few questions. Besides gaining some valuable information from the interviewer, you're also demonstrating your interest in his program.
- If your interview is over the phone, have a few notes to refer to during the call.
- Remember to thank the interviewer. After you rock the interview, you don't want to mess up your chances of acceptance by being rude.

Auditions

Most summer programs in the arts do not require an audition. However, some of the more competitive programs require an audition either in-person or via video or audio tape. If you're considering a program in the arts, turn to chapter eight for a complete discussion of the auditioning process.

A WORLD OF CHOICES

Now for the fun part . . . choosing a program. There are hundreds of summer programs out there, from expensive, month-long, preprofessional courses close to home, to low-cost, week-long, service-oriented programs halfway around the globe. If you're not quite sure what type of program you want, read through the following chapters, which discuss various types of programs: academic, international, community service, outdoor adventure, athletic, arts, and leadership programs. Each chapter offers helpful advice on what to expect from each type of program, as well as tips on how to get in, from admissions directors, faculty members, and past participants.

Near the end of each chapter, you'll find a list of organizations offering programs in a particular subject area. To learn more about any of these programs, just flip to the Program Directory in Part III of this book, which contains a detailed description of each program. It's easy to find the program you're looking for: All of the directory listings are in alphabetical order according to the name of the sponsoring organization. (*Example:* Say you're interested in academic study abroad programs. After reading through chapter four, "Study Abroad and International Travel Programs," choose a program from the list at the end of the chapter—for instance, Camp Norway, which is sponsored by Sons of Norway. Then look up Sons of Norway in the Program Directory, and voilà, you now have a detailed description of Camp Norway and any other programs offered by Sons of Norway.)

If you already have an organization in mind but don't know what types of summer programs it offers, you can go straight to the Program Directory. Since the listings are alphabetized by organization, you can quickly see all of the programs each organization sponsors. (*Example:* You live just two miles from Stanford University in California and would like to know what programs Stanford will be offering for the summer. Just look up Stanford University in the Program Directory, and *bam!*, you now have detailed descriptions of various programs sponsored by Stanford.)

You can also look through the indexes at the back of the book to find programs that fit your particular needs. Cost, location, and program duration are important factors for most applicants. Using these indexes to target California programs under $1,000, for example, is a quick and easy way to create a customized list of programs that bear further investigation.

At the very end of each chapter, you'll find a section called "Enriching Your Summer"—lists of websites, books, and movies you can use to further explore the topics discussed in each chapter. Some of these resources are educational, while others are just for fun, but all of them can help give you a fresh perspective on the subject of your prospective summer program.

Summer may feel like it's still a long way off, but it'll be here before you know it. And many programs have application deadlines several months before the programs actually begin. So let's get started!

Part II: Types of Programs

Academic Programs

OVERVIEW

If you decide to attend an academic summer program, you're in luck. With research universities, two- and four-year colleges, prep schools, and private educational camps all sponsoring programs, there are literally hundreds of opportunities to choose from. While programs differ in size, intensity, and educational focus, all strive to create environments in which learning is fun. Your knowledge of academic subjects will grow, but that's only the tip of the iceberg.

On-campus programs teach essential college-survival skills: how to research substantial papers, study for exams worth 40 to 60 percent of your grade, get along with eccentric roommates, pull all-nighters, and perhaps most important, find restaurants that deliver pizza and wings at 2 A.M. Not surprisingly, most students find they learn as much about themselves as they do about microorganisms, linear algebra, and Margaret Sanger.

"SHOULD I DO AN ACADEMIC PROGRAM?"

There's no question that academic summer programs are the closest approximation to college life you can find as a high school student. Academic programs are great for curing the "smart kid blues": If you're bored by high school classes but intrigued by learning, attending an academic summer session can be a thrilling way to spend the summer. If you enjoy meeting people and thrive in social atmospheres, academic summer programs will yield enough new friends to keep you writing letters and sending e-mails the rest of your high school career. And if you feel socially doomed at school because classmates view you as a brain first and person second, get ready to watch your popularity soar. Academic programs bring unimaginable social freedom. In an environment in which being smart is hip, you'll make friends and foster relationships like you never have before.

You may find that summer program participants are like you in other ways, too. If you attend a school where you're one of only a handful who looks different or worships differently than the rest of the class, you'll be pleasantly surprised by the diversity of race, religion, and ethnic backgrounds represented in summer programs, and on college campuses in general. Regardless of your background, university summer programs allow you to experience the excitement of living and learning amidst a diverse community of scholars. That's right ... scholars. You're in the big leagues now.

But academic programs are not for everyone. If you have limited time and many extracurricular interests, prioritize your summer goals before applying to an academic program. Because most academic programs are at least several weeks long, you may not have time for a job, volunteer work, or other programs during that summer. It is also essential to evaluate your willingness to spend long, sunny afternoons in the library before committing to an academic program. If you end the school year feeling stressed and burned out by final exams, you may not be ready to start summer school a few weeks later. Academic summer programs are fun, but don't kid yourself: They are a lot of work.

SELECTING A PROGRAM

Once you have decided to pursue an academic summer program, you're ready to apply. But where to? Perhaps the first thing to consider is whether content—the classes you take—or location is your top concern. Good cases can be made for both. Some people use academic summer programs as a tool in their college search process. As a high schooler at a New Hampshire boarding school, Sarah Catapano-Friedman was already versed in dorm life and accustomed to being away from home. She attended the Yale Summer Program the summer before her senior year at Phillips Exeter in order to decide if she would apply to Yale early-decision. What did she learn? Not only that she wanted to attend, but that she was fully capable of meeting the university's academic standards: "Yale Summer Programs gave me an excellent opportunity to take advantage of [the university's] facilities and faculty, but also of the Yalies in my classes. During the summer, I became a Yalie, or at least discovered that I could become one."

For those who don't yet have a list of college choices, on-campus programs can still be helpful in the college search. Attending the Indiana State University Summer Honors Seminar—located on a large, bustling campus—will give you a different feel for college life than selecting the Davidson College July Experience. As Daryl Tiggle, associate director of admissions at Union College in New York, said, "University summer programs allow students to try on a school for size. Maybe they will go to one or two

throughout their whole high school career, but they can use those schools as points of comparison. So if they do a program at a large university, they know how that feels and can compare that when they visit a small college."

High school students attending public schools or college preparatory day schools may find attending a boarding school's summer session another way to sample the kind of academic and social life common to college campuses. Leah Pollak, a former teaching intern at the Choate Rosemary Hall Summer Session, said the school's Connecticut grounds provided a beautiful setting reminding her of a small liberal arts college like Williams or Amherst. "Classes are very small and students get a lot of individual attention," Pollak said. "It's really a great opportunity to learn."

Many college transfer students say they left their original institution because it was "too big and impersonal" or "too small and claustrophobic." While attending a summer program as a high school student, you can't truly replicate the college experience—for one, all schools have significantly fewer students on campus during the summer months—but it may help you decide which environment feels most comfortable.

There are other ways to go about selecting a program, however. Especially if you're a freshman or sophomore, it may be premature to choose a program as a means of testing out college campuses. One of the best things about taking classes at a college, university, or well-regarded (and endowed) boarding school is that they offer facilities and equipment the average high school simply cannot: state-of-the art science laboratories, internationally renowned art galleries, and even 120-foot research vessels sailing at sea.

Along with unparalleled resources, these institutions attract some of the world's top scholars, teachers, and students, and their expertise ranges from astrophysics to Zulu. Bored with English, science, and history? Try Latino poetry, physiological psychology, and "The birth of the American film industry." Then add elementary Czech, Russian lit (in translation), and an introduction to gay and lesbian studies. Sound any better? Naturally, there are also excellent foundation courses—from basic college math to freshman prose writing—that can supplement high school lessons. Whichever route you choose, the possibilities are endless. If you have a passion, a curiosity, or an eagerness to expand your intellectual horizons, go for it! Comb through brochures and catalogs until you find the most intriguing classes.

——— **Expert Advice** ———

"I most recommend summer opportunities that allow students to explore [college] major or career interests (i.e., architecture, ecology, marine biology, film, creative writing). It helps tremendously in focusing them in the college process so that they think more about what they are looking for in a school, a program, etc. It can save kids from getting on the 'wrong track' in their college search."

—Cathy Nabbefeld, director of college counseling, Colorado Academy

The Preprofessional Track

Some universities offer more structured precollege summer programs emphasizing career exploration. These "preprofessional" camps—usually featuring law, business, or engineering—combine academic work with field trips, guest speakers, and occasionally, internships. They range in length, but many run only six days, allowing you to combine them with other summer experiences.

Preprofessional programs are great for people seeking a deeper understanding of both the daily life of a professional and the academic and career-related training required for the field. If you ultimately attend a large university for postsecondary work, you may be able to put this knowledge to use when deciding whether to pursue a degree in business or engineering. If a liberal arts college figures in your postgraduation plans, however, you should know that business and prelaw majors are nonexistent, and that even if you declare yourself premed, you'll be required to complete a major "in the liberal arts tradition" as well. So if you're intrigued by habeas corpus and anxious to learn how the courts function, apply for a program. But if you think you want to be a lawyer—eventually—and would rather spend your summer studying linguistics, performing Shakespeare, or whitewater rafting in Colorado, don't feel compelled to attend a prelaw program. It's important to explore all your interests, and there's time enough to worry about careers.

While almost any type of academic major can prepare you for the kind of thought process needed in law school, graduate programs in engineering and medicine demand an earlier commitment. Because universities with strong humanities programs may not be equally competitive in the sciences (and vice versa), it is helpful, although certainly not necessary, to know you want to be an engineer or M.D. before applying to college. To make your way to medical school four years after high school graduation, you really should begin preparing the moment you enter college.

Expert Advice

"Science at Sea (SAS) is open to students who are fifteen to eighteen years old. The program focuses on the marine environment—its scientific nature, its historical and literary significance, how we sail across it, and what it is like to live and work at sea. For the first eleven days of the program, students live and study at SEA's campus in Woods Hole, Massachusetts. They then spend the final ten days of the program onboard one of SEA's sailing oceanographic research vessels, the SSV Westward or the SSV Corwith Cramer. Students get immersed in all aspects of life aboard ship and participate in all operations of the vessel, collecting scientific data, setting and striking sails, navigating in the waters around Cape Cod, and helping in the ship's galley and engine room. The research vessels operate 24 hours per day [and] students are assigned to a watch group of eight people, with whom they rotate through the 24-hour schedule. There's always one watch on duty at sea—and there's lots to see and do!"

—Audrey Meyer, dean, Sea Education Association (SEA)

Student Scoop

"My AP biology teacher came across the University of Colorado Cancer Fellowship in an attempt to place me in an internship involving biotechnology or virology. Daily, I went into the lab, discussed the previous day's experiment with my preceptor, planned the day's lab, and analyzed the results of the lab. Usually, for some reason or another, I had to throw out my data. If the instrument settings were correct, the concentrations were wrong. If the dye took to the cells, the cells died. My favorite example of the frustration of laboratory research involved a few measly yeast cells. They somehow found their way into my lymphoma culture. I spent a week decontaminating the hood and thawing new cells. The rest of the summer I spent more time washing my hands to avoid another catastrophe than I did collecting usable data. Should I consider scientific research as a potential career, I would definitely have to consider my level of patience."

—Kelly Wilhelm, participant, University of Colorado/American Cancer Society Student Cancer Fellowship

Being able to start a premed program on schedule—complete with freshman biology, chemistry, and calculus your first year—is one advantage to knowing your interests in advance. There is another. Undergraduate course work for premed students, as for engineers, is rigorous. University science courses tend to be extremely different from high school ones, primarily because students have access to research laboratories. Therefore, it can be difficult to gauge your ability and desire to complete the premed track while still in high school. Many, many people start their college careers as premed and end up substituting English for chem, political science for bio, and history for calculus by the beginning of sophomore year. Freshman science classes are used as "weed outs," and curves on exams and labs are notoriously brutal. You can save yourself much agony (not to mention disappointing grades) if you learn you prefer essays to problem sets while still in high school.

Then again, a summer program in science or engineering may prove that you can not only handle college science, but that you love doing it. If you have the opportunity to spend a summer working in a research lab, you're lucky indeed. The transition from high school labs—even AP ones—is challenging. You'll gain a real and rare advantage in your college premed courses by working with laboratory technicians or researchers while still in high school. You may even have the opportunity to do actual research—rather than lab exercises—which brings a whole other realm of accomplishment.

Cynthia Osterling spent the summer before her senior year in high school participating in a 10-week program that places high school and college students interested in the sciences at the

Student Scoop

"Some of the work I did in my science program I really didn't understand at the time, but now, taking organic chemistry, I realize 'oh my gosh, I did that as a 16- or 17-year-old.' I was using all this advanced equipment [at Denison University's summer program] I'm not using now as an undergrad at Notre Dame. When you're in small [summer program] groups, you get a lot of opportunity to work one-on-one with professors. Professors really like the students because they're eager to learn, and they teach to that."

—Erin Dunnigan, participant, Summer Science Institute at Denison University

Jackson Laboratory in Bar Harbor, Maine. Between nine and five, students work on their own research projects under the guidance of one of the lab's scientists. In the evening, a bus returns student researchers to their living quarters, an old mansion named "High Seas," where they eat dinner and organize their own social activities. Osterling said that while the program was overwhelming at first, it provided a fantastic introduction to research science. Her project involved classification of obese mouse mutations and at the end of the program, she presented her results at a research symposium. "For anybody who is at all interested in sciences, it is a really wonderful opportunity," Osterling said. "I definitely felt like I knew what I was doing in labs more than other people did my first year at college. This year I'm working on a senior thesis and I feel like Jackson Lab kind of gave me the opportunity to see what it was like to do a research project—how to organize [and how to do] statistics."

Summer program research projects are largely self-directed, but you will always have a supervising scientist or lab technician. This gives you a great opportunity to secure a letter of recommendation from someone who can comment on your motivation and ability to work independently.

CHECKING OUT THE SCENE

All on-campus academic programs provide an introduction to college life, whether you spend the summer living and learning in a boarding school, university, or precollege environment. Which one you choose could depend on the specific classes or opportunities offered or the degree of independence (social and academic) you're ready to handle. Fantastic summers begin with programs that meet your needs and interests. So before you select a summer program based on its prestigious name or beachside location, consider the following: the program's daily schedule (again, academic and social); the program rules and regulations; and the program's method of evaluating and granting credit for academic work.

Schedules, Rules, and Regs

The Boarding School Program

Boarding schools operate the same way during summer sessions as they do during the academic year. There are times set aside for study and times set aside for play. Classes generally meet Monday through Friday as well as half a day on Saturday, making six evenings a week "school nights."

At most boarding school programs, students are expected to eat breakfast, arrive promptly to class, participate in physical education, report to a supervised study hall, and be in bed with lights out at the appointed hour. While structured, the boarding school schedule also allows for socialization. Campuses are small and safe—you'll learn your way around in the matter of days—and students make friends quickly.

The University Summer Session

At large universities' summer sessions, daily activities such as eating, sleeping, going to class, and doing homework are students' own responsibility. While there may be a recommended curfew, there are no bed checks or study halls for high schoolers to report for. Students are usually housed in special, high school-only dorms with counselors, proctors, or resident advisors (R.A.'s) to answer questions, monitor students' physical and emotional well being, organize optional activities and excursions, and prevent alcohol or other drugs from entering the building.

University classes meet Monday through Friday, but depending on your individual course schedule, you may have classes from two to four days a week. A support network of counselors and advisors is available, but you're expected to adjust to college-level work and social freedom with little assistance. It is up to you to fail or succeed, as you will.

The Precollege Experience

Supervision and structured time at specially designated "precollege" programs fall somewhere in between that of boarding schools and university summer sessions. While not all precollege programs are the same, many provide a mixture of required and optional activities. Most have a curfew, and supervision may or may not be strict.

Elizabeth Reynolds, coordinator of the University of Delaware Summer College, said she strives to make the precollege experience at Delaware mirror daily college life. "We try to make the experience as close to what it is like for a freshman as possible," she said. "But because they are minors, we have to give them a little more supervision. We set curfews for them to be in the rooms at night—eleven on weeknights, one on weekends—and the R.A.'s check to be sure that they are on their single-sex floor. But they can stay up all night if they want to. In the beginning they do that, and they get tired. They learn that maybe it's not such a good idea to be writing a paper at four in the morning. The experience is useful for that first [college] semester when everything comes at once."

Student Scoop

"I remember the night two friends and I went for pizza at 2 A.M., later than the recommended 1 A.M. check-in. Having been fed late-night New Haven horror stories, one of my friends insisted I carry my field hockey stick into town. Walking up Broadway to Broadway Pizza, we noted only a police car—no muggers lurking in the dark. We were the ones out of place!"

—Sarah Catapano-Friedman, participant, Yale Summer Program

Because precollege programs are held at colleges or universities, their campuses are generally larger and often more urban than those at boarding schools. This provides students with greater freedom. But as at a boarding school summer program, all activities are geared especially for high school students, and a large staff of counselors stands ready to help you make your way.

Academic Angles

Boarding School Summer Sessions and the Precollege Experience

Boarding school and precollege summer programs provide a more gradual transition from high school to college, academically as well as socially. Teachers at boarding school summer sessions are usually members of the school's regular faculty or high school teachers from other boarding and preparatory schools. At some programs, college students also assist as teaching interns. Because boarding school instructors regularly teach high school students, they are attuned to high school trends and habits and may be more supportive and patient than college professors.

In most—although not all—precollege programs on college or university campuses, instructors are either full- or part-time professors or graduate student teaching assistants (T.A.'s) who modify their courses for high school students. While they may not be as practiced as high school teachers in presenting material to teenagers, these college instructors are nonetheless conscious of their students' age and academic background.

Student Scoop

"We got in a lot of trouble one time because girls weren't allowed to go into guys' rooms and vice versa, and we had curfew at midnight on weekdays and 1:00 on weekends and you couldn't go out of your room even to go to the bathroom after that. And so my roommate and I and the guy next door went across the hall to a guy's room and we were playing spades from two in the morning until 3:30. When my roommate and I were going back to our room, we saw our counselor leave his room. He saw us, so we knew we were in trouble. He asked us what we were doing, and we said 'nothing.' Then he went to the guys' room and talked to them for a while and found out that we had been in there playing spades. So the counselor talked to them for about two hours, during which time the other guy, who lived next door to us, was in their closet because he didn't live there and he couldn't go out of his room past curfew. The counselor was telling them about these rooms on the fourth floor that they could go to if they wanted to be with their girlfriends, which is what he thought we were, but the guy in the closet just wanted him to leave so he could go home. So the next day we all had conferences with the head coordinator of the program and we got grounded for two days, which meant you had to report in every hour from seven o'clock until midnight. Everybody kept making cracks about that guy coming out of the closet."

—Vicky Arias, participant, Georgetown Summer Program for High School Seniors

---

─────────────── Expert Advice ───────────────

"Programs can also boost academic confidence and give students new perspectives on learning because teaching styles are likely to be very different and the peer group is very different than students are accustomed to in high school. Instead of measuring oneself entirely against the students with which they have grown up, students compare themselves to a national or international group. What they know and feel comfortable with knowing is not what they are going to be up against in college. Students begin to approach things in interesting and different ways that can better prepare them for college. They get a preview of the peer group they might be with."

—Jane Schoenfeld, Independent School Placement Service of St. Louis

But make no mistake. Whether modified for high school students or not, the academic work at boarding school summer sessions and precollege programs is challenging. Many summer program courses are accelerated, covering a 13-week semester's worth of material in an 8- or 10-week period. Readings, assignments, and tests come rapidly. Academically, students attending boarding school and precollege programs face many of the same challenges as high school students enrolled in university summer sessions.

For students seeking a less rigorous academic program, some boarding schools and precollege programs offer the alternative option of taking enrichment-only classes. These courses are designed to encourage intellectual exploration and often are not graded. As you might guess, selecting this option will give you more time for recreation and socializing.

The University Summer Session

If you select a summer session at a university that does not offer a special precollege experience, you'll take college classes with college students, completing the same assignments and being graded on the same academic scale. You don't have to show anyone your summer transcript, but you should be prepared to do college-level work in a collegiate atmosphere. There will be significantly more reading than you're accustomed to in high school, and your final grade will probably be determined by no more than two or three assignments—two exams and perhaps a paper or problem sets. If you're ready for that, fine. If not, there are other options. Freshmen at the nation's most competitive colleges and universities often find the adjustment from high school work to college work difficult, so there's no reason to feel you have to handle it as a 16- or 17-year-old.

There are advantages and disadvantages to all three types of on-campus programs, and depending on your age, interests, and prior experience living away from home, you can select the one best for you. Regardless of which option you choose, however, consider leaving your high school friends behind. It always feels safer to travel with someone you know, but most students agree that the best part of an academic summer program is meeting a wide variety of interesting people. It's harder to branch out when you can just fall back on friends you know from home. Going solo will force you to make friends of strangers; you won't be disappointed.

Quick Tips

The Perfect Summer Setting . . . for Studying

Choosing an academic program has as much to do with environment as with subject matter. Keep these points in mind during your research:

Boarding Schools:

- The staff will be familiar with the needs of high school students since most of the faculty members teach at the sponsoring school—or others similar to it—year round.
- The material presented will be geared towards high school students, with tests, quizzes, and homework similar to what you're used to during the school year.
- Their small campuses make it safe and easy to get around and are usually in beautiful natural settings.
- A set schedule means less independence, but also less personal responsibility for time management, etc. They tell you when to eat and sleep, but without the military strictness. Expect a curfew.

University Summer Sessions:

- Remember that you'll be in classes with university students and be expected to keep up with regular college coursework.
- Less structured coursework allows you more freedom.
- Relaxed rules also mean more social freedom. During the summer session, you'll be treated as a regular university student, leaving your schedule—besides classes—entirely up to you.
- The university will have an accessible support network of counselors and RAs.
- Most of your coursework during these sessions will qualify for college credit.

Precollege Programs:

- These programs are the middle ground between heavily supervised boarding school programs and sink-or-swim university summer sessions.
- They may or may not have a strict schedule.
- They may or may not have a set course syllabus.
- They may or may not offer academic credit.
- They may or may not provide structured social activities in addition to special academic classes.

MIXING AND MINGLING

Summer programs are extraordinary in part because no one there knows or cares if you had braces, thick glasses, and a bad haircut in sixth grade. At a high school summer program, you can forge a new identity, become the person you always wanted to be. Leave all your inhibitions and hangups behind! So you're usually shy? Well, no one here knows that, so you don't have to be shy. Are you always the class clown? Do you want to be? Because if you don't, you can try a new role.

Academic programs attract some of the nation's best and brightest. Being smart is par for the course, not something that makes you stand out like a sore thumb. Many students say they find soulmates at academic programs—people who understand them, think like them, and know how to have a good time.

And the people at academic programs are not just smart. They come from all over the state, country, and world. They attend large urban high schools, suburban private schools, and exclusive preparatory academies. They live in worldly cities and small country towns. They are Asian, African American, Latino, and white. They worship as Catholics, Muslims, Protestants, Jews, and Hindus. Or they identify with no religion or faith. They are gay and bisexual as well as straight. In short, academic summer programs are a microcosm of the college population. You'll find you have much in common with other participants—your love for learning and enthusiasm for the program—but you'll also find many differences. This is precisely what makes attending an academic summer program such an exciting, life-changing experience.

The Dorm

Because most academic programs operate on a school campus, you'll be treated to dorm life. If you've never experienced it before, you're in for the ride of your life. From failed electrical equipment to cramped quarters and zany roommates, dorms are an adventure indeed. The high concentration of people is perhaps the most characteristic aspect of a college or boarding school dorm. Think of it this way. If you're home studying on a school night and get stuck on a geometry problem or forget the page numbers of your Spanish assignment, you call up a classmate. Can't concentrate on your Sophocles because you're thinking about Friday's basketball game? Back on the phone. But move school to a dorm and you're suddenly surrounded by your best friends day and night. It can get claustrophobic at times, but there's nothing like having a roommate with whom you can laugh over the day's trials and triumphs.

Assuming you have followed this book's advice and set off to a summer program by yourself, you won't know anyone there. Because everyone is in the same situation, friendships form rapidly. If you're openminded and determined to have the summer of your life, you'll make friends quickly. Be social, especially during the first few days. Smile at everyone, introduce yourself to as many people as possible, and keep the door of your dorm room wide open whenever you're in the room hanging out. People will always stop in to say hello. (Of course, you should always lock the door when you're out of the room.)

Being considerate of others is essential to keeping the friends you make. If you have a roommate, you'll probably be living in close quarters, and this can be a big change for people accustomed to

——— **Student Scoop** ———

"We lived in the dorms and it was really cool because you got to see how the whole dorm environment went."

—Michelle Benitez, participant, Penn Summer Science Academy at the University of Pennsylvania

their own bedroom. Be good-natured about sharing desks, shelves, and closet space—you'll be living together for several weeks or months. If one person listens to music while studying and the other needs quiet, talk it over and find a compromise early. The same goes for level of room cleanliness. Perhaps the music lover can wear earphones and the neat freak can learn to deal with several tee shirts scattered about the floor as long as the trash is taken out regularly. You don't have to be best friends with your roommate, but for your own sanity, it is essential that you get along with him or her.

One of the easiest ways to sour a relationship with your roommate and peers is to be academically competitive with them. Most academic summer programs have admissions requirements, so the applicant pool is self-selected to begin with. Everyone wants to do well and is accustomed to success. Most are used to being the academic stars of the class. While it is exhilarating to be in a group of such dynamic, intelligent people, it can also be intimidating. It is important to remember that summer program students come from a wide range of educational backgrounds and may be differently prepared for the summer program's rigorous academic work. Some students will have benefited from preparation at highly competitive high schools, others will not have.

Be supportive of other students in the program rather than competing with them. At many colleges, it is considered bad form to discuss grades. That's a good policy to adopt at a summer program. But don't confuse academic competition with the friendly exchange of ideas in discussion and debate. It's not cool to be aggressively competitive in academic work, but most summer program environments embrace intellectual exploration. There's no danger of being labeled a "nerd" for having a genuine interest in the program and its classes. After all, that's what you came for.

ADJUSTING TO PRECOLLEGE LIFE

Academic bliss and social utopia. No wonder there doesn't seem to be enough hours in the day. College life (and hence, precollege life) demands good time management. College students are fond of the saying: "We work hard and play hard." The trick is knowing when to do which. There are times—like when the whole floor congregates in the common room across the hall—when you simply have to throw up your hands and put away your reading. Spontaneous "study breaks" are moments to treasure. However there are other times—like the day before a midterm—when you have to put on blinders and walk right by the Frisbee-throwing people in the courtyard. The library is calling your name. When you reach that palace of books, study. Going to the library and then making ten trips to the water fountain each hour is unproductive. Not only are you getting nothing done, you're not with your friends, so the time is doubly wasted. Study when you're studying, and when you're not, have fun.

One thing you learn when living with classmates is that it takes people different lengths of time to do the same amount of work. One person may need ten hours to read a book well, another person only six. If you fall at the longer end, never fear. It doesn't mean you're any less capable, it just means you have to manage time judiciously. Finding a place where you study effectively is key. Some people can read sitting under a tree in the middle of campus. Others need to be in their dorm room where they can wear "studying clothes" and spread everything out on a desk. Still others need to sequester themselves in a library carrel. Finding a spot where you work productively expedites learning, leaving more time to play.

Regardless of where you study, however, do it regularly. Most summer programs teach college-style classes different from anything you've seen before. In theory, high school Advanced Placement classes are college courses. However, many AP instructors teach college material in a high-school style. In other words, they give quizzes, tests, and nightly homework assignments. Such things are nonexistent in the vast majority of college classes. A syllabus will list reading for the entire course and indicate which books complement each lecture or class meeting. Because there's nothing forcing you to complete the work on time, it can be tempting to skip reading for several days, even weeks. Resist. Once you fall behind, it can be difficult to catch up in time for midterms and finals (which, by the way, might account for 50 percent of your grade), and it's impossible to make intelligent contributions to class discussion if you haven't read the material. Learn to skim if necessary.

While you read, write, and calculate, remember that academic summer programs are supposed to be fun. This is your summer vacation. While you want to make wise decisions that will help you prepare for college and life in general, you shouldn't torture yourself. If you feel like playing volleyball on the lawn, do it. Don't stress too much about your grades. As we discussed earlier, you're not required to send them to anyone. If you do well, fantastic—colleges will be pleased to see your transcript. And, if you're in a small class where the professor or instructor knows you well, you can ask for a letter of recommendation. On the other hand, if you struggle a bit but feel you learned a lot about life—if not Napoleon III—you have still come out ahead. Better to falter a little now than during your first year at college. You'll be that much more prepared to make the most of your freshman year.

Oh, and don't forget to sleep. It makes everything better.

Student Scoop

"It helped me prepare for living on my own. It helped me prepare to balance my time between schoolwork and activities, which would later help me in both high school and college. It also humbled me in many ways. The best in every field [was at Center for Talented Youth]. You learn that everyone has that strong point in one or two fields."

—Benjamin Olinsky, participant, Center for Talented Youth (CTY), at Hampshire College and at Franklin and Marshall College

LIST OF PROGRAMS

Here is a list of academic summer programs, grouped by subject. See the Program Directory in Part III of this book for descriptions of each of these programs.

Archeology Programs

Center for American Archeology—Archeological Field School
Crow Canyon Archaeological Center—High School Field School; High School Excavation Program
Earthwatch Institute—Field Research Expedition Internships
University of Wisconsin, La Crosse—Archaeology Field Schools

Aviation/Aeronautics Programs

Embry-Riddle Aeronautical University—ACES Academy (Aviation Career Education Specialization)
Embry-Riddle Aeronautical University—Aerospace Summer Camp
Embry-Riddle Aeronautical University—Engineering Academy
Embry-Riddle Aeronautical University—Flight Exploration
Embry-Riddle Aeronautical University—SunFlight Camps
Foothill College—Academically Talented Youth Program
Mississippi University for Women—Aero-Tech
Oregon Museum of Science and Industry—OMSI Summer Science Camps and Adventures
Randolph-Macon Academy—Randolph-Macon Academy Summer Programs
Saint Louis University—Parks Summer Academy
University of New Hampshire—Project SMART
University of North Dakota—International Aerospace Camp
U.S. Space Camp—Aviation Challenge and Advanced Space Academy
Wright State University—Pre-College Summer Enrichment Programs

Business Programs

Alfred University—High School Academic Institutes
American Collegiate Adventures
American Management Association—Operation Enterprise
Brenau University—Firespark Schools
Columbia College, Leadership Institute—21st Century Leaders
Columbia College, Leadership Institute—Entrepreneurship Camp
Dickinson College—Pre-College Program
Envision EMI, Inc.—NexTech: The National Summit of Young Technology Leaders
Global Institute for Developing Entrepreneurs—IN2BIZ Entrepreneur Camp
Knowledge Exchange Institute—Precollege Business, Law and Diplomacy Program
Knowledge Exchange Institute—Precollege European Capitals Program
Media Workshops Foundation—The Media Workshops

Mississippi University for Women—Business Week
National Student Leadership Conference—Law & Advocacy; International
    Diplomacy; Medicine & Health Care
National Youth Leadership Forum—National Youth Leadership Forum on Medicine
Shad International—Shad Valley
Syracuse University—Summer College for High School Students
University of Notre Dame—Summer Experience
University of Pennsylvania—Precollege Program
Washington and Lee University—Summer Scholars

College Preparation Programs

Academic Study Associates—ASA Pre-College Enrichment Program
Alfred University—High School Academic Institutes
American Collegiate Adventures
Bates College—Edmund S. Muskie Scholars Program
Baylor University—High School Summer Science Research Fellowship Program
Bennington College—Bennington College July Program
Birmingham-Southern College—Summer Scholar Program
Boston College—Boston College Experience
Boston University—Program in Mathematics for Young Scientists (PROMYS)
Brandeis University—Brandeis Summer Odyssey
Brenau University—Firespark Schools
Brown University—Focus Program
Brown University—Pre-College Program
Bryn Mawr College—Writing for College
Calvin College—Entrada Scholars Program
Cambridge College Programme LLC—Cambridge College Programme
Carnegie Mellon University—Pre-College Programs
Catholic University of America—College Courses for High School Students
College Visits
Colorado College—Summer Session for High School Students
Columbia College Chicago—High School Summer Institute
Columbia University—Columbia Summer Programs for High School Students
Cornell University—Cornell University Summer College
Cornell University—Honors Program for High School Sophomores
Davidson College—Davidson July Experience
Dickinson College—Pre-College Program
Duke University—Duke University PreCollege Program
Education Unlimited—College Admission Prep Camp; Prep Camp Excel
Education Unlimited—East Coast College Tour
Education Unlimited—Summer Focus at Berkeley
Evansville Association for the Blind—Summer College Program for Students
    with Disabilities
Foothill College—Academically Talented Youth Program
Georgetown University—Georgetown Summer College
Gould Academy—Young Scholars Program; College Preparatory Program

Harvard University—Harvard Summer School Secondary School Program

Hollins University—Precollege Program

Huntingdon College—Huntingdon College Summer Programs

Irish Centre for Talented Youth

Ithaca College—Summer College for High School Students

Johns Hopkins University—Pre-college Credit Program

Johns Hopkins University Center for Talented Youth—CTY Summer Programs; CAA Summer Programs

Junior Statesmen Foundation—Junior Statesmen Summer School

Knowledge Exchange Institute—Precollege African Safari Program

Knowledge Exchange Institute—Precollege Amazon Exploration Program

Knowledge Exchange Institute—Precollege Business, Law and Diplomacy Program

Knowledge Exchange Institute—Precollege European Capitals Program

Knowledge Exchange Institute—Precollege Research Abroad Program

Lebanon Valley College—Daniel Fox Youth Scholars Institute

Miami University—Junior Scholars Program

Musiker Discovery Programs—Summer Discovery

New Jersey Institute of Technology—Pre-college Academy in Technology and Science for High School Students

Northwestern University—National High School Institute

Oakland University—Oakland University Summer Mathematics Institute

Ohio State University—Ross Young Scholars Program

OxBridge Academic Programs—Cambridge Prep; Cambridge Tradition; Oxford Tradition; Académie de Paris

Pacific Lutheran University—Summer Scholars at PLU

Phillips Academy Andover—Phillips Academy Summer Session

Project PULL Academy—Project PULL Academy Leadership Challenge and College Preview

Purdue University—Seminar for Top Engineering Prospects (STEP)

Putney Student Travel—Excel at Williams and Amherst Colleges; Excel at Oxford/Tuscany and Madrid/Barcelona

Quest Scholars Program—Quest Scholars Programs at Stanford and Harvard

Randolph-Macon Academy—Randolph-Macon Academy Summer Programs

Rochester Institute of Technology—College and Careers

Saint Cloud State University, Ethnic Studies Program—Advanced Program in Technology and Science

Saint Cloud State University, Ethnic Studies Program—Scientific Discovery Program

Shad International—Shad Valley

Skidmore College—Pre-College Program in the Liberal Arts for High School Students at Skidmore

Southern Methodist University—College Experience

Southwest Texas State University—Honors Summer Math Camp

Spelman College—Early College Summer Program

Stanford University—Summer College for High School Students

Stanford University—Summer Discovery Institutes

Stanford University, Education Program for Gifted Youth—Summer Institute in Mathematics and Physics

Summer Institute for the Gifted—College Gifted Program
Summer Study Programs—Summer Enrichment and Summer Study at Penn State
Summer Study Programs—Summer Study at the University of Colorado at Boulder
Summer Study Programs—Summer Study in Paris at The American University of Paris
Syracuse University—Summer College for High School Students
Trinity University—A Trinity Summer
University of California, Los Angeles—College Level Summer Program
University of California, Santa Barbara—Early Start Program
University of California, Santa Barbara—UCSB Summer Research Mentorship Program
University of Colorado Cancer Center—Summer Cancer Research Fellowship
University of Connecticut—Mentor Connection
University of Delaware—Summer College for High School Juniors
University of Denver—Making of an Engineer
University of Florida—UF Student Science Training Program
University of Illinois, Chicago—Health Science Enrichment Program
University of Miami—Summer Scholar Programs
University of Mississippi—Summer College for High School Students
University of New Hampshire—Project SMART
University of Notre Dame—Summer Experience
University of Pennsylvania—Precollege Program
University of Wisconsin, Madison—Engineering Summer Program for High School Students
Western Washington University—SummerQuest
Xavier University of Louisiana—SOAR 1
Yale University—Yale Summer Programs

Computer/Technology Programs

American Collegiate Adventures
American Committee for the Weizmann Institute of Science—Dr. Bessie F. Lawrence International Summer Science Institute
Asheville School—Asheville School Summer Academic Adventures
Brandeis University—Brandeis Summer Odyssey
Columbia University—Columbia Summer Programs for High School Students
Education Unlimited—Computer Camp by Education Unlimited
Envision EMI, Inc.—NexTech: The National Summit of Young Technology Leaders
Foothill College—Academically Talented Youth Program
Gifted and Talented Development Center
Gould Academy—Young Scholars Program; College Preparatory Program
Johns Hopkins University—Pre-college Credit Program
Johns Hopkins University Center for Talented Youth—CTY Summer Programs; CAA Summer Programs
Knowledge Exchange Institute—Precollege Artist Abroad Program
Louisiana State University—Honors High School Credit Program
Miami University—Junior Scholars Program

Milwaukee School of Engineering—Discover the Possibilities; Focus on the
  Possibilities
Mississippi University for Women—Aero-Tech
Mississippi University for Women—Business Week
Mount Holyoke College—SummerMath
National Computer Camps, Inc.—National Computer Camps, Inc.
New Jersey Institute of Technology—Pre-college Academy in Technology and Science
  for High School Students
Oklahoma City Community College—Applying the Skills of Technology in Science
Purdue School of Engineering and Technology, IUPUI—Minority Engineering
  Advancement Program (MEAP)
Randolph-Macon Academy—Randolph-Macon Academy Summer Programs
Rochester Institute of Technology—College and Careers
Saint Cloud State University, Ethnic Studies Program—Advanced Program in
  Technology and Science
Saint Cloud State University, Ethnic Studies Program—Scientific Discovery Program
Seton Hill College—Science Quest II
Shad International—Shad Valley
Southampton College of Long Island University—Summer High School Workshops
Stanford University—Summer College for High School Students
Summer Institute for the Gifted—College Gifted Program
Summer Study Programs—Summer Enrichment and Summer Study at Penn State
Syracuse University—Summer College for High School Students
Transylvania University—Academic Camp with Computer Emphasis
University of California, Los Angeles—College Level Summer Program
University of California, Los Angeles—High School Level Summer Program
University of Connecticut—Mentor Connection
University of Evansville—Options
University of Iowa—Summer Journalism Workshops
University of New Hampshire—Project SMART
University of Notre Dame—Introduction to Engineering
University of Notre Dame—Summer Experience
University of Vermont—Discovering Engineering, Mathematics, and Computer
  Science
University of Virginia —Summer Enrichment Program
Vanderbilt University—Program for Talented Youth
Western Washington University—Adventures in Science and Arts

Engineering Programs

Alfred University—High School Academic Institutes
Carnegie Mellon University—Pre-College Programs
Catholic University of America—Eye on Engineering
Embry-Riddle Aeronautical University—Engineering Academy
Envision EMI, Inc.—NexTech: The National Summit of Young Technology Leaders
Milwaukee School of Engineering—Discover the Possibilities; Focus on the
  Possibilities

Purdue School of Engineering and Technology, IUPUI—Minority Engineering Advancement Program (MEAP)

Purdue University—Seminar for Top Engineering Prospects (STEP)

Rochester Institute of Technology—College and Careers

Saint Louis University—Parks Summer Academy

Shad International—Shad Valley

Smith College—Smith Summer Science Program

Southern Illinois University—Carbondale—Women's Introduction to Engineering

Summer Institute for the Gifted—College Gifted Program

Summer Study Programs—Summer Enrichment and Summer Study at Penn State

Syracuse University—Summer College for High School Students

Transylvania University—Academic Camp with Computer Emphasis

United States Coast Guard Academy—Minority Introduction to Engineering (MITE)

University of California, San Diego—UCSD Academic Connections & Summer Session

University of Cincinnati, College of Engineering—Inquisitive Women Summer Day Camp

University of Dayton—Women in Engineering Summer Camp

University of Denver—Making of an Engineer

University of Evansville—Options

University of Mississippi—Summer College for High School Students

University of New Hampshire—Project SMART

University of Notre Dame—Introduction to Engineering

University of Vermont—Discovering Engineering, Mathematics, and Computer Science

University of Wisconsin, Madison—Engineering Summer Program for High School Students

Language Programs

Academic Study Associates—Language Study Programs

AFS Intercultural Programs—Summer Homestay Language Study

Alliances Abroad—Summer Spanish Program for Youth in Spain; Summer French Programs for Youth in France

American Collegiate Adventures

American International Youth Student Exchange—American International Youth Student Exchange Program

Amerispan Unlimited—Madrid and Marbella Summer Camps; Spanish Language Program in Costa Rica

Asheville School—Asheville School Summer Academic Adventures

Avatar Education Ltd.—Buckswood ARC Summer Programs

Baja California Language College—Baja California Language College

Beloit College—Center for Language Studies

Bordeaux Language School—Teenage Summer Program in Biarritz

Boston College—Boston College Experience

Brown University—Pre-College Program

Center for Cross-Cultural Study—Summer in Seville

Center for Cultural Interchange—Discovery Abroad Programs
Ceran Lingua—Ceran Junior
Choate Rosemary Hall—English Language Institute
Colorado College—Summer Session for High School Students
Comunicare—Study and Share
Concordia College—Concordia Language Villages
Costa Rican Language Academy (CRLA)
Dickinson College—Pre-College Program
Dwight-Englewood School—Dwight-Englewood Summer Programs
EF International Language Schools
Foothill College—Academically Talented Youth Program
Georgetown University—Georgetown Summer College
Georgia Hardy Tours, Inc.—Summer Study
Gould Academy—Young Scholars Program; College Preparatory Program
Hawaii Preparatory Academy—Hawaii Preparatory Academy Summer Session
Humanities Spring in Assisi
Hun School of Princeton—Hun School Summer Programs
Johns Hopkins University—Pre-college Credit Program
Knowledge Exchange Institute—Precollege African Safari Program
Knowledge Exchange Institute—Precollege Amazon Exploration Program
Knowledge Exchange Institute—Precollege Artist Abroad Program
Knowledge Exchange Institute—Precollege Business, Law and Diplomacy Program
Language Link—Intercultura; Spanish Language Institute; CLIC
Language Studies Abroad, Inc.—Language Studies Abroad
Language Study Abroad
Lawrence Academy—International English Institute
LEAPNow—Summer Program in Central America
Lingua Service Worldwide—Junior Classic and Junior Sports Program
Lingua Service Worldwide—Junior Course in Salamanca
Lingua Service Worldwide—Summer Language Adventure
The Masters School —Summer ESL
Nacel Open Door—Summer Programs
National Registration Center for Study Abroad—Summer Language Programs
Northwestern University, Center for Talent Development—Apogee, Spectrum,
    Equinox, Leapfrog
Oak Ridge Military Academy—Academic Summer School
OxBridge Academic Programs—Cambridge Prep; Cambridge Tradition; Oxford
    Tradition; Académie de Paris
Phillips Academy Andover—Phillips Academy Summer Session
Randolph-Macon Academy—Randolph-Macon Academy Summer Programs
Rassias Programs
Sons of Norway—Camp Norway
Southwestern Academy—International Summer Programs
Southwestern Academy—Southwestern Adventures
Summer Institute for the Gifted—College Gifted Program
Summer Study Programs—Summer Enrichment and Summer Study at Penn State
Summer Study Programs—Summer Study at the University of Colorado at Boulder

Summer Study Programs—Summer Study in Paris at The American University of Paris

Tufts University European Center—Tufts Summit

University of Dallas Study Abroad—Shakespeare in Italy; Latin in Rome; Thomas More in England; Winston Churchill in England

University of Southern Mississippi, The Frances A. Karnes Center for Gifted Studies—Summer Program for Academically Talented Youth

Vanderbilt University—Program for Talented Youth

World Learning—Experiment in International Living (EIL)

Liberal Arts Programs

Academic Study Associates—ASA Pre-College Enrichment Program

Adelphi University—Academic Success Program

American Collegiate Adventures

Appalachian State University—Summer Sports and Academic Camps

Asheville School—Asheville School Summer Academic Adventures

Barnard College—Summer in New York: A Pre-College Program

Bennington College—Bennington College July Program

Birmingham-Southern College—Summer Scholar Program

Boston College—Boston College Experience

Brandeis University—Genesis at Brandeis University

Brown University—Focus Program

Brown University—Pre-College Program

Calvin College—Entrada Scholars Program

Carnegie Mellon University—Pre-College Programs

Catholic University of America—College Courses for High School Students

Choate Rosemary Hall—Choate Rosemary Hall Summer Session

Colorado College—Summer Session for High School Students

Columbia University—Columbia Summer Programs for High School Students

Cornell University—Cornell University Summer College

Cornell University—Honors Program for High School Sophomores

Davidson College—Davidson July Experience

Duke University—Duke University PreCollege Program

Dwight-Englewood School—Dwight-Englewood Summer Programs

Education Unlimited—Summer Focus at Berkeley

Foothill College—Academically Talented Youth Program

Georgetown University—Georgetown Summer College

Georgia Hardy Tours, Inc.—Summer Study

Gifted and Talented Development Center

Hargrave Military Academy—Summer School and Camp

Harvard University—Harvard Summer School Secondary School Program

Hawaii Preparatory Academy—Hawaii Preparatory Academy Summer Session

Hollins University—Precollege Program

Humanities Spring in Assisi

Hun School of Princeton—Hun School Summer Programs

Huntingdon College—Huntingdon College Summer Programs

Indiana State University—Summer Honors Program

Irish Centre for Talented Youth

Ithaca College—Summer College for High School Students

Johns Hopkins University—Pre-college Credit Program

Johns Hopkins University Center for Talented Youth—CTY Summer Programs; CAA Summer Programs

Juniata College—Voyages: Summer Camp for Gifted Students

Lebanon Valley College—Daniel Fox Youth Scholars Institute

Leysin American School in Switzerland—Summer in Switzerland

Maine Teen Camp

Miami University—Junior Scholars Program

Minnesota Institute for Talented Youth—Expand Your Mind

Musiker Discovery Programs—Summer Discovery

Northwestern University—National High School Institute

Northwestern University, Center for Talent Development—Apogee, Spectrum, Equinox, Leapfrog

Oak Ridge Military Academy—Academic Summer School

OxBridge Academic Programs—Cambridge Prep; Cambridge Tradition; Oxford Tradition; Académie de Paris

Pacific Lutheran University—Summer Scholars at PLU

Phillips Academy Andover—Phillips Academy Summer Session

Putney School—Putney School Summer Programs

Putney Student Travel—Excel at Williams and Amherst Colleges; Excel at Oxford/Tuscany and Madrid/Barcelona

Randolph-Macon Academy—Randolph-Macon Academy Summer Programs

Saint Paul Academy and Summit School—Summer Programs

Sidwell Friends School—Sidwell Friends Summer Programs

Skidmore College—Pre-College Program in the Liberal Arts for High School Students at Skidmore

Southern Methodist University—College Experience

Southwestern Academy—Southwestern Adventures

Stanford University—Summer College for High School Students

Stanford University—Summer Discovery Institutes

Summer Institute for the Gifted—College Gifted Program

Summer Study Programs—Summer Enrichment and Summer Study at Penn State

Summer Study Programs—Summer Study at the University of Colorado at Boulder

Summer Study Programs—Summer Study in Paris at The American University of Paris

Syracuse University—Summer College for High School Students

Trinity University—A Trinity Summer

University of California, Los Angeles—College Level Summer Program

University of California, Los Angeles—High School Level Summer Program

University of California, Santa Barbara—Early Start Program

University of Connecticut—Mentor Connection

University of Dallas Study Abroad—Shakespeare in Italy; Latin in Rome; Thomas More in England; Winston Churchill in England

University of Delaware—Summer College for High School Juniors

University of Mississippi—Summer College for High School Students

University of Notre Dame—Summer Experience
University of Pennsylvania—Precollege Program
University of Southern Mississippi, The Frances A. Karnes Center for Gifted Studies—
    Summer Program for Academically Talented Youth
University of Virginia —Summer Enrichment Program
University of Washington—Courses for High School Students
University of Wisconsin, Superior—Youthsummer
Vanderbilt University—Program for Talented Youth
Washington and Lee University—Summer Scholars
Western Washington University—Adventures in Science and Arts
Western Washington University—SummerQuest
Wright State University—Pre-College Summer Enrichment Programs
Yale University—Yale Summer Programs
Youth for Understanding International Exchange—Summer Overseas

Marine Science Programs

ActionQuest—ActionQuest Programs
Broadreach, Inc.—Broadreach Summer Adventures for Teenagers
Christchurch School—Summer Programs on the River
Dauphin Island Sea Lab—Discovery Hall Summer High School Program
Earthwatch Institute—Field Research Expedition Internships
ECHO International Educational Expeditions—Australian Biological Adventures
Hawaii Preparatory Academy—Hawaii Preparatory Academy Summer Session
Hobart and William Smith Colleges—Environmental Studies Summer Youth Institute
Knowledge Exchange Institute—Precollege Amazon Exploration Program
Occidental College—High School Oceanology Program
Ocean Educations Ltd.—Marine and Environmental Science Program
Oceanic Society—Bahamas Dolphin Project for High School Students
Oceanic Society—Belize Student Expedition
Odyssey Expeditions—Tropical Marine Biology Voyages
Oregon Museum of Science and Industry—OMSI Summer Science Camps and
    Adventures
Sea Education Association—Science at Sea; Oceanography of the Gulf of Maine
Seacamp Association, Inc.—Seacamp
SeaWorld Adventure Parks—SeaWorld/Busch Gardens Adventure Camps
Southampton College of Long Island University—Summer High School Workshops
University of California, San Diego—UCSD Academic Connections & Summer
    Session
University of Miami—Summer Scholar Programs
University of New Hampshire—Project SMART

Mathematics Programs

Academic Enrichment Institute—Summer Academic Enrichment Institute
American Collegiate Adventures
American Committee for the Weizmann Institute of Science—Dr. Bessie F. Lawrence
    International Summer Science Institute

Asheville School—Asheville School Summer Academic Adventures
Boston College—Boston College Experience
Boston University—Program in Mathematics for Young Scientists (PROMYS)
Brandeis University—Brandeis Summer Odyssey
Brown University—Pre-College Program
Colorado College—Summer Session for High School Students
Columbia University—Columbia Summer Programs for High School Students
Cornell University—Cornell University Summer College
Dwight-Englewood School—Dwight-Englewood Summer Programs
Education Unlimited—Summer Focus at Berkeley
Foothill College—Academically Talented Youth Program
Georgetown University—Georgetown Summer College
Gould Academy—Young Scholars Program; College Preparatory Program
Hampshire College—Hampshire College Summer Studies in Mathematics
Johns Hopkins University—Pre-college Credit Program
Johns Hopkins University Center for Talented Youth—CTY Summer Programs; CAA
    Summer Programs
Juniata College—Voyages: Summer Camp for Gifted Students
Lebanon Valley College—Daniel Fox Youth Scholars Institute
Louisiana State University—Honors High School Credit Program
Mathematics Foundation of America—Canada/USA Mathcamp
Miami University—Junior Scholars Program
Minnesota Institute for Talented Youth—Expand Your Mind
Mount Holyoke College—SummerMath
New Jersey Institute of Technology—Pre-college Academy in Technology and Science
    for High School Students
Northwestern University, Center for Talent Development—Apogee, Spectrum,
    Equinox, Leapfrog
Oak Ridge Military Academy—Academic Summer School
Oakland University—Oakland University Summer Mathematics Institute
Ohio State University—Ross Young Scholars Program
Pacific Lutheran University—Summer Scholars at PLU
Phillips Academy Andover—Phillips Academy Summer Session
Purdue School of Engineering and Technology, IUPUI—Minority Engineering
    Advancement Program (MEAP)
Putney School—Putney School Summer Programs
Randolph-Macon Academy—Randolph-Macon Academy Summer Programs
Rutgers University—Young Scholars Program in Discrete Mathematics
Saint Cloud State University, Ethnic Studies Program—Scientific Discovery Program
Sidwell Friends School—Sidwell Friends Summer Programs
Skidmore College—Pre-College Program in the Liberal Arts for High School Students
    at Skidmore
Southern Methodist University—College Experience
Southwest Texas State University—Honors Summer Math Camp
Spelman College—Early College Summer Program
Stanford University—Summer College for High School Students

Stanford University, Education Program for Gifted Youth—Summer Institute in Mathematics and Physics

Summer Institute for the Gifted—College Gifted Program

Summer Study Programs—Summer Enrichment and Summer Study at Penn State

Summer Study Programs—Summer Study at the University of Colorado at Boulder

Summer Study Programs—Summer Study in Paris at The American University of Paris

Transylvania University—Academic Camp with Computer Emphasis

University of California, Los Angeles—College Level Summer Program

University of California, Los Angeles—High School Level Summer Program

University of California, Santa Barbara—Early Start Program

University of Connecticut—Mentor Connection

University of Delaware—Summer College for High School Juniors

University of Delaware—Upward Bound Math and Science Center

University of Michigan—Michigan Math and Science Scholars

University of Nebraska—Lincoln—All Girls/All Math

University of New Hampshire—Project SMART

University of Pennsylvania—Precollege Program

University of Southern Mississippi, The Frances A. Karnes Center for Gifted Studies—Summer Program for Academically Talented Youth

University of the South—Bridge Program in Math and Science

University of Vermont—Discovering Engineering, Mathematics, and Computer Science

Vanderbilt University—Program for Talented Youth

Wright State University—Pre-College Summer Enrichment Programs

Xavier University of Louisiana—MathStar

Science Programs

Alfred University—High School Academic Institutes

American Collegiate Adventures

American Committee for the Weizmann Institute of Science—Dr. Bessie F. Lawrence International Summer Science Institute

Asheville School—Asheville School Summer Academic Adventures

Baylor University—High School Summer Science Research Fellowship Program

Boston College—Boston College Experience

Brandeis University—Brandeis Summer Odyssey

Brenau University—Firespark Schools

Brown University—Pre-College Program

Carnegie Mellon University—Pre-College Programs

Choate Rosemary Hall —Choate Rosemary Hall Summer Session

Colorado College—Summer Session for High School Students

Columbia University—Columbia Summer Programs for High School Students

Columbia University, Biosphere 2—Exploring Earth, Life & the Summer Sky

Cornell University—Cornell University Summer College

Dauphin Island Sea Lab—Discovery Hall Summer High School Program

Dickinson College—Pre-College Program
Dwight-Englewood School—Dwight-Englewood Summer Programs
Earthwatch Institute—Field Research Expedition Internships
Education Unlimited—Summer Focus at Berkeley
Georgetown University—Georgetown Summer College
Gould Academy—Young Scholars Program; College Preparatory Program
Harvard University—Harvard Summer School Secondary School Program
Hawaii Preparatory Academy—Hawaii Preparatory Academy Summer Session
Hobart and William Smith Colleges—Environmental Studies Summer Youth Institute
Hollins University—Hollinscience Program
Indiana State University—Summer Honors Program
Indiana University, Bloomington—Jim Holland Summer Enrichment Program in Biology
The Island Laboratory
Ithaca College—Summer College for High School Students
Johns Hopkins University—Pre-college Credit Program
Johns Hopkins University Center for Talented Youth—CTY Summer Programs; CAA Summer Programs
Juniata College—Voyages: Summer Camp for Gifted Students
Knowledge Exchange Institute—Precollege African Safari Program
Knowledge Exchange Institute—Precollege Amazon Exploration Program
Knowledge Exchange Institute—Precollege Research Abroad Program
Lawrence Academy—Environmental Field Study
Lebanon Valley College—Daniel Fox Youth Scholars Institute
Louisiana State University—Honors High School Credit Program
Miami University—Junior Scholars Program
Minnesota Institute for Talented Youth—Expand Your Mind
Musiker Discovery Programs—Summer Discovery
National FFA Organization—Agricultural Programs Overseas
National Youth Leadership Forum—National Youth Leadership Forum on Medicine
New Jersey Institute of Technology—Pre-college Academy in Technology and Science for High School Students
Northern Virginia Summer Academy
Northwestern University, Center for Talent Development—Apogee, Spectrum, Equinox, Leapfrog
Ocean Educations Ltd.—Marine and Environmental Science Program
Oklahoma City Community College—Applying the Skills of Technology in Science
Oregon Museum of Science and Industry—OMSI Summer Science Camps and Adventures
Pacific Lutheran University—Summer Scholars at PLU
Phillips Academy Andover—Phillips Academy Summer Session
Purdue School of Engineering and Technology, IUPUI—Minority Engineering Advancement Program (MEAP)
Putney School—Putney School Summer Programs
Quest Scholars Program—Quest Scholars Programs at Stanford and Harvard
Randolph-Macon Academy—Randolph-Macon Academy Summer Programs

Saint Cloud State University, Ethnic Studies Program—Advanced Program in Technology and Science

Saint Cloud State University, Ethnic Studies Program—Scientific Discovery Program

Scandinavian Seminar—Ambassadors for the Environment

School for Field Studies—Environmental Field Studies Abroad

Sea Education Association—Science at Sea; Oceanography of the Gulf of Maine

Seacamp Association, Inc.—Seacamp

SeaWorld Adventure Parks—SeaWorld/Busch Gardens Adventure Camps

Seton Hill College—Science Quest II

Shad International—Shad Valley

Sidwell Friends School—Sidwell Friends Summer Programs

Skidmore College—Pre-College Program in the Liberal Arts for High School Students at Skidmore

Smith College—Smith Summer Science Program

Southampton College of Long Island University—Summer High School Workshops

Southern Methodist University—College Experience

Stanford University—Summer College for High School Students

Stanford University, Education Program for Gifted Youth—Summer Institute in Mathematics and Physics

Summer Institute for the Gifted—College Gifted Program

Summer Study Programs—Summer Enrichment and Summer Study at Penn State

Summer Study Programs—Summer Study at the University of Colorado at Boulder

Summer Study Programs—Summer Study in Paris at The American University of Paris

Transylvania University—Academic Camp with Computer Emphasis

Tufts University School of Veterinary Medicine—Adventures in Veterinary Medicine

University of California, Los Angeles—College Level Summer Program

University of California, Los Angeles—High School Level Summer Program

University of California, San Diego—UCSD Academic Connections & Summer Session

University of California, Santa Barbara—Early Start Program

University of California, Santa Barbara—UCSB Summer Research Mentorship Program

University of Colorado Cancer Center—Summer Cancer Research Fellowship

University of Connecticut—Mentor Connection

University of Delaware—Summer College for High School Juniors

University of Delaware—Upward Bound Math and Science Center

University of Florida—UF Student Science Training Program

University of Illinois—Chicago—Health Science Enrichment Program

University of Miami—Summer Scholar Programs

University of Michigan—Michigan Math and Science Scholars

University of Mississippi—Summer College for High School Students

University of New Hampshire—Project SMART

University of Notre Dame—Summer Experience

University of Pennsylvania—Penn Summer Science Academy

University of Pennsylvania—Precollege Program

University of the South—Bridge Program in Math and Science
University of Southern Mississippi, The Frances A. Karnes Center for Gifted Studies—
Summer Program for Academically Talented Youth
University of Virginia —Summer Enrichment Program
University of Wisconsin, La Crosse—Archaeology Field Schools
University of Wisconsin, Madison—Pre-college Program in Environmental and
Native American Studies
University of Wisconsin, Madison—Summer Science Institute
University of Wisconsin, Superior—Youthsummer
Vanderbilt University—Program for Talented Youth
Washington and Lee University—Summer Scholars
Western Washington University—Adventures in Science and Arts
The Wilds—Safari Camp
World Learning—Experiment in International Living (EIL)
Wright State University—Pre-College Summer Enrichment Programs
Xavier University of Louisiana—BioStar; ChemStar
Xavier University of Louisiana—SOAR 1
Yale University—Yale Summer Programs

Writing Programs

Alfred University—High School Academic Institutes
American Collegiate Adventures
American University—Discover the World of Communication
Asheville School—Asheville School Summer Academic Adventures
Ball State University—Ball State University Journalism Workshops
Barnard College—Summer in New York: A Pre-College Program
Bates College—Creative Writing Workshops
Bennington College—Bennington College July Program
Bryn Mawr College—Writing for College
California Chicano News Media Association—San Jose Urban Journalism Workshop
for Minorities
California State Summer School for the Arts
Capitol Region Education Council and Wesleyan University—Center for Creative
Youth
Carleton College—Summer Writing Program
Choate Rosemary Hall —The Writing Project
Columbia College Chicago—High School Summer Institute
Columbia University—Columbia Summer Programs for High School Students
Cornell University—Cornell University Summer College
Cornell University—Honors Program for High School Sophomores
Denison University—Jonathan R. Reynolds Young Writers Workshop
Georgia Hardy Tours, Inc.—Summer Study
Gifted and Talented Development Center
Hollins University—Precollege Program
Huntingdon College—Huntingdon College Summer Programs
Idyllwild Arts Foundation—Idyllwild Arts Summer Program

Indiana University, Bloomington—High School Journalism Publications Workshops

Interlochen Center for the Arts—Interlochen Arts Camp

Irish Centre for Talented Youth

Johns Hopkins University—Pre-college Credit Program

Johns Hopkins University Center for Talented Youth—CTY Summer Programs; CAA Summer Programs

Kenyon College—Young Writers at Kenyon

Lewis and Clark College, Northwest Writing Institute—Fir Acres Workshop in Writing and Thinking; Writer to Writer

Maine Teen Camp

New York University—Tisch Summer High School Program

Northwestern University—National High School Institute

OxBridge Academic Programs—Cambridge Prep; Cambridge Tradition; Oxford Tradition; Académie de Paris

Phillips Academy Andover—Phillips Academy Summer Session

Rhodes College—Young Scholars and Writers Camp

Simon's Rock College of Bard—Young Writer's Workshop

Southampton College of Long Island University—Summer High School Workshops

Southwest Texas State University—Summer Creative Writing Camp

Spelman College—Early College Summer Program

Spoleto Study Abroad

Stanford University—Summer Discovery Institutes

Summer Study Programs—Summer Enrichment and Summer Study at Penn State

Summer Study Programs—Summer Study in Paris at The American University of Paris

University of Arizona—Summer Institute for Writing

University of California, Los Angeles—College Level Summer Program

University of California, Los Angeles—High School Level Summer Program

University of California, San Diego—UCSD Academic Connections & Summer Session

University of Connecticut—Mentor Connection

University of Iowa—Iowa Young Writers' Studio

University of Iowa—Summer Journalism Workshops

University of Mississippi—Summer College for High School Students

University of Southern California—Summer Production Workshop

University of Southern Mississippi, The Frances A. Karnes Center for Gifted Studies—Summer Program for Academically Talented Youth

Vanderbilt University—Program for Talented Youth

Wright State University—Pre-College Summer Enrichment Programs

Yale University—Yale Daily News Summer Journalism Program

ENRICHING YOUR SUMMER

Here is a list of websites, books, and movies you can use to further explore the academic subjects listed.

Websites

Business

interactive.wsj.com/home.html
Interactive version of the *Wall Street Journal* features exclusive business news updated 24 hours a day.

www.library.upenn.edu/lippincott/
Free access to the resources of the Lippincott Library at the famed Wharton School of Business.

www.fbla-pbl.org/
The Future Business Leaders of America help young people prepare for success as leaders in business, government, and communities.

College Preparation

www.kaptest.com
Your one-stop destination on the Web for test prep, admissions, and success in school and career.

www.ed.gov/offices/OSFAP/Students/
It's never too soon to start planning how to pay for college. This U.S. Department of Education site can help you at every stage of the financial aid process.

www.collegeboard.com
A site stocked with college planning tools from the people who sponsor the SAT.

Computers/Technology

www.hackers.com
Not that any of you are remotely interested in computer hacking ...

www.happypuppy.com
Great gaming site with lots of downloads, news, reviews, and prizes.

www.egghead.com
"The computer store inside your computer."

Language

www.dictionary.com
Online dictionary, thesaurus, translator, word of the day, crossword puzzles and word games, and vocabulary learning resources for many languages.

www.travlang.com
Free translations, useful phrases, and sound files in dozens of foreign languages.

Math

www.mathacademy.com
Comprehensive math resource for students, teachers, and researchers.

www.mathonline.org
A math homework help site for middle and high school students, staffed on school nights by high school math teachers.

www.maa.org
Thinking about a career in math? Check out the Mathematical Association of America's website for a peek at the world of the professional mathematician.

Science

www.nasa.gov
Do you dream of exploring space or working for NASA? Even confirmed land-lovers are sure to find this site fascinating.

www.sci-journal.org
Gives school and college students the chance to publish work they've done in their science classes so that other students around the world can read about it.

biology.about.com/science/biology/msub21.htm
A directory of virtual dissection sites for those of you who may be too squeamish to dissect a real frog, cockroach, or cow's eye . . . Yuck!

Writing

www.writerswrite.com
Actually a resource for writing pros, but there's plenty of stuff for amateurs, too. Features guidelines to paying and nonpaying online publications, writing and publishing news, message boards, writing contests, and more.

www.bartleby.com
Combines the best of both contemporary and classic reference works into the most comprehensive public reference library on the Web.

Books

Business

Atlas Shrugged by Ayn Rand

Who Moved My Cheese? by Spencer Johnson

Hardball for Women by Pat Heim

How to Say it at Work by Jack Griffin

College Preparation

College Catalog and *Guide to the Best Colleges in the U.S.* by the Staff of Kaplan, Inc.

Computers/Technology

The First $20 Million is Always the Hardest by Po Bronson

The Veiled Web by Catherine Asaro

Growing Up Digital by Don Tapscott

Language

The Professor and the Madman by Simon Winchester

2107 Curious Word Origins by Charles Earl Funk

A History of English by Craig Carver

Foundations of Latin by Philip Baldi

Math

A History of Pi by Petr Beckmann

Flatland by Edwin A. Abbott

Miracle Math by Harry Lorayne

Science

The Atom in the History of Thought by Bernard Pullman

Black Holes and Baby Universes by Stephen Hawking

The Demon-Haunted World: Science as a Candle in the Dark by Carl Sagan

One River: Explorations and Discoveries in the Amazon Rain Forest by Wade Davis

A Journey Into Gravity and Spacetime by John Archibald Wheeler

On the Origin of Species by Charles Darwin

Hot Zone by Richard Preston

Einstein's Dreams by Alan P. Lightman

Plague Time by Paul W. Ewald

QED by Richard P. Feynman

Writing

The Writing Life by Annie Dillard

One Writer's Beginnings by Eudora Welty

On Writing Well by William Zinsser

The Art of Fiction: Notes on Craft for Young Writers by John Gardner

Writing Down the Bones by Natalie Goldberg

The Art of Fiction by David Lodge

Simple and Direct: A Rhetoric for Writers by Jacques Barzun

What If: Writing Exercises for Fiction Writers by Anne Bernays

The Elements of Style by William Strunk Jr., E. B. White, Charles Osgood, Roger Angell

Movies

Business

Wall Street
Michael Douglas and Charlie Sheen embody the greed of the '80s.

Working Girl
Melanie Griffith goes from secretary to executive in this tale of a corporate Cinderella.

Office Space
A comedic representation of today's corporate subculture, complete with harried peons and an evil boss.

Clockwatchers
An independent film exploring life as an office temp, with Toni Colette and Lisa Kudrow.

College Preparation

Higher Learning
This drama, directed by John Singleton and starring Omar Epps, turns a critical eye on the effects of racism on college campus life.

Real Genius
Teen geniuses unite to build a laser and wreak havoc at their university. Starring a young Val Kilmer with a rockin' '80s 'do.

Revenge of the Nerds
See nerdy college freshman Anthony Edwards (in his pre-*ER* days) stand up to the mean, bullying jocks.

Dead Poets Society
In this sobering look at the possible consequences of intense academic pressure, Robin Williams teaches his students to "seize the day."

Good Will Hunting
Matt Damon and Ben Affleck wrote and starred in this story about an academic underdog who learns to believe in himself.

Computers/Technology

The Matrix
Amazing special effects upstage Keanu Reeves in this exploration of virtual reality.

War Games
Matthew Broderick achieves every hacker's dream: to start World War III from his own PC.

Apollo 13
True story of astronauts facing impossible odds who survive, not due to technology, but due to teamwork.

2001: A Space Odyssey
This Stanley Kubrick masterpiece warns us that human evolution is tied to an increasing dependence on technology we may not be ready for.

Toy Story
First movie to succeed at creating a completely computer-animated universe. And it's really kinda sweet!

Language

Nell
Liam Neeson and Natasha Richardson try to decipher Jodie Foster's unique language patterns.

My Fair Lady
Rex Harrison, an upper-crust Brit who believes that class differences are based on language and speech patterns, falls in love with Cockney flower seller Audrey Hepburn.

Children of a Lesser God
Marlee Matlin, a deaf woman who has isolated herself from the hearing world, slowly opens up to William Hurt, a new teacher at the school where she works.

Math

Stand and Deliver
Edward James Olmos tries to teach AP Calculus to his East L. A. high school students and succeeds beyond his wildest dreams. Based on a true story.

Rain Man
Tom Cruise learns a little something about compassion from his autistic brother, Dustin Hoffman, who just happens to be a math savant.

Little Man Tate
How do you raise a boy genius? Jodie Foster and Dianne Wiest clash over who can provide the best upbringing for a sensitive math prodigy.

Cube
Six strangers wake up to find themselves trapped in a giant cube and must use their wits (and their math skills!) to escape with their lives.

Science

Contact
An interesting take on science versus faith, starring Jodie Foster.

Jurassic Park
Steven Spielberg and Michael Crichton show us how to use frog DNA to create some really nasty dinosaurs.

Awakenings
Robin Williams is a doctor who rouses Robert DeNiro from his sleeplike existence. But will the cure last?

The Andromeda Strain
An early Michael Crichton work in which scientists fight a deadly outbreak caused by alien elements.

Writing

All the President's Men
Two newspaper journalists take down Nixon's presidency. Starring Robert Redford and Dustin Hoffman.

Finding Forrester
A reclusive novelist mentors a promising young writer from the South Bronx.

Shakespeare in Love
Gwyneth Paltrow stars in this witty fictional account of the writing of *Romeo and Juliet*.

Girl, Interrupted
Based on writer Susanna Kayson's account of her time in a mental hospital and the quirky misanthropes she kept company with. Starring Winona Ryder and Angelina Jolie.

Study Abroad and International Travel Programs

4

OVERVIEW

Can there be a more romantic summer than one spent abroad? From the British aristocracy's Grand Tours to Amy March's continental romance in *Little Women*, overseas travel conjures up 19th-century images of young men's adventures and young women's social transformation. In the past few decades, the prevalence of air travel has made international excursions more accessible for many Americans. Nevertheless, books and movies continue to feed us fairy tales. That first extended trip abroad stands like a beacon of magical life-changing experience. And so it is.

Whether you select "traditional" destinations like London and Paris or explore remote parts of Asia, Africa, Latin America, or the Middle East, international summer programs connect you to new people, cultures, and customs. Whether it is your first trip out of the United States or your tenth, the experience will literally open new worlds.

"SHOULD I TRY AN INTERNATIONAL STUDY OR TRAVEL EXPERIENCE?"

There are many reasons to travel abroad. As airplanes, telephones, and the World Wide Web become increasingly prevalent, governments, economies, and people of all parts of the world are pulled together daily. To succeed in the 21st century, everyone from agrarians to entrepreneurs will need a global consciousness. Medicine is affected by research in Berlin as well as in Berkeley. Stockbrokers watch the Tokyo exchange as closely as the one in New York, and educators compare American children's test results with those from Norway, China, and New Zealand.

Being able to converse in two or three languages is an asset in any profession, but knowledge and appreciation of the world's people proves equally beneficial. Linguistic

fluency becomes valuable only when coupled with appreciation of culture. Most international summer programs provide an opportunity to both strengthen language skills and spend quality time with—not simply among—people of another culture. To laugh with local children and play chess with elderly men—that is the stuff of meaningful travel.

The drawback to international programs—and it can be great—is the cost. Traveling thousands of miles is not cheap, especially during the Northern Hemisphere's hot, summer months when airfare skyrockets. Many students find ways to manage the price tag, however. Some programs offer financial aid or scholarships. In addition, private agencies offer grants and fellowships to students studying in specified countries or regions. By carefully selecting your overseas destination, you can also trim dollars off the cost of extra expenditures like food, entertainment and souvenirs. Prices will always be lower in less developed parts of the world than in the big tourist-attracting cities of Europe. However you scrounge for money, know that the end product merits your effort. Almost all students find study abroad or international travel experience well worth their investment.

— Quick Tips —

Know What You're Looking For

Questions to ask yourself:

- What is the primary goal or purpose of my trip?

- How important is language to my selection process?

- Do I want to receive academic credit for the program?

- What are my housing preferences and/or requirements: hotels, hostels, dormitory, homestay, tents?

- Am I interested in or willing to travel in an underdeveloped region where I might live without running water, electricity, and other modern conveniences?

- Would I rather travel through several countries or settle down in one place?

- Does it matter whether other program participants are from the United States or from countries around the world?

MAKING CHOICES

Weighing Your Options

With so many international programs and destinations, how can you begin to choose one? Examining program specialties should help you narrow the field. Some emphasize language immersion, others cultural exchange, academic study, or outdoor adventure. Still too many options? You may find it helpful to list any "must have" components of your trip as well as anything that would automatically eliminate a program as a possibility. For example, some people want only programs allowing them to use a foreign language they're studying in school. Others want only programs without classroom instruction.

One major distinction to consider when selecting an international summer program is whether the company or educational institution that runs the program is American or foreign. Programs operating from the United States and Canada attract almost all their participants on overseas trips from North America. Programs with international leadership, however, tend to attract students from all over the world. American students typically choose programs based in North America; information about these programs is more widely distributed in the United States and Canada, gaining academic credit for participation is often easier, and both parents and students often feel more

comfortable dealing with directors who share their native language and culture. These are certainly practical and legitimate reasons to select an American-based program.

There are also advantages in selecting a foreign operated one, however, so you shouldn't automatically rule them out. Directors, teachers, and guides of foreign-based programs are more likely to be native-born than those at programs with U.S. leadership. Because of this, every aspect of your overseas experience—from classroom instruction to registration and even the program brochure—provides a cultural experience. Depending on the organization's sponsoring country, summer school teachers may have more or less stringent academic standards, daily schedules may be more or less structured, and menus more or less to your taste than if you attended a program with U.S. leadership. You sacrifice some degree of security and predictability when selecting a foreign-operated program. In exchange, you receive a richer cultural experience. For many, the tradeoff proves worthwhile.

Programs sponsored by schools or camps outside the United States draw teenagers from across the globe—including many from countries that are their geographic neighbors—and encourage interaction among all participants. Enforex: Centro de Estudios Internacionales, an international language school recognized by the Spanish Ministry of Education, attracts students from 32 countries yearly. American students attending its residential summer school divide their time between Spanish language classes and social and cultural activities, including flamenco dancing and broadcast journalism. What is unique, however, is that they share these activities, as well as their dorm, with students from places as far away as Brazil, Germany, and Japan. In addition, native Spanish-speaking students attend camp. The possibility for cultural exchange is tremendous. Similar organizations can be found throughout many parts of the world.

Expert Advice

"I think the student's reason for wanting to go is where it has to start. If it were purely to improve my language skills, I would go to a country where I have some of that language. If it were because I was specifically interested in a particular culture, that would lead me. A student should have an innate interest for being in a program because of the country in which it is located—not just for the community service or for the language immersion, but because they want to learn how [people in that country] live differently than in the U.S. That's something we really accentuate. There are some students who really just want to 'go abroad.' That's not what we're about."

—Annie Thompson, enrollment director, World Learning's Experiment in International Living

---

Expert Advice

"Our assumption is that you won't learn to speak a language in a classroom, so we don't make the mistake of transferring students to classrooms in Europe. We put them in classes during the first ten days of the program to get them over that fear of making a fool of themselves, which is part of the process of learning a foreign language. Students sign a pledge that they must speak the language. When we get to the airport in New York, we begin in the language and don't quit until we get home. The first week is exhausting, but it really starts to click after eight to ten days. It is a fun way to learn a language, and that's why it works."

—Peter Shumlin, admissions director, Putney Student Travel

Both programs operated by U.S. and foreign organizations provide variety in their focus. The most frequent categories include teen travel tours (with or without academic or outdoor adventure components), language instruction, the precollege academic experience, and community service opportunities. Overseas community service opportunities will be fully discussed in the following chapter; descriptions of the other international programs follow.

Language Instruction

Many summer programs make language fluency their primary objective. Some require participants to enter with a minimum ability level; others accept students with no prior experience. All language-oriented programs, however, place students in a location where they can acquire and practice language skills both in the classroom and on the streets. Programs' philosophies about language acquisition, and hence their methodologies, differ. While some programs favor intensive in-class instruction, others dismiss classrooms as artificial and do all teaching in the community. The most intense programs require students to sign a pledge to speak in the target language at all times, even during social hours.

Choosing the program that's right for you will depend on your learning style and personal preferences. Some people insist they can only learn a foreign language if they sit down and memorize rules from a grammar book. Others maintain the only way they learn is by engaging in real conversations with native speakers. While some people are eager to take on the exhausting but exhilarating task of speaking in a foreign language 24/7, others prefer a more leisurely schedule—several hours of language/cultural lessons followed by afternoon activities in English. The choice is yours.

Academic Enrichment

Language practice is certainly not the only reason to go abroad. If people limited their travels to places where they could speak the native language, most could see only a small fraction of the world. Yet there is much to gain from studying architecture in Italy, history in Belgium, and ecology in Ecuador, even if you take Japanese in high school. English-language travel programs emphasizing cultural and academic enrichment can be found all over the world and are particularly prevalent in English-speaking countries. Programs at Oxford and Cambridge Universities, for

---

Quick Tips

Hidden Treasures

Sightseeing is a major part of studying abroad, and often turns out to be the best part of traveling to a foreign country. After all, what would Paris be without the Eiffel Tower? Egypt without the pyramids would be about as exciting as, well, miles of uninterrupted sand dunes. Here's a list of some lesser-known attractions to add to your list of reasons to study abroad.

Australia—Kakadu National Park

Botswana—Moremi Wildlife Reserve

Brazil—Iguacu Falls

Costa Rica—Mote Verde Cloud Forest; Arenal Volcano

Denmark—Legoland

Egypt—Valley of the Kings

Iceland—Geysir (geothermal park)

Kenya—Maasai Mara National Reserve

Indonesia—Prambanam Temples

New Zealand—Tongariro National Park

Norway—Hardanger Fjord

Portugal—The Tower of Belem

South Africa—Table Mountain

Spain—Santiago de Compostela Cathedral

Zambia—Victoria Falls

(From www.travelguide.net)

---

example, allow students to experience British life, visit some of the United Kingdom's many museums, and gain a precollege academic experience by living and learning on a university campus.

Teen Travel Tours

Teen travel tours have often been dismissed as superficial: spoiled American teenagers breezing through Europe without stopping anywhere long enough to do more than snap a photo. While you certainly want to avoid tours that rush you from the Eiffel Tower to Buckingham Palace to the Hague, travel programs that schedule in time for relaxation and reflection can be both highly educational and a lot of fun. Especially if you have never traveled before or are venturing into a region where you know little of the language and culture, tours can serve as a good introduction. While exploring the sights and sounds of another land, you have the comfort of being among people who speak your language and have chosen your activities and accommodations with care.

Most tours have either outdoor adventure or academic enrichment components or both. You might hike in the Swiss Alps, study art history in Italy, then mountain bike across Austria. While the cultural experience won't be as rich as that gained in an academic program with homestays, travel tours foster group leadership and strengthen independent living skills. If you decide to try a teen travel tour, you may want to select one that combines the region's major attractions with visits to out-of-the way places. That way, you'll also get a taste of local color.

GETTING READY

Anticipation is half the joy of travel, so preparing for your trip abroad can be lots of fun. Planning ahead can also save you considerable hassle once you arrive at your destination. This, of course, leaves more time for making friends and exploring cities.

Once you have been accepted to a summer program, you will probably receive a large packet of information in the mail. Be sure to read this carefully before filing it away until summer! Information packets often contain essential descriptions of the things you need to do before departure.

Travel Documents

Most countries outside North America require U.S. and Canadian citizens to show a passport and/or visa upon arrival at airport customs. Those that do not still require proof of citizenship in the form of a birth certificate, driver's license, or other government-issued photo identification card. A few countries require both a passport and birth certificate for underage travelers not accompanied by their parents. Because official travel documents like passports and visas can take several weeks to months to

process, it is crucial not to leave this for the last minute. If you already have a passport, check to see that it is current; Canadian passports expire every five years, as do U.S. passports for minors.

Health Check

After filing for a passport and/or visa(s), carefully read any health and safety guidelines outlined in your summer program information packet. If you are traveling to an underdeveloped country or are visiting remote, sparsely inhabited regions, you may be required or advised to get vaccinated against certain diseases and/or take preventative medication. It's never fun being sick and it is especially unpleasant in a foreign country far from the comforts of home. Some illnesses can be quite severe—even life threatening—so err on the conservative side when deciding which health precautions to follow.

Money

Money is another important matter to consider well before departure. The actual amount you need will depend on your program—the region in which you are located (the cost of living in Switzerland is much greater than in Costa Rica), the focus of the trip (cities are expensive and provide many shopping opportunities, while remote regions of Africa are inexpensive, with little to buy), and the amount of time you spend away from the group or organization with which you travel (the more time you are on your own, the more expenses you will incur). In any case, you should calculate a rough budget and then take more money than you expect to need. It is wise to have a cushion for unknown emergencies.

You may find it helpful to consult the newspaper or Internet for exchange rates and travel books for approximate prices. Be aware, however, that exchange rates fluctuate and may change between the time you arrive in the country and the time you leave. Possible expenses to budget for include food (snacks, and on some programs, daily lunch), laundry services, entertainment, gifts, and souvenirs. If you are attending an international school or camp, you should also check for entry or exit taxes levied by the host country and note whether this is included in your tuition and/or travel package.

Perhaps the greater challenge when it comes to using money abroad is figuring out the best way to carry it. Your local bank won't be around the corner, so you have to find alternative ways to access cash. Several options are discussed below. Which method will work best for you depends greatly on your foreign destination. But it can be difficult to canvass the situation from your North American home. If possible, ask students who participated in the program last year for advice (summer program directors may be able

to give you contacts). They will have the most accurate, up-to-date information. Regardless, you should plan to take several forms of money with you; this will protect you in case one method of securing money proves inconvenient or inaccessible.

Cash and Credit Cards

Carrying a small amount of cash is always a good idea. To be safe, conceal your greenbacks in a money belt or another well-hidden place. If you are traveling for several weeks, however, you will probably want access to more money than is safe to carry in bills. If you don't yet have a credit card, now might be a good time to get one. In an emergency, credit cards will get you money fast. They are also relatively safe. If they are stolen, one call to the credit card company will immediately deactivate your account. Most credit cards also provide some degree of insurance on anything you charge.

One thing to be aware of, however, is that credit card companies require you to pay monthly bills. If you will be out of the country for more than four weeks, this could cause problems. A bill will be sent to your mailing address asking you to pay at least a percentage of the overall amount you have charged. When you fail to send the company a check for the minimum balance, they will levy a fine (late fees) and demand higher interest on the unpaid portion of your bill the following month. To avoid excess charges and building a bad credit history, you have two options. First, you can write the credit card company a check before departure, paying them a lump sum against the charges you plan to make while abroad. You lose some money by doing this—money sent to the company makes no interest—but it is an excellent safeguard. A second option is having your parents pay the bills while you are away. They can either open mail from your credit card company and send a check, or you can simply apply for a credit card that is in both your name and theirs. That way, they will get a bill directly. Of course, regardless of who's paying the bills, it is important to use credit cards responsibly. Even if you're handing cashiers plastic, you're spending real money.

Travelers' Checks

Travelers' checks are another safe way to carry cash. Available through the American Automobile Association (AAA), American Express offices, and many banks, travelers' checks require their owner's signature before they can be cashed. When purchasing travelers' checks, you immediately sign your name on a marked signature space on each check. When you are ready to cash a check, you sign your name on a second signature space. The cashier, who watches you sign, looks to see that the signatures match. If your checks are stolen, you should immediately report the numbers of the missing checks to the company who issued them, and your money will be protected. Many people purchase travelers' checks in U.S. dollars and convert them into local currency when needed. This makes them much harder than a credit card to spend irresponsibly.

ATMs

Bank ATM (automated teller machine) cards provide another way to access cash safely in many areas. ATM cards can be issued from either a savings or checking account at your home bank. When you insert your card in an ATM in a foreign country, the machine will give you local currency at the daily exchange rate without charging commission. Bypassing the commission of exchange bureaus can save considerable cash. It can also save valuable time. Before using an ATM, however, it is vital to check for fees. Some U.S. and Canadian banks charge patrons if they use their ATM card at any ATM machine not owned by their bank. Other banks limit the number of free withdrawals cardholders can make from another bank's ATM. Even if your bank does not issue such charges, a foreign bank may. For example, if you change money in London, the British bank may charge you for use of their ATM. As you can imagine, each time you ask the ATM for British pounds, the American or Canadian dollars in your bank account dwindle at double speed. One other word of caution: while ATMs are prevalent in most large cities, they may be hard to find in remote regions. Never depend exclusively on an ATM card.

Wiring Money

Wiring money—having parents (or a very good friend) take fifties out of their bank account and send them to you care of American Express or other international credit or banking company—is costly and a huge hassle. While it works in an emergency, you should avoid wiring if at all possible. Take enough money to protect yourself against any and all unknowns.

PACKING

So you've got the passport and travelers' checks and you've brushed up on your cultural know-how and language skills (or at least survival phrases). You are ready to go! After you pack, that is.

Before piling your whole wardrobe on your bed, think minimalism. International flights have weight restrictions and levy a hefty penalty against those who go over. It's a pain to lug heavy suitcases anyway, and you'll want to leave plenty of room for souvenirs. Try to pack clothes that are not only light, but also easy to care for. Black, navy, and denim, for example, hide dirt much better than white and khaki. Wrinkle-free shirts and dresses are a must; that way you can spend your time meeting people rather than ironing shirts. Packing according to local weather and customs is key. If you're going to England, bring an umbrella. If you're heading to southern Italy or equatorial Brazil, pack a hat and shades. You should always be respectful of local customs when traveling. If you're touring or studying in Western Europe, that may simply mean dressing for dinner. If you're visiting countries with high Muslim populations, however, it could mean a more significant change of habit. Pack enough conservative clothing—dress pants, long skirts, and dresses—to cover your bases (and any part of the body that might be bare).

Quick Tips

Going Native

Most people find that the more they prepare for an international experience, the more rewarding the trip. There are many different ways to whet your appetite for what lies ahead. Try ones from the list below that match your interests and the kind of international experience you anticipate.

- Read the world or international section of your daily newspaper. If your home paper fails to adequately cover world news, check the *New York Times, Washington Post, Los Angeles Times,* or *Chicago Tribune.* English-language international papers may also be available at your local library or online.

- Peruse travel guidebooks. Read about the sites, museums, or restaurants—anything to give you the flavor of your destination.

- Look at a globe or atlas. Get your destination in perspective by examining both political and topographical maps.

- Watch movies or read books set in the country you're traveling to. They can be silly or serious, as long as they get you in the mood. (Check out our "Enriching Your Summer" guide at the end of this chapter for suggestions.)

- Listen to music popular in your foreign destination(s). This is an especially good idea if you're doing a homestay or attending school or camp with local teenagers. Definitely helps that first night out at the local disco.

- Brush up on your language skills. Tune your radio or TV to the appropriate foreign-language station. Rent a foreign film (with or without subtitles). Read children's books (or the classics if you're ambitious) in your target language. Borrow language tapes from your local library. And dig out those old school vocabulary lists!

- Eat at an ethnic restaurant. Order from the non-English side of the menu for everyone at the table.

- Don't speak the language? Buy a phrase book. Learn to say: "Hello," "Goodbye," "Nice to meet you," "Thank you," "Please," "Excuse me," "I don't understand," "Do you know where _____ is?" "Where is the bathroom?" "Do you speak English?" "How much is this?" "Yes," and "No." Learning the names of basic foods you like and dislike can also be a big help.

Regardless of where you're heading, there are certain things every traveler should carry. Official documents such as passports, visas, airline tickets, and emergency phone numbers should always be stored in a carry-on bag along with money, credit cards, travelers' checks, and prescription medicine. Although you will exchange most of your U.S. or Canadian dollars after you have arrived in the country, it is wise to carry a small amount of local currency—perhaps $25—when traveling. This will cover most incidental or emergency expenses you encounter along the way. U.S. or Canadian dollars can often be exchanged at local banks and can almost always be converted to foreign currency at the international airport from which you depart. Because your carry-on bag will hold all your important documents, it is essential that you keep it with you at all

---

Quick Tips

What to Bring

Worried you will leave something behind? Check to see if these nonclothing essentials are on your packing list:

- A photocopy of any important documents, including the first page of your passport (the part with the photo), your drivers' license or other photo ID, emergency phone numbers, your credit card number, your travelers' check numbers, and your trip itinerary. These backup copies should always be kept separate from original documents to reduce the chance that both would be stolen.

- An extra pair of prescription eyeglasses and/or contact lenses, a second supply of any prescription medication, and a photocopy of all prescriptions

- Unloaded camera and film (both 35 mm film and disposable cameras are usually more expensive abroad)

- Comfortable walking shoes

- Aspirin, sun block, small first aid kit, and moist towelettes or liquid antibacterial soap designed to kill germs without the use of water

- Any cosmetic supplies that might be unavailable outside North America

- Travel guidebook and maps

- Small gifts you can give friends you make along the way as well as larger items for host families and/or foreign tour guides or language instructors. Hometown memorabilia, patriotic trinkets, and coins and postage stamps are especially appropriate.

---

times. Never ever let it out of your grasp, even for a minute. Pickpockets and thieves often work out of international airports, so be wary if someone offers to carry your bags. If you do engage a porter, be sure he or she is wearing an official, easily identifiable uniform, and keep the carry-on bag yourself.

GETTING STARTED

Adjusting to Life Abroad

Your first day in a foreign country can be a little overwhelming: a strange language, a different time zone, maybe even cars driving on the "wrong" side of the road. Will you be safe? Will you run out of money? Can you get help in an emergency? What if you're homesick? What if no one understands you when you speak? What if you hate your host family? These are all justifiable concerns, but with a clear head, you can handle almost anything. If you're traveling from the United States or Canada with a group, your trip coordinators will probably schedule time for you to decompress, ask questions, and settle in. If you arrive alone or are left to your own devices once you've been picked up at the airport, keep your cool and you'll begin to feel relaxed in no time.

Money

Your first priority upon arrival should be exchanging money. Small shops and eateries, tourist attractions, and public transportation may not accept credit cards, so it is never good to be without local currency. Shop around to find the best exchange rate in the area before converting all your dollars in one lump sum (which, by the way, you should never do. Having a six-week supply of cash in your bedroom is not smart or safe). Airport exchange rates are almost always unfavorable and the private exchange bureaus surrounding tourist attractions often charge high commissions. The best bet is usually a local bank. Never exchange money from someone on the street—black-market money exchanging is illegal.

When exchanging money, always get enough cash to carry you through the weekend since banks are often closed on Saturday, Sunday, or Monday, depending on the country. If you are traveling from one country to another, however, exchange only as much as you think you will need. Every time you convert bills from one currency to another, you lose money on the commission charged. The budget you made at home before the start of your trip may be helpful in figuring out how much to convert at a time.

As soon as you have secured your cash and travelers' checks, review your money exchange receipt and figure out how much a pound, peseta, mark, or yen is in dollars. It is very easy to spend money quickly without realizing exactly how much you've spent if you don't do the math. Always round up, not down, when converting in your head so you avoid underestimating prices.

Communication

At some point after landing, you'll want to let your parents know you arrived safely. And no matter how well you're adjusting, there will be times during your stay when you really want to ask them for advice. What is the best way to stay in touch? Communication varies greatly from country to country and region to region. Phone calls may be prohibitively expensive in some parts of the world. However, if you're staying in one place for six or eight weeks, it might be worth having your parents call phone companies and compare international rates. Occasionally there are special deals that can greatly reduce the cost of international calls, making them downright affordable.

Note

International Newspapers on the Web

AUSTRALIA
The Sydney Morning Herald
www.smh.com.au

CHINA
China Daily
www.chinadaily.com.cn

ENGLAND
The London Times
www.the-times.co.uk

FRANCE
Le Monde
tout.lemonde.fr/

GERMANY
Berliner Morgenpost
www.berliner-morgenpost.de

INDIA
The Times of India
www.timesofindia.com

ITALY
La Repubblica
www.repubblica.it

JAPAN
The Japan Times
www.japantimes.co.jp/

MEXICO
Heraldo de Mexico
www.heraldo.com.mx

RUSSIA
Pravda
www.pravda.ru

SCOTLAND
The Scotsman
www.scotsman.com

SPAIN
El Mundo
www.el-mundo.es/index.html

If the high cost of phone calls eliminates that as an option, don't despair. You may find communicating by fax a good alternative. Because they reduce the amount of time you are "online," faxes are much less expensive than phone calls. You can write your parents everything they want to know (or you want them to know), and send the letter off with a few pushes of a button. If you are faxing from a photocopy center or store, you may be limited to communicating during business hours. And of course, fax machines are going to be hard to come by at any hour of the day in remote or undeveloped parts of the world.

Electronic mail is another possibility. E-mail is fast and fairly reliable, and like faxes, allows you to tell as much as you'd like without spending a fortune. Again, this form of communication will be possible in only some areas of the world, and you may be restricted to business hours. Cyber cafés, computer clusters where you rent time online and pay for snacks to accompany your work, may be open limited hours, and often have long lines and high fees.

Part of the study abroad and travel experience is learning to make decisions, difficult decisions, without anyone's help or advice. You may not be able to communicate as often or as easily as you would like, but that's part of the adventure. When all else fails, there's always the good old-fashioned letter or postcard.

Safety

Students' and parents' number one concern about high school programs abroad is safety. In reality, there's little to fear as long as you use good judgment. While you may be more vulnerable to pickpockets and scam artists as a foreigner abroad, physical safety issues are the same in most parts of the world. When in urban areas, you should always protect your belongings and avoid carrying large sums of cash. Be street smart when walking about the city and using public transportation. Know where you're going and ask directions only of responsible people (police officers, transportation coordinators, and store proprietors are usually good choices). Always be aware of the people around you and whenever possible, travel with a companion. Avoid walking in dark streets or alleys at all times. If you suspect that someone is following you, retreat into a nearby store and wait it out. Female students should exercise particular caution. Annoying as it may be, young women should follow discriminatory local customs. If women do not travel in the streets unaccompanied, you should not either—it could put you in serious danger.

In small villages or rural areas, chances are you will be relatively safe. Summer programs choose these locations carefully and check each host family meticulously. Following local customs will generally keep you safe. If your host family allows their children to wander about town with their friends after dark, you can probably follow suit once you know your way about and can communicate adequately with locals.

Regardless of where you are, learn emergency phone numbers and carry them with you. If your passport, credit card, and/or travelers' checks are stolen, report them immediately. Your program director should have the phone number for the U.S. and Canadian embassies readily available, and if you photocopied the numbers of your credit card and travelers' checks, you can take care of those calls quickly.

Timing

With logistical matters out of the way, you're ready to enjoy your trip in full. If you're based in one place—a school, camp, or host family house—shedding that tourist veneer might be your number one goal. That first time you answer correctly when someone asks for directions—wow, what a thrill. But it takes time. Map and guidebook in hand, you'll look nothing like a native your first week abroad. How can you remedy that? As soon as the jet lag wears off and you've stopped sleeping twelve hours a day, nudge your mind and body into local rhythms.

Eating, sleeping, working, and relaxing according to local custom will put you in the right mind set. If everyone takes siestas mid-afternoon, join in. That way you won't be tired when you're at the disco into the early daylight hours. If dinner is served at 9 P.M. and you're accustomed to eating at 5:30 sharp, calm your growling stomach and hold out for the big meal. Adopt a slower pace if that's what's called for—the tourist sites aren't going away. Lifestyles vary greatly from place to place and living the schedule of another people is a golden opportunity. You not only gain insight into their culture, you become better able to evaluate your own.

Homestays

The most difficult, and arguably the most rewarding, adjustment is that associated with host families. When living in a home, you have little opportunity to escape an alien environment by retreating into English. In some instances you may share small living quarters with four or five other people, and thus have little physical privacy. Adapting to an individual family's quirks on top

—————————————— **Expert Advice** ——————————————

"Students and their parents tend to be scared to death of homestays. We don't do it to torture them. If their fear were borne out, we wouldn't do it. We plan homestays because of the tremendous growth they inspire. From our experience, the self-confidence that is gained from having to make it in a family for a week or ten days is immeasurable. It often becomes the subject for college essays. The fact is, you can't really understand a foreign culture until you live it."

— Peter Shumlin, admissions director, Putney Student Travel

of a regional lifestyle can be difficult; however, it is the best way to experience daily life. At a host family's home, you eat real food—not restaurant fare—and listen to real conversation.

Summer programs usually place students in families that have children of their own, and this can help break the ice. Children are easy to talk to, and teenagers are eager to hear about life in your home country as well as your impressions of their culture. If you are considerate of your host family's needs and appreciative of their efforts to entertain and care for you, you will probably grow to like, or even love, your home away from home.

Most summer programs select host families with great care, placing students only with people they know well. Even if a family enthusiastically volunteers to host a student, however, they have to make sacrifices and exert considerable effort to do so. It goes without saying that you should show appreciation for their efforts. Common sense courtesies will see you through. Even if you don't speak well, make an effort to converse, by "sign language" or pantomime if necessary. Try eating all the foods offered, no matter how unfamiliar they appear, so you won't offend the chef. Follow the family's rules and habits. For example, if family members take their shoes off upon entering the house, take yours off too. Clean up after yourself and offer to help with household chores. Also, be conscious of prices. For example, Coke and Pepsi may be very expensive in some countries. If you're accustomed to drinking it by the gallon, limit your intake to match that of other family members. Also note that in many parts of the world people are charged for local as well as long distance phone calls. Always ask permission before using the phone, and make sure your host parents won't be billed if you call friends at other host family houses.

Quick Tips

Summer Shouldn't be Hard to Swallow

If there are certain foods you cannot eat, whether for health, religious, or ethical reasons, your summer program should inform the host family. It is certainly acceptable to remind the family if you are served a dish you cannot or must not consume. However, you should try a taste of anything you can eat.

Many families decide to host foreign students in order to expand their own cultural horizons. While you're soaking in their language, culture, and customs, they may want to learn more about yours. Think of some fun ways to share your heritage. You could try cooking some of your favorite American foods for them. If you are traveling to an area of the world that will not have all

the ingredients you need, you can pack small quantities and take them with you (because of customs laws, you may not be able to take fresh fruits, vegetables, or meats—but they'd spoil anyway). You may also want to bring photographs, postcards, and picture books from home. Audio tapes—especially mixes of your favorite music—and a Walkman™ are also a good, easy-to-pack option.

In the end, you may be glad you have your own family, siblings, and bedroom at home, but you will have had a rare opportunity to peer into daily life in another part of the world. There is nothing else like it.

REVELING IN YOUR ADVENTURE

When it comes to travel, make flexibility your watchword. An element of risk encircles globetrotting—you never know exactly what lies at the other end of an airline flight. The most basic comforts could vanish overnight. Sounds of rushing cars, trains, and late night music may disrupt your sleep. Heat and mosquitoes may make daily excursions nearly unbearable. Local food may disagree with your refined taste or fast-food palette. But these are minor inconveniences when the world lays stretched out before you waiting to be (re)discovered. If you get disappointed or discouraged, remind yourself of the excitement of travel. Look around you and marvel at the history, or the natural beauty, or the resilience of the local people.

If you feel lonely or homesick, seek company rather than brooding alone. Travel is most rewarding when you make friends with those you meet along the way. If you don't speak the language, interaction will be limited, but not impossible. You will find English-speakers in most of the world, especially in large cities and among young people. Search them out, and remember to be patient if their heavy accents or broken sentences make comprehension difficult. If you have any skills in the native language at all, use them! It

doesn't matter if you talk only in the present tense or if your vocabulary resembles that of an eight-year-old. Locals are delighted when you make an effort to address them in their native tongue. And the more you speak, the faster you will improve. "It's kind of hard not to learn while you are there," said Neal Chervin, director of Academic Study Associates, Inc., a program that sends high school students to France and Spain. "But it is important to go into the restaurants, to really ask questions, and to listen in class."

Capitalizing on every opportunity is essential. "You get out of the program what you put into it, which is to say that you have to take advantage of what is offered," said Cassandra Porsch, who attended the Academic Study Associates program in France. "I think it has the potential to be very rewarding if you take advantage of all that is offered. It was definitely rewarding for me." Whether program coordinators organize optional cultural trips or your host brother asks you to join him cruising the streets of town, seize the opportunity. Trying exotic foods, dancing to local bands, and enjoying local rituals all make for a livelier, more exciting experience abroad. Your summer overseas may not be the stuff of legends and fairy tales, but it will be an adventure. Guaranteed.

LIST OF PROGRAMS

Here is a list of international summer programs. See the Program Directory in Part III of this book for a description of each of these programs.

Academic Study Abroad Programs

Academic Study Associates—Language Study Programs
AFS Intercultural Programs—Summer Homestay Language Study
Alliances Abroad—Summer Spanish Program for Youth in Spain; Summer French Programs for Youth in France
American Collegiate Adventures
American Institute for Foreign Study—Pre-College Summer Study Abroad
American International Youth Student Exchange—American International Youth Student Exchange Program
Amerispan Unlimited—Madrid and Marbella Summer Camps; Spanish Language Program in Costa Rica
Avatar Education Ltd.—Buckswood ARC Summer Programs
Baja California Language College

Barat Foundation—Barat Foundation Summer Program
Bordeaux Language School—Teenage Summer Program in Biarritz
Broadreach, Inc.—Broadreach Insights
Broadreach, Inc.—Broadreach Summer Adventures for Teenagers
Cambridge College Programme LLC—Cambridge College Programme
Center for Cross-Cultural Study—Summer in Seville
Center for Cultural Interchange—Discovery Abroad Programs
Ceran Lingua—Ceran Junior
Colorado College—Summer Session for High School Students
Comunicare—Study and Share
Costa Rican Language Academy (CRLA)
Dickinson College—Pre-College Program
Earthwatch Institute—Field Research Expedition Internships
ECHO International Educational Expeditions—Australian Biological Adventures
EF International Language Schools—EF International Language Schools
Georgia Hardy Tours, Inc.—Summer Study
Humanities Spring in Assisi
Irish American Cultural Organization—Irish Way
Irish Centre for Talented Youth
Knowledge Exchange Institute—Precollege African Safari Program
Knowledge Exchange Institute—Precollege Amazon Exploration Program
Knowledge Exchange Institute—Precollege Artist Abroad Program
Knowledge Exchange Institute—Precollege Business, Law and Diplomacy Program
Knowledge Exchange Institute—Precollege European Capitals Program
Knowledge Exchange Institute—Precollege Research Abroad Program
Language Link—Intercultura; Spanish Language Institute; CLIC
Language Studies Abroad, Inc.—Language Studies Abroad
Language Study Abroad
LEAPNow—Summer Program in Central America
Leysin American School in Switzerland—Summer in Switzerland
Lingua Service Worldwide—Junior Classic and Junior Sports Program
Lingua Service Worldwide—Junior Course in Salamanca
Lingua Service Worldwide—Summer Language Adventure
Musiker Discovery Programs—Summer Discovery
Nacel Open Door—Summer Programs
National FFA Organization—Agricultural Programs Overseas
National Registration Center for Study Abroad—Summer Language Programs
New York Film Academy—New York Film Academy Summer Program
Oceanic Society—Bahamas Dolphin Project for High School Students
Oceanic Society—Belize Student Expedition
OxBridge Academic Programs—Cambridge Prep; Cambridge Tradition; Oxford
    Tradition; Académie de Paris
Putney Student Travel—Excel at Oxford/Tuscany and Madrid/Barcelona
Rassias Programs
Scandinavian Seminar—Ambassadors for the Environment
School for Field Studies—Environmental Field Studies Abroad
Sons of Norway—Camp Norway

Summer Study Programs—Summer Study in Paris at The American University of Paris

Tufts University European Center—Tufts Summit

University of Dallas Study Abroad—Shakespeare in Italy; Latin in Rome; Thomas More in England; Winston Churchill in England

World Learning—Experiment in International Living (EIL)

Youth for Understanding International Exchange—Summer Overseas

Community Service Abroad Programs

AFS Intercultural Programs—Summer Community Service/Team Mission

American Farm School—Greek Summer

Amigos de las Americas

Breakthroughs Abroad, Inc.—High School Programs

Broadreach, Inc.—Broadreach Insights

Broadreach, Inc.—Broadreach Summer Adventures for Teenagers

Comunicare—Study and Share

Costa Rican Language Academy (CRLA)

Earthwatch Institute—Field Research Expedition Internships

Global Routes—High School Community Service Programs

Global Volunteers

Global Works International Programs—Summer Programs

Intern Exchange International—Intern Exchange International

Involvement Volunteers Association—International Volunteering; Networked International Volunteering

La Société Française—International Volunteer Program

Latitudes International—Community Service Travel

LEAPNow—Summer Program in Central America; Summer Program in Australia

Legacy International—Global Youth Village

Longacre Expeditions

Nacel Open Door—Summer Programs

National FFA Organization—Agricultural Programs Overseas

Operation Crossroads Africa—Africa & Diaspora Programs

Peacework

Scandinavian Seminar—Ambassadors for the Environment

School for Field Studies—Environmental Field Studies Abroad

Sidwell Friends School—SFS in Costa Rica

Student Safaris International—Zanzibar to the Serengeti; Queensland Explorer

Visions

Volunteers for Peace—VFP International Workcamps

Where There Be Dragons—Summer Programs

World Horizons International

World Learning—Experiment in International Living (EIL)

Youth for Understanding International Exchange—Summer Overseas

Homestay/Cultural Immersion Programs

Academic Study Associates—Language Study Programs

Adventure Ireland

AFS Intercultural Programs—Summer Homestay; Summer Homestay Language
   Study; Summer Homestay Plus
Alliances Abroad—Summer Spanish Program for Youth in Spain; Summer French
   Programs for Youth in France; Culture and Adventure Program for Youth in Ireland
American Collegiate Adventures
American Farm School—Greek Summer
American Institute for Foreign Study—Pre-College Summer Study Abroad
American International Youth Student Exchange—American International Youth
   Student Exchange Program
Amerispan Unlimited—Madrid and Marbella Summer Camps; Spanish Language
   Program in Costa Rica
Amigos de las Americas
Baja California Language College
Barat Foundation—Barat Foundation Summer Program
Bordeaux Language School—Teenage Summer Program in Biarritz
Breakthroughs Abroad, Inc.—High School Programs
Broadreach, Inc.—Broadreach Insights
Broadreach, Inc.—Broadreach Summer Adventures for Teenagers
Center for Cross-Cultural Study—Summer in Seville
Center for Cultural Interchange—Discovery Abroad Programs
Choate Rosemary Hall —Study Abroad
Comunicare—Study and Share
Costa Rican Language Academy (CRLA)
EF International Language Schools
Georgia Hardy Tours, Inc.—Summer Study
Global Works International Programs—Summer Programs
Irish American Cultural Organization—Irish Way
Language Link—Intercultura; Spanish Language Institute; CLIC
Language Studies Abroad, Inc.—Language Studies Abroad
Language Study Abroad
Latitudes International—Community Service Travel
LEAPNow—Summer Program in Central America
Lingua Service Worldwide—Junior Classic and Junior Sports Program
Lingua Service Worldwide—Junior Course in Salamanca
Lingua Service Worldwide—Summer Language Adventure
Nacel Open Door—Summer Programs
National FFA Organization—Agricultural Programs Overseas
National Registration Center for Study Abroad—Summer Language Programs
Peacework
Rassias Programs
Sidwell Friends School—SFS in Costa Rica
Sons of Norway—Camp Norway
Tennis: Europe and More—Tennis: Europe and More
Tufts University European Center—Tufts Summit
Visions
Where There Be Dragons—Summer Programs
Wilderness Ventures—Wilderness Adventure Expeditions; Advanced Leadership
   Expeditions; Offshore Adventure Expeditions

World Horizons International
World Learning—Experiment in International Living (EIL)
Youth for Understanding International Exchange—Summer Overseas

Outdoor Adventures Abroad Programs

AFS Intercultural Programs—Summer Homestay Plus
America's Adventure/Venture Europe
Breakthroughs Abroad, Inc.—High School Programs
Broadreach, Inc.—Broadreach Insights
Broadreach, Inc.—Broadreach Summer Adventures for Teenagers
Center for Cultural Interchange—Discovery Abroad Programs
Earthwatch Institute—Field Research Expedition Internships
ECHO International Educational Expeditions—Australian Biological Adventures
Global Works International Programs—Summer Programs
Interlocken—Crossroads Adventure Travel
International Bicycle Fund—Bicycle Africa Tours; Sbuhbi Lithlal Ti Swatixwtuhd
JCC Maccabi Xperience Israel Programs—Israel Summer Programs
LEAPNow—Summer Program in Central America; Summer Program in Australia
Longacre Expeditions
Musiker Discovery Programs—Musiker Tours
National FFA Organization—Agricultural Programs Overseas
Odyssey Expeditions
Outpost Wilderness Adventure—Outpost Wilderness Adventures
The Road Less Traveled
Sail Caribbean
Sidwell Friends School—SFS in Costa Rica
Student Hosteling Program—Summer Biking Programs
Student Safaris International—Zanzibar to the Serengeti; Queensland Explorer
Visions
Weissman Teen Tours, Inc.—Weissman Teen Tours
Westcoast Connection—Active Teen Tours
Westcoast Connection—European Programs
Westcoast Connection—Golf & Tennis Programs
Westcoast Connection—Israel Experience
Westcoast Connection—On Tour
Westcoast Connection—Outdoor Adventure Programs
Westcoast Connection—Ski & Snowboard Sensation
Where There Be Dragons—Summer Programs
Wilderness Ventures—Wilderness Adventure Expeditions; Advanced Leadership
    Expeditions; Offshore Adventure Expeditions
World Learning—Experiment in International Living (EIL)

Travel/Sightseeing Programs

Adventure Ireland
American Collegiate Adventures
American Farm School—Greek Summer

Comunicare—Study and Share
Education Unlimited—Tour Italy
Interlocken—Crossroads Adventure Travel
Irish American Cultural Organization—Irish Way
JCC Maccabi Xperience Israel Programs—Israel Summer Programs
Knowledge Exchange Institute—Precollege European Capitals Program
Musiker Discovery Programs—Musiker Tours
Putney Student Travel—Excel at Oxford/Tuscany and Madrid/Barcelona
Rassias Programs
University of Dallas Study Abroad—Shakespeare in Italy; Latin in Rome; Thomas
    More in England; Winston Churchill in England
Weissman Teen Tours, Inc.—Weissman Teen Tours
Westcoast Connection—Active Teen Tours
Westcoast Connection—European Programs
Westcoast Connection—Golf & Tennis Programs
Westcoast Connection—Israel Experience
Westcoast Connection—On Tour
Westcoast Connection—Ski & Snowboard Sensation
Where There Be Dragons—Summer Programs

ENRICHING YOUR SUMMER

Here is a list of websites, books, and movies you can use to further explore study and travel abroad.

Websites

Important Info: Passports, Visas, Immunizations

travel.state.gov/
A wealth of helpful info from the Bureau of Consular Affairs, including country-by-country explanations of which documents are needed for U.S. citizens traveling abroad; the process of obtaining/renewing/replacing a passport; a downloadable passport application; and a special "Tips for Students" section.

www.cdc.gov
Center for Disease Control site covers vaccination requirements, food and water precautions, disease outbreaks, etc.

Regional Resources: Research Your Destination

www.excite.com/travel/countries
dir.yahoo.com/Regional/Countries/
Online directories. Click on any country you want to find info about restaurants, tourist attractions, etc.

www.fodors.com
www.lonelyplanet.com
www.frommers.com
Online versions of popular travel guides.

www.actualidad.com
Links to a surprisingly large number of international newspapers available on the web—everything from the *Egyptian Gazette* to the *Bolivian Times* to *Pakistan Today*. Many sites are in English.

www.nationalgeographic.com/traveler/
Contains links to dozens of helpful destination sites.

www.worldtravelguide.net
A general travel website containing airport guides, lists of major attractions, travelers' reviews, and reservation info.

Language Links

www.travlang.com
Free translations and useful phrases for travelers in dozens of languages; downloadable sound files allow you to listen to the correct pronunciation of foreign phrases.

babelfish.altavista.digital.com/translate.dyn
Translates text and webpages from one language to another.

Books

Travel Guides

Lonely Planet series

Let's Go series

Rough Guide series

Eyewitness Travel Guide series

Rick Steves's series

Language Help

Easy Phrase Book series

Barron's Languages at a Glance series

Fodor's Languages for Travelers series

Essays and Memoirs

Maiden Voyage by Tania Aebi and Bernadette Brennan

Dove by Robin Lee Graham and Derek L.T. Gill

A Year in Provence by Peter Mayle

Neither Here Nor There: Travels in Europe by Bill Bryson

Fresh Air Fiend by Paul Theroux

Round Ireland with a Fridge by Tony Hawks

There's No Toilet Paper on the Road Less Traveled: The Best of Travel Humor and Misadventure by Doug Lansky

Femme D'Aventure: Travel Tales From Inner Montana to Outer Mongolia by Jessica Maxwell

Literature and Fiction

Memoirs of a Geisha by Arthur Golden (Japan)

The Kitchen God's Wife by Amy Tan (China)

Sea of Memory by Erri de Luca (Italy)

Tear This Heart Out by Angeles Mastretta (Mexico)

Crazy by Benjamin Lebert (Germany)

Angela's Ashes by Frank McCourt (Ireland)

Les Misérables by Victor Hugo (France)

Anna Karenina by Leo Tolstoy (Russia)

The God of Small Things by Arundhati Roy (India)

Movies

Foreign Films*

Life is Beautiful
Roberto Benigni's masterpiece, classified as a comedy but with some powerful life lessons to offer.

Crouching Tiger, Hidden Dragon
Director Ang Lee achieved critical and popular success with this Chinese martial arts film, which combines spectacular fight scenes with a delicate love story.

Ciao, Professore
Italian comedy featuring the outrageous clash between a strict, no-nonsense teacher and his class of rambunctious, street-smart kids.

Leningrad Cowboys Go America
Absurd road movie from Finland chronicling the world tour of the most mediocre polka band in Siberia.

Tampopo
A group of noodle-obsessed men attempt to help a woman run the best noodle restaurant in Tokyo.

Babette's Feast
Drama about an exiled French housekeeper for a pair of devoutly religious, elderly, Danish sisters.

Children of Heaven
Iranian film about a young boy who loses his sister's only pair of shoes; they must then hatch a plan to share his shoes and keep his negligence a secret from their parents.

To Live
Follows a contemporary family across the turbulent face of modern China, from the Japanese invasion through Mao's Great Leap Forward and the Cultural Revolution.

Walkabout
Mystical story of two English children abandoned in the Australian outback and rescued by an Aborigine boy.

Exotic Locales

Hideous Kinky
British hippie Kate Winslet takes her two young daughters to colorful Morocco in the 1960s and on a subsequent search for enlightment.

Out of Africa
Based on the real-life story of Karen Blixen, who establishes a plantation in Africa. Starring Meryl Streep and Robert Redford.

Hatari!
John Wayne and friends traipse all over Africa capturing animals for a zoo.

The Joy Luck Club
The universal complexity of mother-daughter relationships is explored in this film about four young Chinese-American women and their amazingly strong immigrant mothers.

The Last Emperor
Biography of Pu Yi, who was named Emperor of China at age three but lost his throne during the revolution and ended up as a peasant worker.

Shogun
TV miniseries available on video. A shipwrecked Englishman must create a life for himself in 17th century Japan.

Doctor Zhivago
Romantic epic following the life of a Russian doctor/poet during World War I and the Bolshevik Revolution.

Midnight Express
Based on the true story of an American drug smuggler who faces brutal conditions in a Turkish prison.

A Passage to India
Cultures clash when a young British woman accuses an Indian doctor of attacking her in 1920s India.

The Mission
A Jesuit mission in the jungles of Brazil is threatened by the Portuguese. Starring Robert DeNiro and Jeremy Irons.

A Cry in the Dark
"The dingo's got my baby!" True story of a mother charged with murder when her infant disappears in the Australian outback.

*Some of the foreign film recommendations were provided by 1-World Festival of Films. Website: www.1worldfilms.com.

Community Service Programs

OVERVIEW

Organized volunteer projects compose the fastest growing category of summer programs for high schoolers. In poverty-stricken regions of North America, Latin America, Europe, Africa, and the Caribbean, American teens can be seen swinging hammers and wielding axes in an effort to build homes, clear paths, and improve the lives of those around them.

The work is long, hot, and hard, living conditions rustic to downright primitive. But the personal satisfaction? Phenomenal. Students choose to do it again and again.

"SHOULD I TRY A COMMUNITY SERVICE PROGRAM?"

Throughout the school year, socially conscious high school students manage to find time to serve their communities in countless ways, from collecting food to tutoring children, singing for the elderly to racing for diabetes. When summer begins and academic and extracurricular commitments end, however, students can throw their entire minds and bodies into addressing the societal problems before them. Brawn, high energy, and sheer determination combine to raise houses, erect walls, and halt erosion—all in a matter of weeks. Those who've participated in community service summer programs say the joy of seeing their efforts materialize and the sorrow at bidding newly made friends farewell last long after the final coat of paint has dried.

In almost all cases, community service programs select work projects involving manual labor. If construction, maintenance and repair leave you cold, find a local volunteer program that allows you to tap other skills or talents instead. Similarly, if you are ready to put in 10 hours of hard labor a day only if you can retreat to an air conditioned home and cable TV at night, a local community service program might better serve your needs. Organized community service programs are rewarding, both in the projects completed and the friendships made, but you have to be ready for the working and living environments that come with the territory.

FINDING YOUR PROGRAM

While almost all organized community service programs involve manual labor, the feel of programs differ in several ways. Service can be viewed from the angle of cultural exchange or protecting the environment or social justice and religion; which perspective a program emphasizes will influence the community service experience. Programs also differ in the centrality of volunteer work to the program schedule. Some summer programs make service the all-encompassing focus while others use it as just one of many activities including outdoor sports, travel, and cultural exploration. The greatest distinction among programs, however, is whether they combine service with an overseas experience or not. Thinking about the kind of summer experience you're seeking and the way you want to incorporate volunteer efforts into your daily life will help you select the best program for your needs and interests.

Programs in the United States

Service programs in the United States allow students to address some of the pressing needs they learn about in daily newspapers and the nightly news. From aiding victims of natural disaster to building low-income housing in urban slums or rural villages, student volunteers confront poverty and misfortune head-on. Alternatively, service programs operating in state and national parks provide students with an opportunity to help protect and preserve the country's valuable natural resources. Laying paths, constructing educational sites, and erecting fences are some of the activities that fill volunteers' days.

Student volunteers often labor in remote and isolated places. Environmental service programs may come with breathtaking backdrops—the rugged mountains of the West, sparkling ocean of the East, and clear blue skies of the Midwest. But some programs—like The American Jewish Society for Service—make no promises. Each year they send volunteers to the places most in need of help.

Volunteers generally work five or six days a week for between one and six weeks, enjoying social and recreational activities after work and on the weekends. Student committees usually take turns with daily tasks including shopping, cooking, and house

---

Expert Advice

"The American Jewish Society for Service is an independent national organization that was created in 1950 to give Jewish teenagers and those of other faiths an opportunity to perform humanitarian service in fulfillment of the highest teachings of Judaism, Tzadukka. Over the past forty-eight years, AJSS campers have constructed homes from the foundation up, built classrooms for an outdoor educational center, built community centers, repaired flood and tornado damaged communities, poured concrete for sidewalks, repaired children's playgrounds and [completed] all conceivable home renovations and repairs. We have been in 43 of the contiguous states with an alumni of well over 2,000 teenagers."

—Carl Brenner, executive director, American Jewish Society for Service

---

cleaning. Housing may be cramped—a nearly completed Habitat for Humanity building, a church hall, or four-person tents staked near the work site—but students agree that tight quarters result in intense group bonding.

There are distinct advantages to selecting a community service program within national borders. If your summer goal is simply to help others through service, location becomes irrelevant. There are people in need in all corners of the globe, even in the wealthy USA. Community service programs within the country you live are significantly less expensive than those abroad, primarily because of savings in the cost of transportation. By saving money on airfare, you can fund another week of service. It makes fiscal sense. Service programs in the United States and Canada also have the advantage of reduced health and safety risks. While volunteers may live in rustic environments, they are secure in knowing that food and drinking water are safe, and that emergency health care is within reach.

Programs Abroad

Community service programs abroad enable students to combine volunteer work in areas of acute need with a rich cultural experience in an underdeveloped or poverty-stricken region of the world. Work projects, which consist almost entirely of manual labor, focus on sanitation (building latrines and water systems), housing development, farming, road repair, and environmental protection. While the majority of programs are based in Latin America, projects also dot the Caribbean (including its French-speaking islands), Greece, Ireland, Russia, the Fiji Islands, the West Indies, Eastern Europe, and several African nations.

Depending on the program and sponsoring organization, students may live in host family homes, community centers, or tents. Work projects are usually directed by the group leaders—who travel with students from North America—and may or may not be done alongside native residents. Programs in which students live and work beside a host family provide the richest cultural experience. In a few select programs, students are sent in pairs to tiny villages rather than staying in one village with their traveling companions.

When programs that include host-family-stays function in regions where a language other than English is spoken, there is

—— **Student Scoop** ——

"We spent some time at a government work camp, basically working on a stream restoration project. Then we were flown out by helicopter to the base of Mt. McKinley. I went places I'd never get to go if I was a tourist or just at the park hiking. There was an old road at the base of the mountain, and we constructed check dams to reverse the erosion problems."

—Cynthia Osterling, participant, Student Conservation Association High School Program (Alaska)

—— **Student Scoop** ——

"Landmark is better for people who aren't quite so sure about going out and being away from civilization. It is only two weeks, which helps a lot. The time flies. The program [which engages students in one- or two-week work projects in places of historical, cultural, or social significance to the United States] is ideal for people not ready for a serious time commitment or a drastic lifestyle change."

—Nira Salant, participant, Landmark Volunteers (Maine)

Types of Programs

usually a two-year minimum language requirement. But most find the language barrier a distant second to cultural obstacles. Because life in the small rural villages of developing countries is such a stark contrast to life in industrially advanced nations like the United States and Canada, homestays require a complete opening of the mind. When high school volunteers succeed, they are privy to amazing growth. Anna Moore is one such student. She said she came out of her rustic Paraguayan adventure more intelligent, aware, and sensitive.

"I lived in a thatched roof, dirt floored hut in a four room house with no running water and nothing separating me from the cows outside save a couple of worn boards," said Moore of her Amigos de las Americas experience in Paraguay. "But I had my own room and bed, which was great (conditions vary depending on what country and region you're in. Some volunteers had much more modern conditions). I also had my own chicken that laid eggs under the bed. By the end of my stay I had taken to hoarding the eggs because the food really sucked. Prior to the trip I had been a vegetarian, but the four Paraguayan food groups are grease, oil, fat, and salmonella-infested carrion. It's not really that bad. Sometimes we had vegetables (one of our projects was garden planting) but usually it was mandioca (from the mandioc plant; it has absolutely no nutritional value), greasy noodle type things and chicken or beef. The chicken was whole, but if you pretended not to see the internal organs it really wasn't that bad. Just greasy. I'll never forget my host mom being a little offended that I didn't devour the claws (it's actually the best part; you get used to it) during my first few days. The beef tastes better than the chicken, but watch out: There are animals inside it that like to make happy homes in the stomach. Trust me. Once I got over my fear of meat, which didn't take long because I got really hungry, I started to get into making the food. (I didn't find out it had given me parasites until I got home.) My host mom and I spent lots of time cooking—almost every afternoon when I came back from garden planting and latrine building. I learned how to make some really good Paraguayan dishes, but I don't think I ever convinced my [host] mom that cooking oil is not a staple."

While it may be impossible to prepare for such drastic changes in lifestyle, all intercultural community service programs include orientation and training before immersion into the host culture. The intensity of such preparation usually matches that of the anticipated program experience. Joseph Kim, who participated in an eight-week Amigos de las Americas program in Ecuador, had six months of training before setting off for his small village home. "For our [Amigos] chapter, the training started in November and ended right before we left in June," Kim said. "We learned how to build latrines, we got health tips, and we had some Spanish classes. We learned how to deal with cultural differences and how to deal with culture shock when you get there. We also learned how to deal with culture shock on the way back, when you haven't seen cars in two months. They taught us self-defense, to be safe."

Programs that emphasize a group as well as individual experience place all students in one village or town under the direction of a group leader who travels with them. This allows for continual briefing and training throughout the program, as well as an extended support network. Orientations before departure may include discussions of health precautions and cultural adjustment while an orientation upon arrival in the host country reinforces cultural lessons and addresses any last minute concerns. Once students are settled into a routine in their host village, they meet with leaders and fellow group members regularly to discuss progress and any challenging adjustment issues.

Community service programs in developing countries offer an unsurpassed opportunity to experience a daily lifestyle that is becoming increasingly rare as electricity, running water, and modern farming equipment spreads throughout the world. For anyone interested in public health, sociology, anthropology, or global politics, it is a fascinating opportunity for study and observation. Community service programs also provide an attractive alternative to traditional language programs. It is the rare village in which natives speak English, so you'll be immersed in a foreign language from morning until night. Moreover, these villages are without distractions. In a small, predominately illiterate town, people entertain with stories, news, and gossip. You'll be swept into a highly verbal culture where people pride themselves on their ability to converse well.

Expert Advice

"The students' motivation is high. We work with the young people during the pre-trip orientation to make sure they understand their responsibilities. They need to realize that this isn't simply a four- or six-week vacation. We stress their involvement and purpose during both the departure orientation and in further orientations after they arrive in the host country. We immerse the students in the cultural and day-to-day issues that are key to their experience with the group they're joining. By the time they meet the local group, the students have a very good sense of what it all means."

—Ligia Willmore, region II international coordinator, AFS

A caveat, however: In many remote regions, people speak local dialects distinct from the official state language you study in school. Anna Moore, who went to Paraguay with Amigos de las Americas, said she learned more Guaraní, a Native American dialect, than she did Spanish during her eight-week stay, although her Spanish did improve considerably. If language acquisition is your primary concern, you should choose your program carefully. Even if you are placed in a region that uses the official language, there will probably be significant regional variation. South American and Caribbean Spanish, for example, are quite noticeably different from the Castilian spoken in Spain. In some regions, spoken language is a mixture of Spanish, the language of the European conquistadors, and several indigenous tongues. The same is true of African and Caribbean French—the language is a blend of European French and local dialects. You'll learn many beautiful phrases your foreign language instructors at home may not understand.

If you plan to volunteer in a developing country, you must go in with open eyes. There is no question that the experience of living as a member of a foreign family is special, but it doesn't come without drawbacks. There are the usual difficulties of adapting to a culture as well as an individual family's habits: there may be a lack of privacy and of time to unwind alone; you may crave contact with someone who speaks your language and understands your longing for a milkshake and fries. But on top of the usual challenges, you must consider your health. Receiving the appropriate vaccines before leaving home will protect you to a degree, but sanitation is often poor and water unsafe to drink. Without refrigeration, meat can become infected quickly. You'll be putting in long hours of physical labor, so of course you must eat and stay hydrated. Community service programs in developing countries have a lot to offer, but you must be aware of possible consequences.

THE VOLUNTEERING EXPERIENCE

Because most community service summer programs engage their volunteers in manual labor rather than in teaching or tutoring, students in programs without homestays may have significantly less contact with local residents than they are accustomed to in volunteer work at home. Community service in the form of manual labor is rewarding in its own right. If you have previously served meals at a soup kitchen or tutored a child in an aftercare program, you may have stopped to wonder if you were really making a difference. Are the two hours a week you spend with a lonely and neglected child enough to counterbalance the lack of attention he receives the rest of the week? Are the free meals you're providing hungry homeless women energizing them to seek work the next day, or simply filling their stomachs temporarily?

In many ways, manual labor eliminates the question of impact by providing an immediate, tangible counter to any doubts. If you build a home for a family and watch them move in, you know the family now has permanent shelter. Stepping back at the end of your work program and seeing the concrete progress you have made shows, unequivocally, that you have made a difference.

But progress can be slow and tedious. It may take days to clear a house of debris before you can begin making repairs. What keeps people going when all their muscles ache? Belief in the work and commitment to the cause does wonders. Once you have selected your community service program and know exactly what your project will entail, you may want to do a little research. Find out why the community in which you'll be volunteering requires help. Besides their immediate needs (storm repair, affordable housing, etcetera), what has to be done to get the community back on its feet? Determine, in your own mind, why you want to help. What makes this project special? Of course, you'll be better able to answer this question when you arrive on site and meet the community leaders and residents who greet you. But preparing ahead of time will help smooth your path into the community.

Remember that giving service is a privilege—a community must accept your assistance in order for you to help, and however desperate their need, they will not look favorably on arrogance or ignorance. The more you know and understand about a community, the more appreciative they will be of your volunteer efforts. Many high schools have added a community service component to their graduation requirement, and some students use summer program volunteer work to fulfill that requirement (several summer programs provide students with a certificate detailing the number of community service hours they logged for this express purpose). If you participate in a service program with a requirement in mind, enter the project because you want to help the people you are serving, not because you are required to serve. It is unfair to everyone involved—the community you are helping and other participants who are eager to make a difference—if you make only a half-hearted effort. Most people find that meeting and taking a daily interest in the community in which they work is the best way to extract meaning from a service project. Through discussion with residents, many students discover they are getting as much out of the project as the community they're helping. In spite of their misfortune, residents have much to teach about hope, resilience, and life itself. While it can sometimes be difficult to reach out to community members, the rewards are great.

Student Scoop

"I was really looking for something like this. I wanted to get away from the city and from the normal kinds of community service. I volunteer at the New England Aquarium, which is great, but it is much more of a professional atmosphere. With Landmark, you really get outside and get dirty; you do some real work. Plus you're living there. You don't go home at the end of the day. It was very different."

—Nira Salant, participant, Landmark Volunteers (Maine)

Expert Advice

"Our summer community service programs have been especially good for high school age students. Young people usually want to do something meaningful, yet they don't often have many skills. So we create programs that let them see tangible and immediate results of their service. Instead of becoming frustrated, they clearly see the difference they have made."

—Ligia Willmore, region II international coordinator, AFS

SWEAT, SUN, FRIENDS AND FUN

While organized community service projects are hard work, they're also a lot of fun. Most programs operate within a group structure. Students travel, work, and in many cases, room together. As a result, community service summer programs provide many of the same benefits and rewards as academic, athletic, travel, and adventure programs—they allow participants to meet and work with some of the most exciting, committed high school students in the country. As with other summer programs, students can enter a project knowing no one and find that only two days later, they have a circle of close friends. The intensity of such programs is evident in the fact that participants of some two-week service projects become so attached they organize a reunion the following winter and stay in touch throughout the year.

――――― **Student Scoop** ―――――

"We had to develop activities to bring together Chinese and AFS students. It was really challenging because students tend not to intermingle initially. To be the first one to talk to somebody or to go over to a group of people is really difficult."

—Megan Miller, participant, AFS (China)

Community service programs foster friendships for a multitude of reasons. Participants don old clothes and throw themselves into dumpsters together to stomp out more room for trash. They push and pull and tug in coordinated effort. They meet to discuss the most efficient way to clear a forest path or to cook spaghetti for a hungry swarm of workers. Most important, they rely on each other when they're feeling tired or anxious or down.

While friendships form and laughter flows, each person takes his or her turn leading the group. At the site, in the community, and within the volunteer group, leadership opportunities abound. If one person learns how to do a particular task, he or she teaches the rest of the group. As volunteers move from one phase of a project to the next or from one activity to another, different people step up to direct progress. Program leaders work to help student participants take the lead.

Summer service programs include plenty of time for reflection, whether that means discussing concerns and challenges with other volunteers or mulling over thoughts in your head before you go to sleep at night. "Some team leaders ask the volunteers to keep a small journal," said Kim Tyler, assistant director of Landmark Volunteers. "Each evening there is a 'circling up' process where groups discuss any issues, questions, or complaints. There is always a Landmark staff person who visits the site during the program to meet with the volunteers and ask them if [the experience] was what they expected, and if not, how it differed. They want to know if the project was challenging enough, and if it was meaningful to participants."

Of course, if you participate in a community service project in which you are one of just two foreign volunteers in a small village, your communal experience will be a little bit different. Rather than having a ready group of peers with whom to make friends, you'll learn to depend on the locals for companionship. In most cases you'll become part of a large, close-knit family and active community social life. Integrating yourself into village culture may be challenging at first, but becoming one of the village's young people is an exciting and rewarding project. And as you gain skill in village tasks and competence in the sanitation work you learned in your home country's training sessions, you may even find people looking to you as a leader in the community.

The leadership skills you develop during a community service program, complemented by the cultural interaction with community residents and the personal satisfaction of completing a difficult and meaningful project, give you much to talk about. Regardless of whether you spend two weeks pulling weeds or eight weeks balancing life in a French-speaking host family house with farming in their community's fields, you'll learn a lot about yourself. Taking note of some of your feelings during the first few days of the program can help you later when you may want to relate and comment upon your experience in college essays or interviews.

——— **Student Scoop** ———

"At home I help out at church as a server and basically do community service wherever I can. But Landmark is different. It's more enjoyable because you get to meet all the people in your group and make new friends."

—Jon Markey, participant, Landmark Volunteers (Pennsylvania and New Hampshire)

——— **Student Scoop** ———

"At the end of the eight weeks we had a party. It was so funny because we played this game that was similar to hot potato, using an envelope. Inside the envelope were things to do, and all of them had to do with me or my [Amigos] partner, like kiss them or dance with them. The village people put so much effort into the party."

—Joseph Kim, participant, Amigos de las Americas (Ecuador)

Perhaps the most important thing to take from a community service summer program, however, is the reward of service itself. When you return from the summer, use the skills and energy you've stored away to jump-start a volunteer project in your own community. If you spend the summer building houses, perhaps you'll be interested in joining the local Habitat for Humanity chapter when you return home for school. Or maybe something entirely new—volunteering with the Special Olympics, recording books for the blind, organizing a park cleanup—will pique your interest. If you take the time to look, you'll find service opportunities right in your own backyard.

LIST OF PROGRAMS

Here is a list of community service programs. See the Program Directory in Part III of this book for a description of each of these programs.

AFS Intercultural Programs—Summer Community Service/Team Mission
American Jewish Society for Service—Summer Work Camps
Amigos de las Americas
Birmingham-Southern College—Student Leaders in Service
Birmingham-Southern College—Summer Scholar Program
Brandeis University—Genesis at Brandeis University
Breakthroughs Abroad, Inc.—High School Programs
Broadreach, Inc.—Broadreach Insights
Broadreach, Inc.—Broadreach Summer Adventures for Teenagers
Camp Courageous of Iowa—Volunteer Program
Comunicare—Study and Share
Costa Rican Language Academy (CRLA)
Deer Hill Expeditions
Earthwatch Institute—Field Research Expedition Internships
Friendship Ventures—Youth Leadership Program
Global Routes—High School Community Service Programs
Global Volunteers
Global Works International Programs—Summer Programs
Hugh O'Brian Youth Leadership (HOBY)—HOBY Leadership Seminars
Intern Exchange International
Involvement Volunteers Association—International Volunteering; Networked
    International Volunteering
La Société Française—International Volunteer Program
Landmark Volunteers—Summer Service Opportunity Programs
Latitudes International—Community Service Travel
Lawrence Academy—Global Leaders Workshop
LEAPNow—Summer Program in Central America; Summer Program in Australia
Legacy International—Global Youth Village

Longacre Expeditions
Longacre Leadership—Longacre Leadership Program
Nacel Open Door—Summer Programs
National FFA Organization—Agricultural Programs Overseas
Operation Crossroads Africa—Africa & Diaspora Programs
Peacework
The Pittsburgh Project
Project Sunshine—Project Sunshine Volunteer Programs
Scandinavian Seminar—Ambassadors for the Environment
School for Field Studies—Environmental Field Studies Abroad
Sidwell Friends School—SFS in Costa Rica
Student Conservation Association—High School Conservation Work Crew (CWC)
    Program
Student Safaris International—Zanzibar to the Serengeti; Queensland Explorer
Visions
Volunteers for Peace—VFP International Workcamps
Where There Be Dragons—Summer Programs
The Wilds—Safari Camp
World Horizons International
World Learning—Experiment in International Living (EIL)
Youth for Understanding International Exchange—Summer Overseas

ENRICHING YOUR SUMMER

Here is a list of websites, books, and movies you can use to further explore the idea of community service.

Websites

www.igc.org
A gateway to "progressive sites" through their four networks: Peacenet, Econet, WomensNet, and AntRacismNet.

www.dosomething.org
Site designed especially for teens interested in starting their own community service projects.

www.volunteermatch.org
Online database allows volunteers to search thousands of one-time and ongoing opportunities by zip code, category, and date, and then signup automatically by e-mail for those that fit their interest and schedule.

www.servenet.org
Youth Service America database lets users enter their zip code, city, state, skills, interests, and availability and be matched with organizations needing help.

www.speakout.com/activism/policy
Extensive searchable library of online information and links related to public policy issues.

www.oneworld.net
Huge collection of reports, articles, and opinions on a wide range of issues.

www.idealist.org
Over 20,000 nonprofit and community organizations in 140 countries, which you can search or browse by name, location, or mission.

www.unicef.org/voy/
UNICEF Voices of Youth site provides a forum for young people and adults around the world to share ideas about important world issues.

Books

160 Ways to Help the World: Community Service Projects for Young People
by Linda Leeb Duper

Service Learning in Higher Education: Concepts and Practices
by Barbara Jacoby

Free the Children: A Young Man's Personal Crusade Against Child Labor by Craig Kielburger and Kevin Major

Generation React: Activism for Beginners by Danny Seo

Let Us Now Praise Famous Men by James Agee and Walker Evans

Land of a Thousand Hills: My Life in Rwanda by Rosamond Halsey Carr and Ann Howard Halsey

Cyberpolitics: Citizen Activism in the Age of the Internet by Kevin A. Hill and John E. Hughes

Altars in the Street: A Courageous Memoir of Community and Spiritual Awakening by Melody Ermachild Chavis

Brown Dog of the Yaak: Essays on Art and Activism by Rick Bass

The Legacy of Luna by Julia Butterfly Hill

Children of Israel, Children of Palestine: Our Own True Stories
by Laurel Holliday

Out of War by Sara Cameron

Movies

Gorillas in the Mist
The real-life story of anthropologist Dian Fossey, who spent years studying the endangered gorilla population in the mountains of Africa and tried to protect them from poachers.

Cry Freedom
Based on the true story of newspaper editor Donald Woods' investigation into the murder of South African nationalist leader Steven Biko. Starring Kevin Kline and Denzel Washington.

Gandhi
Celebrates the life of Mohandas K. Gandhi, who gained independence for his homeland of India through a doctrine of nonviolence.

Silkwood
Meryl Streep uncovers dangerous working conditions in the nuclear power plant where she works. Fact-based film.

Norma Rae
Sally Field as a real-life textile worker who stands up for workers' rights and tries to unionize her textile mill.

Erin Brockovich
Julia Roberts fights a power company that's been poisoning a community's water supply in this fact-based film.

Dead Man Walking
A powerful drama starring Susan Sarandon as Sister Helen Prejean, who tries to help convicted killer Sean Penn find peace before he is executed.

National Geographic's America's Endangered Species
Two photographers take us on a road trip to find the rarest animals and plants in the United States and the special people who are determined to save them.

Romero
Raul Julia portrays Archbishop Oscar Romero in his fight against social injustices and government tyranny in El Salvador in the late 1970s.

Outdoor Adventure and Travel Programs

6

OVERVIEW

Waking up with the sun, basking in the beauty of the land, sleeping under the stars. Outdoor adventure programs allow you to do this and more as you wind through some of the most beautiful back country in North America. You may not be the cleanest kid around when you return home with mud- and sand-splattered gear, but you'll definitely have stories to tell.

"SHOULD I TRY AN OUTDOOR OR TRAVEL ADVENTURE?"

Outdoor adventure and travel programs are ideal for those seeking continual challenge while journeying from one breathtaking part of the world to another. Whether the program takes you through the Rockies, down the Appalachian Trail, or across the Alaskan tundra, the views will be magnificent. What participants remember most when school resumes in the fall, however, is the time they've shared with traveling companions around the proverbial campfire.

Because adventure and travel groups are small—sometimes as few as eight and rarely more than twenty—friendships not only form quickly, they form deeply. Lessons about the environment and how to care for it are implicit in the program focus, but group leaders often spend as much time showing students how to care for each other as how to care for the earth. Travel groups become like family, with everyone helping everyone else conquer personal obstacles while meeting group goals.

Expert Advice

"Although all activities are taught from a beginner level, the activities are challenging enough so participants develop confidence, teamwork and leadership. The leadership occurs naturally through our leaders' example. Whenever there are two or three leaders with a small group of twelve, participants come away with the principles of leadership just through the leaders' and activity leaders' example."

—Dave Cohan, director of administration, Wilderness Adventure at Eagle Landing

SURVEYING THE CHOICES

If you've decided this is the summer to get in shape, get outdoors, and gain a new perspective on life, an outdoor adventure or travel program may be right for you. For experienced campers, hikers, rafters, and snorkelers, there are opportunities galore. But there are an equal number of thrilling outdoor adventures for those who've never spent a night lulled to sleep by the flapping of a green canvas tent. Make no mistake, these programs are rustic: Food is often carried in backpacks and prepared over a glowing fire. But both between and within programs, there is significant variety. After all, even the Grand Canyon has a hotel with pristine white sheets at the end of its long descending trails.

Some expeditions carefully map out each night's stay before departure. In fact, they use the same campsites, hotels, and/or youth hostels each year and are confident that upon arrival, they will find the grounds neat and the bathrooms sparkling clean. Other programs make finding overnight shelter part of the adventure. The only known destination is the endpoint of the trip; getting from start to finish is an exercise in group survival. That adds to the fun, said Matt Moran, who went on a fourteen-day wilderness expedition in Colorado with Moondance Adventure. Each full day of travel culminated in the hunt for shelter. "You got up—usually when the sun came up because they took our watches so you really had no sense of time—packed up the area to make sure nothing was left, and hiked about 10 miles a day," Moran said. "That doesn't sound like much, but it's up hills and with different elevations, so it was tough. We'd find a spot where it would be nice to camp for the night. We'd all do that together, looking for a place where we'd be protected if a storm came during the night."

For people who like the great outdoors only if they can have a hot shower and clean sheets at night, there are summer program directors who understand (and probably feel the same way). Several "teen tours" whirl high schoolers up and down the East or West Coast (and sometimes Alaska, Hawaii, or Europe) with action-packed schedules that include such adventure and outdoor sports as whitewater rafting, windsurfing, waterskiing, parasailing, rappelling, and hiking. These trips place relatively less emphasis

---

Expert Advice

"Students have many responsibilities while living aboard the boat. They are learning to sail—that's the focus of our program—but they are also doing all the cooking and cleaning. It's not a cruise ship-type experience. There are 10 or 11 students on board each of our 51-foot boats. It takes a cooperative effort, and the students learn a lot about themselves as they live and work with other people. We start from the beginning, teaching the basics of sailing to everyone, and rotating positions and responsibilities daily. When you're skipper for the day, it's your boat and you take charge. Soon the students are running the boat without help from the staff skipper. It's a huge team accomplishment."

—Mike Liese, founder and director, Sail Caribbean

---

on nature; outdoor sports complement city sight seeing, cultural events, and evening entertainment. Travel programs are a great option for teenagers whose vision of an ideal vacation—outdoor sports by day, dance and comedy clubs by night—clashes with their parents' proclivity for house and garden tours. Programs' daily schedules are in tune with mainstream teenage culture (if you shun the Gap, beware). You're likely to eat at Planet Hollywood or Hard Rock Café and hear whatever rock concerts are in town. One advantage of these teen tours is they tend to attract students from overseas as well as all parts of the United States.

After deciding the degree to which you want to "rough it" this summer, more fun choices lie ahead. Do you want to explore the coastline or woodland? Marine life or the desert? Mountain ranges or prairies? In some cases, program coordinators may send beginners to one geographic region, advanced mountaineers to another. But unless you're applying for a highly advanced program that trains experienced trekkers in leadership and outdoor guiding, most programs will not ask for proof of ability level. Be forewarned: Overestimating your skill can be detrimental to your health and happiness. No, the guides won't leave you to nurse your wounds in the woods alone. But while others are enjoying the scenery, you'll be shifting the weight in your backpack or using your hands to guide sore legs one more time around the bicycle wheel. It's silly to spend your days counting the minutes until sunset. There will be interesting, exciting things to see on all outdoor adventures, and both you and your fellow group members will be happier if you select the right expedition. If you have any doubts, ask a member of the summer program staff for advice on placement. You can always select another trip next year, when you've had more time to get in shape.

THE ADVENTURE EXPERIENCE

Days are never dull on an outdoor adventure program. From sunup to sundown there are tasks to complete, from building a fire on which to fry eggs to locating a campsite and staking down tents. Of course, daily activities generate the biggest challenge and excitement. Typical afternoons may be spent backpacking, caving, canoeing, fly fishing, horseback riding, kayaking, mountain biking, mountaineering, rappelling, rock climbing, SCUBA diving, snorkeling, walking high ropes, skiing, waterskiing, whitewater rafting, or windsurfing. Which challenges your group meets and accepts will depend greatly on the area of the country your expedition explores.

Many programs devote several days or weeks to one activity before moving on to another. Before each new phase of the adventure, instructors review safety procedures and provide expert training in the technical skills demanded. Group warmup exercises and team building activities ready the group for its next challenge. Although each day's projects are designed to be more demanding than the last, adventurers always prove equal to the challenge. The reason? Daily growth in team spirit.

Expert Advice

"We start with an early morning wake up—5:30 or 6 A.M.—on either the vessel Outward Bound or on one of the pulling boats, 30-foot boats run by sail or oar, similar to old whaling boats. They take a dip in the ocean then sort of run themselves through the daily activities from eating to water testing to getting under way and moving along the coast. They also deal with issues within the group; for example, trust issues. A big focus is placed on the relationships between the people and the inner strength within each student. The focus isn't so much on the daily task of getting from point A to point B, but on getting to point B in such a way that develops each person and their sense of each other. The daily schedule can be interrupted by an issue of physical or emotional safety—someone not respecting another person or not keeping watch at the bow, and thus endangering the safety of the group."

—Jobi Hanson, assistant program director, Outward Bound Environmental Leadership Program at Thompson Isle Outward Bound Education Center

---

The most unique aspect of outdoor adventure and travel expeditions is the way physical and social challenges merge. While you push physical limits by scaling mountains and paddling whitewater rafts, it's your communication and leadership skills that are put to the ultimate test. Adventure programs are as much about learning to survive with others as learning to thrive in the wilderness. Your team moves only as fast as the slowest traveler, and who that is changes as you move from rappelling to rafting and from kayaking to skiing.

Many outdoor adventure summer programs make leadership a prime concern, and instructors divide daily responsibilities in such a way that everyone has a turn at the reins. On all Adventure Treks expeditions, students take turns being "leader of the day." As Adventure Treks director John Dockendorf explains, "The leader of the day is in charge of creating a vision for the day with help from the instructors, and of supporting his or her team, delegating appropriately, and keeping things moving. The challenge for the leaders is not to do the tasks themselves, but to motivate others to do them." After completing their leader-of-the-day duties, Adventure Treks students have an opportunity to reflect upon their experience. As part of the evening group discussion, the leader of the day gets feedback from his or her peers. Following the meeting, instructors meet with the leader of the day privately to point out possible areas of improvement.

Instructors are on hand to provide expert training in outdoor skills and insightful advice on interpersonal relations throughout the trip, but the ultimate goal of outdoor adventure programs is to reach a point at which students can and do run the ship themselves. This means they are capable of handling not only basic needs—making food, securing shelter, and completing whatever daily tasks their expedition requires—but also their emotional ones. Jobi Hanson, an assistant program director at the Thompsom Isle Outward Bound Education Center, describes this as inner strength. "The instructors go through the course with a plan to fall back on, but every moment of every day the group makes decisions," Hanson said. "Instructors intervene when needed, but when you have a high-functioning group that knows how to be safe, the instructors really step back."

Courses at Outward Bound schools end with something called "solos," miniadventures that place students in isolation to reflect upon their experience and note the ways in which it helped them grow and change. At the North Carolina Outward Bound School in Asheville, students doing solos are given a tarp, a small but adequate amount of food (some students choose to fast), water, a whistle, and a journal. They are then placed several hundred yards apart from each other and are told where they can find their instructors, who are out of sight but within a half-mile distance. Each day, they go to a check-in point where they leave a marker for their instructor. The length of solos varies according to the duration of the Outward Bound course and the individual needs of students in the group, but most sixteen to twenty-three day courses—the most popular expeditions for high school summer programs—have three day/two night solos. After weeks of group living, the solo offers students time for themselves. Outward Bound adventures provide an intense group experience; solos provide a meaningful individual one.

THE PREPARATION

Outdoor adventure and travel programs specialize in unimaginable experiences impossible to prepare for in full. That's the fun of them. But a little bit of preparation can go a long way to making an outdoor summer the best of your life. Most people have daily routines that involve a time for waking up, going to sleep, exercising, and relaxing. There are times during the day when they like to have the company of family and friends, and times when they prefer to be alone. Outdoor adventure and travel programs quickly break you from these comfortable habits. That can be refreshing, but also unsettling or even irritating. On a camping trip, for example, you may be asked to rise early and fix breakfast for the group. You may be forced to skip your shower some days. You may have to bunk at dark and wake at dawn. At all times, you must mold your personal schedule to meet the needs and interests of the group. Being able to see different as interesting, exciting, and good is critical to your summer happiness. In the weeks before departure, become as flexible as you can.

Getting in Shape

While stretching your mind, it wouldn't hurt to stretch your muscles too. If you don't exercise daily, start now. Make a workout plan that includes warmups, stretching, aerobic exercise, and a cooldown. Follow it religiously. If you're just coming off a high school or

——————— **Expert Advice** ———————

"Students should come prepared to be a part of the group, to meet their needs through the group. Where many kids are used to being able to isolate themselves and watch the TV show they want or go to the store when they want to, here they are really tied to a group of 9 or 10 other people. In order to have a snack, they need to get with the group and say, 'is this a good time for us to have a snack?' All of their needs have to be channeled through the group."

—Jobi Hanson, assistant program director, Outward Bound Environmental Leadership Program

club sports season, you'll probably be in decent shape. Nevertheless, you should prepare for the kinds of sports featured on your trip. If you're biking across eastern Canada, dig your 10-speed out of the garage, gather some friends, and cycle to the park across town. Different activities require different muscles, and conditioning specifically for the trip is a big help. Playing field hockey or lacrosse may increase your stamina, but it won't prepare you for the rigors of climbing uphill with a full pack. Try walking or running with weights. If you build up gradually, you'll be a lot less sore those first few days on the trail.

Gearing Up

Making sure you have the right equipment also reduces the possibility of discomfort and injury. Most programs send participants a detailed packing list as soon as they have processed their applications. Try to follow your program's instructions to the letter. Directors have led many expeditions and know exactly what you will need. If you will be hiking, boots are your number one priority. Wearing well-fitting, well broken-in footwear is essential to prevent blistering. Quality hiking boots take considerable time to break in, so be sure to buy them early and take them out on short trips before starting your summer adventure. Other clothing to consider: lightweight shirts you can layer by day and wash and dry by night; a hat and long pants to protect you from the sun's rays, poisonous plants, and mosquitoes; and rain gear—there's nothing worse than putting on wet clothes in the morning.

——— **Student Scoop** ———

"I had been to hockey and lacrosse camps before, but they were different because you don't really have to depend on the kids like you do on this kind of trip."

—Matt Moran, participant, Moondance Adventure

Expeditions requiring extensive overnight packing usually outfit students before departure by either including equipment in the admissions fee or making high-quality gear available for rent or purchase during the course of the trip. Gear is expensive, so if equipment isn't included in your summer program price, renting may be a good option. If you already have your own gear or plan to buy it at a local camping store, check to see that the size and quality are comparable to the gear provided by the program. When exposing your body to the raw elements, you want sturdy equipment.

GROUP DYNAMICS

Teamwork, determination, and confidence are the building blocks of collective survival, and being considerate of other people in your group is the number one way to achieve this. As each person's individual energy and fighting spirit infuse the group, you will begin working together as if you'd known each other for years. Fellow travelers become more than friends and companions, they grow to be vital sources of help, encouragement, and support.

It's natural to feel vulnerable when you're far away from home and familiar things. The fastest way to counter this is swapping stories with people you meet. Outdoor adventurers frequently come from all parts of the country and world. This makes for many exciting hours discussing the differences between the north, south, east, and west, and the way high schools are seemingly the same the world over. These conversations eat away at feelings of strangeness and unfamiliarity. Knowing about their pet dogs and hideous physics teachers makes it easier to ask a fellow adventurer for a boost.

Everyone on outdoor adventure trips wears old clothes and expects to get soaked in dirt, mud, dust, or sand. This, combined with program emphases on teamwork and trust, makes a person's inner self rather than his or her outer appearance the focal point of identity and relationships. It's a welcome change, and group members tend to bond quickly. Be proactive in team building and friendship making by striving to have a meaningful conversation with every member of your group by the end of your second day on the road. Group instructors and leaders work overtime to prevent the formation of cliques. Join the effort! Exclusivity detracts from the very group experience that makes expeditions so special.

As soon as expedition groups begin to coalesce, they work to establish open communication channels. There is an unwritten understanding that people should feel comfortable sharing their feelings and concerns with other members of the group. If you

---

Expert Advice

"Most of our groups are composed of people who come individually, not in a clique of friends. Coming together with a brand new group of kids is an exciting preoccupation for the first week or so. Then comes the excitement of cycling. Most kids have never toured before. Just the act of doing the biking, setting up the tents, cooking meals, doing everything on their own, presents a neat element for another week or so. The sustaining thing—other than the friendships and daily schedule of living—is the fact that most of the trips go through really great areas. There is a serendipity factor. Things you never expect to happen happen. The other thing, and this is more true for your women, but affects guys too, is the achievement and sense of accomplishment that comes from making a long journey totally by one's own power. The mode of transportation is a 21-speed mechanical object, and participants carry all their own gear with them, including tents."

—Ted Lefkowitz, director, Student Hosteling Program

Quick Tips

Conquering the Great Outdoors, Simplified

- Choose wisely. You don't want an outdoor program that's above your skill or fitness level.
- Decide if you want a completely rustic experience (i.e., no showers or electricity), or a tour that allots time for city sightseeing and cultural events.
- Find out if a program fits your preferences for activities and comfort by talking to past participants.
- Check on safety. Ask directors what safety precautions are in place, and make sure health and physical emergencies are provided for by the program.
- Prepare. Get into the habit of exercising regularly.
- Make sure you have the right gear for your activities. Find out if the program provides the equipment or offers items for rent.
- Once you get out there, adjust to the group's needs. Remember: There is no *I* in *team*.
  —Help out with group chores.
  —Take the lead when it's necessary.
  —Support the other participants and ask for support when you need it.

---

think things aren't going as well as they should be or you feel that rearranging the schedule or division of labor would ease travel, speak up. Similarly, if you notice something people do for each other that makes the day go more smoothly, share your observations so everyone can benefit.

Approaching every activity with gusto is another way to create a top-notch experience for you and the group. If everyone jumps out of bed—or sleeping bag—at daybreak, enthusiastically weaves through the day's activities, and cheers for the chef when dinner is served, it's impossible for anyone to be glum. With an upbeat attitude, each day of your trip yields golden memories. And enjoyment is contagious, so don't be afraid to be the first one to liven things up.

Outdoor adventure and travel programs foster leadership skills and self-confidence. Having thrived in a new environment, you can look back at your tremendous accomplishment with pride. While the lessons you learn are not academic per se, they contribute greatly to who you are as a student and person. The interpersonal and teamwork skills you develop will greatly enhance your ability to lead groups, and you will see the result clearly when you return to your school clubs and sports teams in the fall. The alternative lifestyle explored in the great out-of-doors can also help you evaluate your priorities. This will prove useful when selecting a university, a college major, and down the road, a career. In the meantime, it gives you much to think about. Store these thoughts away—they may prove useful in college applications and interviews, and they will certainly help in daily decision-making.

LIST OF PROGRAMS

Here is a list of outdoor adventure and travel programs. See the Program Directory in Part III of this book for a description of each of these programs.

Adventure Programs

ActionQuest—ActionQuest Programs
Adventure Pursuits—Adventure Pursuits Expeditions & Camps
Adventure Treks, Inc.—Adventure Treks
Adventures Cross-Country
AFS Intercultural Programs—Summer Homestay Plus
Alpine Adventures, Inc.—Alpine Adventures
America's Adventure/Venture Europe
Barefoot International—Barefoot International & Fly High Ski School
Bark Lake Leadership Center—Leadership Through Recreation/Music
Breakthroughs Abroad, Inc.—High School Programs
Broadreach, Inc.—Broadreach Insights
Broadreach, Inc.—Broadreach Summer Adventures for Teenagers
Brush Ranch Camps
Cottonwood Gulch Foundation—Prairie Trek Group I; Prairie Trek Group II; Turquoise Trail
Deep Woods Camp for Boys
Deer Hill Expeditions
ECHO International Educational Expeditions—Australian Biological Adventures
Greenbrier River Outdoor Adventures
Hargrave Military Academy—Summer School and Camp
Horizon Adventures, Inc.—Horizon Adventures
Interlocken—Crossroads Adventure Travel
International Bicycle Fund—Bicycle Africa Tours; Sbuhbi Lithlal Ti Swatixwtuhd
The Island Laboratory
Longacre Expeditions
Longacre Leadership—Longacre Leadership Program
Maine Teen Camp
Marine Military Academy—Summer Military Training Camp
Moondance Adventures
Mount Hood Snowboard Camp—MHSC Summer Sessions
Musiker Discovery Programs—Musiker Tours
National FFA Organization—Agricultural Programs Overseas
National Outdoor Leadership School—Wilderness Leadership Courses
Northwaters—Northwaters Wilderness Programs
Oak Ridge Military Academy—Leadership Adventure Camp
Odyssey Expeditions—Tropical Marine Biology Voyages

Orme School—Orme Summer Camp
Outpost Wilderness Adventure—Outpost Wilderness Adventures
Outward Bound USA
Planet Hockey, Inc.—Planet Hockey Ranch
Rainforest Exploration Associaton—City Lights; Starry Nights
The Road Less Traveled
Sail Caribbean
Sea Education Association—Science at Sea; Oceanography of the Gulf of Maine
Seacamp Association, Inc.—Seacamp
SeaWorld Adventure Parks—SeaWorld/Busch Gardens Adventure Camps
Sidwell Friends School—Deep Creek Adventures; SFS Alaskan Adventures
Sierra Adventure Camps
Student Conservation Association—High School Conservation Work Crew (CWC)
    Program
Student Hosteling Program—Summer Biking Programs
Student Safaris International—Zanzibar to the Serengeti; Queensland Explorer
Tamarack Camps
Trailmark Outdoor Adventures
United States Coast Guard Academy—Academy Introduction Mission (AIM)
United States Coast Guard Academy—Minority Introduction to Engineering (MITE)
University of Rhode Island—W. Alton Jones Teen Expeditions
U.S. Snowboard Training Center—USSTC Allstar Snowboard Camp
U.S. Space Camp—Aviation Challenge and Advanced Space Academy
U.S. Sports Camps—Nike Sports Camps
Visions
Weissman Teen Tours, Inc.—Weissman Teen Tours
Westcoast Connection—Active Teen Tours
Westcoast Connection—European Programs
Westcoast Connection—Golf & Tennis Programs
Westcoast Connection—Israel Experience
Westcoast Connection—On Tour
Westcoast Connection—Outdoor Adventure Programs
Westcoast Connection—Ski & Snowboard Sensation
Western Washington University—Outdoor Challenge Institute
Where There Be Dragons—Summer Programs
Wilderness Experience Unlimited—Explorer Group; Trailblazers
Wilderness Ventures—Wilderness Adventure Expeditions; Advanced Leadership
    Expeditions; Offshore Adventure Expeditions
The Wilds—Safari Camp
Woodward Sports Camp
World Learning—Experiment in International Living (EIL)
YMCA of Metropolitan Hartford—Camp Jewell YMCA Outdoor Center

Domestic Travel/Sightseeing Programs

College Visits
Education Unlimited—East Coast College Tour
The Masters School —Summer in the City
Musiker Discovery Programs—Musiker Tours
Tamarack Camps
Weissman Teen Tours, Inc.—Weissman Teen Tours
Westcoast Connection—Active Teen Tours
Westcoast Connection—Golf & Tennis Programs

ENRICHING YOUR SUMMER

Here is a list of websites, books, and movies you can use to further explore various outdoor activities.

Websites

Comprehensive Sites

www.gorp.com
Great Outdoor Recreation Pages offers lots of info on outdoor activities and destinations, plus a gear store, a full-booking adventure travel service, discussion boards, a section for people with special needs, and much more.

www.siadventure.com
The edgier cousin of the *Sports Illustrated* site, covering everything from fishing to bike tours, with news stories, a gear finder, and destination overviews.

www.altrec.com
Covers camping and hiking, cycling, paddling, snowsports, fly fishing, and conditioning. Site features a gear and clothing shop, travel services, magazine-style articles, and other resources.

outdoorsports.yahoo.com/
Directory of outdoor adventure resources.

www.mountainzone.com
Celebrates those high-elevation activities: climbing, snowboarding, skiing, mountain biking, and hiking.

Individual Activities

www.backpacker.com
Backpacker Magazine site offers news, tips, surveys, discussions, and more.

www.scubaduba.com
Resources for SCUBA divers, including a dive buddy directory, interactive dive logs, photo galleries, discussion boards, etc.

www.e-raft.com
Guide to nearly 175 whitewater rafting trips in the U.S., Canada, Mexico, and Costa Rica.

sailingsource.com
Sailing news updated daily, plus links for regattas, sailboats, marine hardware, club and racing reports, and a nautical books club.

siolibrary.ucsd.edu/preston/kayak/sfaq
Answers to frequently asked questions about sea kayaking.

www.usawaterski.org
National governing body for organized water skiing in the United States provides the latest news plus lists and links to member schools, dealers, clubs, camps, competitions, and other events.

www.rocklist.com
News, articles, editorial commentary, trip reports, area guides, route information, and more for climbing enthusiasts around the world.

www.iceclimb.com
Ice climbing equipment, regional conditions, trips, science, message boards, and more.

www.roadcycling.com
Cycling news, product reviews, training articles, discussion board, and other resources.

Outdoor Locations

www.recreation.gov
Provides info on recreation opportunities on U.S. federal lands, searchable by state and activity.

www.campnetamerica.com
Info on campgrounds and RV sites across the United States.

activetravel.about.com/travel/activetravel/
An About.com guide with lots of travel and location info, plus sections on such unusual activities as llama trekking and dogsledding.

www.wwwdi.com
World Wide Wilderness Directory features links to adventure camps around the world. Searchable by activity or destination.

www.adventureguide.com
Users can search for a destination by country, region, or city, or search by nearly 50 different activities. Lots of other resources for travelers.

Books

Guidebooks

The SAS Survival Handbook: How to Survive in the Wild, in Any Climate, on Land or at Sea by John Wiseman

Handbook of Knots by Des Pawson

Mountaineering: The Freedom of the Hills by Don Graydon

Mountain Biking: Over the Edge by Bill Strickland

The Complete Book of Sea Kayaking by Derek C. Hutchinson

A Sea Vagabond's World by Bernard Moitessier

Scuba Diving by Dennis K. Graver

Surfing: A Beginner's Manual by Wayne T. Alderson

Essential Waterskiing for Teens by Luke Thompson

Essays and Memoirs

Into Thin Air by John Krakauer

Climb: Stories of Survival from Rock, Snow and Ice by Clint Willis and David Roberts (editors)

To the Top of Denali: Climbing Adventures on North America's Highest Peak by Bill Sherwonit and Art Davidson

It's Not About the Bike: My Journey Back to Life by Lance Armstrong

A Walk in the Woods: Rediscovering America on the Appalachian Trail by Bill Bryson

Two for the Summit: My Daughter, the Mountains, and Me by Geoffrey Norman

Solo on Her Own Adventure: Women Going It Alone in the Outdoors by Susan Fox Rogers (editor)

Writing Down the River: Into the Heart of the Grand Canyon by Kathleen Jo Ryan

The Fireside Diver: An Anthology of Underwater Adventure by Bonnie D. Cardone (editor)

Literature and Fiction

Hatchet by Gary Paulsen

Banner in the Sky by James Ramsey Ullman

Solo Faces by James Salter

Two Dog River by Richard Day

Island of the Blue Dolphins by Scott O'Dell

Lord of the Flies by William Golding

Moby-Dick by Herman Melville

Movies

Cast Away
Tom Hanks struggles to survive after his plane crashes on a deserted isle. Costarring Helen Hunt and Wilson the ball.

The Perfect Storm
True story of doomed fishermen caught in the storm of the century and their loved ones watching and waiting back home.

White Squall
Coming-of-age drama about high school students who run into disaster while circumnavigating the globe on a sailboat. Starring Jeff Bridges and Scott Wolf (*Party of Five*).

The River Wild
Meryl Streep encounters some thugs while whitewater rafting with her husband and young son.

Vertical Limit
Chris O'Donnell must overcome a tragic decision from his past and climb the dreaded K-2 in search of his sister, trapped by an avalanche.

Alive
Based on the true story of a plane crash in the Andes in 1972, in which members of a rugby team do what they must in order to survive—including eating the flesh of their dead companions.

Jaws
The sequels are incredibly cheesy, but the original is a masterpiece of storytelling and suspense (though not of special effects).

Point Break
Its ridiculous plot about surfers who rob banks is redeemed by great surfing and skydiving scenes. Starring Keanu Reeves and Patrick Swayze.

The Mosquito Coast
Harrison Ford moves his whole family to the jungles of Central America to create an isolationist utopia. But he can't escape human nature . . .

My Side of the Mountain
A family film about a 13-year old Canadian boy who runs away from home and struggles to survive on his own in the wilderness.

Alaska
Another family film about kids alone in the wilderness. This time, they're trying to rescue their dad, who went down in a plane crash.

Athletic Programs

7

OVERVIEW

Whether you are serious about moving from the high school gym to college arena or determined to make varsity cuts next year, athletic summer programs can help you reach your goal. Sports camps provide a great way to get in shape, make new friends, and sample college campuses. And yes, in some cases, they can give you a real edge in the college recruiting process. As is the case with all summer programs, however, it is important to shop carefully and choose wisely. There are many different programs out there, and they vary greatly in type and quality.

"SHOULD I GO TO A SPORTS CAMP?"

Because there are so many summer sports camps, everyone from the future NFL linebacker to the kid who never managed a pull-up in the Presidential Physical Fitness Test can find a program right for them. Most camps are only a week long, so they provide an excellent way to spice up summer work or study—without a huge time commitment. If you select a program with superior coaching, adequate facilities, a dedicated staff, and the opportunity to be noticed by college coaches, chances are you won't regret the decision. But if you have limited time and many summer opportunities, you should consider personal interest and commitment to your sport(s) when deciding if camp is a good investment of summer time and money.

The Talented High School Athlete

If you plan to play a collegiate team sport, hope to be recruited, or want to earn an athletic scholarship, you should attend at least

--- **Expert Advice** ---

"Although we do take USTA ranked juniors, we also have a team for players who just enjoy tennis recreationally. A lot of times players tend to underestimate their ability. We do say to players and parents that if you're not sure if you're good enough, let Tennis: Europe decide."

—Martin Vinokur, director, Tennis: Europe and More

one sports camp each year of high school. As you probably know, that's where the action is. Summer camps at big-name colleges and universities—as well as independently run programs utilizing sports professionals—attract the best high school athletes in the nation. Only playing in this kind of environment lets you know exactly how good you are, and thus gives you an idea of where you might stand in the recruiting game. And—just as important—the competition at sports camp gives you the push you need to play your best.

Jared Harrison attended high school lacrosse camps at the University of Virginia and Princeton University before heading to play college ball at Lehigh. He said seeing other players helped him evaluate his own level of play: "You saw how good the guys in college were, but also some of the high school players. The kids from my area, Virginia, were good, but I saw a lot of kids from Maryland at the camps who had played since they were young."

In some sports—football, lacrosse, basketball, and field hockey, to name a few—attending camp is almost mandatory for those wanting to be widely recruited. We'll discuss this more later in this chapter (see "Playing the Recruiting Game").

The Average High School Athlete (JV or Varsity)

So you enjoy playing sports and are pretty good, but aren't sure you're Division I material, or even that you want to consider sports when choosing your institute of higher learning. Is camp for you?

Any athletic director will tell you that you don't have to be a superstar to get a lot out of a summer athletic experience. In all likelihood, you will be drilling, scrimmaging, and playing hard for several days straight amidst a group of athletes at or above your playing level. Under such circumstances, you can't help but improve. This pays off ten-fold when you return to your high school playing field or court. "They open you up to different skills," Ella Mason said of the UNC—Chapel Hill and Princeton University elite lacrosse camps she attended while at the Friends School of Baltimore. "You can go back [and] use them at your schools and practices." Nothing impresses high school coaches more.

And while high school programs don't have the budget to hire specialized coaches for each position, large college programs (and hence their sports camps) often do. Such specialized attention can be a godsend for goalies. "Anyone who's playing a specialized position should go because a lot of times coaches in high schools don't know much about those positions," said Ellen Morrow, who attended the New Town Field Hockey Camp in Delaware, a four day clinic for field hockey goalies. The clinic "helped me with positioning, stopping, all kinds of skills I didn't even know before."

Even if you're not sure if you want to play college sports, it can't hurt to find out how college coaches and athletic practices differ from those you've grown accustomed to at home. Most camps will have plenty of college athletes around to help run drills, carry equipment, and most importantly, answer questions. If you're worried about balancing sports and school, who better to give you the low-down than current student-athletes?

Some find the friends and contacts they make at camp the most valuable part of the whole experience. "The best part was just going and meeting new people and also playing with friends that I didn't go to school with and I didn't [end up] go[ing] to college with," said Courtney Lane, who attended field hockey camps throughout New England before entering Yale. "I knew people on almost every single team [Yale] played this year and recognized almost everyone, including a lot of the coaches."

The benefits of camp extend beyond athletics. Many allow high school students to experience college life in much the same way as university-based academic summer programs—they provide dormitory housing, resident advisors (R.A.'s), and cafeteria meals. Just like in freshman dorms, the school mixes you with a group of people from across the country and watches as you make friends, linger over dinner, and travel around campus in herds.

The Young Athlete or Casual Player

If you played a sport or two in middle school/junior high and have not decided if you will play in high school, let alone college, or if you only play sports recreationally, summer sports camps can still be a lot of fun. First of all, they are a great way to get, and stay, in shape. All sports programs run extremely long and full days with physical exertion taking center stage. Then, the very nature of team sports ensures that you will meet a lot of people in an environment emphasizing cooperation and fair play. Finally, taking the time to learn and perfect a sport is a rewarding and meaningful experience at any age (and it's a lot easier when you're young).

When selecting a camp, make sure you choose one that matches your needs and interests. It can be disheartening to walk into a camp and find you're the least skilled athlete there. Sure, you'll be pushed, but if there is too great a disparity between your ability and stamina and that of the other players, you won't have fun, and you probably won't learn much.

Because of National Collegiate Athletic Association (NCAA) regulations, camps sponsored by colleges and universities cannot restrict admission based on ability, ranking, or references from high school coaches. As Steve Mallonee, NCAA director of membership services, explained: "If a college is recruiting a young man or woman, they will send them a brochure and ask the youngster to consider attending their camp. A camp, however, may not be conducted on an invitational basis only, but must be open to any and all entrants (limited only by number and age)." Thus even "elite" camps are open to everyone. Before you commit, think about the level of competition and competitiveness you're comfortable with. A summer program should always leave you feeling good about yourself and your potential.

CHECKING OUT THE SCENE

While some sports camps literally fly in title-winning college coaches and superstar professionals to run daily drills and scrimmages, others recruit their coaching staff from the high school down the street. Either may meet your needs, but it is unlikely both will. As you know, a good summer begins with choosing a good camp. "Consult older friends who have already traveled along the same path," advises Yale basketball player John Kirkouski, who attended Keystone State Camps in Pennsylvania while in high school. "Look at the schedule, consider how much time you will be playing, how much time you will be lectured, [and] decide based on your needs and abilities."

Expert Advice

"We have an unbelievable staff. I played on the national team and have a lot of contacts in the field hockey world. I try to bring in the best coaches I can possibly find, and I give them a lot of help. All they have to do is show up and care about the kids. Six to eight of my [summer camp] coaches are current national team members, and that remains consistent every year. All our head coaches are either current or former national team members."

—Karen Shelton, head coach, UNC-Chapel Hill field hockey

Boarding School and Small College Camps

Programs at boarding schools and small colleges tend to offer excellent instruction, above average to superior facilities, and intense training schedules. However, many such programs rely on high school coaches as much or more than college ones. While campers get the individualized attention and day-in-day-out practice necessary for improvement, they are not seen by as many college coaches as they would be at a big university camp. So if you're not ready for the big leagues, or if you're more interested in just having fun, then boarding school and small college camps are perfect for you.

Independent Camps

In many sports, private or independently run camps—ones not operated by a high school, prep school, college or university—offer an alternative way to hone skills. The many independent tennis and golf camps, for example, provide near round-the-clock instruction by highly trained professional coaches. The sheer number of balls

hit guarantees rapid improvement, especially in an atmosphere where you and everyone you see eats, breathes, and lives the sport. These camps serve as excellent stepping stones into summer programs providing even greater experience and exposure.

University Sports Camps

University-sponsored sports camps comprise the largest category of athletic summer programs for the serious athlete. These camps provide exceptional equipment and facilities, top-notch coaches, and in most cases, the opportunity to be seen by recruiters from several universities, not to mention the thrill of playing in your dream college's stadium or arena. If this is what you want, you'll have to learn to play the recruiting game. But before we go into that, let's take a minute to look at the other aspects of a sports camp for top-level athletes.

If your ultimate goal is college athletics, your selection process junior year will be narrowed to camps at schools you would consider attending, or at least those that have invited coaches from these schools to join their camp staff. But assuming you're realistic (i.e., you're not setting your heart on playing for one institution and one institution only), you still have some degree of choice. In that case, it makes sense to consider two factors. First, does the camp provide instruction that will be useful to you? Scrutinize brochures, comparing drills and clinics. Second, are program coaches as concerned about getting you into a good school as they are about getting good players for their team? Look for camps that encourage you to ask questions and leave plenty of time for you to chat informally with their own college athletes.

Recruitment Camps and Tournaments

In several sports, there are summer programs designed and advertised specifically for recruiting purposes. These recruitment weekends are carefully regulated by the NCAA, and coaches from successful programs and big name schools flock to watch the best high school athletes play. If you're serious about college sports, it is wise to participate in this recruitment frenzy in addition to (not in place of) summer camp. Many, many coaches will see you play, and when it comes to recruitment, being seen is the name of the game. Chris Sailer, head coach of Princeton University women's lacrosse team, explains the importance of both improving skill and showing your stuff:

Note

Making Your Day a Birdie

Here's the daily schedule of the Offense Defense Golf Camp in Winchendon, Massachusetts.

7:30	Breakfast
9:00	Golf instruction, "Tee-to-Green Training Method"
12:00	Lunch break (swim and rest)
2:00	Course play (9 or 18 holes). Golf instruction, "Tee-to-Green Training Method"
5:30	Dinner
6:45	Free play, basketball, volleyball, weight room
8:00	Enrichment Program: SAT prep, ESL, etc. (optional, two nights per week)
9:30	Free time, snacks
10:30	On your floors; lights out
Saturday	Off-campus field trips
Sunday	Sleep late, followed by brunch, shag at the range, laundry, swimming, weights, and basketball. Camp meeting. Testing for all new campers.

Expert Advice

"College coaches certainly are provided an opportunity at institutional camps to see how kids perform. However, such camps may not be conducted simply to evaluate or try out prospects. They must include instructional elements. Coaches are not supposed to actively recruit prospects at their own institution's camps. For example, during an institutional camp, a coach should not be over in the corner talking to the 6'10" sophomore saying 'our school has a great athletics department, you should be looking into going here.'"

—Steve Mallonee, director of membership services, NCAA

"If you're a high school athlete, certainly during your junior year, maybe even during your sophomore year, you want to get exposure. Before that, you want to concentrate on developing your game. Recruiting weekends are good [junior year] because while at camp there are maybe ten to twelve college coaches, there may be forty to fifty coaches watching you play at a recruiting weekend." But, she warns, it is essential that high school upperclassmen continue to work on skill development. "Recruiting weekends are great for exposure, but you're not in a teaching atmosphere with college coaches. In other words, you're showing what you have, but not necessarily improving your game. It is important to do both."

PLAYING THE RECRUITING GAME

Can high school summer camps help you make the grade? Absolutely. But in order to work the system, you'll need to stay attuned to your ability, ambitions, finances, and obviously, the nature of your sport.

Choosing Your Camp(s)

High school student-athletes are busy people, especially in their junior year. Not only is that prime time for athletic recruitment, it's also the best time to be taking SAT prep courses, studying vocabulary, and rounding out college applications with significant experiences outside the world of sports. In order to maximize your potential to see and be seen, choose your sports camp carefully.

Hands down, the best option is attending camp at colleges or universities at which you want to play. This gives you the opportunity to drill under the team's head coach; you can't get any more real than that. College athletes said attending camp at a

Expert Advice

"I think camps definitely help in the recruiting process. Summer camps give the player an opportunity to be exposed to a number of college coaches. Conversely, the coaches get a chance to observe and evaluate a player's skill level, athletic ability, and personality much more closely than they would ordinarily be allowed to do. If a player is proactive in the process and demonstrates a solid attitude and work ethic, camp can only benefit her."

—Don Shaw, head coach, Stanford University women's volleyball

university while in high school gave them the chance to see whether they were a good match for that school. In addition to meeting the coaching staff, they were able to talk with college athletes assisting at camp, and therefore get a sense of the team's collective personality. Some found that their future coaches and teammates were creative, enthusiastic, and dedicated, and that they wanted to play under them. Others discovered they were not a good match for the school, and they sought out additional camps, and ultimately, universities.

If you're unable to attend camp at the schools ranked at the top of your college shopping list, the next best thing is attending a camp at a college or university where your schools are represented by either the head or assistant coach on the camp staff. This still gives you a chance to experience their coaching style, and of course, the opportunity to be noticed.

If you're one of a select few—one of the nation's top recruits—camps may very well come to you. If a coach has a hopeful eye on you, he or she may mail a camp brochure encouraging you to attend. Most coaches relish the opportunity to spend a week with their recruits, not just to win them to their program, but also to make sure they are a good fit for their college team. Chris Sailer, head women's lacrosse coach at Princeton University, said she has benefited from the fact that a number of her players attended camp at Princeton or another school where she or her assistants coached: "It is a great chance to get to know a player and watch her in competitive situations. In an intense program of four to five days, you learn a lot about a player, both on and off the field; you learn a lot more about her than you would seeing [her play] one high school game. We like to see players at a camp we run or at a camp in which one of our [staff members] coaches. It is a great opportunity to evaluate them."

But if you're like most high school athletes, Division I coaches aren't pounding on your door. Be careful. It can be all too easy to dream big if you've been the star of your team from peewee right on through varsity. It's cliché, but true: College sports are a whole other ball game. If you're unrealistic about your ability, you can end up being hurt. Robin Pflugrad, football recruiting coordinator for the Arizona State Sun Devils, stresses

---

Expert Advice

"What happens in the summer time, July 7–31, is that the NCAA has an evaluation period for all the kids to be seen by the college coaches. Throughout that time there are AUU tournaments and camps to check out the talent around the country. Usually there are scouting services that list athletes around the country and try to give them an early rating. The camps are run by the shoe companies. Adidas and Nike have tours, and kids go with either Adidas or Nike and tend to follow that tour throughout the country."

—Jim Saia, assistant coach, UCLA men's basketball

the need for levelheaded practicality: "As a prospect, you have to be somewhat of a realist. You should ask yourself 'Do I have the potential to play in the top ten percent in the country? Or do I go to one of the top camps then go down a notch in terms of where I'm looking to play college football?'" Pflugrad said he has seen kids dash from camp to camp at the best football schools in the country only to come out emptyhanded in the end because they aimed too high. It doesn't take much to figure out that spending a year's worth of college tuition on athletic camps in the hopes of earning a college scholarship may turn out to be a bad investment. This is especially true if you do not play a high profile sport (i.e., one that does not make national television).

That doesn't mean you should give up. If you really want to play college sports, attend many different camps—just select ones that run the gamut of competitiveness. If you decide you must attend a big-name camp, do yourself a favor and check to see that they employ coaches from schools at which you might make the cut. If you're not quite good enough to play for the sponsoring school, you might still spark the interest of another coach. Always be on the lookout for ways to improve your recruitment prospects.

Can Camps Work for Me?

Yes, if you're a good athlete, set realistic goals, and work hard. As Yale field hockey player Courtney Lane said, attending camp is "one of the best things you can do if you want to play in college. If you can get coaches to see you and know your name, you have a step up on the other players. You get a chance to play against [people] you wouldn't normally get to play with, and you have a week or five days for intensive play where you're working six to eight hours a day."

It is important to realize that at this level, competition is intense. Josh Weisfuse said of wrestling camp at East Stroudsburg University in Pennsylvania: "They don't call it intensive for nothing. They work you out like crazy." You may not have much fun at camp, and you certainly will play until you feel that you will drop. Regardless of how you feel, however, you must maintain a positive, upbeat attitude. That includes treating other athletes with consideration and respect.

Coaches value seeing their recruits on campus in part because no one wants a cocky, selfish, or unappreciative player. Camp provides a built-in safety check. As Don Shaw, head coach of Stanford University women's volleyball team said, "If I see a player who is grumpy when she gets up in the morning, is not very nice to the other kids, and doesn't pay attention very well, it can work against her [recruiting prospects]." In almost all cases, attending camp will only help you. But just as surely, the wrong attitude will ruin everything.

Protecting Your Chances

It is unlikely that you will be placed in a compromising situation at camp, but one can never be sure. High profile sports at large universities are big business. You should know that there are strict NCAA guidelines regulating high school recruitment, and it is your responsibility as well as the university's to respect those rules. Every institutional camp is required to uphold NCAA standards, but to be safe, schedule an appointment with your

——— **Quick Tips** ———

Making the Cut

- Familiarize yourself with the skills offered at each camp you're researching. You might want to consider attending a camp that offers training for a special position.

- Make sure the camp has your, not just their, best interests in mind. Are they just looking for a parade of possible recruits, or do they offer legitimate opportunities to improve your playing?

- Be wary of illegal recruiting—you might jeopardize your eligibility. Check with your high school athletic director for more info on NCAA guidelines.

- If you have your eye on getting onto a specific college team, find a camp at that college or one where that college's coaches serve as instructors. Exposure is your best bet in terms of recruiting.

- Be realistic about your abilities. Don't shoot for only the top camps, or you might be left in the dust. Make sure you have a range of camps—and colleges—on your preferred list.

- Attend special recruiting camps when they are available, in addition to programs where you can improve your skills.

high school athletic director before stepping foot on a college campus. Make sure you know and thoroughly understand what constitutes appropriate behavior for both you and college coaches before your first day at camp.

When the regular recruiting season begins in the fall, you might arrive on campus for an official college visit to find a locker filled with team uniforms emblazoned with your name and number. As thrilling as the sight may be, resist temptation. It is illegal for you to take anything home, and doing so will jeopardize your eligibility. While the "gifts" presented at summer camps are usually on a much smaller scale—T-shirts and the like—they are still off-limits. Of course, it is fine to accept camp awards and trophies as well as anything presented to everyone attending camp; these are included in the camp registration fee. But if you're offered anything else, politely thank the coach and say "no."

"What's It Like to Be Recruited?"

Advice from Your (Future) Teammates

While sports camps at colleges and universities give you a taste of your future as a college athlete, it is a sugarcoated sample. While at camp, your only responsibility is to improve your game. Your first day as a college student-athlete, you will be forced to balance sports with school, socializing, and the occasional load of laundry. It's just not the same as high school. The beauty of camp is that for a week, you can throw yourself into basketball or wrestling or hockey. Take advantage of that, but don't make the mistake of thinking life at school X is always like that. You'll want to make time to prepare for the other rigors of college later in the summer (even if that just means learning to separate your whites from your darks before heading to the laundry).

Another important lesson to take from camp is that you will not always be the star. You don't have to go to a Division I school to notice the difference either. College players are several years older, stronger, and wiser, and regardless of whether a school recruits locally or worldwide, their athletes are the cream of the available high school crop. As DePauw football player Aaron Conk said, "Even playing at a Division III school, the difference in effort and talent [is substantial]. In high school, I was a heck of a player. Here, you have to work at it. Even though it's a Division III school, you're still playing against the best kids the high schools have to

offer. If they're not big enough or strong enough to go to Michigan or Notre Dame, they're still good players."

Developing a strong work ethic is key. So too is cultivating a sense of loyalty and camaraderie. Whether the NFL draft or junior varsity lies in your future, it is essential that you learn to be simply a member of the team. Immediately. Any college athlete will tell you that your very survival depends on it. At many universities, your teammates become your roommates, your fraternity brothers, and your best friends. You not only practice together, you study together, live together, eat together, and drink (off-season and after your 21st birthday, of course!) together, too.

While your high school team may be fairly homogenous, your college team probably will not. If you're not yet comfortable with that, camp is the perfect place to change your ways. Reach out to other campers—people like you and different from you—and practice being a team player both on and off the court. By doing so, you may prevent a common first-year mistake: "So many freshmen come to college and they are just out to play for themselves," Yale tennis player Naomi Zeff said. "It's not until later that they realize that they are a part of a team. The team should come first. It's a very hard concept to learn, especially for really competitive junior [tennis] players."

Student Scoop

"Practice hard and don't settle for awards or distinguishments. The best kind of player is a self-motivated, confident individual who is a **team** player!"

—Alicia Kirsten Moore, participant, Emory University basketball and volleyball

---

Student Scoop

"It's kind of a hectic time. A lot of it depends on the demand for you. I know that for me, it was stressful as heck because they have people calling you all day everyday. You get so sick of it you don't even want to talk to them."

— Kasey Gilliss, participant, University of Iowa varsity wrestling

LIST OF PROGRAMS

Here is a list of summer athletic programs. See the Program Directory in Part III of this book for a description of each of these programs.

Baseball/Softball Programs

America's Baseball Camps
Appalachian State University—Summer Sports, Music, and Academic Camps
Cooperstown Baseball Camp
Cornell University Sports School—Summer Sports Camps
Higher Ground Softball Camps—Higher Ground Softball Camps
International Sports Camp
Kutsher's Sports Academy
Princeton University—Summer Sports Camps
Stanford University—Summer Sports Camps
University of Illinois—Fighting Illini Sports Camps
University of Notre Dame—Summer Sports Camps
University of San Diego—Summer Sports Camps
U.S. Sports Camps—Nike Sports Camps

Basketball Programs

Appalachian State University— Summer Sports, Music, and Academic Camps
Bates College—Bates College Basketball Camp
Cornell University Sports School—Summer Sports Camps
Five-Star Basketball Camp
FUN-damental Basketball Camp, Inc.—Basketball Camp at Morrisville
Hargrave Military Academy—Summer School and Camp
International Sports Camp
Kutsher's Sports Academy
The Masters School—Panther Basketball Camp
Princeton University—Summer Sports Camps
76ers Basketball Camp
Southern Vermont College—Summer Sports Camps
Stanford University—Summer Sports Camps
University of Illinois—Fighting Illini Sports Camps
University of San Diego—Summer Sports Camps
University of Sports—Superstar Camp
University of Wisconsin, La Crosse—University of Wisconsin Athletic Camps
U.S. Sports Camps—Nike Sports Camps

Comprehensive Sports Programs

Cornell University Sports School—Summer Sports Camps
French Woods Festival of the Performing Arts—French Woods Festival of the
    Performing Arts
Hargrave Military Academy—Summer School and Camp
International Sports Camp
Kutsher's Sports Academy
Maine Teen Camp
Orme School—Orme Summer Camp
Princeton University—Summer Sports Camps
Stanford University—Summer Sports Camps
University of Illinois—Fighting Illini Sports Camps
University of Notre Dame—Summer Sports Camps
University of San Diego—Summer Sports Camps
University of Wisconsin, La Crosse—University of Wisconsin Athletic Camps
U.S. Sports Camps—Nike Sports Camps

Extreme Sports Programs

Barefoot International—Barefoot International & Fly High Ski School
Mount Hood Snowboard Camp—MHSC Summer Sessions
U.S. Snowboard Training Center—USSTC Allstar Snowboard Camp
Woodward Sports Camp

See also ADVENTURE PROGRAMS **in chapter 6**

Football Programs

Appalachian State University— Summer Sports, Music, and Academic Camps
ASC Football Camps, Inc.—ASC Football Camps
Hargrave Military Academy—Summer School and Camp
Kicking Game
Princeton University—Summer Sports Camps
Stanford University—Summer Sports Camps
University of Illinois—Fighting Illini Sports Camps
University of Notre Dame—Summer Sports Camps
University of Wisconsin, La Crosse—University of Wisconsin Athletic Camps
U.S. Snowboard Training Center—USSTC Allstar Snowboard Camp
U.S. Sports Camps—Nike Sports Camps

Golf Programs

Kutsher's Sports Academy
Offense Defense Golf Camp
Stanford University—Summer Sports Camps
University of Illinois—Fighting Illini Sports Camps
University of Notre Dame—Summer Sports Camps
U.S. Sports Camps—Nike Sports Camps
Westcoast Connection—Golf & Tennis Programs

Gymnastics Programs

Chris Waller's Summer Gymnastics Jam
Kutsher's Sports Academy
Stanford University—Summer Sports Camps
University of Illinois—Fighting Illini Sports Camps
University of Wisconsin, La Crosse—University of Wisconsin Athletic Camps
U.S. Gymnastics Training Centers—U.S. Gymnastics Camp
Woodward Sports Camp

Hockey Programs

Hockey Opportunity Camp
International Sports Camp
Kutsher's Sports Academy
Planet Hockey, Inc.—Planet Hockey Skills Camps; Planet Hockey Ranch
Princeton University—Summer Sports Camps
Stanford University—Summer Sports Camps
University of Notre Dame—Summer Sports Camps
U.S. Sports Camps—Nike Sports Camps

Horseback Riding Programs

French Woods Festival of the Performing Arts
Kutsher's Sports Academy

Lacrosse Programs

Cornell University Sports School—Summer Sports Camps
Kutsher's Sports Academy
Princeton University—Summer Sports Camps
Stanford University—Summer Sports Camps
University of Notre Dame—Summer Sports Camps
U.S. Sports Camps—Nike Sports Camps

Rowing Programs

All-American Rowing Camp, LLC—High School Coed Rowing Camp
Christchurch School—Summer Programs on the River
Stanford University—Summer Sports Camps
United States Naval Academy—Navy Crew Camp for Boys
United States Naval Academy—Navy Rowing Camp for Girls
U.S. Sports Camps—Nike Sports Camps

Soccer Programs

Appalachian State University— Summer Sports, Music, and Academic Camps
Cornell University Sports School—Summer Sports Camps
Foothill College—Academically Talented Youth Program
Hargrave Military Academy—Summer School and Camp
International Sports Camp

Kutsher's Sports Academy
Lake Placid Soccer Centre—Mountain View Soccer Camp
Middle States Soccer Camp—Intermediate and Senior Soccer Camps
No. 1 Soccer Camps—College Prep Academy
Princeton University—Summer Sports Camps
SoccerPlus Camps—SoccerPlus Goalkeeper School and SoccerPlus Field Player
    Academy
Southern Vermont College—Summer Sports Camps
Stanford University—Summer Sports Camps
Tab Ramos Soccer Academy
University of Illinois—Fighting Illini Sports Camps
University of Notre Dame—Summer Sports Camps
University of San Diego—Summer Sports Camps
U.S. Sports Camps—Nike Sports Camps
Vogelsinger Soccer Academy and All-Star Soccer School

Swimming and Diving Programs

Cornell University Sports School—Summer Sports Camps
Foothill College—Academically Talented Youth Program
Hargrave Military Academy—Summer School and Camp
Stanford University—Summer Sports Camps
University of Illinois—Fighting Illini Sports Camps
University of Notre Dame—Summer Sports Camps
University of San Diego—Summer Sports Camps
University of Wisconsin, La Crosse—University of Wisconsin Athletic Camps
U.S. Sports Camps—Nike Sports Camps

Tennis Programs

Carmel Valley Tennis Camp
Cornell University Sports School—Summer Sports Camps
Duke University—Duke Tennis Camp
Foothill College—Academically Talented Youth Program
Hargrave Military Academy—Summer School and Camp
Joel Ross Tennis & Sports Camp
Kinyon/Jones Tennis Camp
Kutsher's Sports Academy
Maine Teen Camp
Palmer Tennis Academy—Junior Camps
Stanford University—Summer Sports Camps
Tennis: Europe and More
University of Illinois—Fighting Illini Sports Camps
University of Notre Dame—Summer Sports Camps
University of San Diego—Summer Sports Camps
University of Wisconsin, La Crosse—University of Wisconsin Athletic Camps
U.S. Sports Camps—Nike Sports Camps
Westcoast Connection—Golf & Tennis Programs

Track and Field Programs

Appalachian State University—Summer Sports, Music, and Academic Camps
Cornell University Sports School—Summer Sports Camps
Kutsher's Sports Academy
Princeton University—Summer Sports Camps
Stanford University—Summer Sports Camps
University of Illinois—Fighting Illini Sports Camps
University of Wisconsin, La Crosse—University of Wisconsin Athletic Camps
U.S. Sports Camps—Nike Sports Camps

Volleyball Programs

Appalachian State University— Summer Sports, Music, and Academic Camps
Durango Camps—Durango Youth Volleyball Camp
International Sports Camp
Kutsher's Sports Academy
Stanford University—Summer Sports Camps
University of Illinois—Fighting Illini Sports Camps
University of Notre Dame—Summer Sports Camps
University of San Diego—Summer Sports Camps
University of Wisconsin, La Crosse—University of Wisconsin Athletic Camps

Wrestling Programs

Appalachian State University—Summer Sports, Music, and Academic Camps
Cornell University Sports School—Summer Sports Camps
Hargrave Military Academy—Summer School and Camp
Princeton University—Summer Sports Camps
University of Illinois—Fighting Illini Sports Camps
University of Wisconsin, La Crosse—University of Wisconsin Athletic Camps
U.S. Sports Camps—Nike Sports Camps

ENRICHING YOUR SUMMER

Here is a list of websites, books, and movies you can use to further explore various sports.

Websites

Comprehensive Sites

sportsillustrated.cnn.com
Sports Illustrated and CNN offer a joint 24-hour sports news website, with scores, stats, highlights, interviews, analysis, and commentary by top sports journalists.

www.sportingnews.com
The Sporting News site offers something for every sports fan, including news and info, fantasy leagues, shopping, and forums for discussion.

cbs.sportsline.com
Extensive coverage of NFL football, NBA basketball, NHL hockey, NCAA college football games, and more.

espn.go.com/main.html
Coverage of professional and collegiate sports, plus games and contests, chat, message boards, analyses, and more.

Especially for High School Athletes

www.myscore.com
Web site featuring high school athletics, including game results, individual player's performance, team performance, league standings, game schedules, game notes, highlights, and upcoming local events.

www.varsityonline.com
An Internet-based media company that promotes high school athletes. Site offers daily scores, stats, rosters, and schedules.

Organizations

www.ncaa.org
The National Collegiate Athletic Association is *the* organization through which U.S. colleges and universities speak and act on sports matters. Site covers all sorts of collegiate athletics info, including eligibility requirements for athletes. For prerecorded messages with general eligibility information or to order free brochures, call the NCAA hotline at (800) 638-3731.

www.usa-gymnastics.org
USA Gymnastics, a not-for-profit organization, is the sole national governing body (NGB) for the sport of gymnastics in the United States. Great site that features lots of updated news and info on the sport and its athletes and coaches, plus a directory of college programs and links to other resources.

www.nba.com
www.wnba.com
Official sites of the National Basketball Association and the Women's National Basketball Association.

www.nhl.com
National Hockey League's official website.

www.nfl.com
National Football League's official website.

www.us-soccer.com/
Official site of U.S. Soccer Federation.

www.pga.com
The Professional Golf Association of America's official site.

www.itftennis.com
International Tennis Federation's official site offers all the latest news, rankings, competitions, and rules and regulations.

www.usfieldhockey.com
Covers field hockey news, with links to USFHA-sponsored programs.

Books

Guidebooks

The Science of Hitting by Ted Williams and John W. Underwood

A Woman's Guide to Better Golf by Judy Rankin, et al

Training a Tiger: A Father's Guide to Raising a Winner in Both Golf and Life by Earl Woods

The Inner Game of Tennis by W. Timothy Gallwey

Soccer Practice Games: 120 Games for Technique, Training, and Tactics by Joe Luxbacher

Smart Soccer: How to Use Your Mind to Play Your Best by Nina Savin Scott

Hoops Nation: A Guide to America's Best Pickup Basketball by Chris Ballard

Football Drill Book by Doug Mallory

Sport Psychology Library: Gymnastics by Karen Cogan and Peter Vidmar

The Fit Swimmer: 120 Workouts and Training Tips by Marianne Brems

Essays, Commentaries, and Memoirs

The Best American Sports Writing of the Century by David Halberstam and Glenn Stout (editors)

Can't Anybody Here Play This Game? by Jimmy Breslin

The Boys of Summer by Roger Kahn

When Pride Still Mattered: A Life of Vince Lombardi by David Maraniss

Pros and Cons: The Criminals Who Play in the NFL by Jeff Benedict and Don Yaeger

Heaven Is a Playground by Rick Telander

Venus Envy by L. Jon Wertheim

Little Girls in Pretty Boxes by Joan Ryan

Breaking the Surface by Greg Louganis and Eric Marcus

Literature and Fiction

Tennis Ace by Matt Christopher

The Contender by Robert Lipsyte

The Fix by Jeff Schneider

The Southpaw by Mark Harris

The Forever Season by Don Keith

Titans by Tim Green

The Greatest Player Who Never Lived: A Golf Story by J. Michael Veron

Once a Runner by John L. Parker Jr.

Movies

Varsity Blues
James Van Der Beek (*Dawson's Creek*) steps up as quarterback when his high school team's star is sidelined with an injury.

The Replacements
During a pro football players' strike, Keanu Reeves and company fill in for coach Gene Hackman. Silliness ensues.

Love and Basketball
Two childhood friends find their paths crossing in both love and basketball after growing apart in their youth.

Brian's Song
Made-for-TV-movie available on video. This tearjerker illustrates the real-life friendship between Chicago Bears teammates Brian Piccolo and Gale Sayers.

Rudy
Feel-good movie about a determined young man's dream to play football for Notre Dame in spite of his questionable size and ability.

Jerry Maguire
Tom Cruise is a sports agent who tries to start his own company with just a cute assistant (Renée Zellwegger) and one loud client (Cuba "Show me the money!" Gooding Jr.).

Hoop Dreams
Involving documentary spans six years in the lives of two inner-city NBA hopefuls.

Hoosiers
Gene Hackman is a high school basketball coach whose team has a long shot at the state championships in the 1950s.

A League of Their Own
Tom Hanks coaches Geena Davis, Rosie O'Donnell, and Madonna, among others, in this comedy based on the real-life Woman's Baseball League of the 1940s.

Eight Men Out
True story of the infamous 1919 "Black Sox" scandal, in which Chicago White Sox players agreed to lose the World Series in exchange for cash.

Field of Dreams
Kevin Costner builds a baseball field on his farm and gets ghostly visits from the aforementioned Chicago "Black Sox" of 1919.

The Pride of the Yankees
Biography of Lou Gehrig, who played in 2,130 consecutive games before he was stricken with ALS, a degenerative nerve disease. Starring Gary Cooper as Gehrig and Babe Ruth as himself.

Tin Cup
A washed-up golf pro is inspired to try to compete in the U.S. Open. Starring Kevin Costner, Renée Russo, and Don Johnson.

Happy Gilmore
A goofball comedy starring Adam Sandler as a mediocre hockey player who finds his swing under the direction of a one-handed mentor, becomes the star of the PGA tour, saves his grandmother from eviction, and gets the girl.

Pat and Mike
Katharine Hepburn as a gifted athlete who catches the eye of sports promoter Spencer Tracy.

Rocky
Sylvester Stallone both wrote and starred in this story of an underdog boxer who gets a shot at the heavyweight title. A much, much better film than the four sequels that followed it.

Chariots of Fire
True story of two British runners—a Scottish missionary and a Jewish student—who compete in the 1924 Olympics.

The Cutting Edge
A spoiled figure skater is forced to pair up with a rough-around-the-edges hockey player for a shot at Olympic gold.

Mystery, Alaska
Local hockey team gets the chance to play the New York Rangers in an exhibition game set in their eccentric hometown.

National Velvet
A young Mickey Rooney helps an even younger Elizabeth Taylor train for the Grand National—England's most prestigious horse race.

The Black Stallion
A much older Mickey Rooney helps a young boy train a magnificent, wild horse who had rescued the boy from a sinking ship. Beautiful cinematography.

Arts Programs

8

OVERVIEW

From pantomiming stories to dancing Swan Lake, composing on the computer to acting on Greek islands, programs in the arts enable you to play, dance, act, and compose amidst some of the most talented artists in the country. Although some programs have highly competitive admission policies, many are open to anybody who loves the arts. Program directors emphasize that in the arts, people help one another by forming environments that encourage and support individual expression. Everyone learns and grows as a result. By summer's end, you will have not only a more professional, polished technique, but also greater self-confidence and that special sparkle which comes from self-assurance.

"SHOULD I PARTICIPATE IN AN ARTS PROGRAM?"

If you are at all inclined to the arts—whether dance, drama, music, or visual art—there are many reasons to answer "yes." The school year is packed with academic commitments, and this often pushes art to the side. It's difficult to develop your full potential if you're distracted during practice and rehearsal. It's nearly impossible to enjoy lessons when your thoughts wander to the physics test scheduled the next day. By attending a summer program, you can devote your entire being to artistic expression, and that is richly rewarding.

The Exceptionally Talented Artist

Attending a summer program or participating in a program's summer festival can be a tremendous experience. You will live as a musician, actor, dancer, or painter in a community of fellow artists. This provides the kind of round-the-clock stimulation you find in a traveling company, troupe, orchestra, or artistic commune, but few places else.

As you live within this artistic enclave, you will train intensively, taking classes and, if you're in the performing arts, rehearsing—in groups, ensembles, and individually—throughout the day.

Most programs have students perform on a regular basis. Because professional artists ultimately exhibit their work before audiences, this experience is essential for anyone considering a career in the arts. Surrounding yourself with the best in the field will propel you toward your personal best. In many cases, it will also allow you to better judge your ability and potential.

The most competitive summer arts programs may also assist you in moving to the next level, whether admission to a conservatory or professional school or the launching of your career.

The Average High School Artist

Summer programs in the arts provide resources and training well beyond that available in most high schools and local communities. Not only do summer programs have theaters and dance studios, concert halls, and professional-quality sound and lighting equipment, they also have the human resources to put on large-scale productions. Whereas it may be difficult to round up enough people for chamber music groups at high school, summer programs have enough musicians and instructors for both ensembles and a full orchestra.

While you enjoy the summer program community, you will also hone skills, expand artistic horizons, and strengthen an extracurricular interest. That always looks good on college applications.

SUMMER PROGRAM ADMISSIONS

Summer programs that champion a noncompetitive admissions policy embrace a philosophy that everyone can improve their life through artistic expression. Their students sometimes range from complete novices to preprofessionals, and their staff

---

Expert Advice

High-school students interested in attending an arts school should spend their summers "being in a festival or preprofessional program, practicing, and becoming familiar with the standard repertoire and audition repertoire. Students should also become comfortable with performing in front of audiences, and take every possible opportunity for gaining auditioning experience."

—Tracey Iorio, associate director of admissions, The Juilliard School

---

members individually challenge each artist. These programs accept any applicants who complete their application and pay tuition before the program fills. Summer programs that restrict their opportunities to intermediate and advanced students, however, usually request that applicants have a specified number of years of training or require students to audition for admission. Their students are at an average to advanced high school performance level. Finally, summer programs emphasizing preparation for a professional career have the most rigorous admissions standards. They select only the best in their nationwide applicant pool, and admission is by audition only.

When considering summer programs in the arts, you can view auditions as a great opportunity to gain experience, not as a deterrent. Many musically, theatrically, or kinesthetically talented high-school students send video or audio tapes to college admissions offices as supplements to their written applications, and some of the nation's most prestigious university arts programs require live auditions for college admission. So if you're artistically inclined, seize the opportunity to audition for a summer program when it comes your way. The sooner you become performance ready, the better.

Of course, knowing that an audition is "good for you" doesn't make it any easier to swallow. There is no question that auditions are stressful—being judged always is. Careful preparation proves the best defense against nerves, so we'll take the next few pages to walk through the audition process from start to finish.

AUDITIONING VIA MAIL

Because of logistics, many summer programs attracting national participation conduct some or all of their auditions by mail. Along with a written application, students may be asked to submit a videotape for admission to dance or drama programs and either an audio tape or videotape for admission to music programs.

Taped auditions have their advantages. For one, they enable you to audition when and where you feel comfortable. And if you don't perform to your potential, you can always erase the tape and begin again. On the down side, however, taped auditions— especially ones prepared on audio tape—are highly impersonal. Because judges can't interact with you, everything depends on the quality of your performance. Therefore, submitting a tape representing your best work is of the utmost importance. If judges don't like what is recorded first, they're under no obligation to view or listen to the rest.

"The first piece you choose to perform at an audition is extremely important because it sets the tone for the rest of the audition," said James Gandre, dean of enrollment and alumni at New York's

Expert Advice

"If they allow video, I would always suggest it over audio tape because it shows the person behind the music and lets the listeners see you as a whole person, not just a sound machine."

—James Gandre, dean of enrollment and alumni, Manhattan School of Music

Manhattan School of Music. "Always do what you love the best and what you feel comfortable performing in a variety of circumstances. Auditions are always stressful and choosing a work that you can perform only under optimal conditions would not be a good first choice. This is especially important for a taped audition. If the listeners don't like what they hear first, they might not listen to any more of the repertoire you've prepared."

You can also personalize your tape by providing a brief introduction. Daryl Kamer, associate director of BalletMet Dance Academy in Ohio, said this helps admission committees obtain a more complete picture of the performer. "One of the things I have found dancers do on their own—we don't require it—is to begin the audition tape by saying their name, age, and how long they have studied," Kamer said. "I find it helpful because it gives us a sense of what they are like as a person."

Getting Started

Taped auditions require considerable preparation, so start early. As soon as you receive application and audition materials in the mail, read the instructions carefully. Most programs require a very specific audition repertoire and will not consider accepting anyone who fails to comply with specifications. Ask your private instructor what you may include on the tape that will both meet requirements and showcase personal strengths. When auditioning, it's important to select only pieces and combinations for which you have fully mastered the technical skills. Performing work above your current level of expertise in an attempt to impress the judges only draws attention to your faults. You want to emphasize your strengths.

A common mistake to avoid in audio and video auditions is recording extensive material beyond that required by the admissions staff. "If it's a demo tape where there is some flexibility in terms of what to record," said Angela Beeching, a director of the New England Conservatory of Music, "don't make the mistake of recording too much. Often recording shorter selections or three contrasting movements gives a better overall representation of a musician's abilities. And frankly, admissions committees have a very limited amount of time. Think short and sweet."

Obviously, you have worked hard to perfect your audition and are eager to share it. The problem is that every other applicant feels the same way. So, to the admissions committee sitting in front of towering stacks of tapes, a concise, well-executed audition is a welcome relief. When preparing a videotaped dance audition, decide beforehand which exercises you want to record from the front and which from the left or right. It's not necessary to shoot every angle of every movement.

Let the Tapes Roll

Once you have selected your audition repertoire and polished it to perfection, you're ready to begin recording. But you cannot focus all your attention on the performance at this point. Taped auditions present an unfortunate reality: the quality of equipment and skill of the recorder can greatly affect judges' perception of your ability. Admissions committees recognize this and try to focus their attention on the artist rather than the recording. Nevertheless, you should take steps to maximize the quality of your recording.

Making a tape in a professional recording studio is expensive, and in almost all cases, unnecessary for admission to a high school summer program. You should, however, strive for professional quality. Many high schools have recording equipment you may borrow, as do local colleges (ask for the fine arts department). Equipment may also be rented for a fairly reasonable fee.

If you choose to do your own recording, there are several things to keep in mind. First, begin with high-quality equipment and learn to use it properly. Before recording, practice taping off a CD or radio so you become comfortable with the equipment. Better yet, ask a teacher or friend familiar with the equipment to assist you in the recording. He or she may also be able to provide feedback about the success of individual "takes" of pieces or movements. Second, to avoid distorting the sound, select a recording space that is neither too live nor too dead. You can test for reverberation by clapping your hands or stomping your feet. Once you have selected a time to make your tape, take steps to ensure the space is traffic-free during recording. After you have mastered the equipment, selected a room, and thoroughly warmed-up, you're ready to record. Congrats! Be sure to use a separate—not built-in—microphone and place it far enough away from your mouth or instrument to allow the music to sound natural. Then, relax and do your best.

Note

Dancing on Video

Here are the guidelines for videotape audition used at BalletMet Dance Academy in Columbus, Ohio.

Students are asked to complete a sample class.

Barre: Plies, tendus (slow and quick), rond de jambe a terre, frappe, developpé, grand battement. You need not show both sides of each exercise.

Center: Adagio, pirouette combination (en dehors and endedans), petite allegro (more advanced students should include beats), grand allegro. Please show right and left side, one time through of each exercise.

For young women: Short demonstration of pointe work—two or three combinations that demonstrate the student's technical strength and level of accomplishment.

For young men: Exercise showing entrechat quatre or entrechat six (depending on level of advancement) and single or double tours.

Expert Advice

"I understand that those auditioning are nervous. When you're the only one being videotaped, you feel that you're really being scrutinized. But it's important to be aware that, in a sense, the video is a performance—the expression on their faces, the way they move musically, those are things that enhance the viewing pleasure for me and give a more complete picture of them as a dancer."

—Daryl Kamer, associate director, BalletMet Dance Academy

When recording a dance or dramatic audition, lighting and angles present additional concerns. Too much or too little light can make it difficult to see movement. So too can a "busy" background. Therefore, before beginning your audition, address these issues by adjusting backdrops and monitoring both natural and artificial light. In addition, be aware of camera angles. Videographers may unknowingly create problems by capturing performers in an unflattering position. For example, if the camera is positioned in such a way that it points down at a dancer, Daryl Kamer of the BalletMet Dance Academy explains, the dancer's body will appear shorter and out of proportion. The one advantage of videotaping is that it can enhance a person's features. Capitalize on that! Before recording an entire audition, make a sample tape. Then, check to see that the lighting is adequate, the picture clear, and most important, that you are represented the way you want to be.

Finally, remember that just because you don't see the judges doesn't mean they aren't there. A taped audition is still an audition, and that means you must perform. The little things count, so be serious as you record. If it helps, visualize an audience mesmerized by your music, dance, or monologue.

Sending it Off

Before mailing your audition tape, listen to and/or watch the entire recording. Believe it or not, people send in blank tapes without realizing their audition didn't record. After you confirm that your audition is indeed there, copy the tape just in case it gets lost in the mail.

The tape you send to the summer program should be rewound, cued up, and neatly labeled both on the box and on the tape itself (they may get separated during the evaluation process). Be sure the labels include all pertinent information about you and your recording.

AUDITIONING IN PERSON

Preparation for a live audition is much the same as preparation for a taped one. You should read directions thoroughly and assemble a repertoire with care. While you don't have to worry about lighting, angles, and background noise, live auditions bring their own concerns. Some people find it nervewracking to watch fellow applicants perform; others dislike seeing judges face-to-face. While these aspects of an audition are unavoidable, you can help yourself feel more relaxed by practicing regularly and preparing emotionally for the rigors of the audition process.

Familiarizing yourself with the audition format is a good place to start. Most high school musicians are unaccustomed to starting a piece and being told to stop part way through. Yet in auditions, people are routinely instructed to play only five minutes of a piece, perhaps beginning at the second or third movement. During the weeks before an audition, it's important to practice under these conditions. James Gandre of the Manhattan School of Music offered advice on preparing for a summer program audition in music:

"Do several run-throughs with friends and family members. The best thing to do is what is called a 'mock' audition. You get up and perform the first piece you plan to perform for each audition, then you have people from the audience choose the next piece or movement of a piece. This will get you accustomed to the practice of standing up in front of people to perform your audition repertoire in a random order, just the way it is in a real audition. Remember, under normal performance situations you know what comes next and you've rehearsed it over and over again in that order. In an audition you usually have control only over the first work or first movement of a work you will perform. For example, if you're a pianist, you may choose to start your auditions with a Bach prelude and fugue. The judges at Summer Program A may then ask for the second movement of a Beethoven sonata, stop you two minutes after you begin playing, ask you to go to the final movement of the Prokofiev and listen to another three minutes and end the audition there, not wanting to hear any of your Brahms. Now you go to audition for Summer Program B and you play the same Bach, but this time the judges ask for the last movement of Beethoven, then the first movement of the Brahms and none of the Prokofiev. And so it goes. As you can see, practicing for the audition process is important."

When the actual audition day arrives, you will probably feel nervous no matter how prepared you are. That is normal, and a little adrenaline will only improve your performance. Being overanxious, however, is detrimental. Try to leave yourself time to relax at the audition site before you go on stage. If you arrive minutes before you're called, you will end up feeling rushed and flustered and are unlikely to perform your best. "It's very important that [dancers] give themselves enough time, that they get [to the audition] early if possible," said Michelle Van Doeren, director of the scholarship program at Steps on Broadway in New

——— **Quick Tips** ———

Dealing with the Pre-Audition Jitters

While you're waiting to be called, try taking your mind off the impending audition through relaxation techniques. One simple exercise involves the relaxation of each of your body's muscles in turn. Start by concentrating on your feet and work all the way up to your head. Breathe deeply as you go.

York City. "If they come ahead of time they can relax, take as much time as they need to fill out the application, warm up, and stretch."

Remember that when auditioning for a summer program, you're being critiqued not only on your technique, but also on your ability to behave professionally. Summer programs are ultimately communities of artists, and directors want students who will contribute in a positive way. So while you're preparing for your own audition, don't forget to be supportive and appreciative of those around you.

Finally, go easy on yourself. Even the world's best performers make mistakes. As you audition more frequently, the process will get easier and your performance will improve. In the meantime, be satisfied knowing you gave your best effort.

Quick Tips
Acing the Audition

Taped:

- Adding a personal touch will make you stick out later in judges' minds. Don't do anything tacky, but do introduce yourself and give some background info, such as your age and range of performance experience.
- Make sure you compile all the materials for your audition well ahead of the application deadline. These auditions might seem easier than live performances, but they do require a good amount of prep time.
- Select your audition pieces carefully. Choose selections you've practiced many times and are comfortable with. Don't try to perform above your level.
- Don't overwhelm the admissions committee with an hour-long performance. Judges have to go through lots of auditions, so make sure your audition is short, but representative of your skills.
- Use professional-level equipment to make your audition tape look and sound as polished as your performance demands. You can borrow cameras and audio devices from local colleges, or you can rent them.
- Practice recording before you tape your final audition.
- Visualize an audience to psych yourself up during your performance.
- Before you mail your tape, play it back to make sure your audition was actually recorded. A blank tape isn't a good first impression to make on the summer program admissions committee!

Live:

- Make sure you are fully prepared for the audition.
- Get used to the typical audition format. You might be asked to stop and start in different places during your performance.
- Relax. Give yourself plenty of time before your audition slot to warm up and prepare mentally.
- Don't beat yourself up over little slips. You will only improve with each audition; be satisfied with a good effort.

THE ARTS EXPERIENCE

Once you have been accepted, you're ready to live the life of an artist—at least for the summer. What will your days be like? Schedules vary according to the type of music, art, dance, or acting in which your camp or program specializes, as well as your level of expertise. However, some features are common to all.

Arts programs pride themselves on supportive atmospheres where students teach and learn from each other. Program directors emphasize that clearing your mind of distractions, doubt, and pressure are important steps to performing your best. Many of the arts programs not located on university campuses operate in remote locations where participants literally have nothing to do or worry about other than improving their technique and expression.

Being in such an environment, surrounded by people committed to expressing themselves creatively, often makes improvement come naturally, almost unnoticeably. Many students say the isolation of arts programs—being away from school, home, and everyday worries—enables them to rediscover their love of the arts, which only accelerates their learning process. With practice several times a day, evening rehearsals, and meal time discussions about songs, dance combinations, and scripts, you get swept up in the excitement, becoming deeply involved and intensely focused, starting on day one. The transformation from schooltime boredom to daily artistic expression can be galvanizing.

A unique aspect of summer programs in the arts is that they are often open to people of all ages. There are practical reasons for this: many plays, musicals, and dance productions call for child as well as adult performers. And instrumental music is virtually ageless—ability, not years, makes for a breathtaking performance. As a result, summer programs in the arts yield experiences distinct from those found at academic or athletic summer programs. While most arts programs house people of the same age together, classes, productions, and ensembles could be intergenerational. In some cases you may be working with young children—10- or 11-year-olds—while in other cases you may study alongside people your parents' age. Because of this, not all arts programs provide that unique precollege experience of living and learning with hundreds of people your age.

Expert Advice

"They don't have to think about homework or parents or having to do duties at home. They can completely and totally devote themselves to dance without any outside interference. [Burklyn Ballet] is the only program in the country where all the students perform every week. It means that what they are doing is having to learn very, very quickly. Many of them say when they go back to school, learning is much easier because of the skills they have learned in the program."

—Angela Whitehill, artistic director, Burklyn Ballet Theatre

But those that don't provide the equally rewarding experience of studying and performing in an environment whose composition closely mirrors that of "real" artistic communities.

Being open to meeting and studying with people at all life stages will greatly enhance your arts experience. Even if you do not plan to play professionally, the experience will prepare you for adult life. Throughout college, you will increasingly have opportunities to interact with older people on an equal basis. Whether you're a museum intern or lead volunteer efforts in the community surrounding your college campus, having experience relating to others on an adult to adult level will prove valuable.

Another commonality among arts programs is their integration of many different forms of artistic expression. Many summer programs provide participants with the choice between several different "majors"—from music to fine arts to dance—and the entire camp assembles regularly to share projects, productions, and concerts. But even summer programs focusing entirely on one art form, say dance, provide forums to experiment with related fields; costume and set design, for example. Still other programs strive to unite the varied forms of art for each participant. Rina Shere, executive director of the Institute for Arts and Humanities, said their summer program, the New Jersey Summer Arts Institute, helps high school students "clarify what art really is." The program is interdisciplinary, with all students painting, writing, and dancing: "Everybody has to do everything. This opens up some hidden talents. Someone might come in as a writer and discover she is an actor," Shere said.

Whether you go to a summer program to strengthen skills in one particular area or dabble in several, be open to exploring all opportunities. It will strengthen your work and broaden your appreciation of the arts.

BEYOND SUMMER

Participating in a summer arts program unquestionably raises your level of performance, both by the continual summer lessons and by inspiring those extra practice sessions once you return to school. For those willing to exert a little extra effort in selecting their program initially and reflecting upon the experience at the summer's end, arts programs can bring additional benefits.

Colleges appreciate applicants who have strong academic profiles, but also have interests outside of school. A college campus full of students who do nothing but study would be a boring place for anyone to live and learn. If you can show admissions officers that you have a real interest in the arts and have taken steps to

—— Student Scoop ——

"I started to look at music more seriously; for a while I wanted to be a musician professionally. Even when I gave that up, it was still my most prominent extracurricular. It's not a hobby I can just screw around with. I try to be as good as I can."

—Arum Park, participant, Marrowstone Music Festival

cultivate your appreciation and knowledge of a particular field, you present a stronger application than a student with similar grades and test scores who has shown limited extracurricular involvement.

There are several ways to illustrate your commitment to the arts. You will, of course, indicate your participation in a summer program on the application itself. But that doesn't do much to distinguish you from other students who have attended summer enrichment programs. If you develop a meaningful relationship with one of your summer program teachers, consider asking him or her for a letter of recommendation. Having known you in a nonacademic environment far away from your hometown, family, and friends, the instructor will provide a different perspective than the teachers and coaches you may ask to write your other letters of recommendation.

You can also tell admissions officers about the program yourself. If you have spent a significant part of your summer on the stage, you have probably devoted many hours to thinking about music, dance, or acting. Not just about how you should hold your head or soften your sound, but how the arts complement your daily life. Has the meaning or significance of art changed for you over the course of the summer? In what ways? Do you find your personal and artistic growth intertwined? Can you describe how you feel when you perform and why that matters? Many people write successful essays about extracurricular passions, and you might find that an experience or conversation you had at a summer program provides an intriguing place to start. These same thoughts can be used in college interviews and scholarship applications.

If you're considering an arts school rather than a liberal arts college or university, attending a summer program at one of the institutions you're considering is politic. It will give you a preview of the school's daily life, which is important because attending an arts school limits your opportunity to experience academic disciplines such as anthropology, political science, and engineering. You want to be absolutely sure the program is right for you, and attending a summer program at the school can help you decide. You will familiarize yourself with the campus, study under members of the college's faculty, and meet the type of students who will be your classmates.

Attending a program in which instructors at your desired postsecondary school teach also gives you an additional opportunity to be evaluated. Some arts schools make admissions decisions based almost exclusively on the quality of an audition. During the course of a summer program, you can prove—to yourself and your instructors—you have the skills and drive to flourish in their year-round program. Tracey Iorio, associate director of admissions at The Juilliard School, explained that while the admissions committee does not take summer program participation into consideration per se, students must have gained the performance and technical experience necessary to succeed at Juilliard. Needless to say, many students acquire such experience at a summer program.

CAREER-BOUND

If you have the ability and desire to move directly from high school into a professional career in the arts, some summer programs can provide training, contacts, and emotional support to help you do that. Because bypassing college is a serious decision, you will want to select a summer program that has fully informed professionals to counsel you about career prospects and the advantages and disadvantages of first continuing your study at a college, university, or arts school. If you're contemplating a professional career directly after high school, you will probably want to attend the same program for several summers.

If an immediate professional career may be a stretch for you, a summer program can still open doors for short-term projects such as appearances in television commercials. Several arts programs regularly invite agents and casting directors to their campus to provide feedback for their students. While they assist with the program, these professionals also watch for new talent; students occasionally land jobs as a result.

LIST OF PROGRAMS

Here is a list of summer arts programs. See the Program Directory in Part III of this book for a description of each of these programs.

Art Programs

Appel Farm Arts and Music Center—Appel Farm's Summer Arts Camp
Art Institute of Boston at Lesley University—Pre-College Summer Program
Asheville School—Asheville School Summer Academic Adventures
Ballibay Camps, Inc.—Camp Ballibay for the Fine and Performing Arts
Bennington College—Bennington College July Program
Blue Lake Fine Arts Camp
Brenau University—Firespark Schools
Brookfield Craft Center—Summer Workshop Series
Buck's Rock Performing and Creative Arts Camp
California College of Arts and Crafts—CCAC Pre-College Program
California State Summer School for the Arts
Capitol Region Education Council and Wesleyan University—Center for Creative Youth
Carnegie Mellon University—Pre-College Programs

Colorado College—Summer Session for High School Students
Columbia College Chicago—High School Summer Institute
Columbia University—Columbia Summer Programs for High School Students
French Woods Festival of the Performing Arts
Gifted and Talented Development Center
Humanities Spring in Assisi
Idyllwild Arts Foundation—Idyllwild Arts Summer Program
Interlochen Center for the Arts—Interlochen Arts Camp
Johns Hopkins University—Pre-college Credit Program
Kingdom County Productions and Fledgling Films—Fledgling Films Summer
    Institute
Knowledge Exchange Institute—Precollege Artist Abroad Program
Maine Teen Camp
Miami University—Junior Scholars Program
Minnesota Institute for Talented Youth—Expand Your Mind
New York University—Tisch Summer High School Program
North Carolina School of the Arts—Summer Session
Otis College of Art and Design—Otis Summer of Art
Parsons School of Design—Summer Intensive Studies
Phillips Academy Andover—Phillips Academy Summer Session
Pratt Institute—Pre-College Summer Program
Rhode Island School of Design—Pre-College Program
Ringling School of Art and Design—PreCollege Perspective
Ringling School of Art and Design—Summer Teen Studios
Savannah College of Art and Design—Rising Star
Southampton College of Long Island University—Summer High School Workshops
Southwestern Academy—International Summer Programs
Spoleto Study Abroad
State University of New York, Oswego—Summer Art Institute
State University of New York, Purchase—Summer Visual Arts Institute
Summer Study Programs—Summer Enrichment and Summer Study at Penn State
Syracuse University—Summer College for High School Students
University of the Arts—PREP, Art Smart, and Media and Communications
    Workshops
University of Maryland, School of Architecture—Design Career Discover (Arch 150)
University of Mississippi—Summer College for High School Students
University of Pennsylvania—Precollege Program
University of Southern California—Summer Production Workshop
University of Wisconsin, Madison—Summer Art Classes
University of Wisconsin, Superior—Youthsummer
Wright State University—Pre-College Summer Enrichment Programs

Computer Graphics Programs

Art Institute of Boston at Lesley University—Pre-College Summer Program
Knowledge Exchange Institute—Precollege Artist Abroad Program
Otis College of Art and Design—Otis Summer of Art

Parsons School of Design—Summer Intensive Studies
Ringling School of Art and Design—PreCollege Perspective
Ringling School of Art and Design—Summer Teen Studios
Southampton College of Long Island University—Summer High School Workshops
State University of New York, Oswego—Summer Art Institute
University of the Arts—PREP, Art Smart, and Media and Communications Workshops
University of Iowa—Summer Journalism Workshops

Dance Programs

Appel Farm Arts and Music Center—Appel Farm's Summer Arts Camp
BalletMet—Summer Workshop
Ballibay Camps, Inc.—Camp Ballibay for the Fine and Performing Arts
Blue Lake Fine Arts Camp
Buck's Rock Performing and Creative Arts Camp
Burklyn Ballet Theatre
California State Summer School for the Arts
Capitol Region Education Council and Wesleyan University—Center for Creative Youth
Carnegie Mellon University—Pre-College Programs
Colorado College—Summer Session for High School Students
Dwight-Englewood School—Dwight-Englewood Summer Programs
French Woods Festival of the Performing Arts
Goucher College—Goucher Summer Arts Institute
Huntingdon College—Huntingdon College Summer Programs
Idyllwild Arts Foundation—Idyllwild Arts Summer Program
Interlochen Center for the Arts—Interlochen Arts Camp
Kutsher's Sports Academy
Maine Teen Camp
The Masters School—Summer Theatre
Minnesota Institute for Talented Youth—Expand Your Mind
North Carolina School of the Arts—Summer Session
Northwestern University—National High School Institute
Princeton Ballet School—American Repertory Ballet's Summer Intensive
Stagedoor Enterprises—Stagedoor Manor Performing Arts Training Center
University of the Arts—Drama and Musical Theater
University of Wisconsin, Superior—Youthsummer
Wright State University—Pre-College Summer Enrichment Programs

Design Programs

Art Institute of Boston at Lesley University—Pre-College Summer Program
Art Institute of Seattle—Studio 101
Auburn University —Design Camp
Carnegie Mellon University—Pre-College Programs
Catholic University of America—Experiences in Architecture
Gifted and Talented Development Center

LaGrange College—Visual Arts Workshop
Otis College of Art and Design—Otis Summer of Art
Parsons School of Design—Summer Intensive Studies
Pratt Institute—Pre-College Summer Program
Rhode Island School of Design—Pre-College Program
Ringling School of Art and Design—PreCollege Perspective
Ringling School of Art and Design—Summer Teen Studios
Savannah College of Art and Design—Rising Star
Syracuse University—Summer College for High School Students
University of the Arts—PREP, Art Smart, and Media and Communications
    Workshops
University of Maryland, School of Architecture—Design Career Discover (Arch 150)
Washington University in St. Louis—Architecture Discovery Program

Fashion Programs

Art Institute of Seattle—Studio 101
Otis College of Art and Design—Otis Summer of Art
Parsons School of Design—Summer Intensive Studies
Pratt Institute—Pre-College Summer Program
Syracuse University—Summer College for High School Students

Media Programs

American University—Discover the World of Communication
Appel Farm Arts and Music Center—Appel Farm's Summer Arts Camp
Art Institute of Seattle—Studio 101
Ballibay Camps, Inc.—Camp Ballibay for the Fine and Performing Arts
Buck's Rock Performing and Creative Arts Camp
California Chicano News Media Association—San Jose Urban Journalism Workshop
    for Minorities
California State Summer School for the Arts
Capitol Region Education Council and Wesleyan University—Center for Creative
    Youth
Catholic University of America—Media and Video Production Workshop
Columbia College Chicago—High School Summer Institute
Hollins University—Precollege Program
Idyllwild Arts Foundation—Idyllwild Arts Summer Program
Indiana University—Bloomington—High School Journalism Publications Workshops
Ithaca College—Summer College for High School Students
Kingdom County Productions and Fledgling Films—Fledgling Films Summer
    Institute
Maine Teen Camp
Media Workshops Foundation—The Media Workshops
New York Film Academy—New York Film Academy Summer Program
North Carolina School of the Arts—Summer Session
Northwestern University—National High School Institute
University of the Arts—PREP, Art Smart, and Media and Communications
    Workshops

University of California, San Diego—UCSD Academic Connections & Summer Session

University of Iowa—Summer Journalism Workshops

University of Miami—Summer Scholar Programs

University of Mississippi—Summer College for High School Students

University of Southern California—Summer Production Workshop

University of Virginia—Summer Enrichment Program

Yale University—Yale Daily News Summer Journalism Program

See also WRITING PROGRAMS **in chapter 3**

Music Programs

Appalachian State University—Summer Sports, Music, and Academic Camps

Appel Farm Arts and Music Center—Appel Farm's Summer Arts Camp

Apple Hill Center for Chamber Music—Apple Hill Summer School and Festival

Aspen Music School—Aspen Music Festival and School

Auburn University—Summer Honor Band Camps

Ballibay Camps, Inc.—Camp Ballibay for the Fine and Performing Arts

Blue Lake Fine Arts Camp

Brevard Music Center—Young Artists Division

Britt Festivals—The Britt Institute

Buck's Rock Performing and Creative Arts Camp

California State Summer School for the Arts

Camp Encore/Coda—Upper Camp

Capitol Region Education Council and Wesleyan University—Center for Creative Youth

Carnegie Mellon University—Pre-College Programs

Catholic University of America—Chamber Music Program

Colorado College—Summer Session for High School Students

Drew University—Drew Summer Music

Dwight-Englewood School—Dwight-Englewood Summer Programs

Eastern Music Festival

Eastern U.S. Music Camp, Inc.—Eastern U.S. Music Camp

French Woods Festival of the Performing Arts

Friends Music Camp

Goucher College—Goucher Summer Arts Institute

Huntingdon College—Huntingdon College Summer Programs

Idyllwild Arts Foundation—Idyllwild Arts Summer Program

Indiana University, Bloomington—College Audition Preparation (CAP); Summer Piano Academy; Summer Recorder Academy; Summer String Academy

Indiana University, Bloomington—Indiana University Summer Music Clinic

Interlochen Center for the Arts—Interlochen Arts Camp

Johns Hopkins University—Pre-college Credit Program

Kincardine Summer Music Festival—KSMF Jazz Camp; KSMF Chamber Music Camp; KSMF Festival Week Music Camp

Kinhaven Music School

Lebanon Valley College—Summer Music Camp
Maine Teen Camp
The Masters School—Summer Theatre
Minnesota Institute for Talented Youth—Expand Your Mind
New York University—Tisch Summer High School Program
North Carolina School of the Arts—Summer Session
Northwestern University—National High School Institute
Power Chord Academy
Saint Olaf College—Saint Olaf Summer Music Camp
Seattle Youth Symphony Orchestra—Marrowstone Music Festival
Southwestern Academy—International Summer Programs
Spoleto Study Abroad
Stagedoor Enterprises—Stagedoor Manor Performing Arts Training Center
Stanford Jazz Workshop—Jazz Camp; Jazz Residency
Summer Sonatina International Piano Camp
Summer Study Programs—Summer Enrichment and Summer Study at Penn State
University of the Arts—Drama and Musical Theater
University of the Arts—Summer Institute of Jazz
University of Iowa—Iowa All-State Music Camp
University of Maine—Maine Summer Youth Music Senior Camp
University of Mississippi—Summer College for High School Students
University of New Hampshire—Summer Youth Music School (SYMS)
University of Wisconsin, Madison—Summer Music Clinic
Walden School—Walden School Summer Music School, Festival, and Camp
The Washington Opera—Opera Institute for Young Singers

Photography Programs

Art Institute of Boston at Lesley University—Pre-College Summer Program
Knowledge Exchange Institute—Precollege Artist Abroad Program
LaGrange College—Visual Arts Workshop
Parsons School of Design—Summer Intensive Studies
Pratt Institute—Pre-College Summer Program
Ringling School of Art and Design—Summer Teen Studios
Southampton College of Long Island University—Summer High School Workshops
Spoleto Study Abroad
State University of New York, Oswego—Summer Art Institute
Summer Study Programs—Summer Enrichment and Summer Study at Penn State
University of the Arts—PREP, Art Smart, and Media and Communications
    Workshops
University of Iowa—Summer Journalism Workshops
University of Wisconsin, Superior—Youthsummer

Theater/Film/TV Programs

ACTeen—ACTeen July Academy, ACTeen August Academy, ACTeen Summer Saturday
    Program
American Academy of Dramatic Arts—Summer Actor Training

Appel Farm Arts and Music Center—Appel Farm's Summer Arts Camp
Ballibay Camps, Inc.—Camp Ballibay for the Fine and Performing Arts
Bethesda Academy of Performing Arts—Summer Repertory Theater; Mid-Summer Shakespeare Company
Blue Lake Fine Arts Camp
Buck's Rock Performing and Creative Arts Camp
California State Summer School for the Arts
Cambridge College Programme LLC—Cambridge College Programme
Capitol Region Education Council and Wesleyan University—Center for Creative Youth
Carnegie Mellon University—Pre-College Programs
Catholic University of America—Media and Video Production Workshop
Columbia College Chicago—High School Summer Institute
Columbia University—Columbia Summer Programs for High School Students
Dwight-Englewood School—Dwight-Englewood Summer Programs
East Carolina University—East Carolina Summer Theatre
Education Unlimited—Acting Workshop at Berkeley
French Woods Festival of the Performing Arts
Goucher College—Goucher Summer Arts Institute
Hun School of Princeton—Hun School Summer Programs
Idyllwild Arts Foundation—Idyllwild Arts Summer Program
Indiana University, Bloomington—Midsummer Theatre Program
Interlochen Center for the Arts—Interlochen Arts Camp
Interlocken—Crossroads Adventure Travel
Ithaca College—Summer College for High School Students
Kingdom County Productions and Fledgling Films—Fledgling Films Summer Institute
Maine Teen Camp
The Masters School—Summer Theatre
Minnesota Institute for Talented Youth—Expand Your Mind
New York Film Academy—New York Film Academy Summer Program
New York University—Tisch Summer High School Program
North Carolina School of the Arts—Summer Session
Northwestern University—National High School Institute
Phillips Academy Andover—Phillips Academy Summer Session
School for Film and Television—Summer in the City
Southwest Texas State University —Summer High School Theatre Workshop
Spoleto Study Abroad
Stagedoor Enterprises—Stagedoor Manor Performing Arts Training Center
Stanford University—Summer Discovery Institutes
State University of New York, Oswego—Summer Theater Institute
Summer Study Programs—Summer Enrichment and Summer Study at Penn State
Syracuse University—Summer College for High School Students
University of the Arts—Drama and Musical Theater
University of California, Los Angeles—UCLA High School Acting and Performance Institute
University of Iowa—Workshop in Theatre Arts

University of Miami—Summer Scholar Programs
University of Mississippi—Summer College for High School Students
University of Southern California—Summer Production Workshop
University of Texas—Summer Theatre Workshop
University of Virginia—Summer Enrichment Program
University of Wisconsin, Superior—Youthsummer
Vanderbilt University—Program for Talented Youth
Vassar College and New York Stage & Film—Powerhouse Theatre Program
Wright State University—Pre-College Summer Enrichment Programs

ENRICHING YOUR SUMMER

Here is a list of websites, books, and movies you can use to further explore various art forms.

Websites

Dance

www.abt.org
American Ballet Theatre site not only has info on the prestigious company itself, but features a multimedia "ballet dictionary"—video demonstrations and explanations of select ballet moves by ABT dancers.

www.danceonline.com
Contemporary dance site includes dance criticism, dance news, opinion pieces, feature articles, interviews, dance performances in Real Video, photo exhibits, multimedia works, links, and discussion areas.

www.voiceofdance.com
Features current national dance news and reviews from major U.S. newspapers, interviews with dancers and choreographers, live chats, and more.

Music

www.classical.net
Contains such useful features as a classical CD buying guide, 2,600 links to other classical music Web sites, and reviews of more than 1,500 CDs.

www.operabase.com
Huge database of artists and performances, plus news and reviews from the world's leading newspapers, info on festivals, and more.

www.sonicnet.com/news/musicnewswire
Guide to music news on the Internet. Links to daily headlines from dozens of sites including Billboard, MTV, VH-1, and more.

Theater/Film/TV

www.playbill.com
Find out what's happening in the world of professional theater. Free enrollment in the Playbill Online Club entitles members to discounts on Broadway tickets as well as other special offers.

www.actorsequity.org
The union of American actors and stage managers in professional theater.

www.tdf.org
The Theatre Development Fund is a nonprofit organization which administers a range of audience development and financial assistance programs that encourage production of new plays and musicals.

www.backstage.com
Online version of *Back Stage*, a weekly publication containing resources that are particularly helpful for the aspiring actor, including both union and non-union casting notices and info on acting classes, head shots, etc.

www.imdb.com
Internet Movie Database contains a wealth of info on movies, including plotlines, reviews, production info, bios, and links.

Visual Arts

www.artlex.com
An online visual arts dictionary for artists, students, and educators, with definitions of more than 3,300 terms used in art production, criticism, history, aesthetics, and education.

www.imagesite.com
Billed as "an index for the visual arts," offers info on agencies, artists' reps, competitions, galleries and museums, organizations, schools, and more.

www.digitaltruth.com
Photography site featuring film development chart, techniques and guides, discussion forum, and links.

Books

Dance

The New York City Ballet Workout: Fifty Stretches and Exercises Anyone Can Do for a Strong, Graceful, and Sculpted Body by Peter Martins

The Tap Dance Dictionary by Mark Knowles

Once a Dancer by Allegra Kent

Dancing on My Grave: An Autobiography by Gelsey Kirkland and Greg Lawrence

Savion: My Life in Tap by Savion Glover

Another Way to Dance by Martha Southgate

Blue Tights by Rita Williams-Garcia

Shiva's Fire by Suzanne Fisher Staples

Music

The Structure of Singing: System and Art in Vocal Technique by Richard Miller

Super Sight-Reading Secrets by Howard B. Richman (editor)

The Art of Practicing: A Guide to Making Music from the Heart by Madeline Bruser

With Your Own Two Hands: Self-Discovery Through Music by Seymour Bernstein

Mozart by Peter Gay

Shostakovich: A Life Remembered by Elizabeth Wilson

Silence by John Cage

As Serious as Your Life: John Coltrane and Beyond by Valerie Wilmer

Visions of Jazz by Gary Giddins

Andrea Bocelli: A Celebration by Antonia Felix

The Sandy Bottom Orchestra by Garrison Keillor and Jenny Lind Nilsson

The Mozart Season by Virginia Euwer Wolff

Theater/Film/TV

An Actor Prepares by Constantine Stanislavski

Respect for Acting by Uta Hagen

True and False: Heresy and Common Sense for the Actor by David Mamet

Audition: Everything an Actor Needs to Know to Get the Part by Michael Shurtleff

How to Be a Working Actor: The Insider's Guide to Finding Jobs in Theater, Film, and Television by Mari Lyn Henry and Lynne Rogers

Monologues for Young Actors by Lorraine Cohen (editor)

One-Act Plays for Acting Students: An Anthology of Short One-Act Plays for One, Two, or Three Actors by Norman Bert (editor)

Technical Theater for Nontechnical People by Drew Campbell

Film Production: The Complete Uncensored Guide to Filmmaking by Greg Merritt

Making Documentary Films and Reality Videos by Barry Hampe

Kazan: The Master Director Discusses His Films by Jeff Young

Conversations With Wilder by Cameron Crowe

Call Me Anna by Patty Duke

The Shakespeare Stealer by Gary L. Blackwood

Good Moon Rising by Nancy Garden

King of Shadows by Susan Cooper

Visual Arts

Concerning the Spiritual in Art by Wassily Kandinsky

The American Century: Art and Culture, 1900–1950 by Barbara Haskell

Homemade Esthetics: Observations on Art and Taste by Clement Greenberg

The Natural Way to Draw: A Working Plan for Art Study by Kimon Nicolaides

Minimal Art: A Critical Anthology by Gregory Battcock (editor)

History of Art for Young People by H. W. Janson

Girl With a Pearl Earring by Tracy Chevalier

The Light Possessed by Alan Cheuse

Movies

Dance

Save the Last Dance
Julia Stiles loses her mother, her suburban lifestyle, and her passion for ballet until Sean Patrick Harris helps her get back on her feet, so to speak.

The Red Shoes
A ballerina is torn between a struggling composer and a possessive ballet impresario. Landmark film for its integration of dance in storytelling.

West Side Story
Gang members sing, dance, and fight to an unforgettable Leonard Bernstein score. Starring Natalie Wood, Richard Beymer, and Rita Moreno.

The Band Wagon
Fred Astaire as a washed-up dancer who gets a shot at a big Broadway comeback, if he can put up with a pretentious artistic director and a prima ballerina costar.

An American in Paris
Gene Kelly dances to the magnificent George Gershwin score.

All That Jazz
The ups and downs of a man modeled after director/choreographer Bob Fosse.

Billy Elliot
A boy in a working-class coal mining district in northern England wants to study ballet instead of boxing.

Center Stage
Three teenage girls study ballet at a prestigious academy in New York City.

The Turning Point
Shirley MacLaine, a former dancer who retired to become a wife and mother, is reunited with Anne Bancroft, a successful dancer nearing the end of her career, when MacLaine's daughter joins Bancroft's ballet company.

Music

Moulin Rouge
This love story, set in the infamous Moulin Rouge of 1899 Paris, samples a range of 20th-century pop music.

Amadeus
Mozart, whose unparalleled musical genius is combined with a vulgar immaturity, upsets the much less talented composer, Salieri.

Immortal Beloved
Beethoven as a mad tyrant, as portrayed by Gary Oldman.

The Red Violin
The life of a special violin is chronicled, from its creation in 17th-century Italy up until present-day Montreal.

Mr. Holland's Opus
Richard Dreyfuss is a high school music teacher who had always aspired to be a great composer. He finally realizes that his "great work" isn't his musical composition but rather his family, friends, and the many students whose lives he touched.

Music of the Heart
Meryl Streep battles the board of education to try to teach underprivileged children to play the violin. Based on a true story.

Fame
Explores the dreams and struggles of a group of students at the New York City High School for the Performing Arts.

Hilary and Jackie
The real-life story of celebrated cellist Jacqueline Du Pré and her complex relationship with her less successful sister, Hilary.

Shine
Based on the true story of Australian pianist David Helfgott, a child prodigy who suffers a breakdown and is able to return to the stage (to popular, though not critical acclaim) only many years later.

Theater/Film/TV

All About Eve
Classic film about a scheming understudy who manages to steal the spotlight from an aging star.

The Dresser
A stagehand devotes himself to the tyrannical but deteriorating star of a Shakespearean touring company.

Vanya on 42nd Street
In director Louis Malle's "filmed theater" piece, actors come to a crumbling midtown Manhattan stage to rehearse Chekhov's *Uncle Vanya*.

Hamlet (1948)
Laurence Olivier's definitive version of the melancholy Dane is a must-see for aspiring actors and directors.

Looking for Richard
Documentary about Al Pacino's staging of *Richard III* includes scenes from the rehearsal process, scenes from the performance, and discussions and interviews with various actors.

Waiting for Guffman
Mock documentary about mounting a community theater production in the small town of Blaine, Missouri.

William Shakespeare's Romeo & Juliet (1996)
MTV-style retelling of the classic tale of the star-crossed lovers. Starring Leonardo DiCaprio and Claire Danes.

The Producers
Mel Brooks comedy about a Broadway producer with a scheme to make money off of a sure-fire flop, a musical called *Springtime for Hitler*.

Tootsie
A solid comedy starring Dustin Hoffman as an actor who poses as a woman in order to land an acting job on a soap opera.

Soapdish
Farcical behind-the-scenes look at a fictional soap, *The Sun Also Sets*. Starring Sally Field, Kevin Kline, Whoopi Goldberg, and Robert Downey Jr.

Network
A satire about the convergence of corporate power, entertainment, and television news.

Visual Arts

Pollock
Ed Harris as Jackson Pollock, whose chaotic personal life was reflected in his abstract works of art.

My Left Foot
Daniel Day-Lewis portrays Irish artist and writer Christy Brown, who was born with cerebral palsy. Fact-based film.

Surviving Picasso
Anthony Hopkins as the ego-driven genius, Pablo Picasso, who had a habit of using women and then tossing them away.

Basquiat
True story of the meteoric rise of youthful artist Jean-Michel Basquiat.

Maya Lin: A Strong Clear Vision
Documentary about the young Chinese American woman who designed the Vietnam War Memorial.

Sunday in the Park with George
Videotaped performance of the Sondheim musical about painter Georges Seurat and his masterpiece, "A Sunday Afternoon on the Island of Le Grande Jatte." Starring Mandy Patinkin and Bernadette Peters.

The Light that Failed
Rudyard Kipling melodrama about an artist who struggles to finish his masterpiece before he loses his sight.

The Agony and the Ecstasy
Charlton Heston's Michelangelo clashes with Rex Harrison's Pope Julius II as he paints the ceiling of the Sistine Chapel.

Leadership Programs

OVERVIEW

Whether you're editing the school newspaper or captaining the track team, running student council or directing the class play, nothing complements your talents more than strong leadership skills (and a sense of humor). Developing expertise in a specific field—journalism, drama, or the 100-yard-dash—increases your effectiveness and credibility, but that alone is not enough to succeed in today's world. Listening, speaking, and mediating skills are equally essential.

You may already possess many leadership qualities. But what separates good leaders from exceptional leaders is that the best know they can always become better, and that leadership improves as the result of practice.

"SHOULD I ATTEND A LEADERSHIP CAMP?"

The core components of leadership—the ability to listen to others, generate ideas, synthesize opinion, integrate different perspectives, and communicate effectively—are also the key to academic success and interpersonal happiness. Leadership programs are specifically designed to strengthen each of these skills and target areas for improvement. For example, people who are excellent listeners and facilitators but terrified of microphones can benefit from training in public speaking.

If you currently hold a school or community leadership position, or would like to do so in the future, camp can help you become a more effective and marketable leader. For people interested in election campaigns and congressional proceedings, leadership camps (especially those in Washington, DC) provide an added perk. Many have a political or governmental focus, offering academic class work in American government and world affairs in addition to an impressive array of guest speakers.

--- **Expert Advice** ---

"From my own observation, one of the things I see is that they leave feeling so good about themselves. Parents have said their daughters became more involved in school after attending the camp. One mother whose daughter was coming from New Jersey said [the girl] cried all the way here because she didn't want to come and cried all the way home because she didn't want to leave. She is coming back this summer!"

—Terry Martinez, director of conferences and leadership programs, Wells College

But it is important to recognize that leadership camps are not the only way to hone skills during summer months. Many other programs, particularly ones with an outdoor focus, make leadership development a priority. So if you have a deep interest in another field, you may also consider searching for other programs with strong leadership components.

CHECKING OUT THE SCENE

When it comes to choosing summer programs with a leadership focus, there are several options, and they differ greatly from each other. Some programs emphasize leadership-in-progress, providing a supportive, soul-searching environment in which there is considerable time for goal setting and self-reflection. Other programs are forums for leadership-in-action, where students test the leadership skills they have already developed by competing in elections, mock trials, and debates. Both strengthen leadership skills, but they have very different feels. You will want to select a program that makes you feel comfortable, yet challenged.

Wells College's Leadership Adventure for Girls is an example of a leadership-in-progress program. Students attending this all-female camp participate in many expressive and reflective exercises while exploring what it means to be a leader. During the course of the camp, each student goes on a personal hike, stopping at prearranged stations to complete journal writing exercises. The goal, said Director Terry Martinez, is for girls to explore who they are and who they want to become. Students spend considerable time talking about the qualities that make a leader and ways they can develop relevant skills. At The Leadership Institute at Columbia College in South Carolina, students choose to attend four of seventeen or eighteen workshops covering a range of areas including stress management, peer mediation, assertiveness, sexual harassment, cultural diversity, body image, and how to conduct a meeting. Director Candy Waites said a seminar on body image was added in 1998 because of the way attitudes toward one's body affect self-confidence, and thus the ability to lead. "The whole idea," Waiters said, "is that you need to know who you are, body and mind, before you can lead." Throughout the two-and-a-half-day conference at Columbia College, emphasis is placed on the relationship between leadership and self-confidence.

Expert Advice

"I have them do personal assessments at the beginning and end of the week. Some students have written about how they become more appreciative of one another's abilities. A lot of them come out of their shell and are no longer afraid to share their thoughts, which is good. I also see a big difference in the way they interact with each other. At the beginning of the week, we tend to have little clusters of people who know each other. At the end of the week, all the walls are down and the little groups have become a mass. They really become a team. They work together to complete tasks. Various members of the group 'take over' as the group leaders as the situation demands their special abilities or leadership style."

—Tricia Renner, instructor, Wright State University Leadership Institute

---

While these programs are for girls only, there are similar coeducational camps that present teamwork, cooperation, and self-esteem as the building blocks of strong leadership. The Wright State Leadership Institute at Wright State University in Ohio is one example. Instructor Tricia Renner said the program begins with an effort to establish a working definition of leadership that all members of the group can agree upon. After the discussion—which usually lasts a good two hours—the emphasis on consensus building continues. "After we've defined leadership and looked at it from a lot of different angles, I teach team building and facilitation. We also talk about leadership versus management, ethics, service-leadership, gender differences, and communication," Renner said. The environment at Wright State is noncompetitive and non-threatening; the idea is to help everyone strengthen skills through a joint effort.

Leadership programs vary in their admissions requirements. Some accept any student interested in improving their leadership while others require applications and/or nominations indicating that the student is already a dedicated leader in his or her community.

Other leadership camps emphasize skill building specifically in the context of government and politics. Prominent guest speakers, academic classes, and visits to courts, law schools, and government buildings characterize these programs. Evening workshops and group projects allow participants to put lessons learned during the day into practical use through speeches, debate, and simulation exercises. These summer programs are high-powered, but generally noncompetitive once students have been accepted for the summer.

The exposure to diverse opinions and expert speakers at government-oriented leadership camps often helps student participants refine their leadership skills and political ambitions. "Just the experience of going to Washington, meeting with congressmen, having speakers throughout the week, and hearing

Student Scoop

"My instructors [at the Public Speaking Institute] were Canon and Andy, and they were absolutely wonderful, really caring and enthusiastic. They made it a lot easier to get up in front of people and say your speech. There was great group morale. You really learned how to speak your mind."

—Tamara Shapero, participant, Public Speaking Institute

others' points of view has helped me as student government president," said Sean Fahey, who attended the Washington Workshops in Washington, DC.

Instead of viewing leadership through the lens of politics, some summer programs tackle specific leadership skills such as public speaking and debate. The Public Speaking Institute is an example of one such program. "The philosophy of the program is to make people more comfortable public speakers in a variety of situations and through that, better leaders," program director Sasha Peterson said. "The program is built around the belief that skill and eloquence in public speaking is the single most important element of leadership." Students hone public speaking skills by attending classroom instruction, preparing a mock trial, researching and delivering an expository speech, and finally, giving an extemporaneous speech for the group.

Quick Tips

To Lead or Not to Lead

If you're not sure how you can benefit from a leadership program, ask yourself the following questions:

- Do I want to improve my public speaking skills or learn how to mediate better?

- Am I interested in networking with other young leaders from diverse backgrounds?

- Do I want to work towards a certain leadership position at my high school?

- Do I want to perform better in a leadership position that I currently hold?

- Do I want to live and socialize in an environment that will give me a good feel for the college experience?

- Do I want to be challenged by mock debates and campaigns?

And always remember, regardless of what you learn at any summer program, it's bound to provide good material for a college admissions essay.

Finally, there are leadership-oriented summer programs that emphasize leadership-in-action rather than leadership-in-progress. Students often have to be nominated to attend, and they go through a rigorous application and interview process before gaining acceptance. Once at the program, students participate in a variety of activities that includes campaigning for a mock election. Students run around campus trying to sway votes and exchange favors. For people interested in hard core, real world politics, these programs provide a fantastic opportunity to gain experience and have a lot of fun.

Because these programs attempt to mirror real life government, they are as likely to nurture backstabbing as team building. People spend hours making strategies and counter strategies. It's an important, realistic lesson in political leadership. Sometimes things work, sometimes they don't, and the most deserving do not always win. "The whole conference that people have worked hard to be chosen for is another big competition—you have three days to show people what a leader you are," said Sherry Tsai of the Hugh O'Brian Youth Foundation Leadership Program (HOBY) in California. "You meet a lot of people from around the area, and some people are pretty amazing. But unless they're really vocal, they don't get picked to go on to the national competition. The winners seemed like the ones most excited about HOBY, not the ones with the best leadership skills."

As you search for a leadership program, pay particular attention to the program descriptions listed in this book's index. Examining brochures and talking with program directors will also help you determine whether the summer program features leadership-in-progress or leadership-in-action, and which is best for you.

THE EXPERIENCE

Leadership programs range from weekend workshops to month-long summer sessions, so students' summer experiences differ greatly. Some programs include academic course work, others only informal discussion and skill-building exercise. All probe the question "What is a leader?" and attempt to define what makes a good one.

Regardless of the length and type of program, many students find meeting and living with other student leaders the most exciting part. As is the case with academic summer programs, leadership camps tend to attract exceptional high school students. The vast majority are high achievers who perform well academically and fill prominent leadership positions in their high school or community. And as is the case with academic summer programs, students have the opportunity to live in a college dormitory setting. Late night discussions become the rule, and some students insist they never sleep. When socializing is over there are papers and projects and speeches to write and by the time those are finished, well, it's time to socialize again.

What do students talk about? There are the inside jokes and plans for the weekend, rumors about the student counselors and stories about the day's mishaps. But it's not all idle chatter. When the people who run the nation's student organizations are put in a room together, there is naturally a lot of exchanging of ideas. Student council presidents discuss how they can go about increasing student input and decreasing faculty interference. Newspaper editors compare censorship problems and brainstorm ways to reinvigorate staff recruitment. Sports captains discuss the difficulty of integrating freshmen and upperclassmen. These conversations can be extremely fruitful. Too often high schools become isolated communities where students do not exchange ideas, discuss frustrations, and make action-plans with similar students across the city, state, and nation. One of the many benefits of leadership programs is the opportunity to network.

While networking, you will find that differences among school policies and students' attitudes make for an intriguing study themselves. Because leadership programs attract students from many different backgrounds and geographic areas, views on important issues can differ greatly. As a result, seemingly straightforward conversations can lead to shocking discoveries. "I went to Washington, DC originally because I was interested in government. I

Expert Advice

"The purpose of The Leadership Program is to help girls develop and strengthen their leadership skills and their self-confidence and to establish their own network. These are girls who have already demonstrated leadership ability in their academic, extracurricular, and community activities. One of the things they take away is that there are other young women who think as they do. They realize, 'you know, I'm not the only one who is smart or who cares about what I'm going to do with my life.'"

—Candy Waites, director, Leadership Institute at Columbia College

---

"The first year I went, I got to be the congressional workshop chair, and it gave me a firsthand experience of constant leadership, like how to handle thirty-five people and how to keep them going and voting. It definitely trained me a lot. The second year, [when I was in with a political communication class], I learned the general problems that come up with people when you work on projects together."

—Andy Katz, participant, Junior Statesmen Summer School

wanted to see Washington from the inside and actually meet some people. Instead, I gained a lot more from the social relationships I formed with others who were with me at the camp. I learned more from them than I did in any part of the program itself," said Patrick Dunnigan, who attended the National Young Leaders Conference in Washington, DC. "I also learned from the disagreements I had with others. For example, I got into an argument with a kid from southern Mississippi over racism and attitudes about racism today. It was amazing to see the differences in opinion on the subject. That was something I would not realize by staying in Columbus [Ohio] or at The Wellington School."

The challenge comes when trying to piece all these different personalities, life experiences, and attitudes together. Organizing and motivating peers in a group project is an endeavor any way you look at it, and that's exactly what you'll be doing in a leadership program. As you research platforms in the library or divide up campaign canvassing areas, you will be practicing the skills you already know—being a good listener, incorporating others' ideas, compromising on difficult points, and giving each person an opportunity to contribute. Practice really does make perfect when it comes to leadership. As Junior Statesmen Summer School participant Andy Katz said, "You learn it over and over, but it's never the same kind of lesson twice."

WORKING WITH SPEAKERS AND PEERS

Camps with a leadership focus are a great way to meet and network with fascinating people—students, professors, government officials, policy experts, and more. Leadership skills are largely a measure of one's ability to understand, reach, and relate to other people, and camps provide an opportunity to practice all three. In fact, the quantity and quality of contacts you make during the course of the program will have a significant bearing on how much you get out of the experience. You will have an opportunity to meet some high quality peers and in some cases, prominent leaders as well. Initiating relationships with important people requires a little chutzpah, but you have nothing to lose, and you never know what you might gain.

The big-wig speakers and guest lecturers who visit summer programs usually don't stick around long after their appearance (they have busy schedules) but they almost always leave a few minutes at the end of their presentation to take questions. If their speech leaves you wondering or questioning, raise your hand. Too many people let the title and fame of the person at the podium intimidate them. If speakers make the time to speak to you, you have to assume they want to hear what you have to say. Afraid you'll stumble

over your words in front of the highest ranking official of X governmental agency? Have no fear. You learn by taking chances.

"While I was asking this political consultant a question, I had to introduce myself and where I was from. So I said 'Emil Dizon, Redwood City.' It turns out the guy thought I said I was a male designer. The entire congregation, some two hundred or so students, erupted into laughter in that hotel conference room," said Dizon, who attended the National Young Leaders Conference in Washington, DC. "But after that, people were more open to me and talked to me more on the bus. I think they felt that it was awful brave of me to take that from the speaker. Getting embarrassed like that made me a little more apt to take risks. And I feel that risk taking is a big part of leadership because only by taking risks can one truly succeed at leading other people."

While famous speakers float in and out, the other students on the program will be with you from start to finish. Many will have impressive résumés of their own. Try to avoid competitive thinking. If you feel others are more prepared than you, don't worry. Leadership is highly personal, and each individual develops a unique style. Some will have stronger debating skills, others stronger mediating skills. Use this to your advantage by setting up a system to teach and tutor each other. As you participate in the summer program, all your leadership skills will improve and you will discover new strengths. Learning to lead well is a lifelong project, so go at your own pace, and don't let others discourage you. Remember, confidence yields success.

THE RESULTS

Regardless of how many leadership positions they held during the previous academic year, students who attend leadership summer programs find they end the summer better leaders than when they began it. Leadership programs help you see and understand yourself as a leader in the broadest sense. One doesn't have to be class president to lead. As summer programs teach, a leader is someone who is confident in his or her opinions and willing to express them. People who have confidence in themselves and the skills to communicate effectively lead regardless of whether they are in a high school classroom or the House of Representatives.

Tamara Shapero learned this lesson well. "The Public Speaking Institute helped me more just in everyday life than it has in really formal situations," she said. "Like in literature class when we are discussing what it means to be human and how that relates to Macbeth. I have no problem raising my hand and saying 'no it doesn't relate that way.' The program builds up your confidence and lets you know that if you have an idea, you shouldn't be afraid to voice it."

LIST OF PROGRAMS

Here is a list of summer leadership programs. See the Program Directory in Part III of this book for a description of each of these programs.

Community Service Leadership Programs

Amigos de las Americas
Birmingham-Southern College—Student Leaders in Service
Brandeis University—Genesis at Brandeis University
Camp Courageous of Iowa—Volunteer Program
Friendship Ventures—Youth Leadership Program
Hugh O'Brian Youth Leadership (HOBY)—HOBY Leadership Seminars
Lawrence Academy—Global Leaders Workshop
Legacy International—Global Youth Village
Longacre Leadership—Longacre Leadership Program
Scandinavian Seminar—Ambassadors for the Environment
School for Field Studies—Environmental Field Studies Abroad
World Learning—Experiment in International Living (EIL)

Cultural and Business Leadership Programs

Abilene Christian University—Kadesh Life Camp
Alfred University—High School Academic Institutes
American Management Association—Operation Enterprise
American Youth Foundation—International Leadership Conference
Auburn University—World Affairs Youth Seminar
Brandeis University—Genesis at Brandeis University
Bridgewater College—High School Leadership Academy
Columbia College, Leadership Institute—21st Century Leaders
Columbia College, Leadership Institute—Entrepreneurship Camp
Columbia University—Columbia Summer Programs for High School Students
Congressional Youth Leadership Council—Global Young Leaders Conference
Envision EMI, Inc.—NexTech: The National Summit of Young Technology Leaders
Global Institute for Developing Entrepreneurs—IN2BIZ Entrepreneur Camp
Hollins University —Leadership Enrichment Program
Hugh O'Brian Youth Leadership (HOBY)—HOBY Leadership Seminars
Indiana University, Bloomington—International Studies Summer Institute for High School Students
JCC Maccabi Xperience Israel Programs—Israel Summer Programs
Junior Statesmen Foundation—Junior Statesmen Summer School
Knowledge Exchange Institute—Precollege Business, Law and Diplomacy Program
Knowledge Exchange Institute—Precollege European Capitals Program
Lawrence Academy—Global Leaders Workshop
Legacy International—Global Youth Village

Marine Military Academy—Summer Military Training Camp

Media Workshops Foundation—The Media Workshops

Mississippi University for Women—Business Week

National Student Leadership Conference—Law & Advocacy; International Diplomacy; Medicine & Health Care

National Youth Leadership Forum—National Youth Leadership Forum on Medicine

Northwestern University—National High School Institute

Project PULL Academy—Project PULL Academy Leadership Challenge and College Preview

Quest Scholars Program—Quest Scholars Programs at Stanford and Harvard

Scandinavian Seminar—Ambassadors for the Environment

School for Field Studies—Environmental Field Studies Abroad

Shad International—Shad Valley

Sidwell Friends School—Women's Leadership

Tufts University European Center—Tufts Summit

United States Coast Guard Academy—Academy Introduction Mission (AIM)

United States Coast Guard Academy—Minority Introduction to Engineering (MITE)

University of Dallas Study Abroad—Shakespeare in Italy; Latin in Rome; Thomas More in England; Winston Churchill in England

University of Mississippi—Summer College for High School Students

University of Notre Dame—Summer Experience

University of Pennsylvania—Precollege Program

University of Southern Mississippi, The Frances A. Karnes Center for Gifted Studies— Leadership Studies Program

University of Wisconsin, Madison—Pre-college Program in Environmental and Native American Studies

Wells College—Student Conference on Leadership and Social Responsibility

World Learning—Experiment in International Living (EIL)

Wright State University—Pre-College Summer Enrichment Programs

Debate and Public Speaking Programs

Bates College—Bates Forensic Institutes

Baylor University—Baylor University Debaters' Workshop

Catholic University of America—Capitol Classic Summer Debate Institute

Championship Debate Enterprises—Lincoln-Douglas and Extemp Institute; Policy Debate Institute

Dwight-Englewood School—Dwight-Englewood Summer Programs

Education Unlimited—Public Speaking Institute by Education Unlimited

Illinois State University—Summer High School Forensic Workshop

Junior Statesmen Foundation—Junior Statesmen Summer School

Michigan State University—Spartan Debate Institute (SDI)

Northwestern University—National High School Institute

Phillips Academy Andover—Phillips Academy Summer Session

Vanderbilt University—Program for Talented Youth

Wake Forest University—Summer Debate Workshop; Fast Track; Policy Project; Policy Analysis Seminar

Outdoor Leadership Programs

Adventure Pursuits—Adventure Pursuits Expeditions & Camps
Adventure Treks, Inc.—Adventure Treks
Bark Lake Leadership Center—Leadership Through Recreation/Music
Broadreach, Inc.—Broadreach Insights
Broadreach, Inc.—Broadreach Summer Adventures for Teenagers
Hargrave Military Academy—Summer School and Camp
The Island Laboratory
Longacre Expeditions
Longacre Leadership—Longacre Leadership Program
Marine Military Academy—Summer Military Training Camp
National Outdoor Leadership School—Wilderness Leadership Courses
Oak Ridge Military Academy—Leadership Adventure Camp
Odyssey Expeditions—Tropical Marine Biology Voyages
Orme School—Orme Summer Camp
Outward Bound USA
Sierra Adventure Camps
United States Coast Guard Academy—Academy Introduction Mission (AIM)
United States Coast Guard Academy—Minority Introduction to Engineering (MITE)
Western Washington University—Outdoor Challenge Institute
Wilderness Ventures—Wilderness Adventure Expeditions; Advanced Leadership
    Expeditions; Offshore Adventure Expeditions

Political Leadership Programs

American Youth Foundation—International Leadership Conference
Auburn University—World Affairs Youth Seminar
Choate Rosemary Hall—John F. Kennedy Institute in Government
Columbia College, Leadership Institute—21st Century Leaders
Columbia University—Columbia Summer Programs for High School Students
Congressional Youth Leadership Council—Global Young Leaders Conference
Congressional Youth Leadership Council—National Young Leaders Conference
Georgetown University—Georgetown Summer College
Hugh O'Brian Youth Leadership (HOBY)—HOBY Leadership Seminars
Indiana University, Bloomington—International Studies Summer Institute for High
    School Students
Junior Statesmen Foundation—Junior Statesmen Summer School
Knowledge Exchange Institute—Precollege Business, Law and Diplomacy Program
Knowledge Exchange Institute—Precollege European Capitals Program
Lawrence Academy—Global Leaders Workshop
Legacy International—Global Youth Village
National Student Leadership Conference—Law & Advocacy; International
    Diplomacy; Medicine & Health Care
Tufts University European Center—Tufts Summit
Washington Workshops Foundation—Washington Workshops Seminars

ENRICHING YOUR SUMMER

Here is a list of websites, books, and movies you can use to further explore various facets of leadership.

Websites

Cultural and Business Leadership

www.teenleader.org
Info about summer camp, college admissions, scholarships, and more.

www.civilrights.org
Contains links to various advocacy groups, such as the NAACP and the Anti-Defamation League, plus news about civil rights issues and movements across the country.

www.bpubs.com/Management_Science/Leadership/
Links to articles on leadership from various business publications.

www.emergingleader.com
Articles and discussions about leadership in today's business world.

Debate/Public Speaking

www.net-benefit.com
Resources specifically for high school and college debaters and coaches, including an evidence database, tournament locator, theory library, topic analysis, and numerous articles and links.

www.forensicsonline.com
Online community for high school debaters, with a case list, message board, chat room, and more.

debate.uvm.edu/
Debate Central on the University of Vermont website offers an extensive set of debate-related links, from instruction to video demonstrations to organizations.

Political Leadership

www.senate.gov
Links to info about individual senators, committees, legislative activities, history, etc.

www.lwv.org
Site of the League of Women Voters, a nonpartisan organization that works to increase the informed and active participation of the public in politics.

www.mclaughlin.com
McLaughlin Group's website features online political discussion groups in which anyone may participate.

Books

Cultural and Business Leadership

Business @ the Speed of Thought by Bill Gates

The 21 Irrefutable Laws of Leadership by John C. Maxwell

Daughters of the Moon, Sisters of the Sun: Young Women & Mentors on the Transition to Womanhood by Linda Wolf and K. Wind Hughes

Ophelia Speaks: Adolescent Girls Write About Their Search for Self by Sara Shandler

Any Girl Can Rule the World by Susan M. Brooks

Girl Power: Young Women Speak Out by Hillary Carlip

Herstory: Women Who Changed the World by Ruth Ashby and Deborah Gore Ohrn (editors)

The Autobiography of Malcolm X by Malcolm X and Alex Haley

The Autobiography of Martin Luther King, Jr. by Clayborne Carson (editor)

Narrative of the Life of Frederick Douglass by Frederick Douglass

Freedom in Exile: The Autobiography of the Dalai Lama by the Dalai Lama

She Said Yes: The Unlikely Martyrdom of Cassie Bernall by Misty Bernall

Generation J by Lisa Schiffman

Debate/Public Speaking

The Debater's Guide by Jon M. Ericson, James J. Murphy, and Raymond B. Zeuschner

Basic Debate by Leslie Phillips, William S. Hicks, and Douglas R. Springer

Forensics: The Winner's Guide to Speech Contests by Brent C. Oberg

101 Secrets of Highly Effective Speakers by Caryl Rae Krannich

The Quick and Easy Way to Effective Speaking by Dale Carnegie

Lend Me Your Ears: Great Speeches in History by William Safire (editor)

Political Leadership

John Adams by David McCullough

Power and the Presidency by Robert A. Wilson (editor)

The Presidential Difference: Leadership Style from Roosevelt to Clinton by Fred I. Greenstein

Profiles in Courage by John F. Kennedy

Reagan on Leadership: Executive Lessons from the Great Communicator by James M. Strock

Thomas Jefferson: Man on a Mountain by Natalie S. Bober

My Early Life: 1874–1904 by Winston Churchill

Hitler: 1936–1945 Nemesis by Ian Kershaw

Lenin: A Biography by Robert Service

Saddam Hussein: Absolute Ruler of Iraq by Rebecca Stefoff

Ten Queens: Portraits of Women of Power by Milton Meltzer

Mary, Bloody Mary by Carolyn Meyer

Abe: A Novel of the Young Lincoln by Richard Slotkin

All the King's Men by Robert Penn Warren

Primary Colors by Anonymous

Movies

Cultural and Business Leadership

Kundun
Chronicles the life of the 14th Dalai Lama, from his "discovery" by the monks when he was two years old up until his exile from Tibet.

Citizen Kane
A reporter tries to figure out the meaning of newspaper tycoon Orson Welles's deathbed utterance, "Rosebud."

Schindler's List
Spielberg's masterpiece about a real-life businessman who becomes an unlikely hero when he uses his factory to save hundreds of Jews during the Holocaust.

Anne Frank Remembered
An intense documentary on the life of the young Jewish girl whose diary has inspired millions around the world.

A Few Good Men
Two Marine privates accused of murdering a colleague claim they were only following orders. Starring Jack Nicholson as their colonel and Tom Cruise as their defense attorney.

Courage Under Fire
When Meg Ryan, an Army captain killed in battle, is nominated for the Medal of Honor, Denzel Washington must determine what really happened in the final moments of her life.

Braveheart
Mel Gibson as William Wallace, a 13th century commoner who unites the Scots in an effort to overthrow English rule.

Spartacus
Kirk Douglas, born and raised a slave, leads a rebellion against the Roman Empire.

The Prince of Egypt
Animated retelling of the early life of Moses. Voices by Val Kilmer, Ralph Fiennes, and Michelle Pfeiffer.

Debate/Public Speaking

Inherit the Wind
Based on the notorious 1925 "Scopes Monkey Trial," with debates between Clarence Darrow and William Jennings Bryan taken largely from actual transcripts.

Abe Lincoln in Illinois
Lincoln's debates with Stephen Douglas are depicted in this 1940 film starring Raymond Massey.

Ah, Wilderness!
A high school valedictorian gets in trouble with his father when he tries to inject anticapitalist ideas into his commencement speech. Adaptation of the play by Eugene O'Neill.

Bulworth
After losing respect for the political system and even losing the will to live, a Democratic senator goes around making speeches in which he—gasp!—tells the truth as he sees it. Starring Warren Beatty and Halle Berry.

Election
A high school teacher tries to sabotage an overly ambitious student who is running for president of the student council. Very funny satire starring Matthew Broderick and Reese Witherspoon.

Political Leadership

Mr. Smith Goes to Washington
Jimmy Stewart stars in this Frank Capra classic about a naive, idealistic man who tries to fight the corruption he finds in the U.S. Senate.

The Best Man
Presidential candidates must decide how far they are willing to go to get the crucial endorsement of the current President. Starring Henry Fonda and Cliff Robertson.

Wag the Dog
A political spin doctor and a Hollywood producer fabricate a war to distract the American public from a Presidential sex scandal. Starring Dustin Hoffman and Robert DeNiro.

JFK
Oliver Stone film embracing numerous conspiracy theories in its investigation of the assassination of President Kennedy.

Nixon
Oliver Stone film presenting Nixon as a man with deep-rooted insecurities that lead to his political downfall. Starring Anthony Hopkins and Joan Allen.

Dick
A comedic take on Watergate, with two clueless teenagers playing pivotal roles in the scandal. Starring Kirsten Dunst and Michelle Williams (*Dawson's Creek*).

Evita
Musical retelling of the life of Eva Peron, who rose from poverty to become Argentina's beloved First Lady in the 1940s. Starring Madonna and Antonio Banderas.

Elizabeth
When Queen Mary I dies, her Protestant half-sister, Elizabeth, inherits the crown and must quickly learn to deal with such obstacles as the Catholic Church, traitorous advisors, and greedy suitors.

The Lion in Winter
King Henry II tries to decide upon his successor while his wife and sons plot treachery. Starring Peter O'Toole and Katharine Hepburn.

The Madness of King George
Follows the evolution of George III's mental disorder and the political repercussions of his decline.

Thy Eternal Summer Shall Not Fade

10

Golden summer mornings eventually slip into crisp autumn afternoons, and you must leave the magical world of summer programs behind. Take comfort in Shakespeare's words (Sonnet 18): "thy eternal summer shall not fade." While you must part from new friends and novel places, an enriching summer remains with you for a lifetime. Granted, the return to school is inevitable, but by living summer fully, you will have memories, and more importantly, personal ideals to carry you through to May.

A NEW YOU, A NEW ME

Summer programs afford a prime opportunity to challenge convention. Exposed to new people, places, and learning environments, you will be enriched by new ideas and new ways of looking at the world. What does that mean? Well, many high schoolers find they change in significant ways during the summer—and that they really like the person they become.

While you may have been sharing class with high school friends for years, maybe even a decade, those you meet during a summer program hold no prior conceptions about you. Friendship is based on who you are right now, in the context of the summer program. It's fun to watch others' surprise when you tell them about activities at home or school they never suspected you would do. Or to get a new nickname from summer program friends that people at home would never dream of. You get such an intriguing look into how others perceive you. The most amazing thing about summer programs, however, is that they allow you to recast your identity if you'd like. You rarely have that chance in high school. So open up, let loose, make friends. Leave all that school year stress behind and explore the collegian you want to become.

Note

Roll on, Envious Season

"Call him now old whose visionary brain
Holds o'er the past its undivided reign,
For him in vain the envious season roll
Who bears eternal summer in his soul."

—Oliver Wendell Holmes Sr., "The Old Player" (1855)

────────────────────────── **Student Scoop** ──────────────────────────

"The conversations that I had and the friendships that I made were the best part of the Junior Statesmen Summer Schools. What was really amazing was the intellectual level, but more than that, everyone's willingness to discuss things and talk. I've never had discussions like the ones I've had at summer school; it was just a whole other level. You really mature over a summer program, and it's an experience you'll remember for the rest of your life."

—Jesse Levey, participant, Junior Statesmen Summer Schools

Forming a new circle of friends does require a significant output of energy, but it is well worth it! Most students say that the people are by far the best part of a summer program. If you're in a large program where students are involved in many different classes or activities, attending extra events like intramural athletic games or evening social hours or study breaks can help you meet lots of intriguing people fast. If you're in a program that has a self-contained group—an outdoor adventure expedition or community service project, for example—you have instant friends, but also the challenge of living in close quarters with little time or space to yourself. This makes for lots of good laughs and a few irritations. Live it up, and know that it gets easier with time—you'll be a pro by the time you move into your freshman dorm.

Regardless of what summer program you choose—academic, athletic, artistic, community service, leadership, outdoor adventure, or study abroad—make participating fully your number one priority. Whether that means staying up all night to prepare a campaign speech at a leadership conference or waking up at dawn to watch the sunrise over the ocean before beginning the day's service project, recruit several friends and do it! Summer goes by amazingly quickly. Come September, you'll want to look back with no regrets.

Right, September. The only downside of having such a wonderful summer is it makes it that much harder to return to school. People come back from summer programs knowing they've grown and changed in profound ways. This makes returning to high school friends who may not see or want to recognize the changes difficult. Not only is the excitement of summer program activities and learning gone, so are the people who understand the magnitude of the loss. "I hated going back to school because it was so much better there," said Illana Poley of Challenges for Youth Talented and Gifted in Ames, Iowa. "It was exciting and challenging. When I went back to school I would just sit and think about when I could go back to CY-TAG for literally months. My friends and I would write to each other about CY-TAG withdrawal. One girl even wrote a poem about it. It wasn't a very good poem, but it showed how important the experience was to her."

────── **Student Scoop** ──────

"Where I live is kind of like a bubble, you always see the same people and do the same things. I wanted to try something new, to get away from all the pressures that go along with school."

—Matt Moran, participant, Moondance Adventure

Staying in touch with summer program friends is one good way to keep the spirit of summer alive within you. If you find that friends at home and school don't understand your newfound fascination with African American literature or your longing to sleep out under the stars, write, call, or e-mail summer program friends who do. You will find the support and intellectual stimulation they provided during the summer just as cheering throughout the academic year. It's so easy to slip back into old high school routines: zoning out in boring classes and getting stuck in a mundane social life of movies, basketball games, and the occasional high school dance. Resist! Fight stagnancy by exploring interests piqued during summer months. Volunteer in your community. Organize weekend camping trips. Take sculpting lessons. If you feel trapped, seek new friends by joining a community youth group or playing a club sport. If you find classes aren't stimulating, ask teachers to recommend additional books in an area that interests you. If you feel overworked and over-programmed, cut back on school activities and make time for relaxation and pleasure.

Bringing summer program ideals to your school by sharing what you learned over vacation can also be a rewarding, albeit challenging, task. Summer program communities are special environments in which a high level of trust and tolerance combine to make spontaneity and intense dedication equally valued. Building such an open, fervent, and accepting community may be impossible in the more competitive social and academic environment of most high schools. But if you succeed in bringing just a taste of the summer program spirit home, you'll improve any organization you touch tenfold. In the worse case scenario—your efforts are frustrated—you will at least be able to see how much you have grown.

"It was an experience unlike anything else I had had," said Anna Mullikin of attending Kinhaven Music School in Weston, Vermont. "It also made coming back to the high school kind of hard. I found my senior year a really hard adjustment because you do feel when you go to Kinhaven that you've shared this experience that people who didn't go can't possibly understand. I tried [to bring the spirit of Kinhaven back to my high school] but it was hard. I didn't see the same kind of respect for other players and the whole endeavor of making beautiful music. Kids at my high school were 'too cool' to invest themselves fully in things that could be really fun. That's what I wrote about in my [college admissions] essay."

Student Scoop

"The [summer program students] were all alike. They all really liked to learn. There were no slackers. Everybody really wanted to be there. They were all really talented and very smart."

—Shan-Estelle Brown, participant, Governor's School for French

---

Student Scoop

"It was probably my first real experience immersing in a new group of people. The first summer it went pretty well, the second summer it went significantly better. It was interesting, this whole kind of group dynamics thing."

—Seth Battis, participant, Prairie Trek and Turquoise Trail Expeditions

---

Student Scoop

"I cut all my hair off when I came back [from France]. Saratoga High was still Saratoga High; I felt like I should come back and it should be vastly different, but so little had changed."

—Alice Armstrong, participant, Nacel Open Door

THE COLLEGE CONNECTION

You already know that high school summer programs help prepare you for college. By providing the tremendous freedom of a new environment and a new group of peers, they allow you to forge a fresh identity and get a feel for the type of environment that allows you to perform at your full potential.

But how exactly can you make a summer program work for you? There are concrete as well as intangible ways. Depending on what type of program you choose, summer experiences can help you secure jobs, win scholarships, and procure letters of recommendation. They may inspire a college admissions essay or help you answer college interview questions. While you should never lose sight of summer programs' purpose—to provide a fun, educational, and/or enrichment experience—it is nevertheless important to take learning seriously. Colleges want to see that you have used your time and energy well.

Summer programs give you the opportunity to work with highly skilled educators in a wide variety of fields. These teachers can be valuable resources in any number of ways. They may inspire academic, athletic, or artistic interests, they may challenge conventional lifestyle choices, or they may point you in the direction of a possible career. Get to know these adults, and don't fool around when it comes to making a good impression. In many cases, summer program teachers, instructors, and guides prove excellent sources of letters of recommendation. Their letters will serve you well regardless of where you apply to college. You may even be lucky enough to form lasting relationships with the summer program staff. Traevena Potter-Hall, director of scholar recruitment at the University of Iowa, said high school students participating in the University of Iowa's summer program sometimes develop mentor relationships with professors that last throughout their undergraduate years.

If you have college students as counselors, teaching assistants, or junior guides, take the time to get to know them too. They can give you a dazzling glimpse of what lies ahead. Ask for advice on the college application process, on choosing a major, and on filling out those horrendous financial aid forms. Ask about the college social scene and how it differs from high school. Ask how they like their school and what they would do differently if they were choosing one again. Well-informed students are much more in touch with today's college admissions game than your parents, many of your teachers, and most college professors because they've just been through it.

--- Student Scoop ---

"I also got a job offer for this summer, based solely on the fact that I went to Governor's School—that's all they knew about me."

—Ben Negin, participant, Governor's School for Science

Some students find their counselors have a major influence on their college decisions. "There are college students who are your actual counselors," said Katie Lindgren of the Governor's School for Public Issues in New Jersey. "And one of the guys was a Yale student. He talked so much about how he loved Yale. Seven of us who went to that public issues camp are at Yale now, and five of

us are majoring in ethics, politics, and environment. I guess the program did have a lasting impact on us for continuing to study public policy issues."

Of course, not every summer program experience is going to be perfect. When you sign up for a summer program, you never know exactly what you're getting into. The more research you do ahead of time, the happier you will be, but there are always unpredictable variables. Think flexible. Maybe you won't love your roommates. Maybe you will discover you are not cut out to be premed, or that you hate creative writing, and you're already committed for the summer. Maybe you'll find that unairconditioned dorms are not the most pleasant places to study on hot July nights. Better to find out your likes and dislikes during a six- or eight-week summer program then after you have selected a college and made a two- or four-year commitment. In the meantime, try using the many tips in this book to make the most of your summer experience. If you don't like your roommates, seek other friends. If you find housing a little under par, buy a fan and move on to other thoughts. Most of all, keep things in perspective. It's summer; avoid all school-year stress and allow yourself to have fun.

FINAL WORDS OF WISDOM

Summer programs offer truly amazing opportunities. Select only those you really want to do, then live them to the fullest. High school summers slip by so quickly that before you know it, you will be off to the crazy world of college with its summer internship searches and even more absorbing academic schedules.

So revel in this time to make friends, see new parts of the world, and taste the freedom that lies just a few short years away. And while you're at it, consider keeping a journal. Reading it when the pleasant days of summer have faded away will remind you exactly what made you so happy, and how you can achieve that feeling again.

Have a wonderful summer. You deserve every minute of it.

Part III: Program Directory

ABILENE CHRISTIAN UNIVERSITY

Kadesh Life Camp

Program Location: Abilene Christian University in Abilene, Texas

Subject Areas: Leadership, religion

Program Description: Bible-based small group experience designed to challenge and strengthen students' faith and inspire action. Carefully selected college-age counselors and adult teaching staff act as strong role models.

Program Dates: June 2–8; June 16–22; June 30–July 6; July 14–20

Duration of Program: 1 week

Cost: $235 (includes room and board, 24-hour supervision, accident insurance, use of campus facilities)

Eligibility: Students entering grades 10–12, as well as 2002 high school graduates

Application Process: Applications accepted starting on January 1. A deposit of $75 along with completed application will reserve the student's place in the program.

Application Deadline: Rolling admissions, but application by early spring is recommended

Academic Credit: None available

Contact:
ACU Leadership Camps Registrar
ACU Box 29004
Abilene, TX 79699-9004
Phone: (915) 674-2033
Fax: (915) 674-6475
leadership.camps@campuslife.acu.edu
www.acucamps.com

ACADEMIC ENRICHMENT INSTITUTE

Summer Academic Enrichment Institute

Program Location: San Jose State University in San Jose, California

Subject Areas: College preparatory mathematics: pre-algebra, algebra I, geometry, algebra II, trigonometry/pre-calculus, AB calculus

Program Description: Puts an entire year of college preparatory math into six weeks during the summer. Students come from different parts of the United States, Canada, Japan, Taiwan, Hong Kong, and the Silicon Valley.

Program Dates: June 24–August 2

Duration of Program: 6 weeks

Cost: $1,200

Financial Aid: Community service scholarships available

Eligibility: Middle and high school students with a 3.0 overall grade point average

Application Process: Application, counselor and math instructor recommendations, one-page essay, transcript

Application Deadline: June 24

Average Number of Applicants: 500

Average Number of Participants: 180

Academic Credit: 10 high school credits

Contact:
Summer Academic Enrichment Institute
3283 Mt. Wilson Drive
San Jose, CA 95127
Phone: (408) 272-2282
Fax: (408) 272-2282
info@thesaei.com
www.thesaei.com

Academic Study Associates

ACADEMIC STUDY ASSOCIATES

ASA Pre-College Enrichment Program;

Language Study Programs

Program Location: University of California at Berkeley; University of Massachusetts at Amherst; Oxford University, England; France; Spain

Subject Areas: Pre-college enrichment, liberal arts, fine arts, study abroad, language immersion

Program Description: ASA offers a variety of academic, arts, and language programs for middle and high school students in the U.S. and abroad. The UC Berkeley, UMass, and Oxford programs provide a precollege experience in a university environment. College and high school-level courses offered. Study-abroad programs offered: homestay and French language program in the seaside resort of Royan, France; dorm-based French language program in Nice, France; homestay travel program in Paris; homestay and Spanish language program in 5 locations in Spain; and dorm-based Spanish language program in Barcelona, Spain.

Program Dates: June–July, August

Duration of Program: 4–5 weeks

Cost: Pre-College Enrichment Program: $3,795–$5,895; Language Study Programs: $4,895–$5,195 (does not include airfare)

Eligibility: Grades 9–12

Application Process: Written application, teacher recommendation, transcript

Application Deadline: Rolling admissions

Average Number of Applicants: 1,200

Average Number of Participants: 1,000

Academic Credit: High school credit; college credit available from the University of Massachusetts and UC Berkeley

Contact:
Academic Study Associates
10 New King Street
White Plains, NY 10604
Phone: (914) 686-7730 or (800) 752-2250
Fax: (914) 686-7740
summer@asaprograms.com
www.asaprograms.com

ACTeen

ACTEEN

ACTeen July Academy;

ACTeen August Academy;

ACTeen Summer Saturday Program

Program Location: New York City

Subject Areas: Acting for film, television, and theater

Program Description: Full or part-time conservatories. Participants choose from 11 different course offerings, including film scene study, acting technique, commercials, speech and voice, movement, musical theater, Shakespeare, script writing, directing, improvisation, audition technique, and industry showcases. Classes meet in modern, multi-camera studios. Professional working instructors and successful working graduates round out the experience.

Program Dates: July 1–26, July 31–August 16, Saturdays between July 13–August 17

Duration of Program: 4 weeks (July program); 2 1/2 weeks (August program); 6 weeks (Summer Saturday program)

Cost: $1,800–$2,300 (full programs); $250–$300 (individual courses)

Financial Aid: None available

Eligibility: Ages 13–20

Application Process: Onsite audition, recommendation letter. Long-distance applicants may send tape; phone interviews are substituted.

Application Deadline: Apply before April 15 for best placement

Average Number of Applicants: 300–400

Average Number of Participants: 90—100 (total for all 3 programs)

Academic Credit: None available

Contact:
ACTeen
35 W. 45th Street
New York, NY 10036
Phone: (212) 391-5915
Fax: (212) 768-8918
rita@acteen.com
www.acteen.com

ActionQuest

ACTIONQUEST

ActionQuest Programs

Program Location: Caribbean, Mediterranean, Galapagos Islands, Australia, South Pacific

Subject Areas: Sailing, SCUBA diving, marine biology

Program Description: Multilevel sailing and SCUBA diving certification programs for teens. Shipmates from the U.S., the Far East, South

America, and Europe live aboard 50-foot yachts. Noncompetitive, supportive atmosphere with a staff/shipmate ratio of 1:4.

Program Dates: Sessions throughout summer

Duration of Program: 3 weeks

Cost: $3,175–$4,575

Eligibility: Ages 13–19, no experience necessary

Application Deadline: Rolling, but apply in January/February to be assured a spot

Academic Credit: High school credit sometimes available

Contact:
ActionQuest Programs
P.O. Box 5517
Sarasota, FL 34277
Phone: (941) 924-6789 or (800) 317-6789
Fax: (941) 924-6075
info@actionquest.com
www.actionquest.com

ADELPHI UNIVERSITY

Academic Success Program

Program Location: Adelphi University in Garden City, New York

Subject Areas: Learning disabilities and AD/HD support services for accepted students

Program Description: Program offering students with learning disabilities comprehensive, structured, professional support. Each student receives both tutoring and counseling. Interdisciplinary staff of clinical educators and clinical social workers with advanced degrees.

Program Dates: July–August

Duration of Program: 5 weeks

Cost: $6,000 (includes room and board)

Financial Aid: None available

Eligibility: Students with a primary diagnosis of a specific learning disability or attention deficit/hyperactivity disorder; other diagnoses will not be considered

Application Process: Application (available on website), two letters of recommendation by professionals in the field (learning specialists, tutors, teachers, educational psychologists), interview

Application Deadline: March 1

Average Number of Applicants: 250

Average Number of Participants: 50

Academic Credit: 7 college credits

Contact:
Adelphi University
Academic Success Program
Chapman Hall
Garden City, NY 11530
Phone: (516) 877-4710
Fax: (516) 877-4711
LDProgram@adelphi.edu
http://academics.adelphi.edu/asp

ADVENTURE IRELAND

Program Location: Ashfield College in Dublin, Ireland

Subject Areas: Irish culture, travel, cultural immersion

Program Description: Family homestays, field trips and tours, and music, dance, language, and history classes give students broad exposure to Irish culture.

Program Dates: Flexible dates depending on groups; contact the program for info

Duration of Program: 1–4 weeks custom built

Cost: $1,995 for 3-week program (includes room and board; does not include airfare)

Eligibility: Ages 10–18

Application Process: Downloadable application pack available on website

Application Deadline: Rolling admissions

Average Number of Applicants: 80

Average Number of Participants: 80

Academic Credit: High school credit upon request

Contact:
Adventure Ireland
Ashfield College, Main Street
Templeogue
Dublin 6W, IRELAND
Phone: 011-353-1-4900246
Fax: 011-353-1-4900871
info@adventure-ireland.com
www.adventure-ireland.com

ADVENTURE PURSUITS

Adventure Pursuits
Expeditions & Camps

Program Location: Pacific Northwest, the Rocky Mountains, Canada, Northwoods, Hawaii, Alaska, New Zealand

Subject Areas: Outdoor adventure, leadership

Program Description: Challenging and fun wilderness adventures for teens and young adults, emphasizing safety and skill development. Inspires leadership, self-confidence, and teamwork. Activities include whitewater rafting, kayaking, backpacking, canoeing, road and mountain biking, horsepacking, canyoneering, mountaineering, rock climbing, rappelling, skiing, and snowboarding. Summer camp programs also offered for younger students (ages 9–14).

Program Dates: Sessions throughout summer

Duration of Program: 1–4 weeks

Cost: $490–$3,790

Eligibility: Ages 12–21 (specific age requirements vary by expedition); no experience necessary; average health and conditioning required

Application Deadline: Rolling admissions

Contact:
Adventure Pursuits
31160 Broken Talon Trail
Oak Creek, CO 80467
Phone: (800) 651-TEEN or (970) 736-8336
Fax: (970) 736-8311
info@apadventures
www.apadventures.com

ADVENTURE TREKS, INC.

Adventure Treks

Program Location: Pacific Northwest, California, Canadian Rockies, Alaska, North Carolina, Idaho, Wyoming, Montana

Subject Areas: Outdoor adventure, leadership

Adventure Treks, Inc.

Program Description: 14–30-day multiactivity adventure programs in Western North America, Alaska, North Carolina, and Canada. Activities include backpacking, whitewater rafting, sea kayaking, mountain climbing, rock climbing, canoeing, and mountain biking. The group will usually stay at an activity site for 2–6 days at a time and then travel on to the next site. Students are given as much responsibility as they can comfortably handle. A 1:4 instructor/student ratio guarantees individual attention and instruction. All programs focus on fun, community building, and outdoor skills.

Program Dates: June 15–August 18

Duration of Program: 2–4 weeks

Cost: $1,895–$3,795

Eligibility: Ages 13–18

Application Process: Application form and personal essay required

Application Deadline: Discounts prior to November 15, December 1, January 31; rolling thereafter

Contact:
P.O. Box 1321
Flat Rock, NC 28731
Phone: (888) 954-5555 or (828) 698-0399
Fax: (828) 696-1663
advtreks@aol.com
www.adventuretreks.com

ADVENTURES CROSS-COUNTRY

Program Location: Mill Valley, California

Subject Areas: Wilderness programs, adventure travel, travel abroad

Program Description: Offers wilderness programs around the world for teens. Activities include backpacking, rafting, sea kayaking, rock climbing, scuba diving, and sailing. Each trip has a different combination of activities. Trips are meant to incorporate life-changing experiences and fun.

Program Dates: Sessions throughout the summer

Duration of Program: 2–7 weeks

Cost: $2,000–$5,000 (includes room and board; transportation included on certain trips)

Financial Aid: Available

Eligibility: Students in grades 7–12. Groups are divided according to age.

Application Process: Application and teacher reference

Application Deadline: Rolling

Academic Credit: None available

Contact:
Adventures Cross-Country
242 Redwood Highway
Mill Valley, CA 94941
Phone: (800) 767-2722
Fax: (415) 332-2130
ARCC@adventurescrosscountry.com
www.adventurescrosscountry.com

AFS INTERCULTURAL PROGRAMS

Summer Homestay;

Summer Homestay Language Study;

Summer Homestay Plus;

Summer Community Service/Team Mission

Program Location: *Summer Homestay:* Argentina, Chile, Costa Rica, Ecuador, Finland, Paraguay, Spain, Thailand, Turkey.
Summer Homestay Language Study: Canada, Chile, Costa Rica, France, Japan, Russia, Venezuela.
Summer Homestay Plus: Australia, Brazil, France, Hungary, Ireland, Italy, Netherlands, New Zealand.
Summer Community Service/Team Mission: Argentina, Bolivia, China, Costa Rica, Ghana, Panama, Russia, Switzerland, Thailand, United Kingdom.

Subject Areas: Study abroad, homestay, language, community service

Program Description: *Summer Homestay:* As members of host families and communities, participants make new friends, gain or improve language skills, and learn first-hand about another culture.

Summer Homestay Language Study: This program offers students at all language levels a total immersion experience through formal instruction and daily informal conversation with the host family or dormmates. Students are placed in small classes according to their language proficiency.

Summer Homestay Plus: Participants enjoy all the benefits of a homestay and also participate in outdoor adventure, arts, or environmental activities. Each country offers unique experiences (e.g., New Zealand program offers rock climbing, caving, canoeing, and other outdoor activities; local artisans in Hungary demonstrate traditional crafts of woodcarving, weaving, and leather and jewelry making; etc.).

Summer Community Service/Team Mission: Participants make a difference and learn new skills through four weeks of volunteer work. Each country offers unique opportunities (e.g., working at an orphanage in Ghana; working on the reconstruction of hiking paths in the Swiss Alps; etc.).

Program Dates: Late June to mid-August (year/semester programs are also available)

Duration of Program: 4–8 weeks

AFS Intercultural Programs

Cost: $3,495–$4,795

Financial Aid: Need-based and merit-based scholarships available

Eligibility: Summer Homestay, Summer Homestay Language Study, Summer Homestay Plus: Ages 15–18. Summer Community Service/Team Mission: Ages 15–21.

Contact:
AFS International Programs/USA
198 Madison Avenue, 8th floor
New York, NY 10016
Phone: (800) AFS-INFO or (212) 299-9000
Fax: (212) 299-9090
afsinfo@afs.org
www.afs.org/usa

ALFRED UNIVERSITY

High School Academic Institutes

Program Location: Alfred University in the Finger Lakes region of New York

Subject Areas: Art and design, astronomy, entrepreneurial leadership, writing, science and engineering

Program Description: High school students get a taste of college life as they live in Alfred's dormitories and take classes with university professors. They have the opportunity to meet with admissions staff and to participate in athletic and recreational activities. Alfred also sponsors football, swimming, and basketball camps that are separate from its Academic Institutes.

Program Dates: June and July

Duration of Program: 1 week

Cost: $400–$700

Financial Aid: None

Eligibility: Grades 10–12

Application Process: Transcripts, essay, and two teacher recommendations are required.

Application Deadline: May 17, 2002

All-American Rowing Camp, LLC

Average Number of Applicants: 30–70 per program

Average Number of Participants: 20–50 per program

Academic Credit: None

Contact:
Summer Programs Office
Saxon Drive
Alfred, NY 14802
Phone: (607) 871-2612
Fax: (607) 871-2045
summerpro@alfred.edu
www.alfred.edu/summer

ALL-AMERICAN ROWING CAMP, LLC

High School Coed Rowing Camp

Program Location: Lake Lemon in Bloomington, Indiana

Subject Areas: Rowing—sweep and sculls

Program Description: Camp activities are divided between on-the-water training—when campers row in eights, fours, pairs, doubles, and singles—and land exercises, including work on the ergometer. Afternoon seminar topics include nutrition, technique, goal-setting, strength training, cross training, and racing strategy. Staff includes James Dietz (National Team Coach), Mark Wilson (National Elite Champion and head coach at Indiana University), and coaches from Yale, Princeton, and the University of Massachusetts. Campers are housed in an air-conditioned dorm at Indiana University.

Program Dates: June 25–29

Duration of Program: 5 days

Cost: $425 (residential), $350 (commuter)

Eligibility: Coed, grades 9–12, all skill levels

Application Process: Simple written application; online registration available on website.

Application Deadline: June 15

Average Number of Applicants: 50+

Average Number of Participants: 50+; limited to 75 participants

Contact:
Mark Wilson, Director
4800 N. McCoy Road
Bloomington, IN 47408
Phone: (812) 856-4485
Fax: (812) 856-5116
WilsonMR@indiana.edu
www.allamericanrowingcamp.com

ALLIANCES ABROAD

**Summer Spanish
Program for Youth in Spain;**

**Summer French
Programs for Youth in France;**

**Culture and Adventure
Program for Youth in Ireland**

Program Location: Marbella or Madrid, Spain; Antibes or Nice, France; Ireland

Subject Areas: Spanish/French language study, cultural immersion

Program Description: The Summer Spanish and French programs both offer language study, sports, cultural, and social activities. The Ireland program offers seminars on Gaelic literature, culture, and dance, and excursions. Students have the option of staying with a host family or in a student dorm.

Program Dates: June–September

Duration of Program: Spain: 2, 4, 6, or 8 weeks; France: 3 or more weeks; Ireland: 3 or more weeks

Cost: Spain: $1,500–$3,500; France: $2,400 (3 weeks); Ireland: $2,088 (3 weeks)

Financial Aid: None available

Eligibility: Spain: ages 8–18; France: ages 14–18; Ireland: ages 14–18

Application Process: Preliminary application; standard application (with information for host family placement). Will receive confirmation packet 3–4 weeks prior to start of program.

Application Deadline: 6 weeks prior to start of program

Academic Credit: None available

Contact:
Alliances Abroad
2423 Pennsylvania Avenue NW
Washington, DC 20037
Phone: (202) 467-9467 or (866) 6ABROAD
Fax: (202) 467-9460
outbound@alliancesabroad.com
www.alliancesabroad.com

ALPINE ADVENTURES, INC.

Alpine Adventures

Program Location: Upstate New York

Subject Areas: Rock climbing, mountaineering, ice climbing, backcountry skiing

Program Description: Intensive training in small, personalized groups with student-to-instructor ratios of 2:1 or 3:1. Students are grouped by ability.

Program Dates: Year-round

Duration of Program: 2 or 5 days

Cost: $299–$1,475

Application Process: Registration by phone: full payment due at the time of registration (credit card only). Registration by mail: completed registration form along with deposit (check or money order) of $50 for 2-day course or $100 for 5-day course.

Application Deadline: Rolling

Eligibility: Ages 14 and older in good to excellent physical condition, although accommodations can be made for those with physical limitations.

Contact:
Alpine Adventures
Dept. 960, P.O. Box 179
Keene, NY 12942
Phone: (518) 576-9881
Fax: (518) 576-9574
mail@alpineadven.com
www.alpineadven.com

AMERICA'S ADVENTURE/ VENTURE EUROPE

Program Location: Colorado, Utah, California, Nevada, Arizona, Washington, Alaska, Hawaii, Costa Rica, Greece, France, Spain, Norway, Sweden, Switzerland, Italy

Subject Areas: Outdoor adventure, travel, language

Program Description: Wide variety of outdoor adventures throughout the U.S. and Europe, as well as some European language immersion/outdoor adventure programs. Activities include rock climbing, whitewater rafting, biking, backpacking, horseback riding, sea kayaking, sailing, and more. Each adventure program consists of an autonomous group of 13 teenagers and two adult leaders. Students in each program are grouped by age, skill level, and aptitude.

Program Dates: Sessions throughout summer

Duration of Program: 2–6 weeks

Cost: $1,588–$4,488

Eligibility: Age and experience requirements vary with program (contact organization for details). Participants must be entering grades 9–12 (except one wilderness basics course, designed for students entering grades 7–8) and have the desire to participate.

Application Process: Completed application, phone interview, two references, $600 deposit are required. Downloadable application and brochure request form are available on website.

Application Deadline: Rolling

Average Number of Participants: 13 students per program

Contact:
AAVE
2245 Stonecrop Way
Golden, CO 80401
Phone: (800) 222- 3595 or (303) 526-0806
info@aave.com
www.aave.com

AMERICA'S BASEBALL CAMPS

Program Location: 45 camps in 18 states

Subject Areas: Baseball

Program Description: America's Baseball Camps offers both day and residential camps. Directed by Ben Boulware, formerly of the Chicago White Sox, ABC boasts that all of its instructors have some affiliation with professional baseball. ABC demands an intense work ethic and gives campers exposure to agents and scouts.

Program Dates: Varies by location

Duration of Program: 1 week

Cost: $100 and up

Eligibility: Ages 11–22

Contact:
America's Baseball Camps
P.O. Box 18865
Fountain Hills, AZ 85269
Phone: (800) 222-8152
Fax: (480) 816-3440
abc@americasbaseballcamps.com
www.abccamps.com

AMERICAN ACADEMY OF DRAMATIC ARTS

Summer Actor Training

Program Location: New York City and Hollywood, California

Subject Areas: Acting conservatory training including acting, voice and speech, and stage movement

Program Description: 6-week program at both the New York and California schools. Program is designed for those just beginning their study of acting and for those who would like to test their interest and ability in an environment of professional training. Students work toward final scene presentations. Classes meet Monday–Thursday, 4 hours per day. Electives available at end of school day and on Fridays.

Program Dates: Early July–mid-August

Duration of Program: 6 weeks

Cost: $1,500 (2001 tuition). Additional fee for electives.

Eligibility: Must be at least age 14 or entering ninth grade. Acceptance based on completed application and audition.

Application Process: Completed application with $50 application fee, and audition consisting of 2 contrasting monologues (comedy/drama) approximately 2 minutes each, 5 minutes total.

Application Deadline: Rolling admissions

Average Number of Applicants: 375

Average Number of Participants: 150

American Academy of Dramatic Arts

Contact:
American Academy of Dramatic Arts
120 Madison Avenue
New York, NY 10016
Phone: (800) 463-8990
Fax: (212) 696-1284
admissions-ny@aada.org
or 1336 N. LaBrea Avenue
Hollywood, CA 90028
Phone: (800) 222-2867
admissions-ca@aada.org
www.aada.org

AMERICAN COLLEGIATE ADVENTURES

Program Location: University of Wisconsin in Madison, Wisconsin; Institute of International Studies in Seville, Spain

Subject Areas: Creative arts, entertainment, writing, languages, ESL, computers, business, math, science, behavioral studies; college preparation; Spanish; study and travel abroad

Program Description: Wisconsin: Students take 2 college-level courses and SAT test prep. College visits include the University of Wisconsin, Northwestern University, University of Minnesota, University of Michigan, University of Notre Dame, University of Chicago, and Michigan State University. Spain: Spanish classes in both Spanish and English. Daily field trips to castles, museums, and famous landmarks. Weekend trips to Madrid, Granada, Cordoba, La Rabida, Matalascanas.

Program Dates: June–August

Duration of Program: Wisconsin: 3- and 6-week sessions; Spain: 4-week session, plus 1-week optional excursion to London and Paris

Cost: Varies; contact ACA for more info

Eligibility: Wisconsin: Students completing grades 9–11; Spain: Students completing grades 10–12, no prior Spanish required

Application Deadline: June

Academic Credit: Wisconsin: High school and college credit available; Spain: 6 hours of transferable college credit awarded

Contact:
American Collegiate Adventures
666 Dundee Road, Suite 803
Northbrook, IL 60062
Phone: (800) 509-7867
Fax: (847) 509-9908
info@acasumr.com
www.acasumr.com

AMERICAN COMMITTEE FOR THE WEIZMANN INSTITUTE OF SCIENCE

Dr. Bessie F. Lawrence International Summer Science Institute

Program Location: The Weizmann Institute of Science in Rehovot, Israel

Subject Areas: Biology, chemistry, physics, mathematics, computer sciences, and biochemistry

Program Description: Participants spend the first three weeks on campus studying and doing lab research in biology, chemistry, physics, mathematics, and computer sciences. All study is in English. Four days are spent at a field school in the Judean desert, hiking and learning the ecological, geographical, geological, archaeological, and zoological characteristics of the area. Students tour Jerusalem for three days; optional trips to Galilee and Eilat offered.

Program Dates: July

Duration of Program: 4 weeks

Cost: Full scholarship, valued at $5,000

Eligibility: Graduating high school seniors with a strong background in science

Application Process: Application, school transcript, 3 recommendation letters, 2 essays, SAT and AP test scores

Application Deadline: March 1

Average Number of Applicants: 100

Average Number of Participants: 20 U.S. participants; many others from around the world

Academic Credit: None available

Contact:
American Committee for the Weizmann Institute of Science
Dr. Bessie F. Lawrence International Summer Science Institute
130 East 59th St., 10th floor
New York, NY 10022
Phone: (212) 895-7906

American Farm School

Fax: (212) 895-7993
Debbie@ACWIS.org
www.weizmann-usa.org

AMERICAN FARM SCHOOL

Greek Summer

Program Location: Thessaloniki, Greece

Subject Areas: Travel abroad, homestay, cultural immersion, community service

Program Description: Students spend five weeks living with village families while completing a much-needed community improvement. Students will also have the opportunity to travel to historical and recreational sites around the country.

Program Dates: June 24–July 31

Duration of Program: 5 or more weeks

Cost: $3,300 plus $1,000 tax-deductible donation (includes room and board)

Financial Aid: Available (February 1 deadline)

Eligibility: Students who have completed their sophomore, junior, or senior year of high school

Application Process: 3 essays, 3 recommendations, interview

Application Deadline: Rolling; program usually full by mid-February

Average Number of Applicants: 50

Average Number of Participants: 35

Academic Credit: High school credit available

Contact:
American Farm School
Greek Summer
1133 Broadway
New York, NY 10010
Phone: (212) 463-8434
Fax: (212) 463-8208
nyoffice@amerfarm.org
www.afs.edu.gr

AMERICAN INSTITUTE FOR FOREIGN STUDY (AIFS)

Pre-College Summer Study Abroad

Program Location: England, France, Russia, Spain

Subject Areas: Study abroad

Program Description: AIFS programs are designed to help students see the world through different eyes, immerse themselves in another culture, learn another language, and develop an understanding of global issues. Students are enrolled in college-level courses, live in double rooms and eat their meals on campus. Homestays are available in Paris, France and Salamanca, Spain. Students spend an average of 15 hours per week in class. In addition, numerous cultural outings are included.

Program Dates: July through August

Duration of Program: 3–9 weeks

Cost: $3,600–$7,000 (includes airfare)

Eligibility: Students at least 16 years old who have completed their junior or senior year in high school and are in good academic standing

Application Process: Application form, transcript, $500 deposit are required. Inquiry form and downloadable application form available on website.

Application Deadline: April 15

Academic Credit: High school and college credit available

Contact:
AIFS
River Plaza
9 West Broad Street
Stamford, CT 06902-3788
Phone: (800) 727-AIFS
Fax: (203) 869-9615
precollege.info@aifs.com
www.aifs.com

AMERICAN INTERNATIONAL YOUTH STUDENT EXCHANGE

American International Youth Student Exchange Program

Program Location: England, Ireland, France, Spain, Germany, Australia, Denmark, Sweden, Austria, Greece, China, Japan, and other countries

Subject Areas: Academic study abroad and/or homestay

Program Description: AIYSEP is a non-profit organization that seeks to promote greater international understanding through cultural and homestay programs. Applicants must exhibit maturity, superior character, and accomplished language skills and may spend a summer, a semester, or a full year abroad.

Program Dates: Summer programs begin in June

Duration of Program: 4-, 6-, or 8-week summer programs

Cost: $1,999 for 4 weeks, $2,200 for 6 weeks, special arrangement for 8 weeks; $3,595 for a semester; $4,095 for a year

Eligibility: High school students ages 14–19; prior knowledge of a foreign language is necessary

Application Process: Registration form, 2-page typewritten essay, 4 letters of recommendation, transcripts, $150 application fee (of which $50 is nonrefundable)

Application Deadline: May 1 for summer; April 10 for semester/year programs

Financial Aid: Available

Academic Credit: High school credit

Contact:
AIYSEP
200 Round Hill Road
Tiberon, CA 94920
Phone: (415) 499-7669 or (800) 347-7575
Fax: (415) 499-5651
AIYSEP@aol.com
www.AIYSEP.org

AMERICAN JEWISH SOCIETY FOR SERVICE

Summer Work Camps

Program Location: Varies each summer

Subject Areas: Volunteer work

Program Description: Most AJSS projects involve constructing homes for the needy, though other projects have included building a school, a gymnasium, a barn, and a community center. Each work camp consists of a director, two counselors, a cook, and a predominantly Jewish group of approximately 16 campers. AJSS has conducted 121 projects in 43 states since 1951.

Program Dates: June–July, August

Duration of Program: 6 weeks

Cost: $2,500 plus transportation

Financial Aid: Scholarships are available.

Eligibility: High school juniors and seniors willing to do sometimes strenuous work

Application Process: Written application, references, personal interview; online application available on website

Application Deadline: March 15

Financial Aid Deadline: March 15

Average Number of Applicants: 70

Average Number of Participants: 50

Academic Credit: None

Contact:
AJSS
15 East 26th Street, Room 1029
New York, NY 10010
Phone: (212) 683-6178
Fax: (973) 443-9199
Aud1750@aol.com
www.ajss.org

AMERICAN MANAGEMENT ASSOCIATION

Operation Enterprise

Program Location: Varies each summer, major universities

Subject Areas: Management, leadership

Program Description: Senior executives and AMA faculty present highly interactive workshops on topics such as Management, Negotiation, Strategic Planning, and Presentation Skills. Delegates practice making presentations and engage in a management simulation. Local sightseeing trips round out the program.

Program Dates: Sessions throughout the summer

Duration of Program: 8 days

Cost: $1,750 (includes room and board)

Financial Aid: Available

Eligibility: Ages 16–18; college-age

Application Process: Application, transcript, recommendation

Application Deadline: March 15

Average Number of Applicants: 300

Average Number of Participants: 120

Academic Credit: College credit (three semester hours)

Contact:
AJSS
American Management Association
1601 Broadway
New York, NY 10019
Phone: (212) 903-8205
Fax: (212) 903-8168
dweinberg@amanet.org
www.amanet.org/oe

AMERICAN TRAILS WEST

Program Location: Various locations in the U.S. (including Hawaii and Alaska), Canada, and Europe

Subject Areas: Outdoor adventure, travel

Program Description: American Trails West offers a wide range of summer adventures, including sightseeing, outdoor activities, and evening entertainment. Trips feature a "triple combo" of camping, hotel, and dorm accommodations, or hotel and dorm only (no camping).

Program Dates: Late June to mid-August

Duration of Program: 3–6 weeks

Cost: $2,450 and up

Eligibility: No special requirements

Application Process: Deposit of $300, online registration via website

Contact:
American Trails West
92 Middle Neck Road
Great Neck, NY 11021
Phone: (800) 645-6260 or (516) 487-2800
Fax: (516) 487-2855
atwtours@americantrailswest.com
www.americantrailswest.com

AMERICAN UNIVERSITY

Discover the World of Communication

Program Location: American University School of Communication in Washington, DC

Subject Areas: 16 mm film production, scriptwriting, video production and editing, multimedia, journalism

Program Description: For students who want a creative, challenging experience, this program offers an opportunity to explore the world of communication. Students select one or more courses in production and writing. Classes are held on the American University campus and are taught by experienced faculty and professionals in various fields of communication.

Program Dates: Mid-June–August

Duration of Program: 2-, 3-, and 5-week courses

Cost: $425–$1,300 (varies by course); limited housing available for an additional fee

Eligibility: Open to all high school students (entering grade 9 through graduating seniors) with an interest in and enthusiasm for creative arts

Application Process: Contact the program for more info

Application Deadline: Rolling

Contact:
AU School of Communication
Mary Graydon Center, Room 300
4400 Massachusetts Avenue, NW
Washington, DC 20016-8017
Phone: (202) 885-2105
Fax: (202) 885-2019
fss@american.edu
www.soc.american.edu

See also National Student Leadership Conference

AMERICAN UNIVERSITY OF PARIS

See Summer Study Programs

AMERICAN YOUTH FOUNDATION

International Leadership Conference

Program Location: Camp Merrowvista in New Hampshire; Camp Miniwanca in Michigan

Subject Areas: Leadership, international relations

Program Description: Participants from 50 states and 30 countries live in one of two camps as part of a global village, actively

learning leadership skills by investigating the world and their relationship to others. Outdoor activities include lakefront swimming, a ropes course, archery, basketball, and fencing.

Program Dates: Camp Merrowvista: June 15–22. Camp Miniwanca: July 24–31, August 4–11

Duration of Program: 1 week

Cost: $625 (includes room and board)

Financial Aid: AYF-sponsored "I Dare You" Leadership Award recipients may apply for scholarships through their high schools or 4-H programs. AYF provides some scholarships for second-, third-, and fourth-year program participants.

Eligibility: Ages 15–18

Application Process: Completed application along with $100 nonrefundable deposit. Online application available through AYF website.

Academic Credit: None available

Contact:
American Youth Foundation
2331 Hampton Avenue
St. Louis, MO 63139-2908
Phone: (314) 772-8626
www.ayf.com

AMERISPAN UNLIMITED

Madrid and Marbella Summer Camps;

Spanish Language Program in Costa Rica

Program Location: Madrid or Marbella, Spain; Alajuela, Costa Rica

Subject Areas: Language, study abroad

Program Description: In Madrid or Marbella, students can attend a Summer Camp that features language classes and outdoor activities, while in Alajuela they can participate in a more in-depth Language Program that also includes a homestay.

Amerispan Unlimited

Program Dates: Summer Camps: July and August; Language Program: year-round, starts any Monday

Duration of Program: Summer Camps: 2 or 4 weeks; Language Program: 2 weeks to 6 months

Cost: Summer Camps: $1,095 (2 weeks); Language Program: $800 (2 weeks); both programs have an additional $100 registration fee

Eligibility: Summer Camps: ages 12 and up; Language Program: ages 15 and up

Application Process: One-page application

Application Deadline: 4 weeks prior to start

Average Number of Applicants: 20 for Summer Camp; 100 for Language Program

Average Number of Participants: 20 for Summer Camp; 100 for Language Program

Academic Credit: Available for Language Program only

Contact:
Amerispan Unlimited
117 S. 17th Street #1401
Philadelphia, PA 19103
Phone: (800) 879-6640
Fax: (215) 751-1986
info@amerispan.com
www.amerispan.com

Amigos de las Americas

AMHERST COLLEGE

See Putney Student Travel; Summer Institute for the Gifted

AMIGOS DE LAS AMERICAS

Program Location: Mexico, Dominican Republic, Honduras, Costa Rica, Nicaragua, Brazil, Bolivia, Paraguay

Subject Areas: Community service, cross-cultural understanding, youth leadership

Program Description: After successfully completing a training program either through a local Amigos chapter or through the Correspondent Volunteer Training Program, volunteers are assigned to ongoing health and environmental programs partnered with sponsoring agencies in the host countries. They typically live with families in small communities in rural areas and are supervised by more experienced volunteers and officials of the host agency.

Eligibility: Must be age 16 by project departure

Program Dates: Mid-June through mid-August

Duration of Program: 6–8 weeks

Cost: Approximately $3,300; most of the cost is paid through the volunteer's fund-raising efforts

Financial Aid: Scholarships are awarded based on financial need and availability of funds.

Application Process: Call international office for application or referral to a local chapter.

Application Deadline: January 15 for those applying through a local chapter, March 15 for correspondent volunteers

Academic Credit: May be available, depending on student's school requirements

Contact:
Amigos de las Americas
5618 Star Lane
Houston, TX 77057
Phone: (800) 231-7796 or (888) AMIGO-SL; (713) 782-5290 (local)
Fax: (713) 782-9267
info@amigoslink.org
www.amigoslink.org

APPALACHIAN STATE UNIVERSITY

Summer Sports, Music, and Academic Camps

Program Location: Appalachian State University in Boone, North Carolina

Subject Areas: Sports camps: baseball, basketball, cheerleading clinics, soccer, cross country, distance running, track and field, football, girls volleyball, girls fast pitch softball, and wrestling; music camp; academic enrichment

Program Description: Offered by faculty and coaches on campus. Students use state-of-the-art facilities. Participants live in university residence halls and take meals in the university cafeteria. Appalachian State University, a member institution of the University of North Carolina, is

located 3,333 ft. above sea level in the Appalachian Mountains.

Program Dates: Information available on website

Cost: Varies, includes room and board

Financial Aid: None available

Eligibility: Varies with each program; check website for eligibility requirements

Application Process: Check website for registration information, program costs, and deadlines.

Academic Credit: None available

Contact:
Appalachian State University
Office of Conferences and Institutes
P.O. Box 32042
Boone, North Carolina 28608
Phone: (828) 262-3045
Fax: (828) 262-4992
grayai@appstate.edu
www.conferences-camps@appstate.edu

APPEL FARM ARTS AND MUSIC CENTER

Appel Farm's Summer Arts Camp

Program Location: Appel Farm, a 176-acre farm in rural southern New Jersey

Subject Areas: Music, theater, dance, media arts, fine arts

Program Description: Based on their interests and experience, campers choose a major and two minor areas of instruction. Areas of instruction include music, dance, theater, fine arts, and media arts. All campers, in selecting a major, are encouraged to choose an area in which they have the strongest interest and/or the most experience. Campers may choose minors in any of the major art areas, as well as in sports and swimming. Camper/staff ratio of 2:1.

Program Dates: June 25 to July 22; July 23 to August 19

Duration of Program: 4 weeks per session (campers may sign up for both sessions)

Cost: $2,050

Financial Aid: Appel Farm Scholarship program available for applicants in financial need

Financial Aid Deadline: April 1

Eligibility: Ages 9–17, all skill levels

Application Process: Completed application; online information request form available on website

Application Deadline: Rolling admissions

Average Number of Participants: 176–200 campers per session

Contact:
Appel Farm Arts and Music Center
P.O. Box 888
Elmer, NJ 08318
Phone: (800) 394-8478
Fax: (856) 358-6513
appelcamp@aol.com
www.appelfarm.org/camp/index

APPLE HILL CENTER FOR CHAMBER MUSIC

Apple Hill Summer School and Festival

Program Location: Nelson, New Hampshire

Subject Areas: Music

Program Description: Chamber music workshops with coaching by Apple Hill Chamber Players and Festival Artists. Performance opportunities for student participants of all ages and skill levels. Offers rustic living, sports, evening entertainment, group activities, orchestral/ensemble sight reading. Public Apple Hill Chamber Players/Festival concerts on Tuesday evenings. Participants may attend 1 to 5 sessions. All session communities include international participants who have been awarded scholarships by the Apple Hill Chamber Players on their worldwide Playing for Peace tours.

Program Dates: June 21–30 (Session I); July 5–14 (Session II); July 19–26 (Session III); August 2–10 (Session IV); August 17–26 (Session V)

Duration of Program: 10 days (5 sessions)

Cost: $910 (1 session); $1,660 (2 sessions); $2,360 (3 sessions); $3,010 (4 sessions); $3,610 (5 sessions); $40 application fee also required

Financial Aid: Available (January 15 deadline)

Eligibility: Ages 11–90; intermediate amateur to professional skill level

Application Process: Application (available on website), audition tape

Application Deadline: January 15

Average Number of Applicants: 350

Average Number of Participants: 275

Contact:
Apple Hill Center for Chamber Music
P.O. Box 217
East Sullivan, NH 03445
Phone: (603) 847-3371 or (800) 472-6677
Fax: (603) 847-9734
applehill@monad.net
www.applehill.org

Art Institute of Boston at Lesley University

ART INSTITUTE OF BOSTON AT LESLEY UNIVERSITY

Pre-College Summer Program

Program Location: Lesley University in Boston, Massachusetts

Subject Areas: Animation, computer graphics, design, photography, fine arts, illustration, papermaking, sculpture, ceramics, mixed media

Program Description: Studies in a college environment with professional artists, for college credit.

Program Dates: July

Duration of Program: 4 weeks

Cost: $50 (non-credit programs); $90 (credit programs). Both include a $35 materials fee.

Eligibility: Must be at least age 15

Application Process: Course registration

Application Deadline: Rolling admissions

Average Number of Applicants: 200

Average Number of Participants: 200

Academic Credit: Both non-credit and credit programs available

Contact:
attn: Dean of Continuing and Professional Education Programs
700 Beacon Street
Boston, MA 02215
Phone: (800) 773-0494, ext. 6724; (617) 585-6724 or (617) 585-6729
Fax: (617) 437-1226
admissions@aiboston.edu
www.aiboston.edu

ART INSTITUTE OF SEATTLE

Studio 101

Program Location: Seattle, Washington

Subject Areas: Design, media, fashion, culinary arts

Program Description: Studio 101 provides students with the opportunity to take classes in an area they may be considering as a career. The program is designed to introduce students to the tools, techniques, and theories that are utilized by professionals in the field.

Program Dates: August

Duration of Program: 1 week

Cost: $450

Average Number of Applicants: 300+

Average Number of Participants: 150

Contact:
Art Institute of Seattle
2323 Elliot Avenue
Seattle, WA 98121
Phone: (800) 275-2471 or (206) 448-6600
Fax: (206) 269-0275
www.ais.edu

Note: The Art Institutes have 24 locations across the United States. For information on each Institute's summer workshops, visit The Art Institutes website at www.aii.edu.

ASC FOOTBALL CAMPS, INC.

ASC Football Camps

Program Location: 2001 Locations: Southwest Texas State University in San Marcos, Texas; Benedictine University in Lisle, Illinois; Shippensburg University in Shippensburg, Pennsylvania; University of Redlands in Redlands, California; San Francisco State University in San Francisco, California; Bakersfield College in Bakersfield, California

Subject Areas: Football (contact and kicking)

Program Description: Contact Camp: Campers learn from NFL coaches and pros, as well as top college coaches. Stresses conditioning and football techniques for every position, both individually and as a team. Campers move from non-contact drills to full contact in a gradual progression, culminating in full contact scrimmage. Kicking Camp: Staff of NFL kickers teach and improve basic fundamentals and techniques. Each camp has at least one current or former NFL kicker or punter as head instructor, who is assisted by college kickers or punters also acting as counselors. At end of program, campers ages 16–18 kick for college coaches for scholarship consideration.

Program Dates: Sessions during June and July

Duration of Program: Contact Camp: 6 days; Kicking Camp: 4 days

Cost: Contact Camp: $525 (overnight), $425 (day camp). Kicking Camp: $425 (overnight), $325 (day camp).

Eligibility: Contact Camp: Boys ages 8–18 who have not started freshman year of college. Kicking Camp: Boys ages 12–18. Beginners to veteran players. Campers need a full set of football equipment—helmet, chin strap, shoulder pads, two jerseys, pants and pads, football shoes (no metal-tip cleats), athletic supporter, cup, and mouthpiece; some equipment can be rented at the camp.

Application Process: Online application form available

Application Deadline: May 1

Contact:
ASC Football Camps
P.O. Box 72
Liberty Corner, NJ 07938
Phone: (800) 260-8055 or (908) 604-0381
Fax: (908) 604-0487
info@ascfootballcamp.com
www.ascfootballcamp.com

Asheville School

ASHEVILLE SCHOOL

Asheville School
Summer Academic Adventures

Program Location: Asheville, North Carolina

Subject Areas: Literature, creative writing, math, history, science, art, ESL, computers

Program Description: An academically challenging summer experience for students entering grades 7–11, providing exciting opportunities for high-achieving students. Appalachian setting provides plenty of opportunities for outdoor activities, including climbing, hiking, kayaking, and swimming. All students live in dorms on the 300-acre campus, with access to state-of-the-art computer labs and other school facilities.

Program Dates: 2 sessions in June–July

Duration of Program: 3 weeks

Cost: TBA

Financial Aid: Limited need-based and merit-based aid available

Eligibility: Gifted students entering grades 7–11

Application Process: Application, academic transcript, 2 teacher recommendations, personal statement, $30 fee

Application Deadline: May 1

Contact:
Asheville School Summer Academic Adventures
360 Asheville School Road
Asheville, NC 28806
Phone: (828) 254-6345
Fax: (828) 252-8666
www.ashevilleschool.org

ASPEN MUSIC SCHOOL

Aspen Music Festival and School

Program Location: Aspen, Colorado

Subject Areas: Classical music

Program Description: The Aspen Music Festival and School dedicates its efforts to superior professional training. Programs are tailored to

individual students. Orchestral participation and private lessons. Programs in opera, piano, guitar, audio recording, vocal performance, quartet studies, composition, conducting.

Program Dates: June 12–August 18, 2002

Duration of Program: 4½- and 9-week sessions (guitar program is offered only during the second 4½-week session)

Cost: $3,350 for 4½-week session; $5,115 for 9-week session

Eligibility: Talent-based

Application Process: Audition tape. Live audition required in some programs.

Application Deadline: February 15, 2002

Average Number of Applicants: 1,000

Average Number of Participants: 800

Academic Credit: College credit available for selected programs from the University of Colorado

Contact:
Aspen Music School
2 Music School Road
Aspen, CO 81611
Phone: (970) 925-3254
Fax: (970) 925-5708
school@aspenmusic.org
www.aspenmusicfestival.com

AUBURN UNIVERSITY

Summer Honor Band Camps

Program Location: Auburn University in Auburn, Alabama

Subject Areas: Performance of symphonic concert band music

Program Description: Three days of instruction, rehearsals, and clinics, culminating in a symphony concert.

Program Dates: June

Duration of Program: 3 days

Cost: $180 (overnight); $140 (commuters)

Eligibility: JHS students must have had at least 1 year of instrument instruction.

Application Process: Completed registration form

Application Deadline: June 7

Average Number of Applicants: 75

Average Number of Participants: 75

Academic Credit: None available

World Affairs Youth Seminar

Program Location: Auburn University in Auburn, Alabama

Subject Areas: International affairs, government

Program Description: Students from the U.S. and other countries come together for a week of seminars, discussions, and activities. A unique opportunity to be a delegate to a model United Nations, participate in a mock international crisis, and sample the food, dance, and art of many different cultures.

Program Dates: July

Duration of Program: 1 week

Cost: $375

Financial Aid: Full scholarships offered by local Rotary Clubs and other service organizations

Eligibility: Students entering grades 10, 11, and 12

Application Process: Application must be endorsed by school principal or counselor.

Application Deadline: June 18

Academic Credit: None available

Design Camp

Program Location: Auburn University in Auburn, Alabama

Subject Areas: Industrial design

Program Description: Creative students interested in a professional career in design are immersed in a workshop that begins with basic

design concepts. Each day is filled with hands-on design activities, technical demonstrations, and professional guest speakers. Participants have access to photo, computer, wood, and plastic fabrication labs. Individual attention and guidance is given by participating faculty and staff from the Industrial Design Department.

Program Dates: June

Duration of Program: 1 week

Cost: $495

Application Deadline: May 30

Academic Credit: None available

Contact:
Outreach Program Office
Auburn University
100 Mell Hall
Auburn, AL 36849-5608
Phone: (334) 844-5100
Fax: (334) 844-3101
opo@auburn.edu
www.auburn.edu/outreach/opose

AVATAR EDUCATION LTD.

Buckswood ARC Summer Programs

Program Location: Locations in the United States and England

Subject Areas: ESL, performing arts, soccer

Program Description: Open to students from around the world. Offers specialist activities, which are part of a general program of recreation, including: fun activities, sports, socials, cultural visits, sightseeing and special trips. Located at lovely campuses in interesting locations.

Program Dates: June 30–August 25

Duration of Program: 2–8 weeks

Cost: Varies according to program (includes room and board; transportation included within program)

Financial Aid: None available

Eligibility: Ages 7–17

Application Process: Booking form, according to availability

Application Deadline: Rolling

Average Number of Applicants: 700

Average Number of Participants: 400

Academic Credit: None available

Contact:
Avatar Education Ltd
Westminster House
Bolton Close
Uckfield, East Sussex TN22 IPH
England
Phone: 44-1825-760-900
Fax: 44-1825-760-911
info@buckswood.com
www.buckswood.com

BAJA CALIFORNIA LANGUAGE COLLEGE

Program Location: Ensenada, Baja California, Mexico

Subject Areas: Spanish language, culture, arts

Program Description: Youth programs are offered throughout the summer. Teen students receive the total immersion experience. Classes are conducted Monday through Friday from 8:30 to 2:30 and students live with Mexican host families. Weekly excursions and walking tours complement the immersion experience.

Program Dates: May through September

Duration of Program: 1–5 weeks

Cost: $240 per week, Monday–Friday

Eligibility: All ages and levels

Application Process: Written application

Application Deadline: 2 weeks prior to start date

Average Number of Applicants: 300

Average Number of Participants: 300

Academic Credit: College credit available

Baja California Language College

Contact:
Baja California Language College
P.O. Box 7556
San Diego, CA 92167
Phone: (619) 758-9711
college@bajacal.com
www.bajacal.com

BALL STATE UNIVERSITY

Ball State University
Journalism Workshops

Program Location: Ball State University in
Muncie, Indiana

Subject Areas: Journalism

Program Description: High school students
interested in journalism participate in
workshops in Muncie, Indiana. The goal of the
workshops is to enhance grammar, journalism,
and writing skills.

Program Dates: July 8–12; July 15–19, 2002

Duration of Program: 4 days

Cost: $295 (application postmarked by June 1),
$325 (application postmarked after June 1)

Eligibility: Open to all high school students

Application Deadline: June 1

Average Number of Applicants: 500

Average Number of Participants: 500

Academic Credit: College credit available

Contact:
Journalism Art Building 304
attn: Journalism Workshops
Ball State University
Muncie, IN 47306
Phone: (765) 285-8900
Fax: (765) 285-7997
workshops@bsu.edu
www.journalism.bsu.edu/

Ball State University

BALLETMET

Summer Workshop

Program Location: Columbus, Ohio

Subject Areas: Ballet

Program Description: Intensive ballet-based workshop that offers a rich and varied curriculum. All students have classes in ballet technique (every day); pointe or variations or men's work (every day); body conditioning, improved alignment, and overall physical well-being; and jazz, modern, Afro-Caribbean, Flamenco or floor barre (assigned according to levels). Students are housed at Capital University in Bexley, Ohio, a 10-minute drive from the dance studios, and are supervised by adult chaperones.

Program Dates: June 25–August 3 (2001 dates)

Duration of Program: 6 weeks

Cost: $1,350 (commuter); $2,850 (residential)

Financial Aid: Scholarship and financial aid info available upon request

Eligibility: Intermediate to advanced dancers, ages 12 and older

Application Process: Audition required, either in person or on tape

Application Deadline: Students will be enrolled according to the date registration materials are received.

Contact:
BalletMet Dance Academy
322 Mount Vernon Avenue
Columbus, OH 43215
Phone: (614) 224-1672
academy@balletmet.org
www.balletmet.org

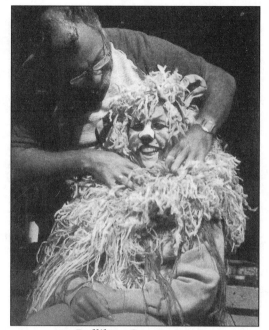

Ballibay Camps, Inc.

BALLIBAY CAMPS, INC.

Camp Ballibay for the Fine and Performing Arts

Program Location: Camptown, Pennsylvania

Subject Areas: Theater performance, studio art, instrumental/vocal music, rock and roll music, dance (ballet, modern, jazz, tap), technical theater, video, radio

Program Description: A coed, individual choice, noncompetitive program. Each camper develops his or her own schedule with the guidance of the staff. Camp produces over thirty shows by campers; also provides all regular camping activities such as swimming, horseback riding, tennis, golf, soccer, and softball.

Program Dates: June 24–August 25

Duration of Program: 2–9 weeks

Cost: $1,475–$4,475

Eligibility: Ages 6–16; experience and training not necessary

Application Process: Completed application

Application Deadline: Year-round

Contact:
Ballibay Camps, Inc.
One Ballibay Road
Camptown, PA 18815
Phone: (570) 746-3223
Fax: (570) 746-3691
jannone@ballibay.com
www.ballibay.com

BARAT FOUNDATION

Barat Foundation Summer Program

Program Location: Provence, France

Subject Areas: French language and culture

Program Description: A total French language and humanities learning experience. Students are grouped according to language proficiency. Provides structured classes conducted in French (or English, depending on student level), taught by French nationals in the following areas: art history, history, literature, architecture, theater, cinema, music, cuisine, fashion, and culture. Students live in a fully equipped, modern French estate in a beautiful, rural setting in Provence, with a large swimming pool, ping-pong, volleyball courts, and indoor and outdoor kitchens and dining facilities.

Program Dates: July through early August

Duration of Program: 4–6 weeks

Cost: $4,995–$7,490

Eligibility: All levels of French from beginner students with no foreign language experience to fluent speakers

Application Deadline: March 1

Average Number of Applicants: 100

Average Number of Participants: 35

Contact:
Barat Foundation
P.O. Box 609
Montville, NJ 07045
Phone: (973) 263-1013
Fax: (973) 263-2287
baratfound@aol.com
www.baratfoundation.org

BAREFOOT INTERNATIONAL

Barefoot International & Fly High Ski School

Program Location: West Palm Beach, Florida

Subject Areas: Barefoot waterskiing

Program Description: Gives high school students a unique opportunity to learn the fundamentals of barefoot waterskiing.

Barefoot International

Program Dates: Year-round

Duration of Program: 1-day, 3-day, and 5-day programs

Cost: $600 (5-day program), $350 (3-day program), $125 (1-day program). Prices do not include room and board.

Eligibility: All skill levels welcome, no equipment required

Average Number of Participants: 3–4 per class, several classes offered per day

Contact:
attn: Mike Seipel
520 S. Country Club Drive
Lake Worth, FL 33462
Phone: (800) 277-5446;
(561) 964-3346 (outside the U.S.)
Fax: (561) 966-2425
msbi5000@aol.com
www.barefootintlflyhigh.com

BARK LAKE LEADERSHIP CENTER

Leadership Through Recreation/Music

Program Location: Irondale, Ontario, Canada

Subject Areas: Leadership

Program Description: Young leaders will have an opportunity to take calculated risks, and demonstrate and develop teamwork and recreational skills while having fun. Programs are led by certified adult instructors, with a 1:12 ratio of instructors to students.

Program Dates: Leadership: July 7–13, July 14–20; Music/Leadership August 18–24

Duration of Program: 1 week

Cost: From $495/week (includes room and board)

Financial Aid: None available

Eligibility: Ages 11–17

Application Process: Transcripts and recommendations

Application Deadline: May 1

Average Number of Applicants: 100

Average Number of Participants: 100

Academic Credit: None available

Contact:
Bark Lake Leadership Center
Irondale, Ontario
Canada K0M1X0
Phone: (705) 447-2447
Fax: (705) 447-2475
info@barklake.com
www.barklake.com

BARNARD COLLEGE

Summer in New York: A Pre-College Program

Program Location: Barnard College in New York City

Subject Areas: Liberal arts curriculum with an emphasis on humanities and social sciences, college preparation

Program Description: Many of the classes that make up this program are adapted from the Barnard College undergraduate curriculum. Classes are small; students receive individual attention, engage in lively discussion, and develop independent projects. Students enroll in two classes, which meet four days a week in morning and afternoon sessions. New York City often becomes an extension of the classroom; in an art history course, for example, students make regular trips to museums and galleries.

Program Dates: June 23–July 27

Duration of Program: 5 weeks

Cost: $2,150 (commuters); $3,350 (residents, includes room and board)

Financial Aid: Available (April 17 deadline)

Eligibility: Students who have completed grades 10 and 11

Application Process: Application, transcript, essay, teacher and guidance counselor recommendations

Application Deadline: May 15

Average Number of Applicants: 300

Average Number of Participants: 150

Academic Credit: High school credit may be available

Contact:
Barnard College
Summer in New York
3009 Broadway
New York, NY 10027
Phone: (212) 854-8866
Fax: (212) 854-8867
pcp@barnard.edu
www.barnard.edu/pcp

Bates College

BATES COLLEGE

Bates College Basketball Camp

Program Location: Bates College in Lewiston, Maine

Subject Areas: Basketball

Program Description: Designed to develop fundamental basketball skills for the appropriate age levels. Participants are divided by age and skill level. Specific emphasis placed on teaching offensive and defensive techniques and strategy and having fun. Both individual and group instruction also emphasized. Daily activities include full court game competition, skill development stations, lectures, demonstrations, and more.

Program Dates: Contact program for summer program dates

Duration of Program: 5 days

Cost: Contact program for further information

Eligibility: Students in grades 3–12

Application Process: Call for application or brochure

Bates Forensic Institutes

Program Location: Bates College in Lewiston, Maine

Subject Areas: Debate (policy and Lincoln-Douglas), speech

Program Description: National Policy Institute: Instruction in proper use of debate handbooks, research techniques; by the third week, students will do at least 2–3 practice debates per day. Lincoln-Douglas Debate Workshop: Daily supervised research labs on a resolution to be debated during the session. Individual Speech Events Workshop: Workshops on interpretive events, original oratory, extemporaneous; students select one event, develop a piece, and participate in many videotaped, critiqued rounds.

Program Dates: June 24–July 13, 2001

Duration of Program: 10 days–3 weeks

Cost: $1,350 (Policy); $950 (Lincoln-Douglas); $575 (Speech). Includes room and board, Institute materials, all copying costs.

Financial Aid: Need-based aid available. Send a copy of parents'/guardians' most recent federal tax returns, a letter explaining any extenuating circumstances, and specific amount of aid requested. Requests for aid will not be considered after the April 1 application deadline.

Eligibility: Students entering grades 9–12. Novices and debaters with one to two years of experience are encouraged to apply.

Application Process: Contact Bates for brochure and application form. Essay required.

Application Deadline: April 1. Institute alumni who apply before April 1 are guaranteed acceptance into the program.

Creative Writing Workshops

Program Location: Bates College in Lewiston, Maine

Subject Areas: Writing

Program Description: Intensive five-day residential program for young writers. The program is divided into time for classroom instruction, individual writing, small group meetings, guest speakers and readers, and individual tutorials. Students are encouraged to explore a range of genres—fiction, poetry, and drama—according to their individual interests.

Program Dates: 2 sessions in mid- and late July

Duration of Program: 1 week

Cost: $375 (includes room and board)

Eligibility: Session I: grades 8–10; Session II: grades 11–12

Application Process: Essay required

Application Deadline: May 1

Average Number of Applicants: 30

Average Number of Participants: 20

Edmund S. Muskie Scholars Program

Program Location: Bates College in Lewiston, Maine

Subject Areas: Post-World War II U.S. political history

Program Description: Program focuses on recent U.S. history and politics, including the civil rights movement, the Vietnam War, rise of environmentalism and current events, with research in the Muskie Archives. The faculty, drawn from Bates College and top high schools, work one-on-one with students to help them develop research methods, writing skills, and study techniques.

Program Dates: June 24–July 6, 2001

Duration of Program: 2 weeks

Cost: $800 (includes room and board)

Eligibility: Outstanding rising high school seniors with a strong interest in post-WW II U.S. history

Application Process: Sample of academic writing, preferably on history topic; teacher recommendation; transcript; nonrefundable $50 fee

Application Deadline: May 15

Average Number of Applicants: 50

Average Number of Participants: 25

Contact:
Bates College
Office of Special Projects and Summer Programs
163 Wood Street
Lewiston, ME 04240-6016
Phone: (207) 786-6077
summer@bates.edu
www.bates.edu/summer

BAYLOR UNIVERSITY

Baylor University Debaters' Workshop

Program Location: Baylor University in Waco, Texas

Subject Areas: Policy and Lincoln-Douglas debate, extemporaneous speaking and oratory

Program Description: The BDW, in existence for over 60 years, trains students in speech and debate by emphasizing research, critical thinking, and writing, speaking, and organizational skills. Classes are small to facilitate one-on-one interaction.

Program Dates: July

Duration of Program: 2–3 weeks

Cost: TBA

Eligibility: Grades 9–12; novice, junior varsity, varsity, and advanced placement debaters

Application Process: Written application, recommendation

Financial Aid Deadline: June 1

Average Number of Applicants: 250

Average Number of Participants: 250

Academic Credit: None

Contact:
Baylor University Debaters' Workshop
Box 97368
Waco, TX 76798
Phone: (254) 710-6919
Fax: (254) 710-1563
www.baylor.edu

High School Summer Science Research Fellowship Program

Program Location: Baylor University in Waco, Texas

Subject Areas: Science research

Program Description: Offers superior high school students hands-on research experience by working with university science professors in many disciplines. Students gain familiarity with the operation of instruments and interpretation of data obtained by techniques not usually available in high school laboratories. They develop effective working relationships with scientists that enhance specific interests in and across scientific disciplines and associate with other exceptional students with similar interests. Students also participate in science and technology seminars and social and recreational activities.

Program Dates: End of May to end of June

Duration of Program: 5 weeks

Cost: $500 (includes room and board)

Financial Aid: Limited aid available

Eligibility: Students in 11th grade at time of application; 5 boys and 5 girls admitted

Application Process: Application, teacher and character references, short essay, PSAT/SAT score, high school transcript

Application Deadline: April 1

Average Number of Participants: Limit of 10

Academic Credit: 1 semester hour college credit

Contact:
Baylor University
500 Speight
P.O. Box 97344
Waco, TX 76798-7344
Phone: (254) 710-4288
Fax: (254) 710-3639
bernice_helpert@baylor.edu
www.baylor.edu/~Research/high_school.html

BELOIT COLLEGE

Center for Language Studies

Program Location: Beloit College in Beloit, Wisconsin

Subject Areas: Languages: Chinese, Czech, Hungarian, Japanese, Portuguese, Russian, Spanish, and ESL

Program Description: Intensive 9-week and 4-week language immersion programs in Chinese,

Czech, Hungarian, Japanese, Portuguese, Russian, and Spanish, as well as a nine-week English as a Second Language program. A computerized language learning center integrates the finest educational technology with language study. Students interact primarily with others studying the same language in the classroom, residence hall, and dining hall. CLS students are housed by language group in air-conditioned residence halls and have access to campus facilities. Ideal for people preparing to work or study abroad.

Program Dates: June–August

Duration of Program: 4- and 9-week programs

Cost: $3,678–$5,881 (includes room and board)

Financial Aid: Scholarships which cover partial tuition are available. CLS students are eligible for financial aid in the form of federal loans through the Stafford, Perkins, and PLUS loan programs, or private loans through the Norwest and Excel loan programs.

Eligibility: Open to high school juniors through adults. No previous knowledge is required for the beginning language programs; appropriate prior instruction or consent of the instructor will determine placement at intermediate and advanced levels.

Application Process: Application form (online application available on website), transcript, 2 letters of recommendation required

Application Deadline: Admission decisions will be made on rolling basis beginning January 1 and will continue until classes are full.

Average Number of Participants: Average class size of 4–8 students

Academic Credit: College credit available

Contact:
Patricia L. Zody, Director
Center for Language Studies
Beloit College
700 College Street
Beloit, WI 53511-5595

Phone: (608) 356-0751
Fax: (608) 363-2082
cls@beloit.edu
beloit.edu/~cls

BENNINGTON COLLEGE

Bennington College July Program

Program Location: Bennington College in Bennington, Vermont

Subject Areas: Performing arts, visual arts, writing and literature, social sciences, natural sciences, interdisciplinary studies

Program Description: A month-long intensive academic experience for students ages 15–18. Students get a taste of the college life through enrolling in two classes of their choosing, living on campus, and being exposed to a variety of cultural and academic activities.

Program Dates: June 29–July 27, 2002

Duration of Program: 4 weeks

Cost: $3,600 (2001 tuition)

Financial Aid: Available

Financial Aid Deadline: May 15, 2002

Eligibility: Motivated students, ages 15–18. Admission based on academic standing and "a display of an excitement for learning."

Application Process: Application form, personal essay, teacher recommendation, parent statement, transcript, and application fee. Certain courses require samples of artwork or writing.

Application Deadline: Rolling admissions

Average Number of Applicants: 270

Average Number of Participants: 225

Academic Credit: College credit available

Bennington College

Contact:
Bennington College July Program
Bennington, VT 05201
Phone: (802) 440-4418
Fax: (802) 447-4269
july_program@bennington.edu
www.bennington.edu

BETHESDA ACADEMY OF PERFORMING ARTS

Summer Repertory Theater; Mid-Summer Shakespeare Company

Program Location: Washington, DC

Subject Areas: Performing arts

Program Description: Summer Repertory: Performers study and rehearse a musical in an intensive theater program with 5 public performances in a professional theater space. Summer Shakespeare: Comprehensive classical

program focusing on text study, voice, movement, and stage combat while rehearsing a Shakespearean play culminating in 5 public performances.

Program Dates: Summer Repertory: June–July; Summer Shakespeare: July–August

Duration of Program: Summer Repertory: 5 weeks; Summer Shakespeare: 4 weeks

Cost: TBA

Eligibility: High school students willing to commit to the entire rehearsal and performance schedule

Application Deadline: Rolling admissions

Contact:
Bethesda Academy of Performing Arts
7300 Whittier Boulevard
Bethesda, MD 20817
Phone: (301) 320-2550
Fax: (301) 320-1860

BIRMINGHAM-SOUTHERN COLLEGE

Student Leaders in Service

Program Location: Birmingham-Southern College in Birmingham, Alabama

Subject Areas: Leadership and service

Program Description: Exposes high school students to leadership theories and provides opportunities to practice leadership through community service projects. During the week, students and Birmingham-Southern faculty members enhance their understanding of self, expand their knowledge of leadership theories, and explore the relationship between leadership and service. They then apply these theories to hypothetical scenarios, experiences with community service projects, and other activities, such as the ropes course.

Program Dates: June 23–28

Duration of Program: 1 week

Cost: $350 (includes room and board and transportation)

Financial Aid: None available

Eligibility: Rising high school juniors and seniors

Application Process: School transcript, teacher recommendation, 200-word essay on leadership, high school résumé of activities

Application Deadline: Mid-April

Average Number of Applicants: 100

Average Number of Participants: 30–35

Academic Credit: None available

Contact:
Birmingham-Southern College
Student Leaders in Service
900 Arkadelphia Road
BSC Box 549008
Birmingham, AL 35254
Phone: (800) 523-5793, x4696
Fax: (205) 226-3074
smancin@bsc.edu
www.bsc.edu/programs/
leadershipstudies/sls1.htm

Summer Scholar Program

Program Location: Birmingham-Southern College in Birmingham, Alabama

Subject Areas: Academics, extracurricular activities, community service

Program Description: Students take two courses with current students in all different areas of study. Along with classes, activities are planned each day, including bowling, movies, physical activities, community service projects, overnight canoeing trip, etc.

Program Dates: June 10–July 27

Duration of Program: 6 weeks

Cost: $1,000 (includes room and board and transportation)

Eligibility: Rising high school seniors

Application Process: Application, transcript, counselor or teacher recommendation

Application Deadline: April 15

Average Number of Applicants: 85

Average Number of Participants: 45

Academic Credit: College credit available

Contact:
Birmingham Southern College
Summer Scholar Program
900 Arkadelphia Road
Box 549008
Birmingham, AL 35254
Phone: (800) 523-5793, x4684
Fax: (205) 226-3074
tfrankli@bsc.edu
www.bsc.edu

BLUE LAKE FINE ARTS CAMP

Program Location: Twin Lake, Michigan

Subject Areas: Music, art, dance, theater

Program Description: Blue Lake caters to students with an interest in music, art, dance, and theater. Students' mornings are filled with classes and rehearsals. After lunch, students have a break for rest, recreation, an elective course, or individual practice. Afternoon classes and rehearsals end around 4:30. Evening activities include arts performances or camp fun. Blue Lake also sponsors a 3-week international exchange program in Europe.

Program Dates: 4 camp sessions run from late June through mid-August

Duration of Program: 2 weeks

Cost: $795 (includes room and board)

Eligibility: Grades 5–12

Application Process: Registration forms available after December 1

Application Deadline: Enrollment on a first come, first served basis

Financial Aid: Scholarships are limited and awarded based on the following criteria: Audition or portfolio, arts instructor recommendations,

and in some cases, financial need. Contact Blue Lake to request a scholarship application. Additionally, each summer, Blue Lake awards a scholarship to the winner of the Student Concerto Competition, who also performs as a guest soloist with the Festival Orchestra in Blue Lake's Summer Arts Festival.

Average Number of Applicants: 5,000

Average Number of Participants: 4,600

Academic Credit: None

Contact:
Blue Lake Fine Arts Camp
300 E. Crystal Lake Road
Twin Lake, MI 49457
Phone: (231) 894-1966 or (800) 221-3796
Fax: (231) 893-5120
www.bluelake.org

BORDEAUX LANGUAGE SCHOOL

Teenage Summer Program in Biarritz

Program Location: Biarritz, France

Subject Areas: French language study, international travel

Program Description: In addition to 15 French classes per week, the Biarritz program offers surfing, beach volleyball, rafting, horseback riding, tennis, golf, and mountain biking in the Pyrenees. Also includes visits to chateaux, Lourdes, a traditional fishing village, and a natural reserve for wild horses.

Program Dates: Every Monday from June 25 to August 25

Duration of Program: 2, 3, and 4+ weeks

Cost: 7,250 FF (French francs) for 2 weeks; 10,000 FF for 3 weeks; 2,500 FF for each additional week

Eligibility: Ages 13–17. All levels of French language proficiency, including those with no previous exposure to the language.

Application Process: BLS requires registration forms and a 3,000 FF deposit at least 3 weeks

prior to the beginning of the session. Participants must also notify BLS of their travel arrangements two weeks before their arrival.

Application Deadline: 3 weeks prior to the start of each session

Average Number of Applicants: 100

Average Number of Participants: 100

Academic Credit: Available

Contact:
Bordeaux Language School
42 Rue Lafaurie de Monbadon
33000 Bordeaux, France
Phone: 33 (0)5 56 51 00 76
Fax: 33 (0)5 56 51 76 15
info@bls-frenchcourses.com
www.juniorfrenchbiarritz.com

BOSTON COLLEGE

Boston College Experience

Program Location: Boston College in Chestnut Hill, Massachusetts

Subject Areas: Academic study, college preparation

Program Description: Talented high school seniors elect 2 classes from a full range of undergraduate courses. Students live in Boston College dormitories and have access to the university's recreational facilities.

Program Dates: June–August

Duration of Program: 6 weeks

Cost: $3,600

Eligibility: Students in grade 12

Application Process: Registration forms, transcripts, recommendations

Application Deadline: June 15

Average Number of Applicants: 150

Average Number of Participants: 125

Academic Credit: College credit

Contact:
Boston College Summer Programs Office
Chestnut Hill, MA 02467
Phone: (617) 552-3800
Fax: (617) 552-3199
romelus@bc.edu
www.bc.edu/bce

BOSTON UNIVERSITY

Program in Mathematics for Young Scientists (PROMYS)

Program Location: Boston University in Boston, Massachusetts

Subject Areas: Mathematics

Program Description: Participants practice the art of mathematical discovery, studying numerical exploration, formulation and critique of conjectures, and techniques of proof and generalization. More experienced participants may also study algorithms, geometry and topology, or combinatorics. Each participant meets with professional mathematicians several times per week for problem-solving and open-ended explorations. Participants live in dorms with college–age counselors who are always available to discuss mathematics with the students.

Program Dates: July 3–August 12, 2002

Duration of Program: 6 weeks

Cost: $1,500 + $100 for books

Financial Aid: PROMYS is dedicated to the principle that nobody will be unable to attend the program because of financial need.

Eligibility: Open to all high school students

Application Process: Applications available starting January 1. Students must solve a collection of math problems included with the application (for examples, see website for math problems used on previous year's application). Also must submit academic transcript and a letter of recommendation from their math teacher.

Application Deadline: June 1

Average Number of Applicants: 100+

Average Number of Participants: 50

Contact:
PROMYS, Department of Mathematics
Boston University
111 Cummington Street
Boston, MA 02215
Phone: (617) 353-2563
Fax: (617) 353-8100
promys@math.bu.edu
www.promys.org

BRANDEIS UNIVERSITY

Brandeis Summer Odyssey

Program Location: Brandeis University in Waltham, Massachusetts

Subject Areas: Precollege study

Program Description: Summer Odyssey offers instruction in math, science, and technology in a fun environment. In addition to classes, students may participate in various instructive or relaxing workshops and trips, including a whale-watching excursion and a Boston Red Sox game.

Program Dates: July–August

Duration of Program: 4–7 weeks

Cost: TBA

Eligibility: Students in grades 10–12 with a B average or better

Application Process: Transcripts, essay, letter of recommendation

Application Deadline: May 15

Financial Aid Deadline: April 1

Average Number of Applicants: 250

Average Number of Participants: 150

Contact:
Brandeis Summer Odyssey
415 South Street
P.O. Box 9110
Waltham, MA 02454
Phone: (781) 736-2111

Genesis at Brandeis University

Fax: (781) 736-2122
odyssey@brandeis.edu
www.brandeis.edu/odyssey

Genesis at Brandeis University

Program Location: Brandeis University in Waltham, Massachusetts

Subject Areas: Arts and humanities, Jewish studies

Program Description: Although not exclusively for Jewish students, Genesis blends academic study and social action with discussions of the importance of Judaism in contemporary culture.

Program Dates: July

Duration of Program: 4 weeks

Cost: TBA

Financial Aid Deadline: March 1

Eligibility: Students in grades 10–12

Application Process: Personal statement, recommendation, transcripts

Application Deadline: March 15

Average Number of Applicants: 110

Average Number of Participants: 75

Contact:
Genesis at Brandeis University
MS 085
Waltham, MA 02454-9110
Phone: (781) 736-8416
Fax: (781) 736-8122
genesis@brandeis.edu
www.brandeis.edu/genesis

BREAKTHROUGHS ABROAD, INC.

High School Programs

Program Location: Costa Rica, Ecuador, Navajo, Nepal, Tanzania, Thailand

Subject Areas: Community service, homestay/cultural immersion, adventure travel, environmental studies, teaching English

Program Description: Courses combine community service, family stays, cross-cultural exchanges, and adventure travel. Through family

stays and work on service projects, students experience firsthand the day-to-day living of people in other cultures. Guided by experienced staff, students have breakthroughs in global awareness, cultural sensitivity, and in their sense of self.

Program Dates: Late June–early August

Duration of Program: 4–6 weeks

Cost: $2,900–$5,900 (room and board and transportation from gateway city included)

Financial Aid: Available (April 15 deadline)

Eligibility: High school and college students, ages 15 and up

Application Process: Application and two letters of recommendation, $400 deposit

Application Deadline: April 15

Average Number of Applicants: 72

Average Number of Participants: 72 total; no more than 12 students with 2 leaders on each trip

Academic Credit: Arranged individually

Contact:
Breakthroughs Abroad, Inc.
1160-B Woodstock
Estes Park, CO 80517
Phone: (970) 577-1908
Fax: (970) 577-9855
info@breakthroughsabroad.org
www.breakthroughsabroad.org

BRENAU UNIVERSITY

Firespark Schools

Program Location: Brenau University in Gainesville, Georgia

Subject Areas: Program one: fine arts, business, communications; Program two: science, health care

Program Description: Offer gifted and talented students the opportunity to have hands-on learning experiences in a safe and nurturing environment.

Program Dates: June 23–July 6 and July 21–August 3

Duration of Program: 2 weeks

Cost: $979 (includes room and board)

Financial Aid: None available

Eligibility: Ages 13–17

Application Process: Application (available on website, or request by mail or phone)

Application Deadline: Rolling

Average Number of Participants: 300

Academic Credit: None available

Contact:
Brenau University
Firespark Schools
1 Centennial Circle
Gainesville, GA 30501
Phone: (800) 252-5119
Fax: (770) 523-6742
firespark@lib.brenau.edu
www.firespark.org

BREVARD MUSIC CENTER

Young Artists Division

Program Location: Brevard, North Carolina

Subject Areas: Music performance and instruction

Program Description: A summer music festival with instrumentalists participating in 2 of 5 orchestras and 3 wind ensembles. Repertoire-based education with concerts, private instruction, master classes, theory. Programs are also available for pianists and composers.

Program Dates: June 20 to August 5

Duration of Program: 6 ½ weeks

Cost: $3,350

Eligibility: Students with musical ability, from age 14 though graduating seniors

Application Process: Audition, live or by tape; auditions begin in December.

Application Deadline: February 28 (for priority applications), April 1 (final deadline)

Academic Credit: College credit available

Contact:
Brevard Music Center
Young Artists Division
P.O. Box 312
Brevard, NC 28712
Phone: (828) 884-2975
Fax: (828) 884-2036
bmcadmission@brevardmusic.org
www.brevardmusic.org

BRIDGEWATER COLLEGE

High School Leadership Academy

Program Location: Bridgewater College in Bridgewater, Virginia

Subject Areas: Leadership training

Program Description: Through workshops, seminars, and outdoor recreational activities, students develop such leadership skills as team building, communication, ethical empowerment, and creative problem solving.

Program Dates: Early August

Duration of Program: 1 week

Cost: $150

Financial Aid: None available

Eligibility: Rising high school juniors and seniors

Application Process: Résumé, two letters of recommendation, essay, and transcripts (optional)

Application Deadline: March 31

Average Number of Applicants: 450

Average Number of Participants: 110

Academic Credit: None available

Bridgewater College Leadership Academy

Contact:
Bridgewater College
402 E. College Street
Bridgewater, VA 22812
Phone: (540) 828-5680 or (540) 828-5347
Fax: (540) 828-5716
hsla@bridgewater.edu
http://hsla.bridgewater.edu

BRITT FESTIVALS

The Britt Institute

Program Location: Jacksonville, Oregon

Subject Areas: Jazz and classical chamber music—history, theory, technique, and performance

Program Description: The Britt Institute is the educational arm of Britt Festivals, which presents classical, country, folk, jazz, pop, and world music concerts every summer on the estate of pioneer photographer Peter Britt in the historic gold rush town of Jacksonville. Summer program offerings include the Chamber Strings Camp, a 2-week string chamber music session with the Cavani String Quartet from the Cleveland Institute of Music; the Chamber Winds Camp, a

1-week woodwind session with Prairie Winds quintet from Chicago; and the Instrumental Jazz Camp, with a faculty comprised of major jazz educators from across the country. Students also attend performances at Britt Festivals, which in recent years have featured such artists as Marilyn Horne, Jean-Pierre Rampal, Chick Corea, and Wynton Marsalis.

Program Dates: Late June through mid-August

Duration of Program: 1–2 week sessions

Cost: $260–$350 per week for classes, additional $250–$350 per week for room and board

Eligibility: Musicians ages 14–19

Application Process: Audition tape and application that can be mailed or completed online

Application Deadline: April 1

Financial Aid Deadline: May 1

Average Number of Applicants: 350

Average Number of Participants: 150

Academic Credit: None available

Contact:
The Britt Institute
P.O. Box 1124
517 West 10th Street
Medford, OR 97501
Phone: (541) 779-0847, ext. 19
Fax: (541) 776-3712
education@brittfest.org
www.brittfestivals.org

Broadreach, Inc.

BROADREACH, INC.

Broadreach Insights

Program Location: Ecuador, Costa Rica, Panama, and Canada

Subject Areas: Each program has a different mix of activities that can include language study, rainforest ecology, marine mammal study, cultural immersion, community service project, wilderness adventure, low impact camping, hiking, sea kayaking, scuba, and leadership training

Program Description: International summer programs for students ages 17–21 that combine small groups and experiential adventure with academics, cultural immersion, homestays and community service. Each course is designed to have five phases in the following sequence: team building through challenging adventure activities; hands-on academic study; cultural immersion and exploration; a community service project; and a final adventure that allows time for reflection.

Program Dates: Sessions throughout the summer

Duration of Program: 5 weeks

Cost: $4,500–$5,899 (airfare not included)

Eligibility: Ages 17–21. Some trips require academic prerequisites such as language or science study.

Application Process: Application form, recent photo, $500 deposit

Application Deadline: Rolling admissions; students should apply early to be assured a spot

Academic Credit: High school and college credit available

Contact:
Broadreach Insights
P.O. Box 27076
Raleigh, NC 27611
Phone: (866) 946-4733
Fax: (919) 833-2129
insights@gobroadreach.com
www.broadreachinsights.com

Broadreach Summer Adventures for Teenagers

Program Location: Caribbean, Australia, Costa Rica, Egypt, Honduras, Ecuador, Galapagos Islands, Bahamas, Fiji, and the Solomon Islands

Subject Areas: Each program has a different mix of activities that can include SCUBA training and certification, sail training and certification, marine science, wilderness and outdoor adventure, leadership training, ecology studies, sea kayaking, whitewater rafting, hiking, rock climbing, surfing, waterskiing, community service, and cultural immersion

Program Description: Broadreach offers a variety of hands-on summer adventures for teens including SCUBA, sailing, marine biology, and wilderness programs all over the world. Small groups allow for a flexible, noncompetitive, and highly supportive atmosphere. No experience is necessary for many trips. Contact Broadreach for more details on program offerings.

Program Dates: Sessions throughout the summer

Duration of Program: 3–4 weeks

Cost: Varies by program

Eligibility: Students in grades 7–12; no experience is necessary for many trips

Application Deadline: Rolling admissions; students should apply early to be assured a spot

Application Process: Application form, recent photo, $500 deposit

Academic Credit: High school and college credit available on some programs

Contact:
Broadreach, Inc.
P.O. Box 27076
Raleigh, NC 27611
Phone: (888) 833-1907
Fax: (919) 833-2129
info@gobroadreach.com
www.gobroadreach.com

Brookfield Craft Center

BROOKFIELD CRAFT CENTER

Summer Workshop Series

Program Location: Brookfield, Connecticut

Subject Areas: Visual arts

Program Description: An arts program for teens and adults, offering a wide range of activities such as ceramics, fabric arts, jewelry making, blacksmithing, woodworking, glass arts, and pottery. Primarily weekend workshops.

Program Dates: June through August

Duration of Program: 2–3 days

Cost: $200

Application Process: Course registration

Application Deadline: Rolling admissions

Average Number of Participants: Limited by size of classes (6–12 students per class)

Contact:
Brookfield Craft Center
P.O. Box 122
Brookfield, CT 06804
Phone: (203) 775-4526
Fax: (203) 740-7815
brkfldcrft@aol.com
www.brookfieldcraftcenter.org

BROWN UNIVERSITY

Brown Pre-College Program

Program Location: Brown University in Providence, Rhode Island

Subject Areas: College preparation, liberal arts

Program Description: Pre-College courses are carefully selected from existing courses in a variety of academic disciplines in the Brown undergraduate curriculum or are newly created for the summer. Living on the Brown campus for 7 weeks gives students a great opportunity to experience college living and to learn how to apportion their time between academic work and social life. Students take 2 courses and receive grades for all coursework.

Program Dates: June–August

Duration of Program: 7 weeks

Cost: Pre-College Program: TBA. Special rate available for Rhode Island students.

Financial Aid: Dean's Scholarships awarded to outstanding students on the basis of accomplishment and financial need

Eligibility: Students who have completed their junior or senior year of high school; exceptional sophomores may also be considered

Application Process: Application and $40 application fee, academic transcripts, 300-word essay, one teacher's recommendation; TOEFL score for international students

Application Deadline: May 31

Academic Credit: College credit available

Focus Program

Program Location: Brown University in Providence, Rhode Island

Subject Areas: College preparation, liberal arts

Program Description: Offers shorter sessions, varying from one to four weeks in duration, and limited to one intensive course per session. Designed to turn students into self-directed learners, helping to prepare them for the challenges and responsibility of college work. While all Focus courses are noncredit, the final Course Performance Report provides a candid evaluation of the student's academic performance.

Program Dates: June–August

Duration of Program: 1–4 weeks

Cost:: Varies by course

Eligibility: Students who have completed at least their freshman year of high school

Application Process: Application and $40 application fee, academic transcripts, 300-word essay, one teacher's recommendation; TOEFL score for international students

Application Deadline: May 31 (Focus courses beginning in June); June 16 (Focus courses beginning in July)

Academic Credit: None available

Contact:
Brown University
Office of Summer Studies
133 Waterman Street
Providence, RI 02912-9120
Phone: (401) 863-7900
Fax: (401) 863-7908
www.brown.edu/Administration/
Summer_Studies/

BRUSH RANCH CAMPS

Program Location: New Mexico

Subject Areas: Outdoor adventure, sports, music, dance, art

Program Description: Each student takes part in a camp and chooses an individual program. Traditional, Trailblazer, Mountaineer, Adventure, and family camps are available.

Program Dates: Sessions throughout summer

Duration of Program: 1–8 weeks

Cost: $700–$5,600

Eligibility: Ages 6–15 (except for family programs)

Application Deadline: Rolling

Contact:
Brush Ranch Camps
P.O. Box 5759
Santa Fe, NM 87502-5759
Phone: (505) 757-8821
Fax: (505) 757-8822
brc@nmfiber.com
www.brushranchcamps.com

BRYN MAWR COLLEGE

Writing for College

Program Location: Bryn Mawr College in Bryn Mawr, Pennsylvania

Subject Areas: Writing

Program Description: This program prepares students to write for college-level courses. Students practice skills of discussion and analysis through the study of assigned texts, writing exercises, and peer review. In private tutorials, faculty members assist students in preparing a portfolio of finished essays, fiction, and poetry. Special seminars offer orientation to computer skills, the college admissions process, financial aid, and time management. Students live in Bryn Mawr dorms and have access to campus facilities.

Program Dates: Last week of June and first two weeks of July

Duration of Program: 3 weeks

Cost: $2,300 (includes tuition, room and board, and all books, supplies, field trips, and recreational activities)

Financial Aid: Limited aid is available; call or write for an application

Eligibility: College-bound females completing their sophomore, junior, or senior year of high school

Application Process: Transcript, recommendation from teacher or guidance counselor, writing sample, nonrefundable $35 application fee

Application Deadline: April 1, June 1

Average Number of Applicants: 65

Average Number of Participants: 30

Contact:
attn: Director, Writing for College
Bryn Mawr College
101 North Merion Avenue
Bryn Mawr, PA 19010-2899
Phone: (610) 896-1159
Fax: (610) 526-7353
writingforcollege@brynmawr.edu
www.brynmawr.edu

See also Summer Institute for the Gifted

BUCK'S ROCK PERFORMING AND CREATIVE ARTS CAMP

Program Location: New Milford, Connecticut

Subject Areas: Performing arts and creative arts

Program Description: Numerous offerings, including dance, glass blowing, metalsmithing, music, painting, recording, sculpture, theater, video, and writing

Program Dates: June 26 to August 17

Duration of Program: 4–8 weeks

Buck's Rock Performing and Creative Arts Camp

Cost: 4-week session: $4,660; 8-week session: $6,790

Eligibility: Ages 12–16

Application Process: Interview and deposit of $1,000

Application Deadline: Rolling admissions

Average Number of Applicants: 800

Average Number of Participants: 400

Contact:
59 Buck's Rock Road
New Milford, CT 06776
Phone: (860) 354-5030
Fax: (860) 354-1355
bucksrock@mindspring.com
www.bucksrockcamp.com

BURKLYN BALLET THEATRE

Program Location: Johnson, Vermont

Subject Areas: Ballet

Program Description: In this performance-based ballet program, dancers take 3 classes daily with international master teachers, and rehearse 4 hours each day for weekly performances in the 600-seat, state-of-the-art Dibden Center for the Arts. Dancers reside at Johnson State College in the safe, rural village of Johnson, Vermont. A 2-week performance experience at the Edinburgh Festival Fringe is also offered.

Burklyn Ballet Theatre

Program Dates: Main program: June 23–August 4, 2001; Edinburgh Festival: August 4–19, 2001

Duration of Program: 2-, 3-, 4-, and 6-week programs

Cost: $1,700–$3,600 (includes room and board)

Eligibility: Ages 12–25

Application Process: Contact the organization for more information.

Application Deadline: Rolling admissions

Average Number of Applicants: 1,200

Average Number of Participants: 175

Contact:
Burklyn Ballet Theatre
P.O. Box 302
Johnson, VT 05656
Phone: (732) 288-2660 or (802) 635-1390
burklyn@aol.com

CALIFORNIA CHICANO NEWS MEDIA ASSOCIATION

San Jose Urban Journalism Workshop for Minorities

Program Location: San Jose State University in San Jose, California

Subject Areas: Local news

Program Description: Students spend two weeks working with professional journalists from the San Jose Mercury News to produce a 12–16-page newspaper.

Program Dates: First half of July

Duration of Program: 2 weeks

Cost: No cost; room and board provided

Eligibility: High school juniors and seniors

Application Process: 2 essays, writing samples, transcript, 2 recommendations

Application Deadline: April or May

Average Number of Applicants: 27

Average Number of Participants: 17

Academic Credit: None available

Contact:
San Jose Urban Journalism Workshop for Minorities
c/o KALA/KLIU/KRTY Radio
750 Story Road
San Jose, CA 95132
Phone: (408) 293-8030
Fax: (408) 293-6124
RHMadrigal@yahoo.com
www.ccnma.org

CALIFORNIA COLLEGE OF ARTS AND CRAFTS

CCAC Pre-College Program

Program Location: Oakland, California

Subject Areas: Visual arts

Program Description: Provides an opportunity for high school students to study art in an art school setting. 12 studio options offered.

Program Dates: July 8–26, 2002

Duration of Program: 3 weeks

Cost: $1,075 (includes supplies, does not include housing)

Eligibility: Students who have completed the sophomore, junior, or senior year of high school.

Application Process: Application, high school transcript, and essay required; $100 tuition deposit is refundable until May 15, 2002

Application Deadline: April 8, 2002 (priority)

Average Number of Participants: Approximately 200

Academic Credit: 2 college credits available

Contact:
Summer Extended Education
5212 Broadway
Oakland, CA 94618
Phone: (800) 447-1ART or (415) 703-9523
Fax: (415) 703-9539
www.ccac-art.edu

CALIFORNIA STATE SUMMER SCHOOL FOR THE ARTS

Program Location: California Institute of the Arts in Valencia, California

Subject Areas: Film and video, creative writing, visual arts, animation, theater, music, dance

Program Description: Four weeks of exploration, discovery, and hard work designed to unleash students' creative power. Intensive training from professionals in music, theater, video and film, visual arts, creative writing, dance, and animation. Participants are named California Arts Scholars and receive the California Arts Scholar Medallion in local ceremonies. All students live in a dormitory on the 60-acre CalArts campus.

Program Dates: July 14 to August 11 (2001 dates)

Duration of Program: 4 weeks

Cost: $1,445 (in-state residents); $3,445 (out-of-state residents). Includes room and board.

Financial Aid: Available based on demonstrated financial need. Aid is restricted to California residents and to first-time attendees.

Eligibility: California residents enrolled in grades 8–12 may apply to CSSSA. Students from outside of California may also apply; a limited number are admitted each year.

Application Process: Application form, artistic assignments (vary by discipline), 2 recommendations, $20 application fee

Application Deadline: February 28 (2001 deadline)

Average Number of Applicants: 1,300

Average Number of Participants: 500

Academic Credit: College credit available

Contact:
California State Summer School for the Arts
P.O. Box 1077
Sacramento, CA 95812-1077
Phone: (916) 227-9444
Fax: (916) 227-9455
application@csssa.org
www.csssa.org

California State Summer School for the Arts

Calvin College

CALVIN COLLEGE

Entrada Scholars Program

Program Location: Calvin College in Grand Rapids, Michigan

Subject Areas: College preparation for ethnic minorities

Program Description: Students are enrolled and earn credit in regular college courses such as history, biology, political science, or sociology. Classes meet each morning, Monday through Friday, followed by less formal afternoon sessions, which provide instruction in how to study for college-level academics. Evenings are filled with study time, small group meetings, and many exciting and challenging activities. A true college experience.

Program Dates: June 23–July 20

Duration of Program: 4 weeks

Cost: Full scholarships provided, covering tuition, room and board, books, supplies, and activities. Students must pay $50 fee to confirm enrollment.

Eligibility: Ethnic minority students who are currently enrolled in their junior or senior year of high school and have a B average or better

Application Process: Written application, high school transcript, written recommendations, ACT or SAT scores (if available), college-administered placement test (if needed to complete the application process), telephone or personal interview

Application Deadline: April 1

Average Number of Applicants: 50

Average Number of Participants: 35

Academic Credit: College credit available

Contact:
Entrada Scholars Program
Calvin College
3201 Burton Street SE
Grand Rapids, MI 49546
Phone: (800) 688-0122 or (616) 957-6106
Fax: (616) 957-8551
admissions@calvin.edu
www.calvin.edu

CAMBRIDGE COLLEGE PROGRAMME LLC

Cambridge College Programme

Program Location: Cambridge University in Cambridge, England

Subject Areas: Travel and study abroad; British history; 33 academic courses, including British Intelligence: The Art of Espionage, Psychology & Law, Philosophy: The Nature & Destiny of Human Beings, Quantum Physics, Egyptology: Famous Discoveries by British Archaeologists, Psychology: The Journey Inwards, Drama: Basic Acting Techniques, and more

Program Description: Academic and cultural enrichment for teenagers. Three 15-hour courses given by British professors. British cultural history course required for all. Students pick two additional courses from 33 offerings. Supervision by Cambridge University graduate students. Sports, movies, plays, concerts, dancing, open-top bus tours, and other activities in the evenings. Trips to Stonehenge, Bath, Stratford-Upon-Avon (including a play), Ely Cathedral, Warwick Castle. Trips to London to see plays, Tower of London, National Gallery, Covent Garden, Buckingham Palace, Cabinet War Rooms, Harrod's, and more. Additional activities include James Bond party, talent show, and barbecue. Optional: SAT review, golf lessons, one-week trip to Paris.

Program Dates: July 18–August 7; August 7–13 in Paris

Duration of Program: 3 weeks (4 weeks with Paris extension)

Cost: $4,975 (includes room and board); additional non-refundable $95 application fee

Financial Aid: None available

Eligibility: Bright teenagers

Application Process: Request brochure containing application form

Application Deadline: Rolling

Average Number of Applicants: 409

Average Number of Participants: 388

Academic Credit: Submit syllabi and evaluations to schools individually for consideration

Contact:
The Cambridge College Programme
John Hancock Building
175 E. Delaware Place, Suite 5518
Chicago, IL 60611
Phone: (312) 787-7477
Fax: (312) 988-7268
MKSCom@concentric.net

CAMBRIDGE UNIVERSITY

See Cambridge College Programme LLC; Musiker Discovery Programs; OxBridge Academic Programs

CAMP COURAGEOUS OF IOWA

Volunteer Program

Program Location: Pictured Rocks area of Jones County, Iowa, five miles southeast of Monticello

Subject Areas: Community service

Program Description: Camp Courageous, open year-round, is a recreational and care facility for individuals with physical or mental disabilities. The camp asks for volunteer counselors who are patient, energetic, and unselfish and who enjoy working with people. Counselors assist in feeding, dressing, and toileting campers and in guiding them through various athletic and artistic activities.

Program Dates: Mid-May through mid-August

Cost: None

Financial Aid: Volunteers can earn a stipend of $25 per week plus room and board

Eligibility: Ages 16–adult

Application Process: Written application, 3 references, interview by phone or in-person

Application Deadline: Rolling

Academic Credit: None available

Contact:
Camp Courageous
12007 190th Street
P.O. Box 418
Monticello, IA 52310
Phone: (319) 465-5916
Fax: (319) 465-5919
www.campcourageous.org

CAMP ENCORE/CODA

Upper Camp

Program Location: 80-acre site on Stearns Pond in Sweden, Maine

Subject Areas: Music (classical, jazz, rock, pop, theater), outdoor activities

Program Description: Students participate in orchestras, wind ensembles, jazz and rock bands, choral music, and chamber music. Private lessons as well as classes in theory, history, and conducting; frequent concerts. Full waterfront and sports program, active theater, and arts and crafts. Staff members are a combination of undergraduates, graduate students, and professional teachers. Same family ownership since 1950.

Program Dates: 2 sessions: June–July and July–August

Duration of Program: 3½ or 7 weeks

Cost: $3,100 (3½ weeks); $5,400 (7 weeks). Includes room and board.

Eligibility: Students finishing grades 7–11, intermediate and advanced levels only

Application Process: Application, placement tape (see application for tape requirements), personal statement, recommendation, deposit required

Application Deadline: Rolling admissions

Average Number of Participants: 100 (Upper Camp only)

Contact:
Camp Encore/Coda
32 Grassmere Road
Brookline, MA 02467
Phone: (617) 325-1541
Fax: (617) 325-7278
jamie@encore-coda.com
www.encore-coda.com

CAPITOL REGION EDUCATION COUNCIL AND WESLEYAN UNIVERSITY

Center for Creative Youth

Program Location: Wesleyan University in Middletown, Connecticut

Capitol Region Education Council and Wesleyan University

Subject Areas: Arts: creative writing, theater/musical theater, filmmaking, photography, instrumental/vocal music, dance, visual arts, technical theater

Program Description: Residential arts program on the campus of Wesleyan University. Taught by working professional artists along with guest artists and artists-in-residence. Students benefit from performing opportunities and exposure to a wide range of concerts, lectures, and performances.

Program Dates: Late June–July

Duration of Program: 5 weeks

Cost: $3,650 (includes room and board)

Financial Aid: Available

Eligibility: Ages 14–18, grades 10–12

Application Process: Application, autobiographical essay, 2 recommendations, audition/interview

Application Deadline: March 1, 2002

Average Number of Applicants: 250

Average Number of Participants: 180

Contact:
Wesleyan University
Center for Creative Youth
350 High Street
Middletown, CT 06459
Phone: (860) 685-3307
Fax: (860) 685-3311
ccy@wesleyan.edu

CARLETON COLLEGE

Summer Writing Program

Program Location: Carleton College in Northfield, Minnesota

Subject Areas: Writing

Program Description: Intensive writing instruction. Emphasizing a writing process approach, the program helps students to learn to compose academic papers that are similar to

Carleton College

those they will write in college. Classes are small and intimate, designed to encourage all students to become active participants in the learning process. Students read both contemporary and traditional literature and are given written evaluations of their three main papers.

Program Dates: July 7–26

Duration of Program: 3 weeks

Cost: $1,600 (includes room and board)

Financial Aid: Available (April 1 deadline)

Eligibility: Rising seniors

Application Process: Registration form, writing sample, transcript

Application Deadline: May 1

Average Number of Participants: 85

Academic Credit: College credit available (6 Carleton credit hours)

Contact:
Carleton College
Summer Writing Program
One N. College Street
Northfield, MN 55057
Phone: (507) 646-4038
Fax: (507) 646-4540
summer@carleton.edu
www.carleton.edu/campus/SAP

CARMEL VALLEY TENNIS CAMP

Program Location: Carmel Valley, California

Subject Areas: Tennis

Program Description: Residential camp focusing on tennis skills and match strategy. Four hours of tennis instruction per day in small groups along with additional match play. Daytime activities include swimming, climbing wall and ropes course, basketball, sand volleyball, games, and arts and crafts. Evening activities include talent shows, team games, game shows, campfires, and dances. Weekend field trips.

Program Dates: Eight sessions throughout June, July, and August

Duration of Program: 1- and 2-week sessions

Cost: Call for rates

Eligibility: Coed, ages 10–17, all skill levels

Application Deadline: No deadline, but programs usually fill up by May

Average Number of Participants: 52 during each 2-week program

Contact:
Carmel Valley Tennis Camp
20805 Cachagua Road
Carmel Valley, CA 93924
Phone: (831) 659-2615
Fax: (831) 659-2840
cvtc1@aol.com
www.carmelvalleytenniscamp.com

CARNEGIE MELLON UNIVERSITY

Pre-College Programs

Program Location: Carnegie Mellon University in Pittsburgh, Pennsylvania

Subject Areas: Programs in architecture, art, design, drama, music; advanced placement/early admission track in engineering, sciences, and the humanities

Program Description: Six-week program offering an opportunity to earn college credit, meet people from all over the country, and enjoy special recreational activities.

Program Dates: End of June through first week of August

Duration of Program: 6 weeks

Cost: TBA

Financial Aid: Available

Eligibility: Academically and/or artistically oriented students ages 16 and older

Application Process: Contact Office of Pre-College Programs for specific program application requirements.

Application Deadline: May 1

Average Number of Applicants: 800

Average Number of Participants: 450

Academic Credit: High school and college credit available

Contact:
CMU Office of Admissions
Pre-College Programs
5000 Forbes Avenue
Pittsburgh, PA 15213
Phone: (412) 268-2082
Fax: (412) 268-8070
www.cmu.edu/enrollment/pre-college

CATHOLIC UNIVERSITY OF AMERICA

Capitol Classic
Summer Debate Institute

Program Location: Catholic University of America in Washington, DC

Subject Areas: Debate, research, speech

Program Description: Offers concentrated instruction in debate at the novice, junior varsity, and varsity level. Instruction includes both lectures and hands-on experience. Lectures focus on debate theory such as

counterplans, critiques, topicality, conditionality, and fiat. Lab groups focus on skill acquisition such as research, argument and brief construction, speaking drills, and plenty of practice debates.

Program Dates: June 23–July 13, 2002

Duration of Program: 2 or 3 weeks

Cost: $1,295–$1,995

Application Deadline: May 15

Chamber Music Workshop

Program Location: Catholic University of America in Washington, DC

Subject Areas: Chamber music; violin, viola, cello

Program Description: Students form string quartets (two violins, viola, and cello) and prepare a complete work for performance at the end of the week. Activities include primary coaching sessions and rehearsal, with some lecture and discussion, plus a master class midweek.

Program Dates: June 24–28, 2002

Duration of Program: 1 week

Cost: $250

Application Process: Audition required (either in person or on tape)

Application Deadline: February 15, 2002

Average Number of Participants: 16

Academic Credit: None available

College Courses for High School Students

Program Location: Catholic University of America in Washington, DC

Subject Areas: College liberal arts and fine arts curriculum

Program Description: Students select two college freshman-level courses from the university's regular summer session curriculum.

Program Dates: May–June, June–August

Duration of Program: 5 or 6 weeks

Cost: Approximately $3,180–$4,240 ($530 per credit hour)

Eligibility: Rising high school seniors with a B average or better; exceptional rising high school juniors will also be considered

Application Process: Transcript and letter of recommendation from counselor are required. Online application available on website.

Experiences in Architecture

Program Location: Catholic University of America in Washington, DC

Subject Areas: Architecture

Program Description: A three-week intensive workshop designed to expose students to both the academic and professional arenas of architecture. Students visit architects' offices and construction sites, and explore subjects as diverse as landscape design, building technology, urban design, history, and theory.

Program Dates: June 17–July 5 or July 8–July 26

Duration of Program: 3 weeks

Cost: $915–$1,035

Application Deadline: Rolling admissions, but enrollment is limited

Average Number of Participants: 16

Eye on Engineering

Program Location: Catholic University of America in Washington, DC

Subject Areas: Engineering

Program Description: Exposes high school students to the world of engineering. Program components include educational information, hands-on research experience, and a taste of campus life.

Program Dates: July 7–12

Duration of Program: 6 days

Cost: $300

Application Deadline: Rolling admissions, but enrollment is limited

Average Number of Participants: 75

Media and Video Production Workshop

Program Location: Catholic University of America in Washington, DC

Subject Areas: Photography, digital photography, multimedia

Program Description: Exposes high school students to the basics of multimedia production, including shooting, sound recording, and editing video, while providing a historical perspective on film and entertainment.

Program Dates: July 8–19, 2002

Duration of Program: 1 or 2 weeks

Cost: $300–$500

Application Deadline: Rolling admissions, but enrollment is limited

Average Number of Participants: 16

Opera Institute for Young Singers

See The Washington Opera

Contact:
CUA
Office of Summer Sessions
330 Pangborn Hall
Washington, DC 20064
Phone: (202) 319-5257
Fax: (202) 319-6725
cua-summers@cua.edu
summer.cua.edu

Center for American Archeology

CENTER FOR AMERICAN ARCHEOLOGY

Archeological Field School

Program Location: Kampsville, Illinois

Subject Areas: Archeology

Program Description: An opportunity to explore the next steps of archeological inquiry while working in the field, working with collections, and assisting with research. Participants learn analytical methods and data recording, description, and manipulation.

Program Dates: July through early August

Duration of Program: 1–5 weeks

Cost: $500 and up

Eligibility: Junior high and high school students

Application Process: Deposit of 30 percent of tuition along with registration form

Application Deadline: 2 weeks prior to start of program

Academic Credit: High school and college credit available

Contact:
Center for American Archeology
Dept. A
P.O. Box 366
Kampsville, IL 62053
Phone: (618) 653-4316
Fax: (618) 653-4232
caa@caa-archeology.org
www.caa-archeology.org

CENTER FOR CROSS-CULTURAL STUDY

Summer in Seville

Program Location: Seville, Spain

Subject Areas: Spanish language, cultural immersion

Program Description: Students with beginner, intermediate, or advanced Spanish skills can increase their proficiency through CCCS's language classes. Speaking ability is assessed on-site during orientation. Homestays, excursions, and social events help introduce students to Spanish culture.

Program Dates: 2 sessions: June 3–June 28, 2001 and July 1–July 25, 2001

Duration of Program: 3½ or 7 weeks

Cost: $1,935 for 3½-week session; $3,585 for 7-week session

Financial Aid: None

Eligibility: Ages 16 and up

Application Process: Registration form, transcripts, one recommendation, $30 application fee

Application Deadline: Session 1: April 15; Session 2: May 15

Average Number of Applicants: 170

Center for Cross-Cultural Study

Average Number of Participants: 140

Academic Credit: 3–6 college credits

Contact:
Center for Cross-Cultural Study
446 Main Street
Amherst, MA 01002-2314
Phone: (800) 377-2621
Fax: (413) 256-1968
YDN@cccs.com
www.cccs.com

CENTER FOR CULTURAL INTERCHANGE

Independent Homestay;

International Youth Camps;

Language School Program

Program Location: Independent Homestay: Argentina, Australia, Chile, Ecuador, France, Germany, Ghana, India, Ireland, Italy, Japan, Mexico, New Zealand, Poland, Spain, Sweden, Switzerland, Thailand, Turkey, United Kingdom, Uruguay.

International Youth Camps: Switzerland and Spain.

Language School Program: Ecuador, France, Germany, Italy, Mexico, Spain; Junior Language

School Programs (ages 14–16) offered in Spain and France.

Subject Areas: Language, homestays, cultural immersion, outdoor activities

Program Description: Independent Homestay: Students and adults who desire full immersion in the culture and language of a particular country live in a host home where they are treated as full members of the family. International Youth Camps: Students take language classes that are appropriate to their ability level in addition to participating in sports such as horseback riding, canoeing, and camping. Language School Program: CCI offers fun language study and cultural opportunities and places students with a host family.

Program Dates: Independent Homestay and Language School Programs: year-round availability; International Youth Camps: June–July

Duration of Program: Independent Homestay: 1–4 weeks; International Youth Camps: 2–3 weeks; Language School Program: 3 or more weeks

Cost: Independent Homestay: $870–$1,400; International Youth Camps: $2,500–$3,500; Language School Program: $1,690–$2,800

Eligibility: Independent Homestay: ages 15 and up; International Youth Camps: ages 10–17; Language School Program: ages 14 and up, no language experience necessary—classes are appropriate to participant's level

Application Process: Pre-application available on website.

Application Deadline: 6 weeks prior to desired departure

Financial Aid: Some aid is available

Average Number of Participants: Independent Homestay: 160; Language School Program: 160

Academic Credit: Depends on U.S. school

Contact:
Center for Cultural Interchange
17 North Second Avenue
St. Charles, IL 60174
Phone: (888) 227-6231
Fax: (630) 377-2307
info@cci-exchange.com
www.cci-exchange.com

CERAN LINGUA

Ceran Junior

Program Location: Belgium, Spain, United Kingdom

Subject Areas: Language study: French, Spanish, Dutch, German, English

Program Description: Offers intensive residential language courses for students. Small classes (maximum 9 students). Highly educated teachers help students practice what they have learned during mealtimes, breaks, and social activities.

Program Dates: June–August

Duration of Program: 2–4 weeks

Cost: $850/week (includes room and board)

Financial Aid: None available

Eligibility: Ages 10–18, all proficiency levels welcome

Application Process: Send registration to contact address below.

Application Deadline: 3 months before program start date

Average Number of Applicants: 1,500

Average Number of Participants: 1,500

Contact:
Languagency
56 Main Street, Suite 207
Northampton, MA 01060
Phone: (413) 584-0334
Fax: (413) 584-3046
eblangcli@aol.com
www.ceran.com

Championship Debate Enterprises

CHAMPIONSHIP DEBATE ENTERPRISES

Lincoln-Douglas and Extemp Institute;

Policy Debate Institute

Program Location: Flagstaff, Arizona

Subject Areas: Debate, extemporaneous speaking, student congress

Program Description: Both the Lincoln-Douglas and Policy Debate institutes are geared toward students who are accustomed to debating at a highly competitive level. Alumni have won 19 national championships and have enrolled at Harvard, Yale, Princeton, Georgetown, Stanford, Berkeley, and Oxford.

Program Dates: July 1–16

Duration of Program: 15 days

Cost: $1,125

Financial Aid Deadline: April 30

Eligibility: Grades 8–12

Application Process: $85 application fee

Application Deadline: First come, first served, but camps are usually full by end of April

Average Number of Applicants: 75 for Lincoln-Douglas; 30 for Policy Debate; 30 for Extemp

Average Number of Participants: 60 for Lincoln-Douglas; 30 for Policy Debate; 25 for Extemp

Academic Credit: None available

Contact:
CDE
attn: William H. Bennett
P.O. Box Z
Taos, NM 87571
Phone: (505) 751-0514
Fax: (505) 751-9788
bennett@laplaza.org
www.cdedebate.org

CHOATE ROSEMARY HALL

Choate Rosemary Hall Summer Session;

English Language Institute;

John F. Kennedy Institute in Government;

The Writing Project;

Study Abroad

Program Location: Wallingford, Connecticut; Paris, France; Spain; Beijing, China

Subject Areas: Academics, science, writing, English, government, homestays abroad

Program Description: Summer Session: More than 80 courses in 10 departments, with an average class size of only 12 students. Students are fully integrated into all athletic, extracurricular, and social activities on campus. English Language Institute (ELI): Students develop their English language skills through writing, speaking, listening, and reading. JFK Institute: Students take 3 courses (the formation of political ideas; the foundation and workings of American government; current domestic issues) and get the chance to meet political leaders during a trip to Washington, DC. The Writing Project: Intensive 2-week course with daily writing and reading assignments and an introduction to computer-assisted writing. Study Abroad: Students live with host families in Paris or Spain, or at a cultural center in Beijing.

Choate Rosemary Hall

Program Dates: June–July

Duration of Program: 2, 4, or 5 weeks

Cost: Varies by program

Financial Aid: Need-based aid is available

Eligibility: Students completing grades 9–12 (programs are also available for students completing grades 6–8; contact Choate for more information)

Application Deadline: May 15

Average Number of Applicants: 530

Average Number of Participants: 500

Academic Credit: High school credit available

Contact:
Choate Rosemary Hall Summer Session
Wallingford, CT 06492
Phone: (203) 697-2365
Fax: (203) 697-2519
www.choate.edu

CHRIS WALLER'S SUMMER GYMNASTICS JAM

Program Location: University of California at Santa Barbara

Subject Areas: Men's and women's gymnastics

Program Description: Up to six hours of training per day, including scheduled event rotations and event-choice workouts. The GymJam staff includes USAG Safety Certified coaches, Olympic coaches, National Team coaches, U.S. Olympic Training Center coaches, and Olympians. Counselors are responsible for no more than 15 campers at a time. Training is at the University of California at Santa Barbara, and housing is at the Tropicana Gardens student residence suites (five minutes from the gym). Recreational activities include: the zip line, rock wall, ropes course, swimming, skit night, beach trip, scavenger hunt, and more.

Program Dates: June–July

Duration of Program: 1 week per session

Cost: $595 (residential); $395 (commuter). Discounts may be available for multiple sessions, siblings, or teams. Before May 1, personal checks will be accepted as payment for all camp fees.

Eligibility: Ages 9 and older, all levels from beginner to elite. Must have medical insurance.

Application Process: Registration form, $125 nonrefundable deposit, medical release form

Application Deadline: Rolling admissions, May 1 priority

Contact:
Chris Waller's Summer Gymnastics Jam
11664 National Boulevard, Suite 365
Los Angeles, CA 90064
Phone: (888) 892-6131
gymjammers@aol.com
http://members.nbci.com/gymjam/index.htm

CHRISTCHURCH SCHOOL

Summer Programs on the River

Program Location: Christchurch School in Christchurch, Virginia

Subject Areas: Crew, sailing, marine science, study skills

Program Description: Programs offered include: sailing camp, crew camp, academic skill-building courses, and marine science courses. Academic skill-building courses consist of math skills, how-to-study skills, and writing skills, and are designed to reinforce and broaden a student's knowledge and academic background. Students live in air-conditioned dormitories on the 125-acre campus on the Rappahannock River.

Program Dates: June 23–July 29

Duration of Program: 1–4 weeks

Cost: $540–$2,200 (includes room and board)

Financial Aid: None available

Eligibility: Ages 10–17

Application Process: Application (available on website)

Application Deadline: Late April

Average Number of Applicants: 200

Average Number of Participants: 175

Academic Credit: None available

Contact:
Christchurch School
Summer Programs on the River
Rt. 33
Christchurch, VA 23031
Phone: (804) 758-2306
Fax: (804) 758-4780
admissions@christchurchva.com
www.christchurchschool.org

COLGATE UNIVERSITY

See Eastern U.S. Music Camp, Inc.

COLLEGE VISITS

Program Location: Tours to various campuses

Subject Areas: College tours

Program Description: Organizes tours to colleges and universities throughout the U.S. Participants have the opportunity to visit several schools in one convenient trip, experience college life firsthand without having to individually coordinate the visit, and become actively involved in getting accurate and reliable information. Arranges meetings with admission representatives, campus tours, meals, transportation, lodging, and recreational activities.

Program Dates: Various

Duration of Program: 1 week

Cost: Various

Financial Aid: Available

Eligibility: High school sophomores, juniors, seniors

Application Process: Registration form

Application Deadline: 30 days before tour start date

Average Number of Applicants: 450

Average Number of Participants: 400

Academic Credit: None available

College Visits (University of North Carolina—Chapel Hill)

Contact:
College Visits
207 East Bay Street, Suite 304
Charleston, SC 29401
Phone: (843) 853-8149
Fax: (843) 577-2813
cvisits@aol.com
www.college-visits.com

COLORADO COLLEGE

Summer Session for High School Students

Program Location: Colorado College in Colorado Springs, Colorado; international locations

Subject Areas: College preparation; liberal arts and sciences: anthropology, art history/studio, Asian studies, biology, chemistry, classics, Chinese, comparative literature, computer science, dance, economics, education, English, environmental science, film, geology, German, history, Italian, Japanese, mathematics, music, natural sciences, neuroscience, physics, philosophy, political science, psychology, religion, Russian, sociology, Spanish, Southwest studies, women's studies

Program Description: Tailored to qualified high school students looking ahead to college. Students in good academic standing may register for any undergraduate Summer Session course at Colorado College. Students who participate fully in the academic life of the College are housed independently of undergraduate and graduate students and are expected to observe special hours. After-class activities, such as hiking, going to movies, visiting tourist hot spots, etc., are planned on request, but participation is not required.

Program Dates: June 10–August 9

Duration of Program: 3–9 weeks

Cost: $1,520 for 3 weeks; room and board approximately $730 for 3 weeks

Financial Aid: None available

Eligibility: High school students looking ahead to college

Application Process: Application, application fee, teacher/counselor recommendation

Application Deadline: Rolling, applying early recommended due to limited class size

Average Number of Applicants: 45

Average Number of Participants: 30

Academic Credit: College credit available

Contact:
Summer Session
Colorado College
14 E. Cache la Poudre Street
Colorado Springs, CO 80903
Phone: (719) 389-6655
Fax: (719) 389-6955
summer@coloradocollege.edu
www.coloradocollege.edu/summersession

COLUMBIA COLLEGE CHICAGO

High School Summer Institute

Program Location: Columbia College Chicago in Chicago, Illinois

Subject Areas: Arts and communications

Program Description: A full slate of classes in the performing, visual, media, and communication arts are offered. All classes taught by Columbia College Chicago faculty.

Program Dates: July–August

Duration of Program: 5 weeks

Cost: $150/credit hour

Financial Aid: Available, May 1 deadline

Eligibility: Students who have completed grades 10–12

Application Process: Registration with payment

Application Deadline: July 1

Average Number of Applicants: 500

Average Number of Participants: 500

Academic Credit: College credit available

Contact:
Columbia College Chicago
High School Summer Institute
600 S. Michigan Ave.
Chicago, IL 60605
Phone: (312) 344-7134
Fax: (312) 344-8024
summerinstitute@popmail.colum.edu
www.colum.edu

COLUMBIA COLLEGE, LEADERSHIP INSTITUTE

Entrepreneurship Camp

Program Location: Columbia College in Columbia, South Carolina

Subject Areas: Leadership training, career development, entrepreneurship

Program Description: This summer camp is structured to provide young women from around the globe with the skills and tools necessary to own and manage a small business. Participants develop and present a business plan to a team of financial leaders and women business owners. Interaction with successful women business owners allows participants to gain insight into small business management and build effective problem-solving and decision-making skills.

Program Dates: July 20–28 (2001 dates)

Duration of Program: 9 days

Cost: $525–$575 (includes room and board)

Eligibility: Girls entering grades 10–12 who have demonstrated leadership ability

Application Process: Application form, recommendation

Application Deadline: March 9 (2001 date)

Academic Credit: None available

21st Century Leaders

Program Location: Columbia College in Columbia, South Carolina

Subject Areas: Leadership training, career development, entrepreneurship

Program Description: Residential summer conference designed to empower high school girls through leadership training, career development and personal and professional growth. High achieving students meet and work with leaders to strengthen their skills, define career opportunities and build their self confidence.

Program Dates: July 15–20 (2001 dates)

Duration of Program: 6 days

Cost: $475–$550 (includes room and board)

Eligibility: Girls entering grades 11 or 12 who have demonstrated leadership ability

Application Process: Application form, recommendation

Application Deadline: March 9 (2001 date)

Academic Credit: None available

Contact:
Center for Women Entrepreneurs
Columbia College
1301 Columbia College Drive
Columbia, South Carolina 29203
Phone: (803) 786-3108
Fax: (803) 786-3375
www.columbiacollegesc.edu/leadinst/leader.html

COLUMBIA UNIVERSITY

Columbia Summer
Programs for High School Students

Program Location: Columbia University in New York City

Subject Areas: An array of study options, including biology, biomedical engineering, physics, politics, computer programming, math, leadership, law, theater studies, urban studies, visual arts, writing, and college prep

Program Description: Classes from Monday–Thursday, 9:30–4:30, with a minimum of four hours of instruction daily. Time is allotted each day for independent study and tutorials, private meetings with instructors, and use of Columbia's libraries, gym, and pool facilities. Grades are not assigned; extensive evaluations of students' work are given throughout and at end of term. Students may choose to live in supervised Columbia dorms.

Program Dates: Session I: July 1–26, 2002; Session II: July 29–August 16, 2002

Duration of Program: Two 4-week sessions

Cost: Residential: $3,725 plus fees and optional expenses ranging from $100 to $930. Commuter: $2,275 plus fees ranging from $100 to $350.

Financial Aid: Financial assistance awarded only to those students who are financially disadvantaged. In order to qualify for assistance, economic need must be demonstrable and significant. Funding is limited; in years past, approximately 35 students per year were awarded assistance.

Eligibility: Highly motivated students entering grades 9–12

Application Process: Completed application form (online or by mail), official transcript, personal statement, $35 nonrefundable application fee, signed behavior standards consent form, two letters of recommendation. Certain programs may have additional requirements (i.e. writing samples, interview).

Application Deadline: May 8, 2002

Academic Credit: No college credit available. Upon completion of program, students receive an official University Statement of Attendance.

Contact:
Columbia University High School Programs
303 Lewisohn Hall
Mail Code 4110
2970 Broadway
New York, NY 10027-6902
Phone: (212) 854-9699
Fax: (212) 854-5861
sp-info@columbia.edu
www.ce.columbia.edu/hs

COLUMBIA UNIVERSITY BIOSPHERE 2

Exploring Earth, Life & the Summer Sky

Program Location: Biosphere 2 Center in Arizona's Sonoran Desert

Subject Areas: Earth science and astronomy

Program Description: Students investigate the following questions: Will we carry our future environment into space? How do we use life on Earth to study the possibilities of life elsewhere in the universe? Participants study how the geology and adaptations of life on Earth give important insights into how life might evolve and exist on other planets. Using the 24-inch research-grade telescope and electronic camera at the Biosphere 2 Observatory, students capture their own images of the moon, Mars, comets, asteroids, and galaxies.

Program Dates: July–August

Duration of Program: 4 weeks

Cost: Approximately $3,995 (includes room and board and transportation to and from Tucson, AZ airport)

Financial Aid: Limited need-based aid available to eligible applicants; downloadable Financial Aid Form available on website

Eligibility: Rising high school juniors and seniors and rising college freshmen; minimum 3.0 GPA is required

Application Process: Transcript, teacher recommendation, application (available on website)

Average Number of Applicants: 200

Average Number of Participants: 50

Academic Credit: Certificate of Completion from Columbia University

Contact:
Columbia University
Biosphere 2 Center
32540 S. Biosphere Road
Oracle, AZ 85623
Phone: (800) 992-4603
Fax: (520) 896-6361
admissions@bio2.columbia.edu
www.bio2.edu/education

COMUNICARE

Study and Share

Program Location: San José, Costa Rica

Subject Areas: Cultural immersion, Spanish language study, volunteer work

Program Description: Comunicare aims to expose participants to both the cultural and geographical diversity of Central America. In the mornings, students attend Spanish classes or lectures, and in the afternoons they engage in

Comunicare

volunteer work or cultural activities. Weekends include field trips to the former capital of Cartago, the rain forest of Monteverde, and the Puerto Viejo and Jacó beaches.

Program Dates: Mid-June through mid-August

Duration of Program: 2–4 weeks

Cost: $1,250–$1,800

Eligibility: Ages 15–19

Application Process: Application forms, preferably submitted by high school counselor, and $150 deposit (deposit is counted toward the program's fee)

Application Deadline: April

Average Number of Applicants: 30

Average Number of Participants: 20

Academic Credit: None available

Contact:
Comunicare
SB #119, P.O. Box 025292
4684 NW 69th Avenue
Miami, FL 33166
Phone: (506) 224-4473
Fax: (506) 224-4473
comunica@sol.racsa.co.cr
www.comunicare.co.cr

Program Dates: Sessions in June, July, and August

Duration of Program: 1, 2, or 4 weeks

Cost: $470 (1 week); $950 (2 weeks); $2,125 (4 weeks)

Financial Aid: Available, March 1 deadline

Eligibility: Ages 7–18; programs available for all levels of language proficiency

Application Process: Application available online

Application Deadline: Rolling admissions

Average Number of Applicants: 6,100

Average Number of Participants: 6,100

Academic Credit: High school or college credit awarded for 4-week sessions

Contact:
Concordia Language Villages
901 South Eighth Street
Moorhead, MN 56562
Phone: (218) 299-4544 or (800) 222-4750
Fax: (218) 299-3807
clv@cord.edu
www.ConcordiaLanguageVillages.org

CONCORDIA COLLEGE

Concordia Language Villages

Program Location: Different locations in Minnesota

Subject Areas: Language and culture study

Program Description: Concordia Language Villages encourage young people's enthusiasm for and interest in other languages and cultures through various hands-on activities involving the target language and culture. Sessions in 12 world languages are offered: Chinese, Danish, English, Finnish, French, German, Japanese, Korean, Norwegian, Russian, Spanish, and Swedish.

Concordia College

CONGRESSIONAL YOUTH LEADERSHIP COUNCIL

Global Young Leaders Conference

Program Location: First half of each program held in Washington, DC, and second half held in New York City

Subject Areas: Global leadership, international relations

Program Description: GYLC offers top high school students from around the world an opportunity to interact with powerful leaders, influential diplomats, and international businesspeople. Students engage in global leadership development activities by role-playing diplomats who represent various countries. They also participate in small group discussions focusing on global issues, a Global Summit simulation held at the United Nations, a peace and security simulation, and a trade activity.

Program Dates: Four separate sessions throughout the summer

Duration of Program: 12 days

Cost: $2,065 (summer 2001 tuition for U.S. students); $2,095 (summer 2001 tuition for international students)

Financial Aid: Limited number of scholarships available, based on financial need, scholastic merit, leadership achievements, and other factors. Call the Admissions Office at (202) 777-4173, or email them at finaid@gylc.org.

Eligibility: High school students from the U.S. and around the world who have shown outstanding qualities in academics, leadership, and citizenship may apply.

Application Process: Competitive admissions through nominations from educators and GYLC alumni, and through tough, college-like admissions process. Students may contact CYLC to obtain application forms.

Contact:
Congressional Youth Leadership Council—GYLC
1110 Vermont Avenue, NW, Suite 320
Washington, DC 20005
Phone: (202) 777-4173
Fax: (202) 638-5218
admissions@gylc.org
www.gylc.org

Congressional Youth Leadership Council—
Global Young Leaders Conference

Congressional Youth Leadership Council—National Young Leaders Conference

National Young Leaders Conference

Program Location: Washington, DC

Subject Areas: Leadership, government

Program Description: A unique leadership development program that offers top high school students from around the country and the world an opportunity to learn from today's leaders. Students meet with the men and women who shape our laws and policies. They also participate in group discussions; small group seminars on leading topics; and detailed simulations which involve an international crisis, a session of Congress, and a Supreme Court case. Carefully selected faculty advisors supervise and instruct students.

Program Dates: Four separate sessions throughout the summer

Duration of Program: 11 days

Cost: $1,745 (summer 2001 tuition)

Financial Aid: Limited number of scholarships available, based on financial need, scholastic merit, leadership achievements, and other factors. Call the Office of Financial Aid at (202) 777-4179, or email them at finaid@cylc.org.

Eligibility: High school students who have shown outstanding qualities in academics, leadership, and citizenship may apply.

Application Process: Competitive admissions, through nominations from educators and NYLC alumni, and through tough, college-like admissions process. Students may contact CYLC to obtain application forms.

Contact:
Congressional Youth Leadership Council—NYLC
1110 Vermont Avenue, NW, Suite 320
Washington, DC 20005
Phone: (202) 638-0009
Fax: (202) 638-5218
admissions@cylc.org
www.cylc.org

COOPERSTOWN BASEBALL CAMP

Program Location: Cooperstown, New York

Subject Areas: Baseball

Program Description: Intensive overnight and day training. Excellent opportunity to sharpen baseball skills. Nightly outings to area attractions, including the Baseball Hall of Fame and Museum, the Baseball Wax Museum, and Oneonta Tigers Game, local batting cages, and Baseball Card and Memorabilia Shops in Cooperstown. Licensed as an overnight children's camp.

Program Dates: Sessions through July and August

Duration of Program: 1 week

Cost: $750 (includes room and board)

Financial Aid: None available

Eligibility: Overnight Camp: boys, ages 8–17; Day Camp: coed, ages 8–17

Application Process: Call or email to request application, at least 30 days in advance.

Average Number of Applicants: 300

Average Number of Participants: 150

Academic Credit: None available

Contact:
Cooperstown Baseball Camp
P.O. Box 704
Cooperstown, NY 13326
Phone: (607) 293-7324
Fax: (607) 293-8131
info@cooperstownbaseball.com
www.cooperstownbaseball.com

Cornell University

CORNELL UNIVERSITY

Cornell University Summer College

Program Location: Cornell University in Ithaca, New York

Subject Areas: Liberal arts, career exploration, college preparation

Program Description: Students take two regular Cornell University courses, participate in a career exploration seminar of their choice, and attend workshops in math, writing, study skills, and college admissions. Students live in a Cornell residence hall and have access to campus facilities.

Program Dates: June–August

Duration of Program: 3 or 6 weeks

Cost: $5,900 (6 weeks); $3,550 (3 weeks). Includes room and board.

Financial Aid: Limited need-based aid available to U.S. citizens only; downloadable financial aid application available on website

Eligibility: Students completing their junior or senior year of high school

Application Process: Application (online and downloadable versions available on website), transcript, standardized test scores, teacher or guidance counselor recommendation, application fee

Application Deadline: May 4 (2001 date)

Academic Credit: Students receive letter grades and college credit for each completed course.

Summer Honors Program for High School Sophomores

Program Location: Cornell University in Ithaca, New York

Subject Areas: Humanities, communications, college preparation

Program Description: College-level work with emphasis on developing analytical and writing skills. Students spend 2½ hours each weekday morning in lectures and discussion sections of their program seminars. Students generally spend four afternoons a week in class and in writing tutorials; one afternoon is left unscheduled for independent study or recreation. Under the guidance of the program directors and their teaching assistants, students write and revise several academic papers. Students also take essay examinations based on the course readings. Students live together in a Cornell residence hall and have access to campus facilities.

Program Dates: July

Duration of Program: 3 weeks

Cost: $3,550 (includes room and board)

Financial Aid: None available

Eligibility: Students completing their sophomore year of high school

Application Process: Application (online and downloadable versions available on website), transcript, standardized test scores, teacher or guidance counselor recommendation, personal statement, application fee

Application Deadline: May 4 (2001 date)

Academic Credit: Students receive a letter grade and college credit for completed coursework.

Contact:
Summer College
Cornell University
B20 Day Hall
Ithaca, NY 14853-2801
Phone: (607) 255-6203
Fax: (607) 255-6665
summer_college@cornell.edu
www.sce.cornell.edu

CORNELL UNIVERSITY SPORTS SCHOOL

Summer Sports Camps

Program Location: Cornell University in Ithaca, New York

Subject Areas: Baseball, basketball, soccer, wrestling, cross country, fencing, field hockey, football, ice hockey, lacrosse, rock climbing, sailing, softball, strength and conditioning, swimming, tennis

Program Description: Morning, afternoon, and evening sessions instructed by Cornell's head coaches, players, and guest coaches. Resident campers receive three meals per day in Cornell's award-winning dining halls. Campers reside in Cornell dormitories, where they are supervised by full-time camp counselors.

Program Dates: Sessions from late June to mid-August

Duration of Program: 1 week

Cost: $139–$699 (includes room and board for resident programs)

Financial Aid: Available for local youths only

Eligibility: Boys and girls of all skill levels, ages 7–18

Application Process: Call for brochure or print application from website.

Application Deadline: Approximately three weeks prior to the individual camps

Average Number of Applicants: 3,000

Average Number of Participants: 3,000

Academic Credit: None available

Contact:
Cornell University Athletics
Sports School Office
103 Bartels Hall
Campus Road
Ithaca, NY 14853-3401
Phone: (607) 255-1200
Fax: (607) 255-2969
camps@cornell.edu
www.athletics.cornell.edu/camps

COSTA RICAN LANGUAGE ACADEMY (CRLA)

Program Location: San Jose, Costa Rica

Subject Areas: Spanish language study, cultural immersion, volunteer opportunities

Program Description: This Costa Rican-owned and operated language school provides a Spanish immersion program in a warm and friendly environment. Teachers have university degrees. Students taught in small groups or private classes. Volunteer opportunities and homestays are available. Included in program cost are airport transportation, Internet access, excursions, Latin dance, Costa Rican cooking, and conversation classes. Also great discounts on tours to beaches, mountains, volcanoes, national parks, and more.

Program Dates: Open enrollment

Duration of Program: 1–12 weeks

Cost: $155 per week or $235 per week with homestay

Application Process: Contact CRLA for more information.

Contact:
Costa Rican Language Academy
P.O. Box 1966-2050
San Jose, Costa Rica
Phone: (800) 854-6057
Fax: 011 (506) 233-5065
crlang@sol.racsa.co.cr
www.learn-spanish.com and
www.spanishandmore.com

Costa Rican Language Academy (CRLA)

COTTONWOOD GULCH FOUNDATION

Prairie Trek Group I;

Prairie Trek Group II;

Turquoise Trail

Program Location: New Mexico, Colorado, Utah, Arizona

Subject Areas: Outdoor adventure

Program Description: Participants of Cottonwood Gulch Expeditions go backpacking, river running, caving, and mountain biking, investigate Indian ruins, track wild animals, and develop group skills on the challenge course.

Program Dates: July–August

Duration of Program: 5 weeks (Prairie Trek Group I and Turquoise Trail); 6 weeks (Prairie Trek Group II)

Cost: $2,670 (Prairie Trek Group I and Turquoise Trail); $3,490 (Prairie Trek Group II)

Financial Aid: Limited aid available

Eligibility: Prairie Trek Group I: Boys only, ages 13–16; Prairie Trek Group II: Coed, ages 15–17; Turquoise Trail: Girls only, ages 13–16

Application Process: Registration form, participant statement, references, deposit required

Average Number of Participants: Maximum of 20 campers per group

Contact:
Cottonwood Gulf Foundation
P.O. Box 3915
Albuquerque, NM 87190
Phone: (800) 246-8735 or (505) 248-0563
www.go-trek.org

Cottonwood Gulch Foundation

CROW CANYON ARCHAEOLOGICAL CENTER

High School Field School;

High School Excavation Program

Program Location: Colorado

Subject Areas: Archaeology

Program Description: Participants experience an intensive, hands-on course in archaeology, working alongside professional archaeologists in the field and lab. Outdoor adventure activities included in the 3-week Field School.

Program Dates: Field School: July 7–27, 2002; Excavation Program: July 28–August 3, 2002

Duration of Program: Field School: 3 weeks; Excavation Program: 1 week

Crow Canyon Archaeological Center

Cost: Field School: $2,500; Excavation Program: $725

Eligibility: Incoming high school freshmen through outgoing seniors. Must be at least 14 years old by September 1, 2002.

Application Deadline: Rolling admissions

Application Process: Application form, essay, teacher's recommendation

Academic Credit: High school and college credit available for 3-week Field School

Average Number of Participants: Field School: 30; Excavation Program: 20

Contact:
Crow Canyon Archaeological Center
23390 Road K
Cortez, CO 81321-9909
Phone: (800) 422-8975;
(970) 565-8975 ext. 130
Fax: (970) 565-4859
ttitone@crowcanyon.org
www.crowcanyon.org

DARTMOUTH COLLEGE

See Kinyon-Jones Tennis Camp; Rassias Programs

DAUPHIN ISLAND SEA LAB

Discovery Hall Summer High School Program

Program Location: Dauphin Island, located in the Mouth of the Mobile Bay in the Gulf of Mexico, 7 miles off mainland Alabama

Subject Areas: A general marine science curriculum that incorporates biology, geology, and chemistry

Program Description: The Discovery Hall Program is designed to stimulate awareness of the ocean, its inhabitants, and the problems that arise as the coastal zone grows in population. Students spend one-third of the course in the field exploring and examining different marine communities; one-third in the classroom; and one-third in the lab. Field activities include the exploration of a salt marsh community, beach profiling, reef fishing, and trawling aboard the Sea Lab's 65-foot research vessel.

Program Dates: June–August

Duration of Program: Two 4-week sessions

Cost: $1,200 (includes room and board)

Eligibility: Students entering grades 10–12 who have completed (by summer) a general biology course

Application Process: Application (downloadable from website), transcript, 2 teacher recommendations, 500-word essay

Application Deadline: May 11 (2001 date)

Average Number of Participants: 30 per session

Academic Credit: The Alabama Department of Education recommends that participants receive 1 year of high school science credit.

Contact:
Dauphin Island Sea Lab
attn: DHP Registrar
101 Bienville Boulevard
Dauphin Island, AL 36528
Phone: (334) 861-7515
Fax: (334) 861-7421
dkeaton@disl.org
www.disl.org

DAVIDSON COLLEGE

Davidson July Experience

Program Location: Davidson College in Davidson, North Carolina

Subject Areas: Liberal arts, precollege program

Program Description: An educational, social, and personal development precollege program. Participants take two academic courses, which vary each year.

Program Dates: July

Duration of Program: 3 weeks

Cost: To be determined for 2002

Financial Aid: Available for minority students with documented financial need

Application Deadline: April 1

Average Number of Applicants: 80

Average Number of Participants: 70

Contact:
Davidson College
P.O. Box 1719
Davidson, NC 28036
Phone: (704) 894-2508
Fax: (704) 894-2645
julyexp@davidson.edu
www.davidson.edu/academic/education/
julyexp.html

Deep Woods Camp for Boys

DEEP WOODS CAMP FOR BOYS

Program Location: North Carolina

Subject Areas: Hiking, backpacking, camping, whitewater canoeing and rafting, rock climbing, mountain biking

Program Description: A camp for boys offering an entire program of wilderness adventure activities.

Program Dates: June, July, and August

Duration of Program: 4, 6, or 10 weeks

Cost: $1,500–$3,750

Eligibility: Boys ages 10–15; no experience necessary

Application Process: Contact the camp to enroll.

Application Deadline: None

Contact:
Deep Woods Camp for Boys
751 Walnut Hollow Road
Brevard, NC 28712
Phone: (828) 885-2268
Fax: (828) 885-2268
www.perigee.net/~moreland/deepwoods

DEER HILL EXPEDITIONS

Program Location: Colorado, Utah, Arizona, New Mexico

Subject Areas: Wilderness, service, and cross-

Deer Hill Expeditions

cultural expeditions

Program Description: Wilderness expeditions, community service, and cross-cultural living. Outdoor activities include whitewater rafting, backpacking, and rock climbing. Service learning is integrated into each program through cross-cultural living and working with Native Americans (Navajo, Hopi and Zuni), or conservation projects with the U.S. Forest Service.

Program Dates: June, July, and August

Duration of Program: 3–5 week sessions

Eligibility: Coed, grades 7–12

Cost: $3,150–$4,850 (includes room and board)

Application Process: Call or write for application.

Application Deadline: Applications accepted at any time, programs close when filled

Academic Credit: Community service credit accepted by high schools

Contact:
P.O. Box 180
Mancos, CO 81328
Phone: (800) 533-7221
Fax: (970) 533-7221
info@deerhillexpeditions.com
www.deerhillexpeditions.com

DENISON UNIVERSITY

Jonathan R. Reynolds Young Writers Workshop

Program Location: Denison University in Granville, Ohio

Subject Areas: Creative writing

Program Description: Designed to give high school students the opportunity to develop their talents as poets and fiction writers. Offers intensive workshops, tutorials, group talks, readings, social encounters with other writers, and many other literary events. Faculty for the

Denison University

workshop include members of the creative writing faculty at Denison and the University of Cincinnati. Cookouts, trips off campus, evening social events, and daily readings by faculty, staff, guest writers, and student participants themselves also planned.

Program Dates: June 16–23

Duration of Program: 8 days

Cost: $900

Financial Aid: Available

Eligibility: Students currently enrolled in grades 10–12

Application Process: Application (and financial aid forms), letter of recommendation, portfolio of recent writing (maximum 10 pages of poetry, or 20 pages of fiction, or 20 pages combined of poetry and fiction)

Application Deadline: April 15

Average Number of Applicants: 60

Average Number of Participants: 30

Academic Credit: None available

Contact:
Dr. Dennis M. Read
Department of English
Denison University
Granville, OH 43023
Phone: (740) 587-6565
Fax: (740) 587-5680
read@denison.edu

See also Summer Institute for the Gifted

DICKINSON COLLEGE

Pre-College Program

Program Location: Dickinson College in Carlisle, Pennsylvania; Queretaro, Mexico

Subject Areas: Business, law, science, language, college preparation

Program Description: Motivated, academically talented students are offered a wide selection of academic, cultural, and social opportunities. Students select 2 college-level courses in business, prelaw, or science; or foreign language programs at Dickinson's overseas centers for a topical immersion experience; or two courses of their choice. Most classes meet every weekday, providing an intensive period of study in a seminar setting. Social and academic field trips and activities enhance this precollege experience.

Program Dates: July–August

Duration of Program: 5 weeks

Cost: On-campus program: $3,950 (includes room and board); Mexico: $4,550 (includes airfare, room and board)

Eligibility: Rising juniors and seniors

Application Process: Transcript, 2 recommendations, essay

Application Deadline: April 15

Average Number of Participants: 50

Academic Credit: College credit available

Contact:
Dickinson College
Pre-College Program
P.O. Box 1773
Carlisle, PA 17013
Phone: (717) 245-1375
Fax: (717) 245-1972
summer@dickinson.edu
www.dickinson.edu/summer

DREW UNIVERSITY

Drew Summer Music

Program Location: Drew University in Madison, New Jersey

Subject Areas: Chamber music

Program Description: A residential and commuter program of chamber music for young vocalists and instrumentalists. The program features small classes; composition and music reviewing are also offered.

Program Dates: Last week of June

Duke University

Duration of Program: 8 days

Cost: $700

Eligibility: Intermediate and advanced players from grade 8 through college

Application Process: Completed application and personal audition

Application Deadline: April 9

Average Number of Applicants: 70

Average Number of Participants: 60

Contact:
Music Department
Drew University
Madison, NJ 07940
Phone: (973) 408-3428
Fax: (973) 408-3885
vschulze@drew.edu
www.depts.drew.edu/music/

See also Summer Institute for the Gifted

DUKE UNIVERSITY

Duke Tennis Camp

Program Location: Duke University in Durham, North Carolina

Subject Areas: Tennis

Program Description: Conducted by Jay Lapidus and Jamie Ashworth, two of the premier coaches in college tennis today, the Duke camp accommodates players from beginner to tournament level. Instruction is offered in a 5:1 camper to counselor ratio to ensure top quality and individual attention.

Program Dates: 3 sessions run from late June to early July

Duration of Program: 1 week

Cost: Available upon request

Eligibility: Ages 8–18

Application Process: Registration form from camp brochure

Application Deadline: First come, first served

Average Number of Participants: 100 per week

Contact:
Duke Tennis Camp
attn: Jay Lapidus
P.O. Box 2553
Durham, NC 27715-2553
Phone: (919) 479-0854
Fax: (419) 793-1508
camp@duketennis.com
www.duketennis.com

Duke University PreCollege Program

Program Location: Duke University in Durham, North Carolina

Subject Areas: Liberal arts, college preparation

Program Description: Students attend college freshman and sophomore courses for credit. The program features small classes and a highly rated residential program.

Program Dates: July–August

Duration of Program: 6 weeks

Cost: $4,850 (includes room and board)

Financial Aid: Limited need-based aid is available

Eligibility: Gifted and talented rising seniors who show promise of success in a college environment

Application Process: Application packet, essay, and standardized test scores required

Average Number of Applicants: 400

Average Number of Participants: 140

Academic Credit: College credit for two courses

Contact:
Duke University PreCollege Program
Box 90747
Durham, NC 27708
Phone: (919) 681-6981
Fax: (919) 681-7921
pwallace@duke.edu
www.tip.duke.edu

DURANGO CAMPS

Durango Youth Volleyball Camp

Program Location: Fort Lewis College in Durango, Colorado

Subject Areas: Coed volleyball

Program Description: All skills covered. Camp staff includes Head Coach Butch May, 1968 USA Men's Volleyball Olympian and a staff of mature former collegiate and USA National team men and women.

Program Dates: July 21–26

Duration of Program: 5 days

Cost: $445 (day camper); $545 (resident, includes room and board)

Financial Aid: None available

Eligibility: Ages 11–18; all skill levels

Application Process: Check website for complete information and application form.

Application Deadline: Rolling, maximum 60 participants

Average Number of Applicants: 50+

Average Number of Participants: 50+

Contact:
Durango Camps
P.O. Box 3782
Durango, CO 81302
Phone: (888) 892-1547
Fax: (970) 382-2519
grambo@rmi.net
www.durangocamps.com

DWIGHT-ENGLEWOOD SCHOOL

Dwight-Englewood Summer Programs

Program Location: Dwight-Englewood School in Englewood, New Jersey

Subject Areas: All academic disciplines, arts, ESL, athletics

Dwight-Englewood School

Program Description: Day programs providing a variety of opportunities for students from public, parochial, and independent schools. A combination of advancement, introduction, and enrichment courses in all academic disciplines, in the arts, and in sports, allows for diversity of study.

Program Dates: June 25–August 3

Duration of Program: 6 weeks

Cost: $100–$2,000

Financial Aid: None available

Eligibility: Preschool through grade 12

Application Process: Check with program for more information

Application Deadline: Rolling

Average Number of Applicants: 1,000

Average Number of Participants: 900

Academic Credit: High school credit available

Contact:
Dwight-Englewood School
Summer Programs
315 E. Palisade Avenue
Englewood, NJ 07631
Phone: (201) 569-9500, x3501
Fax: (201) 569-1676
www.d-e.org

EARTHWATCH INSTITUTE

Field Research Expedition Internships

Program Location: 51 countries throughout the world

Subject Areas: Work abroad, study abroad, outdoor adventure, ecology, anthropology, marine sciences, archaeology

Program Description: Earthwatch matches students and adults with research scientists who need volunteer assistance in the field. This is a hands-on program in seven areas of fieldwork: oceans; endangered ecosystems; biodiversity; cultural diversity; archaeology; global change; and world health. Sample expeditions include researching sea turtles in Costa Rica, studying dolphin behavior in Brazil, or excavating dinosaur bones in Wyoming. Supervising staff work closely with students throughout the program. While these expeditions attract people of all ages, many students find them useful for testing out career possibilities and for practicing a second language. Accommodations are basic, ranging from small research stations to rainforest lodges.

Program Dates: Year-round

Duration of Program: 2 weeks (average)

Cost: $700–$3,000 (airfare not included)

Financial Aid: Some aid is available

Eligibility: Ages 16 and older

Application Deadline: Rolling admission

Academic Credit: Must be arranged independently by the student

Contact:
Earthwatch Institute
3 Clock Tower Place, Suite 100
Box 75
Maynard, MA 01754-0075
Phone: (800) 776-0188 or (978) 461-0081
Fax: (978) 461-2332
info@earthwatch.org
www.earthwatch.org

EAST CAROLINA UNIVERSITY

East Carolina Summer Theatre

Program Location: East Carolina University in Greenville, North Carolina

Subject Areas: Performing arts, theater production

Program Description: Apprenticeships are available for high school seniors to work closely with a professional theater company.

Program Dates: Generally June 1 to July 25, but flexible to meet the student's needs

Duration of Program: 8 weeks

Cost: None. Tuition and housing are free, but meals and transportation are not provided

Eligibility: High school seniors, preferably with some experience in theatrical production techniques

Application Process: Résumé and letter of interest. Application form may be requested.

Application Deadline: April 15

Average Number of Applicants: 30

Average Number of Participants: 10

Contact:
East Carolina University
attn: Jeff Woodruff
Department of Theatre and Dance
Greenville, NC 27858
Phone: (252) 328-1192
Fax: (252) 328-4890
www.theatre-dance.ecu.edu

Eastern Music Festival

EASTERN MUSIC FESTIVAL

Program Location: Guilford College in Greensboro, North Carolina

Subject Areas: Classical music

Program Description: EMF is an internationally acclaimed classical music festival combining a 5-week professional concert series with an intensive training program in piano and orchestral studies. Students participate in orchestral and chamber music rehearsals and performances, private lessons, master classes, and chamber music coaching and classes. Faculty consists of outstanding musicians from leading symphony orchestras and music schools, who perform a weekly series of concerts and share their extensive musical knowledge with students. Small 2.5-to-1 student-teacher ratio.

Duration of Program: 5 weeks

Cost: $3,649

Financial Aid: 90 percent of participants receive financial assistance through merit and work-study scholarships

Eligibility: Ages 14–20

Application Process: Written application and audition

Application Deadline: March 1

Average Number of Applicants: 750

Average Number of Participants: 200

Contact:
Eastern Music Festival
P.O. Box 22026
Greensboro, NC 27420
Phone: (336) 333-7450
Fax: (336) 333-7454
www.easternmusicfestival.com

Eastern U.S. Music Camp

EASTERN U.S. MUSIC CAMP, INC.

Eastern U.S. Music Camp

Program Location: Colgate University in Hamilton, New York

Subject Areas: Music: instrumental, vocal, classical, jazz

Program Description: A music camp providing instruction in symphony orchestra, chamber ensemble, concert band, jazz ensemble, jazz combos, concert choir, vocal jazz, madrigal choir, men's and women's choirs. Classes in music theory, harmony, composition, arranging, and conducting. Weekly recitals and concerts. Private lessons offered in all instruments including voice, piano, guitar, organ, plus daily piano and guitar workshops. Daily recreation.

Program Dates: June 30–July 27, 2002

Duration of Program: 2-, 3-, and 4-week

sessions

Cost: Residential: $1,325 (2 weeks), $1,987 (3 weeks), $2,650 (4 weeks); Commuter: $548 (2 weeks), $822 (3 weeks), $1,094 (4 weeks)

Eligibility: Ages 10–19

Application Process: Application form can be mailed or submitted electronically via website; $295 deposit required.

Application Deadline: Rolling admissions

Average Number of Applicants: 175

Average Number of Participants: 175

Academic Credit: High school credit available for 4-week session

Contact:
Eastern U.S. Music Camp, Inc.
7 Brook Hollow Road
Ballston Lake, NY 12019
Phone: (518) 877-5121
Fax: (518) 877-5121
eusmc@hotmail.com
easternusmusiccamp.com

ECHO INTERNATIONAL EDUCATIONAL EXPEDITIONS

Australian Biological Adventures

Program Location: Australia

Subject Areas: Marine biology, travel abroad, outback camping

Program Description: Participants investigate the biology of the "land down under" by exploring 6 of the continent's unique regions: Ayres Rock, the Outback, the Head of the Bight, the Daintree Rainforest, the Great Barrier Reef, and Kangaroo Island.

Program Dates: July 3–27

Duration of Program: 3 weeks

Cost: $4,850 (includes room and board and round-trip airfare between Los Angeles and Australia)

Financial Aid: None available

Eligibility: Students in grades 8–12

Application Process: Teacher recommendation

Application Deadline: February 28

Academic Credit: College credit available through Bellarmine University

Contact:
Echo International Educational Expeditions
6405 Echo Trail
Louisville, KY 40299
Phone: (502) 266-9795
Fax: (502) 261-1325
aussiebioadv@aol.com
www.homepage.mac.com/aussiebioadv

EDUCATION UNLIMITED

College Admission Prep Camp;

Prep Camp Excel

Program Location: California campuses, including Stanford University, University of California—Berkeley, University of California—Los Angeles, University of California—Davis, University of San Diego

Subject Areas: College admissions and test preparation

Program Description: The Prep Camps are a way to have a great time on a college campus while getting a head start on the college admissions process. The program entails SAT/PSAT prep, essay writing, time management, study skills, and guidance counseling.

Program Dates: June–August

Duration of Program: College Admission Prep Camp: 10 days; Prep Camp Excel: 5 days

Cost: College Admission Prep Camp: $1,550–$1,850; Prep Camp Excel: $975

Financial Aid: Need-based aid available

Eligibility: College Admission Prep Camp: entering grades 11–12; Prep Camp Excel: entering grades 9–10

Application Deadline: May 1

Average Number of Applicants: 700

Average Number of Participants: 700

Computer Camp by Education Unlimited

Program Location: Stanford University, University of California—Berkeley, University of California—Los Angeles, University of California—Davis, University of San Diego

Subject Areas: Web page design, Java programming, desktop publishing, applications

Program Description: The program trains students in both creative and practical computer skills with the goal of providing students with the ability to use computers artistically and creatively while exploring emerging technologies and software.

Program Dates: June–August

Duration of Program: 1–4 weeks

Cost: $895–$970 per week

Financial Aid: Need-based aid available

Eligibility: Entering grades 6–12

Application Deadline: May 1

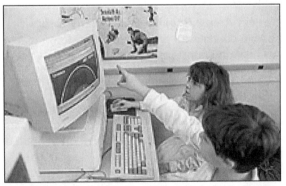

Computer Camp by Education Unlimited

Average Number of Applicants: 700

Average Number of Participants: 700

Public Speaking
Institute by Education Unlimited

Program Location: Stanford University, University of California—Berkeley, University of California—Los Angeles, University of California—Davis, University of San Diego

Subject Areas: Mock trial, Congressional-style speaking, interview simulation

Program Description: The program seeks to instill confidence, articulation, organization, and the ability to deliver a well-crafted speech both in and outside the classroom.

Program Dates: June–August

Duration of Program: 1–4 weeks

Cost: $795–$870 per week

Financial Aid: Need-based aid available

Eligibility: Entering grades 6–12

Application Deadline: May 1

Average Number of Applicants: 700

Average Number of Participants: 700

Summer Focus at Berkeley;
Acting Workshop at Berkeley

Program Location: University of California—Berkeley

Subject Areas: Summer Focus: Introductory college courses for credit, electives, tutoring. Acting Workshop: Basic acting technique, voice, movement, improvisation.

Program Description: Summer Focus: A comprehensive six-week summer academic enrichment program offered in a rare public-private partnership between Education Unlimited and Berkeley Summer Sessions. High school students earn college credit and have a great time through a variety of recreational excursions. Acting Workshop: Designed to give young actors training in several different acting skills, making them more capable and well-rounded actors. Students attend a daily class in basic acting technique, which offers intensive study with one teacher for the duration of the program.

Program Dates: Summer Focus: July–August; Acting Workshop: June–July

Duration of Program: Summer Focus: 6 weeks; Acting Workshop: 2–3 weeks

Cost: Summer Focus: $4,350; Acting Workshop: $1,600–$2,575

Financial Aid: Need-based aid available

Eligibility: Summer Focus: Entering grades 11 and 12 with A or B average. Acting Workshop: Entering grades 7–12.

Application Deadline: May 1

Average Number of Applicants: Summer Focus: 60; Acting Workshop: 100

Average Number of Participants: Summer Focus: 60; Acting Workshop: 100

East Coast College Tour;
Tour Italy

Program Location: College Tour: Boston, Providence, Philadelphia, Washington DC; Tour Italy: Venice, Florence, and Rome

Subject Areas: College Tour: Travel, college admissions and preparation. Tour Italy: International travel, language, culture, art.

Program Description: College Tour: Students will take campus tours of Harvard, Boston College, Yale, Brown University, Georgetown, and more; meet with admissions officers; and receive materials to help them evaluate schools. Once students arrive in Boston, they will travel down the coast in an air-conditioned bus. Tour Italy: Fully chaperoned and guided tour of Italy via train and chartered bus. The itinerary has been carefully designed to balance

EF International Language Schools

the exploration of all the historic sites of these great cities with shopping, bicycling, and relaxation.

Program Dates: College Tour: August; Tour Italy: July–August

Duration of Program: College Tour: 7 days; Tour Italy: 15 days

Cost: College Tour: $1,300 (airfare not included). Tour Italy: $2,450 (airfare not included). (*Note:* For both programs, a chaperoned flight from San Francisco is available at an additional charge.)

Financial Aid: Limited aid available

Eligibility: College Tour: Entering grades 10–12. Tour Italy: Entering grades 10–12 and graduating seniors.

Application Deadline: May 1

Average Number of Participants: College Tour: 20; Tour Italy: 15

Contact:
Education Unlimited
1678 Shattuck Avenue, #305
Berkeley, CA 94709
Phone: (510) 548-6612
Fax: (510) 548-0212
www.educationunlimited.com

EF INTERNATIONAL LANGUAGE SCHOOLS

Program Location: Spain, France, Italy, Germany, Ecuador, Russia, China

Subject Areas: Study abroad, language immersion

Program Description: EF Language Schools offer courses for students with all sorts of interests and objectives, from those looking for a fast course to sharpen language skills to those seeking an enriching summer abroad to those pursuing a full post-graduate semester. Students live with a host family or in a dormitory and may participate in a full range of social, athletic, and cultural activities in addition to their language classes.

Program Dates: Programs begin every 2 weeks throughout the year

Duration of Program: 2–52 weeks

Cost: Starts at $370 per week

Eligibility: Ages 16 to adult

Application Process: Enrollment form

Application Deadline: Rolling admission

Academic Credit: College credit available

Contact:
EF International Language Schools
One Education Street
Cambridge, MA 02141
Phone: (800) 992-1892
Fax: (617) 619-1701
ils@ef.com
www.ef.com

Embry-Riddle Aeronautical University

EMBRY-RIDDLE AERONAUTICAL UNIVERSITY

ACES Academy (Aviation Career Education Specialization)

Program Location: Embry-Riddle Aeronautical University in Daytona Beach, Florida

Subject Areas: Aviation

Program Description: Students explore career opportunities in the fields of air traffic control, avionics, engineering, flight, and maintenance. Students choose the field that most interests them and learn from professionals in the field.

Program Dates: August 9–14

Duration of Program: 6 days

Cost: $800 (includes room and board, linens, dual one-hour flight, educational materials and instruction, and field trips)

Eligibility: High school juniors and seniors ages 16–18 who have an interest in aviation or previous aviation experience

Aerospace Summer Camp

Program Location: Embry-Riddle Aeronautical University in Daytona Beach, Florida

Subject Areas: Aerospace

Program Description: Designed to foster a basic understanding of space and space technology through hands-on projects, classroom lectures, guest speakers, and field trips. Students also learn about the history of space flight, space shuttle operations, and NASA programs.

Program Dates: June 28–July 24

Duration of Program: 4 weeks

Cost: $3,200 (includes room and board, linens, educational materials and instruction, and field trips)

Eligibility: Ages 15–18

Academic Credit: 3 college credits awarded upon successful completion of program

Engineering Academy

Program Location: Embry-Riddle Aeronautical University in Daytona Beach, Florida

Subject Areas: Engineering

Program Description: Introduction to designing, building, and testing aircraft-related components. Hands-on activities in composites, sheet metal, and welding are planned in the project lab. Demonstrations using the wind tunnel and stereo lithography labs follow a computer-aided drafting activity. Observation flight and other field trips are also included.

Program Dates: July 19–24

Duration of Program: 6 days

Cost: $900 (includes room and board, linens, dual one-hour flight, educational materials and instruction, and field trips)

Eligibility: High school juniors and seniors ages 16–18

Flight Exploration

Program Location: Embry-Riddle Aeronautical University in Daytona Beach, Florida

Subject Areas: Introduction to flying

Program Description: Intensive, hands-on introduction to flying in which students practice flight maneuvers as they learn about VFR procedures, how to read weather conditions, and how to comply with aviation regulations. Both residential and non-residential programs are offered.

Program Dates: Residential Camps: June 21–26, July 12–17, July 26–31, August 2–7. Non-Residential Camp: June 7–11.

Duration of Program: Residential: 6 days; Non-Residential: 5 days

Cost: Residential: $1,000 (includes room and board, linens, flight instruction, ground lab instruction, books and materials, a mini-logbook, and field trips). Non-Residential: $800 (includes flight instruction, ground lab instruction, books and materials, mini-logbook).

Eligibility: Ages 12–18

SunFlight Camps

Program Location: Embry-Riddle Aeronautical University in Daytona Beach, Florida

Subject Areas: Flight instruction (all levels)

Program Description: SunFlight Alpha and Bravo Solo Camps: Students learn to fly in ground labs, aircraft simulators, and aircraft. The goal is for all qualified students to solo by the end of the program. SunFlight Eagles Private Pilot Camp: Intensive program allows students to earn their Private Pilot Certificate and earn 6 college credits toward a flight-related degree. SunFlight Instrument Camp: Designed to teach licensed pilots how to fly using instruments, covering the required flight, simulator, and ground hours necessary to take the FAA Instrument Rating knowledge exam, along with oral and flight tests.

Program Dates: SunFlight Alpha: June 21–July 8; SunFlight Bravo: July 19–August 5; SunFlight Eagles and Instrument Camps: June 21–August 16

Duration of Programs: SunFlight Alpha/Bravo: 3 weeks; SunFlight Eagles and Instrument Camps: 8 weeks

Cost: SunFlight Alpha/Bravo: $3,400. SunFlight Eagles: $9,500. SunFlight Instrument Camp: $8,700. (Includes room and board, linens, flight instruction, ground lab instruction, simulator time, average estimated flight fees, books and materials, and field trips. Flight fees may vary depending upon the student's level of ability.)

Eligibility: SunFlight Alpha/Bravo: Students must be age 16 prior to the end of the program. SunFlight Eagles: Students must be age 17 by August 15. SunFlight Instrument Camp: Students must be age 17 and possess a Private Pilot License prior to the start of the program.

Academic Credit: SunFlight Eagles: 6 college credits; SunFlight Instrument Camp: 2 college credits.

Contact:
Embry-Riddle Summer Academy
600 South Clyde Morris Boulevard
Daytona Beach, FL 32114
Phone: (386) 226-6499
Fax: (386) 226-7630
summer@cts.db.erau.edu
www.erau.edu/dce/summer/

ENVISION EMI, INC.

NexTech: The National Summit of Young Technology Leaders

Program Location: Austin, Texas

Subject Areas: Careers in technology

Program Description: Provides a unique learning experience for top students with an intense desire to pursue careers in technology. Throughout the program, students actively

Evansville Summer College Program
for Students with Disabilities

participate in an integrated curriculum encompassing both group work and individual interests. Participants engage in workshops, product demonstrations, campus visits, and tech industry encounters, as well as animated debate and discussion.

Program Dates: One session held in the summer

Duration of Program: 10 days

Cost: $1,965 (summer 2001 tuition)

Eligibility: High school juniors and seniors who have demonstrated academic talent, leadership potential, and a strong interest in technology

Application Process: Competitive admissions process. Students are nominated to attend program; they may also contact NYLF to obtain application forms.

Contact:
NexTech
1110 Vermont Avenue, Suite 420
Washington, DC 20005
Phone: (202) 777-4157
Fax: (202) 777-4176
admissions@nextechsummit.com
www.nextechsummit.com

EVANSVILLE ASSOCIATION FOR THE BLIND

Summer College Program for Students with Disabilities

Program Location: University of Evansville in Evansville, Indiana

Subject Areas: Academic study, college preparation

Program Description: The Summer College Program helps to ease the transition from high school to college life for students with disabilities. Participants enroll in college-level classes, live in university dorms, and learn to improve daily living and social skills.

Program Dates: June 9–July 19, 2002

Duration of Program: 6 weeks

Cost: $3,300

Financial Aid: State Vocational Rehabilitation funds available. Deadline June 2002.

Eligibility: High school seniors and postsecondary students with disabilities

Application Process: Written application

Application Deadline: May 15, 2002

Average Number of Applicants: 20

Average Number of Participants: 16

Academic Credit: College credit available

Contact:
Evansville Association for the Blind
P.O. Box 6445
Evansville, IN 47719
Phone: (812) 422-1181
Fax: (812) 424-3154
EABCDC@evansville.net
www2.evansville.edu/ebaweb

FAIRLEIGH DICKINSON UNIVERSITY

See Tab Ramos Soccer Academy

FIVE-STAR BASKETBALL CAMP

Program Location: Over 30 events nationwide

Subject Areas: Basketball

Program Description: Five-Star is among the most elite camps in the country. Featured on CBS, NBC, ESPN, Sports Illustrated, and USA Today, Five-Star has graduated 250 campers that went on to play in the NBA, including Michael Jordan, Patrick Ewing, Vince Carter, Allan Houston, Alonzo Mourning, Elton Brand, and Grant Hill. Past coaches include Chuck Daly, Dick Vitale, Hubie Brown, Bob Knight, and Rick Pitino, among other famous names.

Program Dates: Various

Duration of Program: 5 1/2 days

Eligibility: Coed, grades 9–12

Application Process: Recommendations required

Application Deadline: First come, first served by June 1

Average Number of Applicants: 9,000

Average Number of Participants: 6,000

Contact:
Five-Star Basketball Camp
attn: Will Klein
569 Kimball Avenue
Yonkers, NY 10704
Phone: (914) 237-1306
Fax: (914) 237-1946
fivestar66@aol.com
www.five-starbasketball.com

FOOTHILL COLLEGE

Academically Talented Youth Program

Program Location: Foothill College in Los Altos, California

Subject Areas: Computer programming, mathematics, foreign languages, laboratory sciences, English writing, PSAT, art, SAT preparation, speed reading, aviation, swimming, water polo, tennis, kickboxing, soccer, karate, badminton

Program Description: Students enroll in one or two academic classes, plus a sport if desired. All classes are part of the Foothill College curriculum and carry Foothill College credit and grades. Youth Program classes are usually separate from other classes but some classes also have adult students. The instruction level is appropriate for bright and eager students. Two Youth Program students are selected to serve as senators in the Foothill Student Government. Field trips and special events offered.

Program Dates: July–August

Duration of Program: 6 weeks

Cost: $28.50 (California residents); $400–$850 (non-residents)

Financial Aid: None available

Eligibility: Students entering grades 8–12

Application Process: Application (available on website), PSAT or SAT scores

Application Deadline: Early June

Average Number of Applicants: 1,000

Average Number of Participants: 1,000

Academic Credit: College credit available

Contact:
Foothill College
Academically Talented Youth Program
12345 El Monte Road
Los Altos Hills, CA 94022
Phone: (650) 949-7638
honors@fhda.edu
www.foothillcollege.org/yo

FRENCH WOODS FESTIVAL OF THE PERFORMING ARTS

Program Location: Catskill Mountains in Hancock, New York

Subject Areas: Specialty programs in music, theater, dance, circus, fine arts, horseback riding, sports, tennis, adventure challenge course, waterfront activities

Program Description: Highly individualized program in which each day consists of six activity periods: three majors and three minors. Majors are chosen at the beginning of each session and are performance- or goal-oriented. Minors are chosen daily to explore new interests. Campers bunk in cabins equipped with modern conveniences such as full bath facilities and ample electrical outlets.

Program Dates: Three intensive 3-week sessions from June 26–August 26

Duration of Program: 3, 6, or 9 weeks

Cost: $3,000 per 3-week session

Eligibility: Ages 7–17

Application Process: By application with deposit. Auditions take place after session begins.

Application Deadline: Rolling admissions

Average Number of Applicants: 1,500

Average Number of Participants: 1,500

Academic Credit: Can provide remedial coursework

Contact:
Summer address:
RR #1, Box 228
Hancock, NY 13783
Phone: (845) 887-5600
Fax: (845) 887-5075
Winter address:
P.O. Box 70100
Coral Springs, FL 33077
Phone: (800) 634-1703 or (954) 346-7455
Fax: (954) 346-7564
admin@frenchwoods.com
www.frenchwoods.com

Friends Music Camp

FRIENDS MUSIC CAMP

Program Location: Olney Friends School in Barnesville, Ohio

Subject Areas: Instrumental and vocal music

Program Description: Students explore classical music and jazz. Private lessons in instruments

and voice; chorus, musical theater, and workshops available. Supportive community experience.

Program Dates: July–August

Duration of Program: 4 weeks

Cost: $1,350

Eligibility: Ages 10–18 with a minimum of 1 year of music lessons

Application Process: Recommendation from a music teacher

Application Deadline: Rolling admissions

Average Number of Applicants: 85

Average Number of Participants: 75

Contact:
Friends Music Camp
P.O. Box 427
Yellow Springs, OH 45387
Phone: (937) 767-1311
Fax: (937) 767-2254
musicsmc@aol.com

FRIENDSHIP VENTURES

Youth Leadership Program

Program Location: Camp Friendship in Annandale, Minnesota; Eden Wood Center in Eden Prairie, Minnesota

Subject Areas: Leadership, community service

Program Description: Participants receive free training, room and board at one of two summer camps, in exchange for assisting counselors in providing a fun and safe camp experience for children and adults with developmental disabilities. Volunteers assist with programs that are designed to build participants' self-esteem and teach them life-enhancing leisure skills such as swimming, fishing, bicycling, dancing, and cooking.

Friendship Ventures

Program Dates: Sessions from June–September; also one week between Christmas and New Year's

Duration of Program: 1 week–12 weeks

Cost: No cost

Eligibility: Ages 14 and older

Application Deadline: Rolling admissions

Academic Credit: High school and college credit available

Contact:
Friendship Ventures
10509 108th Street NW
Annandale, MN 55302
Phone: (800) 450-8376
Fax: (320) 274-3238
fv@friendshipventures.org
www.friendshipventures.org

FUN-damental Basketball Camp

FUN-DAMENTAL BASKETBALL CAMP, INC.

Basketball Camp at Morrisville

Program Location: Morrisville, New York

Subject Areas: Coed basketball

Program Description: Daily skills stations, leagues formed by age and ability, 2 games a day, "knockout," 3-point shoot out, slam dunk contest, foul shooting contest, hot shot contest, guest speaker, recreational swimming, all-you-can-eat meal plan, supervised housing in college dormitories. Awards and trophies presented. Three spacious gymnasiums, air-conditioned auditorium for films and presentations.

Program Dates: July

Duration of Program: 1 week

Cost: $395 (includes room and board and camp T-shirt and basketball)

Financial Aid: None available

Eligibility: Students entering grades 3–12

Application Process: Application (available on website or from brochure), medical form

Application Deadline: 2 weeks prior to camp start date

Average Number of Applicants: 200

Average Number of Participants: 130–150

Academic Credit: None available

Contact:
FUN-damental Basketball Camp at Morrisville
P.O. Box 650
Dewitt, NY 13214
Phone: (315) 637-3861
Fax: (315) 637-1554
basketballcamp@aol.com
www.ebasketballcamps.com

GEORGE MASON UNIVERSITY

See National Student Leadership Conference

GEORGETOWN UNIVERSITY

Georgetown Summer College

Program Location: Georgetown University in Washington, DC

Subject Areas: Liberal arts, college prep, international relations

Program Description: Three programs are offered: the College Prep program, a pre-collegiate program which helps prepare students for college level study; the Summer College for High School Juniors, in which rising seniors may take up to two college courses from the summer session curriculum for credit; International Relations for High School Students, a one week institute dealing with politics and current affairs with distinguished speakers and activities in the Washington, DC area. Commuter students may apply to all programs.

Program Dates: June–July; July–August

Duration of Program: College Prep and Summer College for High School Juniors: 5 weeks; International Relations: 1 week

Cost: TBA

Financial Aid: Limited aid available

Eligibility: Summer College and International Relations Institute open to high school students of academic promise.

Application Process: Application, transcript, essay, test scores, letters of recommendation

Application Deadline: April

Academic Credit: College credit available for Summer College for High School Juniors program

Contact:
School of Summer and Continuing Education
Georgetown University
Washington, DC 20057
Phone: (202) 687-5719
Fax: (202) 687-8954
www.georgetown.edu/ssce

See also Junior Statesmen Foundation; Musiker Discovery Programs

GEORGIA HARDY TOURS, INC.

Summer Study

Program Location: France and England

Subject Areas: Study abroad, language study, homestay

Program Description: The program in France is an intensive language program and students live in a private residence in the south of France. In England, students study history, writing, and literature and stay in dormitory residences at a college in London.

Program Dates: July–August

Duration of Program: 4 weeks

Cost: Contact the organization for current costs

Eligibility: Students in grades 11–12

Application Deadline: Rolling

Academic Credit: High school credit available

Contact:
Georgia Hardy Tours
90 Eglinton Avenue East, Suite 401
Toronto, ON M4P 2Y3 Canada
Phone: (416) 483-7533
Fax: (416) 483-8395
www.ghardytours.com

GIFTED AND TALENTED DEVELOPMENT CENTER

Program Location: Queens College in Charlotte, North Carolina

Subject Areas: Computer programming, animation, fine arts, robotics, law, architecture, Shakespeare, writing

Program Description: A one-week camp for gifted and talented high school students. Students focus on one subject in intensive interest immersion classes.

Program Dates: Early June–early August

Duration of Program: 1 week

Cost: $640

Financial Aid: Limited aid available

Eligibility: Gifted high school students of academic and artistic promise

Application Process: Written application, teacher recommendations, standardized test scores

Application Deadline: Rolling admissions

Average Number of Applicants: 330

Average Number of Participants: 300

Contact:
Gifted and Talented Development Center
Harris House at Queens College
1830 Queens Road
Charlotte, NC 28207
Phone: (704) 366-6039
Fax: (704) 365-8276
www.teenscollege.com

GLOBAL INSTITUTE FOR DEVELOPING ENTREPRENEURS

IN2BIZ Entrepreneur Camp

Program Location: Willamette University in Salem, Oregon

Subject Areas: Business training

Program Description: Guided by entrepreneurs, students investigate various aspects of the business world, including startup and operation, communications, team-building, and leadership, goal-setting, problem-solving, and managing money. The camp also sponsors trips to the beach, Silver Creek Falls State Park, and other destinations.

Program Dates: July

Duration of Program: 2 weeks

Cost: $1,700

Eligibility: Ages 15–18

Application Process: Written application

Application Deadline: May 15

Average Number of Participants: 17

Contact:
Global Institute for Developing Entrepreneurs
800 Welcome Way SE
Salem, OR 97302
Phone: (503) 315-8262; (800) 211-0826
Fax: (503) 315-8262
www.in2biz.com

GLOBAL ROUTES

High School Community Service Programs

Program Location: Navajo Reservation in Arizona and Wind River Reservation in Wyoming; Kenya, Zimbabwe, Ghana, Thailand/Vietnam, Nepal, Belize, Costa Rica, Guadeloupe, Ecuador, Bolivia, St. Lucia

Subject Areas: Community service, international travel

Program Description: A primary focus of the programs for high-school students is to develop the individual student through the experience of working, traveling, and living with a group of peers. An orientation session is followed by a 2–3 week stay in a remote rural village. In all Global Routes high school programs, the entire group lives in one village and students stay in pairs with individual families. Students work with locals on projects such as constructing a school, clinic, or community center, teaching local children, or reforesting surrounding areas. Afterward, students spend 6–10 days exploring the environment and culture of the surrounding country.

Program Dates: July and August

Duration of Program: 3–6 weeks

Cost: $2,550 and up (airfare not included)

Financial Aid: Available; contact Global Routes for financial aid application

Application Process: Completed application

form (including section to be filled out by a parent) and $500 deposit required. Online information request form and printable application form are available on website.

Application Deadline: Rolling admissions, but programs tend to fill by early April

Average Number of Participants: Groups range in size from 13 to 18 students and have from 2 to 5 leaders

Academic Credit: High school community service credits available

Contact:
Global Routes
1814 Seventh Street, Suite A
Berkeley, CA 94710
Phone: (510) 848-4800
Fax: (510) 848-4801
mail@globalroutes.org
www.globalroutes.org

GLOBAL VOLUNTEERS

Program Location: 18 countries, including the United States

Subject Areas: Community service, travel abroad

Program Description: Global Volunteers oversees various service projects throughout the United States. International projects include construction, forestry work, English instruction, and health care assistance.

Duration of Program: 1–3 weeks

Cost: $450 for United States; $1,395–$2,395 for international programs

Eligibility: Any age, but international volunteers under age 18 must be accompanied by an adult

Application Process: Application, references, health questionnaire, skills inventory

Application Deadline: Usually 3 weeks prior to program, sooner for sites requiring visas

Average Number of Applicants: 2,000

Global Volunteers

Average Number of Participants: 2,000

Academic Credit: College credit possible

Contact:
Global Volunteers
attn: Volunteer Coordinator
375 E. Little Canada Road
St. Paul, MN 55117
Phone: (800) 487-1074
Fax: (651) 482-0915
email@globalvolunteers.org
www.globalvolunteers.org

GLOBAL WORKS INTERNATIONAL PROGRAMS

Summer Programs

Program Location: Ireland, Fiji Islands, Czech Republic, Ecuador, Puerto Rico, France, Costa Rica

Subject Areas: Community service, study abroad, outdoor adventure, travel abroad

Program Description: International programs designed for students who want varying degrees of community service projects, adventure/cultural activities, and language immersion. Projects include building a new water system, constructing a playground, educating children about wolves, or rebuilding castles in ruins. Students might live in a small

village in the mountains on Fiji or in castle ruins in the Czech Republic. Some programs include homestays.

Program Dates: June through August

Duration of Program: 4 weeks

Cost: $2,690–$3,665 (airfare not included)

Eligibility: Ages 14–18. For language immersion programs in Ecuador, Puerto Rico, France, and Costa Rica: two years of secondary language.

Application Process: Downloadable application available on website.

Application Deadline: Rolling admissions

Average Number of Participants: 14–23 students per group

Contact:
Global Works
RD2, Box 356B
Huntingdon, PA 16652
Phone: (814) 667-2411
Fax: (814) 667-3853
info@globalworksinc.com
www.globalworksinc.com

GOUCHER COLLEGE

Goucher Summer Arts Institute

Program Location: Goucher College in Baltimore, Maryland

Subject Areas: Performing arts: music, dance, and theater

Program Description: Students participate in small performing arts classes within a college environment. The programs being offered are: brass ensemble, dance, jazz ensemble, and theater.

Program Dates: July 8–20

Duration of Program: 1- and 2-week programs

Cost: $400 and up

Eligibility: Committed middle school and high school students

Application Process: Varies

Application Deadline: May 15

Average Number of Applicants: 200

Average Number of Participants: 150

Contact:
Goucher Summer Arts Institute
1021 Dulaney Valley Road
Baltimore, MD 21204
Phone: (410) 337-6390
Fax: (410) 337-6433
www.gouchercenter.edu

GOULD ACADEMY

Young Scholars Program;

College Preparatory Program

Program Location: Gould Academy in Bethel, Maine

Subject Areas: College preparation, science, writing, algebra, geometry, precalculus, computer programming, Spanish

Program Description: Offers instruction for students seeking academic enrichment. Arts and music integrated into the curriculum. Students take full advantage of the hiking, kayaking, and canoeing provided through the school's beautiful setting.

Program Dates: June to August

Gould Academy

Duration of Program: Young Scholars Program: 4 weeks; College Preparatory Program: 6 weeks

Cost: Young Scholars Program: $2,550; College Preparatory Program: $3,800 (both include room and board and transportation)

Financial Aid: Available

Eligibility: Young Scholars Program: gifted and talented students in grades 7–9; College Preparatory Program: students in grades 10–12

Application Process: Writing sample, parent statement, teacher recommendation, transcript, standardized testing (required for Young Scholars Program only)

Application Deadline: Rolling (preference given to applications received before April 30)

Average Number of Participants: 65

Contact:
Gould Academy
P.O. Box 860
Bethel, ME 04217
Phone: (207) 824-7777
Fax: (207) 824-2926
johnosnt@gouldacademy.org
www.gouldacademy.org

GREENBRIER RIVER OUTDOOR ADVENTURES

Program Location: West Virginia and New England

Subject Areas: Outdoor adventure

Program Description: Programs such as Rock and River, New England Explorer, Wildwater Adventures, and Wilderness Explorer offer a wide range of outdoor activities for teenagers, including whitewater rafting, rock climbing, and mountain biking, focusing on adventure challenge and a community ethic.

Program Dates: Sessions throughout summer

Duration of Program: 1–3 weeks

Eligibility: No special requirements

Greenbrier River Outdoor Adventures

Cost: $715 and up

Application Process: Application form, deposit of $100/week

Contact:
P.O. Box 160
Bartow, WV 24920-0160
Phone: (304) 456-5191 or (800) 600-4752
Fax: (304) 456-3121
groa@groa.com
www.groa.com

HAMPSHIRE COLLEGE

Hampshire College Summer Studies in Mathematics

Program Location: Hampshire College in Amherst, Massachusetts

Subject Areas: Mathematics

Program Description: Working in small classes and individually, students actively engage in the processes of mathematical thought: investigating concrete problems, seeking patterns and generalizations, formulating conjectures in the language of mathematics, and applying insight and experience to the creation of proofs. Four hours of classes each morning and several hours of independent and small group study each evening. Workshops at the start of the summer led by college mathematicians.

Midway through the program, participants choose the direction of their mathematical activities for the remainder of the summer.

Program Dates: June 30–August 10

Duration of Program: 6 weeks

Cost: $1,882 (includes room and board and airport/bus station pickup/dropoff)

Financial Aid: Available

Eligibility: Students in grades 9–12

Application Process: Application, take-home test, sponsor recommendation, and personal statement are required. Transcript and standardized test scores are optional.

Application Deadline: Rolling

Average Number of Applicants: 80

Average Number of Participants: 40

Academic Credit: None available

Contact:
Hampshire College Summer Studies
in Mathematics
Hampshire College
Box NS Hessim
Amherst, MA 01002
Phone: (413) 559-5375
Fax: (413) 559-5448
Dkelly@hampshire.edu

HARGRAVE MILITARY ACADEMY

Summer School and Camp

Program Location: Hargrave Military Academy in Chatham, Virginia

Subject Areas: High school/middle school curriculum, athletics (football, basketball, soccer, swimming, tennis, weightlifting, wrestling), outdoor adventure

Program Description: Program for high school and middle school boys that offers one of the following choices: two repeat classes and one sports activity; or one new class and one sports activity; or one repeat class and two sports activities. Half-credit enrichment courses are offered in such areas as computer applications, drama, leadership, and study skills. Athletic activities are lead by the school's post-graduate and varsity coaches. Outdoor activities include backpacking, rock climbing/rappelling, marksmanship, and canoeing. Integrity and leadership are stressed throughout the program.

Program Dates: June–July

Duration of Program: 5 weeks

Cost: $3,150 for boarders (includes room and board, laundry, activities fee, book rental, and uniforms); cost varies for day students depending on courses and activities chosen

Eligibility: Boys in grades 6–12. Applicants should note that attendance at Sunday morning and Thursday evening church services is mandatory.

Application Process: Nonrefundable fee of $50

Application Deadline: Late June

Academic Credit: High school credit available

Contact:
Hargrave Military Academy
attn: Summer School
200 Military Drive
Chatham, VA 24531
Phone: (800) 432-2480; (804) 432-2481
Fax: (804) 432-3129
admissions@hargrave.edu
www.hargrave.edu/overview/summer/summer.html

HARVARD UNIVERSITY

Harvard Summer School Secondary School Program

Program Location: Harvard University in Cambridge, Massachusetts

Subject Areas: Liberal arts and sciences

Program Description: Students choose from nearly 200 summer session courses in 45 liberal arts and sciences fields and enroll in two

4-unit courses or one 8-unit course. Students receive letter grades for courses, many of which are taught by Harvard faculty. The program includes a College Choices program that sponsors workshops on college admissions and application writing as well as a college fair with representatives from top colleges. Students may commute or live in Harvard dormitories.

Program Dates: June 24–August 10

Duration of Program: 8 weeks

Cost: $3,600 for tuition; additional $3,050 for room and board

Financial Aid: Limited

Eligibility: Applicants must currently be juniors or seniors in high school, and be mature, motivated students who can demonstrate potential for success in a college environment. Current sophomores who can commute to campus may also apply.

Application Process: Application, teacher and counselor recommendations, short essays, standardized test scores, transcript. $40 nonrefundable application fee. Catalog request form and downloadable application form are available on website.

Application Deadline: Applications are reviewed as soon as they are completed; most applicants will receive a decision letter within a week of that time. Some students are placed on a waiting list.

Average Number of Participants: 1,000

Academic Credit: College credits are recorded on an official Harvard transcript and are transferable to most colleges.

Contact:
Harvard Summer School
51 Brattle Street
Cambridge, Massachusetts 02138-3722
Phone: (617) 495-3192
pandey@hudce.harvard.edu
www.ssp.harvard.edu

See also Quest Scholars Program

HAWAII PREPARATORY ACADEMY

Hawaii Preparatory Academy Summer Session

Program Location: Kamuela, Hawaii

Subject Areas: High school/middle school curriculum

Program Description: Over 40 academic and enrichment courses, including ESL, Hawaiian studies, environmental science, marine biology, and videography. Students register for four classes (two morning and two afternoon classes), which they attend Monday–Saturday; morning classes are two hours long, and afternoon classes are one hour in length. Afternoon athletics program includes a nationally recognized equestrian program, SCUBA training, and traditional sports; there are also field trips on Wednesdays and outdoor activities on weekends.

Program Dates: Third week of June through third week of July

Duration of Program: 5 weeks

Cost: $3,500 (boarders); $2,200 (commuters) (2001 rates)

Eligibility: Students entering grades 6–11. Although there are no specific guidelines for acceptance, HPA looks for students who are doing well in their current studies.

Application Process: Application, academic transcript, teacher evaluation form, $20 application fee; online and downloadable application forms are available through website. Once an application file is complete, the review committee considers it and generally makes a decision within 1–2 weeks. Incomplete applications will not be considered.

Application Deadline: May 1

Average Number of Applicants: 200

Average Number of Participants: 120

Academic Credit: None available

Contact:
HPA Summer Session
65-1692 Kohala Mountain Road
Kamuela, HI 96743-8476
Phone: (808) 881-4088
Fax: (808) 881-4071
summer@hpa.edu
www.hpa.edu/SummerSchool/
SummerSchool.html

Contact:
Higher Ground Softball camps
attn: Bobby Simpson
P.O. Box 741
Tifton, GA 31793
Phone: (229) 386-9770
Fax: (229) 386-9774
hgsofbal@surfsouth.com
www.surfsouth.com/~hgsofbal

Higher Ground Softball Camps

HIGHER GROUND SOFTBALL CAMPS

Program Location: Various locations around the world

Subject Areas: Girls' softball

Program Description: Higher Ground coordinates advanced and basic skills camps for individuals and teams around the world.

Program Dates: June–July

Cost: Varies

Financial Aid: None

Eligibility: Girls only, ages 8 and up

Application Process: Registration forms

Average Number of Participants: 1,000

HOBART AND WILLIAM SMITH COLLEGES

Environmental Studies Summer Youth Institute

Program Location: Hobart and William Smith Colleges on Seneca Lake in Geneva, New York

Subject Areas: Environmental studies

Program Description: An introduction to a variety of environmental issues and topics in environmental policy, economics, and ethics. Students learn from and conduct research with full-time HWS faculty in a variety of locations, such as the HWS Explorer (a 65-foot vessel on Seneca Lake), Native American historical sites, quaking bogs, and organic farms. The weekend midway through the program will be spent camping in the Adirondacks.

Program Dates: July–August

Duration of Program: 2 weeks

Cost: TBA

Eligibility: Students entering grades 11–12

Application Process: Application form, personal statement, transcript, SAT or PSAT scores, teacher recommendation

Application Deadline: Rolling admissions, but students should apply early since enrollment is limited

Academic Credit: College credit awarded upon successful completion of program

Contact:
Environmental Studies Summer Youth Institute
Geneva, NY 14456-3397
Phone: (315) 781-3377
Fax: (315) 781-3348
www.hws.edu/

HOCKEY OPPORTUNITY CAMP

Program Location: The Almaquin Highlands of Ontario, Canada

Subject Areas: Hockey

Program Description: Canada's largest residential hockey camp provides daily hockey instruction with a full camp program, including waterskiing, mountain biking, archery, wall climbing, and more.

Program Dates: Early July through late August

Duration of Program: 1–8 weeks

Cost: $460 for one week; $430 for each additional week (U.S. dollars)

Eligibility: Coed, ages 7–16, any skill level

Application Deadline: No deadline, but sessions are usually filled by March 1

Average Number of Participants: 250 per week

Contact:
Hockey Opportunity Camp
Box 448
Sundridge, Ontario CANADA POA 1ZO
Phone: (888) LRN2PLAY
Fax: (705) 386-0179
hoc@learnhockey.com
www.learnhockey.com

HOLLINS UNIVERSITY

Hollinscience Program

Program Location: Hollins University in Roanoke, Virginia

Subject Areas: Science

Program Description: Program features classroom, laboratory, and small project work in areas such as biology, computer science, biochemistry, chemistry, physics, and mathematics. Hollins professors lead lectures, discussions, and workshops in small groups. All participants receive a certificate of participation and the instructor's written evaluation of their progress. Optional college application/ admissions workshop is given by experienced admissions counselors.

Program Dates: June 18–29 (2001 dates)

Duration of Program: 2 weeks

Cost: $900 (includes room and board)

Financial Aid: Limited number of need-based scholarships available; scholarship application available on website

Eligibility: Girls entering grades 11 and 12

Application Process: Application (available on website), official transcript, $40 application fee, recommendation from teacher or guidance counselor

Application Deadline: April 23 (2001 date)

Leadership Enrichment Program

Program Location: Hollins University in Roanoke, Virginia

Subject Areas: Leadership training

Program Description: Program designed to give high school girls the opportunity to assess and develop their leadership skills in small groups. Emphasizes organization, teamwork, communication, ethics, conflict resolution. Instructors and staff work closely with each student throughout the week. Optional college application/admissions workshop is given by experienced admissions counselors.

Program Dates: July 9–13 (2001 dates)

Duration of Program: 5 days

Cost: $475 (residential); $375 (commuter)

Financial Aid: Limited number of need-based scholarships available; scholarship application available on website

Eligibility: Girls entering grades 11 and 12

Application Process: Application (available on website), official transcript, $40 application fee

Application Deadline: May 1 (2001 date)

Precollege Program

Program Location: Hollins University in Roanoke, Virginia

Subject Areas: Precollege arts and academics

Program Description: Precollege courses focus on the theme of creativity, with classes in writing, history and philosophy, psychology, and video production. All participants receive a certificate of participation and the instructor's written evaluation of their progress. Optional college application/admissions workshop is given by experienced admissions counselors.

Program Dates: July 2–13

Duration of Program: 2 weeks

Cost: $900 (residential); $725 (commuter)

Financial Aid: Limited number of need-based scholarships available; scholarship application available on website

Eligibility: Girls entering grades 11 and 12

Application Process: Application (available on website), official transcript, $40 application fee

Application Deadline: April 23 (2001 date)

Average Number of Participants: Maximum class size of 16 students

Contact:
Hollinsummer Programs
Hollins University
P.O. Box 9707
Roanoke, VA 24020-1707
Phone: (800) 456-9595
Fax: (540) 362-6410
huadm@hollins.edu
www.hollins.edu/specprog/hollinsummer/
holsum.htm

HORIZON ADVENTURES, INC.

Horizon Adventures

Program Location: Rocky Mountains of Colorado

Subject Areas: Backpacking, mountain biking, rock climbing, whitewater rafting

Program Description: Wilderness courses held in the Rocky Mountains of Colorado. Each 9-day and 12-day course may include a combination of the following: backpacking, mountain biking, rock climbing, river rafting, 14,000-ft peak ascents. A 6-day specialty course is offered in each of the following: rock climbing, mountain biking, and whitewater rafting. All courses stress backcountry safety, wilderness education, and fun. All course equipment is provided by Horizon Adventures.

Program Dates: June 13–August 11

Duration of Program: 6-day, 9-day, and 12-day courses

Cost: $654–$765 (6 days); $895–$965 (9 days); $1,185–$1,285 (12 days).

Financial Aid: Available

Eligibility: Ages 13–17

Application Process: Application form can be downloaded or submitted online via website; $200 deposit required.

Average Number of Participants: 10 participants per course. Participant-instructor ratio is 3:1 during the technical sections of each course and 5:1 during the backpacking portion of each course.

Contact:
Horizon Adventures
1370 Birch Street
Denver, CO 80220
Phone: (303) 393-7297
Fax: (303) 393-7296
horizon@earthnet.net
www.horizonadventures.com

HUGH O'BRIAN YOUTH LEADERSHIP (HOBY)

HOBY Leadership Seminars

Program Location: 85 different sites nationwide

Subject Areas: Leadership, community service

Program Description: HOBY's mission is to seek out and develop leadership potential in high school sophomores, challenging them to complete 100 hours of community service within one year after they leave the seminar. One boy and one girl are chosen from each of the 85 seminars to attend the World Leadership Conference (WLC) in July.

Program Dates: Varies; WLC in July

Duration of Program: 3 days; 8 days for WLC

Cost: None

Eligibility: Students in grade 10

Application Process: One student per high school per year is selected by the high school principal to attend.

Application Deadline: November

Average Number of Applicants: 14,500

Average Number of Participants: 14,500

Academic Credit: None available

Contact:
HOBY
10880 Wilshire Boulevard, Suite 410
Los Angeles, CA 90024
Phone: (310) 474-4370
Fax: (310) 475-5426
www.hoby.org

HUMANITIES SPRING IN ASSISI

Program Location: Assisi, Italy

Subject Areas: Study abroad; Classical and Italian Renaissance literature, art, and architecture

Program Description: Travel-study program for students interested in art, literature, and Italian

Humanities Spring in Assisi

language and culture. Students learn to use great literature and art as a springboard for poems, prose, sketches, collage, and their own personal development in morning classes and afternoon study-trips. Students also travel to Florence, Venice, Rome, Pompeii, and the Amalfi Coast. Participants also attend operas, ballets, puppet shows, and classical and jazz concerts. Program fosters the spirit of collaboration.

Program Dates: June 23–July 23

Duration of Program: 4 weeks

Cost: $3,200 (includes room and board)

Financial Aid: Available (April 1 deadline)

Eligibility: Ages 15–20

Application Process: Application form

Application Deadline: April 1

Average Number of Applicants: 30–40

Average Number of Participants: 10–12

Academic Credit: High school credit possibly available

Contact:
Humanities Spring in Assisi
Santa Maria di Lignano
2 06081 Assisi (PG)
Italy
Phone: 011-39-075-802400
Fax: 011-39-075-802400
info@humanitiesspring.com
www.humanitiesspring.com

HUN SCHOOL OF PRINCETON

Hun School Summer Programs

Program Location: Princeton, New Jersey

Subject Areas: Academics, ESL, theater, performing arts

Program Description: Offers various programs throughout the session: academics, ESL, theater, day camp, and the Bridge Program. Academic program provides small group instruction, traditional grading, and individual attention. A variety of courses available for enrichment or credit. In the ESL program, international students wishing to improve their English language skills balance academic study and cultural enrichment. American students weak in the English language may also apply.

Program Dates: July 1–August 2

Duration of Program: 5 weeks

Cost: $970–$1,730 (academic day); $4,175 (resident); $2,310 (ESL day); $5,120 (ESL resident);$695 (theater). Bridge Program is free.

Financial Aid: None available

Eligibility: Ages 13–18 (must be 14 to board); dance program requires 2–5 years experience

Application Process: Application, recommendation form, $100 application fee ($500 for boarders), audition for theater program

Application Deadline: Rolling

Average Number of Applicants: 130

Average Number of Participants: 120

Academic Credit: Available

Contact:
The Hun School of Princeton
Summer Programs
176 Egerstoune Rd.
Princeton, NJ 08540
Phone: (609) 689-9392
Fax: (609) 924-2170
summer@hunschool.org
www.hunschool.org

HUNTINGDON COLLEGE

Huntingdon College Summer Programs

Program Location: Huntingdon College in Montgomery, Alabama

Subject Areas: Academics, fiction and poetry writing, opera, dance/choreography

Program Descriptions: Huntingdon College Summer Scholars: Students earn college credit by studying for 5 weeks at Huntingdon College. Creative Writing Workshop: Fundamentals of writing and publishing poetry and fiction. Huntingdon College Summer Opera Camp: Gives talented young singers the opportunity to learn the basics of operatic singing and acting in a carefully managed environment. Intensive Choreography Workshop: Three tracks: junior choreographer, senior choreographer, dancer.

Program Dates: June–July

Duration of Programs: Huntingdon College Summer Scholars: 5 weeks; Creative Writing Workshop: 2 weeks; Huntingdon College Summer Opera Camp: 12 days; Intensive Choreography Workshop: 10 days

Cost: $50 per credit hour with a maximum of 6 credit hours

Application Deadline: Huntingdon College Summer Scholars: May 1. Creative Writing Workshop: July 10. Huntingdon College Summer Opera Camp: April 27. Intensive Choreography Workshop: June 10.

Average Number of Participants: Huntingdon College Summer Scholars: 20; Creative Writing Workshop: 10; Huntingdon College Summer Opera Camp: 15; Intensive Choreography Workshop: 15

Academic Credit: College credit available for Huntingdon College Summer Scholars program

Contact:
Huntingdon College
attn: Summer Programs
1500 East Fairview Avenue
Montgomery, AL 36106
Phone: (256) 834-3300
Fax: (256) 264-2951

IDYLLWILD ARTS FOUNDATION

Idyllwild Arts Summer Program

Program Location: Idyllwild, California

Subject Areas: Dance, music, theater, visual arts, creative writing, video, film

Program Description: Intensive hands-on workshops in all of the visual and performing arts for students of all ages and abilities, including families. Campus located in the spectacular San Jacinto Mountains of Southern California.

Program Dates: June 29–August 18

Duration of Program: 3 days–3 weeks

Cost: $750–$850 per week, depending on program (includes room and board)

Financial Aid: Available, early application recommended

Eligibility: Ages 9 and up

Application Process: Some music and theater programs require an audition tape; contact the organization for more information.

Application Deadline: Rolling

Average Number of Applicants: 1,600

Average Number of Participants: 1,600

Academic Credit: None available

Contact:
Idyllwild Arts Summer Program
P.O. Box 38
Idyllwild, CA 92549
Phone: (909) 659-2171, x365
Fax: (909) 659-5463
summerprogram@idyllwildarts.org
www.idyllwildarts.org

ILLINOIS STATE UNIVERSITY

Summer High School Forensic Workshop

Program Location: Illinois State University in Normal, Illinois

Subject Areas: Forensics, speech individual events, oral interpretation, public address

Program Description: Features two separate workshops: one week is devoted to public address events, while the second week is devoted to oral interpretation. Prepares students for high school speech competition. Students can choose to participate in one or both weeks.

Program Dates: Mid-July

Duration of Program: 1 or 2 weeks

Cost: $450 (1 week) or $760 (2 weeks). Includes room and board and transportation.

Financial Aid: None available

Eligibility: Students entering grades 9–12

Application Process: Application (call to request), recommendation

Application Deadline: June 27

Average Number of Applicants: 100–150

Average Number of Participants: 100–150

Academic Credit: None available

Contact:
Campus Box 4480
Illinois State University
Normal, IL 61790
Phone: (309) 438-7326
Fax: (309) 438-3048

INDIANA STATE UNIVERSITY

Summer Honors Program

Program Location: Indiana State University in Terre Haute, Indiana

Subject Areas: Liberal arts and sciences

Program Description: Students chose from 23 different seminars in liberal arts and sciences in a two-week intensive program.

Program Dates: June and July sessions

Duration of Program: 2 weeks

Cost: $510 (Indiana residents); $865 (out-of-state residents). Includes room and board.

Financial Aid: Limited

Eligibility: Applicants must have completed at least their freshman year of high school, and must be ranked in the top 25 percent of their class or have at least a B average.

Application Process: Application packet, teacher recommendations

Application Deadline: Mid-May

Average Number of Applicants: 1,200

Average Number of Participants: 500

Academic Credit: 2 semester hours of college credit awarded upon successful completion of program

Contact:
Indiana State University
Summer Honors Program
125 Erickson Hall
Terre Haute, IN 47809
Phone: (800) 234-1639 (option 3)
or (812) 237-2335
Fax: (812) 237-3495
extcandy@ruby.indstate.edu
www.indstate.edu/hshonors/

INDIANA UNIVERSITY— BLOOMINGTON

College Audition Preparation (CAP);

Summer Piano Academy;

Summer Recorder Academy;

Summer String Academy

Program Location: Indiana University School of Music in Bloomington, Indiana

Subject Areas: Recorder, piano, violin, viola, cello, bass

Program Description: Intensive instruction in recorder, piano, and string instruments. Includes master classes with outstanding faculty instructors. Piano academy offers two private lessons per week, ensemble coaching, and faculty lectures. String academy offers individual instruction and chamber music instruction, along with private lessons, ensemble classes. All three academies provide performance opportunities. College Audition Preparation furnishes students with information that will increase chances of success during the college audition process. Mock auditions and student ensembles organized, and individual counseling provided.

Program Dates: July (CAP, recorder); June–July (piano, string)

Duration of Program: 5 days (CAP); 3 weeks (piano); 2 weeks (recorder); 4 weeks (string)

Cost: $825 (CAP); $1,800 (piano); $1,340 (recorder); $2,450 (string). All include room and board.

Financial Aid: Available for string (February deadline), piano (March deadline), recorder

Eligibility: Serious instrumental music students in grades 10–12 (CAP); grades 7–12 for piano, recorder, and string academies

Application Process: Application, teacher recommendation, videotape with two contrasting pieces or movements, $50 application fee for Summer String Academy

Application Deadline: May (CAP); March (piano); April (recorder); February (string)

Contact:
Office of Special Programs
School of Music, Indiana University
Bloomington, IN 47405
Phone: (812) 855-6025
musicsp@indiana.edu
www.music.indiana.edu/som/special_programs/

High School Journalism Publications Workshops

Program Location: Indiana University School of Journalism in Bloomington, Indiana

Subject Areas: Journalism

Program Description: Students examine the role of the media, analyze their own school publications, and develop the skills and understanding that will prepare them to meet the challenges of producing quality publications.

Program Dates: July

Duration of Program: 5 days (3 sessions)

Cost: $290 plus meal debit card. $240 commuter fee for each session

Eligibility: High school students who have accepted positions on their newspaper, television, or yearbook staff or simply want to learn about journalism

Application Process: Application form

Application Deadline: June

Contact:
Linda J. Johnson
High School Journalism Institute
School of Journalism, Ernie Pyle Hall 200
Indiana University
Bloomington, IN 47405
Phone: (812) 855-0865
dvorakj@indiana.edu
www.journalism.indiana.edu/workshops/HSJI/students.html

Indiana University Summer Music Clinic

Program Location: Indiana University School of Music in Bloomington, Indiana

Subject Areas: Symphonic band, symphony orchestra, festival choirs, jazz ensemble, show choir, vocal jazz, women's choir

Program Description: Under the leadership of nationally known conductors, students participate in their respective areas. Music theory/applied musicianship taught in small classes, with students participating at their individual level of advancement. Electives include conducting, reed making, leadership/motivation, jazz improvisation, and various small ensembles.

Program Dates: June

Duration of Program: 1 week

Cost: $400

Eligibility: Instrumental and vocal music students in grades 9–12

Application Process: Contact program director for more information on applying and deadlines.

Contact:
Stephen W. Pratt, Director
IU Summer Music Clinic
School of Music, Indiana University
Bloomington, Indiana 47405
Phone: (812) 855-1372
www.indiana.edu/~bands/clinic.htm

International Studies Summer Institute for High School Students

Program Location: Indiana University Center for the Study of Global Change in Bloomington, Indiana

Subject Areas: International studies, globalization, international economics and trade, global environmental change, conflict resolution, populations at risk

Program Description: Exposes high school students to a wide range of international issues, through lectures, seminars, teleconferencing, and simulations utilizing nationally prominent speakers, university faculty, and international organization/NGO representatives. Program designed to expose participants to a university-level curriculum and living experience. Attracts participants from around the globe; in previous sessions, students from Japan, Kyrgyzstan, Netherlands, Netherlands Antilles, Philippines, PRC, South Africa, Spain, Taiwan, and Turkey joined with Americans in the program.

Program Dates: July 7–20

Duration of Program: 2 weeks

Cost: $500 (includes room and board)

Financial Aid: Available, April 1 deadline

Eligibility: High school sophomores, juniors, and seniors (ages 15–18) interested in international issues

Application Process: Completion of a paper or online application form, school transcript, letter of recommendation from teacher or school counselor

Application Deadline: Rolling

Average Number of Applicants: 70

Average Number of Participants: 40

Academic Credit: College credit available (3 credits)

Contact:
Center for the Study of Global Change
201 North Indiana Avenue
Indiana University
Bloomington, IN 47408-4001
Phone: (812) 855-0756
Fax: (812) 855-6271
kgold2@indiana.edu
www.indiana.edu/~globalinstitute.htm

Jim Holland Summer Enrichment Program in Biology

Program Location: Indiana University in Bloomington, Indiana

Subject Areas: Biology

Program Description: Program includes lecture-discussions to expose minority students to ideas in genetics, evolution, environmental biology, molecular biology, plant sciences, and microbiology. A substantial portion of the program is devoted to giving students hands-on lab experience in the area of biology related to the discussions. Instructors in the program consist of teams of IU faculty members and high school teachers. Students are housed on campus; evening activities include other

educational, social, and entertainment events.

Program Dates: July 22–27

Duration of Program: 1 week

Cost: No cost, room and board provided

Eligibility: Rising high school freshmen and sophomores who belong to minority groups

Application Process: Application form

Application Deadline: April 20

Contact:
Margi Lockhart, Associate Director
Biology Undergraduate Initiative
Indiana University, Jordan Hall 127
1015 East Atwater Avenue
Bloomington, IN 47401-3773
Phone: (812) 855-6283
Fax: (812) 855-6705
malockha@bio.indiana.edu

Midsummer Theatre Program

Program Location: Indiana University Department of Theatre and Drama in Bloomington, Indiana

Subject Areas: Theater, production arts

Program Description: Comprehensive program integrating all the theater arts, educating students through the study, appreciation, and application of performance and production arts and crafts. Primary means of instruction is experiential, developing each student's artistic capacity in a demanding but nurturing theater laboratory. Core curriculum focuses on acting, movement, voice, scene study, and dramatic literature. Practical experiences in musical theater; auditioning; playwriting; television; scenic, costume, and lighting design; and makeup. Students attend performances, tour facilities, and meet professional artists and staff at area theaters. Participants are housed on campus.

Program Dates: June 10–23

Duration of Program: 2 weeks

Cost: $850

Financial Aid: None available

Eligibility: Rising sophomores, juniors, and seniors; experience preferred, but not necessary

Application Process: Application

Application Deadline: Contact program for more information

Contact:
Midsummer Theatre Program
Department of Theatre and Drama
Indiana University
Theatre 200
Bloomington, IN 47405-1111
Phone: (812) 855-4502
Fax: (812) 855-4704
theatre@indiana.edu

See also All-American Rowing Camp, LLC

Interlochen Center for the Arts

INDIANA UNIVERSITY—PURDUE UNIVERSITY INDIANAPOLIS (IUPUI)

See Purdue School of Engineering and Technology, IUPUI

INTERLOCHEN CENTER FOR THE ARTS

Interlochen Arts Camp

Program Location: Interlochen, Michigan

Subject Areas: Performing arts, visual arts, creative writing

Program Description: Nestled between two lakes on 1,200 wooded acres, the Interlochen camp offers daily instruction in music, theater, dance, visual arts, and creative writing in addition to more than 500 student and guest artist performances each summer. Participants come from every state and from 45 foreign countries.

Program Dates: Mid-June through mid-August

Duration of Program: 8 weeks

Cost: $4,490

Eligibility: Ages 8–18, grades 3–12

Application Process: Registration forms, $35 application fee, audition materials if required

Application Deadline: February 15

Financial Aid Deadline: February 15

Average Number of Applicants: 3,000

Average Number of Participants: 2, 150

Academic Credit: None

Contact:
Interlochen Arts Camp
P.O. Box 199
Interlochen, MI 49643-0199
Phone: (231) 276-7472
Fax: (231) 276-7464
admissions@interlochen.k12.mi.us
www.interlochen.org

INTERLOCKEN

Crossroads Adventure Travel

Program Location: Italy-Switzerland-France, France-Spain-Portugal

Subject Areas: Outdoor adventure, performing arts, travel abroad

Program Description: The Venice to Paris Cycling Trip involves biking your way through three countries, and includes camping and spending a few final days in Paris. The European Traveling Minstrels tour is intended for students who have a deep enthusiasm for the performing arts. Students become actual members of a traveling theater troupe, moving throughout France, Spain and Portugal. Most nights are spent out of doors in tents, and travel involves long van rides. Students will develop individual skits/dances/mime that they will perform in front of local audiences.

Program Dates: July through August

Duration of Program: 5 to 6 weeks

Cost: $3,850–$4,350. Airfare not included.

Financial Aid: Some scholarships available

Eligibility: Grades 9–12

Application Deadline: Rolling admissions

Academic Credit: None available

Contact:
Interlocken
RR2 Box 16
Hillsboro, NH 03244
Phone: (603) 478-3166
Fax: (603) 478-5260
mail@interlocken.org
www.interlocken.org

INTERN EXCHANGE INTERNATIONAL

Program Location: London, England

Subject Areas: Internships abroad

Program Description: Program offers exciting internships in London at the side of a practicing professional in fields such as law, medicine, finance, and the arts. Students live in dormitories at the University of London, along with IEI staff who are available 24 hours a day. Additional day trips, weekend excursions, and special touring events are included.

Program Dates: June 27–July 26

Duration of Program: 4 weeks

Cost: $5,295 (airfare not included)

Interlocken—Crossroads Adventure Travel

Intern Exchange International

Eligibility: Grades 10–12

Application Process: Application (available on website), personal essay, transcript, $50 application fee, $450 tuition deposit

Application Deadline: Rolling

Average Number of Participants: 215

Contact:
Intern Exchange International
130 Harold Road
Woodmere, NY 11598-1435
Phone: (516) 374-3939
Fax: (516) 374-2104
InternExchange@compuserve.com
www.internexchange.com

INTERNATIONAL BICYCLE FUND

Bicycle Africa Tours;

Sbuhbi Lithlal Ti Swatixwtuhd

Program Locations: Bicycle Africa: various countries in Africa. Sbuhbi Lithlal Ti Swatixwtuhd: Washington State and British Columbia, Canada.

Subject Areas: Cycling, cross-cultural experiences

Program Description: Educational, cross-cultural bicycle tours for ordinarily active people of all ages. Visit development projects, schools, farms, parks, historic sites, and more. Accommodation and food vary with local conditions (no camping).

Program Dates: Bicycle Africa Tours: sessions throughout the year; Sbuhbi Lithlal Ti Swatixwtuhd: July and August

Duration of Program: Bicycle Africa Tours: 2–4 weeks, contact organization for details on different tours; Sbuhbi Lithlal Ti Swatixwtuhd: 2 weeks

Cost: Bicycle Africa Tours: $990–$1,990 (airfare not included); Sbuhbi Lithlal Ti Swatixwtuhd: $1,290 (airfare not included)

Eligibility: Must be in good physical and mental health

Application Deadline: Rolling admissions

Application Process: Waiver form, participant data form, personal health review, $300 deposit

Contact:
International Bicycle Fund
4887 Columbia Drive South
Seattle, WA 98108-1919
Phone: (206) 767-0848
Fax: (206) 767-0848
ibike@ibike.org
www.ibike.org/ibike

INTERNATIONAL SPORTS CAMP

Program Location: The Pocono Mountains of Pennsylvania

Subject Areas: Basketball, baseball, soccer, field hockey, volleyball

Program Description: Offers five specialized sports programs and one all-around sports program that provides the best in athletic

training and camping fun. Provides live-in counselors and well-maintained cabins. Collegiate coaching staff provides in-depth instruction. Additional recreational activities, including the climbing tower and water activities, also offered.

Program Dates: June–August

Duration of Program: 1 week

Cost: $400–$600 (includes room and board)

Financial Aid: None available

Eligibility: Coed, ages 8–18

Application Process: Application form

Application Deadline: Rolling

Average Number of Applicants: 3,000

Average Number of Participants: 2,000

Academic Credit: None available

Contact:
International Sports Camp
1100 Twin Lake Road
Stroudsburg, PA 18360
Phone: (570) 620-2267
Fax: (570) 620-1692
www.international-sports.com

INVOLVEMENT VOLUNTEERS ASSOCIATION

International Volunteering;

Networked International Volunteering

Program Location: Argentina, Armenia, Australia, Bangladesh, Belgium, Cambodia, China, Denmark, Ecuador, England, Fiji, Finland, Germany, Greece, India, Italy, Japan, Kenya, Korea, Lebanon, Mexico, Mongolia, Nepal, New Zealand, Poland, Russia, Sabah (Malaysia), Samoa, South Africa, Spain, Thailand, Turkey, Ukraine, Vietnam, Venezuela

Subject Areas: Volunteer, travel abroad

Program Description: IV offers volunteer opportunities all over the world for those seriously committed to helping others or working to preserve the natural world.

Duration of Program: Minimum of 2 weeks and maximum of 12 months

Cost: Varies with location

Eligibility: Highly mature and committed volunteers only

Application Process: Registration form, passport-sized photos

Application Deadline: Flexible, but 3 months before starting date is preferred

Average Number of Applicants: 400

Average Number of Participants: Nearly 400

Academic Credit: A letter detailing volunteer's participation is provided upon request

Contact:
Involvement Volunteers Association
P.O. Box 218
Port Melbourne, Victoria 3207 AUSTRALIA
Phone: +61 3 9646 9392
Fax: +61 3 9646 5504
ivworldwide@volunteering.org.au
www.volunteering.org.au

IRISH AMERICAN CULTURAL ORGANIZATION

Irish Way

Program Location: Ireland

Subject Areas: Ireland's history and traditions, Gaelic, literature, drama, art, music; homestay; travel abroad

Program Description: Divided into three parts: Irish Education, Home Stay, and Touring. Founded on the belief that fostering an appreciation of other cultures is an important part of an individual's development. An opportunity for young people to explore the rich heritage and tradition of Ireland, while also experiencing the country's distinct culture face-to-face.

Program Dates: July

Duration of Program: 5 weeks

Cost: $2,995 (includes room and board and transportation)

Financial Aid: Available

Eligibility: American high school students

Application Deadline: April

Average Number of Applicants: 100–150

Average Number of Participants: 100

Academic Credit: High school credit available

Contact:
The Irish American Cultural Institute
1 Lackawanna Place
Morristown, NJ 07960
Phone: (973) 605-1991
Fax: (973) 605-8875
irishwaynj@aol.com
www.irishaci.org

IRISH CENTRE FOR TALENTED YOUTH

Program Location: Dublin City University in Dublin, Ireland

Subject Areas: Academic study abroad, including archaeology, architecture, astronomy, aviation studies, classics, creative writing, international relations, global economics, philosophy, politics, psychology, pharmacology

Program Description: Offers highly stimulating and challenging college-level courses for high ability students. Past participants have included students from the U.S., Ireland, other European countries, and Far Eastern countries. Certain aspects of the course material particularly pertain to the Irish setting of the program. For example, the works of Joyce, Beckett, Yeats, and Shaw have been the inspiration of the literature, drama, and writing classes. Students housed in university residence halls. Other campus facilities include a modern and well-equipped library, television and sound studios, computer laboratories, an audio-visual learning resource center, print and graphics studios, research and teaching laboratories, and a modern indoor Sports Complex.

Program Dates: Two sessions: June 16–July 5 and July 7–26

Duration of Program: 3 weeks

Cost: $2,000 (includes room and board)

Financial Aid: Available (two full scholarships available for overseas students)

Eligibility: Ages 12–16, with qualifying SAT scores

Application Process: Application (available on website, or request from Centre)

Application Deadline: April 1

Average Number of Applicants: 550

Average Number of Participants: 550

Academic Credit: Students must arrange credit individually

Contact:
The Irish Centre for Talented Youth
Dublin City University
Dublin 9
Ireland
Phone: (353 1) 700-5634
Fax: (353 1) 700-5693
ctyi@dcu.edu
www.dcu.ie/ctyi

THE ISLAND LABORATORY

Program Location: Connecticut

Subject Areas: Science, environmental studies, outdoor activities, leadership skills, survival skills

Program Description: For 21 years, the Island Laboratory has offered interdisciplinary programs in science, outdoor skills, and leadership. Students take part in laboratory experiments, cook their own meals, and go rafting, canoeing, snorkeling, and spelunking. The program is staffed by volunteers, and all fees go toward food, equipment, and the program.

Program Dates: Early July

Duration of Program: 1 week (Saturday through Saturday)

Cost: $300

Eligibility: Ages 14–19

Application Process: First come, first served. Fill out registration form on webpage or contact by phone; $25 nonrefundable deposit required.

Application Deadline: June 30, but program often fills before that date

Financial Aid: None available

Average Number of Participants: 18; maximum enrollment is 28

Academic Credit: None

Contact:
The Island Laboratory
Harvey Remz, Director
33 Brentley Drive
Huntington, CT 06484
Phone: (203) 929-8746
Harvey.Remz@elizabetharden.com
www.geocities.com/islandlab

ITHACA COLLEGE

Summer College for High School Students

Program Location: Ithaca College in Ithaca, New York

Subject Areas: Theater, musical theater, film, communications, humanities, science, college preparation

Program Description: Offers bright students an opportunity to experience college life during the summer. Classes are taught by Ithaca College faculty, and students live together in a college residence hall. Extracurricular activities include trips to the theater, area parks, a minor league baseball game, dances, etc.

Program Dates: June 30–July 19, or June 30–August 2

Duration of Program: 3 or 5 weeks

Cost: $2,500 (3 weeks, includes room and board); $4,500 (5 weeks, includes room and board)

Financial Aid: Available

Eligibility: Students who have completed grades 10 or 11

Application Process: High school transcript, letter of recommendation, three short essays

Application Deadline: May 1

Average Number of Applicants: 120

Average Number of Participants: 100

Academic Credit: College credit available (3–6 credits)

Contact:
Ithaca College
Summer College for High School Students
120 Towers Concourse
Ithaca, NY 14850-7141
Phone: (607) 274-3143
Fax: (607) 274-1263
cess@ithaca.edu
www.ithaca.edu/summercollege

JCC MACCABI XPERIENCE ISRAEL PROGRAMS

Israel Summer Programs

Program Location: Israel

Subject Areas: Travel abroad, leadership training, outdoor activities

Program Description: Israel Teen Connection takes participants in a thorough tour of Israel, including all of the major cities and archaeological sites. Adventure Israel is an outdoor challenge tour, focusing on adventure, athletics, and outdoor activities. Sports Spectacular combines touring and sports activities, and the Leadership Training Program, which begins in Italy, provides leadership training at various Israeli sites.

Program Dates: July

JCC Maccabi Xperience Israel Programs

Duration of Program: 4–5 weeks

Cost: $3,700–$4,500 (includes airfare)

Financial Aid: Available

Eligibility: Jewish students in grades 9–12

Application Process: Nonrefundable deposit of $180 and interview required.

Application Deadline: May 31

Academic Credit: College credit available

Contact:
JCC Maccabi Xperience Israel Programs
15 East 26th Street
New York, NY 10010
Phone: (212) 532-4949, (800) 732-1266
Fax: (212) 481-4174
info@jccmaccabix.org
www.jccmaccabix.org

JOEL ROSS TENNIS & SPORTS CAMP

Program Location: Kent School in Kent, Connecticut

Subject Areas: Tennis

Program Description: A tennis camp at a prep school at the foot of the Berkshire Mountains. 3–5 hours of daily instruction and match play and 1:4 counselor-camper ratio assures personal attention and quality instruction. Each camper is evaluated and placed in an appropriate group. Offers plenty of other activities and electives, including archery, basketball, biking, canoeing, golf, lacrosse, rollerblading, soccer, and much more.

Program Dates: Late June through mid-August

Duration of Program: 2, 4, 6, or 7 weeks

Cost: $1,795 per session (averages 1 week), $1,195 per minisession

Eligibility: Coed, ages 8–18, all skill levels

Application Process: Online application form available on website. $400 deposit, proof of recent medical exam required.

Contact:
Joel Ross Tennis & Sports Camp
Box 62H
Scarsdale, NY 10583
Phone: (914) 668-3258
Fax: (914) 723-4579
info@joelrosstennis.com
www.joelrosstennis.com

JOHNS HOPKINS UNIVERSITY

Hopkins Pre-college Credit Program

Program Location: Johns Hopkins University in Baltimore, Maryland

Subject Areas: Anthropology, art, biology, chemistry, classics, cognitive science, computer science, earth science, economics, engineering, English, history, languages, mathematics, music, philosophy, physics, political science, psychology, sociology, writing

Program Description: Students interact with a diverse community of advisors, students, faculty, and staff from across the nation and around the world. In the College Preview program, students select any two courses. In the Focus Program, students select two courses that direct them toward a career goal. Both offer extracurricular activities that allow students to explore their interests along with the considerable depth and breadth of the university. Commuter and residential options available.

Program Dates: June–August

Duration of Program: 5 weeks

Cost: $4,750 (residential); $460 per credit plus $100 program fee (commuters)

Financial Aid: Limited merit-based and need-based aid available. Contact the Office of Summer Programs to obtain a financial aid application.

Eligibility: Applicants must be at least 16 and have completed their sophomore year in high school by the time the program takes place.

Application Process: Completed application and residential life forms, test scores (PSAT, SAT, PACT, or ACT), transcript, essay, recommendations (1 from a teacher and 1 from a guidance counselor or principal) required. Downloadable forms available on website.

Application Deadline: April 27 (2001 date)

Academic Credit: College credit available

Contact:
Johns Hopkins University
attn: Academic Program Coordinator
Office of Summer Programs
3003 North Charles Street, Suite 150
Baltimore, MD 21218
Phone: (410) 516-4548; (800) 548-0548
Fax: (410) 516-6017
summer@jhu.edu
www.jhu.edu/summer/pc/

JOHNS HOPKINS UNIVERSITY CENTER FOR TALENTED YOUTH

CTY Summer Programs;

CAA Summer Programs

Program Location: CTY and CAA programs are offered at college campuses throughout the U.S. Past CTY sites have included Johns Hopkins University (Baltimore, MD), Dickinson College (Carlisle, PA), Franklin & Marshall College (Lancaster, PA), Loyola Marymount University (Los Angeles, CA), Skidmore College (Saratoga Springs, NY), and Union College (Schenectady, NY). Past CAA sites have included Roger Williams University (Bristol, RI), Moravian College (Bethlehem, PA), Hood College (Frederick, MD), and University of California at Santa Cruz (Santa Cruz, CA).

Subject Areas: Science, marine science, mathematics, computer science, history and social science, writing, the arts, philosophy, and the classics

Program Description: These programs support and nurture academic talent by providing exceptionally motivated and academically talented students with a chance to study at a pace and depth appropriate for their abilities. Students take only one course—an intense immersion course taught well above grade level that emphasizes active learning and putting knowledge to use in independent and creative ways. Classes are small and are led by an instructor and an instructional assistant. Rather than assign grades, instructors write detailed evaluations describing each student's progress and outlining areas for further growth. Students live on campus and participate in special extracurricular activities.

Program Dates: Session 1: June–July; session 2: July–August

Duration of Program: 3 weeks

Cost: $2,260 (residential); $1,450 (commuter); $2,850 (certain marine science courses)

Financial Aid: Limited assistance awarded based on financial need

Eligibility: Students must be in grade 7 or above but must not turn 17 before September 1 of the year in which they wish to participate in the program. The SAT and the Institute's Spatial Test Battery determine eligibility for the programs. Test scores must place CTY applicants in the top one-half of one percent of their age mates, and must place CAA applicants in the top two percent of their age mates. Visit www.jhu.edu/gifted/ctysummer for more info.

Application Process: Completed application form and medical form; $40 application fee, deposit required

Application Deadline: March 31 (2001 date)

Average Number of Participants: Approximately 2,000

Contact:
Johns Hopkins University
Center for Talented Youth
3400 North Charles Street
Baltimore, MD 21218
Phone: (410) 516-0278
Fax: (410) 516-0325
ctyinfo@jhu.edu
www.jhu.edu/gifted/ctysummer/

JUNIATA COLLEGE

Voyages: Summer Camp for Gifted Students

Program Location: Juniata College in Huntingdon, Pennsylvania

Subject Areas: Arts, humanities, math, science

Program Description: Residential program in the arts, sciences, and humanities, with evening activities, small counselor groupings, and on-campus supervision 24 hours/day.

Program Dates: TBA

Duration of Program: 1 week

Cost: $400 (includes room and board)

Financial Aid: None available

Eligibility: Gifted students entering grades 8–10 in the fall. Students must have high ability, strong school performance, and maturity necessary to live in a residential setting with peers.

Application Process: Application and medical forms

Application Deadline: May 30

Average Number of Participants: 60–80

Academic Credit: None available

Contact:
attn: Dr. Fay Glosenger
Juniata College
1700 Moore Street
Huntingdon, PA 16652
Phone: (814) 641-3655
Fax: (814) 641-3695
glosenger@juniata.edu

JUNIOR STATESMEN FOUNDATION

Junior Statesmen Summer School

Program Location: Georgetown University in Washington, DC; Yale University in New Haven, Connecticut; Princeton University in Princeton, New Jersey; Northwestern University in Evanston, Illinois; Stanford University in Stanford, California

Subject Areas: Debate, speech communication, U.S. foreign policy, constitutional law, American government, economics, comparative government and politics

Program Description: Programs prepare outstanding students for leadership in a democratic society. Students at month-long sessions (Princeton, Yale, Stanford and Northwestern) select two challenging courses, one in Government and the other in Speech. Students who attend the three-week Georgetown session select a single Government course. All programs involve substantial reading, research, and writing. Each three- or four-week class is equivalent to a one-semester, high school honors or AP course. Classes held Monday through Saturday, taught by top university professors. Faculty and college-age resident assistants live on campus with students, providing academic counseling and supervision.

Program Dates: Varies by program

Duration of Program: 3 weeks (Georgetown); 4 weeks (Princeton, Yale, Stanford, and Northwestern)

Cost: $3,100 (2001 cost) (includes room and board)

Financial Aid: Partial scholarships available, based on academic merit and financial need

Eligibility: Any outstanding student entering grades 10–12 may apply. U.S. citizenship not required (assuming excellent command of written and spoken English). Competitive admissions, based on academic achievement, leadership ability, maturity, and interest in politics. Given the demands of the curriculum, the Admissions Committee is especially interested in students who have performed well in their high school English and social studies classes.

Application Process: Application form, personal essay, official transcript, recommendation from school counselor or English/social studies teacher.

Application Deadline: Applications are accepted beginning in February and until all spaces are filled

Average Number of Participants: 800+

Academic Credit: High school and college credit available. Summer school transcripts may be sent to student's high school upon request.

Contact:
Junior Statesmen Summer School
60 East Third Avenue, Suite 320
San Mateo, CA 94401
Phone: (800) 334-5353
Fax: (650) 347-7200
jsa@jsa.org
www.jsa.org/summer/index.html

KENYON COLLEGE

Young Writers at Kenyon

Program Location: Kenyon College in Gambier, Ohio

Subject Areas: Writing

Program Description: An intensive, residential workshop for motivated high school students, Young Writers at Kenyon tries to develop productive writers and insightful thinkers. Students write stories, poetry, personal narratives, dialogues, reflective passages, and experimental pieces. Workshop groups (13–15 students per group) meet for 5 hours each day; sharing and discussion of students' work is a central part of the workshop. Instructors do not assign grades but do meet with each student in individual conferences. Weekend activities include social events and field trips.

Program Dates: June–July

Duration of Program: 2 weeks

Cost: $1,300 (includes room and board)

Financial Aid: Some need-based aid available

Eligibility: Ages 16–18. Competitive admissions, based primarily on the student's application essay and a teacher's recommendation.

Application Process: Written application, essay, transcripts, teacher recommendation

Application Deadline: April 2 (2001 date)

Average Number of Applicants: 100+

Average Number of Participants: 50

Academic Credit: None available

Contact:
Young Writers at Kenyon
Sunset Cottage
Kenyon College
Gambier, Ohio 43022-9623
Phone: (740) 427-5207
Fax: (740) 427-5417
kenyonreview@kenyon.edu
www.kenyonreview.org

THE KICKING GAME

Program Location: Camarillo, California

Subject Areas: Football kicking

Program Description: Offers year-round service for all kickers, with summer camps and private lessons also offered. Also provides help getting players into college, and college players into the NFL.

Program Dates: TBA

Duration of Program: 4 days

Cost: $350 (4-day camp); $60/hr for private lessons

Financial Aid: None available

Eligibility: All ages; mainly high school, college, and professional players

Average Number of Applicants: 100

Average Number of Participants: 100

Contact:
The Kicking Game
P.O. Box 621
Camarillo, California 93011
Phone: (805) 445-8541
Fax: (805) 445-8541
www.greenheart.com/stonehouse/

KINCARDINE SUMMER MUSIC FESTIVAL

KSMF Jazz Camp;

KSMF Chamber Music Camp;

KSMF Festival Week Music Camp

Program Location: Kincardine, Ontario, Canada

Subject Areas: Jazz, chamber music, band, strings, vocal

Program Description: At the Jazz Camp, young musicians enroll in master classes and work in small ensembles with other brass, woodwind, drum, piano, and guitar players and vocalists to develop skills in phrasing and improvisation. A Basic Guitar program was added to the Jazz Camp in 2001 and will continue in 2002. At the Chamber Music Camp, string, wind, and piano players learn the art of performing in small ensembles. At the Festival Week Music Camp, band, string, and choir enthusiasts spend a week working with some of the finest teachers available; beginning level programs are available for both children and adults. None of the camps are residential, but housing for out-of-town students can be arranged.

Program Dates: Jazz: August 4–9, 2002; Chamber Music: August 11–18, 2002; Festival Week: August 11–17, 2002

Duration of Program: 1 week

Cost: Jazz: $300; Chamber Music: $325 for strings and winds, $430 for piano; Festival Week: $150. All are Canadian dollars.

Kincardine Summer Music Festival

Financial Aid: Available. Deadlines: Jazz: June 1, 2002; Chamber Music and Festival Week: until first day of program.

Eligibility: At least a high school level of technical ability is expected for Jazz and Chamber Music Camps, and adults are also welcome. The Festival Week Camp accommodates beginner to advanced musicians, but there are some minimum age limits for the beginner programs.

Application Process: Registration forms, audition for placement only in Jazz and Chamber Music.

Application Deadline: No deadline, but price goes up after June 30. Applications for the Chamber piano program must be received by July 1.

Average Number of Participants: Jazz camp: 55; Chamber Music: 55; Festival Week: 400

Academic Credit: None available

Contact:
Irv Mills
P.O. Box 251
Kincardine, Ontario, CANADA N2Z 2Y7
Phone: (519) 396-2769 or (866) 453-9716
Fax: (519) 396-2769
imills@primeline.net
www.primeline.net/ksmf/

KINGDOM COUNTY PRODUCTIONS AND FLEDGLING FILMS

Fledgling Films Summer Institute

Program Location: Burke Mountain Academy in East Burke, Vermont

Subject Areas: Filmmaking

Program Description: Led by film school interns and professional filmmakers, teens delve into every aspect of filmmaking, from writing, acting, directing, editing, light and sound, production, and camera work.

Program Dates: July

Duration of Program: 3 weeks

Cost: $2,350 (out-of-state boarders); $1,950 (in-state boarders); $1,650 (commuters)

Eligibility: Students in grades 8–12

Application Process: Application with brief résumé and writing sample. Audition required for actors and directors. Recommendations welcomed.

Application Deadline: May

Average Number of Applicants: 50

Average Number of Participants: 30

Academic Credit: College credit available

Contact:
Fledgling Films
949 Somers Road
Barnet, VT 05821
Phone: (802) 592-3190
Fax: (802) 592-3193
www.fledglingfilms.com

KINHAVEN MUSIC SCHOOL

Program Location: Weston, Vermont

Subject Areas: Chamber music

Program Description: Program focusing on chamber music. Large ensembles for brass, winds, and string, and a symphony orchestra. Chorus, folk dance, pottery, hiking, soccer, swimming, and volleyball also available. Senior Session and Junior Session offered.

Program Dates: June 21–August 4 (Senior Session); August 10–25 (Junior Session)

Duration of Program: 6 weeks (Senior Session); 2 weeks (Junior Session)

Cost: $4,500 (Senior Session; includes room and board); $1,825 (Junior Session; includes room and board)

Financial Aid: Available (April deadline)

Eligibility: Students in grades 5–12

Application Process: Application, audition tape

Application Deadline: March

Average Number of Applicants: 350

Average Number of Participants: 90 (Senior Session); 75 (Junior Session)

Academic Credit: None available

Contact:
Kinhaven Admissions
Nancy Bidlack, Admissions Director
1704 Sycamore Street
Bethlehem, PA 18017

Phone: (610) 868-9200
Fax: (610) 868-9200
Kinhavenmusic@aol.com
www.kinhaven.org

KINYON/JONES TENNIS CAMP

Program Location: Dartmouth College in Hanover, New Hampshire

Subject Areas: Tennis

Program Description: Chuck Kinyon and Dave Jones, coaches of the Dartmouth men's tennis team, and other teaching pros guide campers through drills, lectures, and team competition. Extra-help sessions are allotted for campers to work individually with instructors on problematic aspects of their game. During free time, campers have access to squash courts, an Olympic-sized pool, and other recreational facilities. Campers are assigned dorm rooms in either doubles, triples, or quads.

Program Dates: June–August

Duration of Program: Several 1-week sessions

Cost: $625 (residential); $495 (commuter)

Eligibility: Coed, ages 10–17

Application Process: Nonrefundable $200 deposit is due with the application form.

Application Deadline: Rolling admissions

Average Number of Applicants: 300

Average Number of Participants: 300

Contact:
Kinyon/Jones Tennis Camp
24 College Hill
Hanover, NH 03755
Phone: (603) 646-3819
dave.jones@dartmouth.edu
www.dartmouth.edu/~mten/camp.html

Program Directory

Knowledge Exchange Institute

KNOWLEDGE EXCHANGE INSTITUTE

Precollege African Safari Program

Program Location: University of Sahel and National Wildlife Park in Dakar, Senegal-French West Africa

Subject Areas: Environmental studies, wildlife management, ecology, botany, zoology, geology, geography, chemistry, biology, African studies, French language

Program Description: Curriculum includes field studies and laboratory research in environmental studies, wildlife management, ecology, botany, zoology, geology, geography, chemistry, and related sciences. Courses in African studies and French language are also available. Curriculum supplemented with cultural and safari excursions in Senegal and Gambia. Students also visit Goree Island (a reminder of slave trade), USAID, UNICEF, and UNESCO development sites. Program aims to prepare students for the Intel Science Talent Search, Seimens-Westinghouse, and International Science and Engineering Fair while providing a rich cultural environment. Entire program conducted in English.

Program Dates: June 27–August 1

Duration of Program: 5 weeks

Cost: $4,850 (includes room and board and transportation)

Financial Aid: Available (May 15 deadline)

Eligibility: Highly motivated high school students and graduates

Application Process: Application, essay, 2 teacher recommendations, transcript, phone interview

Application Deadline: May 1

Average Number of Applicants: 25

Average Number of Participants: 10

Academic Credit: College credit available

Precollege Amazon Exploration Program

Program Location: Tiputini Biodiversity Station in the Ecuadorian Amazon Rainforest

Subject Areas: Tropical and rainforest ecology, population ecology, environmental studies, botany, zoology, geology, geography, marine biology, Ecuadorian culture, Amazonian society, Spanish language

Program Description: Curriculum includes field studies and research at the Tiputini Biodiversity Station, a research branch of the University of San Francisco de Quito. Research topics are available in tropical ecology, population ecology, environmental studies, wildlife, botany, zoology, geology, geography, and soil science. Spanish language training available. Program aims to prepare students for the Intel Science Talent Search, Seimens-Westinghouse, and International Science and Engineering Fair. Entire program conducted in English.

Program Dates: June 27–August 1

Duration of Program: 5 weeks

Cost: $5,250 (includes room and board and transportation)

Financial Aid: Available (May 15 deadline)

Eligibility: Highly motivated high school students and graduates with an interest in environmental studies, ecology, wildlife and the Rainforest

Application Process: Application, essay, 2 teacher recommendations, transcript, phone interview

Application Deadline: May 1

Average Number of Applicants: 20

Average Number of Participants: 10

Academic Credit: College credit available

Precollege Artist Abroad Program

Program Location: Scuola Internazionale di Grafica in Venice, Italy

Subject Areas: Fine arts, painting, drawing, print-making, photography, computer graphics, web design, book arts, Italian language, history, area studies

Program Description: Students study renowned artists. Curriculum includes courses in painting, drawing, printmaking, photography, computer graphics, web design, book arts, Italian language, history, and society. Coursework supplemented with sightseeing and cultural excursions in Venice, Veneto, Milan, Florence, and Rome. Entire program conducted in English.

Program Dates: June 27–August 1

Duration of Program: 5 weeks

Cost: $5,500 (includes room and board and transportation)

Financial Aid: Available (May 15 deadline)

Eligibility: Motivated high school students and graduates with an interest in the fine arts, graphic design, and Italian culture

Application Process: Application, essay, 2 teacher recommendations, transcript, phone interview

Application Deadline: May 1

Average Number of Applicants: 18

Average Number of Participants: 10

Academic Credit: College credit available

Precollege Business, Law and Diplomacy Program

Program Location: University of International Business and Economics in Beijing, China

Subject Areas: International economics, business, law, politics, diplomacy, China-USA relations, Chinese language, society, martial arts

Program Description: Academic curriculum consists of courses in international economics, business, law, politics, Chinese language, society, martial arts. Courses taught by distinguished professors from the university. Coursework supplemented with professional visits to multinational companies and governing bodies. Curriculum includes cultural excursions in Beijing and a 1-week trip to Hong Kong. Entire program conducted in English.

Program Dates: June 27–August 1

Duration of Program: 5 weeks

Cost: $4,850 (includes room and board and transportation)

Financial Aid: Available (May 15 deadline)

Eligibility: Highly motivated high school students and graduates with an interest in international business, diplomacy, Chinese society

Application Process: Application, essay, 2 teacher recommendations, transcript, phone interview

Application Deadline: May 1

Average Number of Applicants: 22

Average Number of Participants: 10

Academic Credit: None available

Precollege European Capitals Program

Program Location: Europe; hosted by the International Management Institute of Brussels

Subject Areas: European economics, international commerce, Euro currency,

European relations, diplomacy, European history and culture

Program Description: Academic curriculum includes courses in economic policy, international commerce, Euro currency, European relations, diplomacy, European history and culture. Program includes extensive travel to 10 of the following economic and political capitals of Europe: Brussels, Paris, Antwerp, London, Berlin, Vienna, Amsterdam, Rome, Venice, Zurich, Geneva, Copenhagen, Prague, Madrid. Professors from the institute accompany students on all excursions. Entire program conducted in English.

Program Dates: June 27–August 1

Duration of Program: 5 weeks

Cost: $5,250 (includes room and board and transportation)

Financial Aid: Available (May 15 deadline)

Eligibility: Highly motivated high school students and graduates with an interest in European studies

Application Process: Application, 2 teacher recommendations, transcripts, phone interview

Application Deadline: May 1

Average Number of Applicants: 25

Average Number of Participants: 15

Academic Credit: College credit available

Precollege Research Abroad Program

Program Location: Puschino Science Center, Russian Academy of Science, Moscow Region, Russia

Subject Areas: Medical science, molecular biology, genetic engineering, recombinant DNA/RNA technology, cell biology, biochemistry, experimental mathematics, signal transduction, biophysics, astrophysics, radio-astronomy, environmental science, agro-science, ecology, analytical chemistry, plant biology, soil science, cryogenics, virology, bacteriology, other fields of science

Program Description: Curriculum includes laboratory research under the supervision of senior scientists, weekly seminars, preparation for the Intel Science Talent Search (STS), workshops on journal publication, cultural excursions in Moscow, St. Petersburg, and Novgorod. Entire program conducted in English. 40 percent of students advance to the STS semifinals, 5 percent become finalists and do equally well in the Seimens-Westinghouse, International Science and Engineering Fair, and other science contests. 12 students had their work published in prominent science journals and United Nations reports.

Program Dates: July 2–August 7

Duration of Program: 5 weeks

Cost: $4,750 (includes room and board and transportation)

Financial Aid: Available (May 15 deadline)

Eligibility: Highly motivated high school students and graduates

Application Process: Application, essay, 2 teacher recommendations, transcript, phone interview

Application Deadline: May 1

Average Number of Applicants: 50

Average Number of Participants: 20

Academic Credit: College credit available

Contact:
Knowledge Exchange Institute
P.O. Box 332
West Nyack, New York 10994
Phone: (800) 831-5095
Fax: (845) 348-9408
CIS@knowledgeexchange.org
www.knowledgeexchange.org

KUTSHER'S SPORTS ACADEMY

Program Location: Monticello, New York, in the heart of the Catskill Mountains

Subject Areas: Basketball, soccer, volleyball, baseball and softball, roller hockey, floor hockey, lacrosse, mountain biking, gymnastics, aerobics, dance, golf, ice skating, tennis, track and field, creative and performing arts, martial arts, aquatics, horseback riding, and climbing wall

Program Description: A specialty sports camp in which campers choose 1–4 of the sports listed above and receive a full range of instruction. Offers a unique combination of athletics, creative arts, and college preparation instruction taught by experienced professionals. Campers are grouped based on age and skill level. High school campers have the opportunity to meet with specialists in college preparatory planning.

Program Dates: Late June through late August

Duration of Program: 3-, 4-, and 7-week sessions

Cost: $2,700 (3 weeks); $3,500 (4 weeks); $5,400 (7 weeks)

Eligibility: Coed, ages 7–17

Application Deadline: Rolling

Average Number of Participants: 300–500+ during a 4-week session

Contact:
Kutsher's Sports Academy
7 Mine Hill East
Bridgewater, CT 06755
Phone: (888) 874-5400 or (860) 350-3819
info@ksacad.com
www.ksacad.com

LA SOCIÉTÉ FRANÇAISE

International Volunteer Program

Program Location: Various sites in the United States, France, and England

Subject Areas: Community service, travel

Program Description: IVP is a 10-year-old exchange program designed to foster volunteerism and global awareness. The organization provides room and board and provides the opportunity to be more than a tourist.

Program Dates: June 15–August 1 (approximate)

Duration of Program: 6 weeks

Cost: $1,500 (includes airfare from New York City or San Francisco and room and board)

Eligibility: Ages 18 and up; those interested in French program must demonstrate proficiency in French

Application Process: Written application, essays, 3 recommendations, brief interview via phone

Application Deadline: March 15

Financial Aid: None available

Contact:
International Volunteer Program
210 Post Street, Suite 502
San Francisco, CA 94108
Phone: (415) 477-3667
Fax: (415) 477-3669
rjewell@ivpsf.com
www.ivpsf.com

LAGRANGE COLLEGE

Visual Arts Workshop

Program Location: LaGrange College in LaGrange, Georgia

Subject Areas: Visual arts—photography, painting/drawing, sculpture/ceramics, design/graphics

Program Description: Students spend three weeks at the Lamar Dodd Art Center working with LaGrange College art professors and other professional artists and designers. Students also see practical demonstrations, hear guest lecturers, and participate in field trips. The workshop emphasizes a hands-on, studio approach and acquaints students with a broad number of professional and educational opportunities in the arts.

Program Dates: End of June–beginning of July

Duration of Program: 3 weeks

Cost: $1,850

Eligibility: Entering grade 12 with a serious interest in the visual arts

Application Process: Application form, academic transcript, guidance counselor recommendation, and nonrefundable $20 application fee

Application Deadline: May 15

Academic Credit: College credit available

Contact:
LaGrange College
Visual Arts Workshop Coordinator
601 Broad Street
LaGrange, GA 30240-2999
Phone: (706) 880-8005 or (800) 593-2885
http://home.lgc.edu/art/html.pages/vaw.html

LAKE PLACID SOCCER CENTRE

Mountain View Soccer Camp

Program Location: Lake Placid Soccer Centre in Lake Placid, New York; team training and elite training takes place at St. Lawrence University

Subject Areas: Soccer

Program Description: A 1-week soccer camp with instruction based on the Coerver Method to teach campers fundamental individual skills as well as the moves and tactics of soccer's greatest stars and teams. Team, goalkeeping, and elite/advanced programs are also available.

Program Dates: 4 sessions offered in July

Duration of Program: 1 week per session

Cost: Regular sessions: $565/week for overnight camp, $325/week for day campers. Elite programs: $795/week. Goalkeeping: $565/week for regular, $675/week for advanced goalkeeping. Team program: $399/team member.

Eligibility: Coed, ages 8–18. Must be ages 14 and older for elite programs, 15 and older for advanced goalkeeping programs.

Average Number of Participants: 1,500 during the entire month of July

Contact:
Lake Placid Soccer Centre
P.O. Box 847
Lake Placid, NY 12946
Phone: (518) 523-4395 or (800) 845-9959
Fax: (518) 523-9476
lpsoccer@capital.net
www.lakeplacidsoccer.com

Landmark Volunteers

LANDMARK VOLUNTEERS

Summer Service Opportunity Programs

Program Location: Numerous locations in 20 states throughout the U.S.

Subject Areas: Community service

Program Description: Volunteers work in teams of up to 13 members at one of several important historical, cultural, environmental, or social service institutions such as Olympic National Park and Colonial Williamsburg. Work consists mainly of manual labor. Off-duty activities include swimming, hiking, cookouts, movies, or joining in the activities of host families. One day in each session is set aside for expeditions or other organized recreation. Housing and food are arranged in cooperation with the host organizations. A few locations have rustic accommodations with tents or teepees and campfire cooking. In all group situations, the adult team leader lives with the volunteers.

Program Dates: June through August

Duration of Program: 2 weeks

Cost: $750

Eligibility: Must be at least age 14 by June 1 and must be entering grade 10, 11, or 12

Application Process: Admission is merit-based. The application, references, and order of receipt are all influential in determining eligibility.

Application Deadline: Rolling admissions, preferred by May 1

Academic Credit: At the end of the 2-week session, volunteers receive a certificate for 80 hours of community service.

Contact:
P.O. Box 455
Sheffield, MA 01257
Phone: (413) 229-0255
Fax: (413) 229-2050
landmark@volunteers.com
www.volunteers.com

LANGUAGE LINK

Intercultura;

Spanish Language Institute;

CLIC

Program Location: Heredia, Costa Rica (Intercultura); Cuernavaca, Mexico (Spanish Language Institute); Seville, Spain (CLIC)

Subject Areas: Spanish language study, cultural immersion

Program Description: Small classes, homestays, excursions, and cultural activities give students rigorous practice with the Spanish language. Programs are supervised, and students live with families who take responsibility for the teens.

Program Dates: Intercultura: August; Spanish Language Institute: June–August; CLIC: July–August

Duration of Program: Intercultura: 2, 3, or 4 weeks; Spanish Language Institute: number of weeks are chosen by each participant (students arrive any Friday in the specified months and depart on a Sunday); CLIC: 2, 3, or 4 weeks

Cost: Intercultura: $900 (3 weeks); Spanish Language Institute: $955 (3 weeks); CLIC: $1,094 (3 weeks)

Financial Aid: None available

Eligibility: Intercultura: ages 14–17; Spanish Language Institute: ages 13–17; CLIC: ages 15–17. No prior knowledge of Spanish necessary. (Programs for adults only or teens accompanied by a parent or guardian are also offered; contact Language Link or visit their website for more information.)

Application Process: Registration forms

Application Deadline: 3 weeks prior to start of program

Average Number of Applicants: 50 per program

Average Number of Participants: 50 per program

Contact:
Language Link
P.O. Box 3006
Peoria, IL 61612-3006
Phone: (800) 552-2051
Fax: (309) 692-2926
info@langlink.com
www.langlink.com

Language Link—Spanish Language Institute

Language Studies Abroad, Inc.

LANGUAGE STUDIES ABROAD, INC.

Language Studies Abroad

Program Location: Cultural centers of Mexico, Spain, France, Switzerland, Canada, Italy, Costa Rica, Germany, Austria, China, Japan, Russia, Portugal, Brazil, Chile, United States

Subject Areas: Foreign language study, cultural immersion

Program Description: Learning vacations offering 4 or more hours per day of language instruction with highly qualified native teachers in small classes of 5–15 students. Total immersion is enhanced through accommodations in a school residence shared with native youth or in a carefully selected homestay, depending on the location. Students enjoy afternoon and weekend excursions, sports, art, history, and various other cultural activities. All programs promote worldwide cultural understanding, respect, and global friendships.

Program Dates: Summer only to year-round

Duration of Program: 2 weeks or more

Cost: $760 and up

Eligibility: Ages 8–19

Application Process: Apply online, over the phone, or request an application. No previous language experience necessary.

Application Deadline: 1 month prior to start date

Financial Aid: None available

Average Number of Applicants: 500

Average Number of Participants: 500

Academic Credit: Available

Contact:
Christine Coté, President
Language Studies Abroad
1801 Hwy 50 East, Suite I
Carson City, NV 89701
Phone: (800) 424-5522
Fax: (775) 883-2266
info@languagestudiesabroad.com
www.languagestudiesabroad.com

LANGUAGE STUDY ABROAD

Program Location: Cuernavaca, Mexico; Seville, Spain; Paris, France; Vichy, France; Siena, Italy; Rome, Italy

Subject Areas: French, Spanish, Italian

Program Description: Small group language study with native-born teachers. In addition to conversation and grammar practice, students can attend mini-lecture courses on the art, literature, history, government, and business affairs of the host country. Optional films, cultural activities, and visits to museums and tourist attractions on evenings and weekends. Students live with trained and monitored host families or may opt for a hotel or apartment if they seek greater privacy.

Program Dates: Year-round. Classes begin every Monday.

Duration of Program: Minimum of 2 weeks

Cost: Varies with location and duration of program

Eligibility: All ages and levels of language proficiency

Application Process: Email or visit website for registration form; $100 application fee

Application Deadline: Rolling

Average Number of Applicants: 200–300

Average Number of Participants: 200–300

Academic Credit: College credit may be available

Contact:
Language Study Abroad
1960 5th Avenue
San Rafael, CA 94901
Phone: (415) 454-9072
Fax: (415) 455-5332
www.languagestudy.com

LATITUDES INTERNATIONAL

Community Service Travel

Program Location: South Dakota, Mexico, Botswana

Subject Areas: Community service, international travel, cultural exchange

Program Description: A nonprofit, community service, summer program in which participants live and work in Africa, Mexico, or a Native American reservation in South Dakota. Each Latitudes trip includes a group work project, where participants work cooperatively; an afternoon apprenticeship, where students donate their time to a meaningful activity in the community; and cultural immersion through daily interaction with local residents and through weekend travel activities.

Latitudes International

Program Dates: Late June through early August

Duration of Program: 3–5 weeks

Cost: South Dakota: $2,900 (airfare not included); Mexico: $3,750 (includes airfare from Dallas/Fort Worth); Botswana: $4,900 (includes airfare from New York City)

Financial Aid: Financial aid application form can be downloaded or submitted electronically on website; April 1 deadline

Eligibility: Ages 14–19

Application Process: Application form can be downloaded or submitted electronically on website; interview by phone or in person; $400 deposit (includes nonrefundable $100 processing fee).

Application Deadline: April 1

Average Number of Applicants: 30

Average Number of Participants: 20

Academic Credit: None available

Contact:
Jonathan Pearce
Latitudes International
51 First Avenue
East Haven, CT 06512
Phone: (800) 398-4960
Fax: (203) 468-9260
info@latitudesinternational.com
www.latitudesinternational.com

LAWRENCE ACADEMY

Environmental Field Study

Program Location: Groton, Massachusetts

Subject Areas: Environmental science

Program Description: Students from around the world learn about the interrelationships between wildlife, vegetation, water, and human activity through authentic scientific investigation in the field. Fieldwork is supported by classroom theory and by lab work. During Weekabout field trip, students conduct original research in a field station lab of their own creation. Electives available in mathematics, writing and speaking skills, business, and contemporary world issues.

Program Dates: June 28–August 2

Duration of Program: 5 weeks

Cost: $3,375 (includes room and board and transportation to and from airport)

Financial Aid: None available

Eligibility: Ages 13–17; students who are not native speakers of English must have a minimum TOEFL score of 550

Application Process: Contact Lawrence Academy for an application.

Global Leaders Workshop

Program Location: Groton, Massachusetts

Subject Areas: Leadership skills, community service

Program Description: Helps students to develop qualities of true leadership: self-confidence, social responsibility, and communication skills. Includes outdoor challenge, writing and speaking, community service, ethics, drama, and discussion of world problems. Each student designs an implementation plan for making positive changes in their home school. During Weekabout field trip, students travel to a service site to make a positive change in the lives of others. Electives available in mathematics, business, and sciences.

Program Dates: June 28–August 2

Duration of Program: 5 weeks

Cost: $3,375 (includes room and board and transportation to and from airport)

Financial Aid: None available

Eligibility: Ages 13–17; students who are not native speakers of English must have a minimum TOEFL score of 550

Application Process: Contact Lawrence Academy for an application.

International English Institute

Program Location: Groton, Massachusetts

Subject Areas: English as a Second Language (ESL)

Program Description: IEI offers 5 levels of ESL instruction: beginner, intermediate (low, mid, high), and advanced. Prepares students to enter North American boarding schools or colleges. During Weekabout field trip, students visit historic and cultural sites. Electives available in mathematics, business, sciences, study skills, and TOEFL test preparation.

Program Dates: June 28–August 2

Duration of Program: 5 weeks

Cost: $4,900 (includes room and board and transportation to and from airport)

Financial Aid: None available

Eligibility: Ages 13–17; no previous study of English is required

Application Process: Contact Lawrence Academy for an application.

Contact:
Lawrence Academy
Office of Summer Programs
Powder House Road
P.O. Box 992
Groton, Massachusetts 01450
Phone: (978) 448-1520
Fax: (978) 448-1519
summerprograms@lacademy.edu
www.lacademy.edu

LEAPNOW

Summer Program in Central America; Summer Program in Australia

Program Location: Guatemala and Honduras, Central America; Queensland, Australia

Subject Areas: Community service, study abroad, homestay, language study, outdoor adventure

Program Description: The program in Central America begins with 2 weeks of intensive Spanish language study and a homestay with

*LEAP*Now

Guatemalan families. Later activities include house construction, SCUBA diving, and a trek through the Guatemalan highlands. The Australia program also includes diverse activities, such as sea kayaking, snorkeling, horseback-riding, and environmental and community work.

Program Dates: June–July

Duration of Program: 5 weeks

Cost: $3,600, plus $100 application fee

Financial Aid: Available

Eligibility: Ages 15 and up

Application Process: Application, 2 recommendations, telephone interview

Application Deadline: Rolling admissions

Average Number of Applicants: 12 per trip

Average Number of Participants: 8 per trip

Academic Credit: High school or college credit available

Contact:
LEAPNow
P.O. Box 1817
Sebastopol, CA 95473
Phone: (707) 829-1142
Fax: (914) 273-5430
info@leapnow.org
www.leapnow.org

LEBANON VALLEY COLLEGE

Daniel Fox Youth Scholars Institute

Program Location: Lebanon Valley College in Annville, Pennsylvania

Subject Areas: Sciences, math, social sciences, arts, humanities, college preparation

Program Description: Enables exceptional high school students to preview college life. Students take an intensive workshop in the sciences, social sciences, or humanities, choosing from as many as 21 courses. Youth Scholars work closely with college faculty in small groups, and use the science laboratories, computer labs, music facilities, and athletic facilities. Students live on-campus and participate in a number of extracurricular activities.

Program Dates: June 23–28

Duration of Program: 1 week

Cost: $380 (includes room and board)

Financial Aid: Available

Eligibility: Primarily for students enrolled in grades 10–11. Required proficiency level depends on the discipline and is determined by the faculty.

Application Process: Students must be nominated by teacher or counselor.

Application Deadline: End of March

Average Number of Applicants: 400

Average Number of Participants: 180–200

Academic Credit: None available

Contact:
Lebanon Valley College
Daniel Fox Youth Scholars Institute
College Avenue
Anneville, PA 17003
Phone: (717) 867-6213
Fax: (717) 867-6075
erskine@lvc.edu or greenawa@lvc.edu

Lebanon Valley College Summer Music Camp

Program Location: Lebanon Valley College in Annville, Pennsylvania

Subject Areas: Music

Program Description: Faculty members from LVC music department help campers improve individual and group performance in concert band, strings, piano/organ, guitar, with emphasis on chamber music and jazz. Private instruction, master classes, classes in composition, theory, history, MIDI, and music technology. Campers live in a modern, air-conditioned dorm, eat in the college dining hall,

and have access to all campus facilities. Scheduled recreational activities include a picnic, movies, sports, and an evening at Hersheypark.

Program Dates: July 8–13

Duration of Program: 5 days

Cost: $415 (includes room and board)

Eligibility: Grades 9–12

Application Process: Completed application

Application Deadline: June 15

Average Number of Applicants: 100

Average Number of Participants: 100

Contact:
Lebanon Valley College Summer Music Camp
101 N. College Avenue
Annville, PA 17003
Phone: (717) 867-6289
Fax: (717) 867-6390
hearson@lvc.edu
www.lvc.edu

LEGACY INTERNATIONAL

Global Youth Village

Program Location: 20 different countries

Subject Areas: International travel, leadership training, community service, global issues/dialogue, environment, arts

Program Description: An international summer camp for youth and staff from over 20 different countries. Participants delve into topics and explore the customs, traditions, joys, and hardships of their peers around the world. They learn to respect differences and discover similarities that transcend cultural, religious, political, and language barriers.

Program Dates: TBA

Duration of Program: 3 weeks

Legacy International

Cost: $1,800 (U.S.), $2,100 (international); includes room and board

Financial Aid: None available

Eligibility: Ages 14–18

Application Process: Request application online, by mail, or by telephone.

Application Deadline: TBA

Average Number of Applicants: 300

Average Number of Participants: 70

Academic Credit: None available

Contact:
Legacy International
1020 Legacy Dr.
Bedford, VA 24523
Phone: (540) 297-5982
Fax: (540) 297-1860
inquiries@globalyouthvillage.org
www.globalyouthvillage.org

LESLEY UNIVERSITY

See Art Institute of Boston at Lesley University

LEWIS AND CLARK COLLEGE, NORTHWEST WRITING INSTITUTE

Fir Acres Workshop in Writing and Thinking;

Writer to Writer

Program Location: Lewis and Clark College in Portland, Oregon

Subject Areas: Writing

Program Description: Fir Acres Workshop: A residential workshop where students from across the country gather to engage in creative and critical writing, collaborative learning, and reading and writing across the disciplines. This workshop is taught by the faculty associates of the Northwest Writing Institute. Writer to Writer: A seminar encouraging creative writing by high school students through interaction with professional adult writers in fiction, poetry, screenwriting, journalism, and other forms. Draws students from throughout Oregon, but primarily from the Portland metro area.

Program Dates: Mid-July

Duration of Program: Fir Acres Workshop: 2 weeks; Writer to Writer: 5 days

Cost: Fir Acres Workshop: $1,300; Writer to Writer: $300

Financial Aid: Partial scholarships available to early applicants

Eligibility: Open to all high school students

Application Process: Teacher recommendation and writing sample required.

Application Deadline: Mid-April/rolling admissions

Contact:
Northwest Writing Institute
Lewis and Clark College
0165 S.W. Palatine Hill Road
Portland, OR 97219
Phone: (503) 768-7745
Fax: (503) 768-7747
ccollins@lclark.edu
www.lclark.edu/~nwi/

LEYSIN AMERICAN SCHOOL IN SWITZERLAND

Summer in Switzerland

Program Location: Leysin American School in Leysin, Switzerland

Subject Areas: General academic classes, travel, recreation, leadership, performing arts

Program Description: Offers students a unique international experience in the Swiss Alps. Includes solid academics in the morning and extracurricular activities in the afternoon. A range of general and alpine sports activities, a leadership program, cultural excursions (in Switzerland, France, and Italy), and performing arts are offered.

Program Dates: June 29–July 19 and July 20–August 9

Duration of Program: 3 weeks per session

Cost: $2,950 (3 weeks) or $5,550 (6 weeks); includes room and board and transportation

Financial Aid: Available

Eligibility: Ages 9–19

Application Process: School transcript, teacher recommendation

Application Deadline: Rolling admissions

Average Number of Participants: 200

Academic Credit: High school credit available

Contact:
Leysin American School in Switzerland
P.O. Box 7154
Portsmouth, NH 03802
Phone: (888) 642-4142
Fax: (603) 431-1280
usadmissions@las.ch
www.las.ch

LINGUA SERVICE WORLDWIDE

Junior Classic and Junior Sports Program

Program Location: Cap d'Ail, France

Subject Areas: French language and culture, travel abroad, sports

Program Description: Combines the study of French with sports and cultural activities. Students study French for 3 hours daily. After class, students participate in sporting or cultural activities. Sporting classes are taught by European professional players. The school is situated in a vast park on a hillside terrace overlooking the Mediterranean Sea.

Program Dates: Start date on any Monday from mid-June to August

Duration of Program: 2–4 weeks

Cost: $1,025 (2 weeks), $1,425 (3 weeks), $1,795 (4 weeks); includes room and board

Financial Aid: None available

Eligibility: Ages 13–17

Application Process: Application

Application Deadline: Suggested deadline at least 30 days prior to start date

Academic Credit: Available

Junior Course in Salamanca

Program Location: Salamanca, Spain

Subject Areas: Spanish language and culture, travel abroad

Program Description: Designed for students who want to learn the language and experience the culture of Spain. Participants study Spanish in the mornings, four lessons daily, from Monday to Friday. Afternoons are dedicated to cultural or sporting activities, excursions, or field trips.

Program Dates: Start dates in June and July

Duration of Program: 2–4 weeks

Cost: $875 (2 weeks), $1,200 (3 weeks), $1,465 (4 weeks); includes room and board, as well as transportation from Madrid to Salamanca

Financial Aid: None

Eligibility: Ages 14–16

Application Process: Application

Application Deadline: Suggested deadline at least 30 days prior to start date

Average Number of Participants: 80–100

Academic Credit: Available

Summer Language Adventure

Program Location: Montreal, Canada

Subject Areas: French language, travel abroad

Program Description: Small group, total immersion French language course, combined with exploration of Canadian culture and lifestyle. Students attend classes in the mornings and participate in sports and cultural activities in the afternoon.

Program Dates: Start dates on any Monday from the end of June to August

Duration of Program: 2–8 weeks

Cost: $975 (2 weeks), $405/additional week (room and board and transportation in Montreal included)

Financial Aid: None available

Eligibility: Ages 13–17

Application Process: Application

Application Deadline: Suggested deadline at least 30 days prior to start date

Academic Credit: Available

Contact:
Lingua Service Worldwide
75 Prospect Street, Suite 4
Huntington, NY 11743
Phone: (800) 394-5327
Fax: (631) 271-3441
itctravel@worldnet.att.net
www.linguaserviceworldwide.com

LONG ISLAND UNIVERSITY

See Southampton College of Long Island University

LONGACRE EXPEDITIONS

Program Location: Various locations in the United States, Canada, Belize, Iceland, Great Britain, and Ireland

Subject Areas: Outdoor adventure, travel, eco-service, leadership skills

Program Description: An outdoor adventure program, featuring trips in the United States and abroad. The goal of the program is to increase each participant's self-confidence and promote personal growth through both physical challenge and interpersonal interaction.

Program Dates: Late June through mid-August

Duration of Program: 2-, 3-, and 4-week sessions

Cost: $1,595 and up

Application Process: Submit enrollment agreement along with $500 deposit.

Application Deadline: Rolling admissions, but apply early to be assured a spot

Eligibility: Must be a physically fit teen with a good attitude; no experience required. Each expedition specifies its own age requirements.

Average Number of Participants: 10–16 per trip

Contact:
Longacre Expeditions
RD 3, Box 106
Newport, PA 17074
Phone: (717) 567-6790 or (800) 433-0127
Fax: (717) 567-3955
longacre@longacreexpeditions.com
www.longacreexpeditions.com

LONGACRE LEADERSHIP

Longacre Leadership Program

Program Location: Newport, Pennsylvania

Subject Areas: Leadership, community service, outdoor adventure

Program Description: Longacre Leadership has established an underlying philosophy of "growth through challenge." Teens learn independence and self-reliance by taking responsibility for all aspects of community life. The close, caring community promotes respect and acceptance between individuals, emphasizing group dynamics

Longacre Expeditions

and communications skills. Participants learn construction, do community service projects, help run a 300-acre farm, grow organic vegetables, drive tractors, and ride horses. Includes outdoor adventure trips such as rock climbing, mountain biking, backpacking, and rafting.

Program Dates: July 1–August 11

Duration of Program: 4- and 6-week sessions

Cost: $3,280 (4 weeks); $4,560 (6 weeks)

Financial Aid: Available

Eligibility: Ages 12–18

Application Deadline: Rolling

Average Number of Participants: 72

Contact:
Longacre Leadership
RR 3, Box 102A
Newport, PA 17074
Phone: (717) 567-3349
Fax: (717) 567-3955
connect@longacre.com
www.longacre.com

LOUISIANA STATE UNIVERSITY

Honors High School Credit Program

Program Location: Louisiana State University in Baton Rouge, Louisiana

Subject Areas: Honors high school math, science, computer science

Program Description: Enables bright, motivated students to complete an honors-level math, science, or computer course. Residential component available.

Program Dates: June 10–July 19

Duration of Program: 6 weeks

Cost: $1,625 (includes room and board)

Financial Aid: Available (mid-April deadline)

Eligibility: Students entering grades 7–12 with a B average or better

Application Process: Transcript

Application Deadline: May 1

Average Number of Applicants: 250

Average Number of Participants: 200

Academic Credit: High school credit available

Contact:
Honors High School Credit Program
Louisiana State University
177 Pleasant Hall
Baton Rouge, LA 70803
Phone: (800) 388-3883
Fax: (225) 578-6324
youth@doce.lsu.edu
www.doce.lsu.edu

LOYOLA UNIVERSITY

See National Student Leadership Conference

MACALESTER COLLEGE

See Minnesota Institute for Talented Youth

MAINE TEEN CAMP

Program Location: Porter, Maine

Subject Areas: Land and water sports, arts, music, audio and video recording, adventure, academic tutoring

Program Description: An international residential camp for teens 13–17, MTC offers high quality instruction and dozens of choices within the following program areas: fine arts, performing arts and music, land sports, water sports, trips and travel, academics/ESL, and adventure challenge activities. Each camper participates in four electives each day plus an evening program activity. Boys and girls cabins are located at opposite ends of the camp. Accommodations include large contemporary lakeside bunkhouses and both modern and rustic smaller cabins equipped with indoor bathrooms and electricity.

Program Dates: June through August

Duration of Program: 4–8 weeks

Cost: $3,295–$4,995

Eligibility: Coed, ages 13–17

Application Process: Deposit of $500 to secure a spot. Application can be obtained and submitted by mail or downloaded or submitted electronically via website.

Application Deadline: June 15

Average Number of Participants: 250+ per session; approximately 25–30 percent of participants come from countries other than the United States.

Contact:
Maine Teen Camp
481 Brownfield Road
Porter, Maine 04068
Phone: (800) 752-2267 or (207) 625-8581
Fax: (207) 625-8738
mtc@teencamp.com
www.teencamp.com

MARINE MILITARY ACADEMY

Summer Military Training Camp

Program Location: Marine Military Academy in Harlingen, Texas

Subject Areas: Military training, physical fitness

Program Description: Physical fitness and military training for young men. Activities include paintball, marksmanship, mud course, obstacle courses, rappelling, rock climbing, military drills and formations, and team sports.

Program Dates: July

Duration of Program: 4 weeks

Cost: $2,500 (includes room and board)

Financial Aid: None available

Eligibility: Boys, ages 13–17

Application Process: Application (available on website), report of medical history, complete immunization history, medical addendum form (available on website), copy of birth certificate

Average Number of Applicants: 325

Average Number of Participants: 250

Academic Credit: None available

Contact:
Marine Military Academy
320 Iwo Jima Blvd.
Harlingen, TX 78550
Phone: (956) 423-6006
Fax: (956) 412-3848
admissions@mma-tx.org
www.marinemilitaryacademy.com

THE MASTERS SCHOOL

Panther Basketball Camp

Program Location: The Masters School in Dobbs Ferry, New York

Subject Areas: Basketball

Program Description: Participants learn the fundamentals of basketball in this day camp led by acclaimed coach Dominic Malandro. Players focus on skills such as ball handling, shooting, defense, passing, rebounding, and foul shooting, as well as 1-on-1 games, 2-on-2 games, and full-team games. Camp runs Monday through Friday from 9 A.M.—3:30 P.M.

Program Dates: July 8–12, 15–19

Duration of Program: 1–2 weeks

Cost: $250–$450 (1–2 weeks, lunch provided)

Financial Aid: None available

Eligibility: Ages 9–16, coed

Application Process: Application

Application Deadline: Check with program for more information.

Academic Credit: None available

Program Directory

Summer ESL

Program Location: The Masters School in Dobbs Ferry, New York

Subject Areas: English as a second language

Program Description: Students learn and practice the English language, study aspects of American life, and experience New York City in one highly integrated program. Classes held in air-conditioned classrooms on campus during the morning and evening hours. Afternoon activities include art, music, sports and fitness, swimming, tennis, and public speaking. Students visit Ellis Island, The Statue of Liberty, The Empire State Building, The Metropolitan Museum of Art, see Broadway musicals, and more. Students also take advantage of a range of campus facilities and reside in campus dorms.

Program Dates: July 7–26 (Session I), July 28–August 16 (Session II)

Duration of Program: 3–6 weeks

Cost: TBA (includes room and board)

Eligibility: Ages 12–17

Application Process: Application

Application Deadline: June 26 (Session I), July 17 (Session II)

Average Number of Participants: 100–150

Summer in the City

Program Location: The Masters School in Dobbs Ferry, New York

Subject Areas: Learning and exploring New York City

Program Description: Students experience New York City through an educational context. The first week is spent learning about the rich immigrant history of Manhattan with trips to Ellis Island, Lower East Side Tenement Museum, South Street Seaport. The second week students explore different neighborhoods: Greenwich Village, Washington Square Park, Chinatown, Little Italy, the Financial District. The final week of the program focuses on the arts; events include seeing Broadway shows, visiting the Metropolitan Museum of Art, and touring television studios, Lincoln Center, Times Square.

Program Dates: July 7–26

Duration of Program: 3 weeks

Cost: TBA (includes room and board)

Financial Aid: None available

Eligibility: Students in grades 9–12

Application Process: Application

Application Deadline: June 26

Average Number of Applicants: 50

Average Number of Participants: 20

Academic Credit: None available

Summer Theatre

Program Location: The Masters School in Dobbs Ferry, New York

Subject Areas: Acting, singing, dancing, directing, set design, lighting design, costume design

Program Description: Intensive theater camp. Students focus on acting, singing, and dancing, resulting in a final performance at the end of the session. Classes and rehearsals will be held daily. Weekend events include seeing Broadway shows, touring television studios, exploring New York City, and more.

Program Dates: July 28–August 16

Duration of Program: 3 weeks

Cost: TBA (includes room and board)

Financial Aid: None available

Eligibility: Check with program for more information

Application Process: Application, audition

Application Deadline: July 17

Academic Credit: None available

Contact:
The Masters School
49 Clinton Avenue
Dobbs Ferry, NY 10522
Phone: (914) 479-6474
Fax: (914) 693-1230
gcrane@themassersschool.com
www.themassersschool.com

MATHEMATICS FOUNDATION OF AMERICA

Canada/USA Mathcamp

Program Location: TBA; location varies every year. Past locations include the University of Toronto, University of British Columbia, University of Washington at Seattle, and Colby College

Subject Areas: Mathematics

Program Description: Incorporates the fun elements of a camp, making friends who have common interests, and academic goals that range from exposure to new mathematical ideas to preparing students for an early pursuit of mathematical knowledge. Young mathematicians from the continent's top universities—selected for teaching ability and enthusiasm—act as counselors.

Program Dates: Second week of July to second week of August

Duration of Program: 5 weeks

Cost: $20 application fee; $2,995 (residential students); $1,995 (non-residential students); includes room and board. Discount airfare available.

Financial Aid: Available (April 30 deadline, further information available on website)

Eligibility: Ages 13–18

Application Process: Application and qualifying quiz available on website, or request a hard copy via email or post mail. Two recommendations and application fee also required (fee waived upon receipt of explanatory note).

Application Deadline: Rolling admissions, applications must be postmarked by May 15. Late applications accepted until all slots are filled.

Average Number of Applicants: 200

Average Number of Participants: 95

Academic Credit: None available

Contact:
Mathematics Foundation of America
Canada/USA Mathcamp
3560 Pine Grove Avenue
Port Huron, MI 48060
Phone: (519) 672-7990
Fax: (519) 434-6244
info@mathcamp.org
www.mathcamp.org

MEDIA WORKSHOPS FOUNDATION

The Media Workshops

Program Location: Los Angeles, California

Subject Areas: Media

Program Description: Weeklong sessions throughout July and August offering experience in film, television, music, journalism, and the Internet media fields. Includes visits to film studios and media centers, tours, lectures, screenings, and individual career counseling. Students are housed in supervised UCLA residence halls and have complete use of campus facilities.

Program Dates: Sessions in July and August

Duration of Program: 6 days

Cost: $795 (includes room and board)

Application Process: Apply by mail or online via website.

Application Deadline: Rolling admissions

Average Number of Applicants: 100

Average Number of Participants: 100

Contact:
Media Workshops Foundation
291 S. La Cienega Blvd. #735
Beverly Hills, CA 90211
Phone: (800) 223-4561
mworkshop1@aol.com
www.mediaworkshops.com or
www.mediaworkshops.org

MIAMI UNIVERSITY

Junior Scholars Program

Program Location: Miami University in Oxford, Ohio

Subject Areas: Art, architecture, liberal arts, foreign languages, math, sciences, computer science, economics

Program Description: Scholars chosen from the program attend summer classes along with regular Miami undergraduates, earning credit in their chosen area. In addition to a rigorous schedule of classes, participants take part in a special program of recreation, seminars, and social events.

Program Dates: June–August

Duration of Program: 6 weeks

Cost: $1,570–$1,681 (in-state); $2,171–$2,497 (out-of-state); includes room and board

Financial Aid: None available

Eligibility: Academically talented rising seniors who want to learn about university life and earn college credit early

Application Process: Application, transcript, recommendation, achievement test scores

Application Deadline: May 15

Average Number of Applicants: 100

Average Number of Participants: 60

Academic Credit: College credit available (6–8 hours)

Contact:
Junior Scholars Program
Miami University
202 Bachelor Hall
Oxford, OH 45056-3414
Phone: (513) 529-5825
Fax: (513) 529-1498
JuniorScholars@muohio.edu
www.muohio.edu/juniorscholars

MICHIGAN STATE UNIVERSITY

Spartan Debate Institute (SDI)

Program Location: Michigan State University in East Lansing, Michigan

Subject Areas: Policy debate

Program Description: Policy debate for all levels of experience, from top varsity to "pre-novices" with no experience. Commitment to interactive practice debates and extensive individual instruction. One tournament for 2-week session; two tournaments and over 30 practice debates for 3-week session.

Program Dates: July–August

Duration of Program: 2–3 weeks

Cost: $800 (2 weeks); $1,100 (3 weeks). Includes room and board.

Financial Aid: Limited need-based aid available

Eligibility: High school students with all levels of debate experience

Application Process: Application, recommendation from high school debate coach required.

Application Deadline: Rolling

Contact:
Spartan Debate Institute (SDI)
Michigan State University
10 Linton Hall
East Lansing, MI 48824
Phone: (517) 432-9667
Fax: (517) 432-9667
debate@msu.edu
www.msu.edu/~debate/

MIDDLE STATES SOCCER CAMP

Intermediate and Senior Soccer Camps

Program Location: Ursinus College in Collegeville, Pennsylvania; Westtown School in Westtown, Pennsylvania; Episcopal High School in Alexandria, Virginia; Foxcroft School in Middlebury, Virginia; Goucher College in Baltimore, Maryland; West Nottingham Academy on Rising Sun, Maryland; St. Andrew's School in Middletown, Delaware

Program Description: Intermediate program: Skill training combined with a heavy emphasis on tactical understanding. Senior program: Concepts such as off-the-ball running, attacking patterns, defensive coordination, and principles of play in all parts of the field. Advanced players have opportunity for more individualized instruction and competition. Ratio of players to coaches is 7:1. Each player receives a written assessment at end of program. Options include residential program, extended day program (9 A.M.–9 P.M.), or day program (9 A.M.–4 P.M.).

Program Dates: Sessions throughout the summer

Duration of Program: 1-week sessions

Cost: $455 (residential); $345 (extended day program); $235 (day program). Advanced players/goalkeepers: $515 (residential); $395 (extended day program).

Financial Aid: Wendell E. Broad Memorial Scholarship Fund assists economically disadvantaged applicants; contact the Director at (703) 764-0964 for more info.

Eligibility: Intermediates: ages 13–14 with some soccer experience; Seniors: ages 15–18 with soccer experience. Programs are coed except for the All Girls Camp at Goucher College and the Advanced Player/Goalkeeper Camp (boys only) at St. Andrew's.

Application Process: Submit application form and nonrefundable $100 deposit. Applicants to Advanced Player/Goalkeeper Camp must be recommended by a Middle States staff member or submit a letter of reference from their high school or club coach.

Contact:
Middle States Soccer Camp
P.O. Box 2835
Manassas, VA 20108
Phone: (703) 330-3423 or (703) 330-0492
hgoodman@middlestatessoccercamp.com
www.middlestatessoccercamp.com

MILWAUKEE SCHOOL OF ENGINEERING

Discover the Possibilities;

Focus on the Possibilities

Program Location: Milwaukee School of Engineering in Milwaukee, Wisconsin

Subject Areas: Engineering and technology

Program Description: Discover the Possibilities: Designed to accommodate students who want an overview of engineering and technology. Focus on the Possibilities: Designed for those students who already know the specific area of engineering or technology in which they are interested. Students attend academic programming during the day and participate in recreational activities in the evening.

Program Dates: Three sessions in July

Duration of Program: 1-week sessions

Cost: $625 (includes room and board, books and supplies, recreational activities)

Eligibility: High school sophomores, juniors, and seniors

Application Process: Submit an application with a $50 deposit. Application available on MSOE website or can be requested from the Enrollment Management Office. Balance of cost is due 10 days prior to start of program.

Average Number of Participants: 96 per session

Contact:
Milwaukee School of Engineering
1025 North Broadway
Milwaukee, WI 53202
Phone: (800) 332-6763
Fax: (414) 277-7475
explore@msoe.edu
www.msoe.edu/admiss/summer.html

Minnesota Institute for Talented Youth

MINNESOTA INSTITUTE FOR TALENTED YOUTH

Expand Your Mind

Program Location: Macalester College in St. Paul, Minnesota

Subject Areas: Math, science, visual and performing arts, humanities

Program Description: Provides enriched classes for a diverse group of students. Participants explore topics in depth in a hands-on learning environment. Classes have a 15:1 student/teacher ratio.

Program Dates: June 17–28, July 8–19

Duration of Program: 2 weeks (2 sessions)

Cost: $370 (commuter); $890 (resident, includes room and board)

Financial Aid: Available for out-of-state students (April 20 deadline)

Eligibility: Students in grades 7–12

Application Process: Transcript, teacher recommendation, essay, artwork if applicable

Application Deadline: April 20

Average Number of Applicants: 650

Average Number of Participants: 550

Academic Credit: None available

Contact:
Minnesota Institute for Talented Youth
Macalester College
1600 Grande Ave.
St. Paul, MN 55105
Phone: (651) 696-6590
Fax: (651) 696-6592
mity@macalester.edu
www.mity.org

MISSISSIPPI UNIVERSITY FOR WOMEN

Business Week;

Aero-Tech

Program Location: Mississippi University for Women in Columbus, Mississippi

Subject Areas: Business, leadership, aviation/aeronautics, computers/technology

Program Description: Business Week: Students learn about America's free enterprise system by participating in simulations of managing their own companies. Aero-Tech: Students spend half of each day on Columbus Air Force Base learning all aspects of the Air Force. Afternoons are spent on campus at MUW applying technology and discovering skills needed for the careers of the future.

Program Dates: Business Week: June 3–8, 2001; Aero-Tech: July 23–27, 2001

Duration of Program: Business Week: 6 days; Aero-Tech: 5 days

Cost: Business Week: $175; Aero-Tech: $125 (day camp), $360 (residential camp)

Mississippi University for Women

Eligibility: Business Week: Coed, entering grades 8–10; Aero-Tech: Coed, entering grades 7–12

Application Process: Contact MUW for more information.

Average Number of Applicants: Business Week: 150

Average Number of Participants: Business Week: 131

Contact:
Mississippi University for Women
W-Box 1638
Columbus, MS 39701
Phone: (662) 329-7137
Fax: (662) 329-8571
continue@muw.edu
www.muw.edu/summer

MOONDANCE ADVENTURES

Program Location: Various locations in the U.S. including Blue Ridge Mountains, Colorado, Wyoming, Washington, Montana, Alaska; Scandinavia, Costa Rica

Subject Areas: Outdoor adventure

Program Description: Wilderness-based adventure travel programs for teens (family programs are also available). Activities include backpacking, rock climbing, ropes course, mountain biking, whitewater rafting, and sea kayaking. Program is built on individual achievement with a strong sense of teamwork. Students are divided into coed groups of 8–12 students along with two adult leaders. Traveling in small groups ensures that students become valued members of the team and receive significant individual attention.

Program Dates: June–August

Duration of Program: 2–3 weeks

Cost: Varies by program

Eligibility: Age limits and physical fitness levels vary by program

Application Process: Application form, deposit required

Application Deadline: Rolling

Contact:
Moondance Adventures
P.O. Box 20178
Atlanta, GA 30325
Phone: (800) 832-5229
Fax: (404) 367-9419
www.moondanceadventures.com

MOUNT HOLYOKE COLLEGE

SummerMath

Program Location: Mount Holyoke College in South Hadley, Massachusetts

Subject Areas: Mathematics, computer programming

Program Description: Students actively investigate mathematics, computing, and science, with a focus on problem solving, conceptual understanding, and confidence building. Options for applied mathematics study, choosing from such workshops as robotics, architecture, biology, and economics. Students also explore careers and participate in sports, writing, arts and crafts, and weekend trips.

Program Dates: June 30–July 27

Duration of Program: 4 weeks

Cost: $4,000 (includes room and board)

Financial Aid: Available (May 1 deadline)

Eligibility: Girls entering grades 9–12

Application Process: Application, one-page essay

Application Deadline: May 1

Average Number of Applicants: 65

Average Number of Participants: 55–60

Academic Credit: Arranged individually by student

Contact:
SummerMath
Mount Holyoke College
50 College Street
South Hadley, MA 01075-1441
Phone: (413) 538-2608
Fax: (413) 538-2002
summermath@mtholyoke.edu
www.mtholyoke.edu/proj/summermath

MOUNT HOOD SNOWBOARD CAMP

MHSC Summer Sessions

Program Location: Mount Hood, Oregon

Subject Areas: Snowboarding

Program Description: Offers first-timer, beginner, intermediate, and advanced instructional programs in each session. Students snowboard on a glacier which has snow on it all year long. The coaches film students snowboarding; later that day, the groups will review the tape with their coach. Beginning instruction focuses on mastering turns, switch stance, jumping, 180s, and simple tricks. Intermediate and advanced instruction includes riding halfpipe and bigger jumps, as well as advanced spins and tricks. Equipment clinic topics include stance setup, waxing, edge sharpening, and binding adjustment. Dorm-style lodging assigned by age and sex.

Program Dates: June–August (other programs offered year-round)

Duration of Program: 1 week per session

Cost: $1,100–$1,200 (includes room and board)

Financial Aid: Limited number of full scholarships based on demonstrated financial need, community service, academics, and age. Scholarship application request is available online; applicants must also submit transcript and 3 letters of recommendation.

Eligibility: Ages 12 and older, all levels of experience

Application Process: Call MHSC to register. After registration, MHSC will send a complete registration package that includes further details, release forms, etc. $250 deposit required.

Contact:
MHSC
P.O. Box 140
Rhododendron, OR 97049
Phone: (503) 622-3044
mhsc@snowboardcamp.com
www.snowboardcamp.com

Mount Hood Snowboard Camp

MUSIKER DISCOVERY PROGRAMS

Musiker Tours

Program Location: Tours of the United States (including Alaska and Hawaii), Canada, Mexico, Italy, Switzerland, France, Belgium, Holland, England

Subject Areas: Travel and sightseeing, outdoor activities

Program Description: Teen tours that are activity oriented, including excursions to amusement parks; outdoor sports such as rollerblading and mountain biking; and camping. Students choose from programs that feature a combination of camping/hotels/dorms or just hotels/dorms.

Program Dates: June–August

Duration of Program: 3–6 weeks

Cost: Varies; includes room and board. Airfare not included; lowest available airfare can be arranged by Musiker Tours.

Eligibility: Students in grades 7–12

Application Process: Application form (downloadable form available on website), $350 deposit due with application

Application Deadline: Rolling

Academic Credit: None available

Contact:
Musiker Tours
1326 Old Northern Boulevard
Roslyn, NY 11576
Phone: (888) 8-SUMMER
Fax: (516) 625-3438
musiker@summerfun.com
www.summerfun.com

Summer Discovery

Program Location: Georgetown University in Washington, DC; University of California—Los Angeles; University of California—San Diego; University of California—Santa Barbara; University of Michigan; University of Vermont; Cambridge University in England

Subject Areas: Liberal arts and sciences, college preparation, study abroad

Program Description: Precollege residential enrichment programs for high school students at 7 different college campuses. Students choose from up to 10 daily after-class activities, learning to balance work and play. All Summer Discovery students and staff live together in one on-campus residence hall.

Program Dates: June–August

Duration of Program: 3–6 weeks

Cost: Varies

Financial Aid: Limited number of need-based, partial-tuition scholarships available; March 15 deadline (2001 date)

Eligibility: Age requirements vary by program

Application Process: Application (downloadable form on website), $50 application fee, guidance counselor recommendation form. $900 deposit due within 15 days of notification of acceptance into program.

Application Deadline: Rolling

Academic Credit: High school and college credit available

Contact:
Summer Discovery
1326 Old Northern Boulevard
Roslyn, NY 11576
Phone: (888) 8-SUMMER
Fax: (516) 625-3438
discovery@summerfun.com
www.summerfun.com

NACEL OPEN DOOR

Summer Programs

Program Location: Argentina, Australia, Brazil, France, Germany, Ireland, Japan, Mexico, Paraguay, Quebec, Spain

Subject Areas: Travel abroad, homestays, language education, intercultural sharing

Program Description: Not-for-profit program dedicated to promoting international understanding and language education through direct experience in other cultures and languages. Students participate in homestay programs abroad. Some programs involve language study, sports camps, cultural studies, and community service. American families may also host a foreign student for 4-8 weeks in the summer. Organization also offers inbound and outbound academic semester and year programs.

Program Dates: June–August

Duration of Program: 3–7 weeks

Cost: Starting at $2,095 (includes room and board and transportation)

Financial Aid: Up to $250 possible in discounts; fundraising packet available

Eligibility: Ages 13–19; requirements vary by program; many programs require a minimum of 2 years study in the host country's language

Application Process: Application (available on website), interview with a Nacel Open Door representative, two recommendations

Application Deadline: 45 days before program start date

Average Number of Applicants: 300

Average Number of Participants: 250

Academic Credit: Must be arranged individually by student

Contact:
Nacel Open Door
3410 Federal Drive, Suite 101
St. Paul, MN 55122

Phone: (800) 622-3553
Fax: (651) 686-9601
mail@nacelopendoor.org
www.nacelopendoor.org

National Computer Camps, Inc.

NATIONAL COMPUTER CAMPS, INC.

Program Location: University campuses throughout the country

Subject Areas: Computers

Program Description: In operation since 1978, National Computer Camps teach students how to program, write a home page, use the Internet, take apart a computer, create a graphics video, and use PowerPoint and other applications. Classes are taught at the college-prep level, although no prior experience with computers is necessary to enroll. The camps also offer tennis, basketball, soccer, and swimming, although participation is voluntary.

Program Dates: June–August

Duration of Program: 1 or more weeks

Cost: $525–$675 per week

Eligibility: Ages 8–18

Application Process: Call to apply.

Application Deadline: None

Average Number of Applicants: 2,000

Average Number of Participants: 2,000

Academic Credit: None

Contact:
National Computer Camps, Inc
P.O. Box 585
Orange, CT 06477
Phone: (203) 795-9667
Info@NCCamp.com
www.NCCamp.com

NATIONAL FFA ORGANIZATION

Agricultural Programs Overseas

Program Location: Australia, New Zealand, United Kingdom, Austria, Germany, Switzerland, France, Mexico, Costa Rica, and more

Subject Areas: Agricultural education abroad

Program Description: FFA programs are intended to develop students' potential for leadership, personal growth, and career success through agricultural education. Summer programs allow students to study international agricultural projects firsthand. Australian Homestay takes students to a farm in a rural village for one month during the summer. Adventure New Zealand includes a host-family stay and a south island adventure tour. Activities include glacier hiking and caving. Earth Tour focuses on the environment and horticulture, while traveling through Switzerland, France, and Germany. A variety of other programs are offered.

Program Dates: June–July

Duration of Program: 2–4 weeks

Cost: Varies by program

Financial Aid: Scholarships are available

Eligibility: Students in grades 10–12

Application Deadline: March 1

Academic Credit: None available

National FFA Organization

Contact:
FFA Agricultural Programs Overseas
6060 FFA Drive
P.O. Box 68960
Indianapolis, IN 46268
Phone: (317) 802-4220; (888) 332-7853
Fax: (317) 802-5220
www.ffa.org/international

NATIONAL OUTDOOR LEADERSHIP SCHOOL

Wilderness Leadership Courses

Program Location: Wyoming, Idaho, Alaska, Washington, Canada, Mexico

Subject Areas: Leadership, outdoor adventure

Program Description: NOLS offers more than 200 courses nationwide and abroad. Students participate in outdoor activities such as kayaking and backpacking and learn leadership and interpersonal skills.

Program Dates: Varies by trip

Duration of Program: 2–7 weeks

Cost: Varies by trip

Financial Aid: Scholarships are available; scholarship application deadline is 4–6 months prior to start of program. Contact NOLS admissions office for scholarship applications.

Eligibility: Ages 14 and up; age requirements vary by trip. High level of physical fitness and emotional maturity is strongly recommended.

Application Process: Completed application, nonrefundable $50 application fee. Students under 18 need parent's/guardian's written consent. Medical form, acknowledgment of risks form, and insurance form must be returned for final enrollment, along with $250 deposit.

Application Deadline: Rolling admissions; suggested deadline is at least 4 months prior to start of program

Contact:
National Outdoor Leadership School
Admissions Office
288 Main Street
Lander, WY 82520
Phone: (307) 332-5300
Fax: (307) 332-1220
admissions@nols.edu
www.nols.edu

NATIONAL REGISTRATION CENTER FOR STUDY ABROAD

Summer Language Programs

Program Location: Sevilla, Spain; Benalmadene, Spain; Salamanca, Spain; Montreal, Quebec, Canada; Salzburg, Austria; Vienna, Austria; Grun, Germany; Schmockwitz, Germany

Subject Areas: Spanish, French, German language study

Program Description: Options offered: Spanish in Sevilla; Spanish in Andalusia; Spanish in Salamanca; Summer Language Adventure— Montreal; German in Austria; German in Vienna; BWS Germanlingua; International Language Camp GLS. Students learn a foreign language or enhance existing skills and learn about the culture of their host country through small classes, frequent excursions, and cultural activities. Most participants live with host families, although students in the Austria program live in a dormitory with other young people from around the world.

Program Dates: June, July, and August

Duration of Program: 2–4 weeks

Cost: Sevilla: $957–$1,347; Andalusia: $850; Salamanca: $913–$1,460; Montreal: $905; Austria: $1,491; Vienna: $1,095; Germanlingua: $975–$1,775; Language Camp GLS: $1,023

Financial Aid: None

Eligibility: Sevilla: ages 15–17; Andalusia: ages 14–17; Salamanca: ages 14–16; Montreal: ages 13–17; Austria: ages 12–18; Vienna: ages 13–18; Germanlingua: ages 12–17; Language Camp GLS: ages 13–16

Application Process: Registration forms. Language ability will be assessed by host school.

Application Deadline: 40 days prior to start of program

Academic Credit: College credit available for all programs except German in Austria and BWS Germanlingua

Contact:
National Registration Center for Study Abroad
attn: June Domoe
823 North 2nd Street
Milwaukee, WI 53203
Phone: (414) 278-7410
Fax: (414) 271-8884
info@nrcsa.com
www.nrcsa.com

NATIONAL STUDENT LEADERSHIP CONFERENCE

Law & Advocacy;

International Diplomacy;

Medicine & Health Care

Program Locations: All programs are offered in the Washington, DC area (American University, George Mason University, and the University of

Maryland). Law & Advocacy is also offered in Palo Alto, California (Stanford University) and Chicago, Illinois (Loyola University).

Subject Areas: Leadership development, law, trial advocacy, diplomacy, international relations, medicine; college preparation

Program Description: At a National Student Leadership Conference, students learn to unlock their hidden leadership potential while focusing on a specific academic area. Special guest speaker programs allow students to meet with and learn from national and world leaders in the field. Each program offers a hands-on experience through insider tours, off-campus field trips and briefings, and simulations such as a mock trial, medical ethics debate, or model United Nations assembly. Students also experience a preview of college life while staying on a beautiful university campus.

Program Dates: June–August

Duration of Programs: 6 or 11 days

Cost: $997 (6 days); $1,697 (11 days). Includes room and board.

Financial Aid: Scholarships available, based on academic merit and financial need. Contact NSLC for a scholarship application.

Eligibility: Outstanding students, ages 14–18

Application Process: Participants are selected in one of the following ways: school nomination, alumni nomination, talent identification programs, or merit application. Nominated students are sent an invitation to enroll and are preapproved for admission. Students submitting a merit application must have at least a B average and need a recommendation from a school counselor, teacher, or principal.

Application Deadline: Rolling admissions

Academic Credit: Upon graduation, students receive a Certificate of Achievement and Program Transcript which may be submitted for high school credit and as part of the college admissions process. College credit available through American University.

Contact:
National Student Leadership Conference
Office of Admissions
P.O. Box 811086
Boca Raton, FL 33481
Phone: (800) 994-NSLC
Fax: (561) 392-3722
information@nslcinfo.org
www.nslcinfo.org

National Youth Leadership Forum

NATIONAL YOUTH LEADERSHIP FORUM

National Youth Leadership Forum on Medicine

Program Location: Programs held in the following cities: Atlanta, Washington DC, Boston, Houston, San Francisco, Chicago, Philadelphia, and Los Angeles

Subject Areas: Careers in medicine

Program Description: NYLF offers top students from around the world an intense exploration of the field of medicine. Students learn from internationally recognized and respected physicians and healthcare professionals, and participate in on-site visits to medical schools, hospitals, and research facilities. During small group sessions students discuss leading medical issues, and during simulation activities they explore the areas of bio-ethics, clinical decision making, and public health.

Program Dates: 2–4 sessions held throughout the summer in each of the above listed cities

Duration of Program: 10 days

Cost: $1,840 (summer 2001 tuition)

Financial Aid: Limited number of scholarships available, based on financial need, scholastic merit, leadership achievements, and other factors. Call the admissions office at (202) 628-6090 or email them at medicine_adm@nylf.org.

Eligibility: High school students from the U.S. and around the world who possess academic merit, leadership potential, and a strong interest in the field of medicine

Application Process: Competitive admissions process. Students are nominated to attend program; they may also contact NYLF to obtain application forms.

Contact:
National Youth Leadership Forum
2020 Pennsylvania Avenue, NW
Washington, DC 20006-1811
Phone: (202) 628-6090
Fax: (202) 638-4252
info@nylf.org
www.nylf.org

NEW JERSEY INSTITUTE OF TECHNOLOGY

Pre-college Academy in Technology and Science for High School Students

Program Location: New Jersey Institute of Technology in Newark, New Jersey

Subject Areas: Computer science, precalculus, calculus, chemistry, physics, college preparation

Program Description: Participants earn up to eight college credits in small, customized classes taught by committed faculty. Course credits can be applied toward an undergraduate degree at NJIT, and at most other colleges and universities. Students have the option to live on-campus during the week; housing in NJIT'S air-conditioned residence halls runs from Sunday night to Friday during the day.

Program Dates: July 1–August 7

Duration of Program: 5–1/2 weeks

Cost: $216/credit plus $116 student fee; non-refundable $50 application fee also required

Financial Aid: None available

Eligibility: Qualified students in grades 9–12

Application Process: Application, recommendation, transcript, recent test results (PSAT, SAT)

Application Deadline: May 15

Average Number of Applicants: 50

Average Number of Participants: 40

Academic Credit: College credit available

Contact:
New Jersey Institute of Technology
Pre-college Programs
University Heights
Newark, NJ 07102
Phone: (973) 596-3423
Fax: (973) 642-1847
muldrow@adm.njit.edu
www.njit.edu/precollege

NEW YORK FILM ACADEMY

New York Film Academy Summer Program

Program Location: New York, Los Angeles, Massachusetts, New Jersey, Paris, Cambridge, United Kingdom

Subject Areas: Filmmaking, acting

Program Description: Filmmaking program where each student writes, shoots, directs and edits his/her own short films.

Program Dates: First Monday of every month (start date)

Duration of Program: 4-, 6-, and 8-week sessions; 1-year session

Cost: $4,000

Financial Aid: None available

Eligibility: Open door

Application Deadline: One month prior to start date

Average Number of Applicants: 1,000

Average Number of Participants: 700

Academic Credit: Available

Contact:
Alex Millier
New York Film Academy
100 E 17th Street
New York, NY 10003
Phone: (212) 674-4300
Fax: (212) 477-1414
film@nyfa.com
www.nyfa.com

NEW YORK STAGE & FILM

See Vassar College and New York Stage & Film

NEW YORK UNIVERSITY

Tisch Summer High School Program

Program Location: New York University, Lee Strasberg Theatre Institute, and CAP21 in New York City

Subject Areas: Filmmaking: film narrative, animation. Drama: acting, musical theater. Writing: musical theater.

Program Description: Offers high school students the chance to participate in intensive training in a residential arts program. Students receive valuable exposure to their industry as well as to the rich cultural life of New York City. All students in the programs are required to live in a residence hall on the NYU campus. Evenings and weekends feature a variety of group outings,

as well as class preparation and rehearsals.

Program Dates: July–August

Duration of Program: 4 weeks

Cost: $5,402 (includes room and board)

Eligibility: Applicants must be current high school juniors; current sophomores of exceptional maturity may also be considered

Application Process: Application, personal statement, nonrefundable $35 application fee, secondary school recommendation form and personal recommendation form, and official transcript

Application Deadline: March 19 (2001 date)

Academic Credit: College credit available

Contact:
New York University
Tisch School of the Arts
Summer High School Program
721 Broadway, 12th Floor
New York, NY 10003-6807
Phone: (212) 998-1500
tisch.highschool@nyu.edu
www.nyu.edu/tisch/summer

NO. 1 SOCCER CAMPS

College Prep Academy

Program Location: Loomis Chaffee School in Windsor, Connecticut; 8 other locations nationwide

Subject Areas: Soccer

Program Description: Preseason training program for high school players only. Named "top soccer camp" by *Sports Illustrated for Kids*.

Program Dates: July 9–14, August 6–17

Duration of Program: 2 weeks

Cost: $1,480 (includes room and board)

Financial Aid: None available

Eligibility: High school students

Application Process: Apply on website.

Application Deadline: July

Average Number of Applicants: 150

Average Number of Participants: 150

Academic Credit: None available

Contact:
No. 1 Soccer Camps
P.O. Box 389
Isle of Palms, SC 29451
Phone: (800) 622-4646
Fax: (843) 886-0885
info@no1soccercamps.com
www.no1soccercamps.com

NORTH CAROLINA SCHOOL OF THE ARTS

Summer Session

Program Location: North Carolina School of the Arts in Winston-Salem, North Carolina

Subject Areas: Dance, drama, music, film, visual arts

Program Description: Students study with renowned professionals, pushing their talents to the limit and exploring their potential as artists. Offers participants a taste of residential life at an arts conservatory, and the chance to live in a community of artists.

Program Dates: June 24–July 26

Duration of Program: 5 weeks

Cost: $1,864 (in-state high school); $2,665 (out-of-state high school); includes room and board; costs differ for college students

Financial Aid: None available

Eligibility: Ages 12 and up (dance and music); ages 14 and up (film and visual arts); ages 15 and up (drama)

Application Process: Application, application fee, 2 letters of recommendation, statement of purpose

Application Deadline: June 1

Average Number of Applicants: 1,000

Average Number of Participants: 550

Contact:
North Carolina School of Arts
1533 S. Main Street
Winston-Salem, NC 27127
Phone: (336) 770-3290
Fax: (336) 770-3370
admissions@ncarts.edu
www.ncarts.edu

NORTHERN VIRGINIA SUMMER ACADEMY

Program Location: Alexandria, Virginia

Subject Areas: Health care, genetics, biomedical technology

Program Description: Provides the opportunity for academically talented, rising high school juniors and seniors to explore the relationship between health care, technology, genetics, and public policy through research projects, field trips, laboratory experiments, and seminars. Students use a group project to research chosen topics related to science and public policy. In addition to academic work, students participate in theater and music activities, team-building projects, and activities designed to improve their communication and speaking skills.

Program Dates: July

Duration of Program: 3 weeks

Cost: $700 or $1,000 (based on participation of student's school, includes room and board)

Financial Aid Deadline: June 1

Eligibility: Rising high school junior and senior honors students

Application Process: Essay, transcript, 3 recommendations, interview

Northwaters

Application Deadline: Priority deadline May 1, after May 1 admissions based on space available

Average Number of Applicants: 40

Average Number of Participants: 20

Academic Credit: None available

Contact:
Northern Virginia Summer Academy
1503 Wake Forest Drive
Alexandria, VA 22037
Phone: (703) 765-2395
Fax: (703) 765-2395
jkgeary@starpower.net
www.acps.k12.va.us/nvsa

NORTHWATERS

Northwaters Wilderness Programs

Program Location: Temagami Wilderness, Canada

Subject Areas: Outdoor adventure

Program Description: Authentic wilderness experiences for students. Participants go on canoe trips and are taught outdoor living skills with an emphasis on environmental issues and "learning from the land in a spirit of harmony, balance, and trust."

Program Dates: Sessions throughout summer

Duration of Program: 2-, 3½-, and 7-week programs

Cost: $1,250–$4,100

Eligibility: Requirements vary by program. Programs include Langskib (boys, ages 10–19), Northern Lights (girls, ages 11–13), and Northwaters (coed, ages 13–19).

Application Process: Contact organization for details.

Contact:
Northwaters
P.O. Box 477
St. Peters, PA 19470
Phone: (610) 469-4661
Fax: (610) 469-6522
north@northwaters.com
www.northwaters.com

Northwestern University

NORTHWESTERN UNIVERSITY

National High School Institute

Program Location: Northwestern University in Evanston, Illinois

Subject Areas: Liberal arts, media, debate/public speaking, music, theater, dance

Program Description: Students take courses in selected focus tracks in media, music, dance, journalism, arts, theater arts, or leadership. The rigorous program features classwork from 8 A.M. to 10 P.M. in the focus subject chosen.

Program Dates: June–July

Duration of Program: 5 weeks

Cost: $3,000

Eligibility: Varies by program. Academically gifted high school freshmen, sophomores, and juniors.

Application Process: Standardized test scores, essay, résumé, transcript required

Application Deadline: Mid-April

Average Number of Applicants: 2,400

Average Number of Participants: 850

Contact:
Northwestern University—NHSI
617 Noyes Street
Evanston, IL 60208
Phone: (800) 662-NUSI
Fax: (847) 467-1057
nhsi@nwu.edu
www.nwu.edu/nhsi

See also Junior Statesmen Foundation

NORTHWESTERN UNIVERSITY CENTER FOR TALENT DEVELOPMENT

Apogee, Spectrum, Equinox, Leapfrog

Program Location: Northwestern University in Evanston, Illinois

Subject Areas: Math, science, humanities, English, foreign language

Program Description: Offers academic programs for academically talented students. Provides students with opportunities to both learn and socialize with other students with advanced academic interests. Accredited by the North Central Association of Colleges and Schools.

Program Dates: TBA

Duration of Program: 3 weeks

Cost: $2,000 (resident), $1,100 (commuter); includes room and board

Financial Aid: Available (May 15 deadline)

Eligibility: Students from prekindergarten–grade 12

Application Process: Application, SAT/ACT scores, standardized test (other), teacher recommendation, essay

Application Deadline: May 15

Average Number of Applicants: 1,600

Average Number of Participants: 1,400

Academic Credit: High school credit available

Contact:
Northwestern University
Center for Talent Development
617 Dartmouth Place
Evanston, IL 60202
Phone: (847) 467-7884
Fax: (847) 467-4283
ctd@northwestern.edu
www.ctd.northwestern.edu

Oak Ridge Military Academy

OAK RIDGE MILITARY ACADEMY

Academic Summer School

Program Location: Oak Ridge, North Carolina

Subject Areas: Grades 9–12: Camp offers classes in English, algebra, geometry, U.S. and world history, music theory, ESL, photography, and other subjects. Grades 6–8: Students must take all three of the following: math, science, and language arts.

Program Description: Students attend classes for 4 hours each weekday and have 2 hours of supervised study hall 4 nights per week. Classes may be taken for remediation, enrichment or acceleration. Afternoon activities include computer lab, research projects, and leadership training.

Program Dates: June 11–July 1; July 9–July 29 (2000 dates)

Duration of Program: 3 weeks per session; students may register for both sessions

Cost: $2,250 (residential); $2,200 (commuter). Includes books, meals, uniforms, laundry, and haircuts.

Eligibility: Coed, grades 6–12

Application Process: Completed application, school transcripts, recent physical exam and immunization records. Open houses conducted on Mondays from February–June.

Application Deadline: Rolling admissions

Average Number of Applicants: 100

Average Number of Participants: 90

Academic Credit: High school credit available; each 3-week session equals ½ credit

Leadership Adventure Camp

Program Location: Oak Ridge, North Carolina

Subject Areas: Leadership training, outdoor adventure

Program Description: Outdoor adventure training, team sports, and unit activities help to develop leadership skills and promote teamwork. Participants rotate through leadership positions in various challenging situations. Activities include rappelling, paintball, range and target practice, weapon safety. Optional courses in SCUBA, parachuting, and Red Cross lifeguard training.

Program Dates: June 11–July 1; July 9–July 29 (2000 dates)

Duration of Program: 3 weeks per session

Cost: $1,700 (residential); $1,485 (commuter). Includes books, meals, uniforms, laundry, and haircuts.

Eligibility: Coed, grades 6–12

Application Process: Completed application, recent physical exam and immunization records.

Open houses conducted on Mondays from February–June.

Application Deadline: Rolling admissions

Contact:
Oak Ridge Military Academy
P.O. Box 498
Oak Ridge, NC 27310
Phone: (800) 321-7904 or (336) 643-4131;
Fax: (336) 643-1797
ormilitary@aol.com
www.oakridgemilitary.com

OAKLAND UNIVERSITY

Oakland University Summer Mathematics Institute

Program Location: Oakland University Department of Mathematics and Statistics in Rochester, Michigan

Subject Areas: Mathematics

Program Description: Offers two advanced, four-credit mathematics courses to approximately 30 mathematically talented high school students.

Occidental College

Classes taught by regular, full-time, doctorate faculty. Courses are intensive and accelerated and are augmented by problem-solving sessions and opportunities for original work. Day camp only.

Program Dates: TBA

Duration of Program: 6 weeks

Cost: Free; program provides tuition, fees, books, tutoring, counseling, supplies, and lunch.

Eligibility: Students in grades 9–12 with high mathematical ability

Application Process: Transcript, teacher recommendation, completion of problem set given by program

Application Deadline: May 15

Average Number of Applicants: 60

Average Number of Participants: 30

Academic Credit: University credit available (8 semester hours)

Contact:
Oakland University Summer Mathematics Institute
Department of Mathematics and Statistics
Rochester, MI 48309-4484
Phone: (248) 370-3420
Fax: (248) 370-4184
lipman@oakland.edu

OCCIDENTAL COLLEGE

High School Oceanology Program

Program Location: Occidental College in Los Angeles, California

Subject Areas: Marine biology

Program Description: A 5-week course in introductory marine biology, for college students and high school seniors. Lectures, labs, field trips, and research on a 85-foot oceanographic vessel.

Ocean Educations Ltd.

Program Dates: Late June to late July

Duration of Program: 5 weeks

Cost: Tuition: $2,940; Room, board, course fee, books, insurance: $1,500

Eligibility: Students entering grade 12

Application Process: Transcript and teacher recommendations

Application Deadline: May 30 or rolling admissions until full

Academic Credit: College credit available

Contact:
Occidental College
Department of Biology
1600 Campus Road
Los Angeles, CA 90041
Phone: (323) 259-2890
Fax: (323) 341-4974
gmartin@oxy.edu
www.oxy.edu/oxy/marinebiology/

OCEAN EDUCATIONS LTD.

Marine and Environmental Science Program

Program Location: Pearson College in Victoria, British Columbia

Subject Areas: Marine/environmental science

Program Description: Investigation of marine and environmental science topics, including environmental quality assessment and conservation and undersea technology. Students learn to SCUBA dive—or add to existing SCUBA qualifications—in the Juan de Fuca Strait, home to sea lions, harbor seals, and orcas. Once certified, they begin a hands-on investigation of the marine and shoreline ecosystems around them.

Program Dates: 2 sessions in July and August

Duration of Program: 3 weeks

Cost: $2,600 U.S./$3,300 Canadian

Eligibility: Ages 16–19

Application Process: Recommendation from science teacher and guidance counselor

Application Deadline: Rolling admission

Average Number of Applicants: 32

Average Number of Participants: 32

Academic Credit: High school credit

Contact:
attn: Ian Mitchell
Ocean Educations Ltd.
Salt Spring Island, British Columbia
V8K 2E9 CANADA
Phone: (877) 464-6059
ian@oceaned.com
www.oceaned.com

OCEANIC SOCIETY

Bahamas Dolphin Project for High School Students

Program Location: Live-aboard 68-foot yacht in the Bahamas

Subject Areas: Marine biology and ecology

Program Description: This program provides high school students with an intensive, hands-on introduction to dolphin research and marine mammal career opportunities. Based on the Oceanic Society's live-aboard research vessel, students receive instruction in research methods and actively collect data for the Oceanic Society's Bahamas Dolphin Project on spotted dolphins (Stenella frontalis) and bottlenose dolphins (Tursiops truncatus). Although the focus of this program is academic, the course combines scientific inquiry with education and recreation.

Program Dates: July

Duration of Program: 1 week

Cost: $1,650 (does not include airfare)

Eligibility: Ages 16–18

Application Process: Sign up to secure a spot; deposit required.

Application Deadline: Rolling

Average Number of Participants: 8

Academic Credit: Can be used for course credit

Belize Student Expedition

Program Location: Blackbird-Oceanic Society Field Station at the Turneffe Atoll in Belize

Subject Areas: Marine biology and ecology

Program Description: Developed for high school students, this program provides an opportunity for students to expand their classroom education in the sciences with hands-on field experience. Students work with marine biologists to accomplish specific objectives. There will also be an opportunity to exchange ideas with Belizean students at the University of Belize field station.

Program Dates: July 20–27, 2002

Duration of Program: 1 week

Cost: $1,770 (includes airfare from Honolulu)

Eligibility: High school students

Application Process: Sign up to secure a spot; deposit required.

Application Deadline: Rolling

Average Number of Participants: 8

Academic Credit: Credit or non-credit basis

Contact:
Oceanic Society
Fort Mason Center, Building E, Suite 230
San Francisco, CA 94123
Phone: (800) 326-7491
Fax: (415) 474-3395
Tenofsky@oceanic-society.org
www.oceanic-society.org

ODYSSEY EXPEDITIONS

Tropical Marine Biology Voyages

Program Location: British Virgin Islands

Subject Areas: Marine science, SCUBA diving, sailing, leadership training

Program Description: Educational adventure programs exploring sailing, SCUBA diving, and tropical marine biology while living and sailing

Odyssey Expeditions

aboard catamarans in the Caribbean. SCUBA certifications, sailing, marine biology and oceanography instruction, island exploration, sea kayaking, waterskiing, and leadership training.

Program Dates: June 17–August 20

Duration of Program: 3 weeks

Cost: $3,925 (includes room and board)

Financial Aid: None available

Eligibility: Ages 13–17 (high school program); Ages 18–23 (college level)

Application Process: Application (available on website or from brochure)

Application Deadline: None available

Average Number of Participants: 180

Academic Credit: College credit available

Contact:
Odyssey Expeditions
650 SE Paradise Point Road, #100
Crystal River, FL 34429
Phone: (800) 929-7749 or (352) 527-7749
Fax: (801) 504-5000
odyssey@usa.net
www.odysseyexpeditions.org

OFFENSE DEFENSE GOLF CAMP

Program Location: Winchendon, Massachusetts

Subject Areas: Golf

Program Description: A minimum of 24 PGA and USGTA pros teach each day. On practice range, subjects covered include drivers and fairway woods, long irons, short irons, sand play, and putting. While playing the course, each camper receives instruction on course management, shot and club selection, strategy, and mental toughness. Each camper's play on the course is noted by instructors so they can work with pupil on areas requiring most improvement. Campers are housed two or three to a room in spacious living facilities. The campus also provides an

Offense Defense Golf Camp

outdoor swimming pool, tennis courts, athletic fields, a new gym, an aerobics room, and hiking and running trails.

Program Dates: July

Duration of Program: 1–3 weeks

Cost: $840/week (overnight camp); $495/week (day camp)

Eligibility: Junior golfers ages 10–18

Application Process: Downloadable registration form available on website, or write or call for brochure and application. $200 deposit required, $50 of which is refundable before May 1; full tuition balance is due by May 15 and is nontransferable.

Contact:
Offense Defense Golf Camp
P.O. Box 6
Easton, CT 06612
Phone: (800)-T-2-GREEN or (203) 256-9844
Fax: (203) 255-5666
golfcamp@localnet.com
www.offensedefensegolf.com

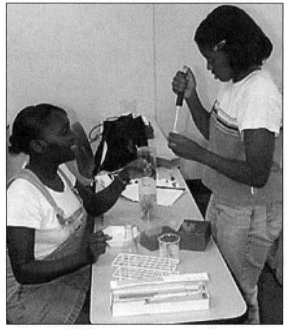

Oklahoma City Community College

OHIO STATE UNIVERSITY

Ross Young Scholars Program

Program Location: Ohio State University in Columbus, Ohio

Subject Areas: Intensive mathematics, with emphasis on number theory

Program Description: The Ross Program offers intensive instruction for academically gifted students with a strong interest in mathematics. Taught by professors, the program includes courses for second-year students and more advanced participants.

Program Dates: June 17–August 11

Duration of Program: 8 weeks

Cost: $2,200

Eligibility: Ages 14–18

Application Process: Transcript, recommendation, mathematical problem set on application form

Application Deadline: May

Average Number of Participants: 30

Academic Credit: College credit available

Contact:
attn: Daniel Shapiro
Department of Mathematics
Ohio State University
231 West 18th Avenue
Columbus, OH 43210
Phone: (614) 292-1569
shapiro@math.ohio-state.edu
www.math.ohio-state.edu/ross

OKLAHOMA CITY COMMUNITY COLLEGE

Applying the Skills of Technology in Science

Program Location: Oklahoma City, Oklahoma

Subject Areas: Science, technology

Program Description: An interactive program for Oklahoma high school students in which students analyze their DNA and publish their results on the Internet.

Program Dates: June

Duration of Program: 3 weeks

Cost: No cost

Eligibility: Open to Oklahoma high school students only

Application Process: Transcript and two recommendations (science teacher and another teacher)

Application Deadline: May 13

Average Number of Applicants: 80

Average Number of Participants: 30

Contact:
Department of Science and Math
Oklahoma City Community College
7777 South May Avenue
Oklahoma City, OK 73159
Phone: (405) 682-1611, x7271
Fax: (405) 682-7805
deanderson@okc.cc.ok.us
www.okc.cc.ok.us/~deanderson/ssa

Operation Crossroads Africa

OPERATION CROSSROADS AFRICA

Africa & Diaspora Programs

Program Location: Africa (7–10 different countries each year) and Brazil

Subject Areas: Community service, international travel

Program Description: Program consists of three orientation days in New York City, six weeks working on a community project, and one week of travel in the host country. Five types of projects: education, health, construction, agriculture, and women's development.

Program Dates: June 18–August 16

Duration of Program: 7 weeks

Cost: $3,500 (includes airfare, orientation, and all expenses abroad)

Financial Aid: Available, February 1 deadline

Eligibility: Ages 17 and older

Application Process: Application form, three references, medical note. Applicant will be notified of acceptance into the program within five weeks of receipt of complete application.

Application Deadline: February 1 (flexible)

Average Number of Applicants: 280 per year

Average Number of Participants: 175 per year

Academic Credit: May be available through student's own school and through SUNY

Contact:
Operation Crossroads Africa
475 Riverside Drive
Suite 1368
New York, NY 10115
Phone: (212) 870-2106
Fax: (212) 870-2644
oca@igc.org
www.igc.org/oca

OREGON MUSEUM OF SCIENCE AND INDUSTRY

OMSI Summer Science Camps and Adventures

Program Location: Throughout the Pacific Northwest, including Yellowstone National Park, Alaska's Chilkoot Trail, California's Redwood National Park, the San Juan Islands, and sites throughout Oregon

Subject Areas: Varied science disciplines, including paleontology, astronomy, marine science

Program Description: OMSI camps are science-oriented with hands-on activities designed to be active, fun, and educational. Settings throughout the West include residential camps, environmental learning centers, state and national parks, and backcountry wilderness areas.

Program Dates: Mid-March through early September

Duration of Program: 1, 2, or 3 weeks

Cost: $350 and up

Financial Aid: Available

Application Deadline: Minimum of 30 days before start of program

Average Number of Applicants: 1,700 for all programs

Average Number of Participants: 1,700 for all programs

Academic Credit: May be available depending on individual school

Contact:
OMSI Summer Science Camps
1945 SE Water Avenue
Portland, OR 97214
Phone: (503) 797-4662
Fax: (503) 239-7800
registrar@omsi.edu
www.omsi.edu

ORME SCHOOL

Orme Summer Camp

Program Location: The Orme School in Mayer, Arizona

Subject Areas: Horseback riding, desert survival, mountain biking, swimming, archery, arts and crafts

Program Description: Activities include horseback riding, rodeo sports, more than a dozen field/gym sports, archery, riflery, southwest travel, and arts and crafts. For older campers ages 13 and up, desert/mountain survival, mountain biking, backpacking, and English riding also offered, as well as other specialized horsemanship classes. Optional academics available, either as a 6-week credit course in high school math, English, intro to computers, or ESL. Non-credit tutoring available by the hour. Located on a 40,000 acre ranch in central Arizona.

Program Dates: Mid-June–mid-August

Duration of Program: 1–7 weeks

Cost: $1,600–$4,400 (includes room and board and transportation from Phoenix, Arizona)

Financial Aid: None available

Eligibility: Ages 7–16

Application Process: Application and deposit

Application Deadline: None available

Average Number of Applicants: 200

Average Number of Participants: 200

Academic Credit: Available

Contact:
The Orme School
Orme Summer Camp
HC63 Box 3040
Mayer, AZ 86333
Phone: (928) 632-7601
Fax: (928) 632-7605
dbartlett@ormeschool.org
www.ormecamp.org

OTIS COLLEGE OF ART AND DESIGN

Otis Summer of Art

Program Location: Otis College of Art and Design in Los Angeles, California

Subject Areas: Visual arts

Program Description: Intensive studio training in a wide range of art and design disciplines, including digital media, life drawing, graphic design, painting, fashion, and toy design.

Program Dates: July–August

Duration of Program: 4 weeks

Cost: $1,255 (housing not included)

Eligibility: Serious young artists accepted on a first come, first served basis

Application Process: Call or write to request a brochure. Register online or via U.S. mail.

Average Number of Participants: 175–200

Academic Credit: College credit available

Contact:
Otis Summer of Art
9045 Lincoln Boulevard
Los Angeles, CA 90045
Phone: (310) 665-6824 or (800) 527-OTIS
Fax: (310) 665-6821
otisart@otisart.edu
www.otisart.edu

OUTPOST WILDERNESS ADVENTURE

Program Location: Colorado, Wyoming, Bolivia, Switzerland, Mexico

Subject Areas: Outdoor adventure

Program Description: A range of small-group adventure programs, featuring rock climbing, mountain biking, fishing, wilderness travel, and more. OWA's summer adventure camps and expeditions are geared specifically to the needs, interests, and abilities of teens, with a focus on activity, fun, state of the art instruction, and expanding young people's horizons. (Programs for adults, families, and groups are offered throughout the year.)

Program Dates: Sessions throughout summer

Duration of Program: 1–6 weeks

Cost: $725 and up

Eligibility: Age requirements vary by program. No experience required for some programs.

Application Process: Register online, or contact OWA via email, phone, or fax to reserve a spot. A $300 deposit is required along with a letter of recommendation for new participants. Full brochure available by request.

Application Deadline: Rolling

Contact:
Outpost Wilderness Adventure
20859 CR 77
Lake George, CO 80827 (summer address)
Phone: (719) 748-3080
Fax: (719) 748-3046
P.O. Box 511
Hunt, TX 78024 (winter address)
Phone: (830) 238-4383
Fax: (830) 238-4788
owa@owa.com
www.owa.com

OUTWARD BOUND USA

Program Location: Various locations in the United States

Subject Areas: Outdoor adventure, leadership training

Program Description: Outward Bound offers more than 600 courses each year through the five Outward Bound schools, including courses in sailing, mountaineering, whitewater, sea kayaking, rock climbing, and more. These safe, adventure-based courses are structured to teach wilderness and survival skills while inspiring self-esteem, self-reliance, concern for others, and care for the environment.

Program Dates: Courses offered year-round

Duration of Program: Varies by course

Cost: $695 and up (varies by course)

Financial Aid: Need-based aid available on a first come, first served basis

Eligibility: No experience required; however, all courses are physically challenging, so Outward Bound does recommend beginning an exercise regime before the start of the course. Students are grouped by age.

Application Process: Online search engine helps match applicants with appropriate courses. Online catalog request form and online application form available on website.

Application Deadline: Rolling

Average Number of Participants: 6–12 per group, plus one instructor and one assistant instructor

Academic Credit: Academic credit available

Contact:
Outward Bound USA
Department P32, R2, Box 280
Garrison, NY 10524
Phone: (888) 882-6863
www.outwardbound.org

OXBRIDGE ACADEMIC PROGRAMS

Cambridge Prep;

Cambridge Tradition;

Oxford Tradition;

Académie de Paris

Program Location: Oxford University, England; Cambridge University, England; Académie de Paris in the Collège Notre-Dame de Sion in Paris, France

Subject Areas: Study abroad; wide range of courses covering humanities, sciences, social sciences, journalism, language immersion, and creative arts

Program Description: These programs offer intensive academic and cultural enrichment at some of the world's most renowned universities. Students live in dormitories, and take a major course (five or six mornings per week) and a minor course (three afternoons per week). Several day trips are included. At the end of the program, students are presented with formal, detailed tutorial reports about their work during the summer.

Program Dates: July–August

Duration of Program: 4 weeks

Cost: Cambridge Prep: $4,295. Cambridge Tradition: $4,695. Oxford Tradition: $4,795. Académie de Paris: $4,695. (Includes room and board, recreation, field trips; does not include airfare.)

Financial Aid: A small number of scholarships are available, based on financial need and the student's ability to contribute to the program. Contact the Oxbridge office to obtain a separate application form.

Eligibility: Cambridge Prep: Grades 8–9. Other programs: Grades 10–12.

Application Process: Deposit of $500 must accompany application.

Application Deadline: Rolling; February 1 for first-choice placement

Average Number of Participants: Cambridge Prep: 150; Cambridge Tradition: 200; Oxford Tradition: 350; Académie de Paris: 150

Academic Credit: High school credit available. Parents and students should determine what their own school requires in order to award credit; in all cases, Oxbridge will seek to meet the needs of individual schools.

Contact:
OxBridge Academic Programs
601 Cathedral Parkway, Suite 7R
New York, NY 10025-2186
Phone: (800) 828-8349 or (212) 932-3049
Fax: (212) 663-8169
info@oxbridgeprograms.com
www.oxbridgeprograms.com

OXFORD UNIVERSITY

See Academic Study Associates; OxBridge Academic Programs

PACIFIC LUTHERAN UNIVERSITY

Summer Scholars at PLU

Program Location: Pacific Lutheran University in Tacoma, Washington

Subject Areas: 40–45 highly diversified subjects, from academics to recreational and cultural courses

Program Description: Encompasses academics, recreation, socialization. Each student designs a personalized program from a wide variety of offered classes. Special evening programs will be held nightly, with trips and leisure activities scheduled for the weekends.

Program Dates: Approximately the last week of July through the first 2 weeks of August

Duration of Program: 3 weeks

Cost: $2,200 (includes room and board and transportation to and from program trips)

Financial Aid: Available, March 1 deadline

Eligibility: Students in grades 4–12, with evidence of academic giftedness

Application Process: Verification of participation in gifted programs, scores on standardized tests, or high recommendation

Application Deadline: July 15

Average Number of Applicants: 100

Average Number of Participants: 100

Academic Credit: Possible credit

Contact:
Pacific Lutheran University
Summer Scholars
Tacoma, WA 98447
Phone: (253) 535-8549
Fax: (253) 536-5103
sumschol@plu.edu
www.plu.edu/~sumschol

PALMER TENNIS ACADEMY

Palmer Tennis Academy Junior Camps

Program Location: Tampa, Florida

Subject Areas: Tennis

Program Description: The program emphasizes fundamental skills and match strategy. Players

Pacific Lutheran University

benefit from the 4:1 player/coach ratio on the court, the commitment to personal attention by the Palmer staff, and the intensive, structured training sessions. SAT tutoring is available at extra cost for high school students. The campers are housed in residences minutes from the Palmer facilities with resident supervision provided by Palmer house parents.

Program Dates: Year-round

Duration of Program: 1 week

Cost: $785 per week (includes room and board)

Eligibility: Coed, ages 9–17 (but the large majority of participants are high school students)

Application Process: $250 deposit. Camps are offered year round, but space availability changes week-to-week. Peak times are summer and December. Interested players should call the Academy for information on the best week to come. Call early to reserve preferred weeks.

Average Number of Participants: Approximately 25 per session

Contact:
Palmer Tennis Academy
14500 North 46th Street
Tampa, FL 33613
Phone: (813) 977-0737
Fax: (813) 971-1180
mail@palmertennis.com
www.palmertennis.com

PARSONS SCHOOL OF DESIGN

Summer Intensive Studies

Program Location: New York City; Paris, France

Subject Areas: Animation design, architecture, design marketing, drawing and painting, fashion design, graphic design, interior design, photography, Web design

Program Description: The Summer Intensive Studies program is open to all students with a serious interest in art and design. All students attend class Monday through Thursday, 9:00 A.M.–4:00 P.M. with a lunch break. All courses are taught by Parsons faculty who are accomplished, New York based practicing artists and designers. Class sizes are very limited, and registrations are accepted in the order in which they are received.

Program Dates: June 26–July 27 (NYC); July 2–28 (Paris)

Duration of Program: 5 weeks

Cost: $ 1,750 tuition and up; $1,350 residence hall. Students are required to provide their own art supplies. A list of required and recommended materials will be sent to each registrant in advance of the summer session. Paris program participants may make their own travel arrangements to and from Paris. U.S.-based participants may find it convenient to fly with the Parsons group, which will be met by Parsons staff upon arrival at the Paris air terminal.

Eligibility: Students who are about to enter their junior or senior year in high school, or have just graduated from high school. Applicants must be at least 16 years old by the start of the program. No prior knowledge is necessary, however it is recommended that students without prior art experience or those developing a portfolio for application, enroll in the Drawing and Painting course. Students whose first language is not English should have a minimum TOEFL score of 500.

Application Deadline: May 1

Academic Credit: 4–5 college credits available

Contact:
Parsons School of Design
Summer Intensive Studies
Office of Special Programs
66 Fifth Avenue
New York, NY 10011
Phone: (212) 229-8925
Fax: (212) 229-5970
schneidr@newschool.edu
www.parsons.edu/sis

PEACEWORK

Program Location: Belarus, Belize, Bolivia, Brazil, Czech Republic, Dominican Republic, El Salvador, Ghana, Guatemala, Guyana, Haiti, Honduras, Mexico, Nicaragua, Russia, United States, Vietnam, Zimbabwe, and more

Subject Areas: Community service, cultural immersion

Program Description: Peacework coordinates international volunteer programs for schools, colleges, service groups, and civic organizations interested in working closely with members of the host community. Most projects involve aid to the poor.

Program Dates: Each organization determines its own program dates

Duration of Program: 1–3 weeks

Cost: Depends on location and duration of program, but generally ranges from $900–$2,200 per person. Each group should also raise a total of $2,000–$3,000 for materials and supplies.

Financial Aid: Peacework provides assistance with fundraising and occasionally bestows grants

Eligibility: Any group of 6 or more with a genuine interest in global volunteer service. Young people must be accompanied by responsible, qualified leadership.

Application Process: Contact Peacework's offices.

Application Deadline: None

Average Number of Participants: 50 groups (600–700 individuals) per year

Academic Credit: Depends on how a program is organized within a school or academic department

Peacework

Contact:
Peacework
305 Washington Street SW
Blacksburg, VA 24060-4745
Phone: (540) 953-1376
Fax: (540) 552-0119
sdarr@compuserve.com
www.peacework.org

PENNSYLVANIA STATE UNIVERSITY

See Summer Study Programs

Phillips Academy Andover

PHILLIPS ACADEMY ANDOVER

Phillips Academy Summer Session

Program Location: Phillips Academy in Andover, Massachusetts

Subject Areas: Academic enrichment

Program Description: Students choose from more than 60 courses, including literature, language, writing, computer science, mathematics, SAT prep, astronomy, marine biology, philosophy, social science, speech and debate, English as a second language, and the arts—theater, filmmaking, ceramics, and visual arts. Students represent a diversity of geography, religion, race, and economic circumstances. With a student-to-faculty ratio of 7:1 and an average class size of 14, this program provides a highly individualized and intensive precollege experience, including an extensive counseling program.

Program Dates: June 25–July 31

Duration of Program: 5 weeks

Cost: $4,600 (resident); $3,200 (day)

Financial Aid: Available (March 1 deadline)

Eligibility: Students in grades 9–12 with strong school records and a serious desire to spend the summer in challenging, disciplined study

Application Process: Counselor recommendation, transcript, available testing, 2 teacher recommendations, corrected English essay, autobiographical essay, audition tape (theater program)

Application Deadline: Rolling (mid-April deadline suggested)

Average Number of Applicants: 1,000+

Average Number of Participants: 500–550

Academic Credit: None available

Contact:
Phillips Academy Summer Session
180 Main Street
Andover, MA 01810
Phone: (978) 749-4400
Fax: (978) 749-4414
summersession@andover.edu
www.andover.edu/summersession

THE PITTSBURGH PROJECT

Program Location: Pittsburgh, Pennsylvania

Subject Areas: Volunteer work

Program Description: Since 1985, over 11,700 students have participated in The Pittsburgh Project's urban service trips. Projects include serving the elderly and providing repairs for shut-in homeowners. Nightly programming, including worship, music, and leadership training, round out the volunteer experience.

Program Dates: 9 sessions, June–August

Duration of Program: 1 week

Cost: $295 per person (includes room and board, staff supervision, tools, and T-shirt)

Financial Aid: Available

Financial Aid Deadline: None

Pittsburgh Project

Eligibility: Grades 9–12. Must come as part of a group with adult leadership.

Application Process: Registration forms, $50 deposit per participant

Application Deadline: None, but many programs fill early

Average Number of Applicants: 120 groups (2,000 individuals)

Average Number of Participants: 95 groups (1,600 individuals)

Academic Credit: Available

Contact:
The Pittsburgh Project
2801 North Charles Street
Pittsburgh, PA 15214-3110

Phone: (412) 321-1678
Fax: (412) 321-3813
headquarters@pittsburghproject.org
www.pittsburghproject.org

PLANET HOCKEY, INC.

Planet Hockey Skills Camps;

Planet Hockey Ranch

Program Location: 50+ locations throughout the United States

Subject Areas: Ice hockey (Skills Camps); Ice hockey, hiking, mountain biking, rock climbing, whitewater rafting, paintball, sand volleyball, and more (Ranch)

Program Description: The Skills Camps are day programs that offer on- and off-ice training, as well as video analysis, nutrition lectures, and hockey consulting ("Life after high school hockey"). The Ranch is a resident camp located in the Colorado Rocky Mountains that incorporates various outdoor sports with traditional hockey training.

Program Dates: Year-round

Duration of Program: 4–5 days (Skills Camps); 1 week (Ranch)

Cost: $99–$975

Financial aid: Available on per-camp basis

Eligibility: Ages 6–adult

Application Process: Call (800) 320-7545 to register.

Application Deadline: First come, first served basis. Limited enrollment.

Contact:
Planet Hockey
Attn: Shawn Killian
9150 County Road 240
Salida, CO 81201
Phone: (800) 320-7545; (719) 539-6273
Fax: (719) 539-6412
info@planethockey.com
www.planethockey.com

POWER CHORD ACADEMY

Program Location: University of Redlands in Redlands, California

Subject Areas: Rock music

Program Description: Musicians write, develop, and refine songs, play in a band, record a CD, and make a music video. A professional touring rock band, chosen by the campers, will appear at each session. Named "Camp of the Year" by 2000MusicCamps.com.

Program Dates: Four sessions in July and August

Duration of Program: 5 days

Cost: $945; $845 for each additional session

Financial aid: Discounts offered for groups (4+ musicians), early applications (full payment before April 30), and honor roll students ("B" average or better on latest report card)

Eligibility: Ages 11–17

Application Process: Application available on website; applicants must submit a tape.

Application Deadline: May 30

Average Number of Applicants: 300+

Average Number of Participants: 200

Contact:
Power Chord Academy
Attn: Brian Wrzesimski
P.O. Box 9953
San Diego, CA 92104
Phone: (800) 897-6677
Fax: (775) 306-7923
info@powerchordacademy.com
www.powerchordacademy.com

PRATT INSTITUTE

Pre-College Summer Program

Program Location: The Pratt Institute in Brooklyn and Manhattan, New York

Subject Areas: Architecture, art history/appreciation, fashion design, foundation arts, graphic design, illustration, painting and drawing, photography, portfolio development

Program Description: The Pre-College Program is an intensive college experience in art, design, and architecture disciplines.

Program Dates: July 12–August 9

Duration of Program: 4 weeks

Cost: $1,560 (does not include housing, fees, and supplies)

Eligibility: High school students who have just completed their sophomore, junior, or senior year

Application Process: Completed application with a $200 deposit and a letter of recommendation from high school art teacher or guidance counselor

Application Deadline: April 2

Average Number of Participants: 200

Academic Credit: 4 college credits available

Contact:
Pratt Institute
Center for Continuing and Professional Studies
Pre-College Program
200 Willoughby Avenue
Brooklyn, NY 11205-9975
Phone: (718) 636-3453
Fax: (718) 399-4410
Prostudy@pratt.edu
www.pratt.edu

PRINCETON BALLET SCHOOL

American Repertory Ballet's Summer Intensive

Program Location: Princeton, New Jersey

Subject Areas: Dance with ballet as the primary focus

Program Description: An intensive workshop for the intermediate to advanced dancer interested in a possible dance career. The students work a

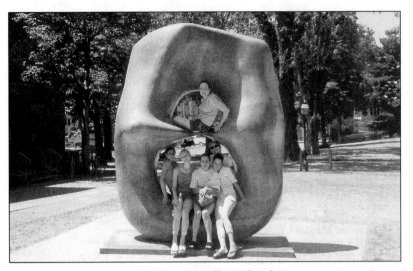

Princeton Ballet School

full day from 9:30 A.M. to 5 P.M. Morning classes in ballet and pointe; afternoon classes in composition, modern, or theater dance.

Program Dates: June 23–July 27

Duration of Program: 5 weeks

Cost: Tuition: $1,250; Room and board: $1,650 (2001 fees)

Eligibility: Students must be at least 13 to audition. To stay in residence, they must be at least 14.

Application Process: A live audition is preferred. Where no live auditions are scheduled, a videotaped audition is acceptable.

Application Deadline: Rolling admissions

Average Number of Applicants: 300

Average Number of Participants: 80

Contact:
Princeton Ballet School
301 North Harrison Street
Princeton, NJ 08540
Phone: (609) 921-7758
Fax: (609) 921-3249
www.arballet.org

PRINCETON UNIVERSITY

Princeton University Summer Sports Camps

Program Location: Princeton University in Princeton, New Jersey

Subject Areas: Coed: track and field, squash, cross country, water polo, ice hockey. Girls: soccer, softball, field hockey, basketball, lacrosse. Boys: baseball, football, basketball, lacrosse, wrestling.

Program Description: The various sports camps provide campers with an opportunity to learn from the Princeton University coaching staff and to use campus facilities. Both day programs and overnight programs available.

Program Dates: Sessions in June, July, and August

Duration of Program: 4 days–2 weeks

Cost: $250–$800

Eligibility: Age requirements vary by program

Application Process: Medical and parental release forms must be completed in full.

Contact:
Center for Visitor and Conference Services
Princeton University
71 University Place
Princeton, NJ 08544
Phone: (609) 258-3369
Fax: (609) 258-4656
cvcs@princeton.edu

See also Junior Statesmen Foundation

PROJECT PULL ACADEMY

Project PULL Academy Leadership Challenge and College Preview

Program Location: Stanford University in Stanford, California

Subject Areas: College and career preparation

Program Description: A residential summer program on the Stanford University campus for motivated students interested in Filipino-American community issues. The program also helps prepare students in college preparation and emphasizes critical thinking, teamwork, and communication skill building, as it relates to effective leadership and success in college.

Program Dates: August

Duration of Program: 1 week

Cost: $385

Financial Aid: Available

Eligibility: High school freshmen, sophomores, and juniors; all ethnicities welcome

Application Process: Two short essays, a recommendation from a teacher/counselor, and a $5 application fee

Application Deadline: April 28

Contact:
Project PULL Academy
2124 Rock Street, #23
Mountain View, CA 94043-2623
Phone: (650) 962-8775
Fax: (650) 962-8775
projectpull@projectpull.org
www.projectpull.org

PROJECT SUNSHINE

Project Sunshine Volunteer Programs

Program Location: Throughout the United States and Canada

Subject Areas: Community service

Program Description: Project Sunshine provides numerous programs and services to brighten the lives of children afflicted with life-threatening diseases. The Mentor Matching program, for example, links hospitalized children with an older student who can provide support, understanding, and fun; the Daytime Buddies program arranges for volunteers to stay with children when family cannot be present at the hospital.

Program Dates: Year-round

Duration of Program: Varies

Cost: None

Eligibility: All ages

Application Deadline: None

Average Number of Participants: Thousands

Academic Credit: Possible high school credit depending on school

Contact:
Project Sunshine
1 Shalvah Place
Monsey, NY 10952
Phone: (212) 348-1200
info@projectsunshine.org
www.projectsunshine.org

PURDUE SCHOOL OF ENGINEERING AND TECHNOLOGY, IUPUI

Minority Engineering Advancement Program (MEAP)

Program Location: Indiana University—Purdue University Indianapolis (IUPUI) in Indianapolis, Indiana

Subject Areas: Engineering and technology

Program Description: MEAP is a daytime program designed to identify minority students who are talented in math and science and introduce them to educational opportunities in engineering- and technology-related fields. Familiarizes students with the prerequisites that aid in preparation for entrance into a college or university when pursuing a technical track. Successful engineers and technologists from industrial and educational fields serve as students' role models. Students also receive instruction in the areas of computer software, hardware, and graphics.

Program Dates: June–July

Duration of Program: 3–5 days

Cost: $40

Eligibility: Minority students in grades 6–11 who are talented in math and science

Application Process: Submit written application, academic transcript, report card, letter of recommendation from math or science teacher or guidance counselor, $5 application fee

Application Deadline: April 9 (2001 deadline)

Contact:
Patrick Gee, Director
Minority Engineering Advancement Program
Purdue School of Engineering and Technology
799 West Michigan Street, ET215
Indianapolis, IN 46202-5160
Phone: (317) 274-2943
Fax: (317) 274-4567
pgee@iupui.edu
www.engr.iupui.edu/meap

PURDUE UNIVERSITY

Seminar for Top Engineering Prospects (STEP)

Program Location: Purdue University in West Lafayette, Indiana

Subject Areas: Engineering, science, technology

Program Description: Provides students with the opportunity to explore the various disciplines of engineering. Students learn about engineering and college life through a series of lab tours, school demonstrations, classroom experiences, trips to local industries, Atoms in Actions (a chemistry show designed to pique a student's interest in the intricacies of chemistry), and various hands-on engineering projects. Students have the opportunity to solve elementary engineering problems using software packages like Microsoft Excel.

Program Dates: Mid-/late July (2 consecutive weeks)

Duration of Program: 1 week

Cost: $450 (includes room and board and transportation within program)

Financial Aid: Available (May 15 deadline)

Eligibility: Rising seniors with high academic ability

Application Process: Application, teacher recommendation, transcript

Application Deadline: May 15

Average Number of Applicants: 250–300

Average Number of Participants: 200

Academic Credit: None available

Contact:
Purdue University
Freshman Engineering STEP
1286 Engineering Administration
West Lafayette, IN 47907
Phone: (765) 494-9713
Fax: (765) 494-5819
step@ecn.purdue.edu
www.fairway.ecn.purdue.edu/FrE/
new/special/step

PUTNEY SCHOOL

Putney School Summer Programs

Program Location: Putney, Vermont

Subject Areas: Academics

Program Description: Located on the 500-acre working farm of The Putney School, the Summer Programs offer small classes, individualized instruction, many outdoor activities, superb arts facilities, and a state-of-the-art computer lab. High school curriculum subjects plus classes in the arts, writing, and international education/ESL.

Program Dates: Sessions in July and late July–August

Duration of Program: Two 3-week sessions

Cost: $2,225 and up

Financial Aid: Limited, April 15 deadline

Eligibility: Ages 14–17

Application Process: $25 fee, application packet, essay, sample of student's work, teacher recommendation

Application Deadline: June 1

Average Number of Applicants: 130

Average Number of Participants: 115

Academic Credit: High school credit available

Contact:
Putney School Summer Programs
Elm Lea Farm
Putney, VT 05346
Phone: (802) 387-6297
Fax: (802) 387-6216
summer@putney.com
www.putney.com

PUTNEY STUDENT TRAVEL

Excel at Williams and Amherst Colleges;

Excel at Oxford/ Tuscany and Madrid/Barcelona

Program Location: Williams College and Amherst College in Massachusetts; Oxford, England; Florence, Italy; Madrid and Barcelona, Spain

Subject Areas: Pre-college enrichment

Program Description: Two Excel United States programs housed at Williams College and Amherst College: Students receive an introduction to college life, taking classes and becoming actively involved in planning and organizing the athletic, artistic, and social events that are a vital part of campus life. Students may also select Excel programs based in Oxford, Florence, Madrid, and Barcelona, and other travel and study abroad options.

Program Dates: June–August

Duration of Program: 3–7 weeks

Cost: $3,695 and up

Application Deadline: Rolling admissions

Average Number of Applicants: 700

Average Number of Participants: 600

Contact:
345 Hickory Ridge Road
Putney, VT 05346
Phone: (802) 387-5885
Fax: (802) 387-4276
excel@goputney.com
www.goputney.com

QUEST SCHOLARS PROGRAM

Quest Scholars Program at Stanford;

Quest Scholars Program at Harvard

Program Location: Stanford University in Stanford, California and Harvard University in Cambridge, Massachusetts

Subject Areas: Environmental science, medicine, community service, college preparation, leadership

Program Description: A summer residence program for talented, low-income, underserved high school students who are interested in the environment or medicine. Quest operates two five-week summer programs—one at Stanford University and a new chapter at Harvard. The intensive summer sessions focus on the environment, medicine, college preparation and skill building, outreach project development, and personal growth. After the summer sessions, Quest works extensively with its graduates during the college application process. Currently, 80% of Quest graduates attend Stanford and 99% attend college.

Program Dates: July and August

Duration of Program: 5 weeks

Cost: Free; room and board and transportation provided by the program

Eligibility: Talented, low-income high school students

Application Process: Application (available online), transcript, teacher recommendations

Application Deadline: Mid-March

Average Number of Applicants: 2,300

Average Number of Participants: 42

Academic Credit: Available

Contact:
Quest Scholars Program
P.O. Box 20054
Stanford, CA 94309
Phone: (650) 854-5200
Fax: (650) 618-1707
questions@syesp.stanford.edu
www.questscholars.org

RAINFOREST EXPLORATION ASSOCIATION

City Lights;

Starry Nights

Program Location: Angel Island State Park, California; Bryce Canyon National Park, Utah

Subject Areas: Hiking, outdoor exploration

Program Description: City Lights: Participants spend three days hiking the trails around Angel Island and hiking to the top of a summit for a 360-degree view of the San Francisco Bay. Participants learn about the history of the island, and spend their two nights camping out. Starry Nights: Participants spend one week backpacking through Bryce Canyon National Park (just north of the Grand Canyon) and three additional days visiting the park's more accessible attractions. The park's diverse scenery includes amazing rock formations, waterfalls, and forests.

Program Dates: City Lights: June 28–30; Starry Nights: July 10–20

Duration of Program: City Lights: 3 days; Starry Nights: 1½ weeks

Cost: City Lights: $125–$475, depending on point of departure; Starry Nights: $500–$1,100, depending on point of departure

Eligibility: City Lights: Anyone is eligible to apply; Starry Nights: Anyone in good physical condition with some hiking/camping experience

Application Process: Application can be accessed on the website or by mailing a self-addressed, stamped envelope. Interview required, either in person, by phone, or via online chat. A $10 nonrefundable deposit secures a space in the program and buys a one-year membership with the REA.

Application Deadline: City Lights: May 1, 2002; Starry Nights: March 15, 2002

Academic Credit: None available

Contact:
Rainforest Exploration Associaton
P.O. Box 151035
San Rafael, CA 94915
Phone: (415) 377-0853
summer@rainforestexploration.org
www.rainforestexploration.org

RANDOLPH-MACON ACADEMY

Randolph-Macon
Academy Summer Programs

Program Location: Randolph-Macon Academy in Front Royal, Virginia

Subject Areas: English, math, science, social studies, history, computer applications, foreign languages, SAT preparation, flight training, ESL

Program Description: Students may take on new course or two repeat courses for credit. They may also take one repeat course while enrolled in the flight program. Students attend supervised study periods in the afternoons. Evening recreational activities include swimming, football, basketball, weightlifting, movies, and other activities. Participants may take trips into town on Saturday afternoons, and to various amusement parks on Sundays.

Program Dates: Call for more information

Duration of Program: 5 weeks

Cost: $2,625 (includes room and board and transportation for academy-sponsored trips)

Financial Aid: None available

Eligibility: Students entering grades 6–12

Application Process: Application, $75 application fee, transcript, teacher recommendation

Application Deadline: Rolling

Average Number of Applicants: 160

Average Number of Participants: 200 (some students enrolled at the academy also participate)

Academic Credit: High school credit available

Contact:
Randolph-Macon Academy
Summer Programs
200 Academy Drive
Front Royal, VA 22630
Phone: (800) 272-1172
Fax: (540) 636-5419
admissions@rma.edu
www.rma.edu

RASSIAS PROGRAMS

Program Location: France and Spain

Subject Areas: Study abroad, language, homestay, travel

Program Description: These programs are based on an intensive language model developed by John Rassias, a Dartmouth College professor. Two programs in France: one in the Loire Valley and one in Provence. Three programs in Spain: one on the North Atlantic coast, one in Castilian Spain, and one in Galicia on the Western Atlantic coast. All programs include two weeks of classes and homestay and two weeks of travel.

Program Dates: Late June–July

Duration of Program: 4 to 5 weeks

Cost: $5,720–$6,320 (includes round-trip airfare from New York)

Eligibility: Students in grades 9–11 with two years of the appropriate language

Rassias Programs

Application Process: Application form, two essays, two recommendations, and interview (in person or by phone). $800 deposit submitted with application (fully refundable less $50 processing fee if applicant is rejected).

Application Deadline: March 31

Contact:
Rassias Programs
P.O. Box 5456
Hanover, NH 03755
Phone: (603) 643-3007
Fax: (603) 643-4249
rassias@sover.net
www.rassias.com

RHODE ISLAND SCHOOL OF DESIGN

Pre-College Program

Program Location: Providence, Rhode Island

Subject Areas: Visual arts and design

Program Description: An intensive experience designed to provide a strong foundation of skills and understanding in the visual arts. Students select a major from one of 14 areas of study and are required to take three foundation courses: drawing, design, and art history. Students attend classes five days per week, six hours per day.

Program Dates: June 24–August 5

Duration of Program: 6 weeks

Cost: $2,550 (tuition); $650–$825 (housing); $620 (meal plan). Lab/model fees and art supplies not included.

Financial Aid: RISD offers two financial aid programs to Pre-College students; one benefits residents of Rhode Island, and the other benefits minority students. For information and application forms for either scholarship, call (401) 454-6209 or write: RISD/CE, Pre-College Scholarship Program, Two College Street, Providence, RI 02903-2787.

Eligibility: High school students who have completed their sophomore, junior, or senior year

Application Process: Application, $30 application fee, $100 tuition deposit, written statement, and letter of recommendation from high school art teacher or guidance counselor. Residential students must also submit $100 housing and dining deposit and completed residence life questionnaire.

Application Deadline: May 26. Since space in each major is limited, early application is advised.

Average Number of Participants: 400

Academic Credit: None available

Contact:
RISD
Two College Street
Providence, RI 02903
Phone: (401) 454-6201; (800) 364-RISD
Fax: (401) 454-6218
summer@risd.edu
www.risd.edu/precollege.cfm

Rhodes College

RHODES COLLEGE

Young Scholars and Writers Camp

Program Location: Memphis, Tennessee

Subject Areas: Writing

Program Description: Gives a select group of high school students the chance to experience college-level study. Participants in the program take one course that includes an intensive writing component.

Program Dates: June 10 to June 22

Duration of Program: 2 weeks

Cost: $1,100

Eligibility: High school juniors and seniors

Application Process: Transcript, personal essay, letter of recommendation from high school counselor or teacher, and $20 registration fee

Application Deadline: Early May

Average Number of Applicants: 80

Average Number of Participants: 70

Academic Credit: College credit available

Contact:
Young Scholars and Writers Camp
Rhodes College
2000 North Parkway
Memphis, TN 38112
Phone: (901) 843-3581
Fax: (901) 843-3728
boswell@rhodes.edu
www.rhodes.edu/writingcamp

RINGLING SCHOOL OF ART AND DESIGN

PreCollege Perspective

Program Location: Ringling School of Art and Design in Sarasota, Florida

Subject Areas: Visual arts and design including illustration, figure sculpture, and animation

Program Description: In this residential program, students study with Ringling faculty in classes that mirror an incoming student's first year at art school. Courses teach and refine skills that form the framework of the visual arts: figure drawing, 2-D and 3-D design studios, color, and computer as an art tool. At the end of the program, students have expanded their portfolios for college admission, scholarships, and other professional career pursuits.

Program Dates: June 23–July 21, 2002

Duration of Program: 4 weeks

Cost: $3,472.98 (includes tuition, room and board, and supplies)

Eligibility: Students ages 16–18 are considered for their potential to benefit from the program

Application Deadline: May 13, 2002; late applications accepted as space allows

Application Process: Statement of purpose, background summary, and letter of recommendation from art teacher or guidance counselor

Average Number of Applicants: 100

Average Number of Participants: 85

Academic Credit: Successful completion of the program may earn three college credits

Summer Teen Studios

Program Location: Sarasota, Florida

Subject Areas: Drawing, figure drawing, painting, web design, illustration and design, color photogrphy, mixing materials, Adobe Photoshop®, and clay animation

Program Description: Summer art classes that allow teens to explore their emerging style in the visual arts and design. Fundamental visual art concepts are emphasized, helping students build a foundation in all areas of interest. Each week of studio experience is a unique session. Ringling School faculty and professional artists bring their artistic talent and enthusiasm to every lesson.

Program Dates: June–July, 2002

Duration of Program: 1-week art classes and 2-week computer classes

Cost: $125–$240 plus registration and lab fees

Eligibility: Students entering grades 7–12

Application Deadline: June 1, 2002

Average Number of Applicants: 250

Average Number of Participants: 250

Academic Credit: None available

Ringling School of Art and Design

Contact:
Ringling School of Art and Design
Continuing and Professional Education
2700 North Tamiami Trail
Sarasota, FL 34234
Phone: (941) 955-8866
Fax: (941) 955-8801
cpe@ringling.edu
www.ringling.edu

THE ROAD LESS TRAVELED

Program Location: Wilderness territories in the United States (including Alaska), Australia, Costa Rica, and Nepal

Subject Areas: Outdoor adventure

Program Description: Wilderness adventure program exploring a remarkable array of wilderness territories in the U.S. and abroad. Provides young people with a life experience that sparks their physical and intellectual growth through the development of wilderness skills and cultural awareness. Activities include backpacking, whitewater rafting, kayaking, desert hiking, ice and snow mountaineering, rock climbing, and trekking.

Program Dates: June–August

Duration of Program: 2–6 weeks

Cost: $1,240–$5,595

Eligibility: Coed, ages 13–19 and families ages 10 and up in average physical condition with a desire to participate

Application Process: Application form, $600 deposit

Application Deadline: Rolling admissions

Contact:
The Road Less Traveled
2331 N. Elston
Chicago, IL 60614
Phone: (800) 939-9839
Fax: (773) 342-5200
rlt1road@aol.com
www.theroadlesstraveled.com

ROCHESTER INSTITUTE OF TECHNOLOGY

College and Careers

Program Location: Rochester Institute of Technology in Rochester, New York

Subject Areas: Career exploration

Program Description: Students explore career options through hands-on workshops, demonstrations, and discussion.

Program Dates: July 19–20 or August 2–3, 2002

Duration of Program: 2 days

Cost: $55 and $65

Financial Aid: None available

Application Process: Application available in June

Application Deadline: July 14 for July 19–20; July 28 for August 2–3

Average Number of Applicants: 500

Average Number of Participants: 500

Academic Credit: None available

Contact:
Rochester Institute of Technology
Admissions Office
60 Lomb Memorial Drive
Rochester, NY 14623-5604
Phone: (716) 475-6631
Fax: (716) 475-7424
admissions@rit.edu
www.rit.edu/admissions

RUTGERS UNIVERSITY

Young Scholars Program in Discrete Mathematics

Program Location: Rutgers University in New Brunswick, New Jersey

Subject Areas: Mathematical sciences

Program Description: Discrete mathematics is a new and growing area of the mathematical

sciences with many applications. Students explore areas such as number theory, algorithms, combinatorics, and fractals.

Program Dates: July 10–August 4

Duration of Program: 4 weeks, with 4 additional meetings during the school year

Cost: $2,600

Eligibility: New Jersey high school students entering grades 11–12

Application Process: Prospective participants must solve a set of math problems on the application

Application Deadline: March 24 for early admission; first come, first served basis after that date

Average Number of Participants: 40

Contact:
Rutgers University
Center for Mathematics, Science, and Computer Education
P.O. Box 10867
Piscataway, NJ 0890-0867
Phone: (732) 445-4065
Fax: (732) 445-3477
micale@dimacs.rutgers.edu
dimacs.rutgers.edu/ysp/

SAIL CARIBBEAN

Program Location: British Virgin/Leeward Islands

Subject Areas: Sailing, SCUBA diving, waterskiing, windsurfing, kayaking, instructor training

Program Description: Participants live coed aboard 50-foot yachts and learn sailing and SCUBA diving. Extensive watersports, island exploration, personal and group challenges, lifeguard training, and U.S. sailing certification. Basic, advanced, and specialty SCUBA certifications.

Program Dates: Early June to late August

Duration of Program: 2–3 weeks

Cost: $3,000 and up

Application Process: Deposit of $500, application form

Application Deadline: Rolling admissions

Eligibility: Ages 13–18, must be able to swim, no other experience necessary

Contact:
79 Church Street
Northport, NY 11768
Phone: (800) 321-0994; (631) 754-2202
Fax: (631) 754-3362
sailcaribb@aol.com
www.sailcaribbean.com

Sail Caribbean

SAINT CLOUD STATE UNIVERSITY, ETHNIC STUDIES PROGRAM

Advanced Program in Technology and Science

Program Location: St. Cloud State University in St. Cloud, Minnesota

Subject Areas: Scientific research

Program Description: For high ability, high potential students who are seriously interested in a future in technology and science. Goals are to focus on scientific research, expose students to career options in technology and science and to provide role models in these fields and encourage mentor-mentee relationships.

Program Dates: Late July–mid-August

Duration of Program: 3 weeks

Cost: Free; room and board provided, as well as some transportation

Eligibility: Students completing grades 11–12; priority given to members of groups underrepresented in science fields

Application Process: Application, teacher recommendation

Application Deadline: May 11 (2001 date)

Average Number of Applicants: 20

Average Number of Participants: 10

Academic Credit: High school credit available

Scientific Discovery Program

Program Location: St. Cloud State University in St. Cloud, Minnesota

Subject Areas: Science, mathematics, computer science, scientific research and method, scientific projects

Program Description: For high ability, high potential students who demonstrate a strong interest in science and/or mathematics. Participants experience biological, chemical, computer, mathematical, social, and statistical sciences through laboratories, special demonstrations, presentations, field trips, and lectures.

Program Dates: Mid-July–August

Duration of Program: 5 weeks

Cost: Free; room and board provided, as well as some transportation

Eligibility: Students completing grades 9–10; priority given to members of groups underrepresented in science fields

Application Process: Application, teacher recommendation

Application Deadline: May 4 (2001 date)

Average Number of Applicants: 40

Average Number of Participants: 25

Academic Credit: High school credit available

Contact:
Ethnic Studies Program
St. Cloud State University
CH 214, 720 Fourth Avenue South
St. Cloud, MN 56301-4498
Phone: (320) 255-4928
Fax: (320) 229-5660
minstudies@stcloudstate.edu
http://pipeline.stcloudstate.edu/applications.html

SAINT LOUIS UNIVERSITY

Parks Summer Academy

Program Location: St. Louis University in St. Louis, Missouri

Subject Areas: Aviation, aviation sciences, aerospace engineering, mechanical engineering

Program Description: Aimed at expanding knowledge of the aviation industry and aviation-related careers. Each year students work in groups to build a project while receiving basic instruction on aerospace theory and engineering.

Program Dates: June 22–28

Duration of Program: 1 week

Cost: $700 (includes room and board)

Financial Aid: Available

Eligibility: High school juniors

Application Process: High school transcript, math/science teacher recommendation, online or paper-based application

Application Deadline: May 1

Average Number of Applicants: 25

Average Number of Participants: 20

Academic Credit: None available

Contact:
Office of Undergraduate Admission
Saint Louis University
Parks Summer Academy
221 N. Grand Boulevard
St. Louis, MO 63103
Phone: (314) 977-3419
Fax: (314) 977-7136
helds@slu.edu
www.imagine.slu.edu

SAINT OLAF COLLEGE

Saint Olaf Summer Music Camp

Program Location: St. Olaf College in Northfield, Minnesota

Subject Areas: Music: instrumental and vocal

Program Description: Provides opportunities for talented vocalists and musicians to do intensive work with St. Olaf faculty. Each camper participates in at least one large ensemble (band, choir, or orchestra), and participation in a second large ensemble is encouraged. Campers also enroll in electives such as jazz ensemble, music theory, instrumental or vocal chamber music, handbells, composition, harp, conducting, musical theater, percussion ensemble, and electronic music. Counselors, who are St. Olaf music students, live in the halls with campers and serve as teaching assistants, music coaches, and recreational directors.

Program Dates: June 18–June 25

Duration of Program: 8 days

Cost: $500 (residential); $400 (commuter) (cost includes two private lessons; an additional two lessons may be scheduled for an extra fee)

Financial Aid: Minnesota residents who meet income guidelines may qualify for a Minnesota Higher Education Scholarship (a full scholarship). Underrepresented minorities who meet income guidelines may qualify for a St. Olaf Minority Scholarship (a partial scholarship).

Eligibility: Students who have completed grades 9–12

Application Process: Registration form, $100 deposit, and music teacher recommendation are required.

Application Deadline: June 1 priority

Contact:
St. Olaf Summer Music Camp
1520 St. Olaf Avenue
Northfield, MN 55057-1098
Phone: (507) 646-3043
Fax: (507) 646-3690
summer@stolaf.edu
www.stolaf.edu/services/conferences

SAINT PAUL ACADEMY AND SUMMIT SCHOOL

Summer Programs

Program Location: St. Paul, Minnesota

Subject Areas: Small group academic tutorials and enrichment classes, multi-arts classes

Program Description: St. Paul Academy's academic program provides small-group instruction in basic skills, and its Artward Bound programs expose students ages 4–14 to the visual, literary, and performing arts.

Program Dates: June 17–July 26

Duration of Program: 6 weeks

Cost: $400–$1,200

Eligibility: Ages 4–adult

Application Process: First come, first served

Application Deadline: Rolling, late fee after June 1

Financial Aid Deadline: May 3

Average Number of Applicants: 800

Average Number of Participants: 800

Academic Credit: High school credit available

Contact:
St. Paul Academy and Summit School Summer Programs
1712 Randolph Avenue
St. Paul, MN 55105
Phone: (651) 696-1355
Fax: (651) 698-6787
www.spa.edu

SAN JOSE STATE UNIVERSITY

See Academic Enrichment Institute; California Chicano News Media Association

SAVANNAH COLLEGE OF ART AND DESIGN

Rising Star

Program Location: Savannah, Georgia

Subject Areas: Visual arts, design, building arts, architecture

Program Description: A 5-week program offering two studio classes per day and 10 hours of college credit which may be applied toward a BFA at SCAD or at other colleges/universities.

Program Dates: 2nd week of July through 2nd week of August

Duration of Program: 5 weeks

Cost: Approximately $4,500

Eligibility: Students who completed their junior year of high school

Application Process: Rising Star application with a nonrefundable $50 fee

Average Number of Applicants: 150

Average Number of Participants: 120

Academic Credit: College credit available

Contact:
Savannah College of Art and Design
342 Bull Street
P.O. Box 2072
Savannah, GA 31402-2072
Phone: (800) 869-7226
Fax: (912) 525-5986
E-mail: admissions@scad.edu
www.scad.edu

SCANDINAVIAN SEMINAR

Ambassadors for the Environment

Program Location: Norway

Subject Areas: Environmental awareness, foreign travel

Program Description: Scandinavian Seminars encourages the development of skills and attitudes that lead to an ecologically sound way of life. Beyond environmental awareness, participants also gain cultural perspective through daily field trips.

Program Dates: June–July

Duration of Program: 4 weeks

Cost: $3,500

Eligibility: Students in grades 9 and above

Application Process: Written application and 2 letters of recommendation

Application Deadline: March 1

Financial Aid Deadline: January 1

Average Number of Applicants: 120

Average Number of Participants: 25

Academic Credit: College credit available

Contact:
Scandinavian Seminar
Attn: Leslie Evans
24 Dickinson Street
Amherst, MA 01002
Phone: (413) 253-9736
Fax: (413) 253-5282
study@scandinavianseminar.com
www.scandinavianseminar.com/environment.htm

SCHOOL FOR FIELD STUDIES

Environmental Field Studies Abroad

Program Location: Australia, British West Indies, Costa Rica, Kenya, Mexico, Pacific Northwest

Subject Areas: Ecology and environmental conservation

Program Description: High school seniors and college students take courses at international field study centers and help local communities solve real-life environmental dilemmas, including preserving species and ecosystems, balancing economic development with conservation, and managing wildlife, marine, and agricultural resources.

Program Dates: 2 sessions, June–July and July–August

Duration of Program: 4 weeks

Cost: $2,975–$3,795

Financial Aid Deadline: First come, first served

Eligibility: Rising high school seniors ages 16 and up. One year of college-level biology or ecology recommended but not required.

Application Process: Registration forms, transcripts, essay, one recommendation

Application Deadline: None

Average Number of Participants: 25–34

Academic Credit: College credit

Contact:
School for Field Studies
16 Broadway
Beverly, MA 01915
Phone: (800) 989-4418
Fax: (978) 927-5127
admissions@fieldstudies.org
www.fieldstudies.org

School for Film and Television

SCHOOL FOR FILM AND TELEVISION

Summer in the City

Program Location: New York City

Subject Areas: Acting intensives

Program Description: Two levels are offered: the Technique Level lets the beginning performer explore the physical, emotional, and vocal life necessary for energized, focused, creative camera performing. The Performance Level gives the more advanced actor a vigorous workout as they make the transition from stage to screen. The curriculum emphasizes on-camera technique in both single camera and multicamera performance. Each level includes: NYC tour, film viewing series, seminars by industry professionals, performance day with invited industry guests, and completion dinner cruise in New York Harbor.

Program Dates: June 24–August 3

Duration of Program: 6 weeks

Cost: $2,975 tuition; $1,700 housing

Eligibility: Motivated and talented student actors, ages 16 and older

Application Process: Phone interview, completed application, letter of interest, and two letters of recommendation. Placement audition required at program orientation.

Application Deadline: Rolling admissions

Average Number of Applicants: 500

Average Number of Participants: 80 total, 12–14 students per section

Academic Credit: College credit available

Contact:
School for Film and Television
39 West 19th Street, 12th Floor
New York, NY 10011
Phone: (888) 645-0030, x108
or (212) 645-0030
Fax: (212) 645-0039
info@filmandtelevision.com
www.filmandtelevision.com/programs/summer.html

SEA EDUCATION ASSOCIATION

Science at Sea;

Oceanography of the Gulf of Maine

Program Location: Science at Sea: Woods Hole and Cape Cod, Massachusetts; Gulf of Maine: Shoals Marine Lab on Appledore Island, Maine

Subject Areas: Oceanography, nautical science, maritime studies

Program Description: The Science at Sea program commences at SEA's campus in Woods Hole, where students learn about oceanography and maritime history in a traditional classroom setting. They then set sail on a research vessel, where they are called upon to implement their knowledge in unfamiliar and often demanding conditions at sea. Oceanography of the Gulf of Maine program is another rigorous academic endeavor that teaches students about marine and coastal environments through hands-on study.

Program Dates: June–July and July–August

Duration of Program: 3 weeks

Cost: $3,300

Financial Aid: Available

Eligibility: Grades 10–12, must have completed at least one high school science and one high school math class

Application Process: Application form and fee, transcript, essay, teacher recommendation

Application Deadline: Rolling admission, but programs usually fill by March

Average Number of Applicants: 120

Average Number of Participants: 60 per session

Academic Credit: Students earn 4 college credits for Gulf of Maine program

Contact:
Sea Education Association
attn: Rafe Parker
P.O. Box 6
Woods Hole, MA 02543
Phone: (800) 552-3633
Fax: (508) 457-4673
admission@sea.edu
www.sea.edu

Sea Education Association

Seacamp Association, Inc.

SEACAMP ASSOCIATION, INC.

Seacamp

Program Location: Big Pine Key, Florida

Subject Areas: Marine science, SCUBA

Program Description: Students get a close look at the mysterious and interesting organisms that live in the unique habitats surrounding the Keys, under the guidance of academically trained instructors who lead explorations, provide help in identification, explain relationships, and teach scientific techniques. Courses specially designed to teach teens to SCUBA dive can lead to NAUI Basic Certification or NAUI Master Certification. Campers certified in SCUBA can use their skills in marine science investigations. Courses available in marine science (24 classes), SCUBA, sailing, windsurfing, and creative expression.

Program Dates: June 24–July 11; July 14–July 31; August 3–August 20

Duration of Program: 18 days

Cost: $2,495, plus $355 for SCUBA

Eligibility: Ages 12–17

Application Process: Deposit of $300

Application Deadline: Rolling

Average Number of Applicants: 500

Average Number of Participants: 450

Contact:
Seacamp
1300 Big Pine Avenue
Dept. Y
Big Pine Key, FL 33043
Phone: (305) 872-2331
Fax: (305) 872-2555
www.seacamp.org

SEATTLE YOUTH SYMPHONY ORCHESTRA

Marrowstone Music Festival

Program Location: Western Washington University in Bellingham, Washington

Subject Areas: Classical music

Program Description: Young musicians from throughout North America gather at the Marrowstone Festival for an intense musical

experience. The curriculum includes master classes taught by world-renowned instructors as well as chamber and orchestral rehearsals and performances.

Program Dates: August

Duration of Program: 2 or 3 weeks

Cost: $1,360 (2 weeks); $1,700 (3 weeks). Includes room and board.

Financial Aid: Available

Eligibility: Ages 13–23. Admission depends upon musical ability, orchestral balance, and housing availability.

Application Process: After receiving the completed application form, MMF will send the applicant a Recording Request Form, which outlines the guidelines for making and submitting a recording. Please do not send a recording prior to receiving the guidelines.

Application Deadline: Rolling

Academic Credit: College credit available

Seattle Youth Symphony Orchestra

Contact:
SYSO
Marrowstone Music Festival
11065 Fifth Avenue NE, Suite A
Seattle, WA 98125
Phone: (206) 362-2300
Fax: (206) 361-9254
marrowstone@syso.org
www.marrowstone.org

SEAWORLD ADVENTURE PARKS

SeaWorld/Busch Gardens Adventure Camps

Program location: Florida, Texas, California, Ohio

Subject areas: Zoology, marine biology, career exploration, outdoor adventure

Program description: SeaWorld/Busch Gardens Adventure Camps offer real-world experiences with amazing animals in the unique settings of their Adventure Parks and in field locations. Adventures include coming face to face with amazing animals like killer whales, giraffes, lions, and dolphins, exploring behind the scenes at Busch Gardens and SeaWorld, enjoying out-of-park excursions to canoe and snorkel in nature preserves, and more.

Program Dates: Camps are available year-round

Duration of Program: 1–2 weeks

Cost: Range from $700–$2,000

Eligibility: Camps at each park have different requirements: programs include adventures for individuals and groups in grades 4–12, adults, teachers, and families

Application Deadline: Rolling

Application Process: Apply directly to park where camp occurs. Nonrefundable deposit of $100–$200 required. Essay, transcripts, and recommendation may be required.

Academic Credit: High school credit available

Contact:
SeaWorld/Busch Gardens Adventure Camps
7007 SeaWorld Drive
Orlando, FL 32821-8097
Phone: (800) 406-2244
Fax: (407) 363-2399
www.seaworld.org/adventurecamp/
pageone.html

SETON HILL COLLEGE

Science Quest II

Program Location: Seton Hill College in Greensburg, Pennsylvania

Subject Areas: Science

Program Description: Science Quest II is a one-week residential camp for young women entering sophomore, junior, or senior year of high school. Hands-on laboratory experiences in biology (mainly ecology), chemistry, and computers. (Science Quest program for girls entering grades 7–9 is also offered; contact the college or visit the website for more info.)

Program Dates: Mid-July

Duration of Program: 1 week

Cost: $400

Eligibility: Girls entering grades 10–12

Application Process: Application form (can be downloaded from website), $50 deposit, teacher recommendation

Application Deadline: June 1

Average Number of Applicants: 20

Average Number of Participants: 15

Contact:
Susan Yochum, Science Quest Director
Seton Hill College
Seton Hill Drive
Greensburg, PA 15601
Phone: (724) 830-1044
Fax: (724) 830-1571
yochum@setonhill.edu
www.setonhill.edu/~msct/camp/index.htm

76ERS BASKETBALL CAMP

Program Location: Stroudsburg, Pennsylvania

Subject Areas: Basketball

Program Description: Established in 1984, the 76ers camp is an intensive training session offered in a traditional private camp ground in the Poconos. Professional, college, and high school coaches instruct campers, and NBA players and coaches make appearances every year.

Program Dates: July 9–August 18

Duration of Program: 6 weeks

Eligibility: Ages 9–17, all levels of proficiency

Application Process: Application and deposit

Application Deadline: June 1

Average Number of Applicants: 5,000

Average Number of Participants: 4,000

Contact:
76ers Basketball Camp
P.O Box 1073
Bala Cynwyd, PA 19004
Phone: (610) 668-7676
Fax: (610) 668-7799
info@sixerscamps.com
www.sixerscamps.com

SHAD INTERNATIONAL

Shad Valley

Program Location: Waterloo, Ontario, Canada

Subject Areas: Science, technology, entrepreneurship

Program Description: Develops innovative leaders, exposing students to innovation and entrepreneurship through an intense leadership and learning experience focusing on science and technology. This unique approach concurrently teaches creative problem solving, effective communication, and teamwork. Students live on campus, attending stimulating and varied lectures, workshops, and group projects. They also have access to high tech

equipment and hands-on labs. Subsequent work term placement for students.

Program Dates: July and August

Duration of Program: 4–9 weeks

Cost: $1,300–$1,950 (includes room and board)

Financial Aid: Available

Eligibility: Students in grades 11–12, ages 16–19

Application Process: Application (available on website)

Application Deadline: December 7

Average Number of Applicants: 1,000

Average Number of Participants: 500

Academic Credit: None available

Contact:
Shad International
8 Young Street East
Waterloo, Ontario
Canada N2J2L3
Phone: (519) 884-8844
Fax: (519) 884-8191
info@shad.ca
www.shad.ca

SIDWELL FRIENDS SCHOOL

Deep Creek Adventures;

SFS Alaskan Adventures

Program Location: Deep Creek Lake, Maryland; Alaska

Subject Areas: Outdoor adventure, sports, arts

Program Description: Outdoor adventure programs for students with a passion for the outdoors. Activities include whitewater rafting, mountain biking, and hiking.

Program Dates: June 20–August 27

Duration of Program: 1–5 weeks

Cost: $550–$2,650 and up

Eligibility: Deep Creek Adventures: Grades 5–10. Alaskan Adventures: Ages 13–16.

Application Process: Application form, nonrefundable deposit

Application Deadline: Rolling admissions

SFS in Costa Rica

Program Location: Costa Rica

Subject Areas: Travel abroad, outdoor adventure, community service

Program Description: While exploring Costa Rica, students participate in such activities as whitewater rafting, homestays, community service, and marine biology.

Program Dates: July

Duration of Program: 16 days

Cost: $2,500 (includes airfare, lodging, meals, transportation)

Eligibility: Ages 13–17

Application Deadline: Rolling admissions

Sidwell Friends Summer Programs

Program Location: Washington, DC

Subject Areas: Middle and high school curriculum

Program Description: A day summer program offering courses in math, science, history, English, keyboarding, SAT preparation for academic enrichment.

Program Dates: June–August

Duration of Program: 4–6 weeks

Cost: $175–$1,200

Eligibility: Grades 7–12

Application Process: Nonrefundable deposit of $200 per course must accompany application. Online application available through website.

Application Deadline: Rolling admissions

Average Number of Participants: 90

Academic Credit: High school credit available

Women's Leadership

Program Location: Tappahannock, Virginia

Subject Areas: Leadership, women's studies

Program Description: Young women learn leadership skills through games and group activities. Focuses on a different aspect of leadership each day, including leadership style, group dynamics, communication, power, flexibility, trust, and responsibility.

Program Dates: Late July–early August

Duration of Program: 8 days

Cost: $725 (includes room and board)

Eligibility: Girls entering grades 8–12

Application Process: Deposit of $250 (nonrefundable) must accompany the application. Online application is available through Web site.

Application Deadline: Rolling admissions

Contact:
Sidwell Friends School
Summer Programs Office
3825 Wisconsin Avenue, N.W.
Washington, DC 20016
Phone: (202) 537-8133
www.sidwell.edu/programs/summer_programs/
summer_prog_main.htm

SIERRA ADVENTURE CAMPS

Program Location: Sierra National Forest in California

Subject Areas: Outdoor adventure, leadership training

Program Description: Canoeing, rappelling, rock climbing, camping, and other outdoor activities are offered on the shore of Bass Lake, a 3½-mile long lake laden with beautiful coves, beaches, and a waterfall inlet. Sleepaway program and aquatic sports day programs are offered. Also offered is a Counselor-in-Training program, giving teens the opportunity to gain leadership

Sidwell Friends School—Women's Leadership

experience while enjoying the full camp program. CITs are included in pre-camp training, staff meetings, and CIT meetings, and are personally taught conflict resolution case studies and leadership skills by the camp directors.

Program Dates: Sessions throughout summer

Duration of Program: Sierra sleepaway: 12 days. Aquatic sports day program: 2 or 3 weeks (campers may attend 2–5 times per week).

Cost: Sierra sleepaway: $875. Includes travel via deluxe air-conditioned charter bus to Bass Lake from initial meeting point in West Los Angeles. Aquatic sports day program: $240–$1,035. Includes door-to-door transportation or daily transportation from designated meeting points in West Los Angeles and the San Fernando Valley.

Eligibility: Ages 8–17, no experience required. Counselors-in-Training must be at least age 13 (aquatic sports) or 14 (Sierra sleepaway) and meet certain other criteria; contact Sierra for more information.

Application Deadline: Rolling admissions

Application Process: Application form, $100 deposit plus $50 nonrefundable registration fee

Average Number of Participants: Sierra sleepaway: Limited to 50 campers and 8 Counselors-in-Training. Aquatic sports day program: Limited to 60 campers and 8 Counselors-in-Training.

Contact:
Sierra Adventure Camps
814 S. Westgate Ave., Suite 117
Los Angeles, CA 90049
Phone: (310) 826-7000 or (818) 385-0200
sierracamp@earthlink.net
www.sierraadventurecamps.com

Simon's Rock College of Bard

SIMON'S ROCK COLLEGE OF BARD

Young Writer's Workshop

Program Location: Simon's Rock College of Bard in Great Barrington, Massachusetts

Subject Areas: Writing

Program Description: Based on Bard College's innovative writing program for entering students, this workshop focuses on using informal, playful, expressive writing as a way to strengthen skills of language and thinking. Students have the opportunity to explore various forms of writing, including poetry, story, and essay, as well as engage in various forms of collaborative learning.

Program Dates: Late June to early July

Duration of Program: 3 weeks

Cost: $1,725

Financial Aid: Available

Eligibility: Open to all high school students

Application Process: Teacher recommendation and essay required.

Application Deadline: Rolling admissions begin in February and run through May. Early application is recommended.

Average Number of Applicants: 150

Average Number of Participants: 78

Contact:
Simon's Rock College of Bard
attn: Jamie Hutchinson
84 Alford Road
Great Barrington, MA 01230
Phone: (413) 528-7231
Fax: (413) 528-7365
jamieh@simons-rock.edu
www.simons-rock.edu

SKIDMORE COLLEGE

Pre-College Program in the Liberal Arts for High School Students at Skidmore

Program Location: Skidmore College in Saratoga Springs, New York

Subject Areas: Liberal arts, college preparation

Program Description: The program offers mature high school students the opportunity to attend regular college credit-bearing courses in the humanities and the social and natural sciences. Allows students to get an early start on their college careers, explore interests not available at their high schools, strengthen their

Smith College Summer Science Program

skills, and experience college life and learning. Numerous social and cultural activities on campus and in historic Saratoga Springs supplement the program.

Program Dates: July to early August

Duration of Program: 5 weeks

Cost: Approximately $3,900

Financial Aid: Available, early May deadline

Eligibility: Academically talented rising high school juniors and seniors

Application Process: $30 fee, application form, written statement of interest, letters of recommendation, transcript

Application Deadline: June

Average Number of Applicants: 60

Average Number of Participants: 45

Academic Credit: College credit granted for all courses

Contact:
Pre-College Program for High School Students
Skidmore College
Saratoga Springs, NY 12866
Phone: (518) 580-5590
Fax: (518) 580-5548
jchansky@skidmore.edu
www.skidmore.edu/summer

SMITH COLLEGE

Smith Summer Science Program

Program Location: Northampton, Massachusetts

Subject Areas: Science and engineering

Program Description: For high school girls with dreams of pursuing a career in science and engineering. Program offers students the opportunity to connect with professionals who will support their efforts, and to make great new friends from all over the world who share their interests.

Program Dates: July 1–28

Duration of Program: 4 weeks

Cost: $3,500

Eligibility: High school girls

Financial Aid: Available

Application Process: School transcript, essay, and deposit of $50

Application Deadline: Rolling

Average Number of Applicants: 200

Average Number of Participants: 80

Contact:
Smith College Summer Science Program
Clark Science Center
Northhampton, MA 01063
Phone: (413) 585-3060
Fax: (413) 585-3068
gscordil@smith.edu
http://smith.escapecs.com

Soccerplus Camps

SOCCERPLUS CAMPS

SoccerPlus Goalkeeper School and SoccerPlus Field Player Academy

Program Location: 25 sites throughout the United States

Subject Areas: Soccer

Program Description: SoccerPlus, which conducts programs across the country, is presented by Tony DiCuccio, Coach of the 1996 Olympic Gold Medal and 1999 World Cup Champion USA Women's National Team. Goalkeeper School and Field Player Academy teach skills in a safe and humanistic environment. Utilizing top instructors and a highly effective curriculum, SoccerPlus presents a series of challenges designed to expand students' physical and mental abilities while delivering success and building self-esteem on and off the field.

Program Dates: June–August

Duration of Program: 6 days

Cost: $545–$975 for day and residential programs

Financial Aid: None available

Eligibility: Ages 10 to adult for goalkeepers, ages 12 to adult for field players. All participants should be proficient in fundamental soccer skills.

Application Process: Registration form available through website or brochure; nonrefundable deposit required

Application Deadline: Rolling

Average Number of Participants: 45–150 per site

Contact:
SoccerPlus Camps
20 Beaver Road, Suite 102
Wethersfield, CT 06109
Phone: (800) KEEPER-1
Fax: (860) 721-8619
info@soccerpluscamps.com
www.soccerpluscamps.com;
www.goalkeeper.com; www.fieldplayer.com

SONS OF NORWAY

Camp Norway

Program Location: Norway

Subject Areas: Study abroad, language

Program Description: Program combines fast-paced learning and the direct experience of living abroad. Emphasis is on learning the Norwegian language. Students live in dormitory-style rooms in a rural setting.

Sons of Norway

Program Dates: June–July

Duration of Program: 4 weeks, plus 1-week optional tour

Cost: $2,750 (summer 2001), airfare not included, additional $595 for optional 1-week tour

Financial Aid: Scholarships available

Eligibility: Grades 11–12 and minimum B grade average

Application Process: Essay and transcripts required.

Application Deadline: Rolling admissions

Academic Credit: High school or college credit available

Contact:
Sons of Norway
1455 West Lake Street
Minneapolis, MN 55408
Phone: (800) 945-8851
Fax: (612) 827-0658
fraternal@sofn.com
www.sofn.com

SOUTHAMPTON COLLEGE OF LONG ISLAND UNIVERSITY

Summer High School Workshops

Program Location: Southampton College in Southampton, New York

Subject Areas: Writing, drawing, environmental studies, marine science, photography, psychobiology, Web design

Program Description: Intensive one-week seminars focusing on one discipline, taught by Southampton College faculty.
Advanced Critical and Creative Composition: A field experience in task-oriented writing. Through a variety of seminars, hands-on experiences, and off-campus trips, participants learn about how writing is used in business, communications, and college.
Introduction to Drawing: Students explore various aspects of drawing in the studio, including still life and live model. Some experimental drawings created.
Introduction to the Environment: Workshop designed to introduce students to the variety of terrestrial and marine environments on Long Island and their collective resources. Trips to pine barrens, salt marshes, and water treatment plants.

Introduction to Marine Science: Program provides field experience and covers topics in marine ecology, coastal geology, oceanography, and ichthyology; approximately one day devoted to the study of each area. Methods of measurement and sampling the marine environment are stressed.

Introduction to Photography: Students focus on work suitable for inclusion in a portfolio. Topics include darkroom techniques, developing and enlarging black and white film, composition and the meaning of imagery, the science behind making a photograph (including building a pinhole camera), and self-expression and creative photography.

Introduction to Psychology/Biology: Participants introduced to topical areas in psychobiology, the study of the biological basis of behavior, learning, and memory. Classroom lectures, lab exercises, and field trips used to demonstrate scientific investigation of human and animal behavior by biologists, psychologists, and neuroscientists.

Introduction to Web Design: Students explore beginning and advanced Web technology and design. Participants focus on developing their own Web presentations and projects. Topics include HTML basics, graphics, and scanning.

Writers and Writing: Through a variety of seminars, workshops, and special events, students meet a number of noted authors, attend readings by distinguished poets and novelists, and develop their own creative writing skills under the guidance of a resident writer who works with each student individually.

Program Dates: Sessions in July and August

Duration of Program: 1 week (Sunday–Friday)

Cost: $420

Eligibility: Rising high school juniors and seniors with a combined PSAT/SAT score of at least 950 or an average of 80 in coursework

Application Process: Application form, high school transcript, PSAT/SAT scores, writing sample, $25 nonrefundable deposit

Application Deadline: Rolling. Applicants are encouraged to apply early for best selection

Contact:
Southampton College
Summer Programs Office
239 Montauk Highway
Southampton, NY 11968-4198
Phone: (631) 287-8175
Fax: (631) 287-8253
summer@southampton.liu.edu
www.southampton.liu.edu/summer/

SOUTHERN ILLINOIS UNIVERSITY—CARBONDALE

Women's Introduction to Engineering

Program Location: Southern Illinois University College of Engineering in Carbondale, Illinois

Subject Areas: Engineering

Program Description: Offers an overview of engineering at the university and professional levels, including hands-on experiences in such popular engineering disciplines as civil engineering, electrical engineering, mechanical engineering, and mining engineering. Offers the opportunity to gain insight from women working as professionals in the field.

Program Dates: Mid-June

Duration of Program: 3 days

Cost: $50 (includes room and board)

Financial Aid: None available

Eligibility: Women who have completed grades 10 or 11

Application Process: Self-nomination with teacher recommendation

Application Deadline: Mid-April

Average Number of Applicants: 90

Average Number of Participants: 48

Academic Credit: None available

Contact:
WIE Coordinator
SIUC College of Engineering
MC 6603
Carbondale, IL 62901-6603
Phone: (618) 453-7730
Fax: (618) 453-4321
www.engr.siu.edu

SOUTHERN METHODIST UNIVERSITY

College Experience

Program Location: Southern Methodist University in Dallas, Texas

Subject Areas: College preparation, variety of college-credit classes

Program Description: Academically talented students get a head-start on college and a taste of campus life during this program. Morning classes consist of college-credit courses that include philosophy, English, math, psychology, history, and government. In the afternoon, all students participate in a "core" class or humanities overview class for three hours of college credit. Students who elect to live in the residence hall participate in special cultural, educational, and recreational activities.

Program Dates: July 1 to August 1

Duration of Program: 4 weeks

Cost: $1,620 (commuter); $2,870 (residential)

Financial Aid: Available (early application suggested)

Eligibility: Students who have completed grades 10 or 11. Participants are selected on the basis of academic ability and motivation as demonstrated by grades.

Application Process: SAT or ACT test scores, teacher recommendations, other application requirements.

Application Deadline: Rolling

Average Number of Participants: 60

Academic Credit: Available

Contact:
Marilyn Swanson, Assistant Director
Gifted Students Institute–TAG
Southern Methodist University
3108 Fondren
P.O. Box 750383
Dallas TX 75275-0383
Phone: (214) 768-5437
Fax: (214) 768-3147
gifted@mail.smu.edu
www.smu.edu/ce

SOUTHERN VERMONT COLLEGE

Summer Sports Camps

Program Location: Southern Vermont College in Bennington, Vermont

Subject Areas: Soccer, basketball

Program Description: Each camp provides information on sport fundamentals, skill development sessions, and individual instruction periods. Students receive personalized attention. Program includes special awards and contests, distinguished guest speakers, camp evaluations, team competitions, and closing day ceremonies.

Program Dates: TBA

Duration of Program: 5 weekdays

Cost: $150 (lunch included)

Financial Aid: None available

Eligibility: Ages 6–17, coed

Application Process: Application

Application Deadline: Rolling

Average Number of Applicants: 50 per camp (200 total)

Average Number of Participants: 50 per camp (200 total)

Contact:
Southern Vermont College
Summer Sports Camps
928 Mansion Drive
Bennington, VT 05201-6002
Phone: (802) 447-4660
Fax: (802) 447-4695
athletics@svc.edu
www.svc.edu

SOUTHWEST TEXAS STATE UNIVERSITY

Honors Summer Math Camp

Program Location: Southwest Texas State University in San Marcos, Texas

Subject Areas: First-time students take courses in elementary number theory and Mathematica computer programming, and returning students study combinatorics, analysis, and abstract algebra

Program Description: Guided by professors, students work cooperatively to explore the mathematical concepts that underlie complex problems. Participants also receive a copy of Mathematica and work on a school-year research project at their home high school supervised by a high school teacher and a faculty mentor from SWT. Extracurricular activities include seminars conducted by guest speakers, afternoon recreation (aerobics, volleyball, basketball, or tennis), picnics, and various weekend excursions.

Program Dates: Begins June 16

Duration of Program: 6 weeks

Cost: $1,200 (includes room, board, book, supplies, and activities)

Eligibility: Grades 10–12

Application Process: Written application, personal essay, teacher recommendation, SAT/PSAT score, transcript, GPA

Application Deadline: Rolling admissions

Financial Aid: Need-based scholarships

Average Number of Applicants: 200

Average Number of Participants: 50

Contact:
Southwest Texas State University
601 University Drive
San Marcos, TX 78666
Phone: (512) 245-3439
Fax: (512) 245-1469
mw07@swt.edu
www.swt.edu

Summer Creative Writing Camp

Program Location: Southwest Texas State University in San Marcos, Texas

Subject Areas: Poetry and fiction

Program Description: The Summer Creative Writing Camp features workshops in fiction and poetry. Students work with established authors and poets and have individual tutorials with the poetry and fiction workshop leaders.

Program Dates: Last week of June

Duration of Program: 1 week

Cost: $250

Application Process: Writing sample, statement, and letter of recommendation required

Application Deadline: Mid-April

Average Number of Applicants: 100

Average Number of Participants: 20

Contact:
Southwest Texas State University
Department of English
San Marcos, TX 78666
Phone: (512) 245-3717
Fax: (512) 245-8546
sw13@swt.edu
www.swt.edu

Summer High School Theatre Workshop

Program Location: Southwest Texas State University in San Marcos, Texas

Subject Areas: Acting, musical theater, and technical theater

Program Description: A 2-week program for high school students. Morning classes in dance, movement, and voice; afternoon classes in acting. Evening rehearsals for a one-act play performed on the last day of the session.

Program Dates: Last 2 weeks of June and last 2 weeks of July

Duration of Program: Two 2–week programs

Cost: $625

Eligibility: Interested high school students

Application Process: Completed application and one letter of recommendation

Application Deadline: June 7 (1st workshop); July 1 (2nd workshop)

Average Number of Applicants: 60–70

Average Number of Participants: 65

Contact:
Southwest Texas State University
Department of Theatre
601 University Drive
San Marcos, TX 78666
Phone: (512) 245-2147
Fax: (512) 245-8440
np01@swt.edu
www.swt.edu

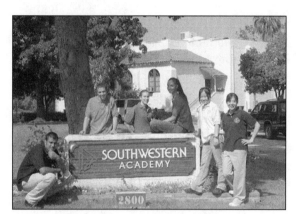

Southwestern Academy

SOUTHWESTERN ACADEMY

International Summer Programs

Program Location: Southwestern Academy in San Marino, California

Subject Areas: ESL, music, art, cultural and recreational field trips

Program Description: Intensive, individualized daily classes in English and other subjects, together with educational and recreational travels to places of interest in Southern California. Students choose from programs that provide between 20–35 hours of English instruction per week. Field trips to Disneyland, Universal Studios, the beach, museums, and art galleries.

Program Dates: June 11–September 21

Duration of Program: 4, 7, or 14 weeks

Cost: $3,950 (4 weeks); $6,750 (7 weeks); $11,500 (14 weeks); all include room and board

Financial Aid: None available

Eligibility: Students in grades 6–12

Application Process: Application (transcript, teacher recommendation required if student wishes to apply for fall also)

Application Deadline: Rolling

Average Number of Applicants: 90

Average Number of Participants: 65

Academic Credit: Available

Southwestern Adventures

Program Location: Beaver Creek Campus in Rimrock, Arizona

Subject Areas: Core subjects, Spanish, art, Native American studies

Program Description: Intensive, individualized morning classes with informal camp-style activities in the afternoon and evening. Remedial and enrichment work available for junior high students, with high school credit for make-up or new courses available for older students. Relaxed environment, with field trips to the Grand Canyon and nearby Native American sites, plus swimming, water skiing, boating, hiking, camping, and other activities.

Program Dates: July 9—August 17

Duration of Program: 6 weeks

Cost: $3,500 plus $500 for incidentals; includes room and board

Financial Aid: Available, April 1 deadline

Eligibility: Students in grades 6–12

Application Process: Application

Application Deadline: June

Average Number of Applicants: 30

Average Number of Participants: 30

Academic Credit: Available

Spelman College

Contact:
Southwestern Academy
2800 Monterey Road
San Marino, CA 91108
Phone: (626) 799-5010 x204
Fax: (626) 799-0407
admissions@southwesternacademy.edu
www.southwesternacademy.edu

SPELMAN COLLEGE

Early College Summer Program

Program Location: Spelman College in Atlanta, Georgia

Subject Areas: College foundation courses (math and English)

Program Description: Students earn college credit in this residential program. Curriculum includes precollege writing, English composition, contemporary mathematics, precalculus, and analysis. Academic enrichment courses in computer skills and African American history and culture offered. Program includes tours to educational and historic sites such as the APEX Museum, the Martin Luther King Jr. Historical District, and the Atlanta History Center.

Program Dates: June–July

Duration of Program: 6 weeks

Cost: $2,950 (includes room and board)

Eligibility: Applicants must have completed at least their junior year, have a GPA of 2.5 or better, and have completed 3 years each of high school math and English.

Application Process: Application packet, standardized test scores required

Application Deadline: March 15

Average Number of Applicants: 130

Average Number of Participants: 50

Academic Credit: College credit available (8 semester hours)

Contact:
Spelman College
Early College Summer Program
350 Spelman Lane SW, Box 849
Atlanta, GA 30314
Phone: (404) 681-3643, ext. 2170
Fax: (404) 215-7768
pdrake@spelman.edu
www.spelman.edu/cont-ed

SPOLETO STUDY ABROAD

Spoleto Study Abroad

Program Location: Spoleto, Italy

Subject Areas: Study abroad, orchestral music, voice, drama, visual arts, photography, creative writing

Program Description: An intensive interdisciplinary program focusing on the arts and the humanities. Students are given the opportunity to grow personally and intellectually while being surrounded by talented and motivated peers and faculty. Music: The program offers students individual lessons, chamber music sessions, and orchestral and vocal ensemble experience. Concerts are given throughout the summer, and there is much interaction with local musicians. Visual Arts: Courses include instruction and practice in drawing, painting, and two-dimensional design. The program also offers visits to works of art found throughout the region. Photography: Students learn camera fundamentals, and move on to more advanced techniques during the session. Creative Writing: Writers' workshop develops students' point of view, voice, tone, and mood through various activities. Students are required to keep a journal. Drama: Students explore acting problems through the work of two theorists: Stanislavsky and Viola Spolin. Includes vocal and physical techniques, character analysis, improvisation skills, and pantomime technique.

Program Dates: Mid-July to mid-August

Spoleto Study Abroad

Duration of Program: 4 weeks

Cost: $5,050 (includes room and board, transportation once in Italy also included)

Eligibility: Ages 15–19

Application Process: Application, two recommendations, portfolio, audition tape, drama resume, writing samples

Application Deadline: February 15

Average Number of Participants: 55

Academic Credit: None available

Contact:
Debbie Schofield
Spoleto Study Abroad
P.O. Box 99147
Raleigh, NC 27624-9147
Phone: (919) 384-0031
Fax: (919) 846-2371
spoleto@mindspring.com
www.spoletostudyabroad.com

Stagedoor Enterprises

STAGEDOOR ENTERPRISES

Stagedoor Manor
Performing Arts Training Center

Program Location: Loch Sheldrake, New York

Subject Areas: Theater, music, dance, modeling

Program Description: Natalie Portman, Jennifer Jason Leigh, and Robert Downey Jr. are among the many famous graduates of "Camp Show Business," as Stagedoor calls itself. Every summer, the camp stages more than 40 shows, and every camper performs in at least one of them. Tennis, volleyball, and horseback riding are offered as well.

Program Dates: June 25–August 26, 2001

Duration of Program: 6 or 9 weeks

Cost: Starts at $3,150

Financial Aid: None

Eligibility: Ages 8–18

Application Process: Registration forms. No auditions necessary.

Application Deadline: Rolling admissions. Applications accepted beginning in September.

Average Number of Participants: 245

Academic Credit: High school credit depending on school

Contact:
Stagedoor Manor
Attn: Carl Samuelson
130 Wood Hollow Lane
New Rochelle, NY 10804
Phone: (888) STAGE88
www.stagedoor.com

STANFORD JAZZ WORKSHOP

Jazz Camp; Jazz Residency

Program Location: Stanford, California

Subject Areas: Jazz (all instruments including strings and vocalists)

Program Description: Students play and study jazz with other players and a faculty of professional musicians. Classes include theory, musicianship, jazz history, jazz ensemble playing, and private lessons. Students are placed in classes with players of similar experience and ability. Resident students stay in Stanford University dorms, under counselor supervision.

Program Dates: Sessions in July and August

Duration of Program: 1 week per session

Cost: $615–$1,190

Financial Aid: Available

Eligibility: Jazz Camp: Ages 12–17, all levels of proficiency (at least 18 months of experience playing the instrument is recommended). Jazz Residency: Ages 12–17, advanced level only (also open to adults of all levels of proficiency).

Application Process: Completed application; online application available through website. First-time applicants applying to intermediate or advanced tracks must submit a recording of their playing.

Application Deadline: June 1

Average Number of Applicants: 220

Average Number of Participants: 200

Contact:
Stanford Jazz Workshop
P.O Box 20454
Stanford, CA 94309
Phone: (650) 736-0324
Fax: (650) 856-4155
info@stanfordjazz.org
www.stanfordjazz.org

STANFORD UNIVERSITY

Summer College for High School Students

Program Location: Stanford University in Stanford, California

Subject Areas: College curriculum

Program Description: The program admits exceptional high school students who are ready to explore a challenging university environment. This includes enrolling in regular Stanford courses, living in Stanford student residences, and interacting with Stanford students and faculty. More than 200 courses offered each summer. Classmates will include other high school students along with undergraduates and the occasional graduate student.

Program Dates: June 23–August 19 (2001 dates)

Duration of Program: 8 weeks

Cost: $6,500 (includes room and board)

Financial Aid: Limited aid available; downloadable financial aid application available on website

Eligibility: Rising high school seniors; commuters who are rising juniors may apply

Application Process: Application (downloadable form available on website), transcript, 2 recommendations, essay, PSAT/SAT scores, $25 application fee

Application Deadline: May 15 (2001 date)

Academic Credit: Letter grades and a maximum of 12 college credits awarded upon completion of coursework

Summer Discovery Institutes

Program Location: Stanford University in Stanford, California

Subject Areas: Creative writing, philosophy, theater, college preparation

Program Description: Designed for exceptional students who have completed at least their sophomore year in high school. Students select one of the available disciplines (2001 disciplines: creative writing, philosophy, and theater) and spend three intensive weeks delving deeply into that field, studying closely with Stanford instructors and other experts in their field. Planned recreational activities and outings provide a welcome balance to the intensive coursework.

Program Dates: July–August

Duration of Program: 3 weeks per Institute

Cost: $3,000–$4,500 (includes room and board)

Financial Aid: Limited aid available; downloadable financial aid application available on website

Eligibility: Rising high school juniors and seniors

Application Process: Application (downloadable form available on website), transcript,

Stanford University—Summer College

recommendation, essay, PSAT/SAT scores, $15 application fee

Application Deadline: May 15 (2001 date)

Academic Credit: 3–6 college credits awarded upon completion of coursework

Contact:
Stanford University
Summer Session (SCHSS)
Building 590, Ground Floor
Stanford, CA 94305-3005
Phone: (650) 723-3109
Fax: (650) 725-6080
summersession@stanford.edu
summersession.stanford.edu

Summer Sports Camps

Program Location: Stanford University in Stanford, California

Subject Areas: Coed: Cross country, golf, tennis, soccer, swimming, track & field, water polo, synchro swim, "All Sports," "Sports Plus," "Teen All Sports," fencing, sailing. Girls: basketball, gymnastics, softball, tennis, volleyball, field hockey, lacrosse, rowing. Boys: baseball, basketball, football, tennis, volleyball, water polo, rowing, lacrosse.

Program Description: An opportunity to learn from top coaches and to use state-of-the-art campus facilities. 28 separate sports camps are offered, including both residential and day programs. All camps offer at least 30 hours of instruction and playing time per week. The goal is for students to gain a complete understanding of the mechanics of their sport. Resident campers live in supervised Stanford dorms and participate in planned recreational activities in the evenings.

Program Dates: Varies by program

Duration of Program: 4 days–2 weeks

Cost: Varies by program

Eligibility: Each program has specific eligibility requirements; contact Stanford Department of Athletics for information. Certain camps are for elite athletes, including Baseball All-Star Camp, High Potential Basketball, National Junior Training Tennis Camp.

Application Process: Contact Stanford Department of Athletics for information on individual camps

Contact:
Stanford University
Summer Sports Camps
Department of Athletics
Stanford, CA 94305-6150
Phone: (650) 723-4591
gostanford.com/camps

See also Education Unlimited; Junior Statesmen Foundation; National Student Leadership Conference; Project PULL Academy; Quest Scholars Program

STANFORD UNIVERSITY, EDUCATION PROGRAM FOR GIFTED YOUTH

Summer Institute in Mathematics and Physics

Program Location: Stanford University in Stanford, California

Subject Areas: Mathematics and physics

Program Description: Provides students with an intense, academically rigorous preview of university-level mathematics or physics. Fosters social and intellectual development centered on the study and enjoyment of mathematics and physics.

Program Dates: June 24–August 15

Duration of Program: 2–4 weeks

Cost: $1,750–$2,950 (includes room and board)

Financial Aid: None available

Eligibility: Students ages 13–18 who meet the prerequisites

Application Process: Application (available on website)

Application Deadline: May 1

Average Number of Applicants: 100

Average Number of Participants: 42

Academic Credit: College credit available

Contact:
EPGY Summer Institute
Ventura Hall, Stanford University
Stanford, CA 94305-4115
Phone: (650) 329-9920 x131
Fax: (650) 745-1143
oas@epgy.stanford.edu
http://epgy.stanford.edu/simp

State University of New York—Oswego

STATE UNIVERSITY OF NEW YORK—OSWEGO

Summer Art Institute;

Summer Theater Institute

Program Location: State University of New York in Oswego, New York

Subject Areas: Studio arts; theater arts

Program Description: Summer Art Institute: Two weeks of college-level instruction. Studio options include ceramics, mixed media, computer graphics, painting, photography, and sculpture. Additionally, students earn college credit, experience campus life, and travel to Canada to visit famous museums. Summer Theater Institute: Students enjoy two weeks totally immersed in theater studies including acting, voice and speech, auditioning technique, unarmed stage combat, improvisation, and movement. Additionally, students earn college credit, experience campus life, and travel to Canada to view the world-famous Shaw Festival.

Program Dates: July 21–August 3, 2002

Duration of Programs: 2 weeks

Cost: $1,795 (includes room and board, supplies, and all field trip expenses)

Financial Aid: Partial scholarships available (need-based)

Eligibility: Good academic standing

Application Process: Application, transcripts, and reference

Academic Credit: 3 undergraduate credits awarded

Contact:
SUNY Oswego
Oswego Summer Youth Programs
214 Swetman Hall
Oswego, NY 13126
Phone: (315) 312-2270
Fax: (315) 312-3078
summer@oswego.edu
www.oswego.edu

STATE UNIVERSITY OF NEW YORK—PURCHASE

Summer Visual Arts Institute

Program Location: State University of New York in Purchase, New York

Subject Areas: Drawing, painting, sculpture, ceramics, collage, and other crafts

Program Description: Students get to explore the creative process through the visual arts. Teachers are highly imaginative art educators who are dedicated to making art "come alive."

Program Dates: July 1–August 25

Duration of Program: 4 weeks

Cost: $1,395 (includes tuition and supplies)

Eligibility: High school students interested in the visual arts

Application Process: Application

Application Deadline: June 3

Average Number of Applicants: 65

Average Number of Participants: 60

Academic Credit: High school credit available

Contact:
State University of New York—Purchase
Youth Programs
735 Anderson Hill Road
Purchase, NY 10577
Phone: (914) 251-6508
Fax: (914) 251-6515
conted@purchase.edu
www.purchase.edu

STUDENT CONSERVATION ASSOCIATION

High School Conservation Work Crew (CWC) Program

Program Location: 70 crews stationed in public lands across the U.S. including Alaska and Hawaii

Subject Areas: Volunteer work, wildlife/environmental conservation

Program Description: Students work outdoors each day on a conservation improvement project, often in remote backcountry settings. Diverse projects may include the following: revegetation, trail construction and maintenance, wildlife habitat improvement, fisheries enhancement, bridge construction, and more. Participants live in tents near the worksite and share all camp duties with other crew members. Week-long hike or canoe trip at the end of each program. A complete listing of available positions is posted online each December/January on www.jobnet.com.

Program Dates: Throughout the summer

Duration of Program: 4–5 weeks

Cost: No tuition; food, shelter, and equipment are also provided

Eligibility: High school students (including graduating seniors) who will be at least 16 years old by the end of the program. No experience necessary; enthusiasm and physical fitness are required.

Application Process: Original application plus two photocopies, two reference forms, application fee of $10–$55 (depending upon date postmarked). SCA will send confirmation packet upon receipt of above materials. Confirmation packet materials must be completed and returned to SCA within three weeks. If applicant is approved, program placement will be determined based upon the following (in order of importance): availability dates, preferred regions, program sites of interest.

Application Deadline: March 31

Average Number of Participants: 500 students per year, 6–10 students per group (equal number of men and women)

Contact:
Student Conservation Association
High School CWC Program
P.O. Box 550
Charlestown, NH 03603
Phone: (603) 543-1700
Fax: (603) 543-1828
cwcmail@sca-inc.org
www.sca-inc.org/vol/cwc/cwc.htm

STUDENT HOSTELING PROGRAM

Summer Biking Programs

Program Location: U.S., Holland, France, England, Italy, Spain, Canada, Ireland, Belgium

Subject Areas: Travel abroad, outdoor adventure travel, athletics

Program Description: Bicycling trips for teenagers through the countrysides and cultural centers of the world. Small coed groups of 8–12 students. Easy, moderate, and challenging trips. Trips are organized according to age/grade. Groups live simply, using campsites, hostels, and other modest facilities. In the countryside, groups buy food at local markets and cook their own meals. In cities, groups frequently eat at restaurants. Trips are somewhat heavier on touring and sightseeing than on bicycling.

Program Dates: Late June through August

Duration of Program: 2–8 weeks

Cost: from $1,450–$5,700

Eligibility: Students in grades 6–12

Application Process: $50 nonrefundable fee

Application Deadline: Rolling admissions

Average Number of Participants: 8–12 per group

Contact:
Student Hosteling Program
1356 Ashfield Road, P.O. Box 419
Conway, MA 01341
Phone: (800) 343-6132; (413) 369-4275
Fax: (413) 369-4257
SHPBike@aol.com
www.biketrips.com or www.bicycletrips.com

STUDENT SAFARIS INTERNATIONAL

Zanzibar to the Serengeti;

Queensland Explorer

Program Location: Tanzania; Australia

Subject Areas: International travel, community service, outdoor adventure

Program Description: Student Safaris tries to broaden the world view of young people through both community service and adventure travel. When participants first arrive in their host country, they get to know local peoples and cultures by participating in a volunteer project. They then embark on an adventure safari through the breathtaking natural scenery. In Tanzania, students might see rhinos, elephants, lions, and other exotic wildlife, while travelers in Australia will explore the Outback and the Great Barrier Reef.

Program Dates: July–August

Duration of Program: 4 weeks

Cost: $5,800–$6,600

Financial Aid Deadline: March 1

Student Safaris International

Eligibility: Ages 14–18. No foreign language required.

Application Process: Written application, short essay, 2 recommendations

Application Deadline: Rolling

Average Number of Applicants: 50

Average Number of Participants: 32

Academic Credit: None available

Contact:
Student Safaris International
attn: Peter Stanley
P.O. Box 3149
Ashland, OR 97520
Phone: (888) 477-7620
Fax: (541) 488-6402
info@studentsafaris.com
www.studentsafaris.com

SUMMER INSTITUTE FOR THE GIFTED

College Gifted Program

Program Location: Amherst College, Bryn Mawr College, Denison University, Drew University, Vassar College

Subject Areas: Liberal arts, physical sciences, languages, robotics, engineering, social sciences, mathematics, computers, SAT preparation, more

Program Description: Residential summer camps for academically gifted students in grades 4–11 on college campuses, blending recreation with high school and college-level study. Extracurricular activities include arts programs, music, photography, Saturday off-campus trips, Sunday creativity programs.

Program Dates: 7 sessions throughout the summer. June 23–July 13 (Sessions I and II at Denison and Vassar); June 30–July 20 (Session III at Drew); July 21–August 10 (Sesson IV and V at Amherst and Vassar); July 28–August 17 (Session VI at Bryn Mawr)

Duration of Program: 3-week sessions

Cost: $2,975

Financial Aid: Available

Eligibility: Students who have been participants in talent searches, students in the 95th percentile in standardized tests or scoring in the gifted range of the ACT, PSAT, or SAT may apply. Students may submit other proofs of giftedness.

Application Process: Application packet, standardized tests

Application Deadline: May 15

Average Number of Applicants: 400 per session

Average Number of Participants: 275 per session

Academic Credit: High school and college credit available

Contact:
Summer Institute for the Gifted
120 Littleton Road, Suite #201
Parsippany, NJ 07054-1803
Phone: (973) 334-6991
Fax: (973) 334-9756
info@cgp-sig.com
www.cgp-sig.com

SUMMER SONATINA INTERNATIONAL PIANO CAMP

Program Location: Bennington, Vermont

Subject Areas: Piano

Program Description: A 2- to 6-week program offering intensive piano instruction.

Program Dates: Sessions in June, July, and August

Duration of Program: 2–6 weeks

Cost: $750 per week

Eligibility: Students 7–17 years old

Application Process: Completed application

Application Deadline: Rolling admissions

Average Number of Applicants: 150 per season

Average Number of Participants: 38 per week

Contact:
Summer Sonatina International Piano Camp
5 Catamount Lane
Old Bennington, VT 05201
Phone: (802) 442-9197
Fax: (802) 447-3175
piano@sonatina.com
www.sonatina.com

SUMMER STUDY PROGRAMS

Summer Enrichment and Summer Study at Penn State

Program Location: Penn State University in State College, Pennsylvania

Summer Study at Penn State

Subject Areas: American literature, ESL, English, French, German, Russian, Spanish, SAT/ACT prep, anthropology, architecture, art, astronomy, biology, business, chemistry, communications, computers, ecology, creative writing, economics, engineering, geology/earth science, government and politics, health sciences, history, math, music, philosophy, photography, physics, psychology, religion, theater, and more

Program Description: Summer Enrichment: Students choose from noncredit enrichment classes and make weekend visits to other college campuses to aid in college selection. Summer Study: Students choose take classes for college credit. All students have full use of all Penn State athletic and recreational facilities (including Penn's 48 tennis courts, 2 golf courses, and a 72-acre lake) and attend scheduled day and night activities.

Program Dates: Summer Enrichment: July 1–July 25. Summer Study: late June–early August.

Duration of Program: 3½ weeks (Summer Enrichment); 6 weeks (Summer Study)

Summer Study in Paris

Cost: Summer Enrichment: $3,195; Summer Study: $5,295. Includes room and board, all expenses on the weekend college visitation trips, all recreational activities, and group photo.

Eligibility: Students completing grades 9–11 (Summer Enrichment). Students completing grades 10–12 (Summer Studies).

Application Process: All applicants are required to submit a current academic transcript with past grades and PSAT/SAT scores. Other diagnostic tests may be requested for applicants who have not taken their PSAT/SAT exams. Foreign students may submit TOEFL scores.

Application Deadline: Rolling admissions (limited enrollment)

Average Number of Participants: 1,000 total (500 per program)

Academic Credit: College credit available for 6-week program

Summer Study in Paris at The American University of Paris

Program Location: The American University of Paris in Paris, France

Subject Areas: Study abroad, American literature, ESL, English, French, SAT/ACT preparation, architecture, art, business, communications, creative writing, economics, film studies, government and politics, history, international law, journalism, math, photography, physics, psychology, speed reading, theater

Program Description: Summer Study: All students choose one college-credit course and one enrichment course. Optional weekend trip to London available. Summer Enrichment: Students choose two non-credit enrichment courses. An in-depth exploration of Paris, athletic and recreational activities, and weekend excursions throughout France included in both programs. Optional French Immersion ("speak only French") experience includes participation in day and night excursions, French classes, dining, roommates, etc.

Program Dates: Early July–mid-August (Summer Study); July (Summer Enrichment)

Duration of Program: 5 weeks (Summer Study); 3 weeks (Summer Enrichment)

Cost: $5,495 (Summer Study); $3,795 (Summer Enrichment); both include tuition, lodging, two meals per day, all expenses on three weekend excursions, unlimited-use Metro Pass, AUP student ID card, group recreational activities, group photo

Eligibility: Students completing grades 10–12 (Summer Study); students completing grades 9–11 (Summer Enrichment)

Application Process: All applicants are required to submit a current academic transcript with past grades and PSAT/SAT scores. Other diagnostic tests may be requested for applicants who have not taken their PSAT/SAT exams. Foreign students may submit TOEFL scores.

Application Deadline: Rolling admissions (limited enrollment)

Average Number of Participants: 300 (Summer Study); 150 (Summer Enrichment)

Academic Credit: College credit available (Summer Study only)

Summer Study at the University of Colorado at Boulder

Program Location: The University of Colorado in Boulder, Colorado

Subject Areas: Anthropology, applied math, biology, chemistry, communication, economics, American Literature, Ethnic studies, fine arts, French, German, Chinese, Japanese, Spanish, Russian, Italian, geography, history, humanities, mathematics, philosophy, physics, political science, psychology, religious studies, sociology, theater

Program Description: A multifaceted program that includes college-credit and enrichment courses, an in-depth exploration of the great outdoors, athletic and recreational activities, weekend excursions. All students experience a taste of college life, along with utilizing the number one sports town in America that offers 200 miles of public hiking and biking trails and approximately 30,000 acres of open space.

Program Dates: Early July–mid-August

Duration of Program: 5 weeks

Cost: $4,995 (Includes room and board, all expenses on outdoor weekend excursions, all recreational activities, group photo)

Eligibility: Students completing grades 10–12

Application Process: All applicants are required to submit a current academic transcript with past grades and PSAT/SAT scores. Other diagnostic tests may be requested for applicants who have not taken their PSAT/SAT exams. Foreign students may submit TOEFL scores.

Application Deadline: Rolling (limited enrollment)

Average Number of Participants: 200

Academic Credit: College credit available

Contact:
Summer Study Programs
900 Walt Whitman Road
Melville, NY 11747
Phone: (800) 666-2556; (631) 424-1000
Fax: (631) 424-0567
precollegeprograms@summerstudy.com
www.summerstudy.com

SYRACUSE UNIVERSITY

Syracuse University Summer College for High School Students

Program Location: Syracuse University in Syracuse, New York

Subject Areas: Liberal arts and sciences, preprofessional studies

Program Description: College-level study and career exploration with seminars and field trips. Summer college programs include courses in: acting/musical theater, architecture, art and

*Syracuse University Summer College for
High School Students*

design, fashion and textile design, engineering, information management and technology, law, liberal arts, management, public communications, social work.

Program Dates: July 1–August 10

Duration of Program: 6 weeks

Cost: $4,400; additional studio fees for arts courses

Financial Aid: Scholarships available

Eligibility: Students who have completed at least their sophomore year of high school

Application Process: Application packet, standardized test scores suggested

Application Deadline: May 1

Average Number of Applicants: 300

Average Number of Participants: 200

Academic Credit: College credit available

Contact:
Syracuse University
111 Waverly Avenue, Suite 240
Syracuse, NY 13244
Phone: (315) 443-5297
Fax: (315) 443-3976
sumcoll@syr.edu
www.syr.edu/summer

TAB RAMOS SOCCER ACADEMY

Program Location: Fairleigh Dickinson University in Madison, New Jersey; Holmdel High School in Holmdel, New Jersey

Subject Areas: Soccer

Program Description: Residential and day camps with a player/staff ratio of 10:1. Players work on dribbling, passing and receiving, defense, and attacking skills, culminating in "Game Day" at the end of the week. Goalkeepers will receive specialized keeper training and then have the opportunity to further develop these skills and tactics in game situations. Also included are activities such as swimming, circuit training, and a college guidance seminar. Students in the Fairleigh Dickinson residential camp live with an age-appropriate roommate in an on-campus dormitory.

Program Dates: July–August

Duration of Program: 5 days

Cost: $495 (Fairleigh Dickinson residential camp); $225–$295 (Fairleigh Dickinson and Homdel day camps). Special group rates are available for 11 or more when registered and mailed together; call for details.

Eligibility: Coed, ages 9–18

Application Process: Online registration available on website

Average Number of Participants: Limit of 120 overnight campers

Contact:
Tab Ramos Soccer Academy
15 Regal Drive
Colonia, NJ 07067
Phone: (732) 382-3895
www.tabramos.com

TAMARACK CAMPS

Program Location: Camp Kennedy in the Upper Peninsula of Michigan; Agree Outpost Camp in Northern Ontario, Canada; Teen Travel Trips in Western U.S. and Alaska

Subject Areas: Outdoor adventure; Judaism

Program Description: Tamarack has been a leader in Jewish camping for over 99 years. Programming encompasses Jewish philosophy and traditions; campers observe dietary laws and Shabbat. Camp Kennedy: Campers live in a hunting lodge on the shores of Nevins Lake, with opportunities to swim, waterski, and learn how to expertly canoe and camp out. The highlight of the program is a thrilling canoe camping trip in the Boundary Waters of Minnesota. Agree Outpost Camp: Opportunities for rock climbing, rappelling, swimming, and sightseeing in Canadian north woods. Teen Travel Trips: Choice of Western trip (bus and camping trip that includes visiting Yellowstone National Park, Grand Tetons, Black Hills) or Alaskan trip (bus, ferry, and camping trip).

Program Dates: June–August

Duration of Program: 2–8 weeks

Cost: Available upon request

Application Deadline: Rolling admissions

Application Process: Application form, deposit of $250. Interview may be required.

Eligibility: Camp Kennedy: entering grades 10–11; Agree Outpost Camp: entering grades 9–11; Teen Travel Trips: entering grades 10–12

Contact:
Tamarack Camps
Fresh Air Society
Max M. Fisher Building
6737 Telegraph Road, #380
Bloomfield Hills, MI 48301 (winter address)
Phone: (248) 647-1100
Fax: (248) 647-1493
tamarack@tamarackcamps.com
http://tamarackcamps.com

TENNIS: EUROPE AND MORE

Program Location: 3–6 European countries (12 different itineraries in all)

Subject Areas: Tennis, cultural immersion

Program Description: Provides a unique opportunity for high school tennis players to compete in sanctioned tournaments and to use tennis to meet, socialize, and even live with European sports families. Players sightsee several afternoons every week.

Tennis: Europe and More

Program Dates: Late June–mid-August

Duration of Program: 16–34 days

Cost: $2,600–$7,000 (includes all expenses except lunches, pocket money, and airfare)

Financial Aid: 2 scholarships worth $2,000 each and 2 scholarships worth $500 each are offered, based on personal character and sportsmanship

Eligibility: Coed, high school varsity-ability and ranked players ages 14–18

Application Process: Three character references required from teachers or guidance counselors, and one playing reference required from a coach.

Application Deadline: June 1, but many teams fill up by early winter

Average Number of Participants: Approximately 160 for the entire summer, with 12 teams of 14 players each

Contact:
attn: Dr. Martin Vinokur
Tennis: Europe and More
73 Rockridge Lane
Stamford, CT 06903
Phone: (203) 322-9803
(800) 253-7486
tenniseuro@aol.com
www.tenniseurope.com

TRAILMARK OUTDOOR ADVENTURES

Program Location: New England, Pacific Northwest, Colorado, Pennsylvania, Northern Rockies

Subject Areas: Outdoor adventure

Program Description: Teen adventure, travel, and community building in New England, Pacific Northwest, Colorado, Pennsylvania, and Northern Rockies.

Program Dates: June 27–August 17

Duration of Program: 1–4 weeks

Cost: $695 and up

Eligibility: Ages 10–17, no experience required

Application Process: Application form, $750 deposit

Application Deadline: None available

Contact:
Trailmark Outdoor Adventures
16 Schuyler Road
Nyack, NY 10960
Phone: (800) 229-0262 or (845) 358-0262
Fax: (845) 348-0437
info@trailmark.com
www.trailmark.com

TRANSYLVANIA UNIVERSITY

Academic Camp with Computer Emphasis

Program Location: Transylvania University in Lexington, Kentucky

Subject Areas: Computers/technology, science, engineering, mathematics

Program Description: Students spend 4 hours each day learning about and programming computers. Two hours each day, students learn about an academic discipline other than computers.

Program Dates: June 9–July 14 (camp #1); June 16–June 21 (camp #2); June 24–June 29 (camp #3)

Duration of Program: 6 days–1 week

Cost: $300

Eligibility: Students in grades 8–10 (session #1), students in grades 10–12 (session #2)

Application Process: Recommendation from a teacher/counselor

Application Deadline: May 1

Average Number of Applicants: 60–70

Average Number of Participants: 50

Contact:
Transylvania University
300 North Broadway
Lexington, KY 40508
Phone: (606) 233-8155
Fax: (606) 233-8171
www.transy.edu

TRINITY UNIVERSITY

A Trinity Summer

Program Location: Trinity University in San Antonio, Texas

Subject Areas: College-level reading, writing, speaking

Program Description: Provides academically gifted students with a humanities-based curriculum. Various on- and off-campus activities, including sightseeing, athletics, and visits to amusement parks, museums, and plays, are offered in addition to classroom work.

Program Dates: June 23–July 12

Duration of Program: 3 weeks

Cost: $1,895

Financial Aid: None available

Eligibility: Rising high school seniors

Application Process: Registration form, transcripts, test scores, recommendations, $25 application fee

Application Deadline: April 15

Average Number of Applicants: 150

Average Number of Participants: 24–27

Academic Credit: None available

Contact:
attn: Dr. Moya Ann Ball
Trinity University
715 Stadium Drive
San Antonio, TX 78212-7200
Phone: (210) 999-8201
Fax: (210) 999-8234
ats@trinity.edu
www.trinity.edu

Trinity University

TUFTS UNIVERSITY EUROPEAN CENTER

Tufts Summit

Program Location: The small village of Talloires, France, in the French Alps

Subject Areas: International relations, French language and culture, leadership training, travel abroad

Program Description: While improving their French language skills, students are introduced to the complex world of international politics and diplomacy through classroom instruction, exploration of French culture, and field trips to local sites of historic importance and natural beauty. Students enroll in two classes: The course in international relations takes students on a journey through international conflicts and resolutions; the daily French classes help students to develop facility with the language through class exercises and exposure to French theater, art, and song. All students live with a French host family. Travel and outdoor activities round out the students' Alpine experience.

Program Dates: July 3–30 (2001 dates)

Duration of Program: 4 weeks

Cost: $4,375 (includes room and board with a carefully selected French family)

Financial Aid: Scholarships available; scholarship application available on website

Eligibility: Students in grades 11–12 with at least 2 years of French instruction

Application Process: Registration form (downloadable form available on website), 2 letters of recommendation, transcript, essay, $40 fee required; also send 4 passport photos for family placement purposes.

Application Deadline: April 10 (2001 date)

Contact:
Tufts University European Center
Tufts Summit for High School Students
108 Packard Avenue
Medford, MA 02155
Phone: (617) 627-3290
Fax: (617) 627-3457
France@tufts.edu
ase.tufts.edu/FrenchAlps/hs.htm

TUFTS UNIVERSITY SCHOOL OF VETERINARY MEDICINE

Adventures in Veterinary Medicine

Program Location: Tufts University School of Veterinary Medicine in North Grafton, Massachusetts

Subject Areas: Veterinary medicine, career preparation

Program Description: Tufts offers separate sessions for middle school and high school students who want to investigate the field of veterinary medicine. The program also accommodates adults interested in changing careers.

Program Dates: April, June–August

Duration of Program: 1–2 weeks

Cost: $500–$2,000

Financial Aid: Available

Eligibility: Grade 7–adult

Application Process: Written application, high school or college transcripts, letters of recommendation, essay. Middle school program requires registration forms only.

Application Deadline: Rolling

Average Number of Applicants: 300

Average Number of Participants: 200

Academic Credit: None available

Contact:
Tufts University School of Veterinary Medicine
200 Westboro Road
North Grafton, MA 01536
Phone: (508) 839-7962
Fax: (508) 839-7953
aum@tufts.edu
www.tufts.edu/vet/avm/index.html

UNITED STATES COAST GUARD ACADEMY

Academy Introduction Mission (AIM)

Program Location: United States Coast Guard Academy in New London, Connecticut

Subject Areas: Military introduction, academics

Program Description: Students live the life of a Coast Guard Academy (CGA) cadet, experiencing the challenges and rewards of the Academy's mix of academics, military, and physical training. Objectives focus on giving participants firsthand knowledge of CGA, empowering them to make informed decisions about applying to and attending CGA. Includes morning calisthenics, sailing, touring a Coast Guard cutter and aircraft, competing in athletics, and working out in the CGA's recreational facilities.

Program Dates: July 20–26 (last full week of July)

Duration of Program: 1 week

Cost: $150

Application Deadline: March 31

Average Number of Applicants: 1,000

Average Number of Participants: 200

Minority Introduction to Engineering (MITE)

Program Location: United States Coast Guard Academy in New London, Connecticut

Subject Areas: Engineering, military introduction

Program Description: All expenses paid trip to the United States Coast Guard Academy to explore the engineering field and its career possibilities. When not in the classroom, students will live the life of a CGA cadet.

Program Dates: June 23–29 (last full week of June); June 30–July 6 (first week of July)

Duration of Program: 1 week

Cost: Free

Application Deadline: April 15

Average Number of Applicants: 500

Average Number of Participants: 180

Contact:
United States Coast Guard Academy
Director of Admissions
31 Mohegan Avenue
New London, CT 06320
Phone: (800) 883-8724; (860) 444-850
Fax: (860) 701-6700

UNITED STATES NAVAL ACADEMY

Navy Crew Camp for Boys

Program Location: United States Naval Academy in Annapolis, Maryland

Subject Areas: Men's crew

Program Description: Individual coaching tailored to each rower's/coxswain's experience level, from complete novice to experienced racer. Access to state-of-the-art training and rowing equipment, including intensive technical ergometer coaching, strength and cardiovascular training, performance enhancement and mental preparation training, and nutrition education.

Program Dates: 3 sessions in June

Duration of Program: 5 days

Cost: $475 (residential camp); $360 (day camp)

Financial Aid: None available

Eligibility: Boys, ages 13–18, all levels of experience

Application Process: Online and downloadable application forms available on website. Medical waiver form must be signed by a parent or guardian.

Application Deadline: Rolling

Contact:
United States Naval Academy
Navy Crew Camp for Boys
566 Brownson Road
Annapolis, MD 21402
Phone: (410) 293-3636
www.navycrewcamp.com

Navy Rowing Camp for Girls

Program Location: United States Naval Academy in Annapolis, Maryland

Subject Areas: Women's crew

Program Description: Rowers are divided into groups according to ability, from complete novices to experienced racers. The 1:10 coach/athlete ratio maximizes individual attention and coaching. Access to state-of-the-art training and rowing equipment, including intensive technical ergometer coaching, strength and cardiovascular training, performance enhancement and mental preparation training, and nutrition education.

Program Dates: 4 sessions in June

Duration of Program: 4 days

Cost: $450 (residential camp); $400 (day camp)

Financial Aid: None available

Eligibility: Girls, ages 12–18, all levels of experience

Application Process: Online and downloadable application forms available on website. A wait list is also available for camps that have already been filled. Medical waiver form must be signed by a parent or guardian.

Application Deadline: Rolling

Contact:
United States Naval Academy
Navy Rowing Camp for Girls
566 Brownson Road
Annapolis, MD 21402
Phone: (410) 293-2419
Fax: (202) 459-2159
www.navyrowingcamp.com

United States Naval Academy—Navy Rowing Camp for Girls

UNIVERSITY OF ARIZONA

Summer Institute for Writing

Program Location: University of Arizona in Tucson, Arizona

Subject Areas: Writing

Program Description: Students, teachers, and staff work as a community, exploring writing as a tool of expression.

Program Dates: Mid- to late July

Duration of Program: 3 weeks

Cost: TBA

Financial Aid: Available for minority students

Eligibility: Open to all high school students

Application Process: Required essay

Application Deadline: May 15

Average Number of Applicants: 100

Average Number of Participants: 45

Contact:
University of Arizona
1201 East Helen Street
Tucson, AZ 85719
Phone: (520) 621-5849
Fax: (520) 621-2222
www.w3.arizona.edu/~wsip

UNIVERSITY OF THE ARTS

Drama and Musical Theater

Program Location: University of the Arts in Philadelphia, Pennsylvania

Subject Areas: Drama program: acting, movement, stage combat. Musical Theater program: acting, dance, voice

Program Description: Drama: Exercises and scene work are used to increase physical and emotional stamina, and to develop a sense of teamwork, discipline, and self-confidence. End-of-course showcase.
Musical Theater: Acting class explores special challenges faced by singing actors. Dance includes ballet, jazz, character, and musical theater dance. Voice class stresses healthy voice projection. Students work on a variety of songs and prepare one song for a mock audition. End-of-course showcase.

Program Dates: July 9–August 3

Duration of Program: 4 weeks

Cost: $1,700 for tuition plus $700 for housing

Eligibility: High school juniors or seniors, ages 16–18

Application Process: Tuition deposit of $100, housing deposit of $100

Application Deadline: May 4

Average Number of Participants: Drama: 25–30; Musical Theater: 30–35

PREP, Art Smart, and Media and Communications Workshops

Program Location: University of the Arts in Philadelphia, Pennsylvania

Subject Areas: PREP: 2-D design, 3-D design, and drawing.
Art Smart: crafts (ceramics and jewelry/metals), design (graphic design and illustration), mixed media (painting and sculpture), figurative (painting and sculpture).
Media & Communications: animation, creative web design, photography, screen directing, video production.

Program Description: PREP: Rigorous 4-week program including drawing and 2- and 3-dimensional design.
Art Smart: Students explore talents and develop their portfolios. Choose one of 4 elective tracks, each of which includes 2 studios, a linked drawing course, and a seminar series.
Media & Communications: Students explore talents and develop portfolio-suitable work. Choose 1 of 5 workshops, some of which include a linked drawing course.

Program Dates: July 10–August 4

University of the Arts

Duration of Program: 4 weeks

Cost: $1,700 for tuition plus $700 for housing

Eligibility: PREP: recent high school graduates; Art Smart and Media & Communications: high school juniors or seniors, ages 16–18

Application Process: Tuition deposit of $100, housing deposit of $100

Application Deadline: May 5

Average Number of Participants: PREP: 20–30; Art Smart: 40–45; Media & Communications: 50–60

Summer Institute of Jazz

Program Location: University of the Arts in Philadelphia, Pennsylvania

Subject Areas: Technique, musical skills, improvisation, reading, performance

Program Description: Coursework includes: private lessons, instrumental workshops, improvisation, jazz skills, and clinics. The second week includes a public concert.

Program Dates: July 9–July 20

Duration of Program: 2 weeks

Cost: $1,050 for tuition plus $400 for housing

Eligibility: High school juniors or seniors, ages 16–18

Application Process: Tuition deposit of $100, housing deposit of $100

Application Deadline: May 5

Average Number of Participants: 50–70

Contact:
University of the Arts
Pre-College Summer Institute Arts Program
320 South Broad Street
Philadelphia, PA 19102
Phone: (215) 717-6430 or (800) 616-ARTS
Fax: (215) 717-6433
precollege@uarts.edu
www.uarts.edu

UNIVERSITY OF CALIFORNIA—BERKELEY

See Academic Study Associates; Education Unlimited

UNIVERSITY OF CALIFORNIA—DAVIS

See Education Unlimited

UNIVERSITY OF CALIFORNIA—LOS ANGELES

College Level Summer Program

Program Location: UCLA in Los Angeles, California

Subject Areas: College curriculum

Program Description: Students enroll in the regular UCLA Summer Sessions and, as a result, can earn credit toward a college degree. Wide range of college level courses taught by regular UCLA faculty and distinguished visiting faculty who bring special expertise and different academic perspectives to the campus.

Program Dates: June–August

Duration of Program: 6–10 weeks

Cost: The tuition fee for most courses is $100 per unit ($400/course). Both on- and off-campus housing are available to all Summer Sessions students at an additional cost; contact the Housing Office at (310) 825-4271 for more info.

Financial Aid: None available

Eligibility: Gifted and high-achieving students entering grades 10–12 who have demonstrated the ability to do college-level work

Application Process: Application form (online application available on website), transcript, PSAT/SAT scores, guidance counselor recommendation, $300 processing/registration fee

Application Deadline: Rolling admissions, but enrollment is limited

Academic Credit: Letter grades and college credit awarded

Contact:
Summer Programs for High School Students
10995 Le Conte Avenue, Room 639
Los Angeles, CA 90024-2883
Phone: (310) 794-8333
Fax: (310) 206-5006
www.summer.ucla.edu/summersessions.html

High School Level Summer Program

Program Location: UCLA in Los Angeles, California

Subject Areas: High school curriculum

Program Description: Courses in math, computers, writing, social sciences, humanities, sciences, and academic skills are taught by middle and high school teachers and professionals from the local community. Some classes include field trips to various local sites, which is included in the tuition.

Program Dates: June–August

Duration of Program: 6 weeks, additional 3-week session may be offered in August

Cost: The tuition fee for most courses is $100 per unit ($400/course). Both on- and off-campus housing are available to all Summer Sessions students at an additional cost; contact the Housing Office at (310) 825-4271 for more info.

Financial Aid: None available

Eligibility: Students entering grades 9–12

Application Process: Application form, transcript, $300 processing/registration fee

Application Deadline: Rolling admissions, but enrollment is limited

Academic Credit: Individual schools determine whether to grant high school credits; the responsibility for obtaining credit rests with the student and must be arranged in advance with his high school counselor.

Contact:
UCLA Extension
P.O. Box 24901
Dept. K
Los Angeles, CA 90024-0901
Phone: (310) 206-7229
Fax: (310) 206-3223
highschool@uclaextension.org
www.uclaextension.org/highschool/
highschool_info.htm

UCLA High School Acting and Performance Institute

Program Location: UCLA in Los Angeles, California

Subject Areas: Acting

Program Description: An intensive program sponsored by the acclaimed UCLA School of Theater, Film and Television. Performance training classes Monday through Friday include: Tai Chi, Acting, Scene Study, Improvisation, and Working with Masks. Afternoon sessions are devoted to performance laboratory, in which a group of 15 students develops a theatrical piece from concept to performance under the supervision of a faculty director. Students also have an opportunity to participate in scheduled workshops and field trips that allow behind-the-scenes understanding of live theater and the Hollywood entertainment industry.

Program Dates: June–August

Duration of Program: 6 weeks

Cost: $1,800. Both on- and off-campus housing are available to all Summer Sessions students at an additional cost; contact the Housing Office at (310) 825-4271 for more info.

Eligibility: Serious theater students completing grades 9–12 who are considering pursuing a major in theater at the college level

Application Process: Online registration available on website. A recommendation must be submitted after the student registers. No audition required: Interviews held the first day of the workshop will determine skill level and placement in the performance classes and laboratories.

Application Deadline: Rolling admissions, but enrollment is limited

Average Number of Participants: 60

Contact:
UCLA High School Acting and Performance Institute
UCLA Summer Sessions
Box 951418
Los Angeles, CA 90095-1418
Phone: (310) 206-7217
Fax: (310) 794-6137
www.summer.ucla.edu/
frame_specialprograms.html

See also Musiker Discovery Programs

UNIVERSITY OF CALIFORNIA—SAN DIEGO

UCSD Academic Connections & Summer Session

Program Location: University of California—San Diego in La Jolla, California

Subject Areas: Sample of subjects: biomedical sciences, cell biology, computer science, cognitive science, engineering, environment, marine biology, media communications, writers' workshop

Program Description: Students have access to university resources and work directly with dedicated instructors who are experts in their respective fields. Courses are designed to be challenging and to emphasize putting knowledge to use in independent and creative ways. A wonderful opportunity for students to explore the best that UCSD has to offer and to be exposed to some of the most exciting fields of research.

Program Dates: Late June to August

Duration of Program: 1–6 weeks

Cost: Varies by course

Eligibility: Grades 9–12, minimum GPA of 3.3

Application Deadline: Rolling admissions

Average Number of Applicants: 400

Average Number of Participants: 300

Academic Credit: High school and college credit available

Contact:
UCSD Academic Connections/Summer Session
9500 Gilman Drive, MC 0176-S
La Jolla, CA 92093-0176
Phone: (858) 534-0804
Fax: (858) 534-8271
barce@ucsd.edu
www.academicconnections.ucsd.edu;
www.ucsd.edu/summer

See also Musiker Discovery Programs

University of California—San Diego

UNIVERSITY OF CALIFORNIA—SANTA BARBARA

Early Start Program

Program Location: University of California—Santa Barbara in Santa Barbara, California

Subject Areas: A full spectrum of all departments and colleges of UCSB

Program Description: Offers highly motivated students the chance to make an early start on a college career and earn college level credit at one of the nation's most distinguished universities.

Program Dates: June 23–August 2

Duration of Program: 6 weeks

Cost: $5,099

Eligibility: Students in grades 10–12 with 3.3 GPA or better

Application Process: Application (available on website), official transcript, two recommendations, personal essay.

Application Deadline: May 1

Average Number of Applicants: 600–700

Average Number of Participants: 250

Academic Credit: Full college credit

UCSB Summer
Research Mentorship Program

Program Location: University of California—Santa Barbara in Santa Barbara, California

Subject Areas: Science

Program Description: Hands-on program for highly motivated students in grades 10–12, who partner with research scientists in the social, life, and physical sciences.

Program Dates: June 24 to August 3, 2001

Duration of Program: 6 weeks

Cost: $5,300 (includes room and board)

Eligibility: High school students in grades 10–12

Application Process: Transcript, recommendation from a teacher and counselor or principal, personal essay, and $35 application fee required.

Application Deadline: May 1

Academic Credit: College credit available

Contact:
Tippi Lawrence
UCSB Summer Sessions
Pre-College Programs
Santa Barbara, CA 93106-2010
Phone: (805) 893-2069
Fax: (805) 893-7306
t.lawrence@summersessions.ucsb.edu
www.summer.ucsb.edu

See also Chris Waller's Summer Gymnastics Jam; Musiker Discovery Programs

UNIVERSITY OF CINCINNATI, COLLEGE OF ENGINEERING

Inquisitive Women Summer Day Camp

Program Location: University of Cincinnati in Cincinnati, Ohio

Subject Areas: Engineering

Program Description: A hands-on engineering program working with departmental projects in the mornings and featuring field trips to major engineering corporations and companies in the afternoons.

Program Dates: June 24–28 and July 8–12

Duration of Program: 5 days

Cost: $125

Eligibility: Females only, grades 9–10

Application Deadline: May 15

Contact:
University of Cincinnati
P.O. Box 210018
Pre-Admission Office
Baldwin Hall
Cincinnati, OH 45221-0018
Phone: (513) 556-0025
Fax: (513) 556-5007
diane.buhr@uc.edu
www.eng.uc.edu/buhr/inquisitivewomen/index.html

UNIVERSITY OF COLORADO—BOULDER

See Summer Study Programs

UNIVERSITY OF COLORADO CANCER CENTER

Summer Cancer Research Fellowship

Program Location: University of Colorado Cancer Center in Denver, Colorado

Subject Areas: Cancer research

Program Description: Students assist doctors and scientists in cancer research in the laboratories and clinics of the University of Colorado Health Sciences Center and other Denver institutions.

Duration of Program: 8–10 weeks

Cost: None

Financial Aid: Students are all paid a small stipend

Eligibility: High school juniors and seniors, college undergraduates, medical students. Minorities are encouraged to apply.

Application Process: Two-page essay, transcripts, letters of recommendation from a teacher and the dean or principal

Application Deadline: Mid-February

Average Number of Applicants: 200

Average Number of Participants: 65

Academic Credit: None

Contact:
University of Colorado Cancer Center
4200 East 9th Avenue
Campus Box B187
Denver, CO 80262
Phone: (303) 315-3000
Fax: (303) 315-5275
Richard.Bakemeier@UCHSC.edu
www.UCHSC.edu/cancer/students

UNIVERSITY OF CONNECTICUT

Mentor Connection

Program Location: University of Connecticut in Storrs, Connecticut

Subject Areas: Science, math, English, social studies, arts, education, psychology, writing, computer science

Program Description: Program for academically talented students. Participants work with a university mentor in an area of mutual interest.

Students choose from over 30 different mentorship sites.

Program Dates: July 8–26

Duration of Program: 3 weeks

Cost: $2,500 (includes room and board)

Financial Aid: Available, May 15 deadline

Eligibility: Academically talented rising high school juniors and seniors

Application Process: Transcript, 2 essays, 2 letters of recommendation

Application Deadline: May 15

Average Number of Applicants: 120

Average Number of Participants: 90

Academic Credit: College credit available (3 credits)

Contact:
University of Connecticut
Mentor Connection
2131 Hillside Road, Unit 3007
Storrs, CT 06269-3007
Phone: (860) 486-0283
Fax: (860) 486-2900
heather.spottiswoode@uconn.edu
www.gifted.uconn.edu

UNIVERSITY OF DALLAS STUDY ABROAD

Shakespeare in Italy;

Latin in Rome;

Thomas More in England;

Winston Churchill in England

Program Location: Italy; England

Subject Areas: Literature, history, philosophy, leadership, political philosophy

Program Description: Dallas' programs strive to avoid "thoughtless tourism"—their goal is to make study and travel mutually enhancing and to awaken a genuine interest in history, politics,

literature, and art. The Shakespeare program focuses on two of the many plays that Shakespeare set in Italy, while the Latin program exposes students to the writings of Livy, Virgil, and Cicero, all in the original Latin. The Shakespeare group travels throughout Rome, Florence, and Assisi, while the Latin group explores Rome and Naples.

Dallas terms both of its England programs "case studies in leadership." Both courses emphasize the importance of historical mindedness and intellectual culture in the shaping of a leader. Academic study is complemented by travel throughout London, Oxford, Cambridge, Bath, and Canterbury.

Program Dates: Shakespeare in Italy and both England programs: July. Latin in Rome: late June–July

Duration of Program: 3 weeks

Cost: $3,900 (includes airfare, room and board, and travel expenses)

Eligibility: Rising high school juniors and seniors. Three years of high school Latin required for Latin program.

Application Process: Registration forms, recommendations (including one from a Latin teacher for latter program), transcripts, test scores

Application Deadline: December 1 (early), January 15 (regular), rolling admission after

Financial Aid Deadline: January 15

Average Number of Applicants: 50–55 for Shakespeare; 65 for Latin; 45–50 for Thomas More; 30–35 for Churchill

Average Number of Participants: 30 for Shakespeare; 35 for Latin; 30 for Thomas More; 20 for Churchill

Academic Credit: 3 transferable college credits

Contact:
Rome and Summer Programs Office
University of Dallas
1845 E. Northgate Drive
Irving, TX 75067

Phone: (972) 721-5206
Fax: (972) 721-5283
udsummer@acad.udallas.edu
www.udallas.edu/udtravel

UNIVERSITY OF DAYTON

Women in Engineering Summer Camp

Program Location: University of Dayton in Dayton, Ohio

Subject Areas: Engineering, career investigation

Program Description: Participants get an insider's look at the field of engineering through classroom activities, participatory experiments, visits to industries, and contact with professional female engineers.

Program Dates: June 16–21

Duration of Program: 1 week

Cost: $325

Financial Aid Deadline: May 31

Eligibility: Females only, grades 10–12

Application Process: Teacher or counselor recommendation

Application Deadline: May 31

Average Number of Applicants: 60–70

Average Number of Participants: 65

Academic Credit: None available

Contact:
University of Dayton
300 College Park
Dayton, OH 45469-0228
Phone: (937) 229-3296
Fax: (937) 229-2756
karen.updyke@notes.udayton.edu
www.engr.udayton.edu/wie

University of Delaware—Upward Bound

UNIVERSITY OF DELAWARE

Summer College for High School Juniors

Program Location: University of Delaware in Newark, Delaware

Subject areas: Liberal arts and sciences, college preparation

Program Description: Students live on campus, take two credit-bearing college-level courses, participate in social, educational, and cultural activities, and generally get a taste of college a year in advance. The 10 available courses, which are limited in size and to Summer College students only in order to encourage discussion and individual attention, are taught by UD faculty members. Each class meets daily for 90 minutes.

Program Dates: Late June–late July

Duration of Program: 5 weeks

Cost: $1,410 (Delaware residents); $3,095 (out-of-state). Includes room and board.

Financial Aid: Available, April 17 deadline (2001 date). Students demonstrating both outstanding academic ability and financial need are given first priority.

Eligibility: Students completing their junior year of high school who have demonstrated strong academic ability, interest, and initiative

Application Process: Application (online application available on website), 2 teacher recommendations, transcript, standardized test scores, $25 application fee, $100 deposit

Application Deadline: May 1 (2001 date). However, by mid-March several classes are nearly closed, and by April waiting lists are common.

Average Number of Participants: 120

Academic Credit: Letter grades and a maximum of 7 college credits awarded upon completion of program

Contact:
University of Delaware Summer College
University Honors Program
186 S. College Avenue
Phone: (302) 831-6560
Fax: (302) 831-4194
summercollege@udel.edu
www.udel.edu/summercollege

Upward Bound Math and Science Center

Program Location: University of Delaware in Newark, Delaware

Subject Areas: Science, math

Program Description: Residential program for qualified high school students interested in science and math.

Program Dates: June–August

Duration of Program: 6 weeks

Cost: Free

Eligibility: High school students (low income and/or first-generation college) in grades 9–11. Must be a resident of Delaware or certain parts of Maryland or Pennsylvania.

Application Process: Essay, transcript, letter of recommendation, family income statement required

Application Deadline: April 15

Average Number of Applicants: 100

Average Number of Participants: 40

Contact:
University of Delaware
Academic Services Center
University of Delaware
5 West Main Street
Newark, DE 19716
Phone: (302) 831-6373
Fax: (302) 831-4128
ud-ubms@udel.edu
www.udel.edu/ASC/

UNIVERSITY OF DENVER

Making of an Engineer

Program Location: University of Denver in Denver, Colorado

Subject Areas: Engineering, career preparation

Program Description: College credit course especially designed for high school students interested in engineering. Includes use of tools, lab equipment, Boolean algebra, logic gates, mechanical dissection, instrumentation, and digital systems to practice engineering design. Numerous lab sessions ensure lots of hands-on experience. Small interactive groups meet with professors and practicing engineers to work on projects (robotics, circuit analysis, electronics, mechanics characterization, history of space, optoelectronics, scanning electron microscopes, etc.) and to discuss engineering ethics and career choices. Field trips and planned social activities are also included.

Program Dates: Mid-June–early July

Duration of Program: 3 weeks

Cost: Tuition: $100 (includes a $2,400 tuition scholarship for all students). Commuter fee: $250. Room and board: $950.

Financial Aid: All accepted students receive a $2,400 tuition scholarship. Room and board and air travel scholarships are also available, based on need. Financial aid deadline: April 19, 2002; after on space and funds available.

Eligibility: Students entering grades 10–12; minimum GPA of 3.0 with strong grades in algebra and geometry

Application Process: Application, transcript, standardized test scores (PLAN, ACT, PSAT, or SAT), letter of recommendation, essay

Application Deadline: April 19, 2002; after on space available

Academic Credit: 4 quarter hours university credit available from the University of Denver. High school credit may be decided by individual high schools.

Average Number of Participants: 65

Contact:
attn: Pam Campbell
Making of an Engineer
University of Denver
1981 S. University Boulevard, Rm #5
Denver, CO 80208
Phone: (303) 871-2663
Fax: (303) 871-2566
www.du.edu/education/ces/moe.html
or www.du.edu/engineering

University of Evansville—Options

UNIVERSITY OF EVANSVILLE

Options

Program Location: University of Evansville in Evansville, Indiana

Subject Areas: Engineering, computer science, career exploration

Program Description: The Options program is designed to get young women excited about careers in engineering and computer science and to encourage them to pursue a challenging math and science curriculum in high school. Students attend minicourses taught by professors and then design their own projects using software techniques taught in class. For at least half a day, they shadow a professional female engineer at her work site. Other activities include a session on financial aid and college selection, a tour of a plant, and a visit to a local water park.

Program Dates: June

Duration of Program: 1 week

Cost: $400

Financial Aid: Need-based aid is available upon request. In many years, outside sponsors donate enough money to reduce the program fee across the board. In 2001, all participants had to pay only $250.

Eligibility: Females only, grades 10–12. Plane geometry required.

Application Process: Application available by phone or e-mail (tn2@evansville.edu), $25 deposit, transcripts, personal essay

Application Deadline: Early-May

Average Number of Applicants: 17–25

Average Number of Participants: 15

Academic Credit: None available

Contact:
University of Evansville
1800 Lincoln Avenue
Evansville, IN 47722
Phone: (812) 479-2651
Fax: (812) 479-2780
pg3@evansville.edu or tn2@evansville.edu
http://csserver.evansville.edu/~options/ad.htm

See also Evansville Association for the Blind

UNIVERSITY OF FLORIDA

UF Student Science Training Program

Program Location: Gainesville, Florida

Subject Areas: Science

Program Description: Students work with faculty performing research in a variety of science fields. Students spend 25 hours each week assisting with research in assigned laboratories. Participants are assigned to small groups of 10–12 which meet three times each week with a facilitator to present and discuss their

research. Participants are matched with mentors according to interest, academic background, and the availability of lab space.

Program Dates: June 9–July 27, 2002

Duration of Program: 7 weeks

Cost: $2,450 (includes room, field trips, planned social activities)

Eligibility: Ages 16–18, current high school juniors or qualified sophomores may apply

Application Deadline: March 31

Average Number of Applicants: Approximately 140

Average Number of Participants: 85

Academic Credit: Available

Contact:
UF-334 Yon Hall
P.O. Box 112010
Gainesville, FL 32611-2010
Phone: (352) 392-2310
Fax: (352) 392-2344
sstp@cpet.ufl.edu
www.cpet.ufl.edu/sstp/sstp.htm

UNIVERSITY OF ILLINOIS—CHICAGO

Health Science Enrichment Program

Program Location: University of Illinois in Chicago, Illinois

Subject Areas: Biomedical research

Program Description: Students receive opportunity to perform biomedical research in a university setting.

Program Dates: June–July

Duration of Program: 6 weeks

Cost: Check with program for more information

Financial Aid: Available to qualified applicants

Eligibility: Students in grades 9–12

Application Process: Application

Application Deadline: Check with program for more information

Average Number of Applicants: 100

Average Number of Participants: 20

Contact:
University of Illinois at Chicago
Early Outreach Program
1101 West Taylor, 3rd floor
Mail Code 969
Chicago, Illinois 60607
Phone: (312) 996-2549
Fax: (312) 996-9446
www.uic.edu/educ/outreach/index.htm

UNIVERSITY OF ILLINOIS—URBANA-CHAMPAIGN

Fighting Illini Sports Camps

Program Location: University of Illinois at Urbana-Champaign

Subject Areas: Boys: baseball, basketball, football, gymnastics, wrestling. Girls: basketball, gymnastics, softball, volleyball. Coed: cheerleading, cross country, golf, soccer, swimming, tennis, track and field.

Program Description: Well-rounded residential and day summer camp programs for girls and boys. Each camp gives the young athlete an opportunity to improve his or her skills and, at the same time, have fun. Campers receive excellent coaching, experience campus life, and have the opportunity to meet athletes from a variety of backgrounds and philosophies.

Program Dates: June–August

Duration of Program: Varies by program

Cost: Varies by program

Eligibility: Age requirements vary by program

Application Process: Downloadable brochures containing application forms available on website.

Contact:
University of Illinois
Summer Camps
Bielfeldt Athletic Administration Building
1700 S. Fourth Street
Champaign, Illinois 61820
Phone: (217) 244-7278
fightingillini.fansonly.com/genrel/camps.html

UNIVERSITY OF IOWA

Iowa All-State Music Camp

Program Location: University of Iowa School of Music in Iowa City, Iowa

Subject Areas: Band, orchestra, chorus, jazz, percussion, organ

Program Description: In addition to ensemble participation and master classes, students have the opportunity to attend classes in music theory, music appreciation, conducting, improvisation, etc. Check website for complete information. Room and board available.

Program Dates: June 9 (start date)

Duration of Program: 1 week (3 programs)

Cost: TBA

Financial Aid: Available (May 3 deadline)

Eligibility: Students in grades 8–12

Application Process: Application (available on website or by request).

Application Deadline: May 3

Average Number of Applicants: 300

Average Number of Participants: 300

Academic Credit: None available

Contact:
The University of Iowa School of Music
Iowa All-State Music Camp
1064 Voxman Music Building
Iowa City, IA 52242
Phone: (319) 335-1635
Fax: (319) 353-2555
rita-schmidt@uiowa.edu
www.uiowa.edu/~bands/asmc/index.html

Iowa Young Writers' Studio

Program Location: University of Iowa, Iowa City

Subject Areas: Creative writing

Program Description: Geared toward students with a strong interest in creative writing, the Young Writers' studio offers small, in-depth classes in fiction, nonfiction, and poetry taught by professional writers and graduate students. On Saturdays and Sundays, students participate in "Dunk Tanks"—one-day, intensive introductions to new kinds of writing, such as screenwriting, playwriting, magazine writing, and journalism. Academic and college essay writing are not part of the curriculum.

Program Dates: July

Duration of Program: 2 weeks

Cost: $1,200

Eligibility: Students who have completed their sophomore year

Application Process: Creative writing sample (8–10 pages of prose or 5 or 6 poems; no academic essays), statement of purpose, school transcript, one letter of recommendation.

Application Deadline: April 9

Financial Aid Deadline: April 9

Average Number of Applicants: 100

Average Number of Participants: 50

Academic Credit: None available

Contact:
Iowa Young Writers' Studio
University of Iowa
100 Oakdale Campus, W-310
Iowa City, IA 52242-5000
Phone: (319) 335-4209
Fax: (319) 335-4039
justin-tussing@uiowa.edu
www.uiowa.edu/~iyws

Summer Journalism Workshops

Program Location: University of Iowa School of Journalism and Mass Communication in Iowa City, Iowa

Subject Areas: Newspaper, yearbook, website design, broadcast, photography, desktop publishing

Program Description: Prepares students to be effective journalists in the media of instruction. Students preparing to work on the staffs of their school media get a jumpstart in this workshop. In addition, students are introduced to college life in an on-campus experience.

Program Dates: July 21–26

Duration of Program: 5 days

Cost: $375 (newspaper and yearbook) to $405 (photography)

Financial Aid: Available (June 15 deadline)

Eligibility: Students in grades 9–12

Application Process: Applications (request from address below)

Application Deadline: June 15

Average Number of Applicants: 140

Average Number of Participants: 140

Academic Credit: Transcript notation

Contact:
Summer Journalism Workshops
W303 Seashore Hall
School of Journalism and Mass Communication
University of Iowa
Iowa City, IA 52242
Phone: (319) 335-3318
Fax: (319) 335-5210
ihspa@uiowa.edu

Workshop in Theatre Arts

Program Location: University of Iowa in Iowa City

Subject Areas: Theater arts

Program Description: Students learn acting, movement, and improvisation while earning college credit. The 2 weeks culminate in a public performance.

Program Dates: July

Duration of Program: 2 weeks

Cost: $700

Eligibility: Interested high school students

Application Process: Completed application form

Application Deadline: May 25

Average Number of Applicants: 25

Average Number of Participants: 16

Academic Credit: College credit available

Contact:
University of Iowa
Theatre Arts Department
107 Theatre Building
Iowa City, IA 52242-1705
Phone: (319) 335-2700
Fax: (319) 335-3568
www.uiowa.edu

UNIVERSITY OF MAINE

Maine Summer Youth Music Senior Camp

Program Location: University of Maine in Orono, Maine

Subject Areas: Instrumental and vocal music

Program Description: Each student participates in either the symphonic band, concert band, or chorus. Additional activities include small ensembles, chamber groups, jazz improvisation, music classes, master classes, piano or guitar instruction, a concert, and off-campus recreation.

Program Dates: July

Duration of Program: 2 weeks

Cost: $600 (residential); $260 (commuter)

Financial Aid: MSYM scholarships available on a limited basis; scholarship applications due June 5

Eligibility: Students entering grades 9–12 and graduating seniors

Application Process: Application and scholarship forms available upon request.

Application Deadline: June 1

Contact:
University of Maine
5788 Class of 1944 Hall
Room 208
Orono, ME 04459-5788
Phone: (207) 581-4702
Fax: (207) 581-4262
www.ume.maine.edu/~spa/page28.html

UNIVERSITY OF MARYLAND

Design Career Discover (Arch 150)

Program Location: University of Maryland School of Architecture in College Park, Maryland

Subject Areas: Architecture and design, career preparation

Program Description: Program organized to help students make an intelligent choice about a possible career in the design professions through an intensive exposure to the characteristics, opportunities, values, and rewards offered by careers in architecture, landscape architecture, and urban planning. Activities include lectures, a hands-on design project, and field trips to design offices and projects in the Baltimore and Washington, DC metropolitan area.

Program Dates: July 15–August 2

Duration of Program: 3 weeks

Cost: $850; housing available for an additional fee; $75–$100 materials and supplies fee

Financial Aid: Available on a need and merit basis; April 15 deadline

Eligibility: Students who have completed grade 9

Application Process: Application, available at www.umd.edu/summer or by contacting SPOC (single point of contact) at summer@umail.umd.edu or (877) 989-SPOC.

Application Deadline: Submit applications by April 15 for best consideration

Average Number of Applicants: 70

Average Number of Participants: 35

Academic Credit: Available (3 credits)

University of Maryland

Contact:
attn: Melissa Weese Goodill
University of Maryland, School of Architecture
College Park, MD 20742
Phone: (301) 405-6284
Fax: (301) 314-9583
mg204@umail.umd.edu
www.inform.umd.edu/arch

See also National Student Leadership Conference

UNIVERSITY OF MASSACHUSETTS—AMHERST

See Academic Study Associates

UNIVERSITY OF MIAMI

University of Miami Summer Scholar Programs

Program Location: University of Miami in Coral Gables, Florida

Subject Areas: Liberal arts

Program Description: Students may select from a range of special programs for college-level study and career exploration in a university atmosphere. Courses include broadcast journalism, chemistry, filmmaking, marine science, earth science, and medicine.

Program Dates: June–July

Duration of Program: 3 weeks

Cost: $3,500

Financial Aid: Available

Eligibility: Rising juniors and seniors with a B average or better

Application Process: Application, letter of interest, recommendations, transcript, $100 application fee (refundable if applicant is not admitted)

Application Deadline: May 12

Financial Aid Deadline: March 1

Average Number of Applicants: 140

Average Number of Participants: 100

Academic Credit: College credit available

Contact:
Summer Scholars Programs
University of Miami
P.O. Box 248005
Coral Gables, FL 33124-1610
Phone: (305) 284-6107 or (800) STUDY-UM
Fax: (305) 284-6279
ssp.cstudies@miami.edu
www.miami.edu/cstudies/ssp/index.html

UNIVERSITY OF MICHIGAN

Michigan Math and Science Scholars

Program Location: University of Michigan in Ann Arbor, Michigan

Subject Areas: College preparatory mathematics and science curriculum

Program Description: Academic exploration program for students interested in pursuing subjects in mathematics and science. Professors teach courses in astronomy, biology, chemistry, geology, mathematics, physics, and statistics. Participants choose one course per session. Hands-on learning emphasized through fieldwork, laboratory experiments, and computer programs. Opportunities to tour research facilities and see scientific and mathematical demonstrations available.

Program Dates: June 30–July 27

Duration of Program: 2–4 weeks

Cost: $700 (tuition); $525 (room and board)

Financial Aid: Available (May 1 deadline)

Eligibility: Students entering grades 10–12 (ages 14–18)

Application Process: Transcript, recommendation, personal statement, course selections.

Application Deadline: May 1

Average Number of Applicants: 200

Average Number of Participants: 138

Academic Credit: None available

Contact:
University of Michigan
Michigan Math and Science Scholars
525 East University, 2082
East Hall
Ann Arbor, MI 48109-1109
Phone: (734) 615-3439
Fax: (734) 763-0937
mmss@umich.edu
www.math.lsa.umich.edu/mmss/

See also Musiker Discovery Programs

UNIVERSITY OF MISSISSIPPI

Summer College for High School Students

Program Location: University of Mississippi in University, Mississippi

Subject Areas: Liberal arts, fine arts, journalism, international studies, premed, engineering

Program Description: Students take at least two college-level courses for credit in the track of their choice. The Summer College includes the PACE Program, the Croft International Studies Program, the Pre-Engineering Program, the Pre-Health-Professions Program, the Art Institute, the Music Institute, the Journalism Institute, and the Theatre Arts Institute. All programs include sports, trips, and recreational activities. Afternoon "exploring sessions" are intended to provide an overview of the University as well as a chance for students to think about majors and careers.

Program Dates: June–July; July–August

Duration of Program: 4 weeks per session

Cost: Approximately $1,000 (includes room and board)

Financial Aid: Several full scholarships, some based on need and others on merit, are available. A financial aid request form is included in the application packet and should be submitted with the completed application.

Eligibility: Students who have completed their junior year. PACE, Croft International Studies Program, Pre-Engineering Program, or Pre-Medicine Program: Student must have a minimum of 25 on the ACT or the SAT equivalent and either have a 3.2 GPA on at least 15 academic courses or have a 3.5 GPA on those courses of the college preparatory curriculum they have completed. Art Institute, Music Institute, Journalism Institute, or Theatre Arts Institute: Student must have a minimum 3.2 GPA in at least 15 academic courses.

Application Process: Application, transcript, letter of permission from high school principal, and teacher recommendations. Each program or institute may have additional requirements such as nomination by the principal, writing samples, or audition.

Application Deadline: May 15

Average Number of Participants: Limit of 25 students per program

Academic Credit: Up to 6 college credits may be awarded

Contact:
Office of Summer School
University of Mississippi
P.O. Box 9
University, MS 38677
Phone: (662) 915-7621
Fax: (662) 915-1535
umsummer@olemiss.edu
www.olemiss.edu/depts/umsummer/

UNIVERSITY OF NEBRASKA—LINCOLN

All Girls/All Math

Program Location: University of Nebraska Center for Science, Math, and Computer Education in Lincoln, Nebraska

Subject Areas: Mathematics

Program Description: Provides a stimulating and supportive environment for girls to develop their math ability and interest. Participants learn about chaos and codes. Students work with female math professors and graduate students, and interact with peers who share an interest in math.

Program Dates: June and July

Duration of Program: 1 week

Cost: $100 for Nebraska residents; $200 for out-of-state participants (includes room and board)

Financial Aid: Available (May 1 deadline)

Eligibility: Females only, grades 10–12 with high ability

Application Process: Application, essay, teacher recommendation, grade transcript

Application Deadline: May 1

Average Number of Applicants: 60

Average Number of Participants: 28

Academic Credit: None available

Contact:
UNL Center for Science, Math, and Computer Education
126 Morrill Hall
Lincoln, NE 68588-0350
Phone: (402) 472-8965
Fax: (402) 472-9311
scimath@unl.edu
www.unl.edu/scimath

UNIVERSITY OF NEW HAMPSHIRE

Project SMART

Program Location: University of New Hampshire in Durham, New Hampshire

Subject Areas: Biotechnology, space science, marine and freshwater science, environmental science

Program Description: Science and Mathematics Achievement through Research Training is an intensive program for enthusiastic students interested in the pursuit of one of the following four areas of science: biotechnology, space science, marine and freshwater science, and environmental science. Students study advanced topics in science, mathematics, and computers through lectures, demonstrations, hands-on labs, and field trips, and learn the process of research with UNH faculty and graduate students. Students reside in the UNH dorms.

Program Dates: July 9–August 3 (2001 dates)

Duration of Program: 4 weeks

Cost: $1,150 (includes room and board)

Eligibility: Students currently enrolled in grade 10 or 11. Selection will be based on a student's interest and aptitude for learning science and mathematics.

Application Process: Formal application, 2 recommendations from science or math teachers or guidance counselor

Application Deadline: April 16 (2001 date)

Average Number of Participants: A maximum of 25 students will be selected to participate in each science area.

Contact:
attn: Director, Project SMART
Department of Plant Biology
University of New Hampshire
Rudman Hall
Durham, NH 03824
Phone: (603) 862-2100
Fax: (603) 862-3784
sminocha@christa.unh.edu
www.smart.unh.edu

Summer Youth Music School (SYMS)

Program Location: University of New Hampshire in Durham, New Hampshire

Subject Areas: Instrumental and vocal music

Program Description: Designed to improve students' technique and musical understanding through master classes, small ensembles, a variety of choruses and jazz groups, and other opportunities. Students concentrate on their major instrument or voice part and choose electives to broaden their experience. Students and faculty members give a variety of free evening recitals throughout the sessions. Each session concludes with a final concert.

Program Dates: Junior Session: July 15–20; Senior Session: July 23–August 4 (2001 dates)

Duration of Program: Junior Session: 1 week; Senior Session: 2 weeks

Cost: Junior Session: $350 (residential); $250 (commuter). Senior Session: $700 (residential); $500 (commuter).

Eligibility: Junior Session: students completing grades 7–8. Senior Session: students completing grades 9–12.

Application Process: Recommendation from music teacher required

Application Deadline: June 5 (2001 date)

Contact:
SYMS
Department of Music
University of New Hampshire
Durham, NH 03824
Phone: (603) 862-2404
www.learn.unh.edu/summer/specinstit.html

UNIVERSITY OF NORTH DAKOTA

International Aerospace Camp

Program Location: Grand Forks, North Dakota

Subject Areas: Aeronautics/aviation

Program Description: A hands-on flight training program. Students fly five aircraft with instructors and visit aerospace career areas.

Program Dates: July 8–17

Duration of Program: 10 days

Cost: $995

Eligibility: High school juniors and seniors

Application Deadline: Rolling admissions

Average Number of Applicants: 62

Average Number of Participants: 30

Contact:
International Aerospace Camp
Department of Continuing Education
P.O. Box 9021
Grand Forks, ND 58202-9021
Phone: (800) 342-8230
Fax: (701) 777-6401
conferences@mail.und.edu
www.conted.und.edu

University of Notre Dame—Engineering

UNIVERSITY OF NOTRE DAME

Introduction to Engineering

Program Location: University of Notre Dame in Notre Dame, Indiana

Subject Areas: All areas of engineering, including computer programming, engineering design, and project building

Program Description: Students with a strong background in mathematics get a glimpse into the field of engineering through hands-on projects and informal classroom lectures given by university professors. Participants have full access to campus facilities, including tennis courts, swimming pools, and a lake, and can take field trips on the weekends.

Program Dates: 2 sessions offered in June and July

Duration of Program: 3 weeks

Cost: $800 plus food

Financial Aid Deadline: April 28

Eligibility: Rising high school seniors; three years of math required

Application Process: Application (available on website or request from program)

Application Deadline: April 28

Average Number of Applicants: 75

Average Number of Participants: 50

Academic Credit: None available

Contact:
attn: Ramzi K. Bualuan
384 Fitzpatrick Hall
University of Notre Dame
Notre Dame, IN 46556
Phone: (219) 631-8320
Fax: (219) 631-9260
iep@nd.edu
www.nd.edu/iep/

Summer Experience

Program Location: University of Notre Dame in Notre Dame, Indiana

Subject Areas: Liberal arts, life sciences, finance/entrepreneurship, literature, psychology, theology, computer science

Program Description: This program for academically gifted students provides participants with an opportunity to explore an academic field of study while in residence on the Notre Dame campus. Courses are college-level and are taught by professors. Includes evening workshops, recreational activities, field trips, and social and community service activities.

Program Dates: July 7–27

Duration of Program: 3 weeks

Cost: TBA

Financial Aid: Limited aid available, May 15 deadline

Eligibility: Rising high school seniors

Application Process: Written application, transcript, standardized test scores, letters of recommendation

Average Number of Applicants: 200

Average Number of Participants: 100

Academic Credit: None available

Contact:
attn: Joan Martel Ball
206 Brownson Hall
University of Notre Dame
Notre Dame, IN 46556
Phone: (219) 631-9381
Fax: (219) 631-8964
jmball@nd.edu
www.nd.edu/~precoll

Summer Sports Camps

Program Location: University of Notre Dame in Indiana

Subject Areas: Boys football, boys basketball, boys baseball, boys soccer, boys lacrosse, girls basketball, girls softball, girls soccer, girls lacrosse, volleyball, hockey, swimming, diving, tennis, golf

Program Description: Notre Dame sponsors both residential and day camps for serious young athletes in a variety of sports.

Program Dates: June–July

Duration of Program: Varies by program

Cost: Varies by program

Eligibility: Age requirements and levels of experience vary by program; also see subject areas above for gender restrictions

Application Process: Call (219) 631-8788 for camp brochures; brochures contain application forms

Application Deadline: Applications will be processed on a first-come, first-served basis until all sessions are filled. Acceptance of a camper will be verified upon receipt of the camp confirmation packet. Note that according to certain NCAA regulations, only members of the camp office (not the coaching staff) may be able to return your calls.

Contact:
Notre Dame Summer Sports Camps
Athletics Department
Notre Dame, Indiana 46556
Phone: (219) 631-8788
und.fansonly.com/genrel/camps/nd-camps.html

UNIVERSITY OF PENNSYLVANIA

Penn Summer Science Academy

Program Location: University of Pennsylvania in Philadelphia, Pennsylvania

Subject Areas: Microbiology, physics/astronomy

Program Description: PSSA is an intensive noncredit program for students interested in research or medicine. Participants choose a concentration in Molecular Biology or Physics & Astronomy. Academic and hands-on courses of study in various subjects, ethical issues, and computers. Upon completion of the program, each PSSA student receives a written evaluation prepared by his instructors as well as a certificate.

Program Dates: July 2–27 (2001 dates)

Duration of Program: 4 weeks

Cost: $3,600 (includes room and board)

Financial Aid: Limited aid available based on need and geared toward students from the Philadelphia region. Downloadable financial aid form available on website.

Eligibility: High school students completing their sophomore or junior year. Minimum academic requirements: for Molecular Biology, one year of high school biology or chemistry; for Physics & Astronomy, one year of high school chemistry or physics.

Application Process: Transcript, 85+ grade average, letter of recommendation from teacher or guidance counselor, essay, $35 application fee

Application Deadline: May 1

Average Number of Applicants: 200

Average Number of Participants: 65

Academic Credit: None available

Precollege Program

Program Location: University of Pennsylvania in Philadelphia, Pennsylvania

Subject Areas: College preparatory courses in prebusiness, international relations, premed, prelaw, cultural studies, behavioral and social sciences, philosophy and religious studies, communications, English, fine arts, sciences, and math

Program Description: High school students are completely integrated into regular college summer courses and campus life. Students take one or two courses during the program and are evaluated by the same academic standards as Penn's undergraduate students. Also includes workshops on college survival strategies and career choices, as well as field trips. Day and residential options available.

Program Dates: July 2–August 10 (2001 dates)

Duration of Program: 6 weeks

Cost: Residential: $3,600 (1 course), $5,500 (2 courses). Commuter: $1,950 (1 course), $3,800 (2 courses).

Financial Aid: Limited aid available based on need and geared toward students from the Philadelphia region. Downloadable financial aid form available on website.

Eligibility: High school students who have completed sophomore or junior year

Application Process: Application (downloadable form available on website), standardized test scores, teacher recommendation, essay, $35 application fee

Application Deadline: May 15

Average Number of Applicants: 300

Average Number of Participants: 200

Academic Credit: Up to 2 course units (6 college credits) available

Contact:
Summer Youth Programs
University of Pennsylvania
3440 Market Street, Suite 100
Philadelphia, PA 19104-3335
Phone: (215) 898-5716
Fax: (215) 573-2053
summer@sas.upenn.edu
www.sas.upenn.edu/CGS/highschool/

UNIVERSITY OF RHODE ISLAND

W. Alton Jones Teen Expeditions

Program Location: Rhode Island and other New England states

Subject Areas: Kayaking, rock climbing, backpacking, canoeing

Program Description: Focus on outdoor activities and recreation. Many trips to choose from during the summer.

Program Dates: Sessions in July and August

Duration of Program: 1 week

University of Rhode Island

Cost: $440–$680

Eligibility: Ages 12–17

Application Deadline: Rolling

Application Process: Application form, deposit of $100

Contact:
University of Rhode Island
W. Alton Jones Campus
401 Victory Highway
West Greenwich, RI 02817
Phone: (401) 397-3304 ext. 6043
Fax: (401) 397-3293
urieec@etal.uri.edu
www.uri.edu/ajc/eec/teen.htm

UNIVERSITY OF SAN DIEGO

University of San Diego Summer Sports Camps

Program Location: University of San Diego in San Diego, California

Subject Areas: Baseball, boys' basketball, girls' basketball, competitive swimming, boys' soccer, girls' soccer, junior soccer, high school soccer, adult tennis, high school tennis, junior tennis, girls' volleyball, coed water polo, masters swim, adult triathlon

Program Description: Residential and day programs led by Division I coaches. Geared specifically for high school students. May include field trips, roller blading/skating, baseball games, beach barbecue, picnics.

Program Dates: TBA

Duration of Program: 5 days

Cost: $195–$350 (day camp); $410–$500 (residential); cost depends on the sport

Eligibility: Ages 8–17. Some programs are for older, high school players only, and some programs require advanced skill levels for participation. Contact program for more information.

Application Process: Full tuition due with registration; information request form and downloadable registration form available on website.

Application Deadline: June 1

Contact:
University of San Diego
Summer Sports Camps
5998 Alcala Park
San Diego, CA 92110-2492
Phone: (619) 260-4593
(800) 991-1873, x2
Fax: (619) 260-4185
sportscamps@acusd.edu
camps.acusd.edu

See also Education Unlimited

UNIVERSITY OF THE SOUTH

Bridge Program in Math and Science

Program Location: The University of the South in Sewanee, Tennessee

Subject Areas: Introductory college calculus, science courses vary (ecology, chaos, fractals, etc.)

Program Description: A residential experience on the campus of The University of the South. Students with strong academic backgrounds who are interested in careers in mathematics or the sciences are encouraged to apply.

Program Dates: June 23–July 13

Duration of Program: 3 weeks

Cost: Free. The program is supported by a foundation grant; no cost to the student for tuition, books, room, or board.

Eligibility: Rising high school seniors of ethnic minorities

Application Process: Application (available on website), two essays, two letters of recommendation, transcript, standardized test scores

Application Deadline: March 15

Average Number of Applicants: 75

Average Number of Participants: 20

Academic Credit: None available

Contact:
The University of the South
The Bridge Program in Math and Science
735 University Avenue
Sewanee, TN 37383
Phone: (931) 598-1997
Fax: (931) 598-1145
mpriestl@sewanee.edu
www.sewanee.edu/MinorityStudentAffairs/
BridgeProgram/

*University of Southern California—Summer
Production Workshop*

UNIVERSITY OF SOUTHERN CALIFORNIA

Summer Production Workshop

Program Location: University of Southern California in Los Angeles, California

Subject Areas: Film production

Program Description: USC, dubbed the top film school in the country by *U.S. News and World Report*, offers summer workshops in production, directing, producing, digital imaging, and screenwriting, all taught by university faculty. In all but 2 years since 1951, a USC graduate has been nominated for an Academy Award.

Program Dates: TBA

Duration of Program: 6–10 weeks

Cost: Varies with duration of program

Financial Aid: None

Eligibility: Ages 17 and up

Application Process: Application forms available online starting in November. No portfolio is necessary.

Application Deadline: Rolling admissions

Academic Credit: College credit

Contact:
University of Southern California
School of Cinema-Television
Summer Production Workshop
850 West 34th Street
George Lucas Building
Los Angeles, CA 90089-2211
Phone: (213) 740-1742
Fax: (213) 740-3326
spw@cinema.usc.edu
cinema-tv.usc.edu/spw

UNIVERSITY OF SOUTHERN MISSISSIPPI, THE FRANCES A. KARNES CENTER FOR GIFTED STUDIES

Leadership Studies Program

Program Location: University of Southern Mississippi in Hattiesburg, Mississippi

Subject Areas: Leadership

Program Description: Leadership I includes those areas necessary for leadership development: fundamentals of leadership, written and oral communication, group dynamics, problem solving, planning, personal skills, and decision making. Leadership II further develops leadership concepts and qualities with emphasis placed on the psychology of leadership, assertiveness training, and situational leadership. Leadership III focuses on the legal aspects of leadership, responsibilities of various positions of leadership, developing personal power, and leadership for the future. These students also have the opportunity for informal interaction with adult leaders. All students are housed in dormitories on the University of Southern Mississippi campus.

Program Dates: June 16–21

Duration of Program: 1 week

Cost: Contact center for further information (includes room, board, recreational activities, and limited accident insurance).

Financial Aid: On a financial needs basis

Eligibility: Students in grades 6–11 who are recommended by school officials and who have a desire to develop and enhance their leadership abilities. Leadership I is a prerequisite for entry into Leadership II; Leadership II is a prerequisite for entry into Leadership III.

Application Process: Application and recommendation of school official

Application Deadline: March 31

Average Number of Participants: 90

Summer Program for Academically Talented Youth

Program Location: University of Southern Mississippi in Hattiesburg, Mississippi

Subject Areas: A variety of courses, including precalculus, geometry, trigonometry, and modern analysis; psychology; nonfiction writing; Southern writers and literature; physics, biology, anatomy/physiology, and other sciences; statistics and probability; and foreign languages.

Program Description: A variety of fast-paced, intensive courses offered. Designed to include appropriate academic, cultural, and recreational experiences. The University of Southern Mississippi offers the program through cooperative efforts with the Duke University Talent Identification Program.

Program Dates: July 7–26

Duration of Program: 3 weeks

Cost: Contact center for further information (includes books, room, board, recreational activities, and limited accident insurance).

Financial Aid: On a financial needs basis

Eligibility: Students in grades 7–10

Application Process: Application, including SAT or ACT scores for those students entering grade 9 or higher

Application Deadline: April 30

Average Number of Participants: 80

Contact:
The University of Southern Mississippi
USM Box 8207
Hattiesburg, MS 39406-8207
Phone: (601) 266-5246/5236
Fax: (601) 266-4978
gifted.studies@usm.edu
www.dept.usm.edu/~gifted

UNIVERSITY OF SPORTS

Superstar Camp

Program Location: University of California, San Diego

Subject Areas: Basketball

Program Description: Top young players compete against other accomplished athletes, get exposure to college scouts, and learn goal-setting and motivation from experienced high school and college coaches.

Program Dates: July

Duration of Program: 4 days

Cost: $495

Financial Aid: Need-based aid available

Eligibility: Separate camps for boys and girls, grades 11–12. Junior division for grades 8–10. Must be nominated by a coach.

Application Process: Coach's nomination, application, $150 deposit

Contact:
University of Sports
attn: Aaron G. Locks
P.O. Box 7507
Cotati, CA 94931-7507
Phone: (707) 585-2302
Fax: (707) 585-3461
camps@uofs.com
www.uofs.com/superstar/superstar.htm

UNIVERSITY OF TEXAS— AUSTIN

Summer Theatre Workshop

Program Location: University of Texas in Austin, Texas

Subject Areas: Performing arts

Program Description: A 5-week program with workshops and performance activities. Classes in acting, movement, makeup, and theater production.

Program Dates: Early June to mid-July

Duration of Program: 5 weeks

Cost: $1,100 (tuition, room and board)

Eligibility: Rising sophomores, juniors, and seniors

Application Process: Standardized test scores, transcripts, a theater teacher recommendation, and a character reference.

Application Deadline: May 1

Average Number of Applicants: 200

Average Number of Participants: 50 (25 boys/25 girls)

Contact:
Department of Theatre and Dance
University of Texas
Austin, TX 78712
Phone: (512) 471-5793
Fax: (512) 471-0824
www.utexas.edu/cofa/theatre/sdnt.html

UNIVERSITY OF VERMONT

Discovering Engineering, Mathematics, and Computer Science

Program Location: University of Vermont in Burlington, Vermont

Subject Areas: Engineering, mathematics, computer science, statistics

Program Description: Teams of students build robotics projects during the week. At the end of the week, a competition is held, with an awards ceremony afterwards. Students explore career opportunities in engineering, mathematics, and computer science. University faculty give presentations on these subjects, as well as on aerospace, biomedical, civil, mechanical, and electrical engineering. Tours of the IBM facility, the Burlington Waste Water Facility, the barn at Shelburne Farms, and the Ben & Jerry's Homemade plant in Waterbury.

Program Dates: July

Duration of Program: 8 days

Cost: $650 (includes room and board and transportation)

Financial Aid: Available for girls and minorities (April 15 deadline)

Eligibility: Students in grades 10–11 who have earned A or B grades in math and science courses

Application Process: In-state applications from Vermont processed through local guidance counselors. Out-of-state applications available on website, or send request to Dawn Densmore.

Application Deadline: May 15

Average Number of Applicants: 120

Average Number of Participants: 65

Academic Credit: None available

Contact:
attn: Dawn Densmore
University of Vermont
Discovering Engineering, Mathematics, and Computer Science
Votey 109, 33 Colchester Avenue
Burlington, VT 05405
Phone: (802) 656-8748
Fax: (802) 656-8802
densmore@emba.uvm.edu
www.emba.uvm.edu/summer/01progr.htm

See also Musiker Discovery Programs

UNIVERSITY OF VIRGINIA

Summer Enrichment Program

Program Location: University of Virginia in Charlottesville, Virginia

Subject Areas: Liberal arts

Program Description: A 2-week intensive academic program for students in high school. Courses in social science, science, computers, and arts and humanities. Students live in groups of 8 in UVA dormitory suites; counselors

live in a separate room in the suite to provide 24-hour supervision.

Program Dates: June 24–July 5; July 8–July 19; July 22–August 2, 2001

Duration of Program: 2 weeks per session

Cost: $830 (includes room and board, accident insurance) (2001 rate)

Financial Aid: Limited aid available through the Summer Enrichment Program and periodically through other funding sources, based on financial need. Contact the program to obtain a Financial Aid Form.

Eligibility: Select students entering grades 9–11

Application Process: Application form, standardized test scores, teacher recommendations, essay required; downloadable application available on website.

Application Deadline: February 15

Average Number of Applicants: 170

Average Number of Participants: 85

Contact:
University of Virginia
Summer Enrichment Program
P.O. Box 400264
Charlottesville, Virginia 22904-4264
Phone: (804) 924-3182
Fax: (804) 924-0747
curry-sep@virginia.edu
curry.edschool.virginia.edu/go/enrich/

UNIVERSITY OF WASHINGTON

Courses for High School Students

Program Location: University of Washington in Seattle, Washington

Subject Areas: Liberal arts

Program Description: A discovery and enrichment program offering the opportunity to explore a variety of academic disciplines, including computing, the arts, sciences, and the humanities. Half-day and full day opportunities.

Program Dates: June–August

Duration of Program: 2 weeks

Cost: Approximately $300–$500 per course

Eligibility: Students in grades 9–12

Application Deadline: Rolling

Contact:
Education Outreach Summer Youth Program
University of Washington
Seattle, WA 98195
Phone: (800) 543-2320 (to request brochure);
(206) 684-6401 (for course information)
Fax: (206) 616-9704
www.outreach.washington.edu

UNIVERSITY OF WISCONSIN— LA CROSSE

Archaeology Field Schools

Program Location: La Crosse, Wisconsin

Subject Areas: Science

Program Description: Three-day to two-week-long field experiences that actively involve students in excavation on an actual archaeological site.

Program Dates: Sessions in June and July

Duration of Program: 3 days to 2 weeks

Cost: $175 (3 days); $250 (1 week)

Financial Aid: Limited scholarships may be available

Eligibility: Open to all high school students

Application Deadline: June 1

Average Number of Applicants: 10

Average Number of Participants: 10

Contact:
The University of Wisconsin—La Crosse
Mississippi Valley Archaeology Center
1725 State Street
La Crosse, WI 54601
Phone: (608) 785-8454
Fax: (608) 785-6474
www.uwlax.edu/mvac

University of Wisconsin Athletic Camps

Program Location: University of Wisconsin in La Crosse, Wisconsin

Subject Areas: Boys' basketball, girls' basketball, distance running, gymnastics, swimming, volleyball, football, tennis, wrestling

Program Description: A variety of athletic camps allowing students to use college facilities and equipment. Overnight and day programs available.

Program Dates: Sessions in June and July

Duration of Program: 2–6 days

Cost: Day camp prices are $100 and up; overnight prices are $200 and up. All camp participants are covered by UW system limited insurance for injury sustained during supervised camp activities.

Eligibility: Age requirements vary by program

Application Process: Completed registration form

Contact:
UW La Crosse Camps/Clinics
1725 State Street
25 Mitchell Hall
La Crosse, WI 54601
Phone: (608) 785-6544
sturh_md@mail.uwlax.edu
perth.uwlax.edu/Athletics/Camps/
campsindex.html

UNIVERSITY OF WISCONSIN— MADISON

Engineering Summer Program for High School Students

Program Location: University of Wisconsin in Madison, Wisconsin

Subject Areas: Engineering

Program Description: A 7-week program for minority high school students interested in engineering.

Program Dates: Mid-June to early August

Duration of Program: 8 weeks

Cost: $50

Eligibility: High school students in grades 10–11

Application Process: Essay, transcript, and letters of recommendation

Application Deadline: Mid-March

Average Number of Applicants: 35

Average Number of Participants: 25

Contact:
University of Wisconsin
1415 Engineering Drive
2640 Engineering Hall
Madison, WI 53706
Phone: (608) 262-7764
Fax: (608) 262-6400

Pre-college Program in Environmental and Native American Studies

Program Location: University of Wisconsin in Madison, Wisconsin

Subject Areas: Environmental studies, Native American studies

Program Description: A 2-week program, priority given to Native American students with an interest in environmental studies.

Program Dates: First 2 weeks in August

Cost: No cost

Financial Aid: Program is free; travel scholarship also available

Eligibility: Ages 14–17 in grades 9–12

Application Process: Letter of recommendation and essay required.

Application Deadline: Rolling admissions (priority: May 15)

Contact:
University of Wisconsin
Institute for Environmental Studies
Science Hall
550 North Park Street
Madison, WI 53706
Phone: (608) 263-1796
Fax: (608) 262-2273
blborns@facstaff.wisc.edu
www.ies.wisc.edu

Summer Art Classes

Program Location: University of Wisconsin in Madison, Wisconsin

Subject Areas: Visual arts

Program Description: Sessions range in length from 1 day to 10 weeks. Students receive instruction in painting, drawing, sculpture, and crafts.

Program Dates: Sessions throughout the summer

Duration of Program: 1–10 weeks

Cost: $60–$160

Eligibility: Varies with the class

Application Process: Completed application form. First come, first served.

Average Number of Applicants: 100

Average Number of Participants: 100

Academic Credit: No credit available

Contact:
University of Wisconsin
Outreach Programs
723 Lowell Hall, 610 Langdon Street
Madison, WI 53703
Phone: (608) 263-7814
Fax: (608) 265-2475
www.wisc.edu/wiscinfo/outreach

Summer Music Clinic

Program Location: University of Wisconsin in Madison, Wisconsin

Subject Areas: Music

Program Description: A week-long music program for high school students, including band, orchestra, choir, musical theatre, jazz ensemble. 40 class offerings available. Performance opportunities. Composition courses.

Program Dates: June 24–30

Duration of Program: 1 week

Cost: $400 (includes room and board)

Eligibility: Students in grades 6–12 at all levels of musical ability

Application Process: Completed application

Application Deadline: May 15

Average Number of Applicants: 500

Average Number of Participants: 500

Contact:
University of Wisconsin
Summer Music Clinic
Rm. 5554 Humanities Building
455 N. Park Street
Madison, WI 53706
Phone: (608) 263-2242
Fax: (608) 265-0452
maaley@facstaff.wisc.edu
www.wisc.edu/smc/

Summer Science Institute

Program Location: University of Wisconsin in Madison, Wisconsin

Subject Areas: Biological sciences

Program Description: A 7-week program for students interested in science. Courses offered in a range of scientific fields. Students participate in collaborative research projects.

Program Dates: June 17 to August 4 (2001 dates)

Duration of Program: 7 weeks

Cost: No cost

Financial Aid: Program is free

Eligibility: High potential minority/underserved high school sophomores or juniors, 2.5 minimum GPA and nomination by science teacher

Application Deadline: April 1

Average Number of Applicants: 120

Average Number of Participants: 30

Academic Credit: ½ elective high school science credit upon approval by local school district

Contact:
University of Wisconsin
Center of Biology Education
1271 Genetics/Biotechnology Building
425 Henry Mall
Madison, WI 53706-1500
Phone: (608) 263-0478
Fax: (608) 262-6748
cbe@mhub.facstaff.wisc.edu
www.wisc.edu/cbe/K12.html

See also American Collegiate Adventures

UNIVERSITY OF WISCONSIN— SUPERIOR

Youthsummer

Program Location: University of Wisconsin–Superior in Superior, Wisconsin

Subject Areas: Liberal arts and sciences, fine arts, career exploration

Program Description: Youthsummer is a fun way for young people to explore careers and sample university life. Over 40 different courses are offered, including classes on aerospace, dance, theater, photography, and freshwater ecology.

Program Dates: June and July

Duration of Program: 1–5 weeks

Cost: $365/week (residential); $220/week (commuters)

Eligibility: Ages 13–17

Application Deadline: Mid-June

Average Number of Applicants: 70/week

Average Number of Participants: 60/week

Academic Credit: None available

Contact:
University of Wisconsin–Superior
Room 50 Rothwell Student Center
Belknap & Catlin—P.O. Box 2000
Superior, WI 54880
Phone: (715) 394-8173
Fax: (715) 394-8454
jspagnol@staff.uwsuper.edu
staff.uwsuper.edu/youth

U.S. GYMNASTICS TRAINING CENTERS

U.S. Gymnastics Camp

Program Location: Mount Holyoke College in South Hadley, Massachusetts (2001 location)

Subject Areas: Men's and women's gymnastics

Program Description: Seven full days of gymnastics, with 6–7 gymnasts per instructor. Includes daily gymnastics classes on all the Olympic events; daily conditioning classes for boys and girls, concentrating on flexibility, strength, and mental preparation; daily dance classes for girls; lectures and demonstrations by elite staff; and optional gymnastics contests. Gymnasts are placed into groups by size and ability; a gymnast who is more advanced on a specific event can move up to the next ability level on that event. At least four Olympians at each session.

Program Dates: 2 sessions in August

Duration of Program: 1 week per session

Cost: $600 for one session; $1,170 for both sessions

Eligibility: All levels from beginners to elite

Application Process: Completed application, $150 deposit; downloadable application available on website. Contact U.S. GTC for full brochure.

Contact:
U.S. GTC
P.O. Box 4088
Tequesta, FL 33469
Phone: (561) 743-8550
Fax: (561) 802-6962
usagtc@aol.com
www.usgymnasticscamps.com

U.S. SNOWBOARD TRAINING CENTER

USSTC Allstar Snowboard Camp

Program Location: Mount Hood, Oregon

Subject Areas: Snowboarding

U.S. Snowboard Training Center

Program Description: Summer training camps feature a 1:5 trainer/athlete ratio, helping campers to reach their maximum potential. Campers are divided into small groups according to ability levels. After a full day on the hill, campers enjoy activities such as skateboarding, trampoline, ping-pong, video games, recreational trips, and more. Summer camp members stay on Mt. Hood at night in a chalet retreat in the woods of Oregon; accommodations are coed but separated, with 24-hour adult supervision.

Program Dates: 8 sessions from June–August

Duration of Program: 8 days per session

Cost: $1,395 (includes room and board, all lift tickets, transportation to and from Portland International Airport)

Eligibility: Open to all ages and all levels of experience

Application Process: Contact USSTC for full brochure; $200 deposit required

Contact:
U.S. Snowboard Training Center
P.O. Box 578
Welches, OR 97067
Phone: (800) 325-4430
Fax: (503) 622-3337
mail@snowboardtraining.com
www.snowboardtraining.com

U.S. SPACE CAMP

Aviation Challenge and Advanced Space Academy

Program Location: Huntsville, Alabama and Atwater, California

Subject Areas: Aviation, space

Program Description: Aviation Challenge: A jet fighter pilot training program for high school. Activities include intense flight simulation, land survival training, water survival activities, and aviation academics. Lessons include aeronautics, aerodynamics, propulsion, flight physiology, aviation history, aircrew equipment, and ejection procedures. Advanced Space Academy: An astronaut training program. Activities include scuba training, intense training missions in the orbiter, space station, and mission control. Alabama only.

Program Dates: Sessions in May, June, July, August (Aviation Challenge); year-round (Advanced Space Academy)

Duration of Program: 5 days

Cost: $899 (depends on camp)

Eligibility: Ages 15–18

Application Process: Registration options: phone, fax, postal service, online

Application Deadline: Late May (Aviation Challenge)

Contact:
U.S. Space Camp Reservations
P.O. Box 070015
Huntsville, AL 35807-7015
Phone: (800) 63-SPACE or (800) 533-7281
Fax: (256) 837-6137
www.spacecamp.com

U.S. SPORTS CAMPS

Nike Sports Camps

Program Location: More than 500 locations across the United States (mostly college campuses)

Subject Areas: Tennis, golf, volleyball, girls' basketball, lacrosse, running, swimming, water polo, softball, rowing, field hockey, soccer, mountain biking, hockey, football, baseball

Program Description: Residential and day camps for athletes of all ability levels. Once in camp, each camper is personally evaluated and placed into a group with other players of similar age and abilities. The Nike camp staff includes many of the most respected coaches and players in each sport. The staff lives on campus and provides 24-hour supervision of all campers.

Program Dates: June–September (most sessions take place in June and July)

Duration of Program: Varies by camp

Cost: Varies by camp

Eligibility: Camps offer different programs for each ability level

Application Process: Online registration available on website; optional refund insurance is available.

Application Deadline: Registrations are accepted right up to the start of any camp with openings

Contact:
U.S. Sports Development
919 Sir Francis Drake Blvd.
Kentfield, CA 94904
Phone: (800) NIKE-CAMP or (415) 459-0459
Fax: (415) 459-1453
www.us-sportscamps.com

VANDERBILT UNIVERSITY

Program for Talented Youth

Program Location: Vanderbilt University in Nashville, Tennessee

Subject Areas: Mathematics, computer science, creative writing, American history, genetics, French, theater, public speaking

Program Description: An intensive, enriched summer residential program for academically talented youth. The goal of the program is to provide a highly challenging, stimulating, and technologically enhanced intellectual environment, while allowing students to have fun and form lasting friendships. Each student enrolls in one academic course for nearly 100 hours of instruction and has access to university libraries and computer labs. Full program of social and recreational activities developed by the residential staff.

Program Dates: June 9–29

Duration of Program: 3 weeks

Cost: $2,200 (includes room and board)

Financial Aid: Available (March 30 deadline)

Eligibility: Academically talented students in grades 8–11

Application Process: Application, ACT or SAT scores required

Application Deadline: March 30

Average Number of Applicants: 110

Average Number of Participants: 90

Academic Credit: None available

Contact:
Vanderbilt University
Program for Talented Youth
Peabody Box 506
Nashville, TN 37203-5701
Phone: (615) 322-8261
Fax: (615) 322-3457
pty.peabody@vanderbilt.edu
http://peabody.vanderbilt.edu/pty

VASSAR COLLEGE AND NEW YORK STAGE & FILM

Powerhouse Theatre Program

Program Location: Vassar College in Poughkeepsie, New York

Subject Areas: Theater arts

Program Description: Apprentices take part in acting, directing, movement, and speech classes taught by Powerhouse Theatre company members and visiting faculty. Summer theater season is comprised of mainstage productions, outdoor Shakespeare, second stage and workshop productions, Powerhouse Radio Theater, cabarets, and playreading festivals.

Program Dates: June 8 to August 2

Duration of Program: 8 weeks

Cost: $2,700 (includes tuition, housing, partial board, and free access to all Powerhouse season productions)

Eligibility: High school seniors–adults with an interest in theater

Application Process: Application form, 3 letters of reference, $35 application fee (nonrefundable)

Application Deadline: April 15

Average Number of Applicants: 200

Average Number of Participants: 50

Vassar College and New York Stage & Film

Contact:
Powerhouse Theatre Program
Vassar College
Maildrop 225
Poughkeepsie, NY 12604
Phone: (845) 437-5907
Fax: (845) 437-7209
Befargislancaster@vassar.edu
www.vassar.edu.powerhouse/appr.html

See also Summer Institute for the Gifted

VISIONS

Program Location: Alaska, Montana, South Carolina, Dominican Republic, Dominica, British Virgin Islands, Guadeloupe, Peru, Australia, Chile

Subject Areas: Community service, cross-cultural living and learning

Program Description: Combination of service work, outdoor adventures, and intercultural activities in locations in and outside the U.S. A small group of teens and staff live together in community settings quite different from mainstream America. Service options in any Visions location always include—but are not limited to—a construction project that benefits the host community. Staff/student ratio is 1:4. Maximum group size is 25 students/6 staff.

Program Dates: June–August

Duration of Program: 3- or 4-week sessions

Cost: $2,480–$3,500

Application Process: Call or e-mail for application. $500 deposit required ($400 refundable until March 15).

Application Deadline: Rolling. Starting as early as October.

Academic Credit: After completing the program, students receive a certificate for 80 to 110 hours of community service.

Visions

Contact:
Visions
P.O. Box 220
110 N. 2nd Street
Newport, PA 17074-0220
Phone: (717) 567-7313 or
(800) 813-9283
Fax: (717) 567-7853
visions@pa.net
www.visions-adventure.com

VOGELSINGER SOCCER ACADEMY AND ALL-STAR SOCCER SCHOOL

Program Location: California, Massachusetts, Texas, Wisconsin

Subject Areas: Soccer

Program Description: Academy is a "soccer retreat" without outside distractions, where players can focus single-mindedly on the development of their game. Players are first placed by age, then re-evaluated daily according to ability. Self-evaluation at the beginning and oral and written evaluation at the end. All-Star Soccer School consists of 1-week intensives on one of the following: individual skills, techniques and tactics; positional play; team play; and combination pre-season preparation and team play.

Program Dates: June–August

Duration of Program: 2 or 3 weeks (Academy); 1 week (All-Star Soccer School)

Cost: $575–$1,995 (includes room and board, uniform)

Eligibility: Academy: ages 12 and up. All-Star Soccer School: varies (Individual Skills, Techniques and Tactics: 9 and up; Positional Play: 10 and up; Team Play: 12 and up; Combination Pre-Season and Team Play: 14 and up)

Application Process: Registration form, nonrefundable deposit $300 for the Academy or $100 for 1-week programs); online registration available on website

Contact:
Vogelsinger Soccer Academy and
All-Star Soccer School
5115 Enelra Place
San Diego, CA 92117
Phone: (800) 822-9053; (858) 541-2036
Fax: (858) 541-2515
Kaasnes1@san.rr.com
www.vogelsingersoccer.com

Volunteers for Peace

VOLUNTEERS FOR PEACE

VFP International Workcamps

Program Location: Western and Eastern
Europe, Africa, Asia, Latin America

Subject Areas: Community service, international
travel

Program Description: Short-term voluntary
service projects arise from the needs of the local

host community, and may include construction
and restoration of low income housing;
environmental projects; park maintenance;
organic farming; social services; working with
children, the elderly, or the handicapped; or
historic preservation. Discussions on issues of
common concern, free-time activities and local
excursions also take place.

Program Dates: June through September

Duration of Program: 2–3 weeks

Cost: Membership in VFP is $20. Program fees
range from $200 to $600. All transportation is
arranged and paid for by the volunteer.

Eligibility: Ages 15 and up

Application Process: VFP membership is
available at any time. Registration for summer
workcamps begins as early as late March. Filled
on first-come, first-served basis.

Academic Credit: May be available, depending
on the student's school's requirements

Contact:
Volunteers for Peace
1034 Tiffany Road
Belmont, VT 05730
Phone: (802) 259-2759
Fax: (802) 259-2922
vfp@vfp.org
www.vfp.org

WAKE FOREST UNIVERSITY

Summer Debate Workshop;

Fast Track; Policy Project;

Policy Analysis Seminar

Program Location: Wake Forest University in
Winston-Salem, North Carolina

Subject Areas: Debate

Program Description: The Summer Debate
Workshop is designed for novice through
advanced high school debaters, while Fast
Track, Policy Project, and Policy Analysis are

designed for highly experienced debaters and have a more competitive application process.

Program Dates: Mid-June through end of July

Duration of Program: 3–6 weeks

Cost: $1,575–$3,175

Eligibility: Students in grades 9–12

Application Process: Registration forms, coach's recommendation, deposit (75% refundable through May 31)

Application Deadline: Rolling admissions

Financial aid deadline: May 31, but rolling decision process so students should apply early

Average Number of Applicants: 250

Average Number of Participants: 160

Academic Credit: None

Contact:
Wake Forest University
attn: Ross Smith
P.O. Box 7324
Reynolda Station, WFU
Winston-Salem, NC 27109
Phone: (336) 758-4848
Fax: (336) 758-4691
bannigva@wfu.edu
www.wfu.edu/~debate

THE WALDEN SCHOOL

Walden School Summer Music School, Festival, and Camp

Program Location: The Walden School in Dublin, New Hampshire

Subject Areas: Music instruction and performance

Program Description: Young musicians with a special interest in composition and improvisation study in small classes with a 4:1 student-faculty ratio. Classes include musicianship, composition, improvisation,

chorus, and more. A concert series, artist residencies, and weekly student composer forums help to enrich the curriculum.

Program Dates: July–August

Duration of Program: 5 weeks

Cost: $4,500

Eligibility: Ages 10–18; must have at least 1 year of private music lessons

Application Process: Submit an application (request via email) with $40 fee. May include tapes or copies of work.

Application Deadline: Early March

Financial Aid Deadline: Early March

Average Number of Applicants: 70–80

Average Number of Participants: 45

Contact:
The Walden School
P.O. Box 320553
San Francisco, CA 94132
Phone: (603) 563-8212
info@waldenschool.org
www.waldenschool.org

WASHINGTON AND LEE UNIVERSITY

Summer Scholars

Program Location: Washington and Lee University in Lexington, Virginia

Subject Areas: Liberal arts

Program Description: Students select three courses from a range of curricula including neuropsychology, the humanities, law, politics, business, premedical studies, and environmental studies. Writing labs and intramural activities designed for college-bound students are included.

Program Dates: June 30–July 26

Duration of Program: 4 weeks

Cost: $2,000

Eligibility: Academically-oriented rising high school seniors

Application Process: Application, standardized test scores, and strong teacher endorsement required.

Application Deadline: Rolling admissions

Average Number of Applicants: 250

Average Number of Participants: 20 per curriculum

Contact:
Washington and Lee University
Summer Scholars
Lexington, VA 24450
Phone: (540) 463-8722; (540) 463-8727
Fax: (540) 463-8113
summerscholars@wlu.edu
http://summerscholars.wlu.edu

The Washington Opera

THE WASHINGTON OPERA

Opera Institute for Young Singers

Program Location: The Benjamin T. Rome School of Music of The Catholic University of America and The Washington Opera studios in Washington, DC

Subject Areas: Opera study and performance training

Program Description: Opera Institute for Young Singers: Unique 3-week program that encourages and nurtures the development of young singers. Training and coursework includes master classes taught by guest artists and master teachers, individual and group vocal coaching, Italian diction, movement and drama classes, audition preparation, ear training and sight singing, Italian art song and opera scene study, and opera history. Classes meet Monday–Friday, 9 A.M.–4 P.M. The program concludes with a recital given by all program participants. A separate program, The Washington Opera Camp for Kids, is designed for younger students (ages 10–14); contact the organization for more information.

Program Dates: July 1–20, 2002

Duration of Program: Opera Institute for Young Singers: 3 weeks

Cost: $900

Financial Aid: Need-based scholarships available

Eligibility: Students ages 15–18 who are already studying voice seriously (specifically, studying a repertoire that includes Italian art songs and opera scenes) and are interested in pursuing a career in opera

Application Process: Contact The Washington Opera to receive an application and schedule an audition. For the audition, students should prepare one Italian art song and one additional art song in any language (spirituals are welcome). Auditions take place in February; an accompanist will be provided. Letter of recommendation from current voice teacher is also required.

Application Deadline: Early February

Academic Credit: One college credit available through The Catholic University of America for an additional $150 fee. Submit a completed CUA application form along with official high school transcript (CUA application forms may be obtained on the day of auditions).

Contact:
The Washington Opera
2600 Virginia Avenue
Suite 104
Washington, DC 20037
Phone: (202) 295-2462
Fax: (202) 295-2478
dvans@dc-opera.org
www.dc-opera.org

Contact:
Architecture Discovery Program
Washington University
Campus Box 1079
One Brookings Drive
St. Louis, MO 63130
Phone: (314) 935-6200
Fax: (314) 935-7656
brennan@architecture.wustl.edu

WASHINGTON UNIVERSITY IN ST. LOUIS

Architecture Discovery Program

Program Location: Washington University in St. Louis, Missouri

Subject Areas: Architecture

Program Description: Designed to introduce the student to every aspect of the study of architecture. The program features lectures; field trips to architect' offices and construction sites; and hands-on assignments, including plans, models, and final review.

Program Dates: June 16–June 29, 2002

Duration of Program: 2 weeks

Cost: $1,500

Financial Aid: None available

Eligibility: Students completing grade 11

Application Process: Transcript, ACT/SAT scores, letter of intent, minimum of 2 letters of reference

Application Deadline: April 15, 2002

Average Number of Applicants: 120

Average Number of Participants: Maximum limit of 50

Academic Credit: None available

WASHINGTON WORKSHOPS FOUNDATION

Washington Workshops Seminars

Program Location: Washington, DC

Subject Areas: U.S. Congress, diplomacy, global affairs

Program Description: The Congressional Seminar and the Diplomacy and Global Affairs Seminar are one-week opportunities to learn more about today's issues and needs firsthand through intimate discussions and meetings with Senators, Representatives, Ambassadors, and Executive Branch officials. Students reside in supervised dormitories at Trinity College.

Program Dates: Sessions throughout the summer

Duration of Program: 1 week

Cost: $900

Eligibility: Schools and teachers are encouraged to select and sponsor students for program attendance; qualified students are also encouraged to apply on their own initiative. The student should possess credible academic standing, an interest in the Seminar issues, and high standards of personal character and integrity.

Application Process: Online application and information request form are available through website.

Application Deadline: Rolling admissions

Average Number of Participants: Limited to 120 students per seminar

Academic Credit: College credit available

Contact:
Washington Workshops Foundation
3222 N Street, NW, Suite 340
Washington, DC 20007
Phone: (800) 368-5688
Fax: (202) 965-1018
www.workshops.org

WEISSMAN TEEN TOURS, INC.

Program Location: England, France, Italy, Switzerland, Belgium, and Holland; Canadian Rockies, Pacific Northwest, National Parks, California, Las Vegas, Colorado

Subject Areas: International and domestic travel, culture, sports

Program Description: Two recreational tours: European tour covers 6 countries in 5 weeks (15 days in Italy); accommodations are at superior 4-star and 5-star hotels throughout Europe. Many unusual cultural and outdoor adventures are included, such as skiing, hiking, parasailing on the Riviera, skiing/snowboarding and whitewater rafting in the Swiss Alps; a moonlight gondola ride in Venice; dance clubs in Paris and London's West End Theatre. U.S./Western Canada tour features stays at first-class hotels, resorts, and National Park lodges. Activities include TV tapings and dance clubs in Los Angeles; water sports on Lake Tahoe; snowmobile adventure over a Canadian glacier, skiing/snowboarding in Whistler. Owners/directors personally escort each tour along with a staff of college graduates and promote a warm "family" atmosphere.

Program Dates: June/July through August

Duration of Program: European tour: 5 weeks; Domestic tour: 6 weeks

Cost: European tour: $8,599; Domestic tour: $7,599. Does not include airfare.

Financial Aid: None available

Eligibility: European tour: grades 10–12; Domestic tour: grades 8–9, 10–11.

Application Process: Two deposits of $800 each, refundable until March 1.

Application Deadline: Rolling admissions

Contact:
Weissman Teen Tours
517 Almena Avenue
Ardsley, NY 10502
Phone: (914) 693-7575 or (800) 942-8005
Fax: (914) 693-4807
wtt@cloud9.net
www.weissmantours.com

Weissman Teen Tours, Inc.

WEIZMANN INSTITUTE OF SCIENCE

See American Committee for the Weizmann Institute of Science

WELLS COLLEGE

Student Conference on Leadership and Social Responsibility

Program Location: Wells College in Aurora, New York

Subject Areas: Leadership training, education

Program Description: Workshops for young women providing practice in problem solving, goal setting, public speaking, and communication. Participants will be able to apply the plans they develop during the conference back at their own high schools. Outdoor activities, such as lakefront swimming and a ropes course, are also available. Participants enjoy three nights' accommodation in residence halls, meals catered by Marriott food service, and use of recreational facilities.

Program Dates: June 24–27 and June 27–30, 2002

Duration of Program: 4 days

Cost: $195 (includes room and board, programming, and materials)

Eligibility: Females only, entering grades 11 or 12 with a B average or above, involved in school and extracurricular activities

Application Process: By invitation only. Chosen from guidance counselor nominations. Contact your high school guidance office, or call Wells to have your guidance counselor's name added to the nomination list.

Academic Credit: None available

Contact:
Wells College
Career and Leadership Programs
Aurora, NY 13026
Phone: (315) 364-3462
Fax: (315) 364-3423
leaders@wells.edu
www.wells.edu/conf/ldprgs1.htm

Wells College

WESLEYAN UNIVERSITY

See Capitol Region Education Council and Wesleyan University

WESTCOAST CONNECTION

Active Teen Tours

Program Location: Various locations in the United States and Canada

Subject Areas: Active travel and sightseeing programs through National Parks and cities

Program Description: Programs available: Eastcoast Encounter; California & Canyons; Northwestern Odyssey; Californian Extravaganza; U.S. Explorer; American Voyager. Trips combine the natural wonders of the great outdoors with the attractions of major cities including Los Angeles, San Francisco, Vancouver, and Seattle. Daytime activities include whitewater rafting, snowboarding/skiing, horseback riding, mountain biking, and hiking. Evening activities include baseball games, TV tapings, comedy clubs, miniature golf, campfires, and more. These trips combine camping, dorm, hotel, and resort stays.

Program Dates: Sessions throughout the summer

Duration of Program: 3–6 weeks

Cost: $3,800 and up

Eligibility: Ages 13–17 (students are grouped compatibly by age)

Application Process: Contact office for materials; deposit required

Application Deadline: Rolling; early registration savings

European Programs

Program Location: France, Italy, Switzerland, England, Belgium, Netherlands

Subject Areas: Touring and adventure abroad

Program Description: Programs available: European Escape; European Discovery; European Experience. All programs balance sightseeing and touring in major cities along with unique recreation and entertainment as well as outdoor activities such as rafting, skiing/snowboarding, biking, and hiking in the French and Swiss Alps. Restful stays on the French and Adriatic Riviera help slow down the pace, helping students enjoy a special experience in Europe.

Program Dates: July–August

Duration of Program: 3–4 weeks

Cost: $3,500 and up

Eligibility: Students finishing grades 9–12 (students are grouped compatibly by age)

Application Process: Contact office for materials; deposit required.

Application Deadline: Rolling; early registration savings

Golf & Tennis Programs

Program Location: Mont Tremblant, Quebec; Park City, Utah

Subject Area: Instruction in golf and tennis as well as other recreational sports

Program Description: Programs available: Mont Tremblant Golf & Tennis, Park City Golf & Tennis. Programs offer golf and/or tennis instruction, supervised play, and an opportunity to visit many exciting cities including Montreal, Toronto, Seattle, and Vancouver. Participants also enjoy many exciting recreational activities including whitewater rafting, skiing/snowboarding, mountain biking, and more.

Program Dates: July–August

Duration of Program: 16–26 days

Cost: $3,500 and up

Eligibility: Ages 13–17

Application Process: Contact office for materials; deposit required.

Application Deadline: Rolling; early registration savings

Israel Experience

Program Location: Israel

Subject Areas: Touring and adventure abroad

Program Description: Participants discover and explore both ancient and modern Israel. The trip balances culture, history, and education with adventure and recreation. Activities include SCUBA diving and snorkeling in the Red Sea,

taking part in an archaeological dig, kayaking the Jordan River, taking a jeep ride in King Solomon's Mountains, riding camelback, and sleeping in a Bedouin tent.

Program Dates: July–August

Duration of Program: 3–4 weeks

Cost: $4,700 and up

Eligibility: Ages 15 and up

Application Process: Contact office for materials; deposit required.

Application Deadline: Rolling; early registration savings

On Tour

Program Location: Europe; Western Canada; Israel

Subject Areas: Touring and adventure

Program Description: Programs available: European Experience; Canadian Mountain Magic; Israel Experience. These programs are designed for students age 17 and older and provide participants with more independence. Although encouraged to join daily group activities, students have the option to explore and discover the ultimate bistro or café on their own.

Program Dates: Sessions throughout the summer

Duration of Program: 3–4 weeks

Cost: $3,700 and up

Eligibility: Ages 17–19, rising high school seniors are eligible

Application Process: Contact office for materials; deposit required.

Application Deadline: Rolling; early registration savings

Outdoor Adventure Programs

Program Location: Various locations in the United States and Canada

Subject Areas: Outdoor adventure

Program Description: Programs available: Eastern Expedition; Great West Challenge; Canadian Mountain Magic; Southwesterner; Western Canadian Adventure. For students seeking a great deal of physical activity, these programs emphasize challenging oneself, developing new skills, and gaining a sense of accomplishment. Programs offer combinations of activities such as whitewater rafting, snowboarding/skiing, rock climbing, mountain biking, canoeing, hiking, and more. Professional guides instruct students and lead specialty activities.

Program Dates: Sessions throughout the summer

Duration of Program: 18–40 days

Cost: $2,600 and up

Eligibility: Ages 13–17 (students are grouped compatibly by age)

Application Process: Contact office for materials; deposit required.

Application Deadline: Rolling; early registration savings

Ski & Snowboard Sensation

Program Location: Mt. Hood, Oregon; Whistler-Blackcomb, British Columbia

Subject Area: Instruction in skiing and snowboarding as well as other recreational sports

Program Description: Program offers skiing and snowboarding instruction and an opportunity to visit many exciting cities including Seattle and Vancouver.

Program Dates: Sessions throughout the summer

Duration of Program: 2–4 weeks

Cost: $3,999

Eligibility: Ages 13–17

Application Process: Contact office for materials; deposit required.

Application Deadline: Rolling; early registration savings

Contact:
Westcoast Connection
154 East Boston Post Road
Mamaroneck, NY 10543
Phone: (800) 767-0227 or (914) 835-0699
Fax: (914) 835-0798
info@westcoastconnection.com
www.westcoastconnection.com

WESTERN WASHINGTON UNIVERSITY

Adventures in Science and Arts

Program Location: Western Washington University in Bellingham, Washington

Subject Areas: Liberal arts and sciences

Program Description: An academic enrichment program for grades 5–12, offering interesting programs in the arts and humanities, computers, and science. Classes meet daily, Monday through Friday, for 5- to 6-hour learning sessions. Each Adventures week is for a specific age group; the fourth week is for students entering grades 9–12. Students may live on campus or commute.

Program Dates: July

Duration of Program: 1 week

Cost: $430

Eligibility: Students entering grades 5–12

Application Process: Downloadable application and catalog request form available on website.

Application Deadline: May 31

Contact:
Adventures in Science and Arts
Western Washington University
Bellingham, WA 98225-5293
Phone: (360) 650-6820
Fax: (360) 650-6858
adventur@wwu.edu
www.wwu.edu/~adventur

Outdoor Challenge Institute

Program Location: Western Washington University in Bellingham, Washington

Subject Areas: Outdoor adventure, leadership training

Program Description: Students build leadership skills through experiential learning in the Pacific Northwest wilderness. Character-building activities are designed to challenge both physical and social comfort zones. Activities include hiking, rock climbing, ropes course, and more. Students are carefully supervised as they take on increasing responsibilities and learn to assess risk. Students may live on-campus or they may commute.

Program Dates: July 30–August 3 (grades 6–8); August 6–10 (grades 9–12) (2001 dates)

Duration of Program: 1 week

Cost: $490 (residential); $260 (commuter)

Eligibility: Students in grades 6–12

Application Process: Downloadable application available on website. Full payment due with application.

Application Deadline: June 15 (2001 date)

Contact:
Western Washington University
Extended Programs—OCI
Mail Stop 5293
Bellingham, WA 98225-5293
Phone: (360) 650-6820
Fax: (360) 650-6858
adventur@wwu.edu
www.ac.wwu.edu/%7Eadventur/outdoor/ociindex.htm

SummerQuest

Program Location: Western Washington University in Bellingham, Washington

Subject Areas: Precollege enrichment

Program Description: An opportunity for college-bound students to sample a college-level course

and engage in curriculum taught by WWU professors. Courses are faculty-designed to enhance your intellectual curiosity, creativity, and critical thinking skills. Workshops on how to succeed in college are also offered. Students live in an on-campus residence hall and participate in group activities that showcase college life.

Program Dates: July 30–August 10 (2001 dates)

Duration of Program: 2 weeks

Cost: $1,200 (includes room and board)

Financial Aid: Two $500 scholarships available for students of color who otherwise could not afford to attend

Eligibility: Students in grades 10–12

Application Process: Application (downloadable form available on website), transcript, 500-word essay, recommendation from teacher or guidance counselor, $100 deposit

Application Deadline: May 30 (2001 date)

Contact:
SummerQuest
Western Washington University
Bellingham, WA 98225-5293
Phone: (360) 650-6820
adventur@wwu.edu
www.ac.wwu.edu/%7Eadventur/quest/index.htm

WHERE THERE BE DRAGONS

Summer Programs

Program Location: China, Silk Road, Thailand, Laos, Vietnam, Tibet, North India, Mongolia

Subject Areas: Travel, wilderness, exploration, service, rugged trekking, peace and conflict studies, philosophy and development studies

Program Description: Travel programs that include rugged travel, home-stays, trekking, and service projects. Features small groups with experienced and qualified program leaders who have undergone extensive training.

Program Dates: June 26—August 6

Duration of Program: 6 weeks

Cost: $5,900 (includes room and board and airfare)

Financial Aid: Available (April 1)

Eligibility: Students who have completed grade 9 and higher

Application Process: Application, personal interview, teacher reference

Application Deadline: Rolling

Average Number of Applicants: 250

Average Number of Participants: 180

Academic Credit: College credit for semester programs

Contact:
Where There Be Dragons
P.O. Box 4651
Boulder, CO 80306
Phone: (800) 982-9203
Fax: (303) 413-0857
dragons@earthnet.net
www.wheretherebedragons.com

WILDERNESS EXPERIENCE UNLIMITED

Explorer Group;

Trailblazers

Program Location: Massachusetts and other New England locations

Subject Areas: Outdoor adventure

Program Description: Explorer Group: An opportunity to gain outdoor living skills and participate in many different outdoor activities. Trailblazers: A trip/resident program held Monday–Friday from 9 A.M.–4 P.M. Each Trailblazer session focuses on a different activity: caving; tubing/kayaking/canoeing; rock climbing/ropes/rescue; kayaking; mountain biking; SCUBA.

Program Dates: July–August

Duration of Program: 3 days–8 weeks

Cost: Explorer Group: $350; Trailblazers: $475 and up

Eligibility: Explorer Group: ages 9–16; Trailblazers: ages 12–17

Application Deadline: May

Application Process: Application form, deposit of 25 percent of cost of program; information request form available on website

Contact:
Wilderness Experience Unlimited
499 Loomis Street
Westfield, MA 01085
Phone: (413) 562-7431 or (888) WE-CLIMB
Fax: (413) 562-7431
adventures@weu.com
www.weu.com

WILDERNESS VENTURES

Wilderness Adventure Expeditions;

Advanced Leadership Expeditions;

Offshore Adventure Expeditions

Program Location: Expeditions throughout the Western United States, Hawaii, Alaska, Canada, Europe, Australia, Central America

Subject Areas: Outdoor wilderness adventure, leadership training, cultural immersion

Program Description: Students choose an expedition based on age, level of prior experience, degree of physical challenge, and geographical areas of interest. All expeditions emphasize wilderness travel and backpacking. Depending on the program, there are also a combination of other activities and skill instruction in sea kayaking, rock climbing, mountaineering, snow and ice climbing, canoeing, whitewater rafting, whitewater kayaking, mountain biking, sailing, snorkeling, and scuba diving. *Wilderness Adventure Expeditions:* Classic adventures, offering varying degrees of challenges. *Advanced Leadership Expeditions:* Designed for either returning

Wilderness Ventures participants or students with similar experience. Involve students more extensively in the planning, decision making, and execution of each activity. *Offshore Adventure Expeditions:* Trips provide opportunities for those who wish to seek a cultural experience in a foreign country in addition to enjoying the same type of outdoor activities offered in the other programs.

Program Dates: June–August

Duration of Program: 16 days—6 weeks

Cost: $2,390–$6,000

Eligibility: Students who have completed grades 7–12 (Wilderness Adventure Expeditions); students who have completed grade 10 through college (Advanced Leadership Expeditions); students finishing grades 8–12 (Offshore Adventure Expeditions)

Application Process: Application (available from website or brochure)

Application Deadline: June (many programs filled by January 30)

Contact:
Wilderness Ventures
P.O. Box 2768
Jackson Hole, WY 83001
Phone: (800) 533-2281
Fax: (307) 739-1934
wv@wildernessventures.com
www.wildernessventures.com

THE WILDS

Safari Camp

Program Location: The Wilds' 9,200-acre wildlife preserve near Cumberland, Ohio

Subject Areas: Wildlife conservation

Program Description: Camp participants develop an appreciation of the natural world as they live and work at North America's largest wildlife conservation facility, home to many species of African, North American, and Asian

mammals that are allowed to roam without the restrictions of pens or cages. Astronomy, boating, hiking, crafts, fishing, and team sports supplement field work and make for a well-rounded camp experience.

Program Dates: July–August

Duration of Program: 1 week

Cost: $325 for members; $360 for nonmembers

Financial Aid: None available

Eligibility: Grades 9–12

Application Process: Email or call for an application.

Application Deadline: May 1

Academic Credit: None available

Contact:
The Wilds
attn: Al Parker
14000 International Drive
Cumberland, OH 43732
Phone: (740) 638-2116
Fax: (740) 638-2287
sparker@thewilds.org
www.thewilds.org

WILLAMETTE UNIVERSITY

See Global Institute for Developing Entrepreneurs

WILLIAMS COLLEGE

See Putney Student Travel

WOODWARD SPORTS CAMP

Program Location: Central Pennsylvania

Subject Areas: Gymnastics and extreme sports (inline skating, skateboarding, BMX freestyle biking)

Program Description: One of the premiere gymnastics camps in the country providing fine facilities, staff, and training. The X-Sports camp provides an aggressive program with modern facilities and radical training ideas.

Program Dates: Fourteen 1-week sessions offered throughout June, July, and August.

Duration of Program: 2-week sessions are recommended; however, 1-week sessions are allowed.

Cost: Gymnastics: $615 per 1-week session, $565 for each additional session. Inline skating, skateboarding, and BMX freestyle biking: $725 per 1-week session, $675 for each additional session.

Eligibility: Both camps are coed for campers ages 7–18. No experience required.

Application Process: Contact Woodward Sports Camp for more info

Contact:
Woodward Sports Camp
P.O. Box 93
134 Sports Camp Drive
Woodward, PA 16882
Phone: (814) 349-5633
Fax: (814) 349-5643
office@woodwardcamp.com
www.woodwardcamp.com

WORLD HORIZONS INTERNATIONAL

Program Location: South Pacific, Costa Rica, Ecuador, Hawaii, Eastern Caribbean, Utah

Subject Areas: Community service, international travel, cross-cultural learning

Program Description: Cross-cultural exchange and community service program for American and Canadian high school students. Wide range of work activities to address the needs of the local communities, such as construction projects, programs to assist senior citizens, tutoring children, and literacy programs for

adults. Volunteers are also invited to pursue an individual internship of their own choosing, working in hospitals, schools, fisheries, bakeries, and local businesses. Weekend activities might include hiking, taking part in a traditional festival, visiting locals in their homes, or sailing to a remote island.

Program Dates: Late June through July

Duration of Program: 4–5 weeks

Cost: Approximately $3,850 to $4,300 (includes airfare from New York City or Miami)

Financial Aid: Scholarship aid available

Application Deadline: Rolling

Academic Credit: Community service credit may be available, depending on the student's school's requirements

World Horizons International

Contact:
World Horizons International
P.O. Box 662
Bethlehem, CT 06751
Phone: (800) 262-5874 or (203) 266-5874
Fax: (203) 266-5874
worhorin@wtco.net
www.world-horizons.com

WORLD LEARNING

Experiment in International Living (EIL)

Program Location: Over 30 programs in Africa, Australia, Asia, and the Americas

Subject Areas: Study abroad, homestays, travel abroad, community service, ecological/outdoor adventure, language study

Program Description: Participants engage in challenging cross-cultural experiences living as members of host families. Activities focus on community service, language study, travel, international ecological problems and strategies, or a combination of these themes. Past programs have included teaching in Kenya, studying Aboriginal culture in Australia, and peace studies in Belfast, Northern Ireland. Intensive language training programs available in France, Japan, Mexico, and Spain. Ecological/outdoor adventure programs explore various remote regions of the world, such as snorkeling in the Great Barrier Reef, examining the fragile ecology of the Galapagos Islands, hiking through tropical rain forests, or biking along the coast of Brittany.

Program Dates: June through August

Duration of Program: 3–5 weeks

Cost: Varies by program, $1,900–$4,975 (includes airfare and room and board)

Financial Aid: Available based on need on a first come, first served basis. To request a financial aid application, send a letter to the attention of the director of financial aid along with the preliminary application and deposit.

Eligibility: Students who have completed grades 9–12; previous language study (1–2 years of Spanish or French) required for certain programs

Application Process: Contact World Learning to obtain catalog and full application. Online information request form and downloadable preliminary application available through website. Supplementary materials required include medical form and international travel documentation/passport verification.

Application Deadline: May 1

Academic Credit: High school credit available

Contact:
The Experiment in International Living
Kipling Road
P.O. Box 676
Brattleboro, VT 05302-0676
Phone: (800) 345-2929 or (802) 258-3447
Fax: (802) 258-3428
eil@worldlearning.org
www.worldlearning.org/ip/summer.html

WRIGHT STATE UNIVERSITY

Wright State University Pre-College Summer Enrichment Programs

Program Location: Wright State University in Dayton, Ohio

Subject Areas: Art, aviation, creative writing, dance, leadership, mathematics, science, space, television, theater

Program Description: Offers students the opportunity to expand their educational and personal horizons by attending residential camps. Each program comprised of a variety of learning experiences, including lectures, hands-on projects, small group discussions, and field trips. Programs taught by university faculty, staff, and experts from the community.

Program Dates: Sessions from late June–early August

World Learning

Duration of Program: 1 or 2 weeks

Cost: $550–$1,200

Eligibility: Rising sophomores, juniors, and seniors

Application Process: High school nomination, application, transcript required.

Application Deadline: Rolling (limited enrollment)

Academic Credit: College credit available from Wright State University

Contact:
Wright State University
163 Millet
3640 Colonel Glenn Highway
Dayton, OH 45435
Phone: (937) 775-3135
Fax: (937) 775-4883
Brenda.Dewberry@wright.edu
www.wright.edu/academics/precollege

XAVIER UNIVERSITY OF LOUISIANA

BioStar;

ChemStar;

MathStar

Program Location: Xavier University in New Orleans, Louisiana

Subject Areas: Biology, chemistry, mathematics

Program Description: Minority students receive preparation in high school biology, chemistry, or algebra. On-campus housing is not available for any "Star" programs.

Program Dates: June (MathStar); June and July (BioStar); July and August (ChemStar)

Duration of Program: 2–3 weeks

Cost: $225 (MathStar); $300 (BioStar and ChemStar)

Eligibility: High school students who are underrepresented in the biomedical sciences, which include African American, American Indian, Mainland Puerto Rican, or Mexican American/Chicano

Application Process: Application, transcript

Application Deadline: Rolling

Average Number of Applicants: 150

Average Number of Participants: 60

SOAR 1

Program Location: Xavier University in New Orleans, Louisiana

Subject Areas: Dentistry, pharmacy, biology, chemistry, medicine

Program Description: Residential program for minorities. Stresses analytical and quantitative reasoning skills for students interested in medicine, denitstry, pharmacy, biology, or chemistry.

Program Dates: June–August

Duration of Program: 6 weeks

Cost: $1,700 (includes housing)

Eligibility: Rising seniors who are underrepresented in the sciences, which include African American, American Indian, Mainland Puerto Rican, or Mexican American/Chicano

Application Process: Application, transcript, standardized test scores

Application Deadline: Rolling

Average Number of Applicants: 500

Average Number of Participants: 80

Contact:
Xavier University
Premedical Office
1 Drexel Dr.
New Orleans, LA 70125
Phone: (504) 483-7437
Fax: (504) 485-7923
number1@xupremed.com
www.xupremed.com

YALE UNIVERSITY

Yale Daily News Summer Journalism Program

Program Location: Yale University in New Haven, Connecticut

Subject Areas: Media/journalism, writing, photography

Program Description: An intensive one-week program for Connecticut high school students interested in journalism. Students participate in workshops to learn the skills of reporting and photography, attend lectures by guest speakers from major national publications, work hands-on reporting a story, and ultimately produce a paper that will be distributed to Connecticut high schools. No housing available; students are expected to return home in the evening after each day's six-hour session.

Program Dates: Mid- to late August

Yale Summer Programs

Duration of Program: 1 week

Cost: No cost

Eligibility: All students who have completed their freshman, sophomore, or junior year in high school; graduating seniors not eligible. Preference given to rising juniors and seniors. Applicants must be residents of Connecticut or attend high school within the state. Writers: No formal experience necessary, though some familiarity with reporting is helpful.
Photographers: Must provide their own camera and have some experience using it.

Application Process: Clips and essay requested

Application Deadline: May 14; inquiries to YDN by April 15

Average Number of Applicants: 45

Average Number of Participants: 30

Contact:
Yale Daily News Summer Journalism Program
P.O. Box 202002

New Haven, CT 06520
Phone: (203) 432-2414
Fax: (203) 432-7425
ydn@yale.edu
www.yaledailynews.com

Yale Summer Programs

Program Location: Yale University in New Haven, Connecticut

Subject Areas: Liberal arts

Program Description: High school students take two college-level courses from a broad range of science, social science, and humanities courses in the summer session curriculum. Students are fully integrated into summer college academic life.

Program Dates: Sessions July–August

Duration of Program: 5 weeks

Cost: Tuition is $1,400 for three semester hours

Eligibility: Applicants must be at least 16 by July 1 and rising or graduating seniors

Application Process: Application, standardized test scores, 2 recommendations, transcript, personal statement

Application Deadline: June

Academic Credit: College credit available

Contact:
Yale University
P.O. Box 208355
New Haven, CT 06520-8355
Phone: (203) 432-2430
Fax: (203) 432-2434
summer.programs@yale.edu
www.yale.edu/summer

See also Junior Statesmen Foundation

YMCA OF METROPOLITAN HARTFORD

Camp Jewell YMCA Outdoor Center

Program Location: Connecticut

Subject Areas: Outdoor adventure

Program Description: Camp offers character-building experiences for boys and girls. Located on 500 acres. Opportunities for backpacking, bicycling, canoeing, caving, and rafting.

Program Dates: Sessions in June, July, and August

Duration of Program: 2 weeks

Cost: $960

Eligibility: Ages 8–16, coed

Application Deadline: Rolling

Application Process: Registration card, deposit of $100

Contact:
Camp Jewell YMCA Outdoor Center
6 Prock Hill Road
Colebrook, CT 06021
Phone: (888) 412-CAMP or (860) 379-2782
Fax: (860) 379-8715
campjewell@ghymca.org
www.ghymca.org/jewell.html

Note: For names and locations of hundreds of other YMCA camps for teens across the United States, visit www.ymca.net.

YOUTH FOR UNDERSTANDING INTERNATIONAL EXCHANGE

Summer Overseas

Program Location: More than 35 countries throughout the world

Subject Areas: Study abroad, adventures abroad, service abroad

Program Description: Educational, non-profit organization that prepares young people for their opportunities and responsibilities in a changing, interdependent world. Students choose a year, semester, or summer program in one of more than 35 countries worldwide. More than 200,000 young people from more than 50 nations in Asia, Europe, North and South America, Africa, and the Pacific have participated in these exchanges. Each exchange coordinated by a worldwide network of national Youth For Understanding organizations and supported by more than 3,500 trained and dedicated volunteers.

Program Dates: June through August

Duration of Program: 3–8 weeks

Cost: $3,175 and up

Financial Aid: Scholarships available

Eligibility: Grades 9–12 and minimum C grade average

Application Process: $75 nonrefundable fee

Application Deadline: May 1

Academic Credit: College credit available

Contact:
Youth For Understanding International Exchange
3501 Newark Street NW
Washington, DC 20016
Phone: (800) TEENAGE
Fax: (202) 895-1104
admissions@us.yfu.org
www.YouthForUnderstanding.org

Youth for Understanding

Part IV: Indexes

Index by Subject Area

This index groups the sponsoring organizations and their programs by subject area. See the Program Directory for the complete program listings.

Archeology

Center for American Archeology—Archeological Field School
Crow Canyon Archaeological Center—High School Field School; High School Excavation Program
Earthwatch Institute—Field Research Expedition Internships
University of Wisconsin, La Crosse—Archaeology Field Schools

Art, Visual

Appel Farm Arts and Music Center—Appel Farm's Summer Arts Camp
Art Institute of Boston at Lesley University—Pre-College Summer Program
Asheville School—Asheville School Summer Academic Adventures
Ballibay Camps, Inc.—Camp Ballibay for the Fine and Performing Arts
Bennington College—Bennington College July Program
Blue Lake Fine Arts Camp
Brenau University—Firespark Schools
Brookfield Craft Center—Summer Workshop Series
Buck's Rock Performing and Creative Arts Camp
California College of Arts and Crafts—CCAC Pre-College Program
California State Summer School for the Arts
Capitol Region Education Council and Wesleyan University—Center for Creative Youth
Carnegie Mellon University—Pre-College Programs
Colorado College—Summer Session for High School Students
Columbia College Chicago—High School Summer Institute
Columbia University—Columbia Summer Programs for High School Students
French Woods Festival of the Performing Arts
Gifted and Talented Development Center

Humanities Spring in Assisi

Idyllwild Arts Foundation—Idyllwild Arts Summer Program

Interlochen Center for the Arts—Interlochen Arts Camp

Johns Hopkins University—Pre-college Credit Program

Kingdom County Productions and Fledgling Films—Fledgling Films Summer Institute

Knowledge Exchange Institute—Precollege Artist Abroad Program

Maine Teen Camp

Miami University—Junior Scholars Program

Minnesota Institute for Talented Youth—Expand Your Mind

New York University—Tisch Summer High School Program

North Carolina School of the Arts—Summer Session

Otis College of Art and Design—Otis Summer of Art

Parsons School of Design—Summer Intensive Studies

Phillips Academy Andover—Phillips Academy Summer Session

Pratt Institute—Pre-College Summer Program

Rhode Island School of Design—Pre-College Program

Ringling School of Art and Design—PreCollege Perspective

Ringling School of Art and Design—Summer Teen Studios

Savannah College of Art and Design—Rising Star

Southampton College of Long Island University—Summer High School Workshops

Southwestern Academy—International Summer Programs

Spoleto Study Abroad

State University of New York, Oswego—Summer Art Institute

State University of New York, Purchase—Summer Visual Arts Institute

Summer Study Programs—Summer Enrichment and Summer Study at Penn State

Syracuse University—Summer College for High School Students

University of the Arts—PREP, Art Smart, and Media and Communications Workshops

University of Maryland, School of Architecture—Design Career Discover (Arch 150)

University of Mississippi—Summer College for High School Students

University of Pennsylvania—Precollege Program

University of Southern California—Summer Production Workshop

University of Wisconsin, Madison—Summer Art Classes

University of Wisconsin, Superior—Youthsummer

Wright State University—Pre-College Summer Enrichment Programs

Aviation/Aeronautics

Embry-Riddle Aeronautical University—ACES Academy (Aviation Career Education Specialization)

Embry-Riddle Aeronautical University—Aerospace Summer Camp

Embry-Riddle Aeronautical University—Engineering Academy

Embry-Riddle Aeronautical University—Flight Exploration
Embry-Riddle Aeronautical University—SunFlight Camps
Foothill College—Academically Talented Youth Program
Mississippi University for Women—Aero-Tech
Oregon Museum of Science and Industry—OMSI Summer Science Camps and Adventures
Randolph-Macon Academy—Randolph-Macon Academy Summer Programs
Saint Louis University—Parks Summer Academy
University of New Hampshire—Project SMART
University of North Dakota—International Aerospace Camp
U.S. Space Camp—Aviation Challenge and Advanced Space Academy
Wright State University—Pre-College Summer Enrichment Programs

Baseball/Softball

America's Baseball Camps
Appalachian State University—Summer Sports, Music, and Academic Camps
Cooperstown Baseball Camp
Cornell University Sports School—Summer Sports Camps
Higher Ground Softball Camps—Higher Ground Softball Camps
International Sports Camp
Kutsher's Sports Academy
Princeton University—Summer Sports Camps
Stanford University—Summer Sports Camps
University of Illinois—Fighting Illini Sports Camps
University of Notre Dame—Summer Sports Camps
University of San Diego—Summer Sports Camps
U.S. Sports Camps—Nike Sports Camps

Basketball

Appalachian State University— Summer Sports, Music, and Academic Camps
Bates College—Bates College Basketball Camp
Cornell University Sports School—Summer Sports Camps
Five-Star Basketball Camp
FUN-damental Basketball Camp, Inc.—Basketball Camp at Morrisville
Hargrave Military Academy—Summer School and Camp
International Sports Camp
Kutsher's Sports Academy
The Masters School—Panther Basketball Camp
Princeton University—Summer Sports Camps
76ers Basketball Camp

Southern Vermont College—Summer Sports Camps
Stanford University—Summer Sports Camps
University of Illinois—Fighting Illini Sports Camps
University of San Diego—Summer Sports Camps
University of Sports—Superstar Camp
University of Wisconsin, La Crosse—University of Wisconsin Athletic Camps
U.S. Sports Camps—Nike Sports Camps

Business

Alfred University—High School Academic Institutes
American Collegiate Adventures
American Management Association—Operation Enterprise
Brenau University—Firespark Schools
Columbia College, Leadership Institute—21st Century Leaders
Columbia College, Leadership Institute—Entrepreneurship Camp
Dickinson College—Pre-College Program
Envision EMI, Inc.—NexTech: The National Summit of Young Technology Leaders
Global Institute for Developing Entrepreneurs—IN2BIZ Entrepreneur Camp
Knowledge Exchange Institute—Precollege Business, Law and Diplomacy Program
Knowledge Exchange Institute—Precollege European Capitals Program
Media Workshops Foundation—The Media Workshops
Mississippi University for Women—Business Week
National Student Leadership Conference—Law & Advocacy; International Diplomacy;
    Medicine & Health Care
National Youth Leadership Forum—National Youth Leadership Forum on Medicine
Shad International—Shad Valley
Syracuse University—Summer College for High School Students
University of Notre Dame—Summer Experience
University of Pennsylvania—Precollege Program
Washington and Lee University—Summer Scholars

College Preparation

Academic Study Associates—ASA Pre-College Enrichment Program
Alfred University—High School Academic Institutes
American Collegiate Adventures
Bates College—Edmund S. Muskie Scholars Program
Baylor University—High School Summer Science Research Fellowship Program
Bennington College—Bennington College July Program
Birmingham-Southern College—Summer Scholar Program
Boston College—Boston College Experience

Boston University—Program in Mathematics for Young Scientists (PROMYS)
Brandeis University—Brandeis Summer Odyssey
Brenau University—Firespark Schools
Brown University—Focus Program
Brown University—Pre-College Program
Bryn Mawr College—Writing for College
Calvin College—Entrada Scholars Program
Cambridge College Programme LLC—Cambridge College Programme
Carnegie Mellon University—Pre-College Programs
Catholic University of America—College Courses for High School Students
College Visits
Colorado College—Summer Session for High School Students
Columbia College Chicago—High School Summer Institute
Columbia University—Columbia Summer Programs for High School Students
Cornell University—Cornell University Summer College
Cornell University—Honors Program for High School Sophomores
Davidson College—Davidson July Experience
Dickinson College—Pre-College Program
Duke University—Duke University PreCollege Program
Education Unlimited—College Admission Prep Camp; Prep Camp Excel
Education Unlimited—East Coast College Tour
Education Unlimited—Summer Focus at Berkeley
Evansville Association for the Blind—Summer College Program for Students with Disabilities
Foothill College—Academically Talented Youth Program
Georgetown University—Georgetown Summer College
Gould Academy—Young Scholars Program; College Preparatory Program
Harvard University—Harvard Summer School Secondary School Program
Hollins University—Precollege Program
Huntingdon College—Huntingdon College Summer Programs
Irish Centre for Talented Youth
Ithaca College—Summer College for High School Students
Johns Hopkins University—Pre-college Credit Program
Johns Hopkins University Center for Talented Youth—CTY Summer Programs; CAA Summer Programs
Junior Statesmen Foundation—Junior Statesmen Summer School
Knowledge Exchange Institute—Precollege African Safari Program
Knowledge Exchange Institute—Precollege Amazon Exploration Program
Knowledge Exchange Institute—Precollege Business, Law and Diplomacy Program
Knowledge Exchange Institute—Precollege European Capitals Program

Knowledge Exchange Institute—Precollege Research Abroad Program

Lebanon Valley College—Daniel Fox Youth Scholars Institute

Miami University—Junior Scholars Program

Musiker Discovery Programs—Summer Discovery

New Jersey Institute of Technology—Pre-college Academy in Technology and Science for High School Students

Northwestern University—National High School Institute

Oakland University—Oakland University Summer Mathematics Institute

Ohio State University—Ross Young Scholars Program

OxBridge Academic Programs—Cambridge Prep; Cambridge Tradition; Oxford Tradition; Académie de Paris

Pacific Lutheran University—Summer Scholars at PLU

Phillips Academy Andover—Phillips Academy Summer Session

Project PULL Academy—Project PULL Academy Leadership Challenge and College Preview

Purdue University—Seminar for Top Engineering Prospects (STEP)

Putney Student Travel—Excel at Williams and Amherst Colleges; Excel at Oxford/Tuscany and Madrid/Barcelona

Quest Scholars Program—Quest Scholars Programs at Stanford and Harvard

Randolph-Macon Academy—Randolph-Macon Academy Summer Programs

Rochester Institute of Technology—College and Careers

Saint Cloud State University, Ethnic Studies Program—Advanced Program in Technology and Science

Saint Cloud State University, Ethnic Studies Program—Scientific Discovery Program

Shad International—Shad Valley

Skidmore College—Pre-College Program in the Liberal Arts for High School Students at Skidmore

Southern Methodist University—College Experience

Southwest Texas State University—Honors Summer Math Camp

Spelman College—Early College Summer Program

Stanford University—Summer College for High School Students

Stanford University—Summer Discovery Institutes

Stanford University, Education Program for Gifted Youth—Summer Institute in Mathematics and Physics

Summer Institute for the Gifted—College Gifted Program

Summer Study Programs—Summer Enrichment and Summer Study at Penn State

Summer Study Programs—Summer Study at the University of Colorado at Boulder

Summer Study Programs—Summer Study in Paris at The American University of Paris

Syracuse University—Summer College for High School Students

Trinity University—A Trinity Summer

University of California, Los Angeles—College Level Summer Program

University of California, Santa Barbara—Early Start Program

University of California, Santa Barbara—UCSB Summer Research Mentorship Program

University of Colorado Cancer Center—Summer Cancer Research Fellowship

University of Connecticut—Mentor Connection

University of Delaware—Summer College for High School Juniors

University of Denver—Making of an Engineer

University of Florida—UF Student Science Training Program

University of Illinois, Chicago—Health Science Enrichment Program

University of Miami—Summer Scholar Programs

University of Mississippi—Summer College for High School Students

University of New Hampshire—Project SMART

University of Notre Dame—Summer Experience

University of Pennsylvania—Precollege Program

University of Wisconsin, Madison—Engineering Summer Program for High School Students

Western Washington University—SummerQuest

Xavier University of Louisiana—SOAR 1

Yale University—Yale Summer Programs

Community Service

AFS Intercultural Programs—Summer Community Service/Team Mission

American Jewish Society for Service—Summer Work Camps

Amigos de las Americas

Birmingham-Southern College—Student Leaders in Service

Birmingham-Southern College—Summer Scholar Program

Brandeis University—Genesis at Brandeis University

Breakthroughs Abroad, Inc.—High School Programs

Broadreach, Inc.—Broadreach Insights

Broadreach, Inc.—Broadreach Summer Adventures for Teenagers

Camp Courageous of Iowa—Volunteer Program

Comunicare—Study and Share

Costa Rican Language Academy (CRLA)

Deer Hill Expeditions

Earthwatch Institute—Field Research Expedition Internships

Friendship Ventures—Youth Leadership Program

Global Routes—High School Community Service Programs

Global Volunteers

Global Works International Programs—Summer Programs

Hugh O'Brian Youth Leadership (HOBY)—HOBY Leadership Seminars

Intern Exchange International

Involvement Volunteers Association—International Volunteering; Networked International Volunteering

La Société Française—International Volunteer Program

Landmark Volunteers—Summer Service Opportunity Programs

Latitudes International—Community Service Travel

Lawrence Academy—Global Leaders Workshop

LEAPNow—Summer Program in Central America; Summer Program in Australia

Legacy International—Global Youth Village

Longacre Expeditions

Longacre Leadership—Longacre Leadership Program

Nacel Open Door—Summer Programs

National FFA Organization—Agricultural Programs Overseas

Operation Crossroads Africa—Africa & Diaspora Programs

Peacework

The Pittsburgh Project

Project Sunshine—Project Sunshine Volunteer Programs

Scandinavian Seminar—Ambassadors for the Environment

School for Field Studies—Environmental Field Studies Abroad

Sidwell Friends School—SFS in Costa Rica

Student Conservation Association—High School Conservation Work Crew (CWC) Program

Student Safaris International—Zanzibar to the Serengeti; Queensland Explorer

Visions

Volunteers for Peace—VFP International Workcamps

Where There Be Dragons—Summer Programs

The Wilds—Safari Camp

World Horizons International

World Learning—Experiment in International Living (EIL)

Youth for Understanding International Exchange—Summer Overseas

Computer Graphics (Arts)

Art Institute of Boston at Lesley University—Pre-College Summer Program

Knowledge Exchange Institute—Precollege Artist Abroad Program

Otis College of Art and Design—Otis Summer of Art

Parsons School of Design—Summer Intensive Studies

Ringling School of Art and Design—PreCollege Perspective

Ringling School of Art and Design—Summer Teen Studios

Southampton College of Long Island University—Summer High School Workshops

State University of New York, Oswego—Summer Art Institute

University of the Arts—PREP, Art Smart, and Media and Communications Workshops

University of Iowa—Summer Journalism Workshops

Computers/Technology (Academics)

American Collegiate Adventures

American Committee for the Weizmann Institute of Science—Dr. Bessie F. Lawrence International Summer Science Institute

Asheville School—Asheville School Summer Academic Adventures

Brandeis University—Brandeis Summer Odyssey

Columbia University—Columbia Summer Programs for High School Students

Education Unlimited—Computer Camp by Education Unlimited

Envision EMI, Inc.—NexTech: The National Summit of Young Technology Leaders

Foothill College—Academically Talented Youth Program

Gifted and Talented Development Center

Gould Academy—Young Scholars Program; College Preparatory Program

Johns Hopkins University—Pre-college Credit Program

Johns Hopkins University Center for Talented Youth—CTY Summer Programs; CAA Summer Programs

Knowledge Exchange Institute—Precollege Artist Abroad Program

Louisiana State University—Honors High School Credit Program

Miami University—Junior Scholars Program

Milwaukee School of Engineering—Discover the Possibilities; Focus on the Possibilities

Mississippi University for Women—Aero-Tech

Mississippi University for Women—Business Week

Mount Holyoke College—SummerMath

National Computer Camps, Inc.—National Computer Camps, Inc.

New Jersey Institute of Technology—Pre-college Academy in Technology and Science for High School Students

Oklahoma City Community College—Applying the Skills of Technology in Science

Purdue School of Engineering and Technology, IUPUI—Minority Engineering Advancement Program (MEAP)

Randolph-Macon Academy—Randolph-Macon Academy Summer Programs

Rochester Institute of Technology—College and Careers

Saint Cloud State University, Ethnic Studies Program—Advanced Program in Technology and Science

Saint Cloud State University, Ethnic Studies Program—Scientific Discovery Program

Seton Hill College—Science Quest II

Shad International—Shad Valley

Southampton College of Long Island University—Summer High School Workshops

Stanford University—Summer College for High School Students

Summer Institute for the Gifted—College Gifted Program
Summer Study Programs—Summer Enrichment and Summer Study at Penn State
Syracuse University—Summer College for High School Students
Transylvania University—Academic Camp with Computer Emphasis
University of California, Los Angeles—College Level Summer Program
University of California, Los Angeles—High School Level Summer Program
University of Connecticut—Mentor Connection
University of Evansville—Options
University of Iowa—Summer Journalism Workshops
University of New Hampshire—Project SMART
University of Notre Dame—Introduction to Engineering
University of Notre Dame—Summer Experience
University of Vermont—Discovering Engineering, Mathematics, and Computer Science
University of Virginia —Summer Enrichment Program
Vanderbilt University—Program for Talented Youth
Western Washington University—Adventures in Science and Arts

Dance

Appel Farm Arts and Music Center—Appel Farm's Summer Arts Camp
BalletMet—Summer Workshop
Ballibay Camps, Inc.—Camp Ballibay for the Fine and Performing Arts
Blue Lake Fine Arts Camp
Buck's Rock Performing and Creative Arts Camp
Burklyn Ballet Theatre
California State Summer School for the Arts
Capitol Region Education Council and Wesleyan University—Center for Creative Youth
Carnegie Mellon University—Pre-College Programs
Colorado College—Summer Session for High School Students
Dwight-Englewood School—Dwight-Englewood Summer Programs
French Woods Festival of the Performing Arts
Goucher College—Goucher Summer Arts Institute
Huntingdon College—Huntingdon College Summer Programs
Idyllwild Arts Foundation—Idyllwild Arts Summer Program
Interlochen Center for the Arts—Interlochen Arts Camp
Kutsher's Sports Academy
Maine Teen Camp
The Masters School—Summer Theatre
Minnesota Institute for Talented Youth—Expand Your Mind
North Carolina School of the Arts—Summer Session
Northwestern University—National High School Institute

Princeton Ballet School—American Repertory Ballet's Summer Intensive
Stagedoor Enterprises—Stagedoor Manor Performing Arts Training Center
University of the Arts—Drama and Musical Theater
University of Wisconsin, Superior—Youthsummer
Wright State University—Pre-College Summer Enrichment Programs

Debate and Public Speaking

Bates College—Bates Forensic Institutes
Baylor University—Baylor University Debaters' Workshop
Catholic University of America—Capitol Classic Summer Debate Institute
Championship Debate Enterprises—Lincoln-Douglas and Extemp Institute; Policy
    Debate Institute
Dwight-Englewood School—Dwight-Englewood Summer Programs
Education Unlimited—Public Speaking Institute by Education Unlimited
Illinois State University—Summer High School Forensic Workshop
Junior Statesmen Foundation—Junior Statesmen Summer School
Michigan State University—Spartan Debate Institute (SDI)
Northwestern University—National High School Institute
Phillips Academy Andover—Phillips Academy Summer Session
Vanderbilt University—Program for Talented Youth
Wake Forest University—Summer Debate Workshop; Fast Track; Policy Project; Policy
    Analysis Seminar

Design

Art Institute of Boston at Lesley University—Pre-College Summer Program
Art Institute of Seattle—Studio 101
Auburn University —Design Camp
Carnegie Mellon University—Pre-College Programs
Catholic University of America—Experiences in Architecture
Gifted and Talented Development Center
LaGrange College—Visual Arts Workshop
Otis College of Art and Design—Otis Summer of Art
Parsons School of Design—Summer Intensive Studies
Pratt Institute—Pre-College Summer Program
Rhode Island School of Design—Pre-College Program
Ringling School of Art and Design—PreCollege Perspective
Ringling School of Art and Design—Summer Teen Studios
Savannah College of Art and Design—Rising Star
Syracuse University—Summer College for High School Students
University of the Arts—PREP, Art Smart, and Media and Communications Workshops

University of Maryland, School of Architecture—Design Career Discover (Arch 150)
Washington University in St. Louis—Architecture Discovery Program

Engineering

Alfred University—High School Academic Institutes
Carnegie Mellon University—Pre-College Programs
Catholic University of America—Eye on Engineering
Embry-Riddle Aeronautical University—Engineering Academy
Envision EMI, Inc.—NexTech: The National Summit of Young Technology Leaders
Milwaukee School of Engineering—Discover the Possibilities; Focus on the Possibilities
Purdue School of Engineering and Technology, IUPUI—Minority Engineering Advancement Program (MEAP)
Purdue University—Seminar for Top Engineering Prospects (STEP)
Rochester Institute of Technology—College and Careers
Saint Louis University—Parks Summer Academy
Shad International—Shad Valley
Smith College—Smith Summer Science Program
Southern Illinois University—Carbondale—Women's Introduction to Engineering
Summer Institute for the Gifted—College Gifted Program
Summer Study Programs—Summer Enrichment and Summer Study at Penn State
Syracuse University—Summer College for High School Students
Transylvania University—Academic Camp with Computer Emphasis
United States Coast Guard Academy—Minority Introduction to Engineering (MITE)
University of California, San Diego—UCSD Academic Connections & Summer Session
University of Cincinnati, College of Engineering—Inquisitive Women Summer Day Camp
University of Dayton—Women in Engineering Summer Camp
University of Denver—Making of an Engineer
University of Evansville—Options
University of Mississippi—Summer College for High School Students
University of New Hampshire—Project SMART
University of Notre Dame—Introduction to Engineering
University of Vermont—Discovering Engineering, Mathematics, and Computer Science
University of Wisconsin, Madison—Engineering Summer Program for High School Students

Fashion

Art Institute of Seattle—Studio 101
Otis College of Art and Design—Otis Summer of Art
Parsons School of Design—Summer Intensive Studies

Pratt Institute—Pre-College Summer Program

Syracuse University—Summer College for High School Students

Football

Appalachian State University— Summer Sports, Music, and Academic Camps

ASC Football Camps, Inc.—ASC Football Camps

Hargrave Military Academy—Summer School and Camp

Kicking Game

Princeton University—Summer Sports Camps

Stanford University—Summer Sports Camps

University of Illinois—Fighting Illini Sports Camps

University of Notre Dame—Summer Sports Camps

University of Wisconsin, La Crosse—University of Wisconsin Athletic Camps

U.S. Snowboard Training Center—USSTC Allstar Snowboard Camp

U.S. Sports Camps—Nike Sports Camps

Golf

Kutsher's Sports Academy

Offense Defense Golf Camp

Stanford University—Summer Sports Camps

University of Illinois—Fighting Illini Sports Camps

University of Notre Dame—Summer Sports Camps

U.S. Sports Camps—Nike Sports Camps

Westcoast Connection—Golf & Tennis Programs

Gymnastics

Chris Waller's Summer Gymnastics Jam

Kutsher's Sports Academy

Stanford University—Summer Sports Camps

University of Illinois—Fighting Illini Sports Camps

University of Wisconsin, La Crosse—University of Wisconsin Athletic Camps

U.S. Gymnastics Training Centers—U.S. Gymnastics Camp

Woodward Sports Camp

Hockey

Hockey Opportunity Camp

International Sports Camp

Kutsher's Sports Academy

Planet Hockey, Inc.—Planet Hockey Skills Camps; Planet Hockey Ranch

Princeton University—Summer Sports Camps

Stanford University—Summer Sports Camps
University of Notre Dame—Summer Sports Camps
U.S. Sports Camps—Nike Sports Camps

Horseback Riding

French Woods Festival of the Performing Arts
Kutsher's Sports Academy

International Homestay/Cultural Immersion

Academic Study Associates—Language Study Programs
Adventure Ireland
AFS Intercultural Programs—Summer Homestay; Summer Homestay Language Study; Summer Homestay Plus
Alliances Abroad—Summer Spanish Program for Youth in Spain; Summer French Programs for Youth in France; Culture and Adventure Program for Youth in Ireland
American Collegiate Adventures
American Farm School—Greek Summer
American Institute for Foreign Study—Pre-College Summer Study Abroad
American International Youth Student Exchange—American International Youth Student Exchange Program
Amerispan Unlimited—Madrid and Marbella Summer Camps; Spanish Language Program in Costa Rica
Amigos de las Americas
Baja California Language College
Barat Foundation—Barat Foundation Summer Program
Bordeaux Language School—Teenage Summer Program in Biarritz
Breakthroughs Abroad, Inc.—High School Programs
Broadreach, Inc.—Broadreach Insights
Broadreach, Inc.—Broadreach Summer Adventures for Teenagers
Center for Cross-Cultural Study—Summer in Seville
Center for Cultural Interchange—Discovery Abroad Programs
Choate Rosemary Hall —Study Abroad
Comunicare—Study and Share
Costa Rican Language Academy (CRLA)
EF International Language Schools
Georgia Hardy Tours, Inc.—Summer Study
Global Works International Programs—Summer Programs
Irish American Cultural Organization—Irish Way
Language Link—Intercultura; Spanish Language Institute; CLIC
Language Studies Abroad, Inc.—Language Studies Abroad
Language Study Abroad

Latitudes International—Community Service Travel

LEAPNow—Summer Program in Central America

Lingua Service Worldwide—Junior Classic and Junior Sports Program

Lingua Service Worldwide—Junior Course in Salamanca

Lingua Service Worldwide—Summer Language Adventure

Nacel Open Door—Summer Programs

National FFA Organization—Agricultural Programs Overseas

National Registration Center for Study Abroad—Summer Language Programs

Peacework

Rassias Programs

Sidwell Friends School—SFS in Costa Rica

Sons of Norway—Camp Norway

Tennis: Europe and More

Tufts University European Center—Tufts Summit

Visions

Where There Be Dragons—Summer Programs

Wilderness Ventures—Wilderness Adventure Expeditions; Advanced Leadership Expeditions; Offshore Adventure Expeditions

World Horizons International

World Learning—Experiment in International Living (EIL)

Youth for Understanding International Exchange—Summer Overseas

Lacrosse

Cornell University Sports School—Summer Sports Camps

Kutsher's Sports Academy

Princeton University—Summer Sports Camps

Stanford University—Summer Sports Camps

University of Notre Dame—Summer Sports Camps

U.S. Sports Camps—Nike Sports Camps

Language

Academic Study Associates—Language Study Programs

AFS Intercultural Programs—Summer Homestay Language Study

Alliances Abroad—Summer Spanish Program for Youth in Spain; Summer French Programs for Youth in France

American Collegiate Adventures

American International Youth Student Exchange—American International Youth Student Exchange Program

Amerispan Unlimited—Madrid and Marbella Summer Camps; Spanish Language Program in Costa Rica

Asheville School—Asheville School Summer Academic Adventures

Avatar Education Ltd.—Buckswood ARC Summer Programs

Baja California Language College

Beloit College—Center for Language Studies

Bordeaux Language School—Teenage Summer Program in Biarritz

Boston College—Boston College Experience

Brown University—Pre-College Program

Center for Cross-Cultural Study—Summer in Seville

Center for Cultural Interchange—Discovery Abroad Programs

Ceran Lingua—Ceran Junior

Choate Rosemary Hall—English Language Institute

Colorado College—Summer Session for High School Students

Comunicare—Study and Share

Concordia College—Concordia Language Villages

Costa Rican Language Academy (CRLA)

Dickinson College—Pre-College Program

Dwight-Englewood School—Dwight-Englewood Summer Programs

EF International Language Schools

Foothill College—Academically Talented Youth Program

Georgetown University—Georgetown Summer College

Georgia Hardy Tours, Inc.—Summer Study

Gould Academy—Young Scholars Program; College Preparatory Program

Hawaii Preparatory Academy—Hawaii Preparatory Academy Summer Session

Humanities Spring in Assisi

Hun School of Princeton—Hun School Summer Programs

Johns Hopkins University—Pre-college Credit Program

Knowledge Exchange Institute—Precollege African Safari Program

Knowledge Exchange Institute—Precollege Amazon Exploration Program

Knowledge Exchange Institute—Precollege Artist Abroad Program

Knowledge Exchange Institute—Precollege Business, Law and Diplomacy Program

Language Link—Intercultura; Spanish Language Institute; CLIC

Language Studies Abroad, Inc.—Language Studies Abroad

Language Study Abroad

Lawrence Academy—International English Institute

LEAPNow—Summer Program in Central America

Lingua Service Worldwide—Junior Classic and Junior Sports Program

Lingua Service Worldwide—Junior Course in Salamanca

Lingua Service Worldwide—Summer Language Adventure

The Masters School —Summer ESL

Nacel Open Door—Summer Programs

National Registration Center for Study Abroad—Summer Language Programs

Northwestern University, Center for Talent Development—Apogee, Spectrum, Equinox, Leapfrog

Oak Ridge Military Academy—Academic Summer School

OxBridge Academic Programs—Cambridge Prep; Cambridge Tradition; Oxford Tradition; Académie de Paris

Phillips Academy Andover—Phillips Academy Summer Session

Randolph-Macon Academy—Randolph-Macon Academy Summer Programs

Rassias Programs

Sons of Norway—Camp Norway

Southwestern Academy—International Summer Programs

Southwestern Academy—Southwestern Adventures

Summer Institute for the Gifted—College Gifted Program

Summer Study Programs—Summer Enrichment and Summer Study at Penn State

Summer Study Programs—Summer Study at the University of Colorado at Boulder

Summer Study Programs—Summer Study in Paris at The American University of Paris

Tufts University European Center—Tufts Summit

University of Dallas Study Abroad—Shakespeare in Italy; Latin in Rome; Thomas More in England; Winston Churchill in England

University of Southern Mississippi, The Frances A. Karnes Center for Gifted Studies—Summer Program for Academically Talented Youth

Vanderbilt University—Program for Talented Youth

World Learning—Experiment in International Living (EIL)

Leadership

Abilene Christian University—Kadesh Life Camp

Adventure Pursuits—Adventure Pursuits Expeditions & Camps

Adventure Treks, Inc.—Adventure Treks

Alfred University—High School Academic Institutes

American Management Association—Operation Enterprise

American Youth Foundation—International Leadership Conference

Amigos de las Americas

Auburn University—World Affairs Youth Seminar

Bark Lake Leadership Center—Leadership Through Recreation/Music

Bates College—Bates Forensic Institutes

Baylor University—Baylor University Debaters' Workshop

Birmingham-Southern College—Student Leaders in Service

Brandeis University—Genesis at Brandeis University

Bridgewater College—High School Leadership Academy

Broadreach, Inc.—Broadreach Insights

Broadreach, Inc.—Broadreach Summer Adventures for Teenagers

Camp Courageous of Iowa—Volunteer Program

Catholic University of America—Capitol Classic Summer Debate Institute

Championship Debate Enterprises—Lincoln-Douglas and Extemp Institute; Policy Debate Institute

Choate Rosemary Hall—John F. Kennedy Institute in Government

Columbia College, Leadership Institute—21st Century Leaders

Columbia College, Leadership Institute—Entrepreneurship Camp

Columbia University—Columbia Summer Programs for High School Students

Congressional Youth Leadership Council—Global Young Leaders Conference

Congressional Youth Leadership Council—National Young Leaders Conference

Dwight-Englewood School—Dwight-Englewood Summer Programs

Education Unlimited—Public Speaking Institute by Education Unlimited

Envision EMI, Inc.—NexTech: The National Summit of Young Technology Leaders

Friendship Ventures—Youth Leadership Program

Georgetown University—Georgetown Summer College

Global Institute for Developing Entrepreneurs—IN2BIZ Entrepreneur Camp

Hargrave Military Academy—Summer School and Camp

Hollins University—Leadership Enrichment Program

Hugh O'Brian Youth Leadership (HOBY)—HOBY Leadership Seminars

Illinois State University—Summer High School Forensic Workshop

Indiana University, Bloomington—International Studies Summer Institute for High School Students

The Island Laboratory

JCC Maccabi Xperience Israel Programs—Israel Summer Programs

Junior Statesmen Foundation—Junior Statesmen Summer School

Knowledge Exchange Institute—Precollege Business, Law and Diplomacy Program

Knowledge Exchange Institute—Precollege European Capitals Program

Lawrence Academy—Global Leaders Workshop

Legacy International—Global Youth Village

Longacre Expeditions

Longacre Leadership—Longacre Leadership Program

Marine Military Academy—Summer Military Training Camp

Media Workshops Foundation—The Media Workshops

Michigan State University—Spartan Debate Institute (SDI)

Mississippi University for Women—Business Week

National Outdoor Leadership School—Wilderness Leadership Courses

National Student Leadership Conference—Law & Advocacy; International Diplomacy; Medicine & Health Care

National Youth Leadership Forum—National Youth Leadership Forum on Medicine

Northwestern University—National High School Institute

Oak Ridge Military Academy—Leadership Adventure Camp

Odyssey Expeditions—Tropical Marine Biology Voyages

Orme School—Orme Summer Camp

Outward Bound USA

Phillips Academy Andover—Phillips Academy Summer Session

Project PULL Academy—Project PULL Academy Leadership Challenge and College Preview

Quest Scholars Program—Quest Scholars Programs at Stanford and Harvard

Scandinavian Seminar—Ambassadors for the Environment

School for Field Studies—Environmental Field Studies Abroad

Shad International—Shad Valley

Sidwell Friends School—Women's Leadership

Sierra Adventure Camps

Tufts University European Center—Tufts Summit

United States Coast Guard Academy—Academy Introduction Mission (AIM)

United States Coast Guard Academy—Minority Introduction to Engineering (MITE)

University of Dallas Study Abroad—Shakespeare in Italy; Latin in Rome; Thomas More in England; Winston Churchill in England

University of Mississippi—Summer College for High School Students

University of Notre Dame—Summer Experience

University of Pennsylvania—Precollege Program

University of Southern Mississippi, The Frances A. Karnes Center for Gifted Studies—Leadership Studies Program

University of Wisconsin, Madison—Pre-college Program in Environmental and Native American Studies

Vanderbilt University—Program for Talented Youth

Wake Forest University—Summer Debate Workshop; Fast Track; Policy Project; Policy Analysis Seminar

Washington Workshops Foundation—Washington Workshops Seminars

Wells College—Student Conference on Leadership and Social Responsibility

Western Washington University—Outdoor Challenge Institute

Wilderness Ventures—Wilderness Adventure Expeditions; Advanced Leadership Expeditions; Offshore Adventure Expeditions

World Learning—Experiment in International Living (EIL)

Wright State University—Pre-College Summer Enrichment Programs

Liberal Arts

Academic Study Associates—ASA Pre-College Enrichment Program

Adelphi University—Academic Success Program

American Collegiate Adventures

Appalachian State University—Summer Sports and Academic Camps
Asheville School—Asheville School Summer Academic Adventures
Barnard College—Summer in New York: A Pre-College Program
Bennington College—Bennington College July Program
Birmingham-Southern College—Summer Scholar Program
Boston College—Boston College Experience
Brandeis University—Genesis at Brandeis University
Brown University—Focus Program
Brown University—Pre-College Program
Calvin College—Entrada Scholars Program
Carnegie Mellon University—Pre-College Programs
Catholic University of America—College Courses for High School Students
Choate Rosemary Hall—Choate Rosemary Hall Summer Session
Colorado College—Summer Session for High School Students
Columbia University—Columbia Summer Programs for High School Students
Cornell University—Cornell University Summer College
Cornell University—Honors Program for High School Sophomores
Davidson College—Davidson July Experience
Duke University—Duke University PreCollege Program
Dwight-Englewood School—Dwight-Englewood Summer Programs
Education Unlimited—Summer Focus at Berkeley
Foothill College—Academically Talented Youth Program
Georgetown University—Georgetown Summer College
Georgia Hardy Tours, Inc.—Summer Study
Gifted and Talented Development Center
Hargrave Military Academy—Summer School and Camp
Harvard University—Harvard Summer School Secondary School Program
Hawaii Preparatory Academy—Hawaii Preparatory Academy Summer Session
Hollins University—Precollege Program
Humanities Spring in Assisi
Hun School of Princeton—Hun School Summer Programs
Huntingdon College—Huntingdon College Summer Programs
Indiana State University—Summer Honors Program
Irish Centre for Talented Youth
Ithaca College—Summer College for High School Students
Johns Hopkins University—Pre-college Credit Program
Johns Hopkins University Center for Talented Youth—CTY Summer Programs; CAA
    Summer Programs
Juniata College—Voyages: Summer Camp for Gifted Students
Lebanon Valley College—Daniel Fox Youth Scholars Institute

Leysin American School in Switzerland—Summer in Switzerland

Maine Teen Camp

Miami University—Junior Scholars Program

Minnesota Institute for Talented Youth—Expand Your Mind

Musiker Discovery Programs—Summer Discovery

Northwestern University—National High School Institute

Northwestern University, Center for Talent Development—Apogee, Spectrum, Equinox, Leapfrog

Oak Ridge Military Academy—Academic Summer School

OxBridge Academic Programs—Cambridge Prep; Cambridge Tradition; Oxford Tradition; Académie de Paris

Pacific Lutheran University—Summer Scholars at PLU

Phillips Academy Andover—Phillips Academy Summer Session

Putney School—Putney School Summer Programs

Putney Student Travel—Excel at Williams and Amherst Colleges; Excel at Oxford/Tuscany and Madrid/Barcelona

Randolph-Macon Academy—Randolph-Macon Academy Summer Programs

Saint Paul Academy and Summit School—Summer Programs

Sidwell Friends School—Sidwell Friends Summer Programs

Skidmore College—Pre-College Program in the Liberal Arts for High School Students at Skidmore

Southern Methodist University—College Experience

Southwestern Academy—Southwestern Adventures

Stanford University—Summer College for High School Students

Stanford University—Summer Discovery Institutes

Summer Institute for the Gifted—College Gifted Program

Summer Study Programs—Summer Enrichment and Summer Study at Penn State

Summer Study Programs—Summer Study at the University of Colorado at Boulder

Summer Study Programs—Summer Study in Paris at The American University of Paris

Syracuse University—Summer College for High School Students

Trinity University—A Trinity Summer

University of California, Los Angeles—College Level Summer Program

University of California, Los Angeles—High School Level Summer Program

University of California, Santa Barbara—Early Start Program

University of Connecticut—Mentor Connection

University of Dallas Study Abroad—Shakespeare in Italy; Latin in Rome; Thomas More in England; Winston Churchill in England

University of Delaware—Summer College for High School Juniors

University of Mississippi—Summer College for High School Students

University of Notre Dame—Summer Experience

University of Pennsylvania—Precollege Program
University of Southern Mississippi, The Frances A. Karnes Center for Gifted Studies—
    Summer Program for Academically Talented Youth
University of Virginia —Summer Enrichment Program
University of Washington—Courses for High School Students
University of Wisconsin, Superior—Youthsummer
Vanderbilt University—Program for Talented Youth
Washington and Lee University—Summer Scholars
Western Washington University—Adventures in Science and Arts
Western Washington University—SummerQuest
Wright State University—Pre-College Summer Enrichment Programs
Yale University—Yale Summer Programs
Youth for Understanding International Exchange—Summer Overseas

Marine Science

ActionQuest—ActionQuest Programs
Broadreach, Inc.—Broadreach Summer Adventures for Teenagers
Christchurch School—Summer Programs on the River
Dauphin Island Sea Lab—Discovery Hall Summer High School Program
Earthwatch Institute—Field Research Expedition Internships
ECHO International Educational Expeditions—Australian Biological Adventures
Hawaii Preparatory Academy—Hawaii Preparatory Academy Summer Session
Hobart and William Smith Colleges—Environmental Studies Summer Youth Institute
Knowledge Exchange Institute—Precollege Amazon Exploration Program
Occidental College—High School Oceanology Program
Ocean Educations Ltd.—Marine and Environmental Science Program
Oceanic Society—Bahamas Dolphin Project for High School Students
Oceanic Society—Belize Student Expedition
Odyssey Expeditions—Tropical Marine Biology Voyages
Oregon Museum of Science and Industry—OMSI Summer Science Camps and
    Adventures
Sea Education Association—Science at Sea; Oceanography of the Gulf of Maine
Seacamp Association, Inc.—Seacamp
SeaWorld Adventure Parks—SeaWorld/Busch Gardens Adventure Camps
Southampton College of Long Island University—Summer High School Workshops
University of California, San Diego—UCSD Academic Connections & Summer Session
University of Miami—Summer Scholar Programs
University of New Hampshire—Project SMART

Mathematics

Academic Enrichment Institute—Summer Academic Enrichment Institute

American Collegiate Adventures

American Committee for the Weizmann Institute of Science—Dr. Bessie F. Lawrence International Summer Science Institute

Asheville School—Asheville School Summer Academic Adventures

Boston College—Boston College Experience

Boston University—Program in Mathematics for Young Scientists (PROMYS)

Brandeis University—Brandeis Summer Odyssey

Brown University—Pre-College Program

Colorado College—Summer Session for High School Students

Columbia University—Columbia Summer Programs for High School Students

Cornell University—Cornell University Summer College

Dwight-Englewood School—Dwight-Englewood Summer Programs

Education Unlimited—Summer Focus at Berkeley

Foothill College—Academically Talented Youth Program

Georgetown University—Georgetown Summer College

Gould Academy—Young Scholars Program; College Preparatory Program

Hampshire College—Hampshire College Summer Studies in Mathematics

Johns Hopkins University—Pre-college Credit Program

Johns Hopkins University Center for Talented Youth—CTY Summer Programs; CAA Summer Programs

Juniata College—Voyages: Summer Camp for Gifted Students

Lebanon Valley College—Daniel Fox Youth Scholars Institute

Louisiana State University—Honors High School Credit Program

Mathematics Foundation of America—Canada/USA Mathcamp

Miami University—Junior Scholars Program

Minnesota Institute for Talented Youth—Expand Your Mind

Mount Holyoke College—SummerMath

New Jersey Institute of Technology—Pre-college Academy in Technology and Science for High School Students

Northwestern University, Center for Talent Development—Apogee, Spectrum, Equinox, Leapfrog

Oak Ridge Military Academy—Academic Summer School

Oakland University—Oakland University Summer Mathematics Institute

Ohio State University—Ross Young Scholars Program

Pacific Lutheran University—Summer Scholars at PLU

Phillips Academy Andover—Phillips Academy Summer Session

Purdue School of Engineering and Technology, IUPUI—Minority Engineering Advancement Program (MEAP)

Putney School—Putney School Summer Programs

Randolph-Macon Academy—Randolph-Macon Academy Summer Programs

Rutgers University—Young Scholars Program in Discrete Mathematics

Saint Cloud State University, Ethnic Studies Program—Scientific Discovery Program

Sidwell Friends School—Sidwell Friends Summer Programs

Skidmore College—Pre-College Program in the Liberal Arts for High School Students at Skidmore

Southern Methodist University—College Experience

Southwest Texas State University—Honors Summer Math Camp

Spelman College—Early College Summer Program

Stanford University—Summer College for High School Students

Stanford University, Education Program for Gifted Youth—Summer Institute in Mathematics and Physics

Summer Institute for the Gifted—College Gifted Program

Summer Study Programs—Summer Enrichment and Summer Study at Penn State

Summer Study Programs—Summer Study at the University of Colorado at Boulder

Summer Study Programs—Summer Study in Paris at The American University of Paris

Transylvania University—Academic Camp with Computer Emphasis

University of California, Los Angeles—College Level Summer Program

University of California, Los Angeles—High School Level Summer Program

University of California, Santa Barbara—Early Start Program

University of Connecticut—Mentor Connection

University of Delaware—Summer College for High School Juniors

University of Delaware—Upward Bound Math and Science Center

University of Michigan—Michigan Math and Science Scholars

University of Nebraska, Lincoln—All Girls/All Math

University of New Hampshire—Project SMART

University of Pennsylvania—Precollege Program

University of the South—Bridge Program in Math and Science

University of Southern Mississippi, The Frances A. Karnes Center for Gifted Studies—Summer Program for Academically Talented Youth

University of Vermont—Discovering Engineering, Mathematics, and Computer Science

Vanderbilt University—Program for Talented Youth

Wright State University—Pre-College Summer Enrichment Programs

Xavier University of Louisiana—MathStar

Media

American University—Discover the World of Communication

Appel Farm Arts and Music Center—Appel Farm's Summer Arts Camp

Art Institute of Seattle—Studio 101

Ballibay Camps, Inc.—Camp Ballibay for the Fine and Performing Arts
Buck's Rock Performing and Creative Arts Camp
California Chicano News Media Association—San Jose Urban Journalism Workshop for Minorities
California State Summer School for the Arts
Capitol Region Education Council and Wesleyan University—Center for Creative Youth
Catholic University of America—Media and Video Production Workshop
Columbia College Chicago—High School Summer Institute
Hollins University—Precollege Program
Idyllwild Arts Foundation—Idyllwild Arts Summer Program
Indiana University, Bloomington—High School Journalism Publications Workshops
Ithaca College—Summer College for High School Students
Kingdom County Productions and Fledgling Films—Fledgling Films Summer Institute
Maine Teen Camp
Media Workshops Foundation—The Media Workshops
New York Film Academy—New York Film Academy Summer Program
North Carolina School of the Arts—Summer Session
Northwestern University—National High School Institute
University of the Arts—PREP, Art Smart, and Media and Communications Workshops
University of California, San Diego—UCSD Academic Connections & Summer Session
University of Iowa—Summer Journalism Workshops
University of Miami—Summer Scholar Programs
University of Mississippi—Summer College for High School Students
University of Southern California—Summer Production Workshop
University of Virginia—Summer Enrichment Program
Yale University—Yale Daily News Summer Journalism Program

Music

Appalachian State University—Summer Sports, Music, and Academic Camps
Appel Farm Arts and Music Center—Appel Farm's Summer Arts Camp
Apple Hill Center for Chamber Music—Apple Hill Summer School and Festival
Aspen Music School—Aspen Music Festival and School
Auburn University—Summer Honor Band Camps
Ballibay Camps, Inc.—Camp Ballibay for the Fine and Performing Arts
Blue Lake Fine Arts Camp
Brevard Music Center—Young Artists Division
Britt Festivals—The Britt Institute
Buck's Rock Performing and Creative Arts Camp
California State Summer School for the Arts
Camp Encore/Coda—Upper Camp

Capitol Region Education Council and Wesleyan University—Center for Creative Youth
Carnegie Mellon University—Pre-College Programs
Catholic University of America—Chamber Music Program
Colorado College—Summer Session for High School Students
Drew University—Drew Summer Music
Dwight-Englewood School—Dwight-Englewood Summer Programs
Eastern Music Festival
Eastern U.S. Music Camp, Inc.—Eastern U.S. Music Camp
French Woods Festival of the Performing Arts
Friends Music Camp
Goucher College—Goucher Summer Arts Institute
Huntingdon College—Huntingdon College Summer Programs
Idyllwild Arts Foundation—Idyllwild Arts Summer Program
Indiana University, Bloomington—College Audition Preparation (CAP); Summer Piano
    Academy; Summer Recorder Academy; Summer String Academy
Indiana University, Bloomington—Indiana University Summer Music Clinic
Interlochen Center for the Arts—Interlochen Arts Camp
Johns Hopkins University—Pre-college Credit Program
Kincardine Summer Music Festival—KSMF Jazz Camp; KSMF Chamber Music Camp;
    KSMF Festival Week Music Camp
Kinhaven Music School
Lebanon Valley College—Summer Music Camp
Maine Teen Camp
The Masters School—Summer Theatre
Minnesota Institute for Talented Youth—Expand Your Mind
New York University—Tisch Summer High School Program
North Carolina School of the Arts—Summer Session
Northwestern University—National High School Institute
Power Chord Academy
Saint Olaf College—Saint Olaf Summer Music Camp
Seattle Youth Symphony Orchestra—Marrowstone Music Festival
Southwestern Academy—International Summer Programs
Spoleto Study Abroad
Stagedoor Enterprises—Stagedoor Manor Performing Arts Training Center
Stanford Jazz Workshop—Jazz Camp; Jazz Residency
Summer Sonatina International Piano Camp
Summer Study Programs—Summer Enrichment and Summer Study at Penn State
University of the Arts—Drama and Musical Theater
University of the Arts—Summer Institute of Jazz
University of Iowa—Iowa All-State Music Camp

University of Maine—Maine Summer Youth Music Senior Camp
University of Mississippi—Summer College for High School Students
University of New Hampshire—Summer Youth Music School (SYMS)
University of Wisconsin, Madison—Summer Music Clinic
Walden School—Walden School Summer Music School, Festival, and Camp
The Washington Opera—Opera Institute for Young Singers

Outdoor Adventure

ActionQuest—ActionQuest Programs
Adventure Pursuits—Adventure Pursuits Expeditions & Camps
Adventure Treks, Inc.—Adventure Treks
Adventures Cross-Country
AFS Intercultural Programs—Summer Homestay Plus
Alpine Adventures, Inc.—Alpine Adventures
America's Adventure/Venture Europe
Barefoot International—Barefoot International & Fly High Ski School
Bark Lake Leadership Center—Leadership Through Recreation/Music
Breakthroughs Abroad, Inc.—High School Programs
Broadreach, Inc.—Broadreach Insights
Broadreach, Inc.—Broadreach Summer Adventures for Teenagers
Brush Ranch Camps
Cottonwood Gulch Foundation—Prairie Trek Group I; Prairie Trek Group II; Turquoise Trail
Deep Woods Camp for Boys
Deer Hill Expeditions
ECHO International Educational Expeditions—Australian Biological Adventures
Greenbrier River Outdoor Adventures
Hargrave Military Academy—Summer School and Camp
Horizon Adventures, Inc.—Horizon Adventures
Interlocken—Crossroads Adventure Travel
International Bicycle Fund—Bicycle Africa Tours; Sbuhbi Lithlal Ti Swatixwtuhd
The Island Laboratory
Longacre Expeditions
Longacre Leadership—Longacre Leadership Program
Maine Teen Camp
Marine Military Academy—Summer Military Training Camp
Moondance Adventures
Mount Hood Snowboard Camp—MHSC Summer Sessions
Musiker Discovery Programs—Musiker Tours
National FFA Organization—Agricultural Programs Overseas

National Outdoor Leadership School—Wilderness Leadership Courses
Northwaters—Northwaters Wilderness Programs
Oak Ridge Military Academy—Leadership Adventure Camp
Odyssey Expeditions—Tropical Marine Biology Voyages
Orme School—Orme Summer Camp
Outpost Wilderness Adventure—Outpost Wilderness Adventures
Outward Bound USA
Planet Hockey, Inc.—Planet Hockey Ranch
Rainforest Exploration Associaton—City Lights; Starry Nights
The Road Less Traveled
Sail Caribbean
Sea Education Association—Science at Sea; Oceanography of the Gulf of Maine
Seacamp Association, Inc.—Seacamp
SeaWorld Adventure Parks—SeaWorld/Busch Gardens Adventure Camps
Sidwell Friends School—Deep Creek Adventures; SFS Alaskan Adventures
Sierra Adventure Camps
Student Conservation Association—High School Conservation Work Crew (CWC) Program
Student Hosteling Program—Summer Biking Programs
Student Safaris International—Zanzibar to the Serengeti; Queensland Explorer
Tamarack Camps
Trailmark Outdoor Adventures
United States Coast Guard Academy—Academy Introduction Mission (AIM)
United States Coast Guard Academy—Minority Introduction to Engineering (MITE)
University of Rhode Island—W. Alton Jones Teen Expeditions
U.S. Snowboard Training Center—USSTC Allstar Snowboard Camp
U.S. Space Camp—Aviation Challenge and Advanced Space Academy
U.S. Sports Camps—Nike Sports Camps
Visions
Weissman Teen Tours, Inc.
Westcoast Connection—Active Teen Tours
Westcoast Connection—European Programs
Westcoast Connection—Golf & Tennis Programs
Westcoast Connection—Israel Experience
Westcoast Connection—On Tour
Westcoast Connection—Outdoor Adventure Programs
Westcoast Connection—Ski & Snowboard Sensation
Western Washington University—Outdoor Challenge Institute
Where There Be Dragons—Summer Programs
Wilderness Experience Unlimited—Explorer Group; Trailblazers

Wilderness Ventures—Wilderness Adventure Expeditions; Advanced Leadership Expeditions; Offshore Adventure Expeditions

The Wilds—Safari Camp

Woodward Sports Camp

World Learning—Experiment in International Living (EIL)

YMCA of Metropolitan Hartford—Camp Jewell YMCA Outdoor Center

Photography

Art Institute of Boston at Lesley University—Pre-College Summer Program

Knowledge Exchange Institute—Precollege Artist Abroad Program

LaGrange College—Visual Arts Workshop

Parsons School of Design—Summer Intensive Studies

Pratt Institute—Pre-College Summer Program

Ringling School of Art and Design—Summer Teen Studios

Southampton College of Long Island University—Summer High School Workshops

Spoleto Study Abroad

State University of New York, Oswego—Summer Art Institute

Summer Study Programs—Summer Enrichment and Summer Study at Penn State

University of the Arts—PREP, Art Smart, and Media and Communications Workshops

University of Iowa—Summer Journalism Workshops

University of Wisconsin, Superior—Youthsummer

Politics/International Relations

American Youth Foundation—International Leadership Conference

Auburn University—World Affairs Youth Seminar

Choate Rosemary Hall—John F. Kennedy Institute in Government

Columbia College, Leadership Institute—21st Century Leaders

Columbia University—Columbia Summer Programs for High School Students

Congressional Youth Leadership Council—Global Young Leaders Conference

Congressional Youth Leadership Council—National Young Leaders Conference

Georgetown University—Georgetown Summer College

Hugh O'Brian Youth Leadership (HOBY)—HOBY Leadership Seminars

Indiana University, Bloomington—International Studies Summer Institute for High School Students

Junior Statesmen Foundation—Junior Statesmen Summer School

Knowledge Exchange Institute—Precollege Business, Law and Diplomacy Program

Knowledge Exchange Institute—Precollege European Capitals Program

Lawrence Academy—Global Leaders Workshop

Legacy International—Global Youth Village

National Student Leadership Conference—Law & Advocacy; International Diplomacy; Medicine & Health Care

Tufts University European Center—Tufts Summit

Washington Workshops Foundation—Washington Workshops Seminars

Rowing/Crew

All-American Rowing Camp, LLC—High School Coed Rowing Camp

Christchurch School—Summer Programs on the River

Stanford University—Summer Sports Camps

United States Naval Academy—Navy Crew Camp for Boys

United States Naval Academy—Navy Rowing Camp for Girls

U.S. Sports Camps—Nike Sports Camps

Science

Alfred University—High School Academic Institutes

American Collegiate Adventures

American Committee for the Weizmann Institute of Science—Dr. Bessie F. Lawrence International Summer Science Institute

Asheville School—Asheville School Summer Academic Adventures

Baylor University—High School Summer Science Research Fellowship Program

Boston College—Boston College Experience

Brandeis University—Brandeis Summer Odyssey

Brenau University—Firespark Schools

Brown University—Pre-College Program

Carnegie Mellon University—Pre-College Programs

Choate Rosemary Hall —Choate Rosemary Hall Summer Session

Colorado College—Summer Session for High School Students

Columbia University—Columbia Summer Programs for High School Students

Columbia University, Biosphere 2—Exploring Earth, Life & the Summer Sky

Cornell University—Cornell University Summer College

Dauphin Island Sea Lab—Discovery Hall Summer High School Program

Dickinson College—Pre-College Program

Dwight-Englewood School—Dwight-Englewood Summer Programs

Earthwatch Institute—Field Research Expedition Internships

Education Unlimited—Summer Focus at Berkeley

Georgetown University—Georgetown Summer College

Gould Academy—Young Scholars Program; College Preparatory Program

Harvard University—Harvard Summer School Secondary School Program

Hawaii Preparatory Academy—Hawaii Preparatory Academy Summer Session

Hobart and William Smith Colleges—Environmental Studies Summer Youth Institute

Hollins University—Hollinscience Program

Indiana State University—Summer Honors Program

Indiana University, Bloomington—Jim Holland Summer Enrichment Program in Biology

The Island Laboratory

Ithaca College—Summer College for High School Students

Johns Hopkins University—Pre-college Credit Program

Johns Hopkins University Center for Talented Youth—CTY Summer Programs; CAA Summer Programs

Juniata College—Voyages: Summer Camp for Gifted Students

Knowledge Exchange Institute—Precollege African Safari Program

Knowledge Exchange Institute—Precollege Amazon Exploration Program

Knowledge Exchange Institute—Precollege Research Abroad Program

Lawrence Academy—Environmental Field Study

Lebanon Valley College—Daniel Fox Youth Scholars Institute

Louisiana State University—Honors High School Credit Program

Miami University—Junior Scholars Program

Minnesota Institute for Talented Youth—Expand Your Mind

Musiker Discovery Programs—Summer Discovery

National FFA Organization—Agricultural Programs Overseas

National Youth Leadership Forum—National Youth Leadership Forum on Medicine

New Jersey Institute of Technology—Pre-college Academy in Technology and Science for High School Students

Northern Virginia Summer Academy

Northwestern University, Center for Talent Development—Apogee, Spectrum, Equinox, Leapfrog

Ocean Educations Ltd.—Marine and Environmental Science Program

Oklahoma City Community College—Applying the Skills of Technology in Science

Oregon Museum of Science and Industry—OMSI Summer Science Camps and Adventures

Pacific Lutheran University—Summer Scholars at PLU

Phillips Academy Andover—Phillips Academy Summer Session

Purdue School of Engineering and Technology, IUPUI—Minority Engineering Advancement Program (MEAP)

Putney School—Putney School Summer Programs

Quest Scholars Program—Quest Scholars Programs at Stanford and Harvard

Randolph-Macon Academy—Randolph-Macon Academy Summer Programs

Saint Cloud State University, Ethnic Studies Program—Advanced Program in Technology and Science

Saint Cloud State University, Ethnic Studies Program—Scientific Discovery Program

Scandinavian Seminar—Ambassadors for the Environment

School for Field Studies—Environmental Field Studies Abroad

Sea Education Association—Science at Sea; Oceanography of the Gulf of Maine

Seacamp Association, Inc.—Seacamp

SeaWorld Adventure Parks—SeaWorld/Busch Gardens Adventure Camps

Seton Hill College—Science Quest II

Shad International—Shad Valley

Sidwell Friends School—Sidwell Friends Summer Programs

Skidmore College—Pre-College Program in the Liberal Arts for High School Students at Skidmore

Smith College—Smith Summer Science Program

Southampton College of Long Island University—Summer High School Workshops

Southern Methodist University—College Experience

Stanford University—Summer College for High School Students

Stanford University, Education Program for Gifted Youth—Summer Institute in Mathematics and Physics

Summer Institute for the Gifted—College Gifted Program

Summer Study Programs—Summer Enrichment and Summer Study at Penn State

Summer Study Programs—Summer Study at the University of Colorado at Boulder

Summer Study Programs—Summer Study in Paris at The American University of Paris

Transylvania University—Academic Camp with Computer Emphasis

Tufts University School of Veterinary Medicine—Adventures in Veterinary Medicine

University of California, Los Angeles—College Level Summer Program

University of California, Los Angeles—High School Level Summer Program

University of California, San Diego—UCSD Academic Connections & Summer Session

University of California, Santa Barbara—Early Start Program

University of California, Santa Barbara—UCSB Summer Research Mentorship Program

University of Colorado Cancer Center—Summer Cancer Research Fellowship

University of Connecticut—Mentor Connection

University of Delaware—Summer College for High School Juniors

University of Delaware—Upward Bound Math and Science Center

University of Florida—UF Student Science Training Program

University of Illinois—Chicago—Health Science Enrichment Program

University of Miami—Summer Scholar Programs

University of Michigan—Michigan Math and Science Scholars

University of Mississippi—Summer College for High School Students

University of New Hampshire—Project SMART

University of Notre Dame—Summer Experience

University of Pennsylvania—Penn Summer Science Academy

University of Pennsylvania—Precollege Program

University of the South—Bridge Program in Math and Science

University of Southern Mississippi, The Frances A. Karnes Center for Gifted Studies—
    Summer Program for Academically Talented Youth
University of Virginia—Summer Enrichment Program
University of Wisconsin, La Crosse—Archaeology Field Schools
University of Wisconsin, Madison—Pre-college Program in Environmental and Native
    American Studies
University of Wisconsin, Madison—Summer Science Institute
University of Wisconsin, Superior—Youthsummer
Vanderbilt University—Program for Talented Youth
Washington and Lee University—Summer Scholars
Western Washington University—Adventures in Science and Arts
The Wilds—Safari Camp
World Learning—Experiment in International Living (EIL)
Wright State University—Pre-College Summer Enrichment Programs
Xavier University of Louisiana—BioStar; ChemStar
Xavier University of Louisiana—SOAR 1
Yale University—Yale Summer Programs

Soccer

Appalachian State University—Summer Sports, Music, and Academic Camps
Cornell University Sports School—Summer Sports Camps
Foothill College—Academically Talented Youth Program
Hargrave Military Academy—Summer School and Camp
International Sports Camp
Kutsher's Sports Academy
Lake Placid Soccer Centre—Mountain View Soccer Camp
Middle States Soccer Camp—Intermediate and Senior Soccer Camps
No. 1 Soccer Camps—College Prep Academy
Princeton University—Summer Sports Camps
SoccerPlus Camps—SoccerPlus Goalkeeper School and SoccerPlus Field Player Academy
Southern Vermont College—Summer Sports Camps
Stanford University—Summer Sports Camps
Tab Ramos Soccer Academy
University of Illinois—Fighting Illini Sports Camps
University of Notre Dame—Summer Sports Camps
University of San Diego—Summer Sports Camps
U.S. Sports Camps—Nike Sports Camps
Vogelsinger Soccer Academy and All-Star Soccer School

Sports, Extreme

Barefoot International—Barefoot International & Fly High Ski School
Mount Hood Snowboard Camp—MHSC Summer Sessions
U.S. Snowboard Training Center—USSTC Allstar Snowboard Camp
Woodward Sports Camp

Sports, Varied

Cornell University Sports School—Summer Sports Camps
French Woods Festival of the Performing Arts—French Woods Festival of the
    Performing Arts
Hargrave Military Academy—Summer School and Camp
International Sports Camp
Kutsher's Sports Academy
Maine Teen Camp
Orme School—Orme Summer Camp
Princeton University—Summer Sports Camps
Stanford University—Summer Sports Camps
University of Illinois—Fighting Illini Sports Camps
University of Notre Dame—Summer Sports Camps
University of San Diego—Summer Sports Camps
University of Wisconsin, La Crosse—University of Wisconsin Athletic Camps
U.S. Sports Camps—Nike Sports Camps

Study Abroad, Academic

Academic Study Associates—Language Study Programs
AFS Intercultural Programs—Summer Homestay Language Study
Alliances Abroad—Summer Spanish Program for Youth in Spain; Summer French
    Programs for Youth in France
American Collegiate Adventures
American Institute for Foreign Study—Pre-College Summer Study Abroad
American International Youth Student Exchange—American International Youth
    Student Exchange Program
Amerispan Unlimited—Madrid and Marbella Summer Camps; Spanish Language
    Program in Costa Rica
Avatar Education Ltd.—Buckswood ARC Summer Programs
Baja California Language College
Barat Foundation—Barat Foundation Summer Program
Bordeaux Language School—Teenage Summer Program in Biarritz
Broadreach, Inc.—Broadreach Insights
Broadreach, Inc.—Broadreach Summer Adventures for Teenagers

Cambridge College Programme LLC—Cambridge College Programme

Center for Cross-Cultural Study—Summer in Seville

Center for Cultural Interchange—Discovery Abroad Programs

Ceran Lingua—Ceran Junior

Colorado College—Summer Session for High School Students

Comunicare—Study and Share

Costa Rican Language Academy—Costa Rican Language Academy (CRLA)

Dickinson College—Pre-College Program

Earthwatch Institute—Field Research Expedition Internships

ECHO International Educational Expeditions—Australian Biological Adventures

EF International Language Schools

Georgia Hardy Tours, Inc.—Summer Study

Humanities Spring in Assisi

Irish American Cultural Organization—Irish Way

Irish Centre for Talented Youth

Knowledge Exchange Institute—Precollege African Safari Program

Knowledge Exchange Institute—Precollege Amazon Exploration Program

Knowledge Exchange Institute—Precollege Artist Abroad Program

Knowledge Exchange Institute—Precollege Business, Law and Diplomacy Program

Knowledge Exchange Institute—Precollege European Capitals Program

Knowledge Exchange Institute—Precollege Research Abroad Program

Language Link—Intercultura; Spanish Language Institute; CLIC

Language Studies Abroad, Inc.—Language Studies Abroad

Language Study Abroad

LEAPNow—Summer Program in Central America

Leysin American School in Switzerland—Summer in Switzerland

Lingua Service Worldwide—Junior Classic and Junior Sports Program

Lingua Service Worldwide—Junior Course in Salamanca

Lingua Service Worldwide—Summer Language Adventure

Musiker Discovery Programs—Summer Discovery

Nacel Open Door—Summer Programs

National FFA Organization—Agricultural Programs Overseas

National Registration Center for Study Abroad—Summer Language Programs

New York Film Academy—New York Film Academy Summer Program

Oceanic Society—Bahamas Dolphin Project for High School Students

Oceanic Society—Belize Student Expedition

OxBridge Academic Programs—Cambridge Prep; Cambridge Tradition; Oxford Tradition; Académie de Paris

Putney Student Travel—Excel at Oxford/Tuscany and Madrid/Barcelona

Rassias Programs

Scandinavian Seminar—Ambassadors for the Environment
School for Field Studies—Environmental Field Studies Abroad
Sons of Norway—Camp Norway
Summer Study Programs—Summer Study in Paris at The American University of Paris
Tufts University European Center—Tufts Summit
University of Dallas Study Abroad—Shakespeare in Italy; Latin in Rome; Thomas More in England; Winston Churchill in England
World Learning—Experiment in International Living (EIL)
Youth for Understanding International Exchange—Summer Overseas

Swimming and Diving

Cornell University Sports School—Summer Sports Camps
Foothill College—Academically Talented Youth Program
Hargrave Military Academy—Summer School and Camp
Stanford University—Summer Sports Camps
University of Illinois—Fighting Illini Sports Camps
University of Notre Dame—Summer Sports Camps
University of San Diego—Summer Sports Camps
University of Wisconsin, La Crosse—University of Wisconsin Athletic Camps
U.S. Sports Camps—Nike Sports Camps

Tennis

Carmel Valley Tennis Camp
Cornell University Sports School—Summer Sports Camps
Duke University—Duke Tennis Camp
Foothill College—Academically Talented Youth Program
Hargrave Military Academy—Summer School and Camp
Joel Ross Tennis & Sports Camp
Kinyon/Jones Tennis Camp
Kutsher's Sports Academy
Maine Teen Camp
Palmer Tennis Academy—Junior Camps
Stanford University—Summer Sports Camps
Tennis: Europe and More
University of Illinois—Fighting Illini Sports Camps
University of Notre Dame—Summer Sports Camps
University of San Diego—Summer Sports Camps
University of Wisconsin, La Crosse—University of Wisconsin Athletic Camps
U.S. Sports Camps—Nike Sports Camps
Westcoast Connection—Golf & Tennis Programs

Theater/Film/TV

ACTeen—ACTeen July Academy, ACTeen August Academy, ACTeen Summer Saturday Program

American Academy of Dramatic Arts—Summer Actor Training

Appel Farm Arts and Music Center—Appel Farm's Summer Arts Camp

Ballibay Camps, Inc.—Camp Ballibay for the Fine and Performing Arts

Bethesda Academy of Performing Arts—Summer Repertory Theater; Mid-Summer Shakespeare Company

Blue Lake Fine Arts Camp

Buck's Rock Performing and Creative Arts Camp

California State Summer School for the Arts

Cambridge College Programme LLC—Cambridge College Programme

Capitol Region Education Council and Wesleyan University—Center for Creative Youth

Carnegie Mellon University—Pre-College Programs

Catholic University of America—Media and Video Production Workshop

Columbia College Chicago—High School Summer Institute

Columbia University—Columbia Summer Programs for High School Students

Dwight-Englewood School—Dwight-Englewood Summer Programs

East Carolina University—East Carolina Summer Theatre

Education Unlimited—Acting Workshop at Berkeley

French Woods Festival of the Performing Arts

Goucher College—Goucher Summer Arts Institute

Hun School of Princeton—Hun School Summer Programs

Idyllwild Arts Foundation—Idyllwild Arts Summer Program

Indiana University, Bloomington—Midsummer Theatre Program

Interlochen Center for the Arts—Interlochen Arts Camp

Interlocken—Crossroads Adventure Travel

Ithaca College—Summer College for High School Students

Kingdom County Productions and Fledgling Films—Fledgling Films Summer Institute

Maine Teen Camp

The Masters School—Summer Theatre

Minnesota Institute for Talented Youth—Expand Your Mind

New York Film Academy—New York Film Academy Summer Program

New York University—Tisch Summer High School Program

North Carolina School of the Arts—Summer Session

Northwestern University—National High School Institute

Phillips Academy Andover—Phillips Academy Summer Session

School for Film and Television—Summer in the City

Southwest Texas State University —Summer High School Theatre Workshop

Spoleto Study Abroad

Stagedoor Enterprises—Stagedoor Manor Performing Arts Training Center
Stanford University—Summer Discovery Institutes
State University of New York, Oswego—Summer Theater Institute
Summer Study Programs—Summer Enrichment and Summer Study at Penn State
Syracuse University—Summer College for High School Students
University of the Arts—Drama and Musical Theater
University of California, Los Angeles—UCLA High School Acting and Performance Institute
University of Iowa—Workshop in Theatre Arts
University of Miami—Summer Scholar Programs
University of Mississippi—Summer College for High School Students
University of Southern California—Summer Production Workshop
University of Texas—Summer Theatre Workshop
University of Virginia—Summer Enrichment Program
University of Wisconsin, Superior—Youthsummer
Vanderbilt University—Program for Talented Youth
Vassar College and New York Stage & Film—Powerhouse Theatre Program
Wright State University—Pre-College Summer Enrichment Programs

Track and Field

Appalachian State University—Summer Sports, Music, and Academic Camps
Cornell University Sports School—Summer Sports Camps
Kutsher's Sports Academy
Princeton University—Summer Sports Camps
Stanford University—Summer Sports Camps
University of Illinois—Fighting Illini Sports Camps
University of Wisconsin, La Crosse—University of Wisconsin Athletic Camps
U.S. Sports Camps—Nike Sports Camps

Travel/Sightseeing, Domestic

College Visits
Education Unlimited—East Coast College Tour
Masters School —Summer in the City
Musiker Discovery Programs—Musiker Tours
Tamarack Camps
Weissman Teen Tours, Inc.
Westcoast Connection—Active Teen Tours
Westcoast Connection—Golf & Tennis Programs

Travel/Sightseeing, International

Adventure Ireland

American Collegiate Adventures

American Farm School—Greek Summer

Comunicare—Study and Share

Education Unlimited—Tour Italy

Interlocken—Crossroads Adventure Travel

Irish American Cultural Organization—Irish Way

JCC Maccabi Xperience Israel Programs—Israel Summer Programs

Knowledge Exchange Institute—Precollege European Capitals Program

Musiker Discovery Programs—Musiker Tours

Putney Student Travel—Excel at Oxford/Tuscany and Madrid/Barcelona

Rassias Programs

University of Dallas Study Abroad—Shakespeare in Italy; Latin in Rome; Thomas More in England; Winston Churchill in England

Weissman Teen Tours, Inc.

Westcoast Connection—Active Teen Tours

Westcoast Connection—European Programs

Westcoast Connection—Golf & Tennis Programs

Westcoast Connection—Israel Experience

Westcoast Connection—On Tour

Westcoast Connection—Ski & Snowboard Sensation

Where There Be Dragons—Summer Programs

Volleyball

Appalachian State University— Summer Sports, Music, and Academic Camps

Durango Camps—Durango Youth Volleyball Camp

International Sports Camp

Kutsher's Sports Academy

Stanford University—Summer Sports Camps

University of Illinois—Fighting Illini Sports Camps

University of Notre Dame—Summer Sports Camps

University of San Diego—Summer Sports Camps

University of Wisconsin, La Crosse—University of Wisconsin Athletic Camps

U.S. Sports Camps—Nike Sports Camps

Wrestling

Appalachian State University—Summer Sports, Music, and Academic Camps

Cornell University Sports School—Summer Sports Camps

Hargrave Military Academy—Summer School and Camp

Princeton University—Summer Sports Camps

University of Illinois—Fighting Illini Sports Camps

University of Wisconsin, La Crosse—University of Wisconsin Athletic Camps

Writing

Alfred University—High School Academic Institutes

American Collegiate Adventures

American University—Discover the World of Communication

Asheville School—Asheville School Summer Academic Adventures

Ball State University—Ball State University Journalism Workshops

Barnard College—Summer in New York: A Pre-College Program

Bates College—Creative Writing Workshops

Bennington College—Bennington College July Program

Bryn Mawr College—Writing for College

California Chicano News Media Association—San Jose Urban Journalism Workshop for Minorities

California State Summer School for the Arts

Capitol Region Education Council and Wesleyan University—Center for Creative Youth

Carleton College—Summer Writing Program

Choate Rosemary Hall—The Writing Project

Columbia College Chicago—High School Summer Institute

Columbia University—Columbia Summer Programs for High School Students

Cornell University—Cornell University Summer College

Cornell University—Honors Program for High School Sophomores

Denison University—Jonathan R. Reynolds Young Writers Workshop

Georgia Hardy Tours, Inc.—Summer Study

Gifted and Talented Development Center

Hollins University—Precollege Program

Huntingdon College—Huntingdon College Summer Programs

Idyllwild Arts Foundation—Idyllwild Arts Summer Program

Indiana University, Bloomington—High School Journalism Publications Workshops

Interlochen Center for the Arts—Interlochen Arts Camp

Irish Centre for Talented Youth

Johns Hopkins University—Pre-college Credit Program

Johns Hopkins University Center for Talented Youth—CTY Summer Programs; CAA Summer Programs

Kenyon College—Young Writers at Kenyon

Lewis and Clark College, Northwest Writing Institute—Fir Acres Workshop in Writing and Thinking; Writer to Writer

Maine Teen Camp

New York University—Tisch Summer High School Program

Northwestern University—National High School Institute

OxBridge Academic Programs—Cambridge Prep; Cambridge Tradition; Oxford Tradition; Académie de Paris

Phillips Academy Andover—Phillips Academy Summer Session

Rhodes College—Young Scholars and Writers Camp

Simon's Rock College of Bard—Young Writer's Workshop

Southampton College of Long Island University—Summer High School Workshops

Southwest Texas State University—Summer Creative Writing Camp

Spelman College—Early College Summer Program

Spoleto Study Abroad

Stanford University—Summer Discovery Institutes

Summer Study Programs—Summer Enrichment and Summer Study at Penn State

Summer Study Programs—Summer Study in Paris at The American University of Paris

University of Arizona—Summer Institute for Writing

University of California, Los Angeles—College Level Summer Program

University of California, Los Angeles—High School Level Summer Program

University of California, San Diego—UCSD Academic Connections & Summer Session

University of Connecticut—Mentor Connection

University of Iowa—Iowa Young Writers' Studio

University of Iowa—Summer Journalism Workshops

University of Mississippi—Summer College for High School Students

University of Southern California—Summer Production Workshop

University of Southern Mississippi, The Frances A. Karnes Center for Gifted Studies—Summer Program for Academically Talented Youth

Vanderbilt University—Program for Talented Youth

Wright State University—Pre-College Summer Enrichment Programs

Yale University—Yale Daily News Summer Journalism Program

Index by Cost of Program

This index groups the sponsoring organizations by the cost of their programs. Room and board, airfare, and other amenities may or may not be included. See individual listings for more information.

No Cost to Participants

California Chicano News Media Association—San Jose Urban Journalism Workshop for Minorities

Calvin College—Entrada Scholars Program

Camp Courageous of Iowa—Volunteer Program

East Carolina University—East Carolina Summer Theatre

Friendship Ventures—Youth Leadership Program

Hugh O'Brian Youth Leadership (HOBY)—HOBY Leadership Seminars

Indiana University, Bloomington—Jim Holland Summer Enrichment Program in Biology

Oklahoma City Community College—Applying the Skills of Technology in Science

Project Sunshine—Project Sunshine Volunteer Programs

Quest Scholars Program—Quest Scholars Program at Stanford; Quest Scholars Program at Harvard

Saint Cloud State University, Ethnic Studies Program—Advanced Program in Technology and Science

Saint Cloud State University, Ethnic Studies Program—Scientific Discovery Program

Student Conservation Association—High School Conservation Work Crew (CWC) Program

United States Coast Guard Academy—Minority Introduction to Engineering (MITE)

University of Colorado Cancer Center—Summer Cancer Research Fellowship

University of Delaware—Upward Bound Math and Science Center

University of the South—Bridge Program in Math and Science

University of Wisconsin, Madison—Pre-college Program in Environmental and Native American Studies

University of Wisconsin, Madison—Summer Science Institute

Yale University—Yale Daily News Summer Journalism Program

$1–$999

Abilene Christian University—Kadesh Life Camp

ACTeen—ACTeen July Academy; ACTeen August Academy; ACTeen Summer Saturday Program

Adventure Pursuits—Adventure Pursuits Expeditions & Camps

Alfred University—High School Academic Institutes

All-American Rowing Camp, LLC—High School Coed Rowing Camp

Alpine Adventures, Inc.—Alpine Adventures

America's Baseball Camps

American University—Discover the World of Communication

American Youth Foundation—International Leadership Conference

Amerispan Unlimited—Madrid and Marbella Summer Camps; Spanish Language Program in Costa Rica

Apple Hill Center for Chamber Music—Apple Hill Summer School and Festival

Art Institute of Boston at Lesley University—Pre-College Summer Program

Art Institute of Seattle—Studio 101

ASC Football Camps, Inc.—ASC Football Camps

Auburn University—Design Camp

Auburn University—Summer Honor Band Camps

Auburn University—World Affairs Youth Seminar

Baja California Language College

Ball State University—Ball State University Journalism Workshops

Barefoot International—Barefoot International & Fly High Ski School

Bark Lake Leadership Center—Leadership Through Recreation/Music

Bates College—Bates Forensic Institutes

Bates College—Creative Writing Workshops

Bates College—Edmund S. Muskie Scholars Program

Baylor University—High School Summer Science Research Fellowship Program

Birmingham-Southern College—Student Leaders in Service

Blue Lake Fine Arts Camp

Brenau University—Firespark Schools

Bridgewater College—High School Leadership Academy

Britt Festivals—The Britt Institute

Brookfield Craft Center—Summer Workshop Series

Brush Ranch Camps

Calvin College—Entrada Scholars Program

Catholic University of America—Chamber Music Workshop

Catholic University of America—Experiences in Architecture

Catholic University of America—Eye on Engineering

Catholic University of America—Media and Video Production Workshop

Center for American Archeology—Archeological Field School

Center for Cultural Interchange—Discovery Abroad Programs (Independent Homestay; International Youth Camps; Language School Program)

Chris Waller's Summer Gymnastics Jam

Christchurch School—Summer Programs on the River

Columbia College, Leadership Institute—21st Century Leaders

Columbia College, Leadership Institute—Entrepreneurship Camp

Concordia College—Concordia Language Villages

Cooperstown Baseball Camp

Cornell University Sports School—Summer Sports Camps

Costa Rican Language Academy (CRLA)

Crow Canyon Archaeological Center—High School Field School; High School Excavation Program

Denison University—Jonathan R. Reynolds Young Writers Workshop

Drew University—Drew Summer Music

Durango Camps—Durango Youth Volleyball Camp

Dwight-Englewood School—Dwight-Englewood Summer Programs

Earthwatch Institute—Field Research Expedition Internships

Eastern U.S. Music Camp, Inc.—Eastern U.S. Music Camp

Education Unlimited—College Admission Prep Camp; Prep Camp Excel

Education Unlimited—Computer Camp by Education Unlimited

Education Unlimited—Public Speaking Institute by Education Unlimited

EF International Language Schools

Embry-Riddle Aeronautical University—ACES Academy (Aviation Career Education Specialization)

Embry-Riddle Aeronautical University—Engineering Academy

Embry-Riddle Aeronautical University—Flight Exploration

Foothill College—Academically Talented Youth Program

FUN-damental basketball camp, inc.—Basketball Camp at Morrisville

Gifted and Talented Development Center

Global Volunteers

Goucher College—Goucher Summer Arts Institute

Greenbrier River Outdoor Adventures

Hockey Opportunity Camp

Hollins University—Hollinscience Program

Hollins University—Leadership Enrichment Program

Hollins University—Precollege Program

Horizon Adventures, Inc.—Horizon Adventures

Hun School of Princeton—Hun School Summer Programs

Idyllwild Arts foundation—Idyllwild Arts Summer Program

Illinois State University—Summer High School Forensic Workshop

Indiana State University—Summer Honors Program

Indiana University, Bloomington—College Audition Preparation (CAP); Summer Piano Academy; Summer Recorder Academy; Summer String Academy

Indiana University, Bloomington—High School Journalism Publications Workshops

Indiana University, Bloomington—Indiana University Summer Music Clinic

Indiana University, Bloomington—International Studies Summer Institute for High School Students

Indiana University, Bloomington—Midsummer Theatre Program

International Bicycle Fund—Bicycle Africa Tours; Sbuhbi Lithlal Ti Swatixwtuhd

International Sports Camp

The Island Laboratory

Juniata College—Voyages: Summer Camp for Gifted Students

Kicking Game

Kincardine Summer Music Festival—KSMF Jazz Camp; KSMF Chamber Music Camp; KSMF Festival Week Music Camp

Kinyon/Jones Tennis Camp

Lake Placid Soccer Centre—Mountain View Soccer Camp

Landmark Volunteers—Summer Service Opportunity Programs

Language Link—Intercultura; Spanish Language Institute; CLIC

Language Studies Abroad, Inc.—Language Studies Abroad

Lebanon Valley College—Daniel Fox Youth Scholars Institute

Lebanon Valley College—Lebanon Valley College Summer Music Camp

Lewis and Clark College, Northwest Writing Institute—Fir Acres Workshop in Writing and Thinking; Writer to Writer

Lingua Service Worldwide—Junior Course in Salamanca

Lingua Service Worldwide—Summer Language Adventure

The Masters School—Panther Basketball Camp

Media Workshops Foundation—The Media Workshops

Michigan State University—Spartan Debate Institute (SDI)

Middle States Soccer Camp—Intermediate and Senior Soccer Camps

Milwaukee School of Engineering—Discover the Possibilities; Focus on the Possibilities

Minnesota Institute for Talented Youth—Expand Your Mind

Mississippi University for Women—Business Week; Aero-Tech

National Computer Camps, Inc.

National Registration Center for Study Abroad—Summer Language Programs

National Student Leadership Conference—Law & Advocacy; International Diplomacy; Medicine & Health Care

New Jersey Institute of Technology—Pre-college Academy in Technology and Science for High School Students

Northern Virginia Summer Academy

Offense Defense Golf Camp

Oregon Museum of Science and Industry—OMSI Summer Science Camps and Adventures

Outpost Wilderness Adventure—Outpost Wilderness Adventures

Outward Bound USA

Palmer Tennis Academy—Palmer Tennis Academy Junior Camps

Planet Hockey, Inc.—Planet Hockey Skills Camps; Planet Hockey Ranch

Power Chord Academy

Princeton University—Princeton University Summer Sports Camps

Project PULL Academy—Project PULL Academy Leadership Challenge and College Preview

Purdue School of Engineering and Technology, IUPUI—Minority Engineering Advancement Program (MEAP)

Purdue University—Seminar for Top Engineering Prospects (STEP)

Rainforest Exploration Association—City Lights; Starry Nights

Ringling School of Art and Design—Summer Teen Studios

Rochester Institute of Technology—College and Careers

Saint Louis University—Parks Summer Academy

Saint Olaf College—Saint Olaf Summer Music Camp

Saint Paul Academy and Summit School—Summer Programs

SeaWorld Adventure Parks—SeaWorld/Busch Gardens Adventure Camps

Seton Hill College—Science Quest II

Sidwell Friends School—Deep Creek Adventures; SFS Alaskan Adventures

Sidwell Friends School—Sidwell Friends Summer Programs

Sidwell Friends School—Women's Leadership

Sierra Adventure Camps

SoccerPlus Camps—SoccerPlus Goalkeeper School and SoccerPlus Field Player Academy

Southampton College of Long Island University—Summer High School Workshops

Southern Illinois University, Carbondale—Women's Introduction to Engineering

Southern Vermont College—Summer Sports Camps

Southwest Texas State University—Summer Creative Writing Camp

Southwest Texas State University—Summer High School Theatre Workshop

Stanford Jazz Workshop—Jazz Camp; Jazz Residency

Summer Sonatina International Piano Camp

Tab Ramos Soccer Academy

The Pittsburgh Project

Trailmark Outdoor Adventures

Transylvania University—Academic Camp with Computer Emphasis

Tufts University School of Veterinary Medicine—Adventures in Veterinary Medicine

United States Coast Guard Academy—Academy Introduction Mission (AIM)

United States Naval Academy—Navy Crew Camp for Boys

United States Naval Academy—Navy Rowing Camp for Girls

University of Cincinnati, College of Engineering—Inquisitive Women Summer Day Camp

University of Dayton—Women in Engineering Summer Camp

University of Denver—Making of an Engineer

University of Evansville—Options

University of Iowa—Summer Journalism Workshops

University of Iowa—Workshop in Theatre Arts

University of Maine—Maine Summer Youth Music Senior Camp

University of Maryland—Design Career Discover (Arch 150)

University of Miami—University of Miami Summer Scholar Programs

University of Michigan—Michigan Math and Science Scholars

University of Nebraska, Lincoln—All Girls/All Math

University of New Hampshire—Summer Youth Music School (SYMS)

University of North Dakota—International Aerospace Camp

University of Notre Dame—Introduction to Engineering

University of Rhode Island—W. Alton Jones Teen Expeditions

University of San Diego—University of San Diego Summer Sports Camps

University of Sports—Superstar Camp

University of Vermont—Discovering Engineering, Mathematics, and Computer Science

University of Virginia—Summer Enrichment Program

University of Washington—Courses for High School Students

University of Wisconsin, La Crosse—Archaeology Field Schools

University of Wisconsin, Madison—Engineering Summer Program for High School Students

University of Wisconsin, Madison—Summer Art Classes

University of Wisconsin, Madison—Summer Music Clinic

University of Wisconsin, Superior—Youthsummer

U.S. Gymnastics Training Centers—U.S. Gymnastics Camp

U.S. Space Camp—Aviation Challenge and Advanced Space Academy

Vogelsinger Soccer Academy and All-Star Soccer School

Volunteers for Peace—VFP International Workcamps

Washington Opera—Opera Institute for Young Singers

Washington Workshops Foundation—Washington Workshops Seminars

Wells College—Student Conference on Leadership and Social Responsibility

Western Washington University—Adventures in Science and Arts

Western Washington University—Outdoor Challenge Institute

Wilderness Experience Unlimited—Explorer Group; Trailblazers

The Wilds—Safari Camp

Woodward Sports Camp

Wright State University—Wright State University Pre-College Summer Enrichment Programs

Xavier University of Louisiana—BioStar; ChemStar; MathStar

YMCA of Metropolitan Hartford—Camp Jewell YMCA Outdoor Center

$1,000–$2,999

Academic Enrichment Institute—Summer Academic Enrichment Institute

ACTeen—ACTeen July Academy; ACTeen August Academy; ACTeen Summer Saturday Program

Adventure Ireland

Adventure Pursuits—Adventure Pursuits Expeditions & Camps

Adventure Treks, Inc.—Adventure Treks

Adventures Cross-Country

Alliances Abroad—Summer Spanish Program for Youth in Spain; Summer French Programs for Youth in France; Culture and Adventure Program for Youth in Ireland

Alpine Adventures, Inc.—Alpine Adventures

America's Adventure/Venture Europe

American Academy of Dramatic Arts—Summer Actor Training

American International Youth Student Exchange—American International Youth Student Exchange Program

American Jewish Society for Service—Summer Work Camps

American Management Association—Operation Enterprise

American Trails West

American University—Discover the World of Communication

Amerispan Unlimited—Madrid and Marbella Summer Camps; Spanish Language Program in Costa Rica

Appel Farm Arts and Music Center—Appel Farm's Summer Arts Camp

Apple Hill Center for Chamber Music—Apple Hill Summer School and Festival

Baja California Language College

BalletMet—Summer Workshop

Ballibay Camps, Inc.—Camp Ballibay for the Fine and Performing Arts

Barnard College—Summer in New York: A Pre-College Program

Bates College—Bates Forensic Institutes

Birmingham-Southern College—Summer Scholar Program

Bordeaux Language School—Teenage Summer Program in Biarritz

Boston University—Program in Mathematics for Young Scientists (PROMYS)

Breakthroughs Abroad, Inc.—High School Programs

Brush Ranch Camps

Bryn Mawr College—Writing for College

Burklyn Ballet Theatre

California College of Arts and Crafts—CCAC Pre-College Program

California State Summer School for the Arts

Carleton College—Summer Writing Program

Catholic University of America—Capitol Classic Summer Debate Institute

Catholic University of America—Experiences in Architecture

Center for Cross-Cultural Study—Summer in Seville

Center for Cultural Interchange—Discovery Abroad Programs (Independent Homestay; International Youth Camps; Language School Program)

Ceran Lingua—Ceran Junior

Championship Debate Enterprises—Lincoln-Douglas and Extemp Institute; Policy Debate Institute

Christchurch School—Summer Programs on the River

Colorado College—Summer Session for High School Students

Columbia University—Columbia Summer Programs for High School Students

Comunicare—Study and Share

Concordia College—Concordia Language Villages

Congressional Youth Leadership Council—Global Young Leaders Conference

Congressional Youth Leadership Council—National Young Leaders Conference

Costa Rican Language Academy (CRLA)

Cottonwood Gulch Foundation—Prairie Trek Group I; Prairie Trek Group II; Turquoise Trail

Crow Canyon Archaeological Center—High School Field School; High School Excavation Program

Dauphin Island Sea Lab—Discovery Hall Summer High School Program

Deep Woods Camp for Boys

Dwight-Englewood School—Dwight-Englewood Summer Programs

Earthwatch Institute—Field Research Expedition Internships

Eastern U.S. Music Camp, Inc.—Eastern U.S. Music Camp

Education Unlimited—College Admission Prep Camp; Prep Camp Excel

Education Unlimited—East Coast College Tour; Tour Italy

Education Unlimited—Summer Focus at Berkeley; Acting Workshop at Berkeley

EF International Language Schools

Envision EMI, Inc.—NexTech: The National Summit of Young Technology Leaders

Friends Music Camp

Global Institute for Developing Entrepreneurs—IN2BIZ Entrepreneur Camp

Global Routes—High School Community Service Programs

Global Volunteers

Global Works International Programs—Summer Programs

Gould Academy—Young Scholars Program; College Preparatory Program
Greenbrier River Outdoor Adventures
Hampshire College—Hampshire College Summer Studies in Mathematics
Hawaii Preparatory Academy—Hawaii Preparatory Academy Summer Session
Hockey Opportunity Camp
Horizon Adventures, Inc.—Horizon Adventures
Hun School of Princeton—Hun School Summer Programs
Idyllwild Arts foundation—Idyllwild Arts Summer Program
Indiana University, Bloomington—College Audition Preparation (CAP); Summer Piano
    Academy; Summer Recorder Academy; Summer String Academy
International Bicycle Fund—Bicycle Africa Tours; Sbuhbi Lithlal Ti Swatixwtuhd
Irish American Cultural Organization—Irish Way
Irish Centre for Talented Youth
Ithaca College—Summer College for High School Students
Joel Ross Tennis & Sports Camp
Johns Hopkins University Center for Talented Youth—CTY Summer Programs; CAA
    Summer Programs
Kenyon College—Young Writers at Kenyon
Kingdom County Productions and Fledgling Films—Fledgling Films Summer Institute
Kinhaven Music School
Kutsher's Sports Academy
La Société Française—International Volunteer Program
LaGrange College—Visual Arts Workshop
Lake Placid Soccer Centre—Mountain View Soccer Camp
Language Link—Intercultura; Spanish Language Institute; CLIC
Latitudes International—Community Service Travel
Legacy International—Global Youth Village
Lewis and Clark College, Northwest Writing Institute—Fir Acres Workshop in Writing
    and Thinking; Writer to Writer
Leysin American School in Switzerland—Summer in Switzerland
Lingua Service Worldwide—Junior Classic and Junior Sports Program
Lingua Service Worldwide—Junior Course in Salamanca
Lingua Service Worldwide—Summer Language Adventure
Longacre Expeditions
Louisiana State University—Honors High School Credit Program
Marine Military Academy—Summer Military Training Camp
Mathematics Foundation of America—Canada/USA Mathcamp
Miami University—Junior Scholars Program
Michigan State University—Spartan Debate Institute (SDI)
Mount Hood Snowboard Camp—MHSC Summer Sessions

Nacel Open Door—Summer Programs

National Registration Center for Study Abroad—Summer Language Programs

National Student Leadership Conference—Law & Advocacy; International Diplomacy; Medicine & Health Care

National Youth Leadership Forum—National Youth Leadership Forum on Medicine

New Jersey Institute of Technology—Pre-college Academy in Technology and Science for High School Students

No. 1 Soccer Camps—College Prep Academy

North Carolina School of the Arts—Summer Session

Northern Virginia Summer Academy

Northwaters—Northwaters Wilderness Programs

Northwestern University Center for Talent Development—Apogee, Spectrum, Equinox, Leapfrog

Oak Ridge Military Academy—Academic Summer School

Oak Ridge Military Academy—Leadership Adventure Camp

Ocean Educations Ltd.—Marine and Environmental Science Program

Oceanic Society—Bahamas Dolphin Project for High School Students

Oceanic Society—Belize Student Expedition

Offense Defense Golf Camp

Ohio State University—Ross Young Scholars Program

Orme School—Orme Summer Camp

Otis College of Art and Design—Otis Summer of Art

Outpost Wilderness Adventure—Outpost Wilderness Adventures

Outward Bound USA

Pacific Lutheran University—Summer Scholars at PLU

Parsons School of Design—Summer Intensive Studies

Peacework

Pratt Institute—Pre-College Summer Program

Princeton Ballet School—American Repertory Ballet's Summer Intensive

Putney School—Putney School Summer Programs

Rainforest Exploration Association—City Lights; Starry Nights

Randolph-Macon Academy—Randolph-Macon Academy Summer Programs

Rhode Island School of Design—Pre-College Program

Rhodes College—Young Scholars and Writers Camp

The Road Less Traveled

Rutgers University—Young Scholars Program in Discrete Mathematics

Saint Paul Academy and Summit School—Summer Programs

School for Field Studies—Environmental Field Studies Abroad

School for Film and Television—Summer in the City

Seacamp Association, Inc.—Seacamp

Seattle Youth Symphony Orchestra—Marrowstone Music Festival

SeaWorld Adventure Parks—SeaWorld/Busch Gardens Adventure Camps

Shad International—Shad Valley

Sidwell Friends School—Deep Creek Adventures; SFS Alaskan Adventures

Sidwell Friends School—SFS in Costa Rica

Sidwell Friends School—Sidwell Friends Summer Programs

Sierra Adventure Camps—Sierra Adventure Camps

Simon's Rock College of Bard—Young Writer's Workshop

Sons of Norway—Camp Norway

Southern Methodist University—College Experience

Southwest Texas State University—Honors Summer Math Camp

Spelman College—Early College Summer Program

Stanford Jazz Workshop—Jazz Camp; Jazz Residency

Stanford University, Education Program for Gifted Youth—Summer Institute in Mathematics and Physics

State University of New York, Oswego—Summer Art Institute; Summer Theater Institute

State University of New York, Purchase—Summer Visual Arts Institute

Student Hosteling Program—Summer Biking Programs

Summer Institute for the Gifted—College Gifted Program

Tennis: Europe and More

Trailmark Outdoor Adventures

Trinity University—A Trinity Summer

Tufts University School of Veterinary Medicine—Adventures in Veterinary Medicine

University of the Arts—Drama and Musical Theater

University of the Arts—PREP, Art Smart, and Media and Communications Workshops

University of the Arts—Summer Institute of Jazz

University of California, Los Angeles—UCLA High School Acting and Performance Institute

University of Connecticut—Mentor Connection

University of Delaware—Summer College for High School Juniors

University of Denver—Making of an Engineer

University of Florida—UF Student Science Training Program

University of Iowa—Iowa Young Writers' Studio

University of Maryland—Design Career Discover (Arch 150)

University of Michigan—Michigan Math and Science Scholars

University of Mississippi—Summer College for High School Students

University of New Hampshire—Project SMART

University of Texas, Austin—Summer Theatre Workshop

University of Wisconsin, La Crosse—University of Wisconsin Athletic Camps

University of Wisconsin, Superior—Youthsummer

U.S. Snowboard Training Center—USSTC Allstar Snowboard Camp

Vanderbilt University—Program for Talented Youth

Vassar College and New York Stage & Film—Powerhouse Theatre Program

Visions

Vogelsinger Soccer Academy and All-Star Soccer School

Volunteers for Peace—VFP International Workcamps

Wake Forest University—Summer Debate Workshop; Fast Track; Policy Project; Policy Analysis Seminar

Washington and Lee University—Summer Scholars

Washington University in St. Louis—Architecture Discovery Program

Westcoast Connection—Outdoor Adventure Programs

Western Washington University—SummerQuest

Wilderness Ventures—Wilderness Adventure Expeditions; Advanced Leadership Expeditions; Offshore Adventure Expeditions

Woodward Sports Camp

World Learning—Experiment in International Living (EIL)

Wright State University—Wright State University Pre-College Summer Enrichment Programs

Xavier University of Louisiana—SOAR 1

Yale University—Yale Summer Programs

$3,000–$4,999

Academic Study Associates—Language Study Programs

Academic Study Associates—Pre-College Enrichment Program

ActionQuest—ActionQuest Programs

Adventure Pursuits—Adventure Pursuits Expeditions & Camps

Adventure Treks, Inc.—Adventure Treks

Adventures Cross-Country

AFS Intercultural Programs—Summer Homestay; Summer Homestay Language Study; Summer Homestay Plus; Summer Community Service/Team Mission

Alliances Abroad—Summer Spanish Program for Youth in Spain; Summer French Programs for Youth in France; Culture and Adventure Program for Youth in Ireland

America's Adventure/Venture Europe

American Farm School—Greek Summer

American Institute For Foreign Study (AIFS)—Pre-College Summer Study Abroad

American International Youth Student Exchange—American International Youth Student Exchange Program

American Trails West

Amigos de las Americas

Apple Hill Center for Chamber Music—Apple Hill Summer School and Festival

Aspen Music School—Aspen Music Festival and School

Ballibay Camps, Inc.—Camp Ballibay for the Fine and Performing Arts

Barat Foundation—Barat Foundation Summer Program

Barnard College—Summer in New York: A Pre-College Program

Beloit College—Center for Language Studies

Bennington College—Bennington College July Program

Boston College—Boston College Experience

Breakthroughs Abroad, Inc.—High School Programs

Brevard Music Center—Young Artists Division

Broadreach, Inc.—Broadreach Insights

Brush Ranch Camps

Buck's Rock Performing and Creative Arts Camp

Burklyn Ballet Theatre

California State Summer School for the Arts

Cambridge College Programme LLC—Cambridge College Programme

Camp Encore/Coda—Upper Camp

Capitol Region Education Council and Wesleyan University—Center for Creative Youth

Catholic University of America—College Courses for High School Students

Center for Cross-Cultural Study—Summer in Seville

Center for Cultural Interchange—Discovery Abroad Programs (Independent Homestay; International Youth Camps; Language School Program)

Ceran Lingua—Ceran Junior

Columbia University—Columbia Summer Programs for High School Students

Columbia University Biosphere 2—Exploring Earth, Life & the Summer Sky

Cornell University—Cornell University Summer College

Cornell University—Summer Honors Program for High School Sophomores

Cottonwood Gulch Foundation—Prairie Trek Group I; Prairie Trek Group II; Turquoise Trail

Deep Woods Camp for Boys

Deer Hill Expeditions

Dickinson College—Pre-College Program

Duke University—Duke University PreCollege Program

Earthwatch Institute—Field Research Expedition Internships

Eastern Music Festival

Eastern U.S. Music Camp, Inc.—Eastern U.S. Music Camp

ECHO International Educational Expeditions—Australian Biological Adventures

Education Unlimited—Summer Focus at Berkeley; Acting Workshop at Berkeley

Embry-Riddle Aeronautical University—Aerospace Summer Camp

Embry-Riddle Aeronautical University—SunFlight Camps

Evansville Association for the Blind—Summer College Program for Students with Disabilities

French Woods Festival of the Performing Arts

Global Routes—High School Community Service Programs

Global Works International Programs—Summer Programs

Gould Academy—Young Scholars Program; College Preparatory Program

Hargrave Military Academy—Summer School and Camp

Harvard University—Harvard Summer School Secondary School Program

Hawaii Preparatory Academy—Hawaii Preparatory Academy Summer Session

Hockey Opportunity Camp

Humanities Spring in Assisi

Hun School of Princeton—Hun School Summer Programs

Interlochen Center for the Arts—Interlochen Arts Camp

Interlocken—Crossroads Adventure Travel

Ithaca College—Summer College for High School Students

JCC Maccabi Xperience Israel Programs—Israel Summer Programs

Joel Ross Tennis & Sports Camp

Johns Hopkins University—Hopkins Pre-college Credit Program

Junior Statesmen Foundation—Junior Statesmen Summer School

Kinhaven Music School

Knowledge Exchange Institute—Precollege African Safari Program

Knowledge Exchange Institute—Precollege Business, Law and Diplomacy Program

Knowledge Exchange Institute—Precollege Research Abroad Program

Kutsher's Sports Academy

Lake Placid Soccer Centre—Mountain View Soccer Camp

Latitudes International—Community Service Travel

Lawrence Academy—Environmental Field Study

Lawrence Academy—Global Leaders Workshop

Lawrence Academy—International English Institute

LEAPNow—Summer Program in Central America; Summer Program in Australia

Leysin American School in Switzerland—Summer in Switzerland

Lingua Service Worldwide—Summer Language Adventure

Longacre Leadership—Longacre Leadership Program

Maine Teen Camp

Mathematics Foundation of America—Canada/USA Mathcamp

Mount Holyoke College—SummerMath

New York Film Academy—New York Film Academy Summer Program

Northwaters—Northwaters Wilderness Programs

Northwestern University—National High School Institute

Occidental College—High School Oceanology Program

Odyssey Expeditions—Tropical Marine Biology Voyages

Operation Crossroads Africa—Africa & Diaspora Programs

Orme School—Orme Summer Camp

OxBridge Academic Programs—Cambridge Prep; Cambridge Tradition; Oxford Tradition; Académie de Paris

Parsons School of Design—Summer Intensive Studies

Peacework

Phillips Academy Andover—Phillips Academy Summer Session

Putney Student Travel—Excel at Williams and Amherst Colleges; Excel at Oxford/Tuscany and Madrid/Barcelona

Rhode Island School of Design—Pre-College Program

Ringling School of Art and Design—PreCollege Perspective

The Road Less Traveled

Sail Caribbean

Savannah College of Art and Design—Rising Star

Scandinavian Seminar—Ambassadors for the Environment

School for Field Studies—Environmental Field Studies Abroad

School for Film and Television—Summer in the City

Sea Education Association—Science at Sea; Oceanography of the Gulf of Maine

Skidmore College—Pre-College Program in the Liberal Arts for High School Students at Skidmore

Smith College—Smith Summer Science Program

Sons of Norway—Camp Norway

Southwestern Academy—International Summer Programs

Southwestern Academy—Southwestern Adventures

Stagedoor Enterprises—Stagedoor Manor Performing Arts Training Center

Stanford University—Summer Discovery Institutes

Student Hosteling Program—Summer Biking Programs

Summer Study Programs—Summer Enrichment and Summer Study at Penn State

Summer Study Programs—Summer Study at the University of Colorado at Boulder

Summer Study Programs—Summer Study in Paris at The American University of Paris

Syracuse University—Syracuse University Summer College for High School Students

Tennis: Europe and More

Tufts University European Center—Tufts Summit

University of Dallas Study Abroad—Shakespeare in Italy; Latin in Rome; Thomas More in England; Winston Churchill in England

University of Pennsylvania—Penn Summer Science Academy

University of Pennsylvania—Precollege Program

Visions

Wake Forest University—Summer Debate Workshop; Fast Track; Policy Project; Policy Analysis Seminar

The Walden School—Walden School Summer Music School, Festival, and Camp

Westcoast Connection—Active Teen Tours

Westcoast Connection—European Programs

Westcoast Connection—Golf & Tennis Programs

Westcoast Connection—Israel Experience

Westcoast Connection—On Tour

Westcoast Connection—Ski & Snowboard Sensation

Wilderness Ventures—Wilderness Adventure Expeditions; Advanced Leadership Expeditions; Offshore Adventure Expeditions

World Horizons International

World Learning—Experiment in International Living (EIL)

Youth for Understanding International Exchange—Summer Overseas

Over $5,000

Academic Study Associates—Language Study Programs

Academic Study Associates—Pre-College Enrichment Program

Adelphi University—Academic Success Program

Adventures Cross-Country

American Committee for the Weizmann Institute of Science—Dr. Bessie F. Lawrence International Summer Science Institute

American Institute For Foreign Study (AIFS)—Pre-College Summer Study Abroad

Aspen Music School—Aspen Music Festival and School

Barat Foundation—Barat Foundation Summer Program

Beloit College—Center for Language Studies

Breakthroughs Abroad, Inc.—High School Programs

Broadreach, Inc.—Broadreach Insights

Brush Ranch Camps

Buck's Rock Performing and Creative Arts Camp

Cambridge College Programme LLC—Cambridge College Programme

Camp Encore/Coda—Upper Camp

Cornell University—Cornell University Summer College

Embry-Riddle Aeronautical University—SunFlight Camps

French Woods Festival of the Performing Arts

Harvard University—Harvard Summer School Secondary School Program

Hun School of Princeton—Hun School Summer Programs

Intern Exchange International—Intern Exchange International

Joel Ross Tennis & Sports Camp

Knowledge Exchange Institute—Precollege Amazon Exploration Program

Knowledge Exchange Institute—Precollege Artist Abroad Program
Knowledge Exchange Institute—Precollege European Capitals Program
Kutsher's Sports Academy
New York University—Tisch Summer High School Program
Rassias Programs
The Road Less Traveled
Sail Caribbean
Southwestern Academy—International Summer Programs
Spoleto Study Abroad
Stanford University—Summer College for High School Students
Student Hosteling Program—Summer Biking Programs
Student Safaris International—Zanzibar to the Serengeti; Queensland Explorer
Summer Study Programs—Summer Enrichment and Summer Study at Penn State
Summer Study Programs—Summer Study in Paris at The American University of Paris
Tennis: Europe and More
University of California, Santa Barbara—Early Start Program
University of California, Santa Barbara—UCSB Summer Research Mentorship Program
University of Pennsylvania—Precollege Program
Weissman Teen Tours, Inc.
Westcoast Connection—Active Teen Tours
Westcoast Connection—European Programs
Westcoast Connection—Golf & Tennis Programs
Westcoast Connection—Israel Experience
Westcoast Connection—On Tour
Where There Be Dragons—Summer Programs
Wilderness Ventures—Wilderness Adventure Expeditions; Advanced Leadership Expeditions; Offshore Adventure Expeditions

Index by Location of Program

This index groups the sponsoring organizations by the location of their summer programs. International programs are at the front of the index, listed by region. U.S. programs follow the international groupings, listed by state.

INTERNATIONAL

Africa

AFS Intercultural Programs—Summer Community Service/Team Mission
Broadreach, Inc.—Broadreach Summer Adventures for Teenagers
Breakthroughs Abroad, Inc.—High School Programs
Center for Cultural Interchange—Discovery Abroad Programs (Independent Homestay; International Youth Camps; Language School Program)
Global Routes—High School Community Service Programs
International Bicycle Fund—Bicycle Africa Tours
Involvement Volunteers Association—International Volunteering; Networked International Volunteering
Knowledge Exchange Institute—Precollege African Safari Program
Latitudes International—Community Service Travel
Operation Crossroads Africa—Africa and Diaspora Programs
Peacework
School for Field Studies—Environmental Field Studies Abroad
Student Safaris International—Zanzibar to the Serengeti
Volunteers for Peace—VFP International Workcamps
World Learning—Experiment in International Living (EIL)

Asia and the Middle East

AFS Intercultural Programs—Summer Homestay
AFS Intercultural Programs—Summer Homestay Language Study
AFS Intercultural Programs—Summer Community Service/Team Mission
American Institute For Foreign Study (AIFS)—Pre-College Summer Study Abroad

American International Youth Student Exchange Program

Breakthroughs Abroad, Inc.—High School Programs

Broadreach, Inc.—Broadreach Summer Adventures for Teenagers

Breakthroughs Abroad, Inc.—High School Programs

Center for Cultural Interchange—Discovery Abroad Programs (Independent Homestay; International Youth Camps; Language School Program)

Choate Rosemary Hall—Study Abroad

EF International Language Schools

Global Routes—High School Community Service Programs

Global Works International Programs—Summer Programs

Involvement Volunteers Association—International Volunteering; Networked International Volunteering

JCC Maccabi Xperience Israel Programs—Israel Summer Programs

Knowledge Exchange Institute—Precollege Business, Law and Diplomacy Program

Knowledge Exchange Institute—Precollege Research Abroad Program

Language Studies Abroad, Inc.—Language Studies Abroad

Peacework

The Road Less Traveled

Volunteers for Peace—VFP International Workcamps

Westcoast Connections—Israel Experience

Where There be Dragons—Summer Programs

World Learning—Experiment in International Living (EIL)

Australia/New Zealand

ActionQuest—ActionQuest Programs

Adventure Pursuits—Adventure Pursuits Expeditions & Camps

AFS Intercultural Programs—Summer Homestay Plus

American International Youth Student Exchange Program

Broadreach, Inc.—Broadreach Summer Adventures for Teenagers

Center for Cultural Interchange—Discovery Abroad Programs (Independent Homestay; International Youth Camps; Language School Program)

ECHO International Educational Expeditions—Australian Biological Adventures

Involvement Volunteers Association—International Volunteering; Networked International Volunteering

LEAPNow—Summer Program in Australia

School for Field Studies—Environmental Field Studies Abroad

Student Safaris International—Queensland Explorer

Visions

World Learning—Experiment in International Living (EIL)

Canada

Adventure Pursuits—Adventure Pursuits Expeditions & Camps
Adventure Treks, Inc.
AFS Intercultural Programs—Summer Homestay Language Study
American Trails West
Bark Lake Leadership Center—Leadership Through Recreation/Music
Broadreach, Inc.—Broadreach Insights
Hockey Opportunity Camp
International Bicycle Fund—Sbuhbi Lithlal Ti Swatixwtuhd
Kincardine Summer Music Festival—KSMF Jazz Camp; KSMF Chamber Music Camp;
    KSMF Festival Week Music Camp
Lingua Service Worldwide—Summer Language Adventure
Longacre Expeditions
Musiker Discovery Programs—Musiker Tours
Nacel Open Door—Summer Programs
National Outdoor Leadership School—Wilderness Leadership Courses
Northwaters—Northwaters Wilderness Programs
Ocean Educations Ltd.—Marine and Environmental Science Program
Shad International—Shad Valley
Student Hosteling Program—Summer Biking Programs
Tamarack Camps
Westcoast Connection—Active Teen Tours; On Tour; Outdoor Adventure Programs; Ski
    and Snowboard Sensation
Wilderness Ventures—Wilderness Adventure Expeditions; Advanced Leadership
    Expeditions; Offshore Adventure Expeditions

Caribbean

ActionQuest—ActionQuest Programs
Amigos de las Americas
Broadreach, Inc.—Broadreach Summer Adventures for Teenagers
Global Routes—High School Community Service Programs
Oceanic Society—Bahamas Dolphin Project for High School Students
Odyssey Expeditions—Tropical Marine Biology Voyages
Peacework
Sail Caribbean
School for Field Studies—Environmental Field Studies Abroad
Visions
World Horizons International

Central/South America

ActionQuest—ActionQuest Programs
AFS Intercultural Programs—Summer Homestay
AFS Intercultural Programs—Summer Homestay Language Study
AFS Intercultural Programs—Summer Homestay Plus
AFS Intercultural Programs—Summer Community Service/Team Mission
America's Adventure/Venture Europe
Amerispan Unlimited—Spanish Language Program in Costa Rica
Amigos de las Americas
Baja California Language College
Breakthroughs Abroad, Inc.—High School Programs
Broadreach, Inc.—Broadreach Insights
Broadreach, Inc.—Broadreach Summer Adventures for Teenagers
Breakthroughs Abroad, Inc.—High School Programs
Center for Cultural Interchange—Discovery Abroad Programs (Independent Homestay;
    International Youth Camps; Language School Program)
Comunicare—Study and Share
Costa Rican Language Academy (CRLA)
Dickinson College—Pre-College Program
EF International Language Schools
Global Routes—High School Community Service Programs
Global Works International Programs—Summer Programs
Involvement Volunteers Association—International Volunteering; Networked
    International Volunteering
Knowledge Exchange Institute—Precollege Amazon Exploration Program
Language Link—Intercultura; Spanish Language Institute; CLIC
Language Studies Abroad, Inc.—Language Studies Abroad
Language Study Abroad
Latitudes International—Community Service Travel
LEAPNow—Summer Program in Central America
Longacre Expeditions
Moondance Adventures
Musiker Discovery Programs—Musiker Tours
Nacel Open Door—Summer Programs
National FFA Organization—Agricultural Programs Overseas
National Outdoor Leadership School—Wilderness Leadership Courses
Oceanic Society—Belize Student Expedition
Outpost Wilderness Adventure
Peacework
School for Field Studies—Environmental Field Studies Abroad

Sidwell Friends School—SFS in Costa Rica

Volunteers for Peace—VFP International Workcamps

Wilderness Ventures—Wilderness Adventure Expeditions; Advanced Leadership Expeditions; Offshore Adventure Expeditions

Visions

World Horizons International

World Learning—Experiment in International Living (EIL)

Europe

Academic Study Associates—ASA Pre-College Enrichment Program; Language Study Programs

Adventure Ireland

AFS Intercultural Programs—Summer Homestay

AFS Intercultural Programs—Summer Homestay Language Study

AFS Intercultural Programs—Summer Homestay Plus

AFS Intercultural Programs—Summer Community Service/Team Mission

Alliances Abroad—Summer Spanish Program for Youth in Spain; Summer French Programs for Youth in France; Culture and Adventure Program for Youth in Ireland

American Collegiate Adventures

American Committee for the Weizmann Institute of Science—Dr. Bessie F. Lawrence International Summer Science Institute

American Farm School—Greek Summer

American Institute For Foreign Study (AIFS)—Pre-College Summer Study Abroad

American International Youth Student Exchange—American International Youth Student Exchange Program

American Trails West

Amerispan Unlimited—Madrid and Marbella Summer Camps

Avatar Education Ltd.—Buckswood ARC Summer Programs

Barat Foundation—Barat Foundation Summer Program

Bordeaux Language School—Teenage Summer Program in Biarritz

Cambridge College Programme LLC—Cambridge College Programme

Center for Cross-Cultural Study—Summer in Seville

Center for Cultural Interchange—Discovery Abroad Programs (Independent Homestay; International Youth Camps; Language School Program)

Ceran Lingua—Ceran Junior

Choate Rosemary Hall—Study Abroad

Education Unlimited—East Coast College Tour; Tour Italy

EF International Language Schools

Georgia Hardy Tours, Inc.—Summer Study

Global Works International Programs—Summer Programs

Humanities Spring in Assisi

Interlocken—Crossroads Adventure Travel

Intern Exchange International

Involvement Volunteers Association—International Volunteering; Networked International Volunteering

Irish American Cultural Organization—Irish Way

Irish Centre for Talented Youth

Knowledge Exchange Institute—Precollege Artist Abroad Program

Knowledge Exchange Institute—Precollege European Capitals Program

La Société Française—International Volunteer Program

Language Studies Abroad, Inc.—Language Studies Abroad

Language Study Abroad

Leysin American School in Switzerland—Summer in Switzerland

Lingua Service Worldwide—Junior Classic and Junior Sports Program; Junior Course in Salamanca

Longacre Expeditions

Moondance Adventures

Musiker Discovery Programs—Musiker Tours; Summer Discovery

Nacel Open Door—Summer Programs

National FFA Organization—Agricultural Programs Overseas

National Registration Center for Study Abroad—Summer Language Programs

New York Film Academy—New York Film Academy Summer Program

Outpost Wilderness Adventure

OxBridge Academic Programs—Cambridge Prep; Cambridge Tradition; Oxford Tradition; Académie de Paris

Putney Student Travel—Excel at Oxford/Tuscany and Madrid/Barcelona

Rassias Programs

Scandanavian Seminar—Ambassadors for the Environment

Sons of Norway—Camp Norway

Spoleto Study Abroad

Student Hosteling Program—Summer Biking Programs

Summer Study Programs—Summer Study in Paris at The American University of Paris

University of Dallas Study Abroad—Shakespeare in Italy; Latin in Rome; Thomas More in England; Winston Churchill in England

Volunteers for Peace—VFP International Workcamps

Weissman Teen Tours, Inc.

Westcoast Connections—European Programs; On Tour

Wilderness Ventures—Wilderness Adventure Expeditions; Advanced Leadership Expeditions; Offshore Adventure Expeditions

World Learning—Experiment in International Living (EIL)

Various (Unspecified) Locations Around the World

Earthwatch Institute—Field Research Expedition Internships
Global Volunteers
Higher Ground Softball Camps
Legacy International—Global Youth Village
Longacre Expeditions
Mathematics Foundation of America—Canada/USA Mathcamp
Project Sunshine—Project Sunshine Volunteer Programs
Tennis: Europe and More
Youth for Understanding International Exchange—Summer Overseas

UNITED STATES

Alabama

Auburn University—Summer Honor Band Camps; World Affairs Youth Seminar; Design Camp
Birmingham-Southern College—Student Leaders in Service; Summer Scholars Program
Dauphin Island Sea Lab—Discovery Hall Summer High School Program
Huntingdon College—Huntingdon College Summer Programs
U.S. Space Camp—Aviation Challenge and Advanced Space Academy

Alaska

Adventure Pursuits—Adventure Pursuits Expeditions & Camps
Adventure Treks, Inc.
America's Adventure/Venture Europe
American Trails West
Musiker Discovery Programs—Musiker Tours
National Outdoor Leadership School—Wilderness Leadership Courses
Sidwell Friends School—Deep Creek Adventures; SFS Alaskan Adventures
Student Conservation Association—High School Conservation Work Crew (CWC) Program
Tamarack Camps
Wilderness Ventures—Wilderness Adventure Expeditions; Advanced Leadership Expeditions; Offshore Adventure Expeditions
Visions

Arizona

America's Adventure/Venture Europe

Champion Debate Enterprises—Lincoln-Douglas and Extemp Institute; Policy Debate Institute

Columbia University Biosphere 2—Exploring Earth, Life, and the Summer Sky

Cottonwood Gulch Foundation—Prairie Trek Group I; Prairie Trek Group II

Deer Hill Expeditions

Global Routes—High School Community Service Programs

Orme School—Orme Summer Camp

Southwestern Academy—Southwestern Adventures

University of Arizona—Summer Institute for Writing

California

Academic Enrichment Institute—Summer Academic Enrichment Institute

Academic Study Associates—ASA Pre-College Enrichment Program; Language Study Programs

Adventure Pursuits—Adventure Pursuits Expeditions & Camps

Adventure Treks, Inc.

Adventures Cross-Country

American Academy of Dramatic Arts—Summer Actor Training

ASC Football Camps, Inc.

Baja California Language College

California Chicano News Media Association—San Jose Urban Journalism Workshop for Minorities

California College of Arts and Crafts—CCAC Pre-College Program

California State Summer School for the Arts

Carmel Valley Tennis Camp

Chris Waller's Summer Gymnastics Jam

Education Unlimited—College Admission Prep Camp; Prep Camp Excel; Computer Camp by Education Unlimited; Public Speaking Institute by Education Unlimited; Summer Focus at Berkeley; Acting Workshop at Berkeley

Foothill College—Academically Talented Youth Program

Idyllwild Arts Foundation—Idyllwild Arts Summer Program

Junior Statesmen Foundation—Junior Statesmen Summer School

Kicking Game

Media Workshops Foundation—The Media Workshops

Musiker Discovery Program—Summer Discovery

National Student Leadership Conference—Law & Advocacy; International Diplomacy; Medicine & Health Care

National Youth Leadership Forum—National Youth Leadership Forum on Medicine

New York Film Academy—New York Film Academy Summer Program

Oakland University—Oakland University Summer Mathematics Institute

Occidental College—High School Oceanology Program

Otis College of Art and Design—Otis Summer of Art

Power Chord Academy

Project PULL Academy—Project PULL Academy Leadership Challenge and College Preview

Quest Scholars Program—Quest Scholars Program at Stanford

Rainforest Exploration Association—City Lights; Starry Nights

SeaWorld Adventure Parks—SeaWorld/Busch Gardens Adventure Camps

Sierra Adventure Camps

Southwestern Academy—International Summer Programs

Stanford Jazz Workshop—Jazz Camp; Jazz Residency

Stanford University—Summer College for High School Students; Summer Discovery Institutes; Summer Sports Camps

Stanford University, Education Program for Gifted Youth—Summer Institute in Mathematics and Physics

University of California, Los Angeles—College Level Summer Program; High School Level Summer Program; UCLA High School Acting and Performance Institute

University of California, San Diego—UCSD Academic Connections and Summer Session

University of California, Santa Barbara—Early Start Program; UCSB Summer Research Mentorship Program

University of San Diego—Summer Sports Camps

University of Southern California—Summer Production Workshops

University of Sports—Superstar Camp

U.S. Space Camp—Aviation Challenge and Advanced Space Academy

Vogelsinger Soccer Academy and All-Star Soccer School

Weissman Teen Tours, Inc.

Colorado

Adventure Pursuits—Adventure Pursuits Expeditions & Camps

Adventure Treks, Inc.

America's Adventure/Venture Europe

Aspen Music School—Aspen Music Festival and School

Colorado College—Summer Session for High School Students

Cottonwood Gulch Foundation—Prairie Trek Group I; Prairie Trek Group II

Crow Canyon Archaelogical Center—High School Field School; High School Excavation Program

Deer Hill Expeditions

Durango Camps—Durango Youth Volleyball Camp
Horizon Adventures, Inc.
Outpost Wilderness Adventure
Summer Study Programs—Summer Study at the University of Colorado at Boulder
Trailmark Outdoor Adventures
University of Colorado Cancer Center—Summer Cancer Research Fellowship
Weissman Teen Tours, Inc.

Connecticut

Brookfield Craft Center—Summer Workshop Series
Buck's Rock Performing and Creative Arts Camp
Capitol Region Education Council and Wesleyan University
Choate Rosemary Hall—Choate Rosemary Hall Summer Session; English Language Institute; John F. Kennedy Institute in Government; The Writing Project
The Island Laboratory
Joel Ross Tennis & Sports Camp
Junior Statesmen Foundation—Junior Statesmen Summer School
No. 1 Soccer Camps—College Prep Academy
United States Coast Guard Academy—Academy Introduction Mission (AIM); Minority Introduction to Engineering (MITE)
University of Connecticut—Mentor Connection
Yale University—Yale Daily News Summer Journalism Program; Yale Summer Programs
YMCA of Metropolitan Hartford—Camp Jewell YMCA Outdoor Center

Delaware

Middle States Soccer Camp—Intermediate and Senior Soccer Camps
University of Delaware—Summer College for High School Juniors; Upward Bound Math and Science Center

District of Columbia

American University—Discover the World of Communication
Bethesda Academy of Performing Arts—Summer Repertory Theater; Mid-Summer Shakespeare Company
Catholic University of America—Capitol Classic Summer Debate Institute; Chamber Music Workshop; College Course for High School Students; Experiences in Architecture; Eye on Engineering; Media and Video Production Workshop; Opera Institute for Young Singers
Congressional Youth Leadership Council—Global Young Leaders Conference; National Young Leaders Conference
Education Unlimited—East Coast College Tour

Georgetown University—Georgetown Summer College
Junior Statesmen Foundation—Junior Statesmen Summer School
Musiker Discovery Program—Summer Discovery
National Student Leadership Conference—Law & Advocacy; International Diplomacy; Medicine & Health Care
National Youth Leadership Forum—National Youth Leadership Forum on Medicine
Sidwell Friends School—Sidwell Friends Summer Programs
The Washington Opera—Opera Institute for Young Singers
Washington Workshops Foundation—Washington Workshops Seminars

Florida

Barefoot International—Barefoot International & Fly High Ski School
Embry-Riddle Aeronautical University—ACES Academy (Aviation Career Education Specialization); Aerospace Summer Camp; Engineering Academy; Flight Exploration; SunFlight Camps
Miami University—Junior Scholars Program
Palmer Tennis Academy—Junior Camps
Ringling School of Art and Design—Pre-College Perspective; Summer Teen Studios
Seacamp Association, Inc.—Seacamp
SeaWorld Adventure Parks—SeaWorld/Busch Gardens Adventure Camps
University of Florida—Student Science Training Program
University of Miami—University of Miami Summer Scholar Programs

Georgia

Brenau University—Firespark Schools
LaGrange College—Visual Arts Workshop
National Youth Leadership Forum—National Youth Leadership Forum on Medicine
Savannah College of Art and Design—Rising Star
Spelman College—Early College Summer Program

Hawaii

Adventure Pursuits—Adventure Pursuits Expeditions & Camps
America's Adventure/Venture Europe
American Trails West
Hawaii Preparatory Academy—Hawaii Preparatory Academy Summer Session
Musiker Discovery Programs—Musiker Tours
Student Conservation Association—High School Conservation Work Crew (CWC) Program
Wilderness Ventures—Wilderness Adventure Expeditions; Advanced Leadership Expeditions; Offshore Adventure Expeditions
World Horizons International

Idaho

Adventure Treks, Inc.
National Outdoor Leadership School—Wilderness Leadership Courses

Illinois

ASC Football Camps, Inc.
Center for American Archeology—Archeological Field School
Columbia College Chicago—High School Summer Institute
Illinois State University—Summer High School Forensic Workshop
Junior Statesmen Foundation—Junior Statesmen Summer School
National Student Leadership Conference—Law & Advocacy; International Diplomacy;
    Medicine & Health Care
National Youth Leadership Forum—National Youth Leadership Forum on Medicine
Northwestern University—National High School Institute
Northwestern University Center for Talent Development—Apogee, Spectrum, Equinox,
    Leapfrog
Southern Illinois University, Carbondale—Women's Introduction to Engineering
University of Illinois, Chicago—Health Science Enrichment Program
University of Illinois, Urbana-Champaign—Fighting Illini Sports Camps

Indiana

All-American Rowing Camp, LLC—High School Coed Rowing Camp
Ball State University—Ball State University Journalism Workshops
Columbus College Chicago—High School Summer Institute
Evansville Association for the Blind—Summer College Program for Students with
    Disabilities
Indiana State University—Summer Honors Program
Indiana University, Bloomington—College Audition Preparation (CAP); Summer Piano
    Academy; Summer Recorder Academy; Summer String Academy; High School
    Journalism Publications Workshops; Indiana University Summer Music Clinic;
    International Studies Summer Institute for High School Students; Jim Holland
    Summer Enrichment Program in Biology; Midsummer Theatre Program
Purdue School of Engineering and Technology, IUPUI—Minority Engineering
    Advancement
Purdue University—Seminar for Top Engineering Prospects (STEP)
University of Evansville—Options
University of Notre Dame—Introduction to Engineering; Summer Experience; Summer
    Sports Camps

Iowa

Camp Courageous of Iowa—Volunteer Program
University of Iowa—Iowa All-State Music Camp; Summer Journalism Workshops; Workshop in Theatre Arts; Iowa Young Writers' Studio

Kentucky

Transylvania University—Academic Camp with Computer Emphasis

Louisiana

Louisiana State University—Honors High School Credit Program
Xavier University of Louisiana—BioStar; ChemStar; MathStar; SOAR 1

Maine

Bates College—Bates College Basketball Camp; Bates Forensic Institutes; Creative Writing Workshops; Edmund S. Muskie Scholars Program
Camp Encore/Coda—Upper Camp
Gould Academy—Young Scholars Program; College Preparatory Program
Maine Teen Camp
Sea Education Association—Oceanography of the Gulf of Maine
University of Maine—Maine Summer Youth Music Senior Camp

Maryland

Goucher College—Goucher Summer Arts Institute
Johns Hopkins University—Hopkins Pre-college Credit Program
Johns Hopkins University Center for Talented Youth—CTY Summer Programs; CAA Summer Programs
Middle States Soccer Camp—Intermediate and Senior Soccer Camps
University of Maryland—Design Career Discover (Arch 150)
United States Naval Academy—Navy Crew Camp for Boys; Navy Rowing Camp for Girls

Massachusetts

Academic Study Associates—ASA Pre-College Enrichment Program; Language Study Programs
Art Institute of Boston at Lesley University—Pre-College Summer Program
Boston College—Boston College Experience
Boston University—Program in Mathematics for Young Scientists (PROMYS)
Brandeis University—Brandeis Summer Odyssey; Genesis at Brandeis University
Education Unlimited—East Coast College Tour
Hampshire College—Hampshire College Summer Studies in Mathematics
Harvard University—Harvard Summer School Secondary School Program

Lawrence Academy—Environmental Field Study; Global Leaders Workshop; International English Institute
Mount Holyoke College—SummerMath
National Youth Leadership Forum—National Youth Leadership Forum on Medicine
Offense Defense Golf Camp
Phillips Academy—Phillips Academy Summer Session
Putney Student Travel—Excel at Williams and Amherst Colleges
Quest Scholars Program—Quest Scholars Program at Harvard
Sea Education Association—Science at Sea
Simon's Rock College of Bard—Young Writer's Workshop
Skidmore College—Pre-College Program in the Liberal Arts for High School Students at Skidmore
Smith College—Smith College Science Program
Summer Institute for the Gifted—College Gifted Program
Tufts University European Center—Tufts Summit
Tufts University School of Veterinary Medicine—Adventures in Veterinary Medicine
U.S. Gymnastics Training Centers—U.S. Gymnastics Camp
Vogelsinger Soccer Academy and All-Star Soccer School
Wilderness Experience Unlimited—Explorer Group; Trailblazers

Michigan

American Youth Foundation—International Leadership Conference
Blue Lake Fine Arts Camp
Calvin College—Entrada Scholars Program
Interlochen Center for the Arts—Interlochen Arts Camp
Michigan State University—Spartan Debate Institute (SDI)
Musiker Discovery Program—Summer Discovery
Tamarack Camps
University of Michigan—Michigan Math and Science Scholars

Minnesota

Carleton College—Summer Writing Program
Concordia College—Concordia Language Villages
Friendship Ventures—Youth Leadership Program
Minnesota Institute for Talented Youth—Expand Your Mind
Saint Cloud State University, Ethnic Studies Program—Advanced Program in Technology and Science; Scientific Discovery Program
Saint Olaf College—Saint Olaf Summer Music Camp
Saint Paul Academy and Summit School—Summer Programs

Mississippi

Mississippi University for Women—Business Week; Aero-Tech
University of Mississippi—Summer College for High School Students
University of Southern Mississippi, The Frances A. Karnes Center for Gifted Studies—
    Leadership Studies Program; Summer Program for Academically Talented Youth

Missouri

Saint Louis University—Parks Summer Academy

Montana

Adventure Treks, Inc.
Visions

Nebraska

University of Nebraska, Lincoln—All Girls/All Math

Nevada

America's Adventure/Venture Europe
Weissman Teen Tours, Inc.

New Hampshire

American Youth Foundation—International Leadership Conference
Apple Hill Center for Chamber Music—Apple Hill Summer School and Festival
Kinyon/Jones Tennis Camp
University of New Hampshire—Project SMART; Summer Youth Music School (SYMS)
The Walden School—Walden School Summer Music School, Festival, and Camp

New Jersey

Appel Farm Arts and Music Center—Appel Farm's Summer Arts Camp
Drew University—Drew Summer Music
Dwight-Englewood School—Dwight-Englewood Summer Programs
Hun School of Princeton—Hun School Summer Programs
Junior Statesmen Foundation—Junior Statesmen Summer School
New Jersey Institute of Technology—Pre-College Academy in Technology and Science
    for High School Students
New York Film Academy—New York Film Academy Summer Program
Princeton Ballet School—American Repertory Ballet's Summer Intensive
Princeton University—Princeton University Summer Sports Camps
Rutgers University—Young Scholars Program in Discrete Mathematics
Summer Institute for the Gifted—College Gifted Program
Tab Ramos Soccer Academy

New Mexico

Brush Ranch Camps
Cottonwood Gulch Foundation—Prairie Trek Group I; Prairie Trek Group II
Deer Hill Expeditions

New York

ACTeen—ACTeen July Academy; ACTeen August Academy; ACTeen Summer Saturday
   Program
Adelphi University—Academic Success Program
Alfred University—High School Academic Institutes
Alpine Adventures, Inc.—Alpine Adventures
American Academy of Dramatic Arts—Summer Actor Training
Barnard College—Summer in New York: A Pre-College Program
Columbia University—Columbia Summer Programs for High School Students
Congressional Youth Leadership Council—Global Young Leaders Conference; National
   Young Leaders Conference
Cooperstown Baseball Camp
Cornell University—Cornell University Summer College; Summer Honors Program for
   High School Sophomores
Cornell University Sports School—Summer Sports Camps
Eastern U.S. Music Camp, Inc.
French Woods Festival of the Performing Arts
FUN-damental Basketball Camp, Inc.—Basketball Camp at Morrisville
Hobart and William Smith Colleges—Environmental Studies Summer Youth Institute
Ithaca College—Summer College for High School Students
Kutsher's Sports Academy
Lake Placid Soccer Centre—Mountain View Soccer Camp
The Masters School—Panther Basketball Camp; Summer ESL; Summer in the City;
   Summer Theatre
New York Film Academy—New York Film Academy Summer Program
New York University—Tisch Summer High School Program
Parsons School of Design—Summer Intensive Studies
Pratt Institute—Pre-College Summer Program
Rochester Institute of Technology—College and Careers
School for Film and Television—Summer in the City
Southampton College of Long Island University—Summer High School Workshops
Stagedoor Enterprises—Stagedoor Manor Performing Arts Training Center
State University of New York, Oswego—Summer Art Institute; Summer Theater Institute
State University of New York, Purchase—Summer Visual Arts Institute
Summer Institute for the Gifted—College Gifted Program

Syracuse University—Syracuse University Summer College for High School Students
Vassar College and New York Stage and Film—Powerhouse Theatre Program
Wells College—Student Conference on Leadership and Social Responsibility

North Carolina

Adventure Treks, Inc.
Appalachian State University—Summer Sports, Music, and Academic Camps
Asheville School—Asheville School Summer Academic Adventures
Brevard Music Center—Young Artists Division
Davidson College—Davidson July Experience
Deep Woods Camp for Boys—Deep Woods Camp for Boys
Duke University—Duke Tennis Camp; Duke University Pre-College Program
East Carolina University—East Carolina Summer Theatre
Eastern Music Festival
Gifted and Talented Development Center
North Carolina School of the Arts—Summer Session
Oak Ridge Military Academy—Academic Summer School; Leadership Adventure Camp
Wake Forest University—Summer Debate Workshop; Fast Track; Policy Project; Policy
    Analysis Seminar

North Dakota

University of North Dakota—International Aerospace Camp

Ohio

BalletMet—Summer Workshop
Denison University—Jonathan R. Reynolds Young Writers Workshop
Friends Music Camp
Kenyon College—Young Writers at Kenyon
Ohio State University—Ross Young Scholars Program
SeaWorld Adventure Parks—SeaWorld/Busch Gardens Adventure Camps
The Wilds—Safari Camp
University of Cincinnati, College of Engineering—Inquisitive Women Summer Day
    Camp
University of Dayton—Women in Engineering Summer Camp
Wright State University—Wright State University Pre-College Summer Enrichment
    Programs

Oklahoma

Oklahoma City Community College—Applying the Skills of Technology in Science

Oregon

Britt Festivals—The Britt Institute
Global Institute for Developing Entrepreneurs—IN2BIZ Entrepreneur Camp
Lewis and Clark College, Northwest Writing Institute—Fir Acres Workshop in Writing and Thinking; Writer to Writer
Mount Hood Snowboard Camp—MHSC Summer Camp
Oregon Museum of Science and Industry—OMSI Summer Science Camps and Adventures
U.S. Snowboard Training Center—USSTC Allstar Snowboard Camp
Westcoast Connections—Ski and Snowboard Sensation

Pennsylvania

ASC Football Camps, Inc.
Ballibay Camps, Inc.—Camp Ballibay for the Fine and Performing Arts
Bryn Mawr College—Writing for College
Carnegie Mellon University—Pre-College Programs
Dickinson College—Pre-College Program
Education Unlimited—East Coast College Tour
International Sports Camp
Juniata College—Summer Camp for Gifted Students
Lebanon Valley College—Daniel Fox Youth Scholars Institute; Lebanon Valley College Summer Music Camp
Longacre Leadership—Longacre Leadership Program
Middle States Soccer Camp—Intermediate and Senior Soccer Camps
National Youth Leadership Forum—National Youth Leadership Forum on Medicine
The Pittsburgh Project
Seton Hill College—Science Quest II
76ers Basketball Camp
Summer Study Programs—Summer Enrichment and Summer Study at Penn State
Trailmark Outdoor Adventures
University of the Arts—Drama and Musical Theater; PREP, Art Smart, and Media and Communications Workshops; Summer Institute of Jazz
Woodward Sports Camp

Rhode Island

Brown University—Pre-College Program; Focus Program
Rhode Island School of Design—Pre-College Program
University of Rhode Island—W. Alton Jones Teen Expeditions

South Carolina

Columbia College, Leadership Institute—Entrepreneurship Camp; 21st Century Leaders Visions

South Dakota

Latitudes International—Community Service Travel

Tennessee

Rhodes College—Young Scholars and Writers Camp
University of the South—Bridge Program in Math and Science
Vanderbilt University—Program for Talented Youth

Texas

Abilene Christian University—Kadesh Life Camp
ASC Football Camps, Inc.
Baylor University—Baylor University Debater's Workshop; High School Summer Science Research Fellowship Program
Envision EMI, Inc.—NexTech: The National Summit of Young Technology Leaders
Marine Military Academy—Summer Military Training Camp
National Youth Leadership Forum—National Youth Leadership Forum on Medicine
SeaWorld Adventure Parks—SeaWorld/Busch Gardens Adventure Camps
Southern Methodist University—College Experience
Southwest Texas State University—Honors Summer Math Camp; Summer Creative Writing Camp; Summer High School Theatre Workshop
Trinity University—A Trinity Summer
University of Texas, Austin—Summer Theatre Workshop
Vogelsinger Soccer Academy and All-Star Soccer School

Utah

America's Adventure/Venture Europe
Cottonwood Gulch Foundation—Prairie Trek Group I; Prairie Trek Group II
Deer Hill Expeditions
Rainforest Exploration Association—City Lights; Starry Nights
Westcoast Connections—Golf and Tennis Programs
World Horizons International

Vermont

Bennington College—Bennington College July Program
Burklyn Ballet Theatre
Kingdom County Productions and Fledgling Films—Fledgling Films Summer Institute

Kinhaven Music School
Musiker Discovery Program—Summer Discovery
Putney School—Putney School Summer Programs
Southern Vermont College—Summer Sports Camps
Summer Sonatina International Piano Camp
University of Vermont—Discovering Engineering, Mathematics, and Computer Science

Virginia

Bridgewater College—High School Leadership Academy
Christchurch School—Summer Programs on the River
Hargrave Military Academy—Summer School and Camp
Hollins University—Hollinscience Program; Leadership Enrichment Program; Precollege Program
Northern Virginia Summer Academy
Randolph-Macon Academy—Randolph-Macon Academy Summer Programs
Sidwell Friends School—Women's Leadership
University of Virginia—Summer Enrichment Program
Washington and Lee University—Summer Scholars

Washington

America's Adventure/Venture Europe
Art Institute of Seattle—Studio 101
International Bicycle Fund—Sbuhbi Lithlal Ti Swatixwtuhd
National Outdoor Leadership School—Wilderness Leadership Courses
Pacific Lutheran University—Summer Scholars at PLU
Seattle Youth Symphony Orchestra—Marrowstone Music Festival
University of Washington—Courses for High School Students
Western Washington University—Adventures in Science and Arts; Outdoor Challenge Institute; SummerQuest

West Virginia

Greenbrier River Outdoor Adventures

Wisconsin

American Collegiate Adventures
Beloit College—Center for Language Studies
Milwaukee School of Engineering—Discover the Possibilities; Focus on the Possibilities
University of Wisconsin, La Crosse—Archaeology Field Schools; University of Wisconsin Athletic Camps

University of Wisconsin, Madison—Engineering Summer Program for High School Students; Pre-College Program in Environmental and Native American Studies; Summer Art Classes; Summer Music Clinic; Summer Science Institute

University of Wisconsin, Superior—Youthsummer

Vogelsinger Soccer Academy and All-Star Soccer School

Wyoming

Adventure Treks, Inc.

Global Routes—High School Community Service Programs

National Outdoor Leadership School—Wilderness Leadership Courses

Outpost Wilderness Adventure

Various (Unspecified) Locations in the United States

America's Baseball Camps

American Jewish Society for Service—Summer Work Camps

American Management Association—Operation Enterprise

American Trails West

Avatar Education Ltd.—Buckswood ARC Summer Programs

College Visits

Earthwatch Institute—Field Research Expedition Internships

Five-Star Basketball Camp

Hugh O'Brian Youth Leadership (HOBY)—HOBY Leadership Seminars

La Société Française—International Volunteer Program

Landmark Volunteers—Summer Service Opportunity Programs

Longacre Expeditions

Mathematics Foundation of America—Canada/USA Mathcamp

Moondance Adventures

Musiker Discovery Programs—Musiker Tours

National Computer Camps, Inc.

Outward Bound USA

Planet Hockey, Inc.—Planet Hockey Skills Camps; Planet Hockey Ranch

Project Sunshine—Project Sunshine Volunteer Programs

The Road Less Traveled

School for Field Studies—Environmental Field Studies Abroad

SoccerPlus Camps—SoccerPlus Goalkeeper School and SoccerPlus Field Player Academy

Student Conservation Association—High School Conservation Work Crew (CWC) Program

Student Hosteling Program—Summer Biking Programs

Trailmark Outdoor Adventures

U.S. Sports Camps—Nike Sports Camps

Weissman Teen Tours, Inc.

Westcoast Connection—Active Teen Tours; Outdoor Adventure Programs

Wilderness Experience Unlimited—Explorer Group; Trailblazers

Wilderness Ventures—Wilderness Adventure Expeditions; Advanced Leadership Expeditions; Offshore Adventure Expeditions

World Learning—Experiment in International Living (EIL)

Index by Duration of Program

This index groups the sponsoring organizations by the duration of each program. Programs may be listed in more than one category, if applicable.

1–7 Days

Abilene Christian University—Kadesh Life Camp
Adventure Ireland
Adventure Pursuits—Adventure Pursuits Expeditions & Camps
Alfred University—High School Academic Institutes
All-American Rowing Camp, LLC—High School Coed Rowing Camp
Alpine Adventures, Inc.—Alpine Adventures
America's Baseball Camps
American Youth Foundation—International Leadership Conference
Art Institute of Seattle—Studio 101
ASC Football Camps, Inc.—ASC Football Camps
Auburn University—Design Camp
Auburn University—Summer Honor Band Camps
Auburn University—World Affairs Youth Seminar
Baja California Language College
Ball State University—Ball State University Journalism Workshops
Barefoot International—Barefoot International & Fly High Ski School
Bark Lake Leadership Center—Leadership Through Recreation/Music
Bates College—Bates College Basketball Camp
Bates College—Creative Writing Workshops
Birmingham-Southern College—Student Leaders in Service
Bridgewater College—High School Leadership Academy
Britt Festivals—The Britt Institute
Brookfield Craft Center—Summer Workshop Series
Brown University—Focus Program
Brush Ranch Camps

Carmel Valley Tennis Camp

Catholic University of America—Chamber Music Workshop

Catholic University of America—Media and Video Production Workshop

Center for American Archeology—Archeological Field School

Center for Cultural Interchange—Discovery Abroad Programs (Independent Homestay; International Youth Camps; Language School Program)

Chris Waller's Summer Gymnastics Jam

Christchurch School—Summer Programs on the River

College Visits

Columbia College, Leadership Institute—21st Century Leaders

Concordia College—Concordia Language Villages

Cooperstown Baseball Camp

Cornell University Sports School—Summer Sports Camps

Costa Rican Language Academy (CRLA)

Crow Canyon Archaeological Center—High School Field School; High School Excavation Program

Duke University—Duke Tennis Camp

Durango Camps—Durango Youth Volleyball Camp

Education Unlimited—College Admission Prep Camp; Prep Camp Excel

Education Unlimited—Computer Camp by Education Unlimited

Education Unlimited—East Coast College Tour; Tour Italy

Education Unlimited—Public Speaking Institute by Education Unlimited

Embry-Riddle Aeronautical University—ACES Academy (Aviation Career Education Specialization)

Embry-Riddle Aeronautical University—Engineering Academy

Embry-Riddle Aeronautical University—Flight Exploration

Five-Star Basketball Camp

Friendship Ventures—Youth Leadership Program

FUN-damental Basketball Camp, Inc.—Basketball Camp at Morrisville

Georgetown University—Georgetown Summer College

Gifted and Talented Development Center—Gifted and Talented Development Center

Global Volunteers

Goucher College—Goucher Summer Arts Institute

Greenbrier River Outdoor Adventures

Hockey Opportunity Camp

Hollins University—Leadership Enrichment Program

Horizon Adventures, Inc.

Hugh O'Brian Youth Leadership (HOBY)—HOBY Leadership Seminars

Idyllwild Arts foundation—Idyllwild Arts Summer Program

Illinois State University—Summer High School Forensic Workshop

Indiana University, Bloomington—College Audition Preparation (CAP); Summer Piano Academy; Summer Recorder Academy; Summer String Academy

Indiana University, Bloomington—High School Journalism Publications Workshops

Indiana University, Bloomington—Indiana University Summer Music Clinic

Indiana University, Bloomington—Jim Holland Summer Enrichment Program in Biology

International Sports Camp

The Island Laboratory

Juniata College—Voyages: Summer Camp for Gifted Students

Kicking Game

Kincardine Summer Music Festival—KSMF Jazz Camp; KSMF Chamber Music Camp; KSMF Festival Week Music Camp

Kinyon/Jones Tennis Camp

Lake Placid Soccer Centre—Mountain View Soccer Camp

Lebanon Valley College—Daniel Fox Youth Scholars Institute

Lebanon Valley College—Lebanon Valley College Summer Music Camp

Lewis and Clark College, Northwest Writing Institute—Writer to Writer

The Masters School— Panther Basketball Camp

Media Workshops Foundation—The Media Workshops

Middle States Soccer Camp—Intermediate and Senior Soccer Camps

Milwaukee School of Engineering—Discover the Possibilities; Focus on the Possibilities

Mount Hood Snowboard Camp—MHSC Summer Sessions

National Computer Camps, Inc.

Oceanic Society—Bahamas Dolphin Project for High School Students

Oceanic Society—Belize Student Expedition

Offense Defense Golf Camp

Oregon Museum of Science and Industry—OMSI Summer Science Camps and Adventures

Orme School—Orme Summer Camp

Outpost Wilderness Adventure—Outpost Wilderness Adventures

Palmer Tennis Academy—Palmer Tennis Academy Junior Camps

Peacework

The Pittsburgh Project

Planet Hockey, Inc.—Planet Hockey Skills Camps; Planet Hockey Ranch

Power Chord Academy

Princeton University—Princeton University Summer Sports Camps

Project PULL Academy—Project PULL Academy Leadership Challenge and College Preview

Purdue School of Engineering and Technology, IUPUI— Minority Engineering Advancement Program (MEAP)

Purdue University—Seminar for Top Engineering Prospects (STEP)

Rainforest Exploration Association—City Lights

Ringling School of Art and Design—Summer Teen Studios

Rochester Institute of Technology—College and Careers

Saint Louis University—Parks Summer Academy

SeaWorld Adventure Parks—SeaWorld/Busch Gardens Adventure Camps

Seton Hill College—Science Quest II

Sidwell Friends School—Deep Creek Adventures; SFS Alaskan Adventures

SoccerPlus Camps—SoccerPlus Goalkeeper School and SoccerPlus Field Player Academy

Southampton College of Long Island University—Summer High School Workshops

Southern Illinois University, Carbondale—Women's Introduction to Engineering

Southern Vermont College—Summer Sports Camps

Southwest Texas State University—Summer Creative Writing Camp

Stanford Jazz Workshop—Jazz Camp; Jazz Residency

Stanford University—Summer Sports Camps

Tab Ramos Soccer Academy

Trailmark Outdoor Adventures

Transylvania University—Academic Camp with Computer Emphasis

Tufts University School of Veterinary Medicine—Adventures in Veterinary Medicine

United States Coast Guard Academy—Academy Introduction Mission (AIM)

United States Coast Guard Academy—Minority Introduction to Engineering (MITE)

United States Naval Academy—Navy Crew Camp for Boys

United States Naval Academy—Navy Rowing Camp for Girls

University of California, San Diego—UCSD Academic Connections & Summer Session

University of Cincinnati, College of Engineering—Inquisitive Women Summer Day Camp

University of Dayton—Women in Engineering Summer Camp

University of Evansville—Options

University of Iowa—Iowa All-State Music Camp

University of Iowa—Summer Journalism Workshops

University of Nebraska, Lincoln—All Girls/All Math

University of Rhode Island—W. Alton Jones Teen Expeditions

University of San Diego—University of San Diego Summer Sports Camps

University of Southern Mississippi, The Frances A. Karnes Center for Gifted Studies—Leadership Studies Program

University of Sports—Superstar Camp

University of Wisconsin, La Crosse—Archaeology Field Schools

University Of Wisconsin, La Crosse—University of Wisconsin Athletic Camps

University of Wisconsin, Madison—Engineering Summer Program for High School Students

University of Wisconsin, Madison—Pre-college Program in Environmental and Native American Studies

University of Wisconsin, Madison—Summer Art Classes

University of Wisconsin, Madison—Summer Music Clinic

University of Wisconsin, Superior—Youthsummer

U.S. Gymnastics Training Centers—U.S. Gymnastics Camp

U.S. Space Camp—Aviation Challenge and Advanced Space Academy

Washington Workshops Foundation—Washington Workshops Seminars

Wells College—Student Conference on Leadership and Social Responsibility

Western Washington University—Adventures in Science and Arts

Western Washington University—Outdoor Challenge Institute

Wilderness Experience Unlimited—Explorer Group; Trailblazers

The Wilds—Safari Camp

Woodward Sports Camp

Wright State University—Wright State University Pre-College Summer Enrichment Programs

Yale University—Yale Daily News Summer Journalism Program

8–21 Days

ACTeen—ACTeen July Academy; ACTeen August Academy; ACTeen Summer Saturday Program

ActionQuest—ActionQuest Programs

Adventure Ireland

Adventure Pursuits—Adventure Pursuits Expeditions & Camps

Adventure Treks, Inc.

Adventures Cross-Country

Alliances Abroad—Summer Spanish Program for Youth in Spain; Summer French Programs for Youth in France; Culture and Adventure Program for Youth in Ireland

America's Adventure/Venture Europe

American Collegiate Adventures

American Institute for Foreign Study (AIFS)—Pre-College Summer Study Abroad

American Management Association—Operation Enterprise

American Trails West

American University—Discover the World of Communication

Amerispan Unlimited—Madrid and Marbella Summer Camps; Spanish Language Program in Costa Rica

Apple Hill Center for Chamber Music—Apple Hill Summer School and Festival

Asheville School—Asheville School Summer Academic Adventures

Avatar Education Ltd.—Buckswood ARC Summer Programs

Baja California Language College

Ballibay Camps, Inc.—Camp Ballibay for the Fine and Performing Arts

Bates College—Bates Forensic Institutes

Bates College—Edmund S. Muskie Scholars Program

Baylor University—Baylor University Debaters' Workshop

Blue Lake Fine Arts Camp

Bordeaux Language School—Teenage Summer Program in Biarritz

Brenau University—Firespark Schools

Britt Festivals—The Britt Institute

Broadreach, Inc.—Broadreach Summer Adventures for Teenagers

Brown University—Focus Program

Brush Ranch Camps

Bryn Mawr College—Writing for College

Burklyn Ballet Theatre

California Chicano News Media Association—San Jose Urban Journalism Workshop for Minorities

California College of Arts and Crafts—CCAC Pre-College Program

Carleton College—Summer Writing Program

Carmel Valley Tennis Camp

Catholic University of America—Capitol Classic Summer Debate Institute

Catholic University of America—Experiences in Architecture

Catholic University of America—Media and Video Production Workshop

Center for American Archeology—Archeological Field School

Center for Cultural Interchange—Discovery Abroad Programs (Independent Homestay; International Youth Camps; Language School Program)

Ceran Lingua—Ceran Junior

Championship Debate Enterprises—Lincoln-Douglas and Extemp Institute; Policy Debate Institute

Choate Rosemary Hall—Choate Rosemary Hall Summer Session; English Language Institute; John F. Kennedy Institute in Government; The Writing Project; Study Abroad

Christchurch School—Summer Programs on the River

Colorado College—Summer Session for High School Students

Columbia College, Leadership Institute—Entrepreneurship Camp

Comunicare—Study and Share

Concordia College—Concordia Language Villages

Congressional Youth Leadership Council—Global Young Leaders Conference

Congressional Youth Leadership Council—National Young Leaders Conference

Cornell University—Cornell University Summer College

Cornell University—Summer Honors Program for High School Sophomores

Costa Rican Language Academy (CRLA)

Crow Canyon Archaeological Center—High School Field School; High School Excavation Program

Davidson College—Davidson July Experience

Deer Hill Expeditions

Denison University—Jonathan R. Reynolds Young Writers Workshop

Drew University—Drew Summer Music

Earthwatch Institute—Field Research Expedition Internships

Eastern U.S. Music Camp, Inc.

ECHO International Educational Expeditions—Australian Biological Adventures

Education Unlimited—College Admission Prep Camp; Prep Camp Excel

Education Unlimited—Computer Camp by Education Unlimited

Education Unlimited—East Coast College Tour; Tour Italy

Education Unlimited—Public Speaking Institute by Education Unlimited

Education Unlimited—Summer Focus at Berkeley; Acting Workshop at Berkeley

EF International Language Schools

Embry-Riddle Aeronautical University—SunFlight Camps

Envision EMI, Inc.—The National Summit of Young Technology Leaders

French Woods Festival of the Performing Arts

Friendship Ventures—Youth Leadership Program

Georgetown University—Georgetown Summer College

Global Institute for Developing Entrepreneurs—IN2BIZ Entrepreneur Camp

Global Routes—High School Community Service Programs

Global Volunteers

Goucher College—Goucher Summer Arts Institute

Greenbrier River Outdoor Adventures

Hobart and William Smith Colleges—Environmental Studies Summer Youth Institute

Hockey Opportunity Camp

Hollins University—Hollinscience Program

Hollins University—Precollege Program

Horizon Adventures, Inc.

Hugh O'Brian Youth Leadership (HOBY)—HOBY Leadership Seminars

Huntingdon College—Huntingdon College Summer Programs

Idyllwild Arts Foundation—Idyllwild Arts Summer Program

Illinois State University—Summer High School Forensic Workshop

Indiana State University—Summer Honors Program

Indiana University, Bloomington—College Audition Preparation (CAP); Summer Piano Academy; Summer Recorder Academy; Summer String Academy

Indiana University, Bloomington—International Studies Summer Institute for High School Students

Indiana University, Bloomington—Midsummer Theatre Program

International Bicycle Fund—Bicycle Africa Tours; Sbuhbi Lithlal Ti Swatixwtuhd

Involvement Volunteers Association—International Volunteering; Networked International Volunteering

Irish Centre for Talented Youth

Ithaca College—Summer College for High School Students

Joel Ross Tennis & Sports Camp

Johns Hopkins University Center for Talented Youth—CTY Summer Programs; CAA Summer Programs

Kenyon College—Young Writers at Kenyon

Kingdom County Productions and Fledgling Films—Fledgling Films Summer Institute

Kinhaven Music School

LaGrange College—Visual Arts Workshop

Landmark Volunteers—Summer Service Opportunity Programs

Language Link—Intercultura; Spanish Language Institute; CLIC

Language Studies Abroad, Inc.—Language Studies Abroad

Language Study Abroad

Latitudes International—Community Service Travel

Legacy International—Global Youth Village

Lewis and Clark College, Northwest Writing Institute—Fir Acres Workshop in Writing and Thinking

Leysin American School in Switzerland—Summer in Switzerland

Lingua Service Worldwide—Junior Classic and Junior Sports Program

Lingua Service Worldwide—Junior Course in Salamanca

Lingua Service Worldwide—Summer Language Adventure

Longacre Expeditions

The Masters School— Panther Basketball Camp

The Masters School—Summer ESL

The Masters School—Summer in the City

The Masters School—Summer Theatre

Michigan State University—Spartan Debate Institute (SDI)

Minnesota Institute for Talented Youth—Expand Your Mind

Mississippi University for Women—Business Week; Aero-Tech

Moondance Adventures

Nacel Open Door

National Youth Leadership Forum—National Youth Leadership Forum on Medicine

No. 1 Soccer Camps—College Prep Academy

Northern Virginia Summer Academy

Northwaters—Northwaters Wilderness Programs

Northwestern University Center For Talent Development—Apogee, Spectrum, Equinox, Leapfrog

Ocean Educations Ltd.—Marine and Environmental Science Program

Odyssey Expeditions—Tropical Marine Biology Voyages

Offense Defense Golf Camp

Oklahoma City Community College—Applying the Skills of Technology in Science
Oregon Museum of Science and Industry—OMSI Summer Science Camps and
    Adventures
Orme School—Orme Summer Camp
Outpost Wilderness Adventure—Outpost Wilderness Adventures
Pacific Lutheran University—Summer Scholars at PLU
Peacework
Princeton University—Princeton University Summer Sports Camps
Putney School—Putney School Summer Programs
Putney Student Travel—Excel at Williams and Amherst Colleges; Excel at
    Oxford/Tuscany and Madrid/Barcelona
Rainforest Exploration Association—Starry Nights
Rhodes College—Young Scholars and Writers Camp
Ringling School of Art and Design—Summer Teen Studios
The Road Less Traveled
Sail Caribbean
Saint Cloud State University, Ethnic Studies Program—Advanced Program in
    Technology and Science
Saint Olaf College—Saint Olaf Summer Music Camp
Sea Education Association—Science at Sea; Oceanography of the Gulf of Maine
Seacamp Association, Inc.—Seacamp
Seattle Youth Symphony Orchestra—Marrowstone Music Festival
SeaWorld Adventure Parks—SeaWorld/Busch Gardens Adventure Camps
Sidwell Friends School—Deep Creek Adventures; SFS Alaskan Adventures
Sidwell Friends School—SFS in Costa Rica
Sidwell Friends School—Women's Leadership
Sierra Adventure Camps
Simon's Rock College of Bard—Young Writer's Workshop
Southwest Texas State University—Summer High School Theatre Workshop
Stanford University—Summer Discovery Institutes
Stanford University—Summer Sports Camps
Stanford University, Education Program for Gifted Youth—Summer Institute in
    Mathematics and Physics
State University of New York, Oswego—Summer Art Institute; Summer Theater Institute
Student Hosteling Program—Summer Biking Programs
Summer Institute for the Gifted—College Gifted Program
Summer Sonatina International Piano Camp
Summer Study Programs—Summer Study in Paris at The American University of Paris
Tamarack Camps
Tennis: Europe and More

Trailmark Outdoor Adventures

Trinity University—A Trinity Summer

Tufts University School of Veterinary Medicine—Adventures in Veterinary Medicine

University of Arizona—Summer Institute for Writing

University of the Arts—Summer Institute of Jazz

University of California, San Diego—UCSD Academic Connections & Summer Session

University of Colorado Cancer Center—Summer Cancer Research Fellowship

University of Connecticut—Mentor Connection

University of Dallas Study Abroad—Shakespeare in Italy; Latin in Rome; Thomas More in England; Winston Churchill in England

University of Denver—Making of an Engineer

University of Iowa—Iowa Young Writers' Studio

University of Iowa—Workshop in Theatre Arts

University of Maine—Maine Summer Youth Music Senior Camp

University of Maryland—Design Career Discover (Arch 150)

University of Miami Summer Scholar Programs—University of Miami Summer Scholar Programs

University of Michigan—Michigan Math and Science Scholars

University of New Hampshire—Summer Youth Music School (SYMS)

University of North Dakota—International Aerospace Camp

University of Notre Dame—Introduction to Engineering

University of Notre Dame—Summer Experience

University of the South—Bridge Program in Math and Science

University of Southern Mississippi, The Frances A. Karnes Center for Gifted Studies—Summer Program for Academically Talented Youth

University of Vermont—Discovering Engineering, Mathematics, and Computer Science

University of Virginia—Summer Enrichment Program

University of Washington—Courses for High School Students

University of Wisconsin, La Crosse—Archaeology Field Schools

University of Wisconsin, Madison—Summer Art Classes

University of Wisconsin, Superior—Youthsummer

U.S. Snowboard Training Center—USSTC Allstar Snowboard Camp

Vanderbilt University—Program for Talented Youth

Visions

Vogelsinger Soccer Academy and All-Star Soccer School

Volunteers for Peace—VFP International Workcamps

The Washington Opera—Opera Institute for Young Singers

Washington University in St. Louis—Architecture Discovery Program

Westcoast Connection—Active Teen Tours

Westcoast Connection—Golf & Tennis Programs

Westcoast Connection—Israel Experience

Westcoast Connection—On Tour

Westcoast Connection—Outdoor Adventure Programs

Westcoast Connection—Ski & Snowboard Sensation

Western Washington University—SummerQuest

Wilderness Experience Unlimited—Explorer Group; Trailblazers

Wilderness Ventures—Wilderness Adventure Expeditions; Advanced Leadership
    Expeditions; Offshore Adventure Expeditions

Woodward Sports Camp

Wright State University—Wright State University Pre-College Summer Enrichment
    Programs

Xavier University of Louisiana—BioStar; ChemStar; MathStar

YMCA of Metropolitan Hartford—Camp Jewell YMCA Outdoor Center

Youth for Understanding International Exchange—Summer Overseas

22–35 Days

Academic Study Associates—ASA Pre-College Enrichment Program; Language Study
    Programs

ACTeen—ACTeen July Academy; ACTeen August Academy; ACTeen Summer Saturday
    Program

Adelphi University—Academic Success Program

Adventure Ireland

Adventure Pursuits—Adventure Pursuits Expeditions & Camps

Adventure Treks, Inc.

Adventures Cross-Country

AFS Intercultural Programs—Summer Homestay; Summer Homestay Language Study;
    Summer Homestay Plus; Summer Community Service/Team Mission

Alliances Abroad—Summer Spanish Program for Youth in Spain; Summer French
    Programs for Youth in France; Culture and Adventure Program for Youth in Ireland

America's Adventure/Venture Europe

American Collegiate Adventures

American Committee for the Weizmann Institute of Science—Dr. Bessie F. Lawrence
    International Summer Science Institute

American Farm School—Greek Summer

American Institute For Foreign Study (AIFS)—Pre-College Summer Study Abroad

American International Youth Student Exchange—American International Youth
    Student Exchange Program

American Trails West

American University—Discover the World of Communication

Amerispan Unlimited—Madrid and Marbella Summer Camps; Spanish Language
    Program in Costa Rica

Appel Farm Arts and Music Center—Appel Farm's Summer Arts Camp
Art Institute of Boston at Lesley University—Pre-College Summer Program
Aspen Music School—Aspen Music Festival and School
Avatar Education Ltd.—Buckswood ARC Summer Programs
Baja California Language College
Ballibay Camps, Inc.—Camp Ballibay for the Fine and Performing Arts
Barat Foundation—Barat Foundation Summer Program
Barnard College—Summer in New York: A Pre-College Program
Baylor University—High School Summer Science Research Fellowship Program
Beloit College—Center for Language Studies
Bennington College—Bennington College July Program
Bethesda Academy of Performing Arts—Summer Repertory Theater; Mid-Summer
    Shakespeare Company
Bordeaux Language School—Teenage Summer Program in Biarritz
Brandeis University—Brandeis Summer Odyssey
Brandeis University—Genesis at Brandeis University
Breakthroughs Abroad, Inc.—High School Programs
Broadreach, Inc.—Broadreach Insights
Broadreach, Inc.—Broadreach Summer Adventures for Teenagers
Brown University—Focus Program
Brush Ranch Camps
Buck's Rock Performing and Creative Arts Camp
Burklyn Ballet Theatre
California State Summer School for the Arts
Calvin College—Entrada Scholars Program
Cambridge College Programme LLC—Cambridge College programme
Camp Encore/Coda—Upper Camp
Capitol Region Education Council and Wesleyan University—Center for Creative Youth
Catholic University of America—College Courses for High School Students
Center for American Archeology—Archeological Field School
Center for Cross-Cultural Study—Summer in Seville
Center for Cultural Interchange—Discovery Abroad Programs (Independent Homestay;
    International Youth Camps; Language School Program)
Ceran Lingua—Ceran Junior
Choate Rosemary Hall—Choate Rosemary Hall Summer Session; English Language
    Institute; John F. Kennedy Institute in Government; The Writing Project; Study
    Abroad
Christchurch School—Summer Programs on the River
Colorado College—Summer Session for High School Students
Columbia College Chicago—High School Summer Institute

Columbia University—Columbia Summer Programs for High School Students
Columbia University Biosphere 2—Exploring Earth, Life & the Summer Sky
Comunicare—Study and Share
Concordia College—Concordia Language Villages
Cornell University—Cornell University Summer College
Costa Rican Language Academy (CRLA)
Cottonwood Gulch Foundation—Prairie Trek Group I; Prairie Trek Group II; Turquoise Trail
Dauphin Island Sea Lab—Discovery Hall Summer High School Program
Deep Woods Camp for Boys
Deer Hill Expeditions
Dickinson College—Pre-College Program
Eastern Music Festival
Eastern U.S. Music Camp, Inc.—Eastern U.S. Music Camp
Education Unlimited—Computer Camp by Education Unlimited
Education Unlimited—Public Speaking Institute by Education Unlimited
Education Unlimited—Summer Focus at Berkeley; Acting Workshop at Berkeley
EF International Language Schools
Embry-Riddle Aeronautical University—Aerospace Summer Camp
Embry-Riddle Aeronautical University—SunFlight Camps
French Woods Festival of the Performing Arts
Friends Music Camp
Friendship Ventures—Youth Leadership Program
Georgetown University—Georgetown Summer College
Georgia Hardy Tours, Inc.—Summer Study
Global Routes—High School Community Service Programs
Global Works International Programs—Summer Programs
Gould Academy—Young Scholars Program; College Preparatory Program
Hargrave Military Academy—Summer School and Camp
Hawaii Preparatory Academy—Hawaii Preparatory Academy Summer Session
Higher Ground Softball Camps
Hockey Opportunity Camp
Humanities Spring in Assisi
Hun School of Princeton—Hun School Summer Programs
Indiana University, Bloomington—College Audition Preparation (CAP); Summer Piano Academy; Summer Recorder Academy; Summer String Academy
Interlocken—Crossroads Adventure Travel
Intern Exchange International
International Bicycle Fund—Bicycle Africa Tours; Sbuhbi Lithlal Ti Swatixwtuhd
Involvement Volunteers Association—International Volunteering; Networked International Volunteering

Irish American Cultural Organization—Irish Way

Ithaca College—Summer College for High School Students

JCC Maccabi Xperience Israel Programs—Israel Summer Programs

Joel Ross Tennis & Sports Camp

Johns Hopkins University—Hopkins Pre-college Credit Program

Junior Statesmen Foundation—Junior Statesmen Summer School

Knowledge Exchange Institute—Precollege African Safari Program

Knowledge Exchange Institute—Precollege Amazon Exploration Program

Knowledge Exchange Institute—Precollege Artist Abroad Program

Knowledge Exchange Institute—Precollege Business, Law and Diplomacy Program

Knowledge Exchange Institute—Precollege European Capitals Program

Knowledge Exchange Institute—Precollege Research Abroad Program

Kutsher's Sports Academy

Language Link—Intercultura; Spanish Language Institute; CLIC

Latitudes International—Community Service Travel

Lawrence Academy—Environmental Field Study

Lawrence Academy—Global Leaders Workshop

Lawrence Academy—International English Institute

LEAPNow—Summer Program in Central America; Summer Program in Australia

Lingua Service Worldwide—Junior Classic and Junior Sports Program

Lingua Service Worldwide—Junior Course in Salamanca

Lingua Service Worldwide—Summer Language Adventure

Longacre Expeditions

Longacre Leadership—Longacre Leadership Program

Maine Teen Camp

Marine Military Academy—Summer Military Training Camp

The Masters School—Summer ESL

Mathematics Foundation of America—Canada/USA Mathcamp

Mount Holyoke College—SummerMath

Musiker Discovery Programs—Musiker Tours

Musiker Discovery Programs—Summer Discovery

Nacel Open Door

National Registration Center for Study Abroad—Summer Language Programs

New York Film Academy—New York Film Academy Summer Program

New York University—Tisch Summer High School Program

North Carolina School of the Arts—Summer Session

Northwaters—Northwaters Wilderness Programs

Northwestern University—National High School Institute

Oak Ridge Military Academy—Academic Summer School

Oak Ridge Military Academy—Leadership Adventure Camp

Occidental College—High School Oceanology Program

Orme School—Orme Summer Camp

Otis College of Art and Design—Otis Summer of Art

Outpost Wilderness Adventure—Outpost Wilderness Adventures

OxBridge Academic Programs—Cambridge Prep; Cambridge Tradition; Oxford Tradition; Académie de Paris

Parsons School of Design—Summer Intensive Studies

Phillips Academy—Phillips Academy Summer Session

Pratt Institute—Pre-College Summer Program

Princeton Ballet School—American Repertory Ballet's Summer Intensive

Putney Student Travel—Excel at Williams and Amherst Colleges; Excel at Oxford/Tuscany and Madrid/Barcelona

Quest Scholars Program—Quest Scholars Program at Stanford; Quest Scholars Program at Harvard

Randolph-Macon Academy—Randolph-Macon Academy Summer Programs

Rassias Programs

Ringling School of Art and Design—PreCollege Perspective

The Road Less Traveled

Rutgers University—Young Scholars Program in Discrete Mathematics

Saint Cloud State University, Ethnic Studies Program—Scientific Discovery Program

Savannah College of Art and Design—Rising Star

Scandinavian Seminar—Ambassadors for the Environment

School for Field Studies—Environmental Field Studies Abroad

76ers Basketball Camp

Shad International—Shad Valley

Sidwell Friends School—Deep Creek Adventures; SFS Alaskan Adventures

Sidwell Friends School—Sidwell Friends Summer Programs

Skidmore College—Pre-College Program in the Liberal Arts for High School Students at Skidmore

Smith College—Smith Summer Science Program

Sons of Norway—Camp Norway

Southern Methodist University—College Experience

Southwestern Academy—International Summer Programs

Spoleto Study Abroad

Stanford University, Education Program for Gifted Youth—Summer Institute in Mathematics and Physics

State University of New York, Purchase—Summer Visual Arts Institute

Student Conservation Association—High School Conservation Work Crew (CWC) Program

Student Hosteling Program—Summer Biking Programs

Student Safaris International—Zanzibar to the Serengeti; Queensland Explorer

Summer Sonatina International Piano Camp

Summer Study Programs—Summer Enrichment

Summer Study Programs—Summer Study at the University of Colorado at Boulder

Summer Study Programs—Summer Study in Paris at The American University of Paris

Tamarack Camps

Tennis: Europe and More

Trailmark Outdoor Adventures

Tufts University European Center—Tufts Summit

University of the Arts—Drama and Musical Theater

University of the Arts—PREP, Art Smart, and Media and Communications Workshops

University of California, San Diego—UCSD Academic Connections & Summer Session

University of Michigan—Michigan Math and Science Scholars

University of Mississippi—Summer College for High School Students

University of New Hampshire—Project SMART

University of Pennsylvania—Penn Summer Science Academy

University of Southern California—Summer Production Workshop

University of Texas, Austin—Summer Theatre Workshop

University of Wisconsin, Madison—Summer Art Classes

University of Wisconsin, Superior—Youthsummer

Visions

Wake Forest University—Summer Debate Workshop; Fast Track; Policy Project; Policy Analysis Seminar

The Walden School—Walden School Summer Music School, Festival, and Camp

Washington and Lee University—Summer Scholars

Weissman Teen Tours, Inc.

Westcoast Connection—Active Teen Tours

Westcoast Connection—European Programs

Westcoast Connection—Golf & Tennis Programs

Westcoast Connection—Israel Experience

Westcoast Connection—On Tour

Westcoast Connection—Outdoor Adventure Programs

Westcoast Connection—Ski & Snowboard Sensation

Wilderness Experience Unlimited—Explorer Group; Trailblazers

Wilderness Ventures—Wilderness Adventure Expeditions; Advanced Leadership Expeditions; Offshore Adventure Expeditions

World Horizons International

World Learning—Experiment in International Living (EIL)

Yale University—Yale Summer Programs

Youth for Understanding International Exchange—Summer Overseas

36–49 Days

Academic Enrichment Institute—Summer Academic Enrichment Institute

ACTeen—ACTeen July Academy; ACTeen August Academy; ACTeen Summer Saturday Program

Adventures Cross-Country

AFS Intercultural Programs—Summer Homestay; Summer Homestay Language Study; Summer Homestay Plus; Summer Community Service/Team Mission

Alliances Abroad—Summer Spanish Program for Youth in Spain; Summer French Programs for Youth in France; Culture and Adventure Program for Youth in Ireland

America's Adventure/Venture Europe

American Academy of Dramatic Arts—Summer Actor Training

American Collegiate Adventures—American Collegiate Adventures

American Farm School—Greek Summer

American Institute For Foreign Study (AIFS)—Pre-College Summer Study Abroad

American International Youth Student Exchange

American Jewish Society for Service—Summer Work Camps

American Trails West

Amerispan Unlimited—Madrid and Marbella Summer Camps; Spanish Language Program in Costa Rica

Amigos de las Americas

Appel Farm Arts and Music Center—Appel Farm's Summer Arts Camp

Aspen Music School—Aspen Music Festival and School

Avatar Education Ltd.—Buckswood ARC Summer Programs

BalletMet—Summer Workshop

Ballibay Camps, Inc.—Camp Ballibay for the Fine and Performing Arts

Barat Foundation—Barat Foundation Summer Program

Birmingham-Southern College—Summer Scholar Program

Boston College—Boston College Experience

Boston University—Program in Mathematics for Young Scientists (PROMYS)

Brandeis University—Brandeis Summer Odyssey

Breakthroughs Abroad, Inc.—High School Programs

Brevard Music Center—Young Artists Division

Brown University—Pre-College Program

Brush Ranch Camps

Buck's Rock Performing and Creative Arts Camp

Burklyn Ballet Theatre

Camp Encore/Coda—Upper Camp

Carnegie Mellon University—Pre-College Programs

Catholic University of America—College Courses for High School Students

Catholic University of America—Eye on Engineering

Center for Cross-Cultural Study—Summer in Seville
Colorado College—Summer Session for High School Students
Cornell University—Cornell University Summer College
Costa Rican Language Academy (CRLA)
Cottonwood Gulch Foundation—Prairie Trek Group I; Prairie Trek Group II; Turquoise Trail
Deep Woods Camp for Boys
Duke University—Duke University PreCollege Program
Dwight-Englewood School—Dwight-Englewood Summer Programs
Education Unlimited—Summer Focus at Berkeley; Acting Workshop at Berkeley
EF International Language Schools
Embry-Riddle Aeronautical University—SunFlight Camps
Evansville Association for the Blind—Summer College Program for Students with Disabilities
Foothill College—Academically Talented Youth Program
French Woods Festival of the Performing Arts
Friendship Ventures—Youth Leadership Program
Global Routes—High School Community Service Programs
Gould Academy—Young Scholars Program; College Preparatory Program
Hampshire College—Hampshire College Summer Studies in Mathematics
Hockey Opportunity Camp
Huntingdon College—Huntingdon College Summer Programs
Interlocken—Crossroads Adventure Travel
Involvement Volunteers Association—International Volunteering; Networked International Volunteering
Joel Ross Tennis & Sports Camp
Kinhaven Music School
La Société Française—International Volunteer Program
Lingua Service Worldwide—Summer Language Adventure
Longacre Leadership—Longacre Leadership Program
Louisiana State University—Honors High School Credit Program
Maine Teen Camp
The Masters School—Summer ESL
Miami University—Junior Scholars Program
Musiker Discovery Programs—Musiker Tours
Musiker Discovery Programs—Summer Discovery
Nacel Open Door
New Jersey Institute of Technology—Pre-college Academy in Technology and Science for High School Students
New York Film Academy—New York Film Academy Summer Program

Oakland University—Oakland University Summer Mathematics Institute

Operation Crossroads Africa—Africa & Diaspora Programs

Orme School—Orme Summer Camp

Outpost Wilderness Adventure

Putney Student Travel—Excel at Williams and Amherst Colleges; Excel at Oxford/Tuscany and Madrid/Barcelona

Rhode Island School of Design—Pre-College Program

The Road Less Traveled

Saint Paul Academy and Summit School—Summer Programs

School for Film and Television—Summer in the City

Shad International—Shad Valley

Sidwell Friends School—Sidwell Friends Summer Programs

Southwest Texas State University—Honors Summer Math Camp

Southwestern Academy—International Summer Programs

Southwestern Academy—Southwestern Adventures

Spelman College—Early College Summer Program

Stagedoor Enterprises—Stagedoor Manor Performing Arts Training Center

Student Hosteling Program—Summer Biking Programs

Summer Sonatina International Piano Camp

Summer Study Programs—Summer Study at Penn State

Syracuse University—Syracuse University Summer College for High School Students

Tamarack Camps

University of California, Los Angeles—College Level Summer Program

University of California, Los Angeles—High School Level Summer Program

University of California, Los Angeles—UCLA High School Acting and Performance Institute

University of California, San Diego—UCSD Academic Connections & Summer Session

University of California, Santa Barbara—Early Start Program

University of California, Santa Barbara—UCSB Summer Research Mentorship Program

University of Delaware—Summer College for High School Juniors

University of Delaware—Upward Bound Math and Science Center

University of Florida—UF Student Science Training Program

University of Illinois, Chicago—Health Science Enrichment Program

University of Pennsylvania—Penn Summer Science Academy

University of Southern California—Summer Production Workshop

University of Wisconsin, Madison—Summer Art Classes

University of Wisconsin, Madison—Summer Science Institute

Wake Forest University—Summer Debate Workshop; Fast Track; Policy Project; Policy Analysis Seminar

Weissman Teen Tours, Inc.

Westcoast Connection—Active Teen Tours
Westcoast Connection—Outdoor Adventure Programs
Where There Be Dragons—Summer Programs
Wilderness Experience Unlimited—Explorer Group; Trailblazers
Wilderness Ventures—Wilderness Adventure Expeditions; Advanced Leadership Expeditions; Offshore Adventure Expeditions
Xavier University of Louisiana—SOAR 1
Youth for Understanding International Exchange—Summer Overseas

50 Days or More

AFS Intercultural Programs—Summer Homestay; Summer Homestay Language Study; Summer Homestay Plus; Summer Community Service/Team Mission
Alliances Abroad—Summer Spanish Program for Youth in Spain; Summer French Programs for Youth in France; Culture and Adventure Program for Youth in Ireland
American Farm School—Greek Summer
American Institute For Foreign Study (AIFS)—Pre-College Summer Study Abroad
American International Youth Student Exchange—American International Youth Student Exchange Program
Amerispan Unlimited—Madrid and Marbella Summer Camps; Spanish Language Program in Costa Rica
Amigos de las Americas
Appel Farm Arts and Music Center—Appel Farm's Summer Arts Camp
Aspen Music School—Aspen Music Festival and School
Avatar Education Ltd.—Buckswood ARC Summer Programs
Ballibay Camps, Inc.—Camp Ballibay for the Fine and Performing Arts
Beloit College—Center for Language Studies
Brush Ranch Camps
Buck's Rock Performing and Creative Arts Camp
Colorado College—Summer Session for High School Students
Costa Rican Language Academy (CRLA)
Deep Woods Camp for Boys
East Carolina University—East Carolina Summer Theatre
EF International Language Schools
Embry-Riddle Aeronautical University—SunFlight Camps
French Woods Festival of the Performing Arts
Friendship Ventures—Youth Leadership Program
Harvard University—Harvard Summer School Secondary School Program
Hockey Opportunity Camp
Interlochen Center for the Arts—Interlochen Arts Camp

Involvement Volunteers Association—International Volunteering; Networked
    International Volunteering
Kutsher's Sports Academy
Lingua Service Worldwide—Summer Language Adventure
Maine Teen Camp
New York Film Academy—New York Film Academy Summer Program
Northwaters—Northwaters Wilderness Programs
Ohio State University—Ross Young Scholars Program
Shad International—Shad Valley
Southwestern Academy—International Summer Programs
Stagedoor Enterprises—Stagedoor Manor Performing Arts Training Center
Stanford University—Summer College for High School Students
Student Hosteling Program—Summer Biking Programs
Tamarack Camps
University of California, Los Angeles—College Level Summer Program
University of Wisconsin, Madison—Summer Art Classes
Vassar College and New York Stage & Film—Powerhouse Theatre Program
Wilderness Experience Unlimited—Explorer Group; Trailblazers
Youth for Understanding International Exchange—Summer Overseas

How Did We Do? Grade Us.

Thank you for choosing a Kaplan book. Your comments and suggestions are very useful to us. Please answer the following questions to assist us in our continued development of high-quality resources to meet your needs.

The title of the Kaplan book I read was: _____

My name is: _____

My address is: _____

_____

My e-mail address is: _____

What overall grade would you give this book?	Ⓐ	Ⓑ	Ⓒ	Ⓓ	Ⓕ
How relevant was the information to your goals?	Ⓐ	Ⓑ	Ⓒ	Ⓓ	Ⓕ
How comprehensive was the information in this book?	Ⓐ	Ⓑ	Ⓒ	Ⓓ	Ⓕ
How accurate was the information in this book?	Ⓐ	Ⓑ	Ⓒ	Ⓓ	Ⓕ
How easy was the book to use?	Ⓐ	Ⓑ	Ⓒ	Ⓓ	Ⓕ
How appealing was the book's design?	Ⓐ	Ⓑ	Ⓒ	Ⓓ	Ⓕ

What were the book's strong points? _____

How could this book be improved? _____

Is there anything that we left out that you wanted to know more about?

Would you recommend this book to others? ☐ YES   ☐ NO

Other comments: _____

_____

_____

Do we have permission to quote you? ☐ YES   ☐ NO

Thank you for your help.
Please tear out this page and mail it to:

Managing Editor
Kaplan, Inc.
888 Seventh Avenue
New York, NY 10106

KAPLAN®

Thanks!

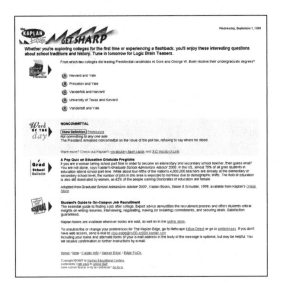

About Kaplan

KAPLAN TEST PREPARATION & ADMISSIONS

Kaplan's nationally recognized test prep and admissions courses cover more than 30 standardized tests, including secondary school, college and graduate school entrance exams, foreign language, and medical and professional licensing exams. In addition, Kaplan offers a college admissions seminar course, one-on-one college admissions counseling, private tutoring and a variety of free information and services for students applying to college and graduate programs. Kaplan offers its services at centers worldwide and online at **www.kaptest.com**. Kaplan Learning Services partners with schools and districts to increase student success on a broad range of standardized assessments including state-wide tests and college admissions.

SCORE! LEARNING, INC.

SCORE! Educational Centers help K-10 students build confidence along with academic skills in a motivating, sports-oriented environment. *SCORE!* **Prep** provides in-home, one-on-one tutoring for high school academic subjects and standardized tests. **eScore.com** is the first educational services Web site to offer parents and kids newborn to age 8 personalized child development and educational resources online.

THE KAPLAN COLLEGES

The Kaplan Colleges system (**www.kaplancollege.com**) is a collection of institutions offering an extensive array of online and traditional educational programs for working professionals who want to advance their careers. Learners will find programs leading to professional, bachelor and associates degrees, certificates and diplomas in fields such as business, IT, paralegal studies, legal nurse consulting, criminal justice and law. The Kaplan Colleges system also includes Concord Law School (**www.concordlawschool.com**), the nation's first online law school, offering J.D. and Executive J.D.™ degrees for working professionals, family caretakers, students in rural communities, and others whose circumstances prevent them from attending a fixed facility law school.

QUEST EDUCATION

Kaplan's Quest Education unit (**www.questeducation.com**) is a leading provider of post-secondary education. Quest offers bachelor and associate degrees and diploma programs primarily in the fields of healthcare, business, information technology, fashion and design.

KAPLAN PUBLISHING

Kaplan Publishing (**kaplan.simonsays.com**) produces retail books and software. Kaplan Books, published by Simon & Schuster, includes titles in test preparation, admissions, education, career development, and life skills; Kaplan and Newsweek jointly publish guides on getting into college, finding the right career, and helping children succeed in school.

KAPLAN INTERNATIONAL

Kaplan International (**kaptest.com**) serves students and professionals, providing intensive English instruction, university preparation, test preparation programs, and housing and activities at three campuses and eight city centers in the U.S. and one center in London. Kaplan also has a strong presence overseas, with 34 centers in 16 countries outside of North America.

KAPLAN COMMUNITY OUTREACH

Kaplan provides educational career resources to thousands of financially disadvantaged students annually, working closely with educational institutions, not-for-profit groups, government agencies and grass roots organizations on a variety of national and local support programs. These programs profiled at **www.kaplan.com** help students from a variety of backgrounds achieve their educational and career goals.

KAPLAN PROFESSIONAL

Kaplan Professional provides licensing and continuing education training, certification, and professional development courses for securities, insurance, financial services, legal, IT, and real estate professionals and corporations. In addition, Kaplan Professional provides solutions to businesses to meet the demanding needs of professional education, tracking and regulatory compliance. The portal to all services is **www.kaplanprofessional.com.**

Self Test Software is a world leader in exam simulation software and preparation for technical certifications including Microsoft, Novell, Oracle, Lotus, Cisco and A+ and Network+, serving businesses and individuals.

Perfect Access Speer is the leading provider of software training and consulting to the legal market in North America.

The Schweser Study Program is the largest worldwide provider of training tools for the Chartered Financial Analyst (CFA®) examination.

Dearborn is a leading provider of licensing and continuing education training and certification for securities, insurance and financial services professionals as well as corporations, independent schools and colleges, and conducts classes in more than 160 locations throughout the U.S. and abroad (**www.dearborn.com**).

Dearborn Trade publishes more than 250 titles specializing in finance, business management and real estate, plus well-read consumer real estate books to help home buyers, sellers and real estate investors make informed decisions.

Real Estate Education Company is the nation's most comprehensive source of real estate materials for pre-and post licensing, continuing education and professional development, with training materials available in print, software, CD-ROM, and through **RECampus.com**, its online real estate campus.

Want more information about our services, products or the nearest Kaplan center?

1 Call our nationwide toll-free numbers:

1-800-KAP-TEST for information on our test prep courses, private tutoring and admissions consulting

1-800-KAP-ITEM for information on our books and software

1-888-KAP-LOAN* for information on student loans

2 Connect with us online:

On the web, go to:
www.kaptest.com
Via email:
info@kaplan.com

3 Write to:

Kaplan
888 Seventh Avenue
New York, NY 10106

KAPLAN®

*Kaplan is not a lender and does not participate in determination of loan eligibility.

Other Kaplan Books for High School Students

High School Success

High School 411

Math Power
Grammar Power
Learning Power
Writing Power
Word Power

Test Preparation

ACT
Fast Track ACT

SAT & PSAT
SAT Math Workbook
SAT Verbal Workbook
SAT Math Mania
SAT Verbal Velocity
Fast Track SAT & PSAT

SAT II
Biology, Chemistry, Mathematics, Physics, Spanish, U.S. History

AP
Biology, Calculus, Statistics, U.S. Government & Politics

College Admissions

Conquer the Cost of College
Kaplan/Newsweek College Catalog
Parent's Guide to College Admissions
Scholarships
Yale Daily News Guide to Succeeding in College
Yale Daily News Guide to Writing College Papers

KAPLAN